Implementing Persistent Object Bases

Principles and Practice

*The Fourth
International Workshop
on Persistent Object Systems*

Senior Editor   *Bruce M. Spatz*
Production Editor   *Sharon E. Montooth*
Cover Designer   *Victoria Ann Philp*
Production and Composition   *Technically Speaking Publications*

Library of Congress Cataloging-in-Publication Data

```
International Workshop on Persistent Object Systems (4th : 1990 :
  Martha's Vineyard, Mass.)
    Implementing persistent object bases : principles and practice /
  the Fourth International Workshop on Persistent Object Systems ;
  edited by Alan Dearle, Gail M. Shaw, Stanley B. Zdonik.
       p.    cm.
    Workshop was held 9/23-27/90, Martha's Vineyard, Mass., USA.
    Includes bibliographical references and index.
    ISBN 1-55860-168-6
    1. Object-oriented data bases--Congresses.  2. Object-oriented
  programming (Computer science)--Congresses.   I. Dearle, Alan.
  II. Shaw, Gail M.   III. Zdonik, Stanley Benjamin.   IV. Title.
  QA76.9.D3I59   1990
  005.1--dc20                                          90-24455
                                                           CIP
```

ISBN 1-55860-168-6
MORGAN KAUFMANN PUBLISHERS, INC.
Editorial Office:
        2929 Campus Drive, Suite 260
        San Mateo, California 94403
Order from:
        P.O. Box 50490
        Palo Alto, CA 94303-9953

94 93 92 91 90 5 4 3 2 1-EB

Implementing Persistent Object Bases

Principles and Practice

The Fourth International Workshop on Persistent Object Systems

Acknowledgements

Co-chairs and Editors

Alan Dearle	*University of Adelaide*
Gail Shaw	*Brown University*
Stan Zdonik	*Brown University*

Program Committee

Malcolm Atkinson	*Altaïr/INRIA and University of Glasgow*
Alan Dearle	*University of Adelaide*
Ron Morrison	*University of St. Andrews*
John Rosenberg	*University of Newcastle*
Gail Shaw	*Brown University*
David Stemple	*University of Massachusetts*
Stan Zdonik	*Brown University*

Secretary

Page Elmore	*Brown University*

Treasurer

Alan Ewald	*Digital Equipment Corporation*

Local Arrangements

Gail Shaw	*Brown University*
Page Elmore	*Brown University*

September 23–27, 1990

Martha's Vineyard
Massachusetts, USA

Sponsored in part by
Digital Equipment Corporation
and
International Business Machines, Inc.

digital™   IBM

CONTENTS

Foreword

In 1985 and 1987 two workshops on persistent object systems were held in Appin, Scotland. The third workshop in this series was held in Newcastle, Australia in January 1989. The most recent workshop in this series was held in September 1990 on Martha's Vineyard in Massachusetts, USA. This book contains the proceedings of the 1990 workshop.

The workshop was organized as a series of working sessions which included short paper presentations followed by a group discussion of the topics addressed by the papers. These proceedings reflect the workshop format. Each chapter contains the papers from one workshop session and is introduced by a summary of the presentations and discussion for the session. These chapter introductions were prepared by the session chairs, often with feedback from participants in the session. After this Foreword you'll find an Introduction to this volume that discusses the research covered by this workshop. At the end of the book you'll find some Concluding Remarks – reflections on the way the field has developed since the first workshop and on where it is heading. We've also included some pictures of the work, and play, on Martha's Vineyard. We hope this organization will help give the reader a sense of the atmosphere of the workshop and a better understanding of the important issues in persistent object systems.

The papers contained in this volume were chosen from a group of 82 proposals submitted to the program committee in the spring of 1990. The committee chose 31 of these papers to include in the workshop. The organizers wanted to keep the workshop small to encourage interaction between the participants and, as a result, many good proposals were not accepted. We feel this turned out to be a good decision; we have a good variety of topics covered in the sessions, with many excellent papers representing work in those areas; the sessions all included active discussions; and the time outside the sessions was filled with participants discussing their work and new ideas, and getting acquainted and re-acquainted.

The organizers are extremely grateful for financial support provided by International Business Machines, Inc. and Digital Equipment Corporation, and for administrative support provided by Brown University. We would also like to thank Page Elmore for her assistance in making local arrangements for the workshop. Special thanks are due to all of the people who served as session chairs and contributed the chapter introductions for this book, to Malcolm and Dave for sharing their thoughts as the Concluding Remarks, and to the workshop attendees for their participation, making this all possible.

Alan Dearle
Gail Shaw
Stan Zdonik

Introduction

The purpose of this workshop is to bring together leading researchers in the areas of programming languages and databases to present and discuss recent research in the area of persistent object systems. Persistent object systems support the uniform creation and manipulation of objects, regardless of their lifetimes. This is in direct contrast with conventional systems in which temporary objects are created and manipulated using one mechanism (typically programming language data structures) and permanent objects are maintained using a different mechanism (usually a filestore or database).

The Persistent Object Systems (POS) workshops are complemented by the workshops on Database Programming Languages (DBPL) held in 1987 and 1989. While the DBPL Workshop focuses on semantic issues of types and persistent data, the POS Workshop focuses on implementation concerns for systems such as DBPLs. Although some POS papers discuss language issues, we are primarily interested in how decisions at the language level affect the implementations. The papers in this proceedings represent the most current research and developments in implementation techniques.

The theme of the workshop is the design, implementation and use of persistent object bases. In keeping with this theme, the workshop (and this book) was organized into ten sessions covering the following interrelated areas:

- types

- language mechanisms

- architectures

- heterogeneity

- transactions and concurrency

- implementation

- optimization

The goal of much of this work is to provide the supporting technology for a programming language and environment that treats data uniformly. For example, it should be possible to query any set object regardless of whether it is persistent or transient. Current practice allows querying only in the persistent store (i.e., the database). Similarly, mechanisms such as data abstraction, which are currently provided by programming languages, should also be available for persistent data.

Such a system would also eliminate the existing *impedance mismatch* between the type system of the programming language and the type system of the data store. This has two advantages. The first is ease of application development; not having to translate between two different representations simplifies the programmer's task. The second is that there is no loss of type protection when moving from transient to long term data storage.

Many workstation-based applications, like office information systems, electrical and mechanical CAD, and programming environments (i.e., CASE), place new requirements on data storage systems. These applications typically require the creation, storage and manipulation of large cyclic structures of heterogeneous objects. Such data structures are supported inadequately by conventional databases and file systems. In applications such as these, both associative retrieval (i.e., query) and graph traversal (i.e., navigation) must be supported with very high performance. It must also be possible to accommodate many new application-specific types directly in the object store.

A persistent object system must also permit objects to be created at a semantic level that is appropriate for the application at hand. For example, if the application is an electronic CAD tool, then the persistent store must be able to create and manage circuits and circuit components. It is also highly desirable to create and manipulate these objects in a way that retains the application semantics. In contrast to this position, a file system allows programs to create persistent objects but, for the most part, the file system is blind to their meaning. Issues such as these are discussed, in particular, in the sessions on *Types* and *Language Mechanisms*.

The implementation of persistent object systems presents many technical challenges. In particular, in order to make them useful they must execute efficiently, they must be easily integratable with existing code that was not written in such an environment, and they must provide support for sharing and correctness.

Much of the research in this area is influenced by the need to make persistent object systems run fast. A persistent object system hides the details of the persistent storage medium from the users of the store. The system automatically moves objects, on demand, from the persistent medium into main memory. Following pointers or relationships from one object to another is a common type of access for the applications that persistent object systems address. The fact that an object can refer to any other object, including those that still reside on a slow secondary storage medium (e.g., a disk), means that pointer traversal could be extremely slow. In the worst case, it could involve a disk seek per traversal. One of the themes of this workshop includes experimenting with techniques to reduce this overhead. Such techniques are discussed in the sessions titled *Clustering and Tools*, *Optimization*, and *By the C*.

Since information in a persistent object system may often exist for many years, the need to support evolution and heterogeneity is more acute than it is in a traditional programming system. Old data might no longer conform to an evolving set of type definitions (i.e., schema). Two programs that are created independently and at different points in time might have difficulty exchanging data, even when the names of the types remain unchanged. These issues are explored, in particular, by presentations in the *Architectures* and *Heterogeneity* sessions.

A persistent object store should also be accessible by many programs or users simultaneously. Arbitrary simultaneous access to such a store or unpredictable system failure can potentially cause inconsistencies in the data. Transactions are a response to this observation.

Current transaction processing is usually based on the notion of serializability as the only correctness criterion. This means that transactions are forced to interleave their steps in such a way that the result is equivalent to some serial ordering of the transactions. Researchers are currently discussing the kinds of protocols that should be supported by future persistent object systems. Should they be based purely on serializability or should they be made more flexible? Should a particular view of correctness be mandated by the system, or should it be possible to program the transaction manager? The papers in the *Transactions* session discuss these issues.

The maintenance of integrity constraints is another aspect of correctness . An integrity constraint is a predicate on the database that must be maintained across updates. Support for constraint management in the object store is an important problem. Active databases (*Heterogeneity* session) are one way to address these concerns.

Another topic of debate is where in the architecture facilities such as versioning, transaction control, and integrity constraints should reside. Should they reside at the very lowest levels of the system, or should they be layered on top of some more primitive object storage facility? Such issues are discussed in the *Architectures* session.

The overriding theme of this workshop is the implementation of persistent object systems. In the five years since the first persistent object systems workshop the field has progressed from a few prototype implementations to the dozens of implemented systems represented in the papers submitted to this fourth workshop. Papers in all of the sessions discuss experimentation with currently implemented systems. In the two *Systems Implementation* sessions the focus is on more specific issues that arise when implementing a persistent object system. These papers delve into such issues as memory management techniques and operating system support. For example, the memory management discussions center on two main issues: what is an appropriate unit of memory to manipulate in a persistent system, and what is the best way to handle space/identifier reclamation.

Early persistent systems used a technique which has become known as *pointer swizzling*. This technique involves moving objects from disk storage to local memory one object at a time and overwriting the embedded disk address which caused the fault with the new virtual memory address of the object. This technique may be expensive due to the fact that address translation hardware cannot be employed to perform necessary translation. This has caused some researchers to build persistent systems on top of paged virtual memory systems. While this technique has some problems, there may be performance gains from exploiting available hardware. Some of the latest systems discussed at this workshop use hybrid solutions performing *pointer swizzling* and demand paging.

Many persistent languages abstract over the concept of store by attempting to provide a conceptually infinite persistent object space. Since these systems are implemented using finite resources, space and identifiers may have to be reused. Reusing memory and identifiers is known as garbage collection. Some interesting questions discussed in the contributions in the *Systems Implementation* sessions are: 'How may parallel garbage collection be performed?', 'Is generation based garbage collection a good technique in persistent systems?', and 'How does garbage collection interact with issues such as stability and transactions?'.

The ideal support that operating system might provide persistent programming systems has been debated since the first POS Workshop. Some reseachers believe that persistent systems will subsume the role of operating systems. Others believe that we must design new operating systems, and even hardware, to support persistent systems. Meanwhile the pragmatists are attempting to make the best out of the operating systems currently provided. There was definitely a feeling at the workshop that the newer operating systems, such as Mach and Chorus, are providing a much closer approximation to the kind of support necessary for persistent systems than their cousins of five years ago.

The papers included in this Fourth Persistent Object Systems Workshop represent the most current research and developments in the design and implementation of persistent object bases. The issues discussed and systems presented illustrate the advances that have been made in the five years since the first workshop. The research presented here is the basis for even greater advances as we continue research and development in the field of persistent object systems.

Part I

Optimization

Chair: John Rosenberg

It was perhaps appropriate that the first session of this Workshop was devoted to optimisation techniques for persistent object systems. We have progressed to a stage where there are a number of operational persistent languages and systems. However, performance is becoming an important issue. It is encouraging to see a number of groups concentrating on this area and attempting to apply various optimisation techniques in order to improve performance. This is essential if persistent systems are to be accepted by the general computing community.

Two papers were presented in this session and both of these concentrated on compile-time optimisations. In a persistent system there is usually an object manager which is responsible for managing objects in both primary and secondary storage. Before an object can be accessed it must be brought into primary memory. This necessarily involves some overhead, particularly in terms of residency checks and calls to the object manager. The papers presented in this session tackle this problem and attempt to minimise the cost of these residency checks.

In the first paper Joel Richardson describes a compilation technique for generating and optimising object load/store code in a persistent language (E). The broad analogy is with register allocation in a conventional language, i.e. the compiler's job is to produce code which moves data into and out of fast memory so that the program may perform its computations. The major difference is that for persistent data, slow memory (disk) is several orders of magnitude slower than fast memory (RAM). Compiled Item Faulting takes advantage of this difference by introducing simple dynamic checks to avoid superfluous calls to the object manager. This is combined with static dataflow analysis to keep data in fast memory for as long as possible.

In the second paper Tony Hosking and Eliot Moss address the more general question of developing compile-time optimisations that provide significant performance improvements for persistent programs. The work is described in the context of a proposed persistent version of Modula-3, but applies equally well to any type-safe imperative language. They concentrate on what they consider to be the two most important issues, namely reduction of CPU time overheads, especially in comparison with non-persistent languages, and I/O costs. The paper focuses on reducing the CPU overheads for object residency checks under the assumption that no special hardware is used. It is argued that by the use of dataflow analysis and additional static information about co-residency of objects the overheads of residency checks can be reduced to a very low level. It is also shown how the same kind of information supports clustering and is promising for reducing I/O costs, which may well be much more significant than the reductions in CPU overhead.

Discussion following the presentations concentrated on two main issues. The first related to the assumptions in both papers of no hardware support. It was argued that it was unrealistic to expect high performance from persistent systems on conventional hardware and that, in the long term, hardware support would be essential. The difficulty appears to be the long development time for hardware, and compatibility issues. It is also clear that even with specialisd hardware, compile-time optimisations will still be important. The effectiveness of such a combination has been demonstrated by the various RISC machines now commercially available.

The second issue discussed was co-residency of objects and clustering. There appear to be several difficulties. In languages such as C and Modula-3 the co-residency information has to be provided by the programmer via pragmas. It is perhaps possible that this could be derived automatically with higher-level languages. Another problem is the question of data evolution. The co-residency information must be modified as the schema evolves and it is not clear how this can be achieved.

The two papers presented have provided essential ground work in this important area and hopefully will set us on the path towards a production quality persistent system.

Compiled Item Faulting: A New Technique for Managing I/O in a Persistent Language

Joel E. Richardson[†]
IBM Almaden Research Center
San Jose, California 95120-6019
joelr@ibm.com

Abstract

In a persistent language, object I/O is transparent to the programmer. Therefore, some mechanism in the system must cause I/O to occur as the program runs. Compiled Item Faulting (CIF) is a new technique that allows a program to interact efficiently with the runtime storage layer. CIF statically identifies expressions (items) denoting objects that may require I/O at runtime, and it decides points in the program where storage layer calls may be needed. Simple dynamic checks are then used to determine if the calls are actually needed.

1 Introduction

In the past decade, many researchers have sought to integrate programming languages and database systems, e.g., [Schm77,Atki83,Alba85,Maie87,Rich87,Morr89,Agra89]. This interest is spurred partly by the significant problems that arise when a program written a conventional language manipulates persistent data. For example, the programmer must include code to move data between disk and main memory and must translate between structures suitable for the persistent store and those expected by the program. As a result, the programmer must remember two representations of each type of object, and the additional code needed to translate between those representations presents additional opportunities for error. Moreover, since persistent objects are not language objects, there is no way for the compiler to aid in type checking; the programmer must include dynamic checks in the translation code to ensure that the object being read is indeed a valid external representation.

A persistent language addresses these problems by allowing a program to manipulate transient and persistent objects in a uniform manner. A given function, for example, may take its arguments from the stack in one invocation and from the disk in another. One of the hallmarks of a persistent language, therefore, is that object I/O is transparent to the programmer. Accordingly, one of the most important challenges in the implementation of such a language is to ensure that I/O is managed efficiently.

Compiled Item Faulting (CIF) is a new technique that was developed and implemented as part of a compiler for the E programming language [Rich87,Rich89a]. CIF is designed to meet several goals. First, we wish to reduce the number of times a running program calls the storage layer since such calls are expensive. Second, we desire a mechanism that is appropriate for use in a multiprogrammed environment. For example, the buffer pool is a shared resource, and it should be easy to release space that is no longer needed. Third, we are interested in allowing programs to manipulate very large objects without necessarily reading them whole. If a program touches only a small portion of a large object, only that portion should be read. The main contributions of CIF are that it provides a framework for meeting these goals and that it introduces a new model for understanding I/O in a persistent language.

CIF combines static analysis and simple dynamic checking. The compiler identifies expressions whose evaluation may require that persistent data be brought into memory. We use the word "may" because a given expression may actually denote a nonpersistent object and because control flow may be such that the object has already been brought into memory. Since neither of these possibilities is decidable at compile time, dynamic checks are inserted to determine when a storage layer call is needed.

[†]This work was done while the author was a student at the University of Wisconsin. This research was partially supported by the Defense Advanced Research Projects Agency under contract N00014-85-K-0788, by the National Science Foundation under grant IRI-8657323, by Fellowships from IBM and the University of Wisconsin, by DEC through its Incentives for Excellence program, and by grants from GTE Laboratories, Texas Instruments, and Apple Computer.

The remainder of this paper is organized as follows. The next section describes related work and compares CIF with object faulting systems. Section 3 presents the context in which this technique was developed. We briefly describe the E language, the EXODUS Storage Manager, and the E compiler. The relationship between the three is illustrated by showing a simple E program and its translation into C code. Then Section 4 describes CIF. We present an example that illustrates several of the important issues in compiling an E program, and we show how CIF addresses these issues. In Section 5, we describe a mechanism for handling buffer space overflow. Finally, Section 6 concludes with a summary and directions for future work.

2   Related Work

Previous work in the implementation of persistent languages has concentrated primarily on object faulting, e.g., [Cock84,Ford88]. Such systems may be viewed as providing virtual memory for persistent objects. As in demand paging, an object faulting system reads objects into memory as they are referenced by a program. There appear to be two main variations of this approach. The implementation of PS-Algol [Cock84] employs a mechanism called "pointer swizzling." In this system, a pointer has two representations: an external, permanent form and an internal, temporary one. When an external pointer is dereferenced, an object fault occurs, the object is read into (or is discovered in) memory, and the faulting pointer is overwritten with the internal form. Subsequent accesses through the overwritten pointer cause no further faults. The variation explored in Zeitgeist [Ford88] uses object "stubs" to represent nonresident objects. When an object is read into memory, it replaces its stub. In addition, each pointer within the object is converted into a reference to a stub (if the referenced object is nonresident) or to the actual object.

Object faulting is appealing for a number of reasons. It is conceptually simple, and by design, it adapts to the object referencing pattern of any particular program execution. In light of our requirements, however, object faulting also has some drawbacks. One problem is that object faulting is constrained to read whole objects. If a pointer is swizzled or if a stub is replaced, then the entire object must be memory resident. As stated earlier, we wish to support applications that manipulate large objects.

Another problem with object faulting is that the translation of an object's format can degrade performance both directly—because of the cycles needed to do the translation—and indirectly—because of the constraints on other actions in the system. For example, in the pointer swizzling approach, freeing memory is expensive. In order to remove an object from memory, we must first "unswizzle" the pointers in that object as well as all pointers *to* that object. That is, we must locate all other objects in memory that have swizzled pointers to the object being removed and then unswizzle those references. Using object stubs alleviates this problem, since an object may be removed from memory simply by leaving a stub in its place. Memory management becomes complicated, however, if the size of an object can be different from the size of a stub, as would be the case in E. This problem does not arise for Zeitgeist, since it is based on Lisp, and a stub is simply a special kind of cons cell.

CIF displays both advantages and disadvantages compared with object faulting. It is able to retrieve portions of objects, and there is no representation conversion when an object is read into memory. Since it depends on static analysis, however, it may tend to be less responsive to the referencing patterns of a particular execution. Currently we can make only qualitative comparisons between CIF and object faulting. A very interesting avenue of future research would be a thorough investigation of the tradeoffs in the two approaches. It may even be possible to develop a hybrid approach combining the best features of both mechanisms.

3   Context

In this section, we briefly describe three parts of the system in which CIF was developed. We outline the main features of the E programming language [Rich87,Rich89a] and show a simple example of a program using a persistent object. The EXODUS Storage Manager [Care86a] provides the runtime storage layer for E programs. We review the interface to this layer. Finally, the E compiler maps an E program into a C program running against the Storage Manager. We describe the organization of the compiler and show the result of compiling the example E program.

```
persistent dbint counter = 0;
main() {
    printf("This program has been run %d times.", counter);
    ++counter;
}
```

Figure 1: An E program that counts the number of times it has been run.

3.1   The E Programming Language

The E programming language was developed in the context of the EXODUS extensible database system project [Care86a]. The original intent was to design a language tailored for writing database system code. The result is an extension of C++ [Stro86] that adds generic classes, iterators, persistent objects, and several predefined classes. C++ provided a good starting point with its class structuring features and its expanding popularity as a systems programming language. Generic classes (generators [Lisk77]) were added for their utility in defining database container types, such as sets and indices. Iterators [Lisk77] were added as a useful programming construct in general and as a mechanism for structuring database queries in particular. Persistence—the ability of a language object to survive from one program run to the next—was added because it is an essential attribute of database objects. In addition, by describing the database in terms of persistent variables, one may then manipulate the database in terms of natural expressions in the language.

Persistence in E is realized via three related constructs: database types (db types), the **persistent** storage class, and the predefined db class **collection**. A type definition may optionally include the **db** (database) attribute. This is a signal that objects of the type can (but are not required to) persist. E provides db classes as well as the fundamental db types: dbint, dbfloat, etc. If a variable of a db type is declared with the **persistent** storage class, the object bound to that variable will persist across program runs. (Db type objects may also be volatile; i.e., they may be allocated on the stack or heap.) Named persistent objects form the roots of an E database. Finally, there is a predefined **collection** class which supports the dynamic creation and destruction of collection elements. An object created within a persistent collection will itself persist.

As a simple example, consider the E program in Figure 1. The counter is a persistent db integer and is initialized to zero at creation time. Each time the program is run, it prints the current value of the counter and then increments it. As promised, the program contains no calls to perform I/O. Since all of the low-level interaction with the storage layer is transparent, the programmer may concentrate on the algorithm at hand.

3.2   The EXODUS Storage Manager

The runtime storage layer for E programs is the EXODUS Storage Manager. The basic abstraction provided by the Storage Manager is the *storage object*, which is an uninterpreted byte sequence of virtually any size. Whether the size of an object is several bytes or several gigabytes, clients of the Storage Manager see a uniform interface. Each object is named by its object ID (OID), which is its physical disk address. Two operations, **ReadObject** and **ReleaseObject**, are the basic means of moving data in and out of memory; i.e., they are the analogues of load and store, respectively. (The Storage Manager "machine" has a cache, however, so a release operation does not actually return the data to disk.) The read call specifies an OID, an offset, and a length. The Storage Manager reads the specified byte sequence into the buffer pool and then returns the address of the first byte of this sequence to the caller.[1] Because the Storage Manager supports atomic, recoverable transactions, the client updates data by calling **WriteObject**. This procedure updates the target object and performs the appropriate logging. When the client program is finished with the data, it calls **ReleaseObject**.

Note that the data requested in a read call is *pinned* in the buffer pool until the client releases it. Pinning is a two-way contract: the Storage Manager guarantees that it will not move the data (e.g., page

---

[1] The Storage Manager actually returns the address of a *user descriptor* to the caller. The user descriptor contains a pointer to the data. This extra level of indirection is needed for technical reasons that do not concern us here. We will therefore ignore the presence of user descriptors in this paper.

```
struct DBREF counter = { ... };
void main()
{
    char *      _counter;
    int         _tmp000;

    ReadObject( counter.oid, counter.offset, sizeof(int), &_counter );
    printf("This program has been run %d times.", *(int*)_counter );
    _tmp000 = *(int*)_counter + 1;
    WriteObject( _counter, 0, sizeof(int), & _tmp000 );
    ReleaseObject( _counter );
}
```

Figure 2: Translation of the counter program.

it out) while it is pinned, and the client promises not to access anything outside the pinned byte range. In addition, the client promises to release (unpin) the data in a "timely" fashion, because data that remains pinned unnecessarily can degrade performance by reducing the effective size of the buffer pool.

3.3   The E Compiler

The E compiler is an extension of version 1.2.1 of the AT&T C++ compiler[2]. The heart of the E compiler is a source-to-source translator that takes E code as input and produces C as output. This translation occurs in multiple phases. The parser consumes one external declaration at a time, e.g., one function definition or one global variable declaration, and produces an abstract syntax tree. Subsequent phases then type check the tree, simplify E/C++ constructs into equivalent C constructs, and finally walk the tree, producing C code. The simplification phase is further divided into two phases. The first transforms all constructs that do *not* concern persistence, e.g., virtual function calls and iterator invocations. CIF occurs in the second simplification phase, which handles all constructs related to db types and persistence. Thus the input to the CIF code generator is essentially a C syntax tree in which certain type nodes are decorated with the "db" attribute and certain variables are marked as having the persistent storage class. The output of the code generator is a C syntax tree in which the db-related constructs have been replaced with equivalent C constructs. In particular, the code generator grafts Storage Manager calls onto the tree at appropriate points, replaces each use of a persistent variable with an expression to reference the object in the buffer pool, and transforms arithmetic on db pointers into expressions involving OIDs and offsets.

Let us make this discussion more concrete by showing how the compiler translates the E program in Figure 1 into a C program that uses the Storage Manager. Figure 2 shows the translated program.[3] Because E is based on C++, every byte of an object is addressable. Thus a reference to a persistent object contains both an OID and a byte offset into the object. An OID/offset pair is packaged together into a structure called a DBREF. A persistent object declaration is translated into an initialized reference to the actual object. In this example, the persistent counter variable has become a DBREF containing the counter's OID and an offset of zero. The initialization of this DBREF is not important for this discussion.

The call to ReadObject pins the counter in the buffer pool. The first two parameters to the call are the counter's oid and offset. In general, calls to ReadObject are preceded by an address calculation which results in a DBREF; the DBREF's OID and offset then form the first two parameters of the call. The length parameter is deduced from the object's type; in this case, the object being read is an integer. The variable _counter, a pointer allocated by the compiler, is passed by reference as the last parameter to ReadObject. When ReadObject returns, _counter points to the first byte of the counter object. The occurrence of the variable counter in the call to printf is then replaced with an expression that dereferences through

---

[2] The E compiler is currently being ported to version 2.

[3] In all cases where we show translated code, we will omit details that are not necessary for the discussion. For example, we do not show the initialization of the Storage Manager subsystem or the allocation of buffer space. Also, the calls that are shown actually require more parameters than illustrated here.

```
persistent dbint X;
dbstruct listNode {
    dbint    data;
    listNode *      next;
};
int count( listNode * list ) {
    int n = 0;
    while( list != NULL ) {
        if (list->data == X) n++;
        list = list->next;
    }
    return n;
}
```

Figure 3: A program that traverses a list.

_counter. The expression includes a cast to produce a value of the appropriate type. To increment the counter, the compiler inserts a call to WriteObject. The parameters to this call include the pointer to the bytes being updated, an offset into the pinned byte range, the number of bytes to be written, and the address of the new bytes to be copied in. Because this last parameter is an address, the compiler must allocate a temporary variable, _tmp000, in which to compute the new counter value. Finally, the counter is unpinned with a call to ReleaseObject.

4   Compiled Item Faulting

While the example in the last section served to illustrate how the E compiler targets code for the Storage Manager interface, we did not explain how the compiler chooses where to place the pin and unpin calls. In this section, we present the main ideas behind Compiled Item Faulting, the technique used to make such decisions.

4.1   An Example

To convey the essential features of CIF, we introduce another example. Consider the program fragment in Figure 3. The fragment begins with a declaration of a persistent integer, X, and the definition of listNode, the type of a node in a linked list. Each node contains an integer data field and a pointer to the next node in the list; the last node in a list contains a NULL pointer. Finally, the function count traverses a list argument, returning the number of nodes in the list with a data field equal to the persistent integer X.

This example illustrates some important issues in the general problem of code generation for E. Consider the use of X. First, the compiler knows from X's declaration that it is a persistent object. As in the example from the last section, a call to ReadObject—a pin operation—must precede the use of X and a call to ReleaseObject—an unpin operation—must follow. But where should those calls be placed? If they simply surround the statement that uses X, then the program will execute a pin/unpin pair for every iteration of the loop. Noting that the problem of pinning X is in some ways like a register allocation problem, we might consider applying techniques developed for that domain. Standard techniques such as usage counts [ASU86] or graph coloring [Chai81] would move the pin and unpin operations outside the loop, keeping X pinned for the duration. However, if an execution does not enter the loop, then it will perform an unnecessary pin/unpin operation. While the cost of an unnecessary register load and store is a few instructions, the cost of an unnecessary pin and unpin is at least a hundred (and potentially thousands of) instructions.

Because pinning is so expensive (and therefore a wrong decision carries a huge penalty), CIF can profitably invest in some runtime checking to address the pinning problem. The compiler introduces a Boolean flag, _X_pinned, associated with the variable X. The flag is set to TRUE when X is pinned and to FALSE when X is released. Each pin operation first tests the flag's state; if the flag is FALSE, then the Storage

```
                int count( listNode * list ) {
                    int     n = 0;
                    /* compiler-generated variables */
                    char *  _X = NULL;
                    int     _X_pinned = FALSE;

                    while( list != NULL ) {
                        /* This is a pin operation. */
                        if( _X_pinned == FALSE ) {
                            _X_pinned = TRUE;
                            ReadObject(  X.oid, X.offset,
                                             sizeof(int), &_X);
                        }
                        if( list->data == *(int*)_X ) n++;
                        list = list->next;
                    }

                    /* This is an unpin operation. */
                    if( _X_pinned == TRUE ) {
                        _X_pinned = FALSE;
                        ReleaseObject( _X );
                    }
                    return n;
                }
```

Figure 4: Showing pin and unpin operations for X.

Manager is called to read the object. The compiler places a pin operation immediately before the use of an item in an expression.[4] Likewise, each unpin operation calls the Storage Manager to release the object only if the flag is TRUE; the flag is then cleared. Unpin operations are placed at points in the program where the object is not subsequently needed.

Figure 4 approximates the code produced for the count function. We are ignoring the handling of list for the moment, and the code as shown omits all but the essential details. At the price of a Boolean test, this code displays the characteristics that we desire. If control enters the loop, then X will be pinned once and will remain pinned until the loop exits. If control never enters the loop, X will never be pinned.

The example so far has presented the simplest case—that of a named, persistent variable appearing in an expression. In so doing, we have given the general flavor of CIF without too much detail. There are several important issues that we must address, however, in generalizing these ideas.

4.2 Items

Compiled Item Faulting relies on compile-time identification of expressions in a program that could require accessing the persistent store. We define an *item* to be an expression that denotes an addressable object. Informally, an item is any expression that may legally appear on the left-hand side of an assignment. Given an expression tree, one may determine whether it is an item simply by looking at the operator in the root node. An item is either a named variable or an expression whose root node operator is a pointer dereference (*), a record field selection (. or ->), or an array index ([]). The items in Figure 3 include the expressions n, X, list, list->data, and list->next. We note that the compiler will also identify *list as being an item. Internally, all expressions of the form *expr → name* are converted to into (*expr).name.

It is important to distinguish an item, which is a syntactic entity, from the actual object that it denotes; a given item may denote different objects during a program run. (By "object," we mean a region of persistent

---

[4] Actually, there are numerous complications related to flow of control through C expressions that make this statement only an approximation. For the sake of clarity, we will omit these details. The interested reader may refer to [Rich89b].

```
void foo( dbint * p )
{                  // scope 1
    {              // scope 2
        int n;
        ... *(p + n) ...
    }
}
```

Figure 5: Illustrating the Scope of Items.

memory, which may correspond to a Storage Manager object or to a portion thereof.) For example, suppose p is a pointer to a structure containing an array, a. Then the object denoted by the item p->a[n] depends on the current values of both p and n at the time that the expression is evaluated. Let us define the *value of an item* to be the value of the object denoted by the item at a given point during the program's execution and the *address of an item* to be the actual address of that object. An item i is said to be *address-dependent* on item j if a change in the value of j can change the address of i. For example, p->a is address-dependent on p and p->a[n] is address-dependent on both p and n. Note that if i is address-dependent on j, then i is also address-dependent on any items that are aliases for j. For example, if pp is a pointer to p, then p->a is also address-dependent on the item *pp. (We shall have more to say about aliases shortly.) Finally, note that named variables are not address-dependent on any other items.

Every item is defined over a lexical scope. In particular, an item associates with the innermost scope of any of the named variables that it contains. Consider the function in Figure 5. A named variable associates with its normal scopes, so p associates with scope 1 and n with scope 2. The item *(p + n) contains both p and n and therefore associates with scope 2.

4.3   Pinning Regions

The compiler inserts pin and unpin operations into the program based on *pinning regions*. A pinning region R_i, for an item i, is a region of the program such that i might possibly be pinned as long as control stays within the region and such that i is definitely *not* pinned when control leaves the region. A pinning region is defined by a block (scope) or by a sequence of one or more statements in the program.[5] A pinning region for an item i may be no larger than the scope of i.

Let R_i be a pinning region for item i. The essential property of R_i is that pin operations are fixed at points where the program uses i, while unpin operations are moved to the end of R_i and to points following certain assignments and procedure calls within R_i. As control flows through the region, each use of i is preceded by a pin operation. Only those that discover i to be unpinned actually do significant work; the remainder simply perform a Boolean test. Similarly, an unpin operation occurs as control leaves R_i or passes through points that might change the address of i. Only those that find i to be pinned do any work. Let us state this description more precisely.

1. The compiler allocates a Boolean flag, _i_pinned, for item i. Within R_i, if _i_pinned is TRUE, then the object denoted by i is currently pinned in the buffer pool. Otherwise the object is not pinned. When control first enters R_i, _i_pinned is FALSE.

2. Each use of i is preceded by a pin operation. A pin operation first tests _i_pinned and proceeds only if it is FALSE. After a pin operation, _i_pinned is TRUE.

3. An unpin operation immediately follows the exit point of R_i. An unpin operation first tests _i_pinned and proceeds only if it is TRUE. After an unpin operation, _i_pinned is FALSE.

4. An unpin operation precedes each flow-of-control construct (e.g. break) that transfers control to a point outside the pinning region.

---

[5] Again, for reasons related to flow of control through C expressions, a pinning region may actually span only a single subexpression. And again, for reasons of clarity, we will avoid such cases for this discussion.

5. An unpin operation follows each point in R_i at which the address of i might change due to an assignment or procedure call.

In Figure 4, the while loop is a pinning region for X. A pin operation precedes "each" use of X (there is only one), and an unpin operation immediately follows the region.

One question is how large should a pinning region be. If we define the pinning region for every item to be the entire scope in which the item is defined, then the program will perform as few pin operations as static analysis will allow. To see this, imagine that control has reached a use of an item; therefore, the item is pinned. If control leaves the current pinning region and flows to another use, then the program will execute another pin operation at the second use. However, if control stays within the same pinning region (i.e., if the region is large enough to contain both uses), then no additional pin is required. If control flows through an intervening point which changes the address of the item, then the second pin will be performed in either case.

The compiler does not take quite so simplistic an approach, however. Although the Storage Manager's buffer pool is large, it is still finite, and it is unnecessarily wasteful of space to keep an item pinned when it is no longer needed. Accordingly, the compiler defines the pinning region for an item i to be the smallest region (block or sequence of statements) of the program that includes all uses of the item. This approach still results in the "minimum" number of pin operations, but it reduces the program's buffer space requirements.

4.4   Coalescing Pinning Regions

In most cases where a program accesses different pieces of the same object, it is more efficient to pin the whole object rather than to pin each piece individually. Consider the items list->next and list->data in Figure 3, for example. Let us assume for now that list points to a persistent list node. (Section 4.6 will consider the general case where a pointer can reference either a persistent or a nonpersistent object.) Each iteration of the while loop uses the values of both items. Since a list node is small, the compiler should insert a single pin/unpin pair for the whole record, rather than a separate pin/unpin pair for each item. In cases where the size of the whole record is very large, however, such combining of read requests may not be appropriate. As we stated in the introduction, one of the goals of CIF is to allow the manipulation of very large objects.

We say that item i *contains* item j if the object denoted by i physically includes the object denoted by j. For example, the item *list contains both list->data and list->next. Currently, containment is based on the syntactic forms of i and j:

- If e is an item denoting a structure, and n is the name of a field in that structure, then e contains $e.n$.

- If a is an item denoting an array and e is an integer-valued expression, then a contains $a[e]$.

The compiler determines pinning regions by initially placing a pinning region around each use of an item and then propagating this information up the syntax tree. If the compiler discovers two pinning regions for item i, it merges them into one larger pinning region. If the compiler discovers two pinning regions R_i and R_j for items i and j, respectively, such that i and j are both contained by item k, and if the size of k is below a specified threshold, then the compiler *coalesces* R_i and R_j into R_k. R_k spans the smallest region of the program that contains R_i and R_j. If the size of k exceeds the threshold, then R_i and R_j are not coalesced, and i and j are pinned separately. In computing the pinning regions, then, for the program in Figure 3, the compiler will initially create $R_{list \to data}$ spanning the first statement inside the while loop and $R_{list \to next}$ spanning the second. Since the size of *list is small, the compiler will later coalesce these regions into R_{*list} spanning both statements. When possible, the compiler also promotes pinning regions inside a loop to span the entire loop. Thus, both R_{*list} and R_X finally span the while loop.

When a pinning region is coalesced, the form of the pin operations that it contains changes. When R_i is coalesced into R_k, any pin operation for i becomes a pin operation for k. In addition, the expressions to produce the value of i (i.e. by dereferencing through a compiler-generated pointer) are amended to include the proper offset into the pinned byte range.

In the list traversal example, the pinning regions $R_{list \to data}$ and $R_{list \to next}$ are coalesced into R_{*list}. A pin operation for *list has the following form:

```
if( _list_pinned == FALSE ){
        _list_pinned = TRUE;
        ReadObject( list.oid, list.offset,
                sizeof(listNode),
                &_list)
}
```

Given that a list node is pinned, then the individual components are accessed at the appropriate offset. For example, the expression

```
*((struct DBREF*) (_list + sizeof(int)))
```

produces the value of `list->next`. That is, `_list` is a pointer to the first byte of the list node. We increment the pointer by the size of the data field, cast the result as a pointer to a DBREF structure[6], and dereference. Figure 6 shows the form of the translated count function. For readability, we only mark the locations where the actual pin and unpin operations are inserted. The effect of this code is to pin each list node at the top of the `while` loop and to unpin the node at the bottom of the loop.

Figure 6 also illustrates a weakness in the current implementation of CIF. The second instance of `PIN( *list )` and the second `UNPIN( *list )` are superfluous. The extra pin arises because every use of an item is preceded by a pin, and the extra unpin arises because the exit point of every pinning region has an unpin operation. Eliminating redundant operations such as these requires additional flow analysis and has not been implemented. While this would not be difficult, there are reasons for leaving at least the pin operations; these reasons concern a mechanism for handling buffer space overflow that will be described in Section 5. In any case, these extra operations cost only a Boolean test and can therefore be tolerated while we pursue more profitable optimizations.

```
int count( listNode * list ) {
    int n = 0;
    /* compiler-generated variables */
    char *      _X;
    int         _X_pinned = FALSE;
    char *      _list;
    int         _list_pinned = FALSE;

    while( list != NULL ) {
        PIN( X );        /* Following statement uses */
        PIN( *list );    /*    X and list->data.     */
        if( *(int*)_list == *(int*)_X ) n++;

        PIN( *list );    /* Following uses list->next. */
        list = *((struct DBREF*) (_list + sizeof(int)));
        UNPIN( *list ); /* Because list was assigned. */
    }
    UNPIN( X );       /* End of X's pinning region. */
    UNPIN( *list ); /* End of *list's pinning region. */
    return n;
}
```

Figure 6: Showing pin and unpin operations for *list.

---

[6]Recall that all db type pointers (e.g. `list->next`) are represented internally by DBREFs.

4.5   Alias and Side Effect Analysis

For correctness, it is essential that an item be unpinned if its address changes. While the assignment to list in our example program is a particularly easy side effect for the compiler to detect, we must be concerned in general with aliases and with the side effects of procedure calls. The general problem is to compute, for each assignment and procedure call, the set of items whose address could change as a result. These are the items that should be unpinned. To obtain this set, we first compute the set of items whose value could change, i.e., the def-set [ASU86]. Our answer is then the set of items, i, such that i is address-dependent on some item j in the def-set.

The current implementation of CIF uses a naive heuristic that nevertheless captures an interesting set of common cases. We say that an item is *reachable through a pointer*, or simply *reachable*, if any of the following are true:

- the item involves a pointer dereference. For example, the items list->next->data and *p are reachable because each involves at least one pointer dereference.

- the item is a global variable. Since the current implementation does not perform "real" alias analysis, we assume that the address of any global variable could have been assigned to a pointer.

- the item is a local variable whose address is taken somewhere in its scope. For example, if p is a local variable and the expression &p occurs somewhere in p's scope, then p is considered reachable.

Given this definition, we can then compute the def-set of items potentially updated by an assignment or procedure call as follows:

- An assignment in which the left operand is a named variable assigns to that item only.

- An assignment in which the left operand involves a pointer dereference assigns to every item reachable through a pointer.

- A function or procedure call assigns to every item reachable through a pointer.

From this def-set, we then derive the set of items whose address could change due to the assignment or call; this is simply the set of items that are address-dependent on some item in the def-set.

The net result of these rules is that items involving a single pointer dereference generally can remain pinned across assignments through a pointer and across procedure calls. This is because the pointer at which such an item is rooted often is *not* reachable; such a pointer is only included in the def-set of a direct assignment to that pointer. Fortunately, such cases appear to be quite common. For example, a class method accesses the components of an instance through an implicit pointer parameter, this. That is, a reference to an instance component x is translated into this->x. As long as the method code does not compute &this, then the instance can remain pinned for the duration of the invocation.

In any event, we do not mean to suggest that more comprehensive alias analysis is not needed, but rather that our simple heuristic is a reasonable first approximation and that it can be surprisingly successful in a number of common cases. Both alias analysis and interprocedural side-effect analysis have been under development for some time, e.g. [Alle74,Weih80]. Recent work by Larus [Laru88] and Pfeiffer [Pfei89] promises to extend alias analysis techniques to languages having structures and heap allocation. Such results would be useful in the context of CIF.

One other issue concerning aliases is worth noting here. Suppose pointers p and q reference the same object. What happens when *p and *q are pinned separately? Because of the Storage Manager interface, the answer, fortunately, is "the right thing." If the Storage Manager receives multiple requests for the same range of bytes, it hands out multiple pointers referencing those bytes. In this case, *p and *q will reference the same set of bytes in the buffer pool; an update to one is visible to the other. Although this issue does not present a correctness problem for E, better alias analysis could certainly improve performance. If the compiler can determine that two items (e.g., *p and *q) are definitely aliases, then one set of pin operations can be eliminated.

```
/*** an E procedure ***/
void f( dbint * p ) { int n = *p; }

/*** the C translation ***/
void f( p )
DBREF p;
{
    int         n;

    /* compiler-generated variables */
    char *      _p = NULL;
    int         _p_pinned = FALSE;
    int         _p_volatile;

    if( _p_pinned == FALSE ) {      /*   PIN( *p )   */
        _p_pinned = TRUE;
        _p_volatile = VOLATILE( p.oid );
        if( _p_volatile )
            _p = (char*) p.offset;
        else
            ReadObject(p.oid, p.offset, sizeof(int), &_p);
    }

    n = *(int*)_p;                  /*   assign *p to n   */

    if( _p_pinned == TRUE ){        /*   UNPIN( *p )   */
        _p_pinned = FALSE;
        if( _p_volatile == FALSE )
            ReleaseObject( _p );
    }
}
```

Figure 7: Handling both persistent and nonpersistent objects.

4.6 Pinning Nonpersistent Objects

One of the key features of a persistent language is orthogonality [Atki83], that is, that a program should be written independently of the lifetime of the data that it manipulates. For E programs, this means that a given db pointer may at one time refer to a Storage Manager object and at another to a volatile object in the heap or stack. Thus far, we have implicitly assumed that all references are to persistent objects. We now complete the picture by describing how a pin operation deals with references to nonpersistent objects.

Section 3.3 stated that a db pointer is represented internally by a DBREF structure, which contains the object's OID and an offset. A db pointer that references a volatile object has a special OID indicating virtual memory and an offset equal to the object's virtual memory address. During a pin operation, the OID format is checked. If the object is persistent, then the Storage Manager is called as previously described. If the object is volatile, then the virtual memory address is simply copied into the compiler-allocated pointer. The result of the OID check is also recorded in a Boolean flag for later use; the subsequent unpin operation does nothing if the object is volatile. These added steps require an integer compare and an assignment. This adds somewhat to the cost of referencing a nonpersistent object, but is negligible when the result is to call the Storage Manager. Figure 7 summarizes this discussion with one last example.

5   Coping with Finite Buffer Space

One final but important point needs to be addressed. We have implicitly assumed that the amount of available buffer space is sufficient to handle all pin requests. Of course, the buffer pool is finite, and it is possible for a pin request to fail for lack of space. This section describes a mechanism that has been implemented for handling such events.

The basic idea behind the mechanism is simple. First, we expect that the majority of pin requests will succeed; if a request fails, we are willing to run a relatively expensive algorithm in order to continue the program. This continuation algorithm will descend the run-time stack, unpinning items bottom-up, i.e. beginning with the deepest stack frame. After each unpin, the failed pin request is then retried. If it succeeds, then the program continues normally. If the top stack frame is reached without success, the transaction is aborted. In this event, the user can rerun the program with more buffer space.

There are two essential requirements for this mechanism to work. First, it must be safe to unpin an item in a suspended activation. The fact that a pin operation precedes each use of an item ensures this safety in most cases (we consider the exception below). That is, before a resumed activation uses an item that was unpinned by the handler, it will first execute a pin operation.

The second requirement is that the exception handler be able to find all of the pointers to pinned items in all existing stack frames. Furthermore, among the pinned items, it must be able to distinguish the persistent ones from the nonpersistent ones, since unpinning a nonpersistent item will not help to reclaim buffer space. Thus, we revise our description of the implementation of CIF one last time. Instead of allocating the pointers and Boolean flags as individual variables, the compiler allocates them in a record (one per item). All of the records for a given procedure are allocated in an array, and the arrays in successive stack frames are then threaded together, with a global variable pointing to the array in the top frame. By traversing this structure, the exception handler can find the pointers to all pinned items at runtime. Furthermore, it can distinguish persistent and nonpersistent items by checking the value of the associated volatile flags. The cost of maintaining this structure is a few pointer manipulations at procedure entry and exit.

There are two related problems that complicate our approach, one of which we have solved in a reasonable manner. Although we also have a solution to the second problem, it is not entirely satisfactory. The following code fragment illustrates the two problems:

```
x = y + f() + z;
```

Assume that y and z are both persistent. The compiler will produce code from this statement with the following form:

```
pin(_y); pin(_z); x = *_y + f() + *_z; unpin(_y); unpin(_z);
```

The first problem is that, within the call to f, we may attempt a pin operation that fails for lack of space. If the exception handler unpins either y or z, then depending on how the C compiler chooses to compile this statement, the program will either run normally, crash, or produce undetected errors. We can solve this problem by putting the call to f in a separate statement and assigning its result to a temporary variable:

```
_tmp001 = f();
pin(_y); pin(_z); x = *_y + _tmp001 + *_z; unpin(_y); unpin(_z);
```

The second problem is not so easily solved. Assume in this example that pinning y succeeds but that pinning z fails. If the exception handler unpins y in order to pin z, we will again have an error. The current solution is that the exception handler ignores the top stack frame in its search for items to unpin. While this approach avoids the error just described, it also implies that the handler will fail to consider items in the top frame that really could be unpinned safely. As a result, there may be situations in which the exception handler will give up in failure prematurely. Given that the search starts at the bottom of the stack, this event should be rare. Nevertheless, a cleaner solution would be somehow to recognize that, for a given region of the program, a *group* of items must be pinned simultaneously; the problem just described arises because we consider items individually.

6   Conclusion & Future Work

This paper has introduced Compiled Item Faulting, a new technique for managing object I/O in a persistent language. CIF is based on the identification of *items* and *pinning regions*. Simple dynamic checks are used within pinning regions to determine whether a storage layer call is actually needed for any given use of an item. Side effect analysis is used to decide which items should be unpinned because of an assignment or procedure call. The main contribution of CIF is that it presents a new framework for understanding I/O in a persistent language.

CIF as described in this paper has been fully implemented, and early indications are that it can significantly improve the performance of E programs. The initial implementation is lacking in several important respects, however. As we indicated, our "alias analysis" is crude (even though it does handle a number of common cases). More comprehensive analysis would allow CIF to be more accurate in its estimation of side effects, and would also expand the opportunities for coalescing. If we can deduce, for example, that pointers p and q point to the same object, then we could coalesce pinning regions for *p and *q. Currently, coalescing is based solely on syntactic form, and such a case results in separate pin operations for the two items.

Another area for improvement concerns the handling of arrays. The current implementation will coalesce pinning regions for individual array elements into a pinning region for the whole array, provided that the array's size is below the given threshold. As a result, performance suffers greatly when the array size crosses the threshold. A better solution for many applications would be to process the array in chunks. Such an extension would require induction variable analysis and loop restructuring.

7   Acknowledgments

I would like to thank Toby Lehman, Jim Stamos, and Bruce Lindsay, all of whom provided many helpful comments. Thanks especially to Jim whose careful scrutiny greatly improved the quality of this paper.

References

[Agra89] Agrawal, R., and Gehani, N., "ODE (Object Database and Environment): The Language and the Data Model," *Proc. ACM-SIGMOD Int'l. Conf. on Management of Data*, Portland, OR, June 1989.

[Alba85] Albano, A., Cardelli, L., and Orsini, R., "Galileo: A Strongly-Typed, Interactive Conceptual Language," *ACM Trans. on Database Systems*, 10(2), June 1985.

[Alle74] Allen, F.E., "Interprocedural Dataflow Analysis," *Information Processing 74*, North-Holland, Amsterdam, 1974.

[Atki83] Atkinson, M.P., Bailey, P.J., Cockshott, W.P., Chisholm, K.J., and Morrison, R., "An Approach To Persistent Programming," *Computer Journal*, 26(4), 1983.

[ASU86] Aho, A.V., Sethi, R., and Ullman, J., *Compilers: Principles, Techniques, and Tools*, Addison-Wesley, Reading, MA, 1986.

[Care86a] Carey, M.J., DeWitt, D.J., Richardson, J.E., and Shekita, E.J., "Object and File Management in the EXODUS Extensible Database System," *Proc. of the 12th Int'l VLDB Conference*, Kyoto, Japan, August 1986.

[Care86b] Carey, M., DeWitt, D., Frank, D., Graefe, G., Richardson, J., Shekita, E., and Muralikrishna, M., "The Architecture of The EXODUS Extensible DBMS," *Proc. of the Int'l. Workshop on Object-Oriented Database Systems*, Pacific Grove, CA, Sept 1986.

[Chai81] Chaitin, G.J., Auslander, A., Chandra, A.K., Cocke, J., Hopkins, M.E., and Markstein, P.W., "Register Allocation via Coloring," *Computer Languages*, v.6, 1981.

[Cock84] Cockshott, W.P., Atkinson, M.P., Chisholm, K.J., Bailey, P.J., and Morrison, R., "Persistent Object Management System," *Software—Practice and Experience*, vol. 14, 1984.

[Ford88] Ford, S., Joseph, J., Langworthy, D.E., Lively, D.F., Pathak, G., Perez, E.R., Peterson, R.W., Sparacin, D.M., Thatte, S., Wells, D.L., Agarwala, S., "Zeitgeist: Database Support for Object-Oriented Programming," *Proc. of 2nd Int'l Workshop on Object-Oriented Database Systems,* Bad Münster, West Germany, September 1988.

[Kern78] Kernighan, B.W., and Ritchie, D.M., *The C Programming Language,* Prentice-Hall, Englewood Cliffs, NJ, 1978.

[Laru88] Larus, J.R., and Hilfinger, P.N., "Detecting Conflicts Between Structure Accesses," *Proc. SIG-PLAN'88 Conf. on Programming Language Design and Implementation,* Atlanta, GA, 1988.

[Lisk77] Liskov, B., Snyder, A., Atkinson, R., and Schaffert, C., "Abstraction Mechanisms in CLU," *Communications of the ACM,* 20(8), August 1977.

[Maie87] Maier, D., and Stein, J., "Development and Implementation of an Object-Oriented DBMS," in *Research Directions in Object-Oriented Programming,* B. Shriver and P. Wegner, Eds., MIT Press, 1987.

[Maie87b] Maier, David, personal communication, November, 1987.

[Morr89] Morrison, R., Brown, A., Carrick, R., Connor, R., Dearle, A., and Atkinson, M.P., "The Napier Type System," *Proc. of the Workshop on Persistent Object Systems,* Newcastle, Australia, January 1989.

[Moss88] Moss, J.E.B., and Sinofsky, S., "Managing Persistent Data with Mneme: Issues and Application of a Reliable, Shared Object Interface," COINS Technical Report 88-30, University of Massachusetts—Amherst, April 1988.

[Pfei89] Pfeiffer, P., "Integrating Non-Interfering Versions of Programs in Languages with Heaps," Thesis Preliminary Proposal, Computer Sciences Department, University of Wisconsin—Madison, 1989.

[Rich87] Richardson, J.E., and Carey, M.J., "Programming Constructs for Database System Implementation in EXODUS," *Proc. ACM-SIGMOD Int'l. Conf. on Management of Data,* San Francisco, May 1987.

[Rich89a] Richardson, J.E., Carey, M.J., and Schuh, D.T., "The Design of the E Programming Language," Computer Sciences TR#824, University of Wisconsin—Madison, February 1989.

[Rich89b] Richardson, J.E., *E: A Persistent Systems Implementation Language,* Ph.D. Dissertation, University of Wisconsin—Madison, August 1989.

[Schm77] Schmidt, J.W., "Some High Level Language Constructs for Data of Type Relation," *ACM Trans. on Database Systems,* 2(3), 1977.

[Stro86] Stroustrup, Bjarne, *The C++ Programming Language,* Addison-Wesley, Reading, MA, 1986.

[Weih80] Weihl, W.E., "Interprocedural Dataflow Analysis in the Presence of Pointers, Procedure Variables, and Label Variables," *Proc. 7th ACM Symp. on Principles of Programming Languages,* 1980.

Towards Compile-Time Optimisations for Persistence[*]

Antony L. Hosking
hosking@cs.umass.edu

J. Eliot B. Moss
moss@cs.umass.edu

Department of Computer and Information Science
University of Massachusetts
Amherst, MA 01003

Abstract

We consider how a persistent programming language might offer performance competitive with that of non-persistent languages, at least on memory resident data. We are concerned with object-oriented languages, and with implementing persistence via *object faulting*, where the system detects uses of non-resident objects and fetches them on demand. We present some background on object faulting and means for implementing it, and describe a specific language we are developing, namely Persistent Modula-3. Then we explore approaches to optimising persistence aspects of Persistent Modula-3, and outline techniques under consideration in our compiler development effort.

1 Introduction

The Object Oriented Systems Group at the University of Massachusetts is engaged in research exploring the integration of programming languages with database technology. As a part of this work, we are involved in the development of *persistent programming languages*, as popularised by the PS-Algol effort [Atkinson *et al.*, 1981; Atkinson and Morrison, 1985].

We approach the problem of language-database integration from the object-oriented standpoint. Our particular approach to persistence is to integrate existing programming languages with our own persistent object store, Mneme [Moss and Sinofsky, 1988; Moss, 1989]. While there is some difference in functionality between Mneme and other object storage systems such as the Exodus storage manager [Carey *et al.*, 1986; Carey *et al.*, 1989] or Observer [Skarra *et al.*, 1987; Hornick and Zdonik, 1987], our integration techniques would extend to them.

We have chosen two object-oriented languages for integration with Mneme: Smalltalk [Goldberg and Robson, 1983] and Modula-3 [Cardelli *et al.*, 1989]. Our reasons for choosing these are as follows. First, they are relatively well-known. Smalltalk was the first object-oriented programming language to gain widespread recognition. Modula-3 is less widely known, but its ancestry is quite familiar, as it derives from the class of languages including Pascal [Jensen and Wirth, 1974], Modula-2 [Wirth, 1983], and Oberon [Wirth, 1988a; Wirth, 1988b]. Second, they represent quite different philosophies. In Smalltalk there is no static type checking. In fact, the Smalltalk class hierarchy provides only a very weak notion of type. Calls are bound at run time using a hierarchical method lookup mechanism, based on the class of the object on which the method is being invoked. If the lookup fails then a run-time error is signalled, indicating that the method is undefined for that class. On the other hand, while retaining dynamic binding of methods, Modula-3 does guarantee type-correctness of programs at compile time—the compiler will detect the invocation of methods that are undefined, or whose arguments are of the wrong type. By choosing two such different languages we hope to explore the generality of our techniques, and identify alternatives arising out of their differences.

When a program manipulates persistent data a decision must be made as to when that data should be fetched from stable storage into memory. One extreme is to require all persistent data to be made memory resident before the program begins manipulating any of it. In the case that a program accesses only a small fraction of the persistent data, such indiscriminate preloading is clearly undesirable.

Rather than preloading, we can dynamically check the residency of a persistent data item, fetching it if necessary. In this way the subset of all persistent data that is resident grows dynamically, as more and more data items are

---

[*]This project is supported by National Science Foundation Grants CCR-8658074 and DCR-8500332, and by Digital Equipment Corporation, GTE Laboratories, and the Eastman Kodak Company.

accessed by the program. This approach incurs a run-time overhead in that each access to a persistent data item requires an explicit residency check, resulting in its retrieval if it is non-resident. In the case where a persistent data item is always accessed by dereferencing some kind of *pointer* to it, this approach reduces to a technique that we call *object faulting*. A residency check is performed every time a persistent pointer is dereferenced, resulting in an *object fault* to retrieve the data item if it is non-resident. We can consider all such referenced data items (both persistent and volatile) as a kind of virtual heap. Object faulting does not preload the entire heap; rather, objects are faulted on demand.

Our design of Persistent Smalltalk makes object faulting the responsibility of the run-time system [Hosking *et al.*, 1990]. All references to non-resident objects are trapped by the Smalltalk virtual machine. Certain heuristics are used to restrict residency checks to just the send bytecodes and some primitives. This approach is purely dynamic in that no changes are made to the Smalltalk compiler or image. Our approach with Modula-3 is to have the *compiler* generate in-line code to perform the residency check, along with a call to the object fault handler if the check fails, wherever a persistent pointer is dereferenced. Note that in contrast with Smalltalk, this does not impose the burden of residency checks on the run-time system. Rather, the compiler statically determines where the checks will occur.

Of particular interest to us is that our persistent programming languages exhibit good *performance*. There are two aspects to the performance of a persistent program. We have already mentioned that persistence usually implies some sort of residency check to ensure data items are memory resident before their contents are accessed. We would like to minimise this overhead, so that in the case that all of its data is resident, a persistent program can approach the performance of its non-persistent counterpart. The second aspect of performance pertains to the *fetching* of non-resident data from stable storage. In this case, good performance is more difficult to define, but can be characterised as that which makes the best use of system resources. To sum up, there are two costs to persistence:

- the cost of residency checks, and

- the cost of fetching, storing, and managing non-resident data.

In this paper we focus on mitigating the cost of residency checks, through the application of what are typically considered to be compiler techniques. Addressing the second aspect of performance would seem to require techniques most often used in databases to cluster data for retrieval.

Our approach to improving performance is to devise and exploit compile-time optimisations that will eliminate or circumvent residency checks. With this emphasis on static techniques we concentrate on their realisation for Modula-3, which submits to stronger compile-time analysis than Smalltalk, and for which we must already modify a compiler to support persistence. This approach is complicated by the dynamic call binding that occurs with object methods in Modula-3—methods are bound to an object when it is created. Such late binding means that at any particular call site the actual code to execute cannot be statically determined. This prohibits such standard optimisations as inlining of method code.

The contributions of this paper are as follows. First, we have begun to frame the issues regarding the *performance* of persistent programming languages. Second, we offer several approaches to implementing persistence, and identify some potential performance problems with those approaches. Finally, we have begun to identify compile-time optimisations for bringing the performance of some aspects of persistent programming languages very close to the performance of their non-persistent counterparts.

The remainder of the paper is organized in the following way. We first review object faulting and some of the requirements it imposes, and then consider techniques for implementing object faulting. Following this background, we describe the Modula-3 programming language, the changes we are making to move from Modula-3 to Persistent Modula-3, and sketch some straightforward techniques for implementing Persistent Modula-3. Finally, we consider compile-time optimisations for improving the performance of persistence, using Persistent Modula-3 as a specific language for concreteness.

2   Requirements for Object Faulting

We have indicated that object faulting requires that there be a mechanism for checking the residency of an object. While we would wish that this check be as cheap as possible we assume that it does incur some marginal cost. That is, we do not assume any special hardware support, for example from paging hardware. Furthermore, so that residency checks may be machine independent we do not assume any particular hardware architecture.

Given that there is *some* mechanism for detecting the need for an object fault, we must have some way of handling the fault. We assume the existence of an underlying *object manager* that, given some unique *object identifier*, will return a pointer to the object in its buffers, retrieving it from the persistent object store if necessary. There is an issue here of format mismatch between objects as they are represented in the store and objects as they are represented in memory. This is especially significant when an object contains references to other objects. These references will typically be represented as object identifiers in the store, but may need to be converted to memory pointers when the object is made resident. This conversion process, known as *swizzling*, can be performed in two ways: *in-place* or by *copying*. In-place swizzling simply overwrites the object in the object manager's buffers with the converted version of the object. This requires that all objects in a buffer be *un*swizzled before the buffer is written back to disk. Unswizzling is complicated by the fact that some of the objects in the buffer may now have pointer references to volatile objects in the heap. These objects and all objects accessible from them must be made persistent.

Copy swizzling maintains a separate converted version of the object in the volatile part of the heap, corresponding to the unconverted version in the object manager's buffers. There is some cost to maintaining this correspondence since every update to the in-heap version of the object eventually results in a corresponding update to the buffer version, and may involve making some volatile objects persistent, as for in-place unswizzling.

The relative advantages of each scheme are obvious: in-place swizzling demands less memory, but may involve more work when unswizzling. Copy swizzling does have the added benefit that buffers may be removed more easily, since only modified objects must be unswizzled. Of more importance is the fact that some persistent object stores will not allow in-place swizzling since applications are denied access to objects in the store's buffers.

One aspect of buffer removal that we have not yet addressed is that any direct pointers to buffer objects from other parts of the heap must be located and updated to reflect the fact that the objects they refer to are no longer resident. Locating the pointers requires that a *remembered set* be maintained for each buffer, indicating all memory locations that contain pointers into the buffer. Whenever a pointer to an object in the buffer is stored in some memory location, we must check to see if the buffer's remembered set should be updated to reflect the store. Techniques such as this are employed by *generation scavenging* garbage collectors [Ungar, 1984]. Such garbage collectors have been shown to have superior performance for interactive systems such as Smalltalk [Ungar, 1987]. Given this performance reputation we assume that generation scavenging will be the garbage collector of choice, so that maintaining remembered sets for the buffers of the object manager will require little additional mechanism. One unfortunate drawback of this is that there will always be the overhead of performing store checks; they cannot be eliminated. However, the overall performance of generation scavenging for persistence is not known at this point in time. In systems such as Smalltalk remembered sets do not seem to grow very large. For persistence, remembered sets will probably be much larger (since it is highly likely that more data will be persistent than volatile). How larger remembered sets will affect the performance of generation scavenging remains to be seen.

3   Techniques for Fault Detection

In the previous sections we have identified the need for some mechanism to check the residency of an object, to detect when an object fault should occur. The object manager handles a fault by returning a direct memory pointer to the desired object, first retrieving it from the store if it is non-resident. Here we elaborate on how residency checks may be performed. Let us consider the virtual heap to be a *directed graph*. The *nodes* of the graph are the objects, and the *edges* of the graph are the references from one object to another. A computation traverses the object graph, which is only partially resident in memory. Traversing an edge from a resident object to a non-resident object causes an object fault, and the link is *snapped* to point to the resident object. It is important to note here that merely naming an object does not cause an object fault. Only when the *contents* of the object need to be accessed, and so the link to the object must be traversed, is it required that the object be made resident.

We need to be able to detect the traversal of a link from a resident object to a non-resident object. There are effectively just two ways of achieving this:

- *Mark the edges* of the graph that are links to non-resident objects, distinguishing them from links to resident objects (see Figure 1(a)).

- *Mark the nodes* of the graph to distinguish resident objects from non-resident objects (see Figure 2(a)).

Edge marking is relatively easy to implement by tagging pointers. Checking whether a pointer refers to a resident object or not is simply a matter of checking the tag. When a marked link is traversed, an object fault occurs and is

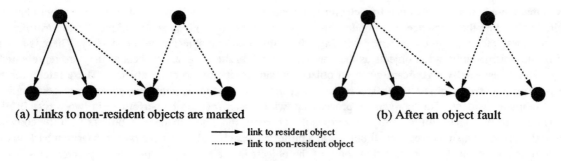

(a) Links to non-resident objects are marked   (b) After an object fault

⟶ link to resident object
┈┈➤ link to non-resident object

Figure 1: Edge Marking

handled by the object manager, which returns a pointer to the resident object. The marked link is then snapped to point to the resident object (see Figure 1(b)). Note that it is legal (though suboptimal) for a marked edge to refer to a resident object, but an unmarked edge may never refer to a non-resident object.

Node marking is complicated by the fact that the non-resident objects are just that, non-resident, and must (paradoxically) be in memory for them to be checked. Solving this problem is simple. Specially marked resident pseudo-objects called *fault blocks* stand in for non-resident objects. Every reference from a resident object to a non-resident object is actually a pointer to a fault block (see Figure 2(b)). When a link is traversed to a fault block a fault occurs and is handled by the object manager. "Snapping the link" in this case involves setting the fault block to point to the object in memory (see Figure 2(c)). Note that there is now a level of indirection via the fault block; this may be bypassed by also updating the traversed link to point to the object in memory (see Figure 2(d)).

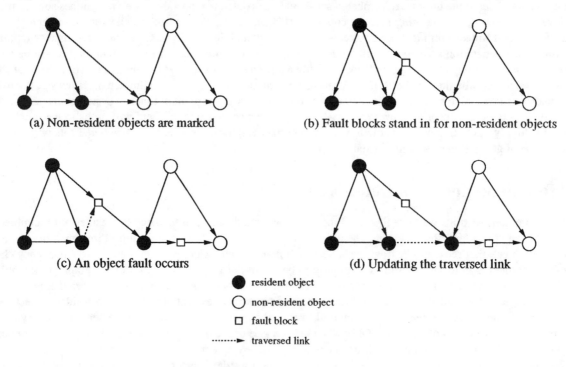

(a) Non-resident objects are marked   (b) Fault blocks stand in for non-resident objects

(c) An object fault occurs   (d) Updating the traversed link

● resident object
○ non-resident object
□ fault block
┈┈➤ traversed link

Figure 2: Node Marking

The preceding discussion assumes that we have an object identifier available to present to the object manager to handle a fault. In the edge marking scheme we store this identifier in the bits of the pointer that are not reserved for the tag. In the node marking scheme we store it in the fault block.

Each of these schemes has its particular advantages and disadvantages. In node marking, a particular fault block may be referenced by many resident objects. This means that the object manager need only be called once per fault block, to obtain a memory pointer to the corresponding object, when the first link to the fault block is traversed. The memory address is then cached in the fault block so that subsequent traversals of links to that fault block can pick it up from there, without additional calls to the object manager. However, there are overheads associated with fault blocks: storage and management for fault blocks; creation of fault blocks for all the objects referred to by a non-resident object when it is swizzled; and the extra level of indirection that fault blocks imply.

Edge marking has the advantage of eliminating the space consumed by fault blocks, and the level of indirection associated with them. Its disadvantage is that the only link that is "snapped" when an object fault occurs is the link that is traversed. All other links to the object are still marked as pointing to a non-resident object. This means that every traversal of a marked link will result in a call to the object manager to determine the object's address, regardless of whether the object is already resident or not.

Snapping the link has been mentioned as one way of reducing the overhead of object faulting. In the edge marking scheme this will usually be of little benefit, since the marked link that ends up getting snapped will probably be in a register or perhaps some other temporary location. The compiler may be of some help here if it can statically determine the source of the marked reference, making sure that it also gets updated when the link is snapped.[1]

4 Modula-3

Modula-3 consists primarily of Modula-2 with extensions for threads (lightweight processes in a single address space), exception handling, objects and methods, and garbage collection, while dispensing with variant records, and the ability to nest modules. Exception handling and threads do not raise any novel issues, so we will not discuss them further. Understanding the remaining extensions requires some understanding of the type system of Modula-3.

Modula-3 is *strongly-typed*: every expression has a unique type, and assignability and type compatibility are defined in terms of a single syntactically specified subtype relation, written <:. If T is a subtype of U, then every instance of type T is also an instance of type U. Any assignment satisfying the following rule is allowed: a T is assignable to a U if and only if T is a subtype of U. In addition there are specific assignment rules for ordinal types (integers, enumerations, and subranges), references (pointers), and arrays. We discuss only the specifics of reference types here.

A reference type may be *traced* or *untraced*. A traced reference (of type REF T) refers to storage (of type T) that is automatically reclaimed by the garbage collector whenever there are no longer any (traced) references to it. Untraced references (of type UNTRACED REF T) are just like Pascal pointers—the storage they refer to must be explicitly allocated and deallocated. The type REFANY contains all traced references, while ADDRESS contains all untraced references. The type NULL contains only the reference value NIL.

Object types are also reference types. An *object* is either NIL or a reference to a data record paired with a method suite, which is a record of procedures that will each accept the object as a first argument. Since they are references, objects may also be either traced or untraced. Every object type has a supertype, *inherits* the supertype's representation and implementation, and optionally may extend them by providing additional fields and methods, or overriding the methods it inherits with different (but type correct) implementations. When an object is created, one may supply specific methods for that individual object (again, they must be type correct), overriding the default implementations supplied by the object's type.

This scheme is designed so that it is (physically) reasonable to interpret an object as an instance of one of its supertypes. That is, a subtype is guaranteed to have all the fields and methods defined by its supertype, but possibly more, and it may override its supertype's method implementations with its own. In addition, an object's method values are not determined until the object is allocated, although the values cannot be changed after that.

An object type is specified by the following syntax:

```
T OBJECT fields METHODS methods END
```

This specifies an object subtype of T, with additional fields `fields` and additional or overriding methods `methods`. An object inherits its traced-ness from its supertype. There are two built-in object types, one traced and the other untraced, having no fields or methods, from which all object types are descended: ROOT and UNTRACED ROOT.[2]

We can summarise the subtype rules for references as follows:

---

[1] We may also apply certain heuristics to this problem. For details see [Hosking *et al.*, 1990].

[2] Shorthands OBJECT...END and UNTRACED OBJECT...END may be used for the forms ROOT OBJECT...END and UNTRACED ROOT OBJECT...END, object types inheriting from ROOT and UNTRACED ROOT, respectively.

```
NULL <: REF T <: REFANY
NULL <: UNTRACED REF T <: ADDRESS
NULL <: T OBJECT...END <: T, for some object type T
ROOT <: REFANY
UNTRACED ROOT <: ADDRESS
```

Finally, for garbage collection we must be able to find all references to traced data. This means that an *untraced* data item cannot contain any *traced* references. For this reason, records and arrays containing traced references are implicitly traced. These restrictions are summarised in the following table:

↗	untraced	traced
untraced	√	×
traced	√	√

That is, a traced data item may contain both traced and untraced references, but an untraced data item may contain only untraced references.

Let us briefly consider an implementation for objects. Because an object can be interpreted according to many different types, it must somehow carry a type code with it so that we can tell what its actual type is. Further, since the methods vary by object type, and possibly even by object, we need some way to find the methods when they are invoked. The expected implementation is for the object fields to be preceded by a pointer to the method suite. The method suite is simply a vector of addresses of procedures, preceded by the type code. Since the offset of a given method within the method suite is static, no run-time search is required to find the code to run on method invocation. Similarly, field offsets are statically known. This implementation approach is illustrated in Figure 3.

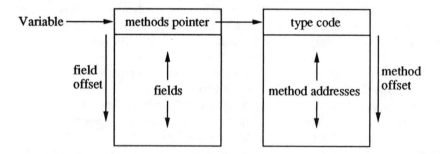

Figure 3: An implementation of Modula-3 objects

5   Persistent Modula-3

The previous section gave an introduction to the Modula-3 type system. In this section we extend that type system to incorporate persistence by adding a third class of reference types: *persistent* references, similar to the **db** types of the E database programming language [Richardson and Carey, 1987]. A persistent reference type is indicated by the keyword PERSISTENT, analogous to UNTRACED. A persistent reference indicates a specific object, but that object may or may not be resident in memory. In addition, we permit any top-level variable[3] to be qualified by the PERSISTENT keyword, since a program must have at least one persistent data item to start with, from which other persistent data can be reached. These may be thought of as implicit persistent references to known root objects in the persistent store.

Our new reference types have subtype rules analogous to traced reference types as follows:

```
NULL <: PERSISTENT REF T <: PERSISTENT REFANY
PERSISTENT ROOT <: PERSISTENT REFANY
```

Once again, an object inherits persistence from its supertype. A variable at top-level may be declared persistent using the PERSISTENT VAR construct just as VAR is used for non-persistent variables.

---

[3] A top-level variable is a variable declared in the outermost scope of a module.

Finally, analogous to traced data, anything reachable from a top-level persistent variable via persistent references will itself persist, so that we must be able to find all references to persistent data. Thus, an untraced data item may not contain persistent references. Whether a persistent data item may refer to non-persistent data is another question. At first glance this may seem to be a little strange, since the data referred to by the persistent data item will disappear when the program ceases execution, leaving dangling references. However, we can give such references special semantics, allowing them to be used to refer to volatile data while the program is running, but setting them to NIL when the persistent data item is written back to stable storage (or when it is loaded from stable storage). We augment the table from the previous section to summarise these rules:

↗	untraced	traced	persistent
untraced	√	×	×
traced	√	√	√
persistent	†	†	√

† ≡ special semantics

This design is admittedly non-orthogonal: orthogonality would require that any data item be able to contain persistent references and, vice versa, every persistent data item be able to contain references to volatile data, making them persist by transitivity. However, non-orthogonality *is* consistent with the traced/untraced distinction, and as with the overhead of garbage collection, allows programmers to indicate explicitly whether or not they accept the overhead of persistence. Furthermore, it makes it easier for us to perform experiments to evaluate the relative performance of using persistent references over ordinary references. Later on we could collapse the persistent and traced distinction, as is done in Smalltalk where all references are potential references to persistent data. Whether or not we do this will depend on performance—if persistence imposes little performance degradation then there is no need for the distinction.

6 Implementation

We have indicated the syntax and semantics of persistent types and variables for Modula-3. Now we turn to the straightforward implementation of these extensions, using the techniques of object faulting. For PERSISTENT REF types the simplest implementation is to perform a residency check every time a given reference is used. We may use either of the node or edge marking schemes. Node marking simply implies the use of fault blocks, marked with some tag bit to enable the check. The overhead of the extra indirection can be removed later by the scavenger: if it detects a reference to a fake object that has a real object attached to it, the reference is updated to point to the real object. The fault block's storage may eventually be reclaimed.

Edge marking is more of a problem, since we need to be able to tag persistent references, to enable the check. On byte-addressed architectures this can be achieved by ensuring that all persistent data is word-aligned, leaving a low-order bit free to be used as the tag. Alternatively, we might use the sign bit to distinguish memory pointers from persistent object identifiers. Both of these techniques make certain assumptions about machine architecture. In some cases tagging may simply be impossible.

We can implement field access for persistent OBJECT types similarly to PERSISTENT REF types. For method invocation, however, we can use the following technique to eliminate conditional code in the residency check. Given that we have a fault block standing in for the resident object, we can supply a fake method suite for the fault block. The fake method suite would contain only procedures that will fault in the real object. At fault time, when the fault block is updated to point to the real object, we would also update the fault block's fake method suite to forward calls to the real object. This technique could also be used for field access if we are prepared to turn field access into method invocation.

As for PERSISTENT VAR, we can treat every persistent variable as if it is an implicit PERSISTENT REF, and use the same implementation techniques.

We have not yet mentioned that the methods (code) of persistent objects must also persist. Clearly ordinary code will persist by virtue of the fact that it is in some program on disk. The question here is whether the code implementing the methods should reside in the persistent object store instead of in the program. Ideally, objects should carry their methods with them wherever they go, even if they are used in a different program from the one that created them. For this, method code must reside in the store. We then face the problem of *dynamically* linking method code with a running program. This does not appear to present any fundamental difficulties, but we have no specific design at this time.

7   Optimisations

The previous section indicated a straightforward implementation of persistence for Modula-3. In this section we look at improving the performance of persistent programs by using compile-time optimisation techniques to eliminate residency checks. Assuming that a resident object is never made non-resident (during a program's execution), then performing a residency check once for a given reference is as good as performing it many times. Further occurrences of the check are thus superfluous and may be eliminated. To eliminate checks we can apply the traditional static analysis techniques used by compilers. We first discuss optimisations that may be enabled by both local (basic block) and global (intra-procedural) analysis, to eliminate redundant residency checks within a procedure. Then we consider less traditional optimisations, requiring inter-procedural analysis, that make use of co-residency properties of persistent data items to amalgamate their residency checks into just one check. Two data items are said to be *co-resident* if, whenever one of them is resident, then so is the other.

Local optimisations are those that may be performed by examining only the statements within a basic block (a section of straight-line code having just one entry point and one exit point). A typical local optimisation is common subexpression elimination. We can use a similar approach to eliminate redundant residency checks within a basic block. If we consider a residency check as evaluating a boolean expression, then the first residency check performed for a reference makes the expression true. All later checks can be replaced by the value TRUE.

This approach will extend to global (intra-procedural) analysis. Furthermore, global analysis enables other optimisations such as dead code elimination and code motion. Given that we can reduce some residency checks to TRUE, then the fault handling code (which is executed when the check evaluates to FALSE), becomes dead and may be eliminated. Also, code motion can be used to move a loop invariant residency check out of a loop. Code hoisting can be used to replace two residency checks that occur in different paths of the program by just one. Techniques similar to these were shown to be quite effective in E [Richardson, 1989].

Procedure inlining replaces a full call to a procedure with the code that implements that procedure. This allows the called code to be optimised in the context of the call site, integrating its analysis with that of the calling procedure. However, inlining is more difficult for methods, because dynamic binding implies that in general we cannot know which specific method will be invoked. It is clear that allowing objects to override their type's default methods at creation time poses some difficulty. Rather than eliminating the feature from the language, we could make use of *pragmas* inserted by the programmer in an object type declaration indicating that a particular method will never be overridden by an individual object instance of that type. Let us consider inlining of a method call in three particular cases. In the first, suppose that data-flow analysis reveals the exact type of the object on which the method is being invoked, and that we can determine (either by pragma or analysis) that the object does not override the type's default implementation for that method. Then we can inline the default code. In the second, we assume that the object's exact type is known, but that it may override the method. We can still inline the default code, preceding it with a check of the object's method suite to make sure that the method's slot contains the default method), and generate code to do a full call in the failure case. In the third case we make no assumptions, but replace the call with conditional code, branching on the type of the object, and inline the default methods as for the second case. This technique is known as *message splitting* and has been applied in other object-oriented languages such as SELF [Chambers and Ungar, 1989; Chambers and Ungar, 1990].

If we are prepared to do some inter-procedural analysis, we can use *customised compilation* to tailor the compilation of a procedure to the characteristics of a particular call site. Just as inlining allows the compiler to optimise a procedure in the context of a particular call site, so does customised compilation, but without the additional space cost that inlining imposes, since the customised version is out of line. The customised compiled procedure can only be used at call sites having appropriate characteristics. Again, this has been used previously in SELF and also in Trellis[4]/Owl [Schaffert *et al.*, 1986]. Applying customised compilation to persistence, we can compile customised versions of procedures based on assumptions about the residency of their arguments. A particular customised version can then be used at any call site where its residency requirements are satisfied.

All of these techniques make use of information gleaned from the *code* at compile-time. Going back to our analogy of the virtual heap as a directed graph, the code establishes possible *traversals* of the graph. We can also derive

---

[4]Trellis is a trademark of Digital Equipment Corporation.

information from the *types* as to the potential *structure* of the graph. If we have co-residency information available attached to the types, then we can *amalgamate* the retrieval of data items that are indicated as being co-resident, reducing the number of residency checks needed. We can best explain this with an example. Consider the following persistent reference type declaration:

```
TYPE
  PRecord = PERSISTENT REF RECORD
    field1 : PERSISTENT REF foo;
    field2 : PERSISTENT REF bar;
  END;
```

Suppose that we know that a `PRecord` should be co-resident with the `foo` object named by `field1`. Then, whenever we fault a `PRecord` data item we simultaneously fault the `foo` item, and ensure that the `PRecord` points directly to the `foo` item. Therefore, the compiler does not need to generate a residency check for uses of `field1` components of a `PRecord`.

One way to represent co-residency information is via annotations to the *type graph*. The nodes of this graph are the types of the program, and the edges indicate uses of one type in defining another. In the above example, there would be nodes for the types `PRecord`, `foo`, and `bar`, and edges from `PRecord` to `foo` and `PRecord` to `bar`. To indicate co-residency we mark edges of the type graph. For example, we could mark the edge from `PRecord` to `foo`, to indicate the co-residency assumption discussed above. In order to provide more precise information we can distinguish edges based on the name of the record component, etc., to which they correspond.

Of course, there is the question of where the co-residency information comes from. One option is to allow programmers to annotate their type declarations with pragmas indicating desired co-residency properties. More preferable would be the automatic derivation of these properties. Static analysis of a procedure can determine some information about desirable co-residency properties for types used in the procedure. For example, intra-procedural analysis can say whether a path through the type graph will *definitely* be traversed, *may* be traversed, or is *never* traversed, when executing the procedure. It is not obvious how to combine analyses of individual procedures to annotate a global type graph with co-residency assumptions. Even so, a global type graph might be desirable, since it would allow the same assumptions to be made throughout the program. This would ensure that optimisations are applied consistently. Further, the global type graph is a relatively simple data structure for the run-time system to use in enforcing co-residency assumptions when handling object faults.

The global type graph is not without problems, though, since each assumption represents a compromise between procedures that follow long paths through the type graph and procedures that follow short ones. If a procedure follows shorter paths, then the global type graph assumptions may cause unnecessary fetches. If a procedure follows longer paths, then it will need to perform more residency checks.

Another problem with the global type graph approach is that a single object may have an unbounded number of objects required to be co-resident with it. For example, large, homogeneous data items such as arrays have many references to the same type, causing a combinatorial explosion because of the potentially high branching factor. Recursively defined types also pose difficulties since they create cycles in the type graph, and thus introduce co-residency paths of unbounded length. For example, consider the singly-linked list type:

```
TYPE
  SLList = PERSISTENT REF RECORD
    next : PERSISTENT REF SLList;
    ...
  END;
```

If the `next` field is marked for co-residency, then fetching any item in the list will fetch all subsequent items.

The shortcomings of the single global type graph may be overcome by putting each use of a type in context. For example, we might specialise the annotation on a type for each variable of the type. We can view this as annotating the variables instead of the types. Each variable has attached to it a subgraph of the full type graph; the root of the subgraph is the variable's type. This subgraph indicates what co-residency assumptions can be made about data reachable from the variable.

So far we have only considered the use of statically obtained co-residency information. There is also the possibility of including statistics obtained by dynamic profiling. If the types define the possible structure of the virtual heap, and the programs define the potential traversals of that structure, then profiling can approximate the probability that a particular traversal will occur. This information can be fed back into the compiler so that more intelligent co-residency decisions can be made based on actual usage patterns. This style of optimisation is similar to that used in some database systems for tuning indexing, clustering, etc.

We have briefly sketched techniques to determine when a number of potential faults can be merged together, so that they each share just one residency check. An interesting further use of co-residency characteristics would be to communicate them to the object manager for *clustering* purposes. Clustering places objects physically close together on disk, so that they may be retrieved with just one disk access. If data items that are co-resident can be clustered, then retrieving those items will be performed with fewer disk accesses. This seems to indicate the potential for even further gains, since it allows us to address the other aspect of performance with persistence: fetching, storing, and managing non-resident data. Even more interesting is the potential to turn things around. Whereas we have indicated that co-residency information may be used for clustering, we could have clustering information drive the co-residency analysis phase of the compiler. Co-residency analysis would still serve as input for *initial* data clustering, but thereafter decisions could be made using profiles of *entire suites* of programs. These clustering decisions could then be used in the compiler's co-residency analysis.

8   Conclusions

We have identified some of the issues regarding the performance of persistent programming languages, and introduced several approaches to implementing persistence. We have discussed how these approaches may be used in implementing Persistent Modula-3, through modification of the compiler. Finally, we have indicated possibilities for improvement of the performance of persistent programs through compile-time optimisations. Of particular interest is the role that co-residency analysis might play in eliminating residency checks and in obtaining clustering criteria for the underlying object store.

Acknowledgements

The Modula-3 implementation group at the University of Massachusetts consists of Rick Hudson and Amer Diwan, in addition to the authors. This group's regular design meetings generated many of the ideas for incorporating persistence in Modula-3.

References

[Atkinson and Morrison, 1985] Malcolm P. Atkinson and Ronald Morrison. Procedures as persistent data objects. *ACM Trans. Program. Lang. Syst. 7*, 4 (Oct. 1985), 539–559.

[Atkinson *et al.*, 1981] M. P. Atkinson, K. J. Chisolm, and W. P. Cockshott. PS-Algol: an Algol with a persistent heap. *ACM SIGPLAN Notices 17*, 7 (July 1981).

[Cardelli *et al.*, 1989] Luca Cardelli, James Donahue, Lucille Glassman, Mick Jordan, Bill Kalsow, and Greg Nelson. Modula-3 report (revised). Tech. Rep. DEC SRC 52, DEC Systems Research Center/Olivetti Research Center, Palo Alto/Menlo Park, CA, Nov. 1989.

[Carey *et al.*, 1986] M. J. Carey, D. J. DeWitt, J. E. Richardson, and E. J. Shekita. Object and file management in the EXODUS extensible database system. In *Proceedings of the Twelfth International Conference on Very Large Databases* (Kyoto, Japan, Sept. 1986), ACM, pp. 91–100.

[Carey *et al.*, 1989] Michael J. Carey, David J. DeWitt, Joel E. Richardson, and Eugene J. Shekita. Storage management for objects in EXODUS. In *Object-Oriented Concepts, Databases, and Applications*, Won Kim and Lochovsky Frederick H, Eds., Frontier Series. Addison-Wesley, ACM Press, New York, NY, 1989, ch. 14, pp. 341–369.

[Chambers and Ungar, 1989] Craig Chambers and David Ungar. Customization: Optimizing compiler technology for SELF, a dynamically-typed object-oriented programming language. In *Proceedings of the SIGPLAN '89*

Conference on Programming Language Design and Implementation (Portland, OR, June 1989), vol. 24, no. 7 of *ACM SIGPLAN Notices*, ACM, pp. 146–160.

[Chambers and Ungar, 1990] Craig Chambers and David Ungar. Iterative type analysis and extended message splitting: Optimizing dynamically-typed object-oriented programs. In *Proceedings of the SIGPLAN '90 Conference on Programming Language Design and Implementation* (White Plains, NY, June 1990), vol. 25, no. 6 of *ACM SIGPLAN Notices*, ACM, pp. 150–164.

[Goldberg and Robson, 1983] Adele Goldberg and David Robson. *Smalltalk-80: The Language and its Implementation*. Addison-Wesley, 1983.

[Hornick and Zdonik, 1987] Mark F. Hornick and Stanley B. Zdonik. A shared, segmented memory system for an object-oriented database. *ACM Trans. Office Inf. Syst. 5*, 1 (Jan. 1987), 70–95.

[Hosking *et al.*, 1990] Antony L. Hosking, J. Eliot B. Moss, and Cynthia Bliss. Design of an object faulting persistent Smalltalk. COINS Technical Report 90-45, Department of Computer and Information Science, University of Massachusetts, Amherst, MA, May 1990.

[Jensen and Wirth, 1974] Kathleen Jensen and Niklaus Wirth. *Pascal User Manual and Report*, second ed. Springer-Verlag, 1974.

[Moss and Sinofsky, 1988] J. Eliot B. Moss and Steven Sinofsky. Managing persistent data with Mneme: Designing a reliable, shared object interface. In *Advances in Object-Oriented Database Systems* (Sept. 1988), vol. 334 of *Lecture Notes in Computer Science*, Springer-Verlag, pp. 298–316.

[Moss, 1989] J. Eliot B. Moss. The Mneme persistent object store. COINS Technical Report 89-107, Department of Computer and Information Science, University of Massachusetts, Amherst, MA, Oct. 1989. Submitted for publication as "Design of the Mneme Persistent Object Store".

[Richardson and Carey, 1987] Joel E. Richardson and Michael J. Carey. Programming constructs for database system implementations in EXODUS. In *Proceedings of the ACM SIGMOD International Conference on Management of Data* (San Francisco, CA, May 1987), vol. 16, no. 3 of *ACM SIGMOD Record*, ACM, pp. 208–219.

[Richardson, 1989] Joel Edward Richardson. *E: A Persistent Systems Implementation Language*. PhD thesis, Computer Sciences Department, University of Wisconsin, Madison, WI, Aug. 1989. Available as Computer Sciences Technical Report #868.

[Schaffert *et al.*, 1986] Craig Schaffert, Topher Cooper, Bruce Bullis, Mike Kilian, and Carrie Wilpolt. An introduction to Trellis/Owl. In *Proceedings of the Conference on Object-Oriented Programming Systems, Languages, and Applications* (Portland, OR, Sept. 1986), vol. 21, no. 11 of *ACM SIGPLAN Notices*, ACM, pp. 9–16.

[Skarra *et al.*, 1987] Andrea Skarra, Stanley B. Zdonik, and Stephen P. Reiss. An object server for an object oriented database system. In *Proceedings of International Workshop on Object-Oriented Database Systems* (Pacific Grove, CA, Sept. 1987), ACM, pp. 196–204.

[Ungar, 1984] David Ungar. Generation scavenging: A non-disruptive high performance storage reclamation algorithm. In *Proceedings of the ACM SIGSOFT/SIGPLAN Software Engineering Symposium on Practical Software Development Environments* (Pittsburgh, PA, Apr. 1984), ACM SIGPLAN Notices, ACM, pp. 157–167.

[Ungar, 1987] David Michael Ungar. *The Design and Evaluation of a High Performance Smalltalk System*. ACM Distinguished Dissertations. The MIT Press, Cambridge, MA, 1987. Ph.D. Dissertation, University of California at Berkeley, February 1986.

[Wirth, 1983] Niklaus Wirth. *Programming in Modula-2*, second, corrected ed. Springer-Verlag, 1983.

[Wirth, 1988a] Niklaus Wirth. From Modula to Oberon. *Software: Practice and Experience 18*, 7 (July 1988), 661–670.

[Wirth, 1988b] Niklaus Wirth. The programming language Oberon. *Software: Practice and Experience 18*, 7 (July 1988), 671–690.

Part II
Language Mechanisms

Chair: Alan Dearle

This session on persistent languages contains four very different papers on persistent programming languages. The first of these was presented by Suad Alagić from Yugoslavia, the second by Florian Mattes from Germany, the third by Dave McNally (who played the bagpipes incessantly at the conference) from Scotland and the last by Peri Tarr from The United States of America.

The paper presented by Suad Alagić discussed the need for meta-level constructs in a language. Suad is investigating the extent to which it is possible to reconcile the differences between the relational and object-oriented programming styles. Examining the limitations of these classical data models has lead him to explore the meta-level and indeed the meta-meta level!

The work is based on earlier work on the MODULEX system. This system provides large grain persistent objects (relations), abstract data types and polymorphism. The paper identifies the need to be able to manipulate the meta-level data in much the same way as the programmer can manipulate persistent data. The system described supports a meta-object hierarchy similar to the object hierarchy found in many object-oriented systems. Furthermore, Alagić argues that the separation of specification from implementation is as important at the meta-level as it is at the data level.

The paper by Joachim Schmidt and Florian Matthes discusses the language DBPL, which is based on Modula-2, and is the successor to Schmidt's last language Pascal/R. Schmidt states that DBPL aims to integrate two different technologies, namely strong type systems for programming languages and relational database modelling. The language supports bulk data management (through relations), sharing, recovery and concurrency control based on serialisability. Persistence in DBPL is realised through database modules.

The paper deals with the issue of naming and name space management in DBPL. The authors develop two different naming schemes, namely key-based naming and associative naming. Unlike many persistent and object-oriented programming languages, DBPL has no object identity on which to base a naming scheme. The naming scheme described in this paper therefore represents a novel approach to naming in persistent systems.

Dave McNally's paper addresses the question *What can persistence offer the applicative programming community?*. The answer would appear to be much. McNally points out that traditional function programming language environments provide no support for long term data, and any objects which are re-used must be re-evaluated during each program execution.

The STAPLE system described in this paper, provides orthogonal persistence whilst preserving static typechecking, static binding and referential transparency. The underlying support system preserves evaluated data between program instantiations and indeed between interactive sessions. McNally claims a total performance degradation on individual operations of about 10overall performance of one functional system he tested increased by an order of magnitude. This can be explained by the removal of the requirement to re-evaluate values required by the computation.

The last paper in the session was presented by Peri Tarr. This paper discusses the PGRAPHITE system. PGRAPHITE was designed and constructed as part of the Arcadia project. This project aims to support software development environments. In such environments, the construction of large persistent directed graphs (such as abstract syntax trees) is commonplace.

The persistence model used by PGRAPHITE is that of persistence by reachability. One problem encountered by the experimenters using this model was that often too much data becomes persistent. Peri presented a novel scheme which is designed to allow the programmer control over how much data becomes persistent. This is achieved through a construct called a relationship. Relationships provide a weak binding between data items, across which the reachability based persistence mechanism cannot follow. This provides a natural way of allowing the programmer to define the extent of persistent data without compromising orthogonality.

The discussion at the end of the session was lively and mostly revolved around two topics, namely evolution in functional systems and what semantics relations should have.

The first half of the discussion focused on the paper by McNally. Some people wondered how an applicative system could evolve. McNally responded by pointing out that applicative systems were, by definition, referentially transparent and therefore the only kind of evolution possible was evolution through recompilation. This statement abruptly concluded the debate!

The system described in the paper by Matthes and Schmidt features copy semantics for relations, that is it is impossible to create an explicit reference to an object of type relation. This kind of semantics is alien to many of the attendees of the conference who are from the object-oriented community. This difference in mind-set catalysed a far reaching but inconclusive debate on the correct semantics for a relation type in a programming language. Central to the debate was the need for aliases to data and the need to be able to evolve data. The debate continued after the session had ended with all the participants moving out onto the hotel balcony to take in the fine Cape Cod sunshine and enjoy a cup of coffee.

Persistent Metaobjects

Suad Alagić
Department of Computer Science and Informatics
Faculty of Electrical Engineering
University of Sarajevo
71000 Sarajevo - Lukavica, Yugoslavia
fax +38 71 525182

Abstract

Specification and representation of persistent metaobjects in a multiparadigm environment that supports both the object- oriented and the relational models are investigated. The advantages of the proposed approach to persistent metaobjects are based on the variable level of exposure of metaobjects to their users, encapsulation and persistence of actions, separation of specification and representation abstractions and abstract, procedural and functional types of attributes of such objects. Hierarchies of persistent objects and persistent metaobjects and their pragmatic relevance are discussed.

1. Introduction

Large scale persistent objects are managed through persistent objects that provide a conceptual, user-oriented view of persistent objects and enable a mapping of that conceptual view to the level of persistent objects. We show that conceptual modelling of such metaobjects demonstrates clearly that classical data models are not sufficient for that purpose. Metaobjects represent a perfect proof of all the limitations of the classical approaches to data models.

Persistent metaobjects

Persistent objects

Typical persistent objects in the object-oriented approach are large, persistent sets of data values together with actions applicable to those values. Persistence of actions is a fundamental difference of the object-oriented approach in comparison with the relational and other classical database technologies. Typical persistent meta-objects are persistent sets of specifications of objects, their attributes, types, actions, integrity constraints, images etc.

The limitations of the classical data models become obvious when considering such metaobjects as specifications of actions and integrity constraints. They can hardly be adequately modelled by flat tables. Apart from signatures for actions the essential part of their specification is their semantics expressed by, for instance, pre and post conditions.

At the meta level the relevance of some features of the object-oriented approach can be nicely investigated. For example, two levels of abstraction, specification and representation are important for metaobjects. While their conceptual, action-oriented view is exposed to the users their actual representation should be separated from the users' view. That representation may in fact be relational. The required object-oriented specification language should be expressive enough in order to specify both the users' view and its representation. A particular sort of flexibility is variable level of exposure of a metaobject to its users. If the relational representation is suitable it may be exposed to the users. If it is not it may be partly or completely hidden. A strict object-oriented case is obtained when a metaobject is seen from the users through a collection of actions applicable to it.

Research supported by SIZ nauke Bosne i Hercegovine under grant Information Technologies (Productica).

This particular aspect is related to the problem of the query language. Queries on metaobjects are particularly important. They refer to properties of attributes, actions and integrity constraints of persistent objects. Since specifications of actions and integrity constraints are metadata and are not standard (such as those that can be suitably represented by flat tables) that poses special problems and requirements on the query language which now must handle properly not only standard properties of persistent objects but also such non-standard objects as their associated actions and integrity constraints. The relational query language on metaobjects is suitable only in a particular case of those metaobjects whose relational representation is natural and may be exposed to the users to operate upon it by relational primitives. Examples of such metaobjects are specifications of attributes, images etc.

The paper investigates the approach to persistent metaobjects outlined above within a specific multiparadigm environment (MODULEX, Alagic (1988)) that supports both the object-oriented and the relational approaches to large scale persistent objects as particular cases. Specific motivation for these considerations come from the design problems related to the object-oriented database catalog and its higher-level conceptual (user-oriented) view which represents an object-oriented data dictionary. The associated problems are those related to the type system of the MODULEX system, the polymorphism problems and static type checking facilities.

The MODULEX environment has the following fundamental features:

(i)   Large scale persistent objects.
(ii)   Encapsulation of object attributes together with the associated actions.
(iii) Information hiding, i.e. separation of two levels of abstraction, object specification and its representation.
(iv)   Control of the level of exposure of an object and its representation to the users.
(v)   Identifiers of persistent objects and their system-oriented management.
(vi)   Complex persistent objects particularly those modelled via a collection of standard conceptual-level abstractions.
(vii) Abstract data types and object types represented in terms of modules.
(viii) Object type hierarchies and inheritance via extended record types like in (Wirth (1988)) and modules.
(ix)   Polymorphic facilities related to (viii), but also based on identifiers of persistent objects, opaque types and properties of modules.
(xi)   Extensibility of the environment based on the module concept.
(xii) Low-levels of the architecture supporting large scale persistent sets, images (indices) upon them and streams.
(xiii) Concurrency control, transactions and recovery.
(xiv) High-level specification, query and transaction language and a database programming language designed in a unified environment and its type system.

2. Specification of persistent metaobjects

A persistent object type is an instance of the generic metaobject type (which is also persistent) called Object. Conceptual modelling of the metaobject type Object involves problems typical for non-standard, complex objects. The design decisions in that process have implications on the suitability of the model for the users as well as for the underlying system support. Because of that separation of specification and implementation (representation) levels of abstraction is of fundamental importance since only the specification abstraction should be revealed to the users.

Our approach (Alagic (1988), Alagic et al. (1989)) offers a particular type of flexibility for the designer of any object, and thus to the designer of metaobjects as well. It is up to the designer of a metaobject to decide about the level of exposure of that object to its users. The level of exposure of an object may vary from the strict action-oriented case (where an object is seen only through a collection of actions applicable to it) to the relational case where a metaobject is represented as a relation so that all the relational primitives (queries in particular) may be applied to it. We present an intermediate level of exposure first in which the record structure representing instances of the metaobject Object is exposed together with a predefined collection of actions (rather than arbitrary insertions, deletions and updates) applicable to this generic metaobject.

The complex metaobject Object has an associated set of attributes of the persistent objects as well as sets of actions applicable to those objects under specified integrity constraints. In order to simplify the presentation we will associate those constraints (in the form of pre and post conditions) with actions, while a set of attributes and a set of actions applicable to instances of a persistent object type are represented via opaque types (Wirth (1983)) in the definition module of the generic metaobject type Object.

```
DEFINITION MODULE Object;

FROM Attribute IMPORT AttributeId;
FROM Action IMPORT ActionId;

TYPE ObjectId; SetOfAttributes; SetOfActions;

    ObjectType = RECORD name:        STRING[30];
                        cardinality: CARDINAL;
                        attributes:  SetOfAttributes;
                        actions:     SetOfActions
             END;

PROCEDURE GetObject(VAR object: ObjectType);
PROCEDURE DisplayObject(object: ObjectType);
PROCEDURE ObjectExists(object: ObjectType): ObjectId;
PROCEDURE SelectObject(name: STRING): ObjectId;

PROCEDURE CreateObject(object: ObjectType): ObjectId;
PROCEDURE DropObject(o: ObjectId);
PROCEDURE UpdateCardinality(o: ObjectId;
                            increment: INTEGER);
PROCEDURE AddAttribute(o: ObjectId;
                    a: AttributeId);
 PROCEDURE DropAttribute(o: ObjectId;
                      a: AttributeId);
PROCEDURE AddAction(o: ObjectId;
                a: ActionId);
PROCEDURE DropAction(o: ObjectId;
                a: ActionId);
....

END Object.
```

A higher and very typical level of exposure of a metaobject is obtained when the actual set of meta instances is exposed. That set is hidden in the implementation part of the above definition module. Consider now putting the following declaration in the definition part:

```
TYPE ObjectSetType = ENTITY SET OF ObjectType;
VAR  ObjectSet : ObjectSetType;
```

The implication is that the relational primitives are exposed as well. Of course, the above example is a relation with abstract (in fact opaque) types of attributes. An example of a client performing relational-like queries is given below:

```
MODULE DisplayLargeObjects;

FROM Object IMPORT ObjectType, ObjectSet, DisplayObject;
FROM InOut  IMPORT WriteString, ReadCard;

VAR o: ObjectType; size: CARDINAL;

BEGIN WriteString("object size =");
    ReadCard(size);
    FOREACH o IN ObjectSet
    WHERE  o.cardinality  > = size
    DO      DisplayObject(o)
    END
END DisplayLargeObjects.
```

If we apply the object-oriented paradigm to metaobjects then other types of metaobjects would be derived from them by specialization. For example, an image may be modelled as a subobject of Object which inherits all the attributes of that metaobject as well as the applicable actions. In MODULEX this situation is captured by extended record types as in (Wirth (1988)) and by the associated subtype polymorphism which permits an instance of the extended record type to appear at a place where an instance of the generic (base) type is expected. A similar type of flexibility applies to the object identifiers of a base type and its extended type. The underlying operation is projection. In spite of the limitations of this type of inheritance it has an important advantage: no dynamic binding is necessary.

```
DEFINITION MODULE Image;

FROM Object IMPORT ObjectType, ObjectId;

TYPE ImageId = IDENTIFIER OF ImageType;
    ImageType = SUBTYPE OF ObjectType
                    RECORD unique:    BOOLEAN;
                               clustering: BOOLEAN
                    END;
    ...

PROCEDURE CreateImage(o: ObjectId;
                             image: ImageType): ImageId;
PROCEDURE DropImage(i: ImageId);

    ...

END Image.
```

3. Implementation of persistent metaobjects

In order to illustrate the representation level we present the implementation module corresponding to the given definition module of the metaobject Object hidden from all other users of that metaobject other than its creator (designer). The implementation module contains a relational- like decomposition of the complex Object structure. However, object-oriented identifiers, rather than user-oriented keys are used for linking inter-related components. This level also contains complete decompositions of actions whose signatures appear in the definition module Object. As an illustration, such decomposition is presented for the action CreateObject. This action, as well as the other ones, operates on the representation level. The difference in the level of detail in comparison with the definition module is obvious in spite of the fact that the latter was not designed in a particularly abstract form.

```
IMPLEMENTATION MODULE Object;

FROM Action IMPORT ActionType, ActionSetType,
                   ActionSet, ActionId, ActionExists;

FROM Attribute IMPORT AttributeType, AttributeSetType,
                   AttributeSet, AttributeId, AttributeExists;

TYPE ObjectId = IDENTIFIER OF ObjectTuple;

  SetOfAttributes = AttributeSetType;
  SetOfActions = ActionSetType;

  ObjectTuple = RECORD name:      STRING[30];
                       cardinality: CARDINAL
               END;

  ObjectSetType = ENTITY SET OF ObjectTuple;
  ObjectAction  = RECORD object: ObjectId;
                         action: ActionId
              END;
  ObjectAttribute = RECORD object: ObjectId;
                           attribute: AttributeId
              END;
  ObjectActionSetType = ENTITY SET OF ObjectAction;
  ObjectAttributeSetType = ENTITY SET OF ObjectAttribute;

VAR ObjectSet: ObjectSetType;
  ObjectActionSet: ObjectActionSetType;
  ObjectAttributeSet: ObjectAttributeSetType;

PROCEDURE CreateObject(object: ObjectType): ObjectId;

VAR o: ObjectTuple; OID: ObjectId;
  a: ActionType; b: AttributeType;
  x: ObjectAction; y: ObjectAttribute;

BEGIN o.name := object.name;
  o.cardinality := object.cardinality;
  OID := NewId(o,ObjectSet);
  x.object := OID;

  FOREACH a IN object.actions
  DO x.action := ActionExists(a);
    IF x.action := NIL
    THEN x.action := NewId(a,ActionSet)
    END;
    Insert(x,ObjectActionSet)
  END;
```

```
        y.object := OID;
        FOREACH b IN object.attributes
        DO y.attribute := AttributeExists(b);
          IF y.attribute = NIL
          THEN y.attribute = NewId(b, AttributeSet)
          END;
          Insert(y,ObjectAttributeSet)
        END;
        RETURN(OID)
   END CreateObject;


   ...


   END Object.
```

4. Actions as persistent metaobjects

A fundamental difference between the object-oriented and the classical data models (relational in particular) is persistence of actions. Because of that the meta-level reflects that difference. A number of subtle problems related to the environments of these actions are discussed in (Connor et al. (1990)). We present a simplified view of our approach to the representation of actions at the meta level which is similar to the approach in the previous section. It is based on abstract (in fact opaque) set-oriented types of attributes for parameters, procedural type of attribute for expressing the actual code for the action and functional types of attributes for the associated pre and post conditions.

```
   DEFINITION MODULE Action;

   FROM Object IMPORT ObjectId;
   FROM Parameter IMPORT ParameterId;

   TYPE SetOfParameters;
       Assertion: PROCEDURE(SetOfParameters): BOOLEAN;

       ActionId = IDENTIFIER OF ActionType;
       ActionType = RECORD name:        STRING[30];
                           code:         PROCEDURE;
                           parameters:   SetOfParameters;
                           preCondition: Assertion;
                           postCondition: Assertion
                 END;
     ...


   PROCEDURE CreateAction(action: ActionType): ActionId;
   PROCEDURE DropAction(a: ActionId);
   PROCEDURE ActionExists(action: ActionType): ActionId;
   PROCEDURE GetObject(a: ActionId): ObjectId;
   PROCEDURE DisplayAction(a: ActionId);

   PROCEDURE AddParameter(a: ActionId;
                               p: ParameterId);
   PROCEDURE DropParameter(a: ActionId;
                               p: ParameterId);
```

```
PROCEDURE ChangePreCondition(a: ActionId;
                                    p: Assertion);
PROCEDURE ChangePostCondition(a: ActionId;
                                    p: Assertion);
PROCEDURE ChangeCode(a: ActionId;
                            c: PROCEDURE);
PROCEDURE ChangeName(a: ActionId;
                            NewName: STRING);

    ...

END Action.
```

A related object hierarchy is introduced as an illustration in which parameters inherit all the properties and actions of attributes. Of course, other ways of modelling this aspect are possible and the presented one is merely an illustration.

```
DEFINITION MODULE Attribute;

FROM Type IMPORT TypeId;

TYPE AttributeId = IDENTIFIER OF AttributeType;
    AttributeType = RECORD name: STRING[30];
                            atype: TypeId
                END;
    ...

END Attribute.



DEFINITION MODULE Parameter;

FROM Attribute IMPORT AttributeType;

TYPE ParameterId = IDENTIFIER OF ParameterType;
    ParameterType = SUBTYPE OF AttributeType
                    RECORD variable: BOOLEAN
                    END;
    ...

END Parameter.
```

5. Persistent objects

An object type becomes persistent when an associated instance of the metaobject type Object is created. In view of the complex structure of this metaobject creation of such an instance is accompanied with creation of other instances representing attributes, actions, images etc. associated with the persistent object. While on the level of objects this may be viewed as a primitive action, its implementation involves references to the meta level as illustrated below by the decomposition of the action CreateProductObject which is represented as a module to make explicit references to the relevant metaobjects.

```
MODULE CreateProductObject;

FROM Object IMPORT ObjectType, ObjectId, CreateObject,
                   AddAttribute, AddAction;

FROM Attribute IMPORT AttributeType, AttributeId, CreateAttribute;

FROM Action IMPORT ActionType, ActionId, CreateAction;

FROM Parameter IMPORT ParameterType, ParameterId,
                      CreateParameter, AddParameter;

FROM Type IMPORT SelectType;

(* DeleteProcedure declaration *)

VAR object: ObjectType; OID: ObjectId;
    attribute: AttributeType; ATTID: AttributeId;
    action: ActionType; ACTID: ActionId;
    parameter: ParameterType; PID: ParameterId;
BEGIN object.name : = "Product";
    object.cardinality : = 0;
    ...
    OID : = CreateObject(object);
    attribute.name : = "name";
    attribute.type : = SelectType("STRING");
    ATTID : = CreateAttribute(attribute);
    AddAttribute(OID,ATTID);
  ...
    action.name : = "DeleteProduct";
    action.object : = OID;
    action.code : = DeleteProcedure;
    ACTID : = CreateAction(action);
    AddAction(OID,ACTID);
    ...
    parameter.name : = "p";
    parameter.type : = SelectType("ProductId");
    PID : = CreateParameter(parameter);
    AddParameter(ACTID,PID);

    ...
END CreateProductObject.
```

6. Persistent meta^{2}objects

A fundamental question is what makes metaobjects persistent. There obviously must exist the root of persistence (see for example (Connor et al. (1990))) which is, of course, persistent. The first generalization step now leads to the generic meta^2 object, whose instances are objects of any type. So the object of all objects becomes the root of persistence. Such an object type at the meta^2 level may be defined in a very abstract manner such as the one given below. The definition contains only one type which is an identifier (a reference) to this generic object type. But neither the nature of the generic object type nor the nature of its identifier are revealed. Some basic, very general actions on generic objects are also defined. The previously given definition module Object (section 2.) now becomes the implementation of the generic object specification in terms of the facilities at the lower level.

```
DEFINITION MODULE Object;

TYPE ObjectId;

PROCEDURE CreateObject(): ObjectId;
PROCEDURE DropObject(o: ObjectId);
PROCEDURE DisplayObject(o: ObjectId);
...
END Object.
```

The meta^2 level defined in this way is important since it permits a high degree of polymorphism. Indeed, we can now specify actions that act on any object type taking as parameters and results references to the generic meta^2 object type. In a similar manner general relationships among object types may be expressed at the meta^2 level. Indeed, it is always possible to express those relationships in terms of the generic object identifiers. An example (definition and implementation) is given below (we assume no multiple inheritance).

```
DEFINITION MODULE Object;

TYPE ObjectType;
        ObjectId = IDENTIFIER OF ObjectType;

PROCEDURE GetObject(VAR object: ObjectType);
PROCEDURE DisplayObject(o: ObjectId);

PROCEDURE CreateObject(object: ObjectType): ObjectId;
PROCEDURE DropObject(o: ObjectId);

PROCEDURE AddSubObject(object,subobject: ObjectId);
PROCEDURE DropSubObject(object, subobject: ObjectId);

PROCEDURE DisplayObjectHierarchy(o: ObjectId);
 ...

END Object.


IMPLEMENTATION MODULE Object;

TYPE ObjectType = RECORD name: STRING[30];
                              cardinality: CARDINAL
                  END;
    AssociationType = RECORD object: ObjectId;
                              subobject: ObjectId
                  END;
    ObjectSetType = ENTITY SET OF ObjectType;
    AssociationSetType = ENTITY SET OF AssociationType;
  VAR ObjectSet: ObjectSetType;
    AssociationSet: AssociationSetType;

 ...
```

```
PROCEDURE DisplayObjectHierarchy(o: ObjectId);

 VAR a: AssociationType;
BEGIN DisplayObject(o);
    FOREACH a IN AssociationSet
    WHERE  a.object = o
    DO  DisplayObjectHierarchy(a.subobject)
    END
END DisplayObjectHierarchy;
   ...
```

END Object.

The meta^2 level may be enriched in a number of ways. Indeed, metaobjects may be viewed in the same manner that the first-level objects were. Meta objects are equipped with the associated actions performed under some integrity constraints. If metaobjects are large scale then the reasons of efficiency justify creation of images on top of metaobjects. More conceptual views may be defined on top of metaobjects. Generalizations of types called kinds (Cardelli (1988)) also belong to the meta^2 level. If a data dictionary or a database catalog is an example of a persistent metaobject, then in a distributed database system a catalog that represents the interface to the users and hides the distribution details from them is an example of a persistent meta^2 object.

Specifications of various types of object hierarchies and their associated semantics seem to belong naturally to the meta^2 level. In other words, attributes of objects, their applicable actions, the associated integrity constraints and images are defined on the meta level, but higher-order relationships (such as object type hierarchies) are specified on the meta^2 level. Following (Cardelli (1988)), the generic type Type whose instances are particular types would in fact belong to the meta^2 level and not to the meta level.

While the advantages of the three level hierarchy are discussed above an obvious question is whether it is necessary and what happens if it is collapsed. Consider first the most dramatic change to the presented approach when the whole hierarchy is collapsed to one level only. It then becomes impossible to distinguish among various types of objects and thus the object-oriented approach, at least as we see it (as strongly typed), becomes impossible.

Untyped persistent objects

　　　　　　　　.　　　　　　*Persistent root*

　　　_____　　　*Persistent objects*

With two levels we can support many features of the strongly typed object-oriented approach such as types and object types, encapsulation of object properties and the associated actions, information hiding through separation of two levels of abstraction, object identifiers etc.

Monomorphic persistent objects

　　　　　　　　.　　　　　　*Persistent root*

　　　_____　　　*Persistent metaobjects*

　　　_____　　*Persistent objects*

Although some, limited types of polymorphism (such as the subtype polymorphism) may in fact be supported within the two level hierarchy, higher types of polymorphism require the third level. Other justifications for the third level are given in the paper (generic, complex object relationships, higher-level views, catalogs for distributed and multi data bases etc.). A particularly interesting candidate for the meta^2 level are transactions since they represent compositions of actions specified at the meta level.

Polymorphic persistent objects

$$Persistent\ root$$

$$Persistent\ meta^2 objects$$

$$Persistent\ metaobjects$$

$$Persistent\ objects$$

Of course, it is possible to extend the hierarchy further to higher levels, but that obviously produces nothing new in the overall approach.

7. Conclusions

Perhaps the major contribution of this paper is its attempt to shift the focus of interest from persistent objects to persistent metaobjects. The pragmatic justifications are various design, implementation and user-oriented problems related to data dictionaries or database catalogs, particularly in object-oriented, distributed and multi database systems.

While the limitations of the classical data models, the relational in particular, have been clearly indicated in complex, non-standard applications (Kemper et al. (1987)), we showed that conceptual modelling of persistent metaobjects indicates those limitations as well. And the metaobjects are essential for the architecture of the coming generation of database systems.

Although the paper presents one particular approach to metaobjects, it indicates some advantages of the object-oriented approach. Those advantages are control of the metaobject type safety achieved through encapsulation of applicable actions to metaobjects, separation of specification and representation (implementation) of metaobjects, their abstract data types of attributes and procedural (functional) attributes.

In comparison with the previous (and very small number of) publications on (semantic) data dictionaries, such as for example (Cammarata (1988)), this paper is probably one of the first to address those issues within the object-oriented paradigm.

Among the subtle problems that we did not address specifically are scopes of identifiers and environments. Those problems are discussed in detail in (Connor et al. (1990)). In our approach they follow from the related rules for modules.

The hierarchy of objects and metaobjects shares some similarities with the type hierarchy of (Cardelli (1988)). The hierarchy presented in this paper is much more specific and related to persistent objects. It certainly indicates the relevance of the quoted reference for the particular problems dealt with in this paper. That observation is one of the contributions of this paper.

Perhaps the major novelty of this paper is its multiparadigm (multi-model) approach to persistent metaobjects which permits coexistence of the (extended) relational and the object-oriented approaches in a unified and consistent environment. It is achieved by the flexibility offered to the designer of metaobjects who is in position to control the level of exposure of a metaobject to its users. The option to expose the relational-like view is of obvious importance since it permits (extended) relational queries on metaobjects. This is at the same time a major difference in comparison with (Connor et al. (1990)).

Acknowledgment

I would like to thank my research assistants Dragan Jurković and Nadira Krdžalić-Rogović for their valuable comments and suggestions.

References

S. Alagic, *Object-Oriented Database Programming*, Springer- Verlag, New York, 1988.

S. Alagic, *Relational Database Technology*, Springer-Verlag, New York, 1986.

S. Alagic, D. Jurkovic and M. Kandic, Object-Oriented Database Programming Environment Based on Modula-2, First International Modula-2 Conference, 1989.

M. P. Atkinson, O.P. Buneman, Types and Persistence in Database Programming Languages, *ACM Computing Surveys*, 19, (2), 105-190, 1987.

M. P. Atkinson, P. Buneman and R. Morrison, *Data Types and Persistence*, Springer-Verlag, 1988.

M. Atkinson, F. Bancilhon, D. DeWitt, K. Dittrich, D. Maier, and S. Zdonik, The Object-Oriented Database System Manifesto, Technical Report 30-89, GIP ALTAIR, INRIA, 1989.

S.J. Cammarata, An Intelligent Information Dictionary for Semantic Manipulation of Relational Databases. Advances in Database Technology - EDBT '88. *Lecture Notes in Computer Science* 303, 1988.

L. Cardelli and P. Wegner, On Understanding Types, Data Abstraction and Polymorphism, *Computing Surveys*, 17, (4), 471-522, 1985.

L. Cardelli, Types for Data Oriented Languages, in Advances in Database Technology - EDBT '88, *Lecture Notes in Computer Science*, 303, Springer-Verlag, Berlin, 1988, pp. 1-15.

E.F Codd, Extending the Database Relational Model to Capture More Meaning, *ACM TODS*, 4, (4), 397-434, 1979.

Connor, R., Dearle, A., Morrison, R. and Brown, F. Existentially Quantified Types as a Database Viewing Mechanism. Advances in Database Technology - EDBT '90. *Lecture Notes in Computer Science* 416, 1990.

J. Eckhardt, J. Edelmann, J. Koch, M. Mall and J.W. Schmidt, Draft Report on the Database Programming Language DBPL, Fachbereich Informatik, J.W. Goethe Universitat, Frankfurt, 1985.

A. Kemper, P.C. Lockemann and M. Wallrath, An Object- Oriented Database System for Engineering Applications, Proceedings of the ACM SIGMOD Conference, San Francisco, 299-310, 1987.

M. Mall, M. Reimer and J.W. Schmidt, Data Selection, Sharing and Access Control in a Relational Scenario, in M.L. Brodie, J. Mylopoulos and J.W. Schmidt (eds.), *On Conceptual Modelling*, Springer-Verlag, New York, 411-440, 1984.

M. Reimer, Implementation of the Database Programming Language Modula/R on the Personal Computer Lilith, *Software Practice & Experience*, 14, (10), 945-956, 1984.

A. Rosental, S. Heiler, U. Dayal and F. Manola, Traversal Recursion: A Practical Approach to Supporting Recursive Applications, Proceedings of the ACM SIGMOD Conference, Washington, D.C., 166-176, 1986.

L.A. Rowe and K.A. Shones, Data Abstractions, Views and Updates in Rigel, Proceedings of the ACM SIGMOD Conference on Management of Data, Boston, 71-81, 1979.

J.W. Schmidt, Some High-Level Language Constructs for Data of Type Relation, *ACM TODS*, 2, (3), 247-261, 1977.

M. Stonebraker and L. Rowe, The POSTGRESS Papers, Memorandum No. UCB/ERL M86/85, Electronics Research Laboratory, College of Engineering, University of California, Berkeley, 1987.

N. Wirth, *Programming in MODULA-2*, Springer-Verlag, Berlin, 1983.

N. Wirth, Type Extensions, *ACM TOPLAS*, 10, (2), 204-284,1988.

N. Wirth, From Modula to Oberon, *Software Practice & Experience*,18, (7), 661-670, 1988.

N. Wirth, Modula-2 and Object-Oriented Programming. First International Modula-2 Conference, 1989.

Naming Schemes and Name Space Management in the DBPL Persistent Storage System *

Joachim W. Schmidt   Florian Matthes

Department of Computer Science
Hamburg University
Schlüterstraße 70
D-2000 Hamburg 13
`schmidt@rz.informatik.uni-hamburg.dbp.de`

Abstract

Database applications must be capable of dynamically creating large quantities of names based on a scheme that can be communicated to and shared by some user community. The paper concentrates on this particular aspect of the set- and predicate-based Data Base Programming Language DBPL. It re-interprets the key and view mechanisms of relational database systems as naming schemes by introducing the concept of a *selector* for user-defined associative naming of partitions of large data sets. The DBPL approach results in a novel interpretation of relations as scopes with variable extents of named and typed data objects. The consequences of associative naming schemes on typing and binding mechanisms are discussed and various extensions required by data-intensive applications are introduced. The paper also describes the system support that the DBPL implementation provides for efficient name space management.

1   Introduction

The choice of a naming scheme is particularly crucial for any system in which names have to be communicated between a variety of users and where the use of names may extend over large time intervals and spatially distributed locations. Database applications require additional naming support for bulk data identification and for the representation of dynamic relationships between individual data objects.

The main objective of this paper is to present the naming scheme of DBPL [SEM88], a persistent language that provides – in addition to conventional types inherited from its algorithmic kernel Modula-2 [Wir83] – an advanced data model. This model includes first-order predicates and large data sets ("relations") and aims for type completeness and orthogonality.

The DBPL naming scheme allows the dynamic creation of object names from values and guarantees the uniqueness of names within the scope of a relation. This approach leads to a novel interpretation of relations as scopes with variable extents of named and typed data objects, as well as to a re-interpretation of database views and queries as mechanisms for scope restriction and iteration.

The paper presents in detail the language support provided by DBPL for such naming schemes and the naming and binding mechanisms realized by the DBPL persistent object store. In addition, it discusses the impact of DBPL's specific predicate-oriented approach to bulk data handling on the overall architecture of the system, on its low-level storage structures, its concurrency control protocols and its ability to support distribution and schema evolution.

2   Language Technology for Large Data Sets

Computer languages introduce *names* as tokens to be bound to computational entities for the purpose of their identification. Traditionally, a *binding* consists of a name-value pair [Str67]. Bindings have been augmented

---

*This research was supported in part by the European Commission under ESPRIT BRA contract # 4092 (FIDE).

by a type component [BL84] and then by an indication whether the value is constant or mutable [AM88]. Such augmentations serve to restrict the use of entities to those computational contexts that preserve the entities' intended semantics – and to formally, and effectively, assure such semantics. Binding can be made at compile time (static binding) or during program execution (dynamic binding) [MAD87,Dea89].

A binding is always performed within a particular environment. The *scope* of a name determines those parts of a program where the name can be used (e.g. to define other bindings). In static scoping, the scope can be determined by a static analysis of program texts, whereas in dynamic scoping these parts may vary from one program execution to another.

2.1   Elementary Naming and Typing in DBPL

Starting from its definitional context, a programming language object, e.g. a set variable, can be introduced into a computational context (expression, statement) or a communication position (parameter) by using its name. It can be protected by analysing its type and mutability status. Computations are based on its value.

```
MODULE m1;
  TYPE Digits = SET OF [0..9];
  CONST allDigits = Digits{0..9};
  VAR d: Digits;
BEGIN
  d:= allDigits;
END m1.
```

The module m1 defines the following (value) bindings:

< name= *allDigits*, value= {*0,1,2,3,4,5,6,7,8,9*}, type= *Digits*, access= {*read*} >
< name= *d*, value= ?, type= *Digits*, access= {*read, assign*} >

Programming languages provide naming and binding mechanisms not only for entities of base types (like int, bool, char) or atomic types (like strings, sets or files), but also for structured objects (e.g. of type record or array). Such (built-in) type constructors provide naming schemes for nested object components, e.g. named selection for record fields or indexed selection for array elements, and allow binding to homogeneous (arrays) or heterogeneous (records) component types.

```
MODULE m2;
  TYPE Mass = RECORD value: REAL; unit: (g, kg, lb) END;
  TYPE Color = (red, green, blue);
  TYPE PartRecType = RECORD name: String; mass: Mass; color: Color END;
  VAR firstPart, nextPart: PartRecType;
BEGIN
  firstPart.mass.unit:= kg;
END m2.
```

Module m2 defines nested name spaces with the following bindings:

< name= *firstPart*, value= ?, type= *PartRecType*, access= {*read, assign*} >
< name= *firstPart.name*, value= ?, type= *String*, access= {*read,assign*} >
< name= *firstPart.mass*, value= ? , type= *Mass*, access= {*read,assign*} >
< name= *firstPart.color*, value= ? ,type= *Color*, access= {*read,assign*} >
< name= *nextPart*, value= ?, type= *PartRecType*, access= {*read,assign*} >

By allowing recursive application of these nested naming schemes, modern programming languages are able to identify and bind a variable and unlimited number of data objects with a fixed set of (statically declared) names.

```
TYPE PartList = POINTER TO RECORD r:PartRecType; next: PartList END;
VAR p: PartList;
```

< name= *p*, value= ?, type= *PartList*, access={*read, assign*} >
< name= *p↑.r*, value= ?, type= *PartRecType*, access= {*read, assign*} >

$< \text{name}= p{\uparrow}.next, \text{value}= ?, \text{type}= PartList, \text{access}= \{read, assign\} >$
$< \text{name}= p{\uparrow}.next{\uparrow}.r, \text{value}= ?, \text{type}= PartRecType, \text{access}= \{read, assign\} >$
$< \text{name}= p{\uparrow}.next{\uparrow}.next, \text{value}= ?, \text{type}= PartList, \text{access}= \{read, assign\} >$
$\ldots$

The rationale behind such a variety of naming and binding mechanisms is derived from application demands: manipulating descriptions of aggregated commercial records [Hoa68] requires different schemes than evaluating matrices in scientific computations. However, there are other issues involved in the design of a particular naming scheme that seem to be independent of the particular application area:

- Orthogonality: All language objects should be named in a uniform way [Lan66,DD79].

- Modularity: The consequences of name changes should be limited to well-defined scopes [L$^+$77,BL84, Har88,Wir83]. Modularity is supported by nested scopes in block-structured languages or by compilation units with explicit import interfaces. A flat name space for "external" names as in C may serve as a counter-example.

- Abstraction: A key feature of a naming scheme is the possibility to introduce new bindings based on existing bindings by abstracting from selected aspects of a the original binding and thereby only revealing "partial" (e.g. type) information about declared objects [L$^+$77,Car89,DCBM89]. A similar motivation underlies view mechanisms [CDMB90] in database systems.

Naming and binding mechanisms in standard programming languages have also been employed for bulk data handling in persistent and shared environments. DBPL [MS89] provides a built-in type constructor for the definition of large data sets (relations). The following declaration

```
TYPE PartRelType = RELATION name OF PartRecType;
VAR Parts: PartRelType;
```

introduces, for example, a binding between the relation name Parts, the relation type PartRelType and a mutable (and initially undefined) relation value.

$< \text{name}= Parts, \text{value}= value, \text{type}= PartRelType, \text{access}= \{read,assign\} >$

The relation value always has to be a set (in the mathematical sense) of objects of the element type (in this case PartRecType) with the additional constraint expressed by the invariant

$$\forall p_1, p_2 \in value(p_1.name = p_2.name) \Rightarrow (p_1 = p_2)$$

2.2   Expressions and Statements in DBPL

Names which are bound to values of type relation may appear in the "standard contexts" provided by an imperative programming language:

- on the left-hand-side of an assignment operator;

- in right-hand-side expressions;

- as value parameters (call by value);

- as variable parameters (call by reference).

DBPL also provides the means to refer to a value of a relation type without introducing a name. The following syntax denotes relations by enumerating their elements:

```
PartRelType{}                          (* the empty relation of type PartRelType*)
PartRelType{firstPart, nextPart}
```

$< \text{name}= \quad, \text{value}= \{\}, \text{type}= PartRelType, \text{access}= \{read\}>$
$< \text{name}= \quad, \text{value}= \{firstPart, nextPart\}, \text{type}= PartRelType, \text{access}= \{read\}>$

The type identifier in a relation constructor is necessary to type check relation expressions using the standard type equivalence rules of Modula-2. These are based on name equivalence and not on structural equivalence.

To evaluate relations in expressions, DBPL provides specialized set-oriented *query expressions* for relation types. There are three kinds of query expressions, namely boolean expressions, selective and constructive query expressions.

Quantified expressions yield a boolean result by evaluating a boolean predicate for all elements of a relation:

```
SOME p IN Parts (p.name = "Table")
ALL p IN Parts (p.mass.unit = kg)
```

Selective query expressions in a relation constructor select a subrelation of a single relation value:

```
PartRelType{EACH p IN Parts: p.mass.unit = kg}
```

creates a relation of type PartRelType that contains (copies of) all elements of the relation variable Parts that fulfil the selection predicate p.mass.unit = kg.

Constructive query expressions construct relations based on the values of other relations:

```
TripleRelType{{pmin.color, pmin.price, pmax.price} OF
    EACH pmin IN Parts, EACH pmax IN parts:
    (pmin.color = pmax.color) AND
    ALL p IN Parts ((p.color <> pmin.color) OR
       (p.price >= pmin.price) AND (p.price <=pmax.price))}
```

The constructive query expression above defines how to derive a relation consisting of triples from the relation Parts. Each triple consists of the color of a part and the minimal and maximal costs for parts of that color. The type of the result relation is given by

```
TYPE TripleRelType = RELATION OF RECORD c: Color; min,max: REAL END;
```

In general, the evaluation of a constructive query expression yields a relation that contains the values of the target expression (preceding the keyword OF), evaluated for all combinations of the element variables (pmin, pmax) that fulfil the selection expression (pmin.color = pmax.color) AND ALL ...

To simplify the manipulation of large data sets, DBPL offers specialized relational update operators that are equivalent to more complicated relation assignments:

```
parts:+ newParts;            (* relation insertion *)
parts:= PartRelType{ EACH p IN parts: TRUE,
               EACH np IN newParts: NOT SOME p IN parts (np.name = p.name)}


parts:- newParts;            (* relation deletion *)
parts:= PartRelType{ EACH p IN parts: NOT SOME np IN newParts (np.name = p.name)}


parts:& newParts;             (* relation update *)
parts:= PartRelType{ EACH p IN parts: NOT SOME np IN newParts (np.name = p.name),
               EACH np IN newParts: SOME p IN parts (np.name = p.name)}
```

2.3   Scopes and Lifetime in DBPL

Depending on the specific demands of an application area, bindings may include additional attributes that regulate, for example, object lifetime, sharability, recovery, clustering, mobility and object access rights (see also Section 3.3).

In general, each of these additional attributes can be determined at various points in time and at different levels of granularity. As is the case with type judgements [Mat87], it is often preferable to trade in the flexibility of fully dynamic modifications of these object properties for the simplicity and efficiency of an early, mostly static decision at object declaration or creation time. Similarly, many binding decisions are not taken on a per-object basis but for composite objects or for entire scopes like modules or directories.

In addition to non-shared, transient variables as found in Modula-2, DBPL allows the declaration of shared and persistent database variables. This is achieved by extending the concept of a module to *database modules* (i.e. name spaces subject to separate compilation). All variables declared within a database module are persistent, i.e. in contrast to program variables in other modules their lifetime exceeds a single program execution. To be precise, the lifetime of a persistent variable is longer than that of any program importing it.

Persistent variables are shared objects and can thus be accessed by several programs simultaneously. An access to a persistent variable must be part of the execution of a transaction [MRS84,RS81]. Database modules can therefore be viewed as self-contained, statically declared, persistent, serializable and recoverable scopes.

In the operations explained above it is sufficient to treat relations as entire indivisable objects that can be named and typed without any visible substructure. Neglecting some syntactic pecularities (listfix notation for relation constructors or infix notation for some operators) the built-in relation types of DBPL could therefore be easily implemented by means of generic, parameterized abstract data types in a sufficiently rich type system. In Quest [Car89], the signature of a generic relation type with similar operations as in DBPL could be defined as follows. (Note that the create operation has an equality predicate as an additional parameter that is needed to maintain the key uniqueness in subsequent operations on the relation.)

```
interface Relation
export
  RelType::ALL(ElemType::TYPE) TYPE        (* a type operator *)

  create(A::TYPE elem:Array(A) equality(:A :A):Bool) :RelType(A)

  :==, :+, :-, :& (A::TYPE var lhs :RelType(A) rhs :RelType(A)) :Ok

  some,all(A ::TYPE range :RelType(A) predicate(:A) :Bool) :Bool

  each(A::TYPE range :RelType(A) predicate(:A) :Bool) :RelType(A)

  each2(A,B,C::TYPE range1 :RelType(A) range2 :RelType(B)
        predicate(:A :B) :Bool projection(:A :B) :C) :RelType(C)
end;
```

As it turns out, this view of a bulk data structure as an "abstract" named entity is too coarse for data-intensive applications requiring naming schemes which support the identification of specific subsets or individual elements of a collection.

3   Extended DBPL Naming Schemes

The previous section outlined predefined standard naming schemes in DBPL that enable programmers to declare and manipulate relation variables. The following subsections will study three extensions of these naming schemes that are mainly motivated by the particular needs of data-intensive applications in a persistent multi-user environment:

- Refinement of the granularity of values that can be named and bound;

- Language support for user-defined parameterized naming schemes;

- Extension of the set of attributes that can be bound to a name.

3.1   Key-Based Naming Schemes

The uniqueness constraint on relation key values expressed by the constraint

$$\forall p_1, p_2 \in value(p_1.name = p_2.name) \Rightarrow (p_1 = p_2)$$

allows the extension of the traditional notion of relations as value spaces (bulk data structures). It also permits the viewing relations as name spaces consisting of sets of bindings between key values and their associated relation elements.

For example, the two-element relation constructed with

Parts:= PartRelType{ {"Table", {10.0, kg}, red}, {"Chair", {2.0, kg},blue} }

defines the following bindings

< name= *Parts*, value= {*firstPart, nextPart*}, type= *PartRelType*, access= {*read,assign*} >
< name= *Parts["Table"]*, value= {*"Table"*, {*10.0, kg*}, *red*}, type= *PartRecType*, access= {*read, assign*} >
< name= *Parts["Chair"]*, value= {*"Chair"*, {*2.0, kg*}, *blue*}, type= *PartRecType*, access= {*read, assign*} >

The syntax of DBPL therefore allows (analogous to the selection of array elements) a denotation of relation elements by a relation name followed by a key value in square brackets. Parts["Table"] is a name for the relation element with the key value "Table" in the relation Parts. Note that Parts["Table"] does not simply denote a copy of a relation element, but that it is a name for an updateable subcomponent of the relation variable Parts (reference semantics). These names can therefore be used on the left-hand-side of an assignment operator, in right-hand-side expressions, as well as value and variable parameters. These are examples of selected relation element variables:

InOut.ReadReal(Parts["Chair"].mass.value);
Parts["Table"].mass.value := Parts["Chair"].mass.value * 4;

The built-in key selector that comes with every relation type may be viewed as a generic *naming scheme* that creates an object name for a given object value:

"Table" → Parts["Table"]
"Chair" → Parts["Chair"]

This is a generic naming scheme since DBPL (as a consequence of the principle of type-completeness) allows the definition of relation types with arbitrary element types, lists of key components and key components of simple or constructed DBPL types[1].

VAR Suppliers: RELATION name, address OF
    RECORD name: String; address: RECORD city, country: String END;
        employees: RELATION OF String;
    END;
VAR Table: RELATION key OF RECORD key, value: INTEGER END;
VAR Grid: RELATION [1],[2] OF ARRAY [1..3] OF Real;
TYPE SparseVector = RELATION col OF RECORD col:INTEGER; val: REAL END;
VAR SparseMatrix: RELATION row OF RECORD row: CARDINAL; val: SparseVector END;

Companies["Bayer","Leverkusen","Germany"]
Table[i]
Grid[1.75, 1.9]
SparseMatrix [1342] [99].val

These examples illustrate that key selectors permit the definition of *problem-oriented* naming schemes which support the identification and manipulation even of individual attributes of deeply nested structures. The set-oriented operations presented in Section 2.2 can now be re-interpreted as operations on name spaces that add, remove, update und query sets of bindings and, in addition, guarantee the uniqueness of names (based on keys) within a given name space (relation value).

A selection based on a non-existent key value (Parts["Cupboard"]) or attempts to change the key value of a selected relation element variable Parts["Table"].name:= "Chair" are illegal and will be detected at runtime leading to a transaction abort. A formalization and generalization of the underlying constraints on selected relation elements will be given in Section 3.2.

---

[1] The current implementation of DBPL does not support relations as key components. This restriction is based on purely engineering decisions, since the semantics of "deep equality" are well understood.

The main conceptual and pragmatic advantages of a value-based naming scheme can be summarized as follows:

- A rich set of value constructors (records, arrays, sets, . . .) implies an equally rich set of naming schemes.

- The unrestricted availabilty of dynamic creation and deletion mechanisms for names allows programmers to implement their own centralized or decentralized, traced or untraced, static or dynamic naming policies.

  However, this freedom can also become a burden, as soon as it becomes necessary to trace the propagation of names to determine whether a name can be safely deleted or not. This deletion can take place when no other objects contain references to a name. As it turns out, DBPL greatly simplifies this task by supporting arbitrary nested quantified predicates. For example, the following update operation deletes all suppliers that no longer supply any part:

  Suppliers :- SupplierRelType{EACH s IN Suppliers: NOT SOME p IN Parts (p.supplier = s.name)};

  Using recursive query expressions as supported by recursive constructors in DBPL [MRS89], it is possible to extend this approach to transitive reachability rules.

- "Printable" names are a must for the communication of identifiers across system boundaries (e.g. at the user-interface or for data exchange between autonomous persistent stores).

- A crucial point observed in long-lived information systems is the fact that values can be "detected" to be names (e.g. the ZIP code of a city used in an early version of a shipment database can be used to obtain additional attributes of a city in a later version of the system) or uniqueness assumptions about names cease to be valid (e.g. two persistent name spaces need to be merged and duplicate names have to be identified).

In a language that does not provide an associative naming scheme, programmers usually resort to one of the following standard solutions to identify elements in a bulk data structure:

Explicit Navigation: In a first step, an "invisible" cursor is positioned within the bulk data structure and subsequent update and read operations operate implicitly on the selected element. As soon as there is a need to manipulate several cursors, this approach becomes impractical because of the overhead to open, close and identify the cursors themselves [Dat89].

Separate Get and Update Operations: Every access to an element of the bulk data structure has to pass a key value as an additional parameter. Update operations tend to be inefficient because of the duplicate key lookup in the get and update operation. Particular problems arise in the selection of deeply nested components since unnecessary large intermediate structures have to be retrieved and locked. For example, a simple operation like INC(SparseMatrix [1342] [99].val) has to be implemented as

```
VAR row1342: SparseVector;
VAR element: REAL;
row1342:= GetByIntKeyvalue(SparseVector, 1342);
element:= GetByIntKeyvalue(row1342.val, 99);
INC(element.val)
PutByIntKeyvalue(row1342.val,99, element);
PutByIntKeyvalue(SparseVector, 1342, row1342);
```

Indirect Access via References: The bulk data structure simply consists of an index that maps key values to references which point to the objects of the element type. All read and update operations are performed using references. The main disadvantage of this approach is the unrestricted scope and lifetime of the references. The uncontrolled proliferation of identifiers prohibits efficient storage management, access control, concurrency control, and recovery strategies to be utilized for element-oriented access.

3.2   Association-Based Naming Schemes

A serious shortcoming of the key-based naming scheme is its restriction to single-element access. What is still missing is a value-based naming mechanism with a granularity that mediates between full relation variables and individual relation elements. A first step towards a generalization of the key selection mechanism is the observation that in an expression context the following equality holds:

PartsRelType{Parts["Table"]} = PartsRelType{EACH p IN Parts: p.name = "Table"}

A key-based selector can therefore be viewed as an abbreviation for a specific parameterized selective query expression (see Section 2.2), EACH p IN Parts: p.name = keyvalue. The following *selector* declaration makes the underlying naming mechanism explicit:

SELECTOR ByKey ON (P: PartRelType) WITH (keyvalue: String): PartRecType;
BEGIN EACH p IN P: p.name = keyvalue END ByKey;

Given this declaration, the selector ByKey declares a parameterized naming scheme that maps from key values to names and Parts[ByKey("Table")] is the name for the (unique) element of type PartRecType in the relation Parts that fulfils the selection predicate p.name = keyvalue. The two names, Parts["Table"] and Parts[ByKey("Table")], always refer to the same relation element since the former is considered a shorthand for the latter.

Since the syntax of selective access expressions already allows a much richer set of selection predicates to be used in place of x.keyattribute = keyvalue, the generalization of key-based to general predicate-based naming schemes is straightforward.

SELECTOR ByColor ON (P: PartRelType) WITH (colorvalue: Color): PartRelType;
BEGIN EACH p IN P: p.color = colorvalue END ByColor;

The selector ByColor allows the selection of a *set* of parts with a given value for the color attribute: Parts[ByColor(red)] is therefore a name for that subrelation of the relation variable Parts, that contains only those elements that fulfil the selection predicate p.color = red. Note that the result type of the selector ByColor is PartRelType and no longer PartRecType. This reflects the fact that the selection yields a set of parts, i.e. there is no implicit de-setting operation as in the case of the selector ByKey.

Again, such *selected relation variables* can be used like plain relation names in expressions and assignments, and as parameters for all standard and user-defined procedures and functions. The semantics of the use of selected relation variables in such contexts can be deduced from the semantics of selected relation assignment. Since the formal definition of selective set assignment [Sch88] goes beyond the scope of this paper, only an intuitive presentation of DBPL selector semantics is provided.

In its most general form a selector declaration can be based on arbitrary selective access expressions:

SELECTOR sp ON (Rel: RelType) WITH (*parameter list*): RelType;
BEGIN EACH r IN Rel: p(r, *parameter list*) END sp;

The goal of assigning an expression, rex, selectively to a relation, i.e., R[sp(...)] := rex, is to substitute the selected part of R by the r.h.s.-expression, rex, while keeping the non-selected part of the l.h.s.-variable invariant with respect to its pre-value, 'R. In terms of non-selective assignments we aim for a post-value, R', such that

R'[sp(...)] = rex   and
R'[*not*sp(...)] = 'R[*not*sp(...)]

This goal can be reached by an implementation such as

R := {EACH r IN rex: TRUE, EACH r IN R: NOT p(r,...)}

However, as already demonstrated in Section 3.1 through examples of key-based selectors, this implementation does not consider possible constraint violations. In the example

Parts["Table"] := PartRecType{ PartName, {5.0, kg}, blue}

we do not intend to replace tables by chairs and therefore have to protect the assignment by an appropriate conditional:

```
IF PartName = "Table" THEN
  Parts:= {{PartName, {5.0, kg}, blue}, EACH p IN Parts: p.name<>"Table"}
ELSE exception END
```

Without going into a deeper case analysis, this semantics can be shown to generalize to conditionals that are universally quantified over arbitrary r.h.s. set expressions rex and to arbitrary first-order selection predicates p.

The signature of the above declared selectors defines a name for the selector, an ON-parameter that defines the range relation for the selector and a WITH-parameter that is used in the selection predicate. The ON-parameter allows the application of selectors to different (selected) range relations of a given type, for example

```
VAR OldParts: PartRelType;

OldParts[ByColor(red)]
OldParts[ByColor(red)] [ByKey("Table")]
```

It is possible to omit this parameterization:

```
SELECTOR RedParts: PartRelType;
BEGIN EACH p IN Parts: p.color = red END RedParts;

OldParts:= PartRelType{EACH p IN [RedParts]: p.mass.unit = lb};
```

The last example emphasizes the similarity between the use of selectors in DBPL and the use of *views* in database systems. Both allow the derivation of new named collections from other collections (or views) by means of value-based restrictions that abstract from any detail of the selection process.

The previous examples only make use of propositional predicates. However, quantified predicates are also admissable in selector declarations and provide mechanisms for bulk data identification based on *dynamic relationships* that involve names of different name spaces:

```
SELECTOR SuppliedFrom ON (P: PartRelType) WITH (city: String): PartRelType;
BEGIN
  EACH p IN Parts: SOME s IN Suppliers ((s.name = p.supplier) AND (s.city = city))
END SuppliedFrom;

Parts[SuppliedFrom("Hamburg")]
```

An important application for selectors is the enforcement of referential integrity between multiple name spaces. The basic idea is to define selectors on relation variables that only select "consistent" elements, i.e. those that fulfil the referential integrity constraint. The semantics of selective relation assignment then guarantee that updates using the selector will be rejected if they violate the integrity constraint.

```
SELECTOR ConsistentParts: PartRelType;
BEGIN EACH p IN Parts: SOME s IN Suppliers (s.name = p.supplier) END ConsistentParts;
```

According to the semantics of selected relation updates sketched above, the selected assignment [ConsistentParts] := OldParts is equivalent to the following conditional unselected assignment:

```
IF ALL p IN OldParts SOME s IN Suppliers (s.name = p.supplier) THEN
  Parts:= OldParts;
ELSE exception END
```

To summarize, the use of selectors for the definition of parameterized and value-based naming schemes, for scope restriction and for constraint maintenance has been presented. Since selectors are named and typed language objects, they can be stored as components of arbitrary data structures or passed as parameters to procedures or other selectors. [RM87] illustrates how the use of (non-parameterized) query expressions as first-class language citizens allows the user to simulate complex objects and to avoid explicit joins to materialize object relationships. DBPL separates parameter substitution and application of selectors (i.e. to "curry"selectors) . The latter is especially useful in conjunction with the module concept of DBPL and allows the refinement from parameterized and unbound (permissive) to non-parameterized and bound (restrictive) selectors to take place in different scopes.

Finally, it should be noted that DBPL generalizes the concept of selectors (which are based on selective access expressions) to constructors that abstract over arbitrary constructive or selective access expressions (see Section 2.2). Recursive constructor definitions have fixed point semantics and thereby integrate the essence of logic-based query languages in a strongly typed and imperative framework [MRS89]. By storing sets of constructors in persistent relation variables, it is possible to arrive at a uniform (dynamic) management of data and rules [SL85,SGLJ89].

3.3   Extended Binding Attributes

In persistent, large-scale and shared environments it becomes necessary to extend the classical notion of a binding (see Section 2) by attributes that describe additional important object properties (like lifetime, accessability or site in distributed environments). Since there is a wide range of binding alternatives (like binding time and binding granularity) the following paragraphs will only highlight the specific decisions made in the DBPL language and system, and compare them with selected approaches of other PPLs and DBPLs.

3.3.1   Object value constraints

A first extension of binding attributes was already introduced in the previous sections: Relation elements denoted by a key selector application and selected relation variables are associated with object value constraints expressed by (first-order) predicates that have to be preserved on updates:

< name= *Parts["Table"]*, value= {*"Table"*, ... }, type= *PartRecType*, access= {*read, assign*},
    assertion= *(Parts["Table"].name = "Table")* >
< name= *Parts[SuppliedFrom("Hamburg")]*, value= ..., type= *PartRelType*, access= {*read, assign*},
    assertion= *(ALL p IN Parts[SuppliedFrom("Hamburg")]*
        SOME s IN Suppliers ((s.name = p.supplier) AND (s.city = city))) >

A similar mechanism for the declaration of object value constraints can be found in Galileo [AGO89] and enables programmers to attach assertions (boolean-valued functions) to instances of classes. However, these assertions are only checked at instance creation time.

3.3.2   Object lifetime

Modern languages infer the lifetime of an object from the scope of its name(s). Typical examples are local objects in block structured languages that are created at block entry and cease to exist at block exit time, and dynamically allocated objects on a heap that are managed according to a transitive reachability rule [Coh81]. Persistent programming languages apply these rules uniformly to transient and persistent data objects [But87,ACC81,Bro89,Car86].

As illustrated in Section 3.1 and 3.2, DBPL provides in addition to these automatically managed scopes other naming schemes that decouple object lifetime from object naming and allow, in addition, explicit object creation and deletion. As a consequence, these naming schemes do not enforce that every name in a scope be bound to an associated object value.

3.3.3   Object sharability

In an environment where multiple threads of control access the same scope (e.g. in a multi-user environment), it becomes possible to attach different values to the same name, depending on the dynamic context in which the name is used. This is the approach taken by conventional programming languages, where each invocation of a program is equipped with its own, private global variables.

The notion of multiple programs accessing a common shared database can be captured in a language context by interpreting databases as scopes for global names that are bound to non-replicated values and that are furthermore associated with specialized concurrency control mechanisms that guarantee serializable schedules for concurrent read and write accesses.

DBPL uses standard transaction-oriented concurrency control mechanisms on all persistent variables in all database modules. However, if different modules implement data structures at different levels of abstraction, it becomes useful to have a finer control of the access control mechanisms (unrestricted access, mutual exclusion, monitor-like protocols, ...).

3.3.4 Object consistency and recovery

In persistent systems it is particularly useful to be able to define the notion of a "consistent" view of a name space. In DBPL (like in conventional database systems) this is accomplished by first defining an initial consistent state. All states that can be derived by applying a transaction to a consistent state are considered to be consistent themselves [Gra81,RS81,SWBM89].

A more implementation-oriented consistency and recovery mechanism can be found in languages based on the concept of a persistent heap. They support atomic and durable state transitions by means of a built-in commit or stabilize [Bro89] operation that affects the whole uniform persistent store and all active processes.

Since DBPL provides a (mostly) static partitioning of the store into a multiplicity of persistent and volatile name spaces (modules), the effects of recovery mechanisms (e.g., automatic UNDO of the effects of partially executed transactions in case of system failures or automatic REDO in case of transaction aborts caused by deadlocks) can be limited to specific name spaces. In the current implementation of DBPL, only persistent variables are subject to automatic recovery mechanisms. More experience is required to evaluate the advantages and disadvantages of this particular binding alternative.

3.3.5 Object clustering, placement and mobility

The performance of storage managers of large, disk-based address spaces can be dramatically improved by exploiting knowledge about the access patterns of programs running against the store. In addition to dynamic clustering algorithms, a primary source of static information about the locality or "relatedness" of data objects is the scope in which their names are visible and accessible. The particular mapping from scopes in DBPL to address spaces of the storage manager is described in more detail in Section 4.1.

In the distributed version of DBPL [JLRS88,JGL+88], database modules are (dynamically) bound to (local- or wide-area) network nodes that serve as repositories for the persistent data. The import of procedure, transaction or variable names from remote hosts allows the unification of a wide range of database access mechanisms like remote procedure call, database procedures (sagas [GMS87]), or database access with full distribution transparency, by means of a single language concept, the export of names from autonomous scopes.

3.3.6 Object access rights

Access rights may depend on a subject, an object and an operation performed by the subject on an object. Operating systems usually distinguish between read, write and execute operations on persistent or volatile data objects. [AM88] argues for separate access rights for read und write access to named and typed locations in a persistent store. For relation variables it is possible to distinguish read, assign, insert, delete and update operations.

In the construction of large scale database applications written in DBPL, selectors can be utilized to define at the module interface value-based access restrictions on database relations [MRS89]. By hiding the database relations in a local scope, clients of such a module are forced to perform updates and read operations through the views provided by the exported selectors. As it turns out, it is often useful to attach additional *access restrictions* to selectors, e.g. to allow only insert and read operations on a given data set. For example, take the integrity constraint ALL p IN Parts SOME s IN Suppliers (s.name = p.supplier) that can be violated only by insertions into the set of parts or deletions in the set of suppliers. DBPL therefore allows the user to attach statically access restrictions to selector declarations. These access restrictions are checked at compile-time (by a straight-forward extension of the type checker).

```
SELECTOR SecureSuppliers FOR (==, :&, :+): SupplierRelType;
BEGIN EACH s IN Suppliers: TRUE END SecureSuppliers;

[SecureSuppliers]:+ SupplierRelType{...};    (* OK *)
[SecureSuppliers]:- SupplierRelType{...};    (* compile-time error *)
```

4   Name Space Management in DBPL

This section describes how the design and implementation of the DBPL persistent store was influenced by the particular choice of naming and binding mechanisms present in DBPL.

In the DBPL project there is a strong commitment to implementability. A multi-user DBPL system under VAX/VMS is used at the Universities of Frankfurt and Hamburg since 1985 for lab courses on database programming. Based on this continuing implementation effort, there exist several prototype extensions for concurrency (optimistic, pessimistic and mixed strategies) [BJS86], integrity [Böt90], storage structures for complex objects, recursive queries [JLS85,SL85] and distribution [JLRS88,JGL+88] . The construction of a distributed DBPL system is based on ISO/OSI communication standards and involves a re-implementation of the DBPL compiler to generate native code for the IBM-PC/AT.

During the last year a substantial effort was made to integrate the experience gained with these prototype extensions into a new, portable implementation of the DBPL runtime system [SBK+88a] under VAX/VMS and Unix. Furthermore, a current project aims to interface the DBPL compiler to Suns optimizing compiler backend thereby enhancing the performance and interoperability of the DBPL system.

The overall architecture of the DBPL system [SBK+88b] is shown in Figure 1.

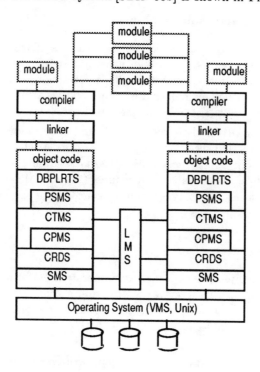

Figure 1: Architecture of the DBPL system

The DBPL compiler translates DBPL modules into object code of the target computer. A program may be comprised of several modules. Many constraints like type compatibilities and access restrictions are checked during compilation. In the object code, most of the DBPL extensions are realized by calls to the upper layer of the runtime system (DBPLRTS).

The layer DBPLRTS represents the interface to the runtime system, thereby abstracting from the internal representation of the objects defined within it. It provides support for iterations and is responsible for the access to persistent variables that are not of type RELATION. Each executing DBPL object program is (conceptually) equipped with its own copy of the runtime system. Multiple executing DBPL programs (on a single machine or on different nodes in a LAN) communicate with a centralized concurrency control process (LMS).

The layer PSMS (predicate set management system) treats predicates (i.e. query expressions) as first-class objects. For selectors and constructors, it performs parameter substitution, expansion of nested predicates, and binding to program variables. Recursive constructors are computed by repeated evaluation of relation-valued expressions according to a fixpoint algorithm.

The layer CTMS (complex transaction management system) is responsible for concurrency control at the abstraction level of DBPL expressions and statements. According to the concept of multi-level synchronization [BSW88], it abstracts from lower-level conflicts arising from implementation details of storage structures or access path support provided by the layer CRDS and SMS.

The layer CPMS (complex predicate management system) implements data structures for the internal representation of queries over NF^2-relations. Internally, queries are represented by augmented syntax trees. They are transformed to simplify the subsequent evaluation. Set-oriented read and write operations are resolved into operations on complex relation elements.

The layer CRDS (complex relational data system) provides a navigational and element-oriented access, based on logical access paths. It contains means for synchronization and recovery, which are realized by primitives provided by the SMS.

On the basis of a block-oriented access, the storage management system SMS offers, in addition to the record and page management, page-overlapping long fields as data objects. The direct support of long fields on the storage level enhances the efficient implementation of complex objects and their access paths.

4.1 Dynamic Bulk Binding and Access Path Management

A fundamental difference between DBPL and implementations of other persistent programming languages is the fact that DBPL does not rely on a physically or conceptually centralized persistent store. On the contrary, the DBPL storage manager tries to exploit the notion of separate or nested name spaces (modules, relations) and to take advantage of the static distinction between persistent and volatile, recoverable and non-recoverable, shared and non-shared scopes.

As a first consequence, the layer SMS does not map all persistent data objects to a single huge database file (as it is done in the PS-algol, Napier, Galileo or O_2 implementations) but maps top-level database variables of relation types to individual files of the operating system. Furthermore, it maps all database variables of other types (like integers, arrays or records) that are declared within the same database module to a single file that also contains all meta information pertaining to that module and which therefore acts as a kind of distributed database dictionary. At a next higher level of granularity, database modules are mapped to operating system directories. Non-persistent bulk data variables are also stored in individual address spaces that are in general mapped to main memory by the buffer manager and are only paged out to files if the system runs out of main memory resources.

Despite the increased complexity of the low-level storage management, this modularization at the file and directory level significantly increases the usability of the DBPL system in today's operating system environments since it allows dynamic access control for different users and user groups, incremental database backups and reorganizations, distribution across multiple volumes and even the use of distributed file systems to store database variables on different network notes.

The lower levels of the DBPL system (SMS and CRDS) identify atomic fragments (i.e. records without relation-valued subcomponents) by means of tuple identifiers (TIDs) consisting of a page identifier and a record number within the page. Subrecords of arbitrary deeply nested relations are identified by a fixed-sized identifier called super-TID. This super-TID consists of TID for a map structure that is allocated for each complex relation element and a relative offset within that map, identifying a map entry that finally points to the atomic fragment (see Figure 2). The sizes of the three components of a super-TID allow the identification of 2^{32} pages with up to 2^8 objects each. The total number of nested elements of a top-level relation element

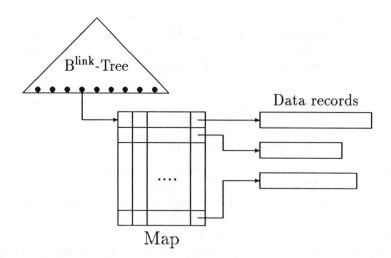

Figure 2: Access path management for nested name spaces

may not exceed 2^{32}.

These implementation-oriented names (super-TIDs) are only made visible to the query evaluator to give support for direct-access join algorithms. All other operations of the CRDS either work on full relations or on single relation elements identified by their key-value. The layer CRDS enforces copy semantics for updates (e.g. it performs a deep-copy of a relation element prior to relation insertion). DBPL therefore does not make use of the possibility to implement shared or circular data structures using super-TIDs.

The built-in key selectors (see Section 3.1) for relation variables are implemented by means of B-link trees (extended B-Trees allowing for concurrent updates [LY81]) that map from (composite) key values to TIDs. Hierarchical and key-based access to NF^2-relations is implemented through map structures that are stored for each complex root relation element and that describe the hierarchic relationships between the atomic fragments of all nested relation elements. Each map entry is augmented by a fixed-sized (8 Byte) key fragment to speed up key-based element selection. By separating data records from access structures (maps) and by choosing appropriate chaining techniques within the map, a high degree of parallelism can be achieved for update and lookup operations.

The CRDS level furthermore supports secondary index structures (generalized B-link trees) that map from (composite) attribute values to sets of TIDs. That means, that in contrast to key-selectors, no uniqueness constraint is enforced. Secondary indices can be created dynamically and are intended to accelerate user-defined naming schemes (e.g. like those defined by the selectors ByColor or RedParts).

4.2   Associative Binding and Query Optimization

A distinguishing property of the predicate-based binding mechanisms introduced in Section 3.2 is the strict separation between the specification of bulk data identification (by a first-order predicate in the language) and its implementation by the system in terms of access structures or explicit iterations. Following the approach of relational database systems, DBPL completely hides the implementation of selected relation access from the programmer. Decisions about access path support, clustering and distribution are made dynamically, outside the scope of the language since such decisions have to be based on the evolving access patterns of a multitude of application programs and on the varying sizes of the bulk data structures involved.

This should be seen in contrast to the prevailing notions of "pointers", "mutable values" or "object identifiers" found in other PPLs and DBPLs that correspond more closely to the implementation concept of storage locations allowing for constant-time direct access. Similarly, user-defined iterators as present in E [Ric89], CLU [LAB+81] or Trellis/Owl [SCB+86] are only a first step towards an abstraction from the strict control flow enforced by imperative programming languages. Since users of an iterator still have to consider the order in which iterators are nested or the point in time when selection predicates are evaluated.

Due to the dynamic nature of conditions which determine the choice of an "optimal" access strategies, the DBPL compiler does not generate directly executable code for selector applications (like Parts[SuppliedFrom ("Hamburg")], see section 3.2) but merely passes an augmented syntax tree of the query expression EACH p IN Parts: SOME s IN Suppliers ((s.name=p.supplier) AND (s.city="Hamburg")) to the DBPL runtime system. The layer PSMS is capable of performing symbolic manipulations on such augmented syntax trees. These transformations are necessary to pass parameters to a selector, to bind variable names occurring within a query expression to a global value or to nest, assign and duplicate selectors and constructors.

A selector application appearing in an expression context, e.g.,

SOME p IN Parts[SuppliedFrom("Hamburg")] (p.name = "Chair")

can simply be replaced by the query expression of the selector body.

SOME p IN
{EACH p IN Parts: SOME s IN Suppliers ((s.name=p.supplier) AND (s.city="Hamburg"))}
(p.name = "Chair")

It should be noted that query expressions are *not* evaluated by repeatedly substituting subexpressions by their value. In place of such a "strict" evaluation order, the DBPL system delays "lazily" the evaluation of such expressions until the final context for the expression is known. The rationale behind this strategy is that larger expressions give the query optimizer more flexibility to choose an advantageous execution order for subexpressions and to exploit "semantic" knowledge derived from the full expression context[2]. For example, the DBPL query optimizer (within the layer CPMS) simplifies the above boolean expression to the following expression which only requires two primary key accesses.

Suppliers[Parts["Chair"].supplier].city = "Hamburg"

The DBPL query optimizer normalizes and simplifies a query expression given by an augmented syntax tree by eliminating negations as well as redundant and constant subexpressions. In a next step, standard algebraic optimizations are performed (pushing selections and projections, range nesting for decoupled sub-queries [JK83]). Finally, an "optimal" nesting of quantifiers (SOME, ALL, EACH) is chosen. The latter optimization is equivalent to the determination of the join order in algebra-based optimizers and is guided by the existence of index structures provided by the layer CRDS. The support for direct hierarchic access within NF^2-relations (sometimes called "materialized joins") in the DBPL data model gives rise to additional possibilities for access optimization. The simple cost model of the query optimizer is the estimated number of accesses to persistent variables (i.e. the size of intermediate results is not taken into account).

The output of the query optimizer is (conceptually) still a (nested) DBPL expression that becomes subject to "strict" evaluation. The syntax tree for the expression is adorned with attributes that determine which subexpressions are to be evaluated by which evaluation algorithm of the layer CPMS. The current implementation for nested relations provides three evaluation strategies (nested loop, index-based joins, hierarchic access); a previous implementation of DBPL for flat relations also supported grid files for multi-dimensional range queries and semi-join programs. The evaluation either yields a boolean result (for existentially or universally quantified expressions) or a temporary relation. In many cases (e.g. in the assignment Parts:+ rex where Parts does not appear in rex) the selected relation elements of rex do not have to be stored in a temporary relation but can be "pipelined" directly to another part of the system that processes them (e.g. performs element insertions).

The previous descriptions illustrate that the use of selectors in an expression context is roughly equivalent to the concept of "query modification" employed in relational database systems. The basic idea for the implementation of a selected relation *update* R[sp(...)]:= rex is again to pass a symbolic description of sp and rex to the DBPL runtime system that transforms the selected update conceptually into a guarded non-selected relation update (see Section 3.2). The specific structure of the guarded update may allow significant simplifications of the integrity checking code based on knowledge about the structure of rex. For example, if it can be inferred that each element in rex fullfils the selection completely.

To summarize, DBPL delegates the implementation of user-defined naming schemes to the query optimization component of the runtime system that makes heavy use of

- the well-understood semantics of first-order predicates;

---

[2]This "lazy" expansion of nested predicates is also essential for the optimization of recursive constructor applications.

- the advantageous algebraic properties of relations as bulk data type constructors;

- the strict separation between side-effect free query expressions and arbitrary DBPL procedures and functions enforced in DBPL.

4.3   Extended Naming Schemes and Transaction Management

As mentioned in Section 2.3, DBPL guarantees that concurrent transactions are executed in a serializable schedule. The underlying concurrency control theory [BHG87] assumes data objects to be abstract *named* entities that can be used as arguments in read or write operations. By using different naming schemes one arrives at different definitions of a conflict which finally lead to concurrency control protocols that allow substantially different degrees of parallelism. For example, multi-level concurrency control protocols [BSW88,EM82] utilize fine-grained naming schemes at the lower system levels and more application-oriented naming schemes at the higher system levels. The goal is to reduce the number of conflicts at the application-level by abstracting from details of lower-level naming schemes.

DBPL utilizes a three-level concurrency control and recovery scheme. Names within the lower layer SMS are page identifiers and file identifiers. The medium layer CRDS makes use of super-TIDS to perform synchronization for data records and access structures. The transaction management at the highest abstraction level of the DBPL data model (within the layer CTMS) identifies components of persistent variables (like SparseMatrix[1][4].val) through a path consisting of

- a system-wide unique database module identifier (essentially a time stamp generated at compile-time),

- an identification of a persistent variable within that module (e.g., SparseMatrix), and

- a (possibly empty) path consisting of key values and attribute identifiers (e.g., 1 , 4, val).

Due to the nested structure of persistent variables in DBPL, this naming scheme leads to a multi-granularity concurrency control protocol at the CTMS level. It is therefore possible to name individual data elements as well as large collections of subcomponents of a composite object. Multi-granularity locking protocols [GLP75] allow both, a high degree of concurrency between transactions that operate at a fine level of granularity, and a small synchronization overhead for transactions that access large portions of the database.

The DBPL transaction manager CTMS resides above the query evaluation component CPMS in order to be able to avoid the well-known "phantom problem" [EGLT76]. Roughly speaking, the "phantom problem" occurs if set-oriented naming schemes are mapped to element-oriented naming schemes and synchronization is performed solely on individual data elements. For example, during the execution of a transaction that contains the access expression

EACH p IN Parts: p.color = red

it is not enough to lock all stored red elements in Parts, but it is also necessary to avoid the possibility that other concurrent transactions insert new elements in Parts making the selection predicate p.color = red true. Such predicative synchronization schemes for DBPL are discussed in more detail in [BJS86].

5   Concluding Remarks

The set- and predicate-oriented approach of DBPL to bulk data identification and manipulation differs considerably from the predominating identification mechanisms of persistent programming languages based on system-generated "object identifiers". This paper emphasizes the need for application-oriented and modular naming schemes with non-standard binding mechanisms as they are provided by the declarative selector mechanism of DBPL. The paper furthermore links the DBPL approach to more conventional naming and binding mechanisms by describing implementation aspects of DBPL's name space management in a persistent multi-user environment.

The authors expect that next generation database programming languages will support a broader spectrum of identification mechanisms. A challenging goal is to maintain DBPL-like associative access without resorting to an "omniscient" runtime system, i.e. to implement the functionality of the DBPL access path management, query optimizer and integrity checker in a language with only basic built-in identification and structuring mechanisms. This will require a powerful type system to capture the highly polymorphic nature of the query optimizer, reflection capabilities [SSS90] to reason about the structure of selection expressions and language constructs to achieve iteration abstraction [LG86].

References

[ACC81]   M.P. Atkinson, K.J. Chisholm, and W.P. Cockshott. PS-Algol: An Algol with a Persistent Heap. *ACM SIGPLAN Notices*, 17(7), July 1981.

[AGO89]   A. Albano, G. Ghelli, and R. Orsini. Types for Databases: The Galileo Experience. In *Proc. of the 2nd Workshop on Database Programming Languages, Portland, Oregon*, June 1989.

[AM88]   M.P. Atkinson and R. Morrision. Types, Bindings and Parameters in a Persistent Environment. In M.P. Atkinson, P. Buneman, and R. Morrison, editors, *Data Types and Persistence*, Topics in Information Systems. Springer-Verlag, 1988.

[BHG87]   P.A. Bernstein, V. Hadzilacos, and N. Goodman, editors. *Concurrency Control and Recovery in Database Systems*. Addison-Wesley, 1987.

[BJS86]   S. Böttcher, M. Jarke, and J.W. Schmidt. Adaptive Predicate Managers in Database Systems. In *Proc. of the 12th International Conference on VLDB*, Kyoto, 1986.

[BL84]   R. Burstall and B. Lampson. A kernel language for abstract data types and modules. In *Semantics of Data Types*, volume 173 of *Lecture Notes in Computer Science*. Springer-Verlag, 1984.

[Böt90]   S. Böttcher. Improving the Concurrency of Integrity Checks and Write Operations. In *Proc. ICDT 90*, Paris, December 1990.

[Bro89]   A.L Brown. Persistent Object Stores. PPRR 71-89, Universities of Glasgow and St Andrews, March 1989.

[BSW88]   C. Beeri, H.-J. Schek, and G. Weikum. Multi-Level Transaction Management, Theoretical Art or Practical Need? In *Advances in Database Technology, EDBT '88*, volume 303 of *Lecture Notes in Computer Science*, pages 134–154. Springer-Verlag, 1988.

[But87]   M.H. Butler. Storage Reclamation in Object Oriented Database Systems. In *Proc. of SIGMOD Conf., San Francisco*, 1987.

[Car86]   L. Cardelli. Amber. In *Combinators and Functional Programming Languages*, volume 242 of *Lecture Notes in Computer Science*. Springer-Verlag, 1986.

[Car89]   L. Cardelli. Typeful Programming. Digital Systems Research Center Reports 45, DEC SRC Palo Alto, May 1989.

[CDMB90] R. Connor, A. Dearle, R. Morrison, and F. Brown. Existentially Quantified Types as a Database Viewing Mechanism. In *Advances in Database Technology, EDBT '90*, volume 416 of *Lecture Notes in Computer Science*, pages 301–315. Springer-Verlag, 1990.

[Coh81]   J. Cohen. Garbage Collection of Linked Data Structures. *ACM Computing Surveys*, 13(3), September 1981.

[Dat89]   C.J. Date. *A Guide to the SQL Standard*. Addison-Wesley, second edition, 1989.

[DCBM89] A. Dearle, R. Connor, F. Brown, and R. Morrison. Napier88 – A Database Programming Language? In *Proc. of the 2nd Workshop on Database Programming Languages, Salishan Lodge, Oregon*, June 1989.

[DD79]   A. Demers and J. Donahue. Revised Report on Russel. TR 79–389, Computer Science Department, Cornell University, 1979.

[Dea89]   A. Dearle. Environments: a flexible binding mechanism to support system evolution. In *Proc. HICSS-22, Hawaii*, volume II, pages 46–55, January 1989.

[EGLT76]   K.P. Eswaran, J.N. Gray, R.A. Lorie, and I.L. Traiger. The Notion of Consistency and Predicate Locks in Database Systems. *Communications of the ACM*, 19(11):624–633, November 1976.

[EM82]   J. Eliot and B. Moss. Nested Transactions and Reliable Distributed Computing. In *Symposium on Reliability in Distributed Software and Database Systems*, pages 33–39, 1982.

[GLP75]   J.N. Gray, R.A. Lorie, and G.R. Putzolu. Granularity of Locks in a Shared Data Base. In *Proc. VLDB Conference*, Boston, Mass., September 1975.

[GMS87]   H. Garcia-Molina and K. Salem. Sagas. In *ACM-SIGMOD International Conference on Management of Data*, pages 249–259, San Francisco, May 1987.

[Gra81]   J.N. Gray. The Transaction Concept: Virtues and Limitations. In *Proc. 7th VLDB Conference*, pages 144–154, Cannes, France, September 1981.

[Har88]   R. Harper. Modules and Persistence in Standard ML. In M.P. Atkinson, P. Buneman, and R. Morrison, editors, *Data Types and Persistence*, Topics in Information Systems. Springer-Verlag, 1988.

[Hoa68]   C.A.R. Hoare. Record Handling. In F. Genuys, editor, *Programming Languages*, pages 291–347. Academic Press, London, 1968.

[JGL+88]   W. Johannsen, L. Ge, W. Lamersdorf, K. Reinhard, and J.W. Schmidt. Database Application Support in Open Systems: Language Support and Implementation. In *Proc. IEEE 4th Int. Conf. on Data Engineering*, Los Angeles, USA, February 1988.

[JK83]   M. Jarke and J. Koch. Range Nesting: A Fast Method to Evaluate Quantified Queries. In *ACM-SIGMOD International Conference on Management of Data*, pages 196–206, San Jose, May 1983.

[JLRS88]   W. Johannsen, W. Lamersdorf, K. Reinhard, and J.W. Schmidt. The DURESS Project: Extending Databases into an Open Systems Architecture. In *Advances in Database Technology, EDBT '88*, volume 303 of *Lecture Notes in Computer Science*, pages 616–620. Springer-Verlag, 1988.

[JLS85]   M. Jarke, V. Linnemann, and J.W. Schmidt. Data Constructors: On the Integration of Rules and Relations. In *11th Intern. Conference on Very Large Data Bases, Stockholm*, August 1985.

[L+77]   B. Liskov et al. Abstraction Mechanisms in CLU. *Communications of the ACM*, 20(8), August 1977.

[LAB+81]   B. Liskov, R. Atkinson, T. Bloom, E. Moss, J.C. Schaffert, R. Scheifler, and A. Snyder. *CLU Reference Manual*. Springer-Verlag, 1981.

[Lan66]   P.J. Landin. The next 700 programming languages. *Communications of the ACM*, 9(3):157–166, 1966.

[LG86]   B. Liskov and J. Guttag. *Abstraction and Specification in Program Development*. The MIT Electrical Engineering and Computer Science Series. MIT Press, 1986.

[LY81]   P.L. Lehmann and S.B. Yao. Efficient Locking for Concurrent Operations on B-Trees. *ACM Transactions on Database Systems*, 6(4):650–670, December 1981.

[MAD87]   R. Morrison, M.P. Atkinson, and A. Dearle. Flexible Incremental Bindings in a Persistent Object Store. Persistent Programming Research Report 38, Univ. of St. Andrews, Dept. of Comp. Science, June 1987.

[Mat87]   D. Matthews. Static and Dynamic Type Checking. In *Proc. of the Workshop on Database Programming Languages, Roscoff, France*, pages 43–52, September 1987.

[MRS84]   M. Mall, M. Reimer, and J.W. Schmidt. Data Selection, Sharing and Access Control in a Relational Scenario. In M.L. Brodie, J.L. Myopoulos, and J.W. Schmidt, editors, *On Conceptual Modelling*. Springer-Verlag, 1984.

[MRS89]   F. Matthes, A. Rudloff, and J.W. Schmidt. Data- and Rule-Based Database Programming in DBPL. Esprit Project 892 WP/IMP 3.b, Fachbereich Informatik, Johann Wolfgang Goethe-Universität, Frankfurt, West Germany, March 1989.

[MS89]   F. Matthes and J.W. Schmidt. The Type System of DBPL. In *Proc. of the 2nd Workshop on Database Programming Languages, Salishan Lodge, Oregon*, pages 255–260, June 1989.

[Ric89]   J.E. Richardson. E: A Persistent Systems Implementation Language. Technical Report 868, Computer Sciences Department, University of Wisconsin-Madison, August 1989.

[RM87]   L. Rowe and Stonebraker M. The POSTGRES Data Model. In *Proc. 13th VLDB, Brighton*, pages 83–96, September 1987.

[RS81]   M. Reimer and J.W. Schmidt. Transaction Procedures with Relational Parameters. Report 45, Institut für Informatik, ETH Zürich, Switzerland, October 1981.

[SBK+88a]   J.W. Schmidt, M. Bittner, H. Klein, H. Eckhardt, and F. Matthes. DBPL System: The Prototype and its Architecture. Esprit Project 892 WP/IMP 3.2, Fachbereich Informatik, Johann Wolfgang Goethe-Universität, Frankfurt, West Germany, November 1988.

[SBK+88b]   J.W. Schmidt, M. Bittner, H. Klein, H. Eckhardt, and F. Matthes. DBPL System: The Prototype and its Architecture. DBPL Memo 111-88, Fachbereich Informatik, Johann Wolfgang Goethe-Universität, Frankfurt, West Germany, November 1988.

[SCB+86]   C. Schaffert, T. Cooper, B. Bullis, M. Kilian, and C. Wilpolt. An Introduction to Trellis/Owl. In *Proc. of 1st Int. Conf. on OOPSLA*, pages 9–16, Portland, Oregon, October 1986.

[Sch88]   J.W. Schmidt. Semantics of Selective Set Assignment. (technical note), December 1988.

[SEM88]   J.W. Schmidt, H. Eckhardt, and F. Matthes. DBPL Report. DBPL-Memo 111-88, Fachbereich Informatik, Johann Wolfgang Goethe-Universität, Frankfurt, West Germany, 1988.

[SGLJ89]   J.W Schmidt, L. Ge, V. Linnemann, and M. Jarke. Integrated Fact and Rule Management Based on Database Technology. In J.W. Schmidt and C. Thanos, editors, *Foundations of Knowledge Base Management*, Topics in Information Systems. Springer-Verlag, 1989.

[SL85]   J.W. Schmidt and V. Linnemann. Higher Level Relational Objects. In *Proc. 4th British National Conference on Databases (BNCOD 4)*. Cambridge University Press, July 1985.

[SSS90]   L. Stemple, D. Fegaras, T. Sheard, and A. Socorro. Exceeding the Limits of Polymorphism in Database Programming Languages. In *Advances in Database Technology, EDBT '90*, volume 416 of *Lecture Notes in Computer Science*, pages 269–285. Springer-Verlag, 1990.

[Str67]   C. Strachey, editor. *Fundamental concepts in programming languages*. Oxford University Press, Oxford, 1967.

[SWBM89]   J.W. Schmidt, I. Wetzel, A. Borgida, and J. Mylopoulos. Database Programming by Formal Refinement of Conceptual Designs. *IEEE – Data Engineering*, September 1989.

[Wir83]   N. Wirth. *Programming in Modula-2*. Springer-Verlag, 1983.

Persistent Functional Programming

David J. McNally
Department of Computational Science
University of St Andrews
St Andrews, Fife, Scotland
djm%uk.ac.st-and.cs@ukc

Stef Joosten
Department of Computer Science
University of Twente
Enschede, Holland
joosten@cs.utwente.nl

Antony J. T. Davie
Department of Computational Science
University of St Andrews
St Andrews, Fife, Scotland
ad%uk.ac.st-and.cs@ukc

Abstract

The authors of this paper have been working on the use of functional languages as tools for rapid prototyping and on the integration of such languages with a persistent object store. This work has been carried out as part of an Esprit I research project — the STAPLE project (Esprit 891). We have implemented several large prototypes using various functional programming languages. These prototypes involve major programming effort and are examples of large real life applications of functional programming. Whilst development of these prototypes has been relatively quick, progress has been hindered by a major shortcoming of current functional languages — the lack of support for long term data. The problem manifests itself in two ways. Firstly, it occurs where there is a need to create, evaluate and access large, possibly unbounded, data structures. Secondly, the problem arises where there is a requirement to construct and develop large programs. This paper describes these problems, and presents the use of persistence as a general solution to them. The implementation of this solution, based on persistent modules, is then described.

1 Introduction

Functional programming is an attractive programming paradigm for a number of reasons, one important one being the static nature of data from a user's point of view. Because functional objects do not change their values we would like to make sure that they are not needlessly evaluated or re-evaluated. In lazy functional programming systems no object will be evaluated unless it needs to be. However, in existing implementations, work done during evaluation is usually lost at the end of each session.

The problem with existing functional programming systems is their lack of support for storage of long term data. This manifests itself, for example, in large functional programs where considerable run-time effort is expended building the data structures over which many subsequent computations are to take place. An ad-hoc technique to solve this problem is to flatten that data structures to the file system and unflatten them again when they are needed. This is inefficient because the reconstruction of these data structures may be as expensive as calculating them in the first place. It also requires explicit programmer effort and will usually result in loss of sharing and topology.

We describe here a lazy functional system in which persistence[atki84,morr85,atki87] ensures that objects will not be needlessly re-evaluated even over execution sessions and that their topology is automatically preserved as long as they are accessible. Accessibility is controlled using a very simple persistent module structure.

In section 2, we present two problems showing the significance of persistence of state. The first of these is connected with the commonly used programming technique of lazy evaluation, which we illustrate with examples where longevity is important. The second concerns the persistence of objects grouped together into modules for large scale program development.

In section 3 we present an example to show that these problems occur and are serious ones in the development of large scale software. We show that systems up till the present have either had to program round the difficulties in a somewhat unnatural way or that they are not able to cope at all.

In section 4 we present a user's view of the STAPLE persistent functional programming system, showing how they create modules containing lazy objects and how they can use them in the construction of other modules and for executing functional programs interactively. We show what types of objects users are allowed to manipulate.

In section 5 we give details of our implementation of the STAPLE system showing how objects of various system types are represented in the persistent store and how lazy reduction is carried out. We show how the STAPLE universe is organised into modules and how these are implemented.

Section 6 reports measurements we have made on the persistent system and suggests some improvements that we hope to make in the near future, and section 7 gives our conclusions.

2   The Problems

Building large functional programs is hindered by two problems which will be examined in this section. Both are connected with the longevity of programs and data. The first problem, which arises from lazy evaluation, is the potential loss of information about the state of evaluation of objects between runs of functional programs. As examples of where this trouble can occur, we examine two programming techniques common in functional programming, partial evaluation and memoising. The second problem, an aspect of modularity, which is not unique to functional programming, is the lack of support for long term storage of large data structures without the need to reconstruct them each time they are needed. Such support is provided in database programming languages such as Napier88[morr89], but is not normally found in existing functional programming systems.

2.1   The State-Loss Problem

2.1.1   Evaluation Strategy

Data in functional programs is *referentially transparent*. This means that the value of an expression describing a data object depends only on the values of its sub-expressions. It does not depend on other factors and in particular it does not depend on the order in which evaluation takes place. These facts contain the implication that no object ever changes its value (otherwise order would be important in evaluation). The property of referential transparency has certain advantages, therefore, for the choice of evaluation strategy. In particular, it allows a delay in evaluation of certain objects, possibly indefinitely. Unevaluated objects are called *suspensions* This leads to a strategy known as *lazy evaluation* or, where function calls are involved, *call by need*, because suspension allows a strategy in which no object is ever evaluated until it is needed. As well as being suspended, objects may also be in partially evaluated states and an object proceeds through a spectrum of states of evaluation (without ever changing its value as far as the user is concerned!) and may, if needed, finally arrive at a fully evaluated state, a *normal* or *canonical* form. Lazy evaluation has some interesting programming techniques associated with it, for instance the ability to manipulate infinite data objects (which are never fully evaluated). For example the definition

```
from( n ) = n : from( n+1 )
```

allows us to define the infinite list of positive integers from(1) (: is the list forming operator). This object starts life being represented by a graph representing the application of from to 1. Depending on how much of the infinite list is needed later, it can be in any of the states:

```
from( 1 ) = 1 : from( 1+1 )
          = 1 : (1+1) : from( (1+1)+1 )
          = 1 : (1+1) : ((1+1)+1) : from( ((1+1)+1)+1 )
          ...
```

and of course any of the additions may be replaced by the integers that they represent at any time they are needed.

The ability to suspend objects leads to a method of implementation called *graph reduction*[peyt87] in which the states of evaluation are represented by graphs. Any graph can be *overwritten* by or reduced to another representing a more evaluated state. Where such graphs contain named objects, they will share sub-graphs when the names are overwritten by the graphs to which they are bound.

When a lazy evaluation strategy is adopted, suspension is made to happen in three situations. Firstly, when structured objects are created, there is no need to evaluate their fields because they may never be accessed. Secondly, when a function is applied to an argument, the evaluation of the function's body may take a course that does not need the value of the argument. For example the function

```
f( x,y ) = if x>0 then y+1 else 0
```

may not need to evaluate y. Thirdly, when bindings are made directly in definitions, a name should be bound to a suspended value since that value may never be needed.

Sharing will be created in a number of ways. For instance, aliases for the same object may be created with different names and it would clearly be advantageous if evaluation of any of the names implied that the others would not need further evaluation. In any situation in which sharing arises, overwriting a suspension will have an effect felt by all graphs which share it.

2.1.2 Partial Application and Memoising

A general and quite common phenomenon in functional programming uses so called Curry'd functions to allow *partial evaluation*. Curry'd functions are defined in such a way that each argument supplied to the function (except the last) makes it produce another function ready to consume further arguments. The advantage of this method is that only some of the arguments need be supplied at an initial call and this allows early binding to these arguments. To take advantage of this, lazy evaluation should ensure that the associations made by this binding should only be evaluated (at most) once. Such objects will only be evaluated once per session. However, it is desirable that this evaluation should persist as long as the object remains accessible.

Consider a small example. Numerical integration is often carried out using a Gaussian quadrature scheme where the integral over a range is replaced by a weighted finite summation taken at n points in the range (n is the order). The calculation of the weights and positions of the points relative to the range is complicated and time-consuming but need only be done once (for a given order) as they are independent of the function being integrated. Thus we can define

```
gauss n f range = ...
```

and expect to carry out partial applications of gauss to particular orders, n.

Providing that these partial values remain reachable from a name in a module, they need never be calculated again. In fact if we use a memo-function technique, we can store an infinite number of values of gauss n in a lazy associative data structure so that the weights and points will only be calculated as and when needed for a particular value of n. To do this, all that needs to be done is to replace calls of gauss n by accesses to the data structure memo which contains suspended calls to gauss. That is

```
memo = [ gauss i | i <- 1,2.. ] -- the infinite list of gauss's
        where
        gauss n f range = ...      -- the function above
gauss n = memo ! n                 -- select the n'th element of memo
```

With this solution, an attempt to use gauss 5, say, will cause significant work to be done the first time, but on subsequent occasions in the same program, will only involve selecting the value from the list memo.

It would again be advantageous, from the point of view of reuseability, if the effects of this hard work were to persist.

2.1.3 The Failure of Existing Systems

It is an unfortunate fact that in most implementations of functional languages, once execution of an interactive expression has completed, the state of evaluation of suspended objects is usually lost. In Miranda[turn85] for example, evaluation of an expression more than once causes exactly the same amount of computation to take place each time. This is because each expression is compiled and then linked with a global environment or script which is loaded into the run-time system at the beginning of each interactive evaluation even though objects in the script may have undergone mutation in previous interactions. Our solution presented below in sections 4 and 5 makes the effects of such evaluations persist.

2.2 Modularity

A prime requirement when constructing large scale software systems is that of modularity. It is clearly desirable to be able to compartmentalize a problem into its logical sub-problems in a structured way. At the same time a mechanism must be provided for the export and import of objects described in such modules so that they may be used in others.

Support for modularity is provided by most existing functional programming systems, but when linking modules together, no account is taken of work that may have been done during previous sessions which may have used the modules involved. All bound objects in these systems start off by being unevaluated. With laziness in mind, it would be advantageous for the state of evaluation of objects to be retained when control passes from one module to another. That is, any bindings made to already evaluated objects in a module will not cause further unnecessary evaluation when used in another. The solution which we present in section 4.2 allows modules to be bound together taking advantage of the most recent evaluation state of each bound object.

3 A Large Scale Example

We have used functional programming languages to build several prototypes and believe that functional languages are particularly suited to this activity[joos89a,joos89b]. These prototypes have exhibited the problems described in Section 2 and we shall examine how and why they occurred by describing one particular prototyping experiment in detail. We shall show how functional programming systems up till now fail to meet the needs of programming in the large even though, in certain cases, it is possible to program around the difficulties encountered. Of course, these ad-hoc techniques can still only partially alleviate the problems. We believe that adding persistence to functional systems provides a useful solution to these problems.

3.1 A Transportation Network Prototype

Transportation network problems arise frequently in town-planning situations. Our partners in the STAPLE project, Concept ASA, are a small database company based in Frankfurt who have a great deal of expertise in constructing such systems. Before building a persistent system, an experiment was jointly undertaken to build a prototype of the Frankfurt transportation network using the Miranda[turn85] functional programming system. Public transport in the city of Frankfurt is organised by the Frankfurt Verkehrs und Tarifverbund (FVV). It consists of a number of methods of transport, subways (U-bahn), trams (Straßenbahn), trains (S-bahn) and buses. There are several hundred stations and stops on tens of routes in this network.

Leaving aside the reasons why functional languages are good for prototyping which is not our main thesis here, current functional languages fail to meet the needs of large scale programming problems. Problems of scale have shown themselves in systems such as Miranda which has shown considerable strain as the Frankfurt system has grown. Indeed Miranda has not been able to cope with the magnitude of the latest developments of the prototype particularly because useful work has been lost between runs and complex objects have had to be re-evaluated every time.

3.2 The Cost of Transitory Evaluation

Using the raw data for the network which specifies these transport routes throughout the city, further information such as the distance between nodes is specified algorithmically. This information is needed by a number of route searching algorithms. However construction of a data structure holding the extra information accounts for a significant proportion of total run time which is incurred every time the prototype is executed. Ideally, we would wish to calculate this data structure only once since it does not change from one run of the system to the next.

3.3   A Provisional Expedient

One stopgap solution which was adopted when Miranda was used to develop the Frankfurt network was to evaluate the data structure and print it to a file in the form of a Miranda definition which was then compiled. This removed the overhead of generating the data structure more than once. The following example shows how this was done:

```
fVVnet = ...         || definition of a huge data structure
output               || definition of the string to be stored on file
 = "fVVnet = " ++ show fVVnet
```

The string `output` contains Miranda source code representing the fully evaluated structure `fVVnet`. After compilation of this source, expressions can use this data-structure without having to re-evaluate it's components. This technique does not solve the problem completely, however, since compilation of the new definition generates code to build the network data structure, but this code has to be executed every time the prototype is run. An even more serious problem is that sharing is lost. The sharing, that is inherent to lazy functional languages, keeps large data structures quite manageable. The flattening process causes all sharing to be discarded with source code being generated many times for the same object. This yields a severe penalty in space and time performance of subsequent evaluations. There is an ad-hoc solution to this problem as well. We could write a formatting function (`show`) to generate a shared structure by using auxiliary definitions. Instead of printing for instance:

```
fVVnet = [ ("456231","335210",5,"u1","456231")
         , ("335210","456231",13,"u1","556231")
         ]
```

one could generate

```
fVVnet = [ (s456231,s335210,5,u1,s456231)
         , (s335210,s456231,13,u1,s556231)
         ]
         where
           s335210 = "335210"
           s456231 = "456231"
           s556231 = "556231"
           u1      = "u1"
```

Being applied systematically on a large scale, this technique would allow sharing to be preserved, but the cost of doing all this would have increased considerably in the meantime. Writing a function to generate the textual representation of the data-structure is no longer a simple task. In addition, it is a task that has nothing to do with the problem we are solving. Users of functional programming languages should not have to expend such irrelevant effort in performing program transformations by hand[†] . This kind of problem is common to large scale software development. Many applications need to build large data-structures which should only be constructed once and persist thereafter.

The ad hoc technique described above is not good enough to cope with the general problem. If a data structure is recursively defined, and contains any cycles, then flattening will not terminate.

4   Persistent Functional Programming

Persistent programming languages already provide support for many of the things we are trying to achieve. In STAPLE[davi90], as we shall see below in section 5, lazy functional objects are implemented as graphs containing evaluated and suspended (still to be evaluated) nodes which often point at each other with highly convoluted topologies and persistent systems are well known to be able to cope with the storage of such non-linear structures[brow89]. During interactive sessions, some further evaluation of persistent objects may take place. Any

---

[†] Systems exist (e.g. PGraphite[tarr89]) though not functional ones, where similar transformations have been automated.

suspended nodes which are consequently evaluated will be overwritten, in place, by their values. In this way, expressions are evaluated at most once.

The STAPLE persistent functional programming environment provides support for persistent objects and has a flexible binding system which allows evolution in the system to be facilitated and controlled.

4.1   The STAPLE Persistent Functional Programming Environment

In order to facilitate the development of functional programs, the STAPLE system, which is built on a persistent store, provides an integrated environment in which objects, grouped together into modules, are stored. The recursive nature of functional languages, particularly with a lazy evaluation strategy allowing infinite data objects, leads to many such objects being partially evaluated. Objects may be completely unevaluated if not yet needed, evaluated enough to determine which pattern they match in some definition, evaluated enough to print the first 30 elements ... right through a spectrum leading eventually (in the case of finite objects) to complete evaluation in a normal form. Because of the insistence on functional purity, referential transparency is maintained and no object changes its value, except in the above sense of being partially reduced on the road to normal form. It is clear therefore, that the state of evaluation of partially or wholly evaluated objects should be made to persist for as long as possible, not only from one evaluation to the next in any given login session, but also across sessions so that evaluation work done on an object will not have to be redone.

Each STAPLE persistent store is organised as a set of modules each of which can contain a number of definitions. This set of modules is organised into a directory structure within the store and modules can be accessed via their name. A module constitutes the unit of compilation. Any module can be compiled in an environment created by importing the definitions exported by other previously compiled modules. An interactive session can also run in such an environment.

We have thus extended the benefit of lazy evaluation in conventional functional language implementations to multiple execution of any programs which use the object.

4.2   Persistent Modules

The module system we have implemented is a particularly simple one which was designed in such a way that users of the existing non-persistent STAPLE system did not need to make any changes to existing source programs, but could utilise the persistent store by the use of two main commands at the operating system level:

- A command to create a module in a persistent store
- A command to interact with a module or modules

4.2.1   Creating a New Module in the Persistent Store

The command

```
mkmodule mname [ othermodulenames ]
```

places a module named *mname* into the persistent store by compiling the source file called *mname*. This module imports all definitions from *othermodulenames* which must already be in the persistent store. A module exports all names defined at its own top level of definitions. If *mname* already exists in the store, this command will overwrite it and any objects defined in the old version will become candidates for garbage collection unless they have been imported by another module in the store. If there is a clash of names in *othermodulenames* and/or *mname* , these are resolved by considering each module as a block in which the previous ones appear as sub-blocks and letting lexical scoping resolve the conflicts.

E.g. Suppose module A defines x and y, module B exports y and z and that module C exports z and w, then the following variables are in scope inside A when the command mkmodule A B C is executed: w from C, z from B and x and y from A.

Note that this rule means that modules cannot be mutually recursive. All recursion must be expressed within modules where the defined objects can be mutually recursive. Further note that modules do not export any names that they import from elsewhere. In the particularly simple set-up described here, the names declared at the top level of a module (and only those names) are exported by that module.

4.2.2 Interacting with the Persistent Store

The command

```
staple [ modulenames ]
```

allows the user to evaluate expressions interactively, in an environment defined by *modulenames* which must be in the persistent store already. Expressions evaluated during the interactive session may prompt the (partial) evaluation of objects defined in the environment being used and this will be reflected in a permanent (referentially transparent) change in state of the persistent store.

5   Persistent Lazy Functional Objects

Our implementation uses the stable persistent object store[brow89] for storing objects. We have chosen to use an existing object store implementation because it provides the functionality we require and has been thoroughly tested and is being used in the implementation of two other persistent systems – Napier88[morr89] and Galileo[alba85]. All run-time objects are created in a stable heap and conform to the stable store object format. This means that any run-time object can be made to persist by making it accessible from the root of persistence. A stabilise operation which occurs at module compilation time, on exit from an interactive session or before a garbage collection, causes all objects reachable from the root to be made to persist.

The STAPLE system maintains a flat name space which binds names to modules. A module is just an object like any other, but is not a run-time object in that it cannot be manipulated by functional programs other than by having evaluation take place on its components. The components of modules are indeed run-time objects and can be bound to as described above. Evaluation taking place on the objects in a module will persist (see section 5.2).

5.1   Run-Time Object Representation

Access to the stable store is carefully controlled by the use of a well defined interface described in [brow90]. This provides functions for creating, accessing, writing and destroying objects in the stable store. Every object in the store has several fields some of which are pointers to other objects, and some of which are scalar values such as integers, machine instructions etc. All objects begin with a header field which indicates the number of pointers in the object and some house keeping information and a size field which contains the total size of the object in words. The general stable store object format is shown diagrammatically as follows:

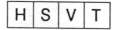

where Pi are the pointer fields and Si are the scalar or non-pointer fields.

STAPLE run-time objects conform to this format, but in addition, we utilise an extra tag field to indicate that the object is an evaluated object or that it is a suspended value. This field is, by convention, the last non-pointer field of the object. In fact this field is used to hold the system type of evaluated objects which eases the printing of results and for debugging. Ideally we should have used a single bit in the header field of the object to indicate that it is suspended, but these bits are reserved for use by the stable store itself – in particular for garbage collection.

5.1.1 Literals

STAPLE has four literal types: `Int`, `Char`, `Bool` and `Real`. The first three of these are represented by objects of the following kind:

$$\boxed{H \mid S \mid V \mid T}$$

Where H and S are the header and size fields, V contains the value and T is the tag which indicates the system type of the object. Real literal objects are represented similarly but have two words which contain the value.

5.1.2 Closures

Function values are represented as closure objects. A closure consists of code for the body of the function, and an environment in which the function is to be executed. The object format is as follows.

Here C is a pointer to a code vector object and E is a pointer to an environment object. When a function is applied to an object, a new environment is created consisting of the environment from the closure, and the argument of the function which is placed in the argument register. The code form the function is then executed in this environment. The tag indicates the system type (closure) of the object. It does not give any further information about the user type of the object (e.g. its domain or range type) which is factored out at compile time.

5.1.3 Environments

Environments are pointed to by closures and suspension and provide the context in which their evaluation takes place. An environment object with 4 components, for example, will have the following format:

where A,B,C and D are pointers to other objects which are the graphs representing the values of non-local variables used by the closure or suspension and T indicates that this is an environment object. The machine instruction to load an object from an environment simply indexes this object which yields a constant access time for environment lookup[davi79].

5.1.4 Suspensions

An unevaluated object is represented by a suspension at run-time. The suspension object contains a code vector, C, and an environment, E, in which to execute the code. A suspension differs from a closure, however, in that the full environment is present in the suspension. A suspension has an additional field which holds the argument, A, which was in the argument register when the suspension was created. For details of the use of the argument register see [davi89]. The format of a suspension object is as follows.

$$\boxed{H\;S\;C\;A\;E\;T}$$

The suspension object's tag is used when the value of the object is required (see section 5.2).

5.1.5 Data Structures

STAPLE provides tuples as standard data structures and allows the user to define algebraic data types. The system also provides lists as a built-in algebraic type.

   In order to facilitate ease of overwriting suspension objects with objects of a different kind, we have implemented compound data structures as two level objects (but see section 6). Structured objects contain a single pointer field pointing to an environment object which contains the fields. In objects of algebraic type, a variant tag is stored as a scalar field in addition to the usual system type tag. For instance, the format of a structure with four fields A,B,C and D is as follows.

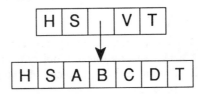

Where V is the variant tag. The variant tag is used in pattern matching to discriminate between cases.

5.1.6 Code Vectors

A code vector object contains executable machine code (which may be abstract or real) and pointers to sub code vectors which are used during the execution of this code vector to construct new closures. For example, a code vector object with 2 sub code vector fields and n words of executable code would be represented by

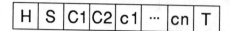

Here C1 and C2 are pointers to the sub code vectors and $c_1 \ldots c_n$ make up the executable code. This differs from conventional implementations of functional languages where the code is stored separately from the program's run-time heap and code addresses in the heap are just integer offsets into the code vector.

5.2 Lazy Reduction

When the value of an object is required strictly, for example when two integers are to be added, the run-time system examines the tag of the object to see if it is a suspension. If the object is not a suspension, it simply proceeds accessing the field or fields of the object as required. If, however, the object is a suspension, a process similar to a function call is initiated. The code from the suspension is executed in an environment created by loading the argument and environment fields of the suspension into the appropriate machine registers. When the execution of this code returns, an evaluated object is left on top of the stack with the suspension immediately below it. Next, the evaluated object is used to overwrite the suspension object in place so that any other objects which shared the suspension object will, in future, see the newly evaluated object. We know that all objects can overwrite a suspension object in place since the size of all run-time values is less than or equal to the size of a suspension.

5.3 STAPLE Modules

A compiled module must be capable of being stored in the persistent store and executed within it. It must therefore conform to the object formats described above. A module descriptor is represented as a stable store object with five pointer fields –

$$\boxed{H\;S\;1\;2\;3\;4\;5\;T}$$

1)   points to a string containing a *textual description* of the module. (A user supplied comment).

2)   points to the *source* of the module.

3)   points to a *symbol table* for the module, this associates names defined in the module with their type and an offset into the environment object pointed to by field 5.

4)   points to a *types table* which contains definitions of all algebraic data-types and type synonyms defined in the module. Fields 3 and 4 together form the module's interface.

5)   this field points to the *value* of the module which is an environment object with one entry for each value exported by the module.

Each entry in the environment initially points to a *suspension* as described in section 5.1.4. In many cases, however, a compile time optimisation can be used to generate the objects themselves[mcna89].

The environment part of a module is created by converting its `definitions` into an expression as follows

```
let definitions in loadenv
```

The expression **loadenv** is only recognised by the module compilation system and has the effect, at run-time, of loading the current environment onto the stack. An environment object is not normally found on the stack during execution of programs, but in this case it allows us simply to execute the above program, and fill in the fifth field of the module with the result found on top of the stack.

5.4   The STAPLE Universe

As mentioned above, the STAPLE system maintains a flat name-space mapping names to modules. This is shown in figure 1.

All objects which are reachable from the stable root object (a special object in the stable store) will persist provided a stabilise operation has taken place. Our universe consists of a STAPLE root object which contains several objects particular to the STAPLE system. One of these is the module name-space. The second is a global nil object, the third is a special module which contains functions for STAPLE's built in operators and finally there is a machine state object which is used to preserve the state of execution of the entire machine over a garbage collection or stabilise operation. Figure 1 shows the organisation of the STAPLE stable store.

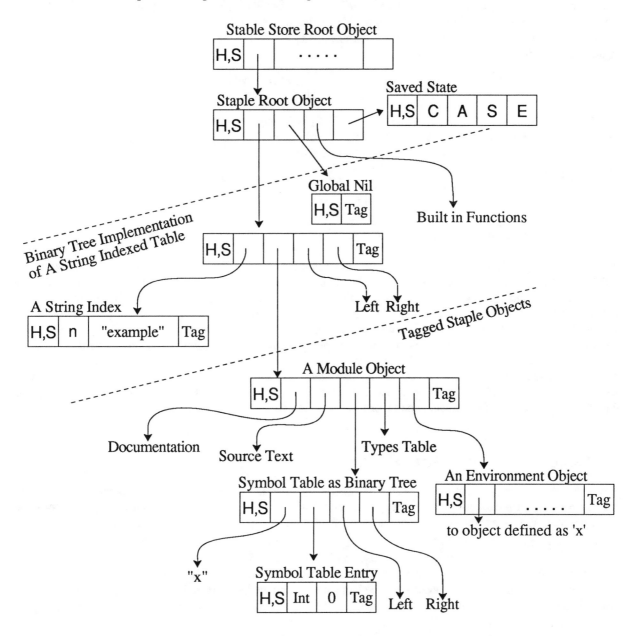

Figure 1 – The STAPLE stable store organisation

6   Measurement and Optimisation

We compared our persistent functional language implementation with an earlier non-persistent one both of which use the CASE abstract machine and are different only in that they have a different run-time heap. Our measurements indicate that the persistent implementation is 10% slower than the non-persistent implementation. Given that we have not breached the stable store interface, we were pleasantly surprised with this result. Our system also compares well with Miranda for programs which are not heavy on access of data structures. We found that our persistent system was twice as fast as Miranda for nfib, 15% faster when calculating the primes less than 1000 but twice as slow for a hidden line removal program which created and accessed a lot of intermediate data structures. The reason for this is clear from our choice of implementation of data structures. In order to facilitate the overwriting of suspensions which are 6 words in size with any other kind of object, data structure objects are two level objects and a double dereference is needed to access a field of a data structure – one to get the fields (an environment object) and one to access the field itself. There is a simple optimisation to this technique which is to have data structure objects in the following format:

where V is the variant tag and F_i are the fields. This makes accessing a field much less expensive, but we need then to deal with the problem of overwriting suspensions with objects which are greater in size. Two techniques can be used to solve this. The first, used by Miranda, is to have a new kind of object called an indirection object which is of the following format.

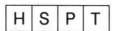

P is a pointer to a value. When an overwrite is executed, the size of the value is examined. If it is less than or equal to the size of a suspension, then the suspension is simply overwritten with the object as before. However, if the object is bigger than a suspension, then the suspension is overwritten by an indirection object whose single pointer field points to the value. All stack load instructions must now check if the object being loaded is an indirection node and if so, dereference the indirection node to access the value. This is expensive, but a garbage collector can remove all indirection nodes by making all pointers which point at indirection nodes point to the values themselves. Another strategy which can be used to solve this problem is to make suspension objects variable size. The type of the object is known at compile time, and a suspension can be created which is known statically to be big enough to be overwritten by a value of the statically determined type. The only overhead present here is one of space in which a suspension which may evaluate to a very large object will occupy a large amount of space. If such a suspended value is never accessed, then the space is wasted. However, this is much less serious than the cost of our existing implementation, or the indirection node strategy. We intend to implement this scheme at an early stage.

7   Conclusions and Future Work

We have described a problem which occurs in existing functional programming systems, namely their lack of support for long term data, which makes it difficult and in some cases impossible to use these languages for large scale systems. We have shown how the problem can arise in real-life prototyping examples.

We have described the STAPLE functional programming system which can be used for large scale functional programs development and prototyping and uses an implementation which preserves the state of evaluation of functional objects from one session to another thus allowing work done in earlier runs to be made available. We have shown how a simple module system can be implemented and we have given details of the persistent objects of which it is made. We have presented measurements of the system, pointed out the optimisations we have made and suggested some for the future.

The STAPLE functional programming system preserves referential transparency even over the persistent store. Functional programs cannot access or manipulate the store directly. We intend to investigate a method based on the stream I/O of HASKELL[huda90] of allowing functional programs to access and manipulate objects in the persistent store.

8   References

[alba85]   Albano, A., Cardelli, L. and Orsini, R., *Galileo: A Strongly Typed Interactive Conceptual Language*, ACM Transactions on Database Systems 10(2), June 1985

[atki85]   Atkinson, M.P. and Morrison, R., *First Class Persistent Procedures*, ACM TOPLAS 7(4), October 1985

[atki87]   Atkinson, M.P. and Buneman, O.P., *Types and Persistence in Database Programming Languages*, ACM Computing Surveys, 19(2), June 1987

[brow89]   Brown, A., *Persistent Object Stores*, Persistent Programming Research Report 71, Department of Computational Science, University of St Andrews, Scotland, March 1989

[brow90]   Brown, A., *Persistent Object Store Library*, Internal Document, Department of Computational Science, University of St Andrews, Scotland, April 1990

[davi79]   Davie, A.J.T., *Variable Access in Languages in which Procedures are First Class Citizens* — research report CS/79/2, Department of Computational Science, University of St. Andrews, Scotland, 1979

[davi89]   Davie, A.J.T. and McNally, D.J., *CASE – A Lazy Version of an SECD Machine with a Flat Environment*, in Proceedings TENCON '89, Bombay, India, 1989

[davi90]   Davie, A.J.T. and McNally, D.J., *STAPLE User's Manual* — research report CS/90/12, Department of Computational Science, University of St. Andrews, Scotland, 1990

[huda90]   Hudak, P. et al., *Report on the Programming Language Haskell*, University of Glasgow, 1990

[joos89a]   Joosten, S.M.M., *The Use of Functional Programming in Software Development*, PhD. Thesis, University of Twente, The Netherlands, 1989

[joos89b]   Joosten, S.M.M., *Public Transport in Frankfurt — an Experiment in Functional Programming*, STAPLE Research Report, University of Twente, The Netherlands, 1989

[mcna89]   McNally, D.J., *Code Generating Functional Language Modules for a Persistent Object Store*, STAPLE project research report STAPLE/StA/89/2, Department of Computational Science, University of St. Andrews, Scotland, 1989

[morr85]   Morrison, R., Dearle, A., Brown, A.L. and Atkinson, M.P., *The Persistent Store as an Enabling Technology for Integrated Support Environments*, in Proc. 8th International Conference on Software Engineering (London, August) IEEE New York, 1985

[morr89]   Morrison, R., Brown, A.L., Connor, R.C.H. and Dearle, A., *The Napier88 Refernce Manual*, Persistent Programming Research Report 77, Department of Computational Science, University of St Andrews, Scotland, March 1989

[peyt87]   Peyton Jones, S., *The Implementation of Functional Programming Languages*, Prentice Hall, 1987

[tarr89]   Tarr, P.L., Wilden, J.C. and Wolf, A.L., *A Different Tack to Providinig Persistence in a Language*, in Proc. of Second International Workshop on Database Programming Languages, Oregon, 1989, Hull, R., Morrison, R. and Stempel, D. (Eds.), Morgan Kaufmann Publishers Inc., San Mateo, California

[turn85]   Turner, D.A., *Miranda: A Non-Strict Functional Language with Polymorphic Types*, in Proc. IFIP International Conference on Functional Programming Languages and Computer Architecture, Nancy, France, LNCS 201, Springer-Verlag, 1985

Extending and Limiting PGRAPHITE-style Persistence

Peri L. Tarr
Jack C. Wileden
Lori A. Clarke

Software Development Laboratory
Department of Computer and Information Science
University of Massachusetts
Amherst, Massachusetts 01003

Abstract

We have been working on both extending and limiting the approach to persistence embodied in our PGRAPHITE system. The extensions include implementing automated support for persistent objects of classes other than directed graphs, notably relationships and relations, and porting our system to storage managers other than Ada Direct_IO, notably Mneme, ObServer II, and the Exodus Storage Manager. The work on restrictions has focused on defining and implementing principled ways to specify the "limits" of the reachability-based persistence model employed by PGRAPHITE. The approach that we have taken relies on using potentially persistent relationships and relations to specify the "boundaries" that (de)limit persistence in complex connected structures. In this paper we describe both of these aspects of our recent work, our implementations of them and our experience with them.

This work was supported in part by the National Science Foundatation (CCR–87–04478) with cooperation from the Defense Advanced Research Projects Agency (ARPA order 6104).

1   Introduction

The PGRAPHITE system [3, 5] is a prototype realization of a particular approach to including persistence in modern programming languages. By "modern", we mean languages that are strongly typed and that provide rich support for the definition and use of abstract data types — Ada is our standard exemplar.

Given such a language, our approach to persistence is to augment the set of operations provided by any and all types in a program to include operations that can make individual instances of the types persist. From the programmer's perspective, this introduces two new abstractions, one for persistent objects and one for persistent stores, that can be smoothly integrated with the other abstractions used in the program. The result is an orthogonal, transparent persistence mechanism that permits late binding on persistence decisions. Most other approaches force a much earlier decision concerning persistence, e.g., at type-definition or instance creation time.

While the approach is fully general (as we have demonstrated by applying it manually and as has been demonstrated by the Persi system [6], which automates the approach for most of C++), our original PGRAPHITE prototype only provided automated support for the approach for a limited set of types. Because PGRAPHITE was developed as part of our work on object management support for software development environments (in the Arcadia project [4]), that set of types was abstract directed graphs, which are among the most frequently used types in such environments. This particular set of types forced us to address the interesting question of "extent" of persistence — if a given graph node is made persistent, what other objects, if any, should become persistent as a result?

Our experience with PGRAPHITE over the last couple of years has indicated that our approach to persistence and to determining the extent of persistence is appropriate for many environment applications. It has also led us to develop automated support for creating additional abstract types that embody our approach to persistence, to explore alternative definitions for the extent of persistence, and to develop an interface definition that modularizes our implementation architecture. In the remainder of the paper we will briefly review the PGRAPHITE approach and its prototype implementation, and then describe our recent work in each of these areas.

2   Review of PGRAPHITE

The PGRAPHITE approach to providing persistence, and the prototype PGRAPHITE processor that produces Ada interface packages that implement the approach for arbitrary abstract directed graph types, have been described in detail elsewhere ([5], [3]). Here we briefly review two central features of the PGRAPHITE approach — PGRAPHITE's name space model and its reachability-based definition of the extent of persistence — then provide an example to illustrate the approach.

2.1   Side-by-side Name Spaces

Every language provides some way of referring to instances of types. But in most languages, this mechanism is somewhat restrictive. In particular, the validity of such references typically is not guaranteed outside of a single program execution. Moreover, the references form a name space that is normally not controllable by anything other than the run-time system of the language. To achieve a name space of object references that is valid within and between separate program executions, one must gain control over the name space. This is usually accomplished by modifying the run-time system or by custom-building a name space on top of the one provided by the programming language.

Our model of persistence addresses this issue instead by using *side-by-side* name spaces and defining a mapping between references in the two spaces. One of the name spaces is made up of the "normal" references to objects provided by the run-time system. We refer to these as *non-persistent* references (NPRs) because they cannot be preserved. The other name space is used to refer to persistent objects in a more enduring way. We call references in this name space *persistent identifiers* (PIDs). When application programs manipulate objects, they use NPRs to refer to those objects, whether or not the objects persist. If a program wants to obtain a reference to an object that will be valid at some, perhaps indeterminate, time in the future, it must request a PID for the object. This has the appropriate side-effect of making the object persistent, if it is not already.

2.2   Reachability-based Persistence

As noted in the introduction, when "specializing" our model of persistence for directed graph objects, we had to choose some semantics for what happens when a node that becomes persistent has attribute values that represent references to other nodes. Since we believe that the meaning or value of a node includes the values of that node's attributes, we employ a *reachability-based* model of persistence for our graph objects. That is, if a node has attributes that represent references to other nodes, those other nodes will persist. This means that explicitly making a node persist will result in making all objects reachable from that node persist implicitly. Since node attributes can be of any type, we generalize the model by stating that the value of any composite object, of which nodes are an example, is derived from the values of its components, so that any object to which a composite object refers will persist.

2.3   A Graph Example

To demonstrate how PGRAPHITE's side-by-side name space and persistence model work for directed graph abstract data types, we will define a simple binary tree ADT and show how a developer would make instances of that ADT persistent.

Consider a simple binary tree object type. Each node in this kind of tree contains a string and references to the node's left and right children. The definition of such a type would include a type for nodes in the tree and operations to create nodes and to set or retrieve the values stored in the nodes (i.e., the node attribute values).

Figure 1 shows a possible definition of a binary tree in GDL (**G**raph **D**escription **L**anguage), the Ada-like input language of PGRAPHITE. The GDL specification describes one node kind, Data_Node, which has attributes called Data (for the string value that each node will contain), Left_Child, and Right_Child. This specification is given as input to the PGRAPHITE preprocessor, which produces an Ada package (called an *interface package*) that defines the binary tree ADT.

One section of the specification part of the PGRAPHITE-generated interface package for the binary tree ADT described in Figure 1 appears in Figure 2. Using the types and operations defined in the interface package, a program could create a binary tree such as the one shown in Figure 3.

At some point, the program might decide that the tree should persist. The only reference to the tree that the program has is the value of the variable Root. Root represents a "normal," run-time system defined, non-persistent reference to the tree, however, so it cannot be preserved. Therefore, the program can use the GetPID operation defined by the PGRAPHITE-generated interface package to retrieve a persistent reference to the root of the tree, thus implicitly causing the root to become persistent. The persistent reference returned by GetPID is guaranteed to identify the root of this tree uniquely throughout its lifetime (unlike

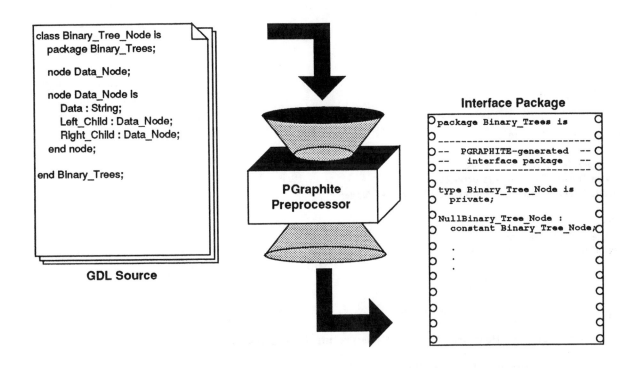

Figure 1: Using PGRAPHITE To Generate A Potentially Persistent Binary Tree ADT.

the non-persistent reference Root, which lasts only as long as the program continues executing), and so the program can save that reference and use it during some later execution to retrieve the root of the tree, or it can pass the reference to any other programs that will need to manipulate the object. Retrieving a persistent object from stable storage is actually nothing more than mapping a persistent reference to a non-persistent reference. Therefore, if a program has a persistent reference to an object that it wants to manipulate, it need only use the GetNPR operation to map the persistent reference to a non-persistent reference. If the persistent object to which the persistent reference is assigned is already in memory, GetNPR will return a non-persistent reference to the in-memory object, which the program can then manipulate normally. If the object is not in memory, GetNPR will retrieve it from stable storage and return a non-persistent reference to it.

As discussed in Section 2.2, we believe that the value of a node includes the values of its attributes, and if an attribute value happens to be a reference to another node, then that other node should persist as well. Therefore, in the course of saving Root in stable storage, when the interface package finds the non-persistent references to other nodes in the root node, it simply uses the GetPID operation to retrieve persistent references to the root node's left and right children, and saves those persistent references with the root node on the stable storage device. This, of course, has the effect of making the children persist. The process continues recursively, and bottoms out when both children are null. Thus, asking for a persistent reference to the root of the tree is equivalent to making the entire tree persist.

```
package Binary_Trees is

-- Non-persistent reference type:
   type Binary_Tree_Node is private;
   Null_Binary_Tree_Node : constant Binary_Tree_Node;

-- Persistent reference type:
   type PID is private;
   NullPID : constant PID;

...

-- Operations to define and manipulate nodes:

   function Create ( TheNodeKind : NodeKindName ) return Binary_Tree_Node;

   procedure PutAttribute ( TheNode : Binary_Tree_Node;
                            TheAttribute : AttributeName;
                            TheValue : String );
   function GetAttribute ( TheNode : Binary_Tree_Node;
                          TheAttribute : AttributeName )
                          return String;

   procedure PutAttribute ( TheNode : Binary_Tree_Node;
                            TheAttribute : AttributeName;
                            TheValue : Binary_Tree_Node );
   function GetAttribute ( TheNode : Binary_Tree_Node;
                          TheAttribute : AttributeName )
                          return Binary_Tree_Node;

...

-- Persistent object abstraction:
   procedure GetNPR ( TheNode : out Binary_Tree_Node;
                      ThePID : in PID );
   procedure GetPID ( ThePID : out PID;
                      TheNode : in Binary_Tree_Node );

...

end Binary_Trees;
```

Figure 2: Part Of The PGRAPHITE-generated Interface Package For The Binary Tree Definition.

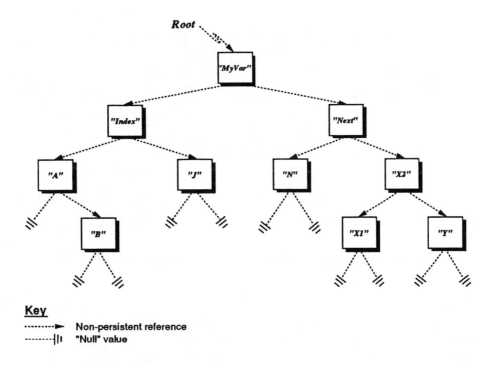

Key

```
-------▶    Non-persistent reference
-------┤|ı    "Null" value
```

Figure 3: An Instance Of The Binary Tree ADT.

3   Extending PGRAPHITE With Relations and Relationships

The model of persistence embodied by PGRAPHITE has proven to be both useful and very flexible in terms of meeting the needs of our users. In particular, graphs are appropriately used to describe relatively regular, anticipated patterns of connections among entities. That is, the type definition of a graph node indicates exactly what connections one *expects* to find at every such node (where "null" is, in fact, a legitimate node attribute value). We have also found, however, that graphs are less appropriate for describing more irregular, or perhaps unanticipated, patterns of connections. In our binary tree example, for instance, every program that manipulates binary trees expects to find connections to the data stored in the node and to the node's children. It is therefore always correct to set or retrieve the values of any of these attributes. On the other hand, different programs might or might not expect to find such information as execution counts, analysis data, or display information such as how a particular node is depicted (if at all), and if they do expect to find any of this information, they might or might not expect every node to have it.

In experimenting with PGRAPHITE and with the APPL/A system [2], we became convinced that relation and relationship are suitable for representing these kinds of irregular or unanticipated connections. Therefore, we have extended PGRAPHITE to automate the generation of persistent object management support for these types as well. By *relationship*, we are referring conceptually to a (possibly n-ary) connection between entities. For example, a relationship between a source code module and one or more executables created from it might exist. We use the term *relation* to refer to an unordered collection of relationships. A relation type, in our current implementation, is defined on instances of only one type of relationship.

Our model of relations and relationships has the following salient features:

OPERATIONS TO MANIPULATE A RELATIONSHIP TUPLE	
Create	creates a new tuple of a given kind
Get Field	retrieves the value of a tuple field of a given type
Put Field	sets the value of a tuple field of a given type
OPERATIONS TO MANIPULATE A RELATION	
Create	creates a collection of a given type
Insert	inserts a tuple into a relation
Remove	removes a tuple from a relation
Select Tuples	retrieves a (collection of) tuple(s) from a relation
Union	unions two relations
Exclude	removes the intersection of two relations
Iterate	steps through the tuples in a relation

Table 1: The relation/relationship abstraction operations.

- **Equal status for all**

   The traditional relational database model of relations defines relationships to be second-class entities, while relations are first-class entities. That is, relationships are defined only in the context of a specific relation — the same relationship instance cannot be shared by multiple relations, and all manipulation of relationships must be done through the relation.

   In our model, both relations and relationships are first-class objects. Instances of relationships can be created that do not belong to a relation; similarly, relationships can be part of multiple relations or can be shared by other objects. Relationships can connect *any* objects, including other relationships or relations. Table 1 shows the operations defined on both data types.

- **Persistence model**

   We have applied the PGRAPHITE model of persistence to relation and relationship types. Since both relations and relationships are first-class entities, this means that users can request PIDs for instances of either type of object. Because both relations and relationships are composite objects, we apply the reachability-based model to these objects as well. Thus, all relationships in a persistent relation will persist, as will all entities connected by a persistent relationship.[1]

   We note here that since relations and relationships are just abstract data types, we can define graph nodes with relations or relationships as attributes, and can define relationships that connect graphs with other entities. We believe that this further supports our claim that our persistence model (a) is orthogonal, and (b) extends to any arbitrary abstract data type.

- **Constraints**

---

[1] We have not yet decided on any specific semantics for what happens if objects connected by persistent relationships are destroyed. Several possiblities exist, ranging from stating that if any of the endpoints of a relationship cease to exist, the relationship will be destroyed, to just leaving the relationship in place with no value for the destroyed endpoint. We are currently exploring these options.

A *constraint* on a relation is a condition that must hold true for the relation to be considered to be in a consistent state. The user can statically define constraints and specify constraint violation recovery procedures. Constraint enforcement and relaxation can be dynamically controlled.

- **Triggers**

    Triggers are operations that are invoked when some event occurs. Triggers are generally used to make relationships active instead of passive — for example, a user can define a trigger that compiles and links source code when the source code is modified so that the executable code to which it is related will be up-to-date. We provide a trigger specification mechanism as part of the set of extensions to PGRAPHITE.

We note here that to simplify the process of experimenting with the new relation/relationship abstraction, we ended up defining a separate tool (which we call R&R) to generate implementations of potentially persistent relation and relationship ADTs. The structure of R&R parallels that of PGRAPHITE: it consists of a preprocessor that accepts type definitions in an Ada-like notation and produces corresponding Ada interface packages that implement the specified (relation and relationship) object types, augmented by the PGRAPHITE-style persistence mechanism.[2] The following example illustrates its structure and use.

3.1   Using The Relation/Relationship Abstraction: An Example

To illustrate how this model of relations and relationships can be used, we present an example that is very typical for software development environments. As noted earlier, directed graphs are extremely common structures in software development environments. In fact, many programs written to support the software development process work almost exclusively with graphs. Graphical[3] user interfaces to such programs often must be able to depict nodes of graphs in various ways to show human users of the tool what the tool is doing.

One of the pieces of information a graphical user interface needs is the location of the depiction of any given node on the display device (usually in terms of its X and Y coordinates), if the node is currently displayed. A user interface must therefore be able to determine whether or not any given node is currently displayed, and if so, it must be able to find out the coordinates at which it is displayed (note that any given object may be displayed at multiple locations, depending on the program and on the user interface).

We might therefore use RIDL (**R**elation/relationship **I**nterface **D**escription **L**anguage, the input language to R&R) to define the relation type shown in Figure 4. This relation type will allow a user interface for the binary tree ADT that we produced with PGRAPHITE in Figure 1 to maintain relationships between binary tree nodes and the coordinates at which the nodes are displayed. R&R takes this definition and produces an interface package, complete with operations to create and manipulate instances of relation and relationship types, as shown in Figure 5. Note that although the operations to manipulate relations and relationships are somewhat different from the operations to manipulate graphs (as would be expected), the GetPID and GetNPR operations for translating between the side-by-side name spaces are the same as the ones defined on graph types, and so instances of the new relation and relationship type can be made persistent or retrieved from stable storage in the same way that graph instances are.

---

[2] After we have completed our experimentation, the PGRAPHITE and R&R preprocessors will be combined.

[3] Here "graphical" refers to "using graphics and graphics display devices," not "related to graphs."

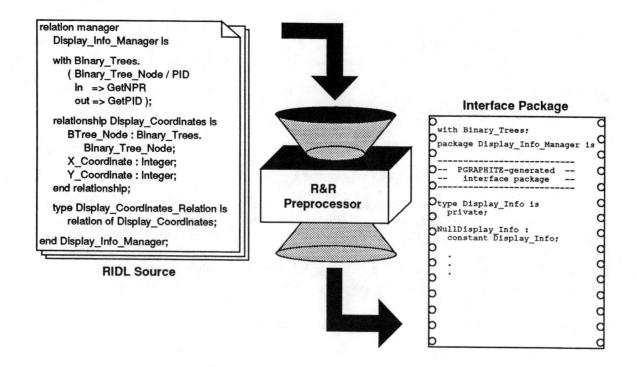

Figure 4: Using R&R To Generate A Potentially Persistent Display Information Relation ADT.

A user interface for the binary tree ADT might be asked to display the tree shown in Figure 3. In a small display window, it might only be able to display the root node and its two children. Therefore, the user interface will only create Display_Coordinates relationships for the root and its children, as shown in Figure 6, and place that limited set of relationship instances into a relation (where the variable Display_Info represents a non-persistent reference to the relation).

There are several points to note here. First, the display information may or may not be made to persist at some point, and whether or not it becomes persistent will depend entirely on the user interface utility, *not* on whether or not the graph persists. Second, all of the display information can be made persistent by making the relation in which it is stored persistent; thus, using the GetPID operation on the relation referenced by Display_Info in Figure 6 will have the expected effect of making all of the relationships in the relation persistent as well (since the value of a relation includes the values of all of the tuples in that relation). Finally, because relationships are first-class objects, it is not necessary to make *all* of the display information persistent — the user interface utility might decide that it only needs to save the display information for the root of the tree, and it can do so simply by asking for a persistent reference to that particular tuple instead of asking for a persistent reference to Display_Info.

With these points in mind, we can now present our approach to limiting the extent of persistence.

```
with Binary_Trees;
package Display_Info_Manager is

-- Non-persistent reference types:
    type Display_Coordinates is private;
    Null_Display_Coordinates : constant Display_Coordinates;
    type Display_Coordinates_Relation is private;
    Null_Display_Coordinates_Relation : constant Display_Coordinates_Relation;

-- Persistent reference type:
    type PID is private;
    NullPID : constant PID;
...
-- Operations to define and manipulate relationships:

    function Create return Display_Coordinates;

    procedure PutField ( TheRelationship : Display_Coordinates; TheField : FieldName;
                         TheValue : Binary_Trees.Binary_Tree_Node );
    function GetField ( TheRelationship : Display_Coordinates; TheField : FieldName )
                     return Binary_Trees.Binary_Tree_Node;

    procedure PutField ( TheRelationship : Display_Coordinates; TheField : FieldName;
                         TheValue : Integer );
    function GetField ( TheRelationship : Display_Coordinates; TheField : FieldName )
                     return Integer;
...
-- Operations to define and manipulate relations:

    function Create  return Display_Coordinates_Relation;
    procedure Insert ( TheRelation : Display_Coordinates_Relation; TheTuple : Display_Coordinates );

    function Select_Tuples ( TheRelation : Display_Coordinates_Relation; TheFieldName : FieldName;
                            Binary_Tree_Node_Value : Binary_Trees.Binary_Tree_Node )
                         return Display_Coordinates_Relation;
    function Select_Tuples ( TheRelation : Display_Coordinates_Relation; TheFieldName : FieldName;
                            Integer_Value : Binary_Trees.Binary_Tree_Node )
                         return Display_Coordinates_Relation;
...
-- Persistent object abstraction:
    procedure GetNPR ( TheRelationship : out Display_Coordinates; ThePID : in PID );
    procedure GetPID ( ThePID : out PID; TheRelationship : in Display_Coordinates );
    procedure GetNPR ( TheRelation : out Display_Coordinates_Relation; ThePID : in PID );
    procedure GetPID ( ThePID : out PID; TheRelation : in Display_Coordinates_Relation );
...
end Display_Info_Manager;
```

Figure 5: Part Of The R&R-generated Interface Package For The Display Information Relation Definition.

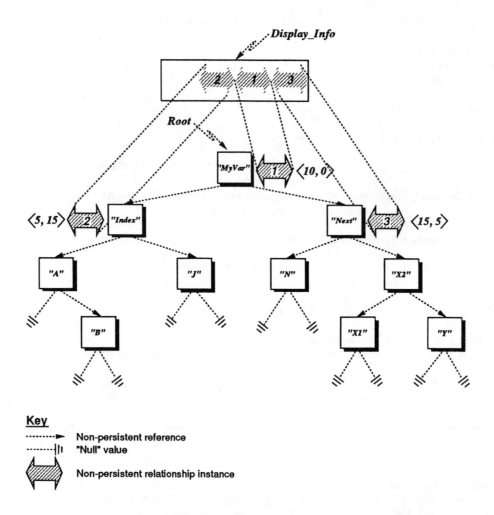

Figure 6: An Instance Of The Binary Tree ADT With Display Position Information.

4   An Approach to Limiting Persistence

One of the lessons that we have learned from experimentation with our PGRAPHITE prototype is that although a reachability-based definition of persistence is often appropriate, applications sometimes need to specify "bounds" on what actually persists. That is, certain information that could be viewed as "part of," or at least "associated with," a graph node should not necessarily become persistent just because that node does. The user should have control over the specification of these boundaries. One obvious way of providing such a capability is to force the user to differentiate between persistent and non-persistent parts of objects when defining the object's type (as has been done, for example, in the Ergo system [1]) by explicitly designating some components as "persistent" and others as "non-persistent." The problem with this solution is that it violates the orthogonality property that we desire for persistent object management systems by introducing distinctions based directly and solely on persistence properties into type definitions. It also means that the same object instance will look different after being retrieved from stable storage than it did before it was stored, since some of its parts may no longer exist. What we want instead is a principled way of controlling the bounds of persistence that preserves orthogonality and transparency. In particular, we want all persistent object instances to look the same, independent of whether or how often they have been saved or retrieved from stable storage.

The approach that we have developed is based on the observation that objects often have two kinds of parts: core parts and associated parts. *Core parts* are those components of an object that must always be present for the object to have any meaning. For example, any node in a binary tree must, by definition, have data and must have (possibly null) left and right children. *Associated parts* are pieces of information that some instances of a type have while others do not. As shown by our example in Section 3.1, a node in a graph that is being depicted on a display device might have associated with it the coordinates on the display at which the node appears, but no such information exists for nodes that are not displayed. Associated information is not less important than core data — the difference, for example, is that our user interface utility does not expect every node to have position information, and nodes that don't have it are still meaningful.

This distinction provides a basis for principled introduction of "bounds" or "limits" in our persistence mechanism. We take the position that core attributes must persist if the object to which they belong persists, and so should be subject to a reachability-based persistence model. Associated parts, on the other hand, need not persist. The user interface utility, for example, might or might not need to preserve any or all of the position information it creates, depending perhaps on whether or not the user asked to have some parts (or all) of the display saved for use at a later time. Therefore, associated parts should be *potentially* persistent — that is, they can be made persistent explicitly, but they will not become persistent automatically simply because the object with which they are associated persists.

This leaves us with a very natural way of letting the user specify the bounds of persistence that does not violate orthogonality or transparency. The user simply defines associated parts using relationships, while core attributes are represented as "normal" node attributes. Since relationships are potentially persistent entities, the persistence of associated parts is thus under explicit program control. Such control can be exercised at the level of individual associations (by making particular relationship instances persist) or at the level of collections of associations (by making a relation that contains a set of relationship instances persist).

Acknowledgements

We would like to thank Alex Wolf and Stan Sutton for all the helpful comments they have provided us over the years.

References

[1] Peter Lee, Frank Pfenning, Gene Rollins, and Dana Scott. The Ergo Support System: An Integrated Set of Tools for Prototyping Integrated Environments. In *Proceedings of SIGSOFT '88: Third Symposium Software Development Environments*, pages 25–34, November 1988.

[2] Stanley M. Sutton, Jr. *APPL/A: A Prototype Language for Software-Process Programming*. PhD thesis, University of Colorado, August 1990.

[3] Peri L. Tarr, Jack C. Wileden, and Alexander L. Wolf. A Different Tack To Providing Persistence In A Language. In *Proceedings of the Second International Workshop on Database Programming Languages*, pages 41–60, June 1989.

[4] Richard N. Taylor, Frank C. Belz, Lori A. Clarke, Leon Osterweil, Richard W. Selby, Jack C. Wileden, Alexander L. Wolf, and Michal Young. Foundations for the Arcadia Enviroment Architecture. In *Proceedings of SIGSOFT '88: Third Symposium on Software Development Environments*, November 1988.

[5] Jack C. Wileden, Alexander L. Wolf, Charles D. Fisher, and Peri L. Tarr. PGRAPHITE: An Experiment in Persistent Typed Object Management. In *Proceedings of SIGSOFT '88: Third Symposium on Software Development Environments*, pages 130–142, November 1988.

[6] Alexander L. Wolf. Abstraction Mechanisms and Persistence. In *Proceedings of the Fourth Workshop on Persistent Object Systems*, September 1990. (To appear.).

Part III

System Implementation I

Chair: Barbara Liskov

The four papers in this session discussed various issues that arise in implementing object-oriented databases. The paper on Cricket, presented by Michael Zwilling, described an experiment in providing support for an object-oriented database by using the virtual memory mechanisms of Mach. Two questions raised by this presentation are: Is virtual memory a good basis for an object store? And, if so, are the Mach mechanisms appropriate; for example, do they provide adequate performance, and do they allow sufficient control?

The second paper was presented by Alan Dearle. It concerned the management of "transient garbage", i.e., objects that have a short lifetime. It is desirable that such objects not enter the persistent store, since if they do, garbage collecting them will be more expensive. The paper described a mechanism that moves objects into the persistent heap only if some client other than the one that created the object uses it. An obvious question here is what effect the mechanism had on the performance of the system.

The third paper described an architecture for an object store; it was presented by Ifor Williams. The goal was to avoid having to do translations via the object table for frequently used objects. Instead such objects would reside in a cache that could be used to access them directly. In addition, object table entries could also be cached to speed translations in the case of a cache miss. The performance of various cache organizations was studied under a workload taken from Smalltalk programs. A major question here is the relevance of these results to persistent object bases, since the architecture did not address persistence and the workload did not reflect applications that required persistence.

The final paper was presented by Gilbert Harrus. It discussed ways of organizing the architecture at workstations to provide efficient access to the persistent store in the O_2 system. It focussed on one organization in which data was brought over to the workstations in pages. Such an organization is particularly appropriate when objects are clustered. However, performance studies are needed to determine the right unit of access.

The discussion was focussed primarily on details of the particular systems presented in these papers. With respect to the transient garbage avoidance scheme, there was concern that the "copy out" mechanism used when a new object was shared would lead to pages with unused portions; the response was that this usually would not happen, and if it did, it could be corrected during garbage collection of the persistent heap. Another problem was how to handle very large objects that required many copy-out pages and exhausted the supply; in this case, they could "persistify" the entire local heap. This system does not provide any concurrency control, so there was concern about its semantics in the presence of concurrency; the answer was that it provided the illusion of a single shared memory store with atomic update.

Elliot Kolodner expressed concern that Cricket might generate "false deadlocks" due to its page level locking. The response was that page-level locking was what could be done with Mach, but perhaps a different approach is more appropriate. Eliot Moss said that a possible solution is to organize objects in pages so that the unit of locking corresponds to logical requirements. However, Alan Dearle said that this can lead to problems if unforeseen sharing occurs later; this approach caused problems in PS-Algol.

A discussion at a higher level ensued because of a question by Alex Wolf about the efficacy and appropriateness of the client-server model that seemed to underlie these systems. Using a server on top of the operating system gives the client only a "thin wire" connection and may prevent it from using features essential for good performance. This question brought about various defenses of the model. Malcolm Atkinson pointed out that the systems are distributed, and if we try to do all computations at a centralized machine, this will lead to a bottleneck, so it seems that we really do not have an alternative. Therefore, the client/server model seems to be needed in a distributed system, but perhaps in a centralized system the database could run directly on the operating system.

This led to a discussion of operating system support for databases. Dave Maier said that in the case of O_2, one server architecture (using files) did attempt to take advantage of things the operating system already did, but they needed locking information so they backed off to the page server approach. Alan Dearle asked why virtual memory has been considered inadequate to support databases. Eliot Moss replied that one issue was the need to control I/O buffers so that the proper recovery semantics could be obtained and, in addition, the operating system defined certain policies (e.g., page replacement) that could not be changed and were inappropriate. Elliot Kolodner said that one possibility was to not abandon virtual memory entirely, but instead control it a little (e.g., by pinning pages); this may be sufficient to cause it to work as needed, and would allow us to avoid the double buffering problem. However, Eliot Moss pointed out that double buffering is not all bad: by copying (from the DB buffer to the OS buffer) we may get better performance due to clustering. Dave Maier said that at any rate we need to move many objects at a time between primary and secondary storage.

Dave Maier also pointed out that things have changed with the advent of operating systems like Mach, which allow users to control certain aspects of operation systems. However, even Mach does not give as much control as the database implementer would like. For example, it still controls page replacement, although Michael Zwilling noted that it pays some attention to hints supplied by the user. Also, Eliot Moss pointed out the need for experiments: we do not have the data at this point to indicate whether building databases in this way will result in better performance than just using the operating system directly.

Cricket: A Mapped, Persistent Object Store

Eugene Shekita
Computer Sciences Department
University of Wisconsin
Madison, WI 53706
shekita@provolone.cs.wisc.edu

Michael Zwilling
Computer Sciences Department
University of Wisconsin
Madison, WI 53706
zwilling@barney.cs.wisc.edu

Abstract

This paper describes Cricket, a new database storage system that is intended to be used as a platform for design environments and persistent programming languages. Cricket uses the memory management primitives of the Mach operating system to provide the abstraction of a shared, transactional single-level store that can be directly accessed by user applications. In this paper, we present the design and motivation for Cricket. We also present some initial performance results which show that, for its intended applications, Cricket can provide better performance than a general-purpose database storage system.

1. Introduction

In recent years, there has been a great deal of research in extending database technology to meet the needs of emerging database applications such as text management and multi-media office systems (see [DBE87] for a good survey). Out of this research has come a variety of new storage systems that attempt to provide more functionality as well as improved performance for these emerging applications. Examples of such systems include [Care86, Horn87, Lind87, Moss88, Sche90, Ston90]. While these storage systems will undoubtedly meet the performance demands of many new applications, our view is that for some applications there is still considerable room for improvement. In particular, we feel that for design environments [Katz87, Chan89], persistent programming languages [Cock84, Atki87], and other applications in which response time rather than throughput is often the key concern, different storage techniques that those currently in use can provide better performance.

Towards this goal, we have designed a new database storage system called Cricket.[1] Cricket uses the memory management primitives of Mach [Acce86] to provide the abstraction of a shared, transactional, single-level store. One advantage of a single-level store is that it provides applications with a uniform view of volatile and non-volatile (i.e., persistent) memory. This in turn can lead to improved performance by eliminating the need for applications to distinguish and convert between non-persistent and persistent data formats [Cope90].

Although storage systems based on a single-level store have been proposed as far back as Multics [Bens72], Cricket offers several features that have not been combined in one system before. One of Cricket's key features is the ability to let applications directly access persistent data, but at the same time maintain the applications in separate (and potentially distributed) protection domains. Cricket also offers transparent concurrency control and recovery, and since it runs as a user-level process on Mach, it is easily ported to a variety of machines. We believe that these features distinguish Cricket from other recent proposals based on a single-level store [Chan88, Ford88, Spec88, Cope90] and make it an attractive platform for design environments and persistent languages.

The remainder of this paper provides a detailed description of Cricket. In the next section, we present the motivation for Cricket, and then in Section 3, we argue why a single-level store is the right approach. This is followed by Section 4, where we review Mach's external pager facilities [Youn87], which play a central role in Cricket's design. Cricket's system architecture is then described in Section 5, and in Section 6, we provide some preliminary performance results that compare Cricket to the EXODUS Storage Manager [Care86]. These preliminary results show that for its intended applications, Cricket can provide better performance than a general-purpose database storage system. Finally, related work is mentioned in Section 7, and conclusions are drawn in Section 8.

This research was partially supported by DARPA under contracts N00014-88-K-0303 and NAG 2-618, NSF under grant IRI-8657323, and donations from Texas Instruments and Digital Equipment Corporation.

[1] As the reader shall see, the flow of control really hops around in our storage system!

2. The Motivation Behind Cricket

While traditional database storage systems are extremely good at retrieving large groups of related objects and performing the same operation on each object, they are generally ill-suited for design environments. To illustrate why, it is useful to step through the execution of a design transaction in a CAD/CAM system [Katz87]. There, transactions can be broken down into three basic phases: 1) a loading phase, when the design is loaded into memory from disk, 2) a work phase, during which the design is repeatedly changed, and 3) a saving phase, when design changes are committed. As noted in [Maie89], this load/work/save paradigm is substantially different from a traditional database workload. During the work phase, accesses are unpredictable and fast response time is the key performance criteria rather than system throughput. Moreover, the data objects that make up the design may be traversed and updated hundreds, even thousands of times before the design is saved.

Unfortunately, traditional database storage systems are not geared for these sort of access patterns. Among other things, the procedure-based interface that must typically be used to traverse and update persistent objects is too slow [Moss90]. And as noted in [Maie89], the recovery protocols are often inappropriate. For example, generating a log record for each update in the work phase of a design transaction would obviously have a negative impact on response time (not to mention the volumes of log data that could be generated). For these reasons, CAD transactions often use a database system in more of a batch mode by loading a whole design into their virtual address space, converting it to an in-memory format, working on it, converting it back to a disk format, and then committing the entire design as changed at end-of-transaction. In general, we would argue that these problems are not just limited to design environments. Implementors of persistent languages have already run up against many of the same problems [Rich89, Schu90].

More recently, a number of new database storage systems have been proposed to address some of these issues, e.g., [Care86, Horn87, Lind87, Moss88, Sche90, Ston90]. But our feeling is that for design environments and persistent languages, many of these systems will still fall short of the mark. This is due to the fact that many of them still use a procedure-based interface to access persistent data. Moreover, many of them still use fairly traditional recovery techniques based on write-ahead logging [Moh89a]. It was these observations and also our experiences with the EXODUS Storage Manager [Care86] and the persistent language E [Rich89, Schu90] that motivated us to design Cricket.

3. The Argument For a Single-Level Store

As mentioned earlier, Cricket provides the abstraction of a single-level store to applications, and we advertise this as one of its key features. With a single-level store, the database itself is mapped into the virtual address space, allowing persistent data to be accessed in the same manner as non-persistent data. This is in contrast to a conventional two-level store, where access to persistent data is less direct and a user-level buffer pool is typically maintained to cache disk pages.

Single-level stores are nothing new, of course. Their origins can be traced back almost 20 years to Multics [Bens72], and many operating systems provide mapped file facilities that effectively implement a single-level store. But more importantly, database implementors have repeatedly rejected the idea of using the mapped file facilities offered by operating systems and instead have chosen to manage buffering and disk storage themselves. There are a variety of reasons given why this is so (see [Ston81, Trai82, Ston84]). Among the most notable are:

- Operating systems typically provide no control over when the data pages of a mapped file are written to disk, which makes it impossible to use recovery protocols like write-ahead logging [Moh89a] and sophisticated buffer management [Chou85].

- The virtual address space provided by mapped files, usually limited to 32 bits, is too small to represent a large database.

- Page tables associated with mapped files can become excessively large.

As pointed out in [Eppi89] and [Cope90], however, these criticisms may no longer be as valid as they once were. The above items can be countered by arguing that:

- With the right operating system hooks, it is possible to control when the data pages of a mapped file are written to disk. Mach, for example, provides many of the necessary hooks with its notion of *memory objects* [Youn87]. More will be said about this shortly.

- For many emerging database applications, a 32-bit address space is sufficient. Moreover, with the rapid increase in memory sizes and with shared-memory multiprocessors becoming more commonplace, processors with large virtual address spaces may soon become available. In fact, IBM's RS/6000 [Bako90] already supports a 52-bit address space, and HP's Precision Architecture [Maho86] supports a 64-bit address space (although strictly speaking, these are both segmented architectures).

- As the cost of memory decreases, large page tables will become less of a concern. Furthermore, inverted page tables such as those found in IBM's RS/6000 and HP's Precision Architecture may become more common with the increase in memory sizes. Inverted page tables exhibit the desirable property of growing in proportion to the size of physical memory rather than the size of virtual memory.

Despite these compelling arguments (see [Eppi89] for several more), the jury is still out on whether a single-level store offers any advantages for traditional database applications. And although Eppinger tried to claim otherwise in his Ph.D thesis, the performance results presented there and in [Duch89] argue that it may not be a good idea for transaction processing. Interestingly enough, the real problem with a using single-level store for transaction processing appears to be the high cost of handling page faults for persistent data rather than the criticisms mentioned above.

3.1. Why a Single-Level Store is Right for Cricket

Given the known problems with a single-level store, why do we think it is the right choice for Cricket? The answer is that we are primarily interested in supporting non-traditional applications where, in our opinion, the advantages of using a single-level store outweigh its disadvantages. In the following paragraphs, we briefly mention some of these advantages.

One advantage is that a single-level store can eliminate the need for applications to distinguish and convert between non-persistent and persistent data formats. In most database storage systems, the format of persistent data and the access to it usually differs from that of non-persistent data. Moreover, the cost of accessing persistent data is generally more expensive, even after it has been brought into memory [Moss90, Schu90]. As a result, applications often convert persistent data to a more efficient in-memory format before operating on it. Unfortunately, this can involve copying costs, added buffering requirements, and format conversions. With a single-level store, non-persistent and persistent data can have a uniform representation and these costs can be eliminated [Cope90]. This has obvious benefits in applications like design environments, where the real-time cost of accessing and updating persistent data is a key concern.

For similar reasons, we feel that a single-level store will also simplify the job of implementing a persistent language. To reduce the cost of accessing persistent data, persistent languages often use "pointer swizzling" [Cock84, Moss90, Schu90]. In pointer swizzling, the embedded object identifiers (i.e., pointers) that are stored in persistent objects are typically converted to virtual addresses while they are in memory. This is done to reduce the cost of traversing objects. Unfortunately, swizzling is not as simple as it sounds. There are the issues of what identifiers to swizzle, when to swizzle them, and how to unswizzle them. And in persistent languages based on C [Agra89, Rich89], it is often difficult to know where identifiers are located, when they change, and when they need to be reswizzled [Schu90]. With a single-level store, object identifiers become virtual memory addresses, so all this effort (and its associated cost) can be eliminated.

Yet another advantage of using a single-level store is that persistence and type can be kept orthogonal [Atki87]. That is, application code can be written without concern for whether it is operating on non-persistent or persistent data. This simplifies code development and also allows binaries that were originally designed to operate on non-persistent data to be used with persistent data — which, of course, has obvious practical and commercial advantages.

Finally, a single-level store can simplify the management of persistent objects that span multiple disk pages. Because a single-level store makes use of MMU hardware, multi-page objects can be made to appear in memory as though they were contiguous without actually requiring physical contiguity. This is in contrast to the EXODUS Storage Manager [Care86], where considerable effort was required to implement contiguous buffering of multi-page objects.

4. External Pagers In Mach

In the next section, we will describe Cricket's system architecture. Before we can do that, however, we need to briefly go over Mach's *external pager* interface [Youn87], since it plays a central role in Cricket's design.

Among other things, Mach provides a number of facilities that allow user-level tasks (i.e., processes) to exercise control over virtual memory management. Mach provides the notion of a *memory object*, which is simply a data repository that is managed by some server (in this case Cricket). Such a server is called an *external pager*. An external pager is in charge of paging the data of a memory object to and from disk.

In Mach, tasks can associate (i.e., map) a given region of their address space to a memory object using the *vm_map* kernel call. After doing so, the external pager for that memory object will be called by the Mach kernel when a page in the mapped region needs to be read or written to disk. Physical sharing of data occurs when more than one task maps the same memory object into its address space. The Mach kernel and external pagers coordinate their activity through a message-based interface, which is summarized in Table 1.

Mach Kernel to External Pager Interface

memory_object_data_request ( )	request for data page of a memory object
memory_object_data_write ( )	request to write page of a memory object to disk

External Pager to Mach Kernel Interface

memory_object_data_provided ( )	supplies kernel with data page
memory_object_data_unavailable ( )	tells kernel to use zero-filled page

Table 1: External Pager Interface

Figure 1 illustrates how the Mach kernel and an external pager coordinate their activity on a page fault for a memory object M. At startup, the external pager acquires a *port* (i.e., capability) from the Mach kernel and associates it with M. Through an exchange of messages, the capability for M is passed to the client task, which then calls *vm_map* to map M into its address space. (Alternatively, the external pager can call *vm_map* on behalf of the client if it has the right permissions.) When the client attempts to access a page P in the mapped region, a page fault is generated. The page fault is caught by the Mach kernel, which verifies the client's access permissions and then sends a *memory_object_data_request* message to the external pager, asking it to supply the data for P. The external pager reads the data from disk and provides it to the kernel via *memory_object_data_provided*. The kernel then locates a free page frame, copies the data into the frame, and resumes the client. Subsequent accesses to P will not generate a page fault.

By default, Mach uses an LRU replacement algorithm to manage kernel memory. If its free-page list starts to run low and page P is at the top of the inactive list, then P will be replaced. If P is clean, its contents are simply discarded. Otherwise, the kernel sends a *memory_object_data_write* message to the external pager with a pointer to P, at which point the external pager is expected to write P to disk.

In addition to the interface calls mentioned above, Mach also provides the means for an external pager to force a page of a memory object to be cleaned or flushed. This effectively allows the external pager to control (to some extent) the replacement policy used for a memory object. Furthermore, *memory_object_data_provided* can be called asynchronously, so prefetching data for a memory object is also possible.

5. Cricket's System Architecture

This section describes Cricket's system architecture. The section is broken into two parts. In the first part, we discuss Cricket's basic design, and in the second part we discuss more advanced design issues that are largely unresolved at this point in time.

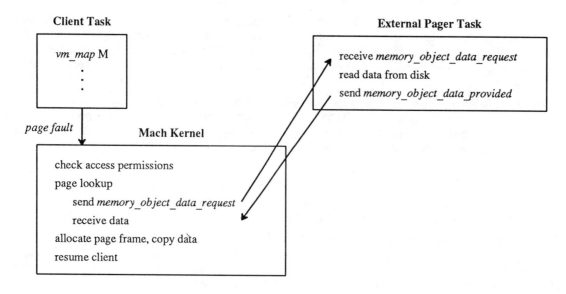

Figure 1: Handling a Page Fault on a Memory Object

5.1. Basic Design

5.1.1. Architecture Overview

Figure 2 illustrates what the single-site architecture of Cricket looks like. As shown, Cricket follows a client/server paradigm. Client applications run as separate tasks, each in their own protection domain, and they use an RPC interface to request basic services from Cricket. The RPC interface includes *connect* to establish a connection with Cricket, *disconnect* to break a connection, *begin_transaction* to begin a transaction, and *end_transaction* to end a transaction. For efficiency, some of Cricket's functionality is split between the Cricket server itself and a runtime library that gets linked with the application code at compile time. The runtime library includes RPC stubs as well as code for allocating persistent data. More will be said about this shortly.

The Cricket server is multi-threaded to permit true parallelism on multiprocessors and also to improve throughput by permitting threads to run even when others are blocked on synchronous events like I/O. The Mach C-Threads package [Drav88] is used to create and manage threads. When Cricket starts up, it creates a pool of threads which all line up on the same central message queue waiting to service client or kernel requests. A given thread is not tied to any particular function or transaction. When a thread finishes servicing a request, it puts itself on the central message queue again and waits for yet another request. Mach takes care of preemptively scheduling individual threads.

As mentioned earlier, client applications are allowed direct (shared) access to persistent data. This is accomplished using Mach's external pager facility. We simply treat the database as a memory object and have the Cricket server play the role of its external pager. When a client first *connects* to Cricket, a *vm_map* call is executed by Cricket on behalf of the client to map the database into the client's virtual address space. The *connect* call returns the virtual address that corresponds to the start of the database, as mapped in the client's address space. Using this address, the client can then access the database just as if it were in virtual memory — ala a single-level store. To ensure that pointers to persistent data remain valid over time, Cricket always maps the database to the same range of virtual addresses

It is important to note that database I/O is completely transparent to client applications as a result of using Mach's external pager facility. By default, the same holds true for concurrency control and recovery — although for efficiency, we are also experimenting with options that make those functions less transparent.

5.1.2. On Protection verses Performance

As shown in Figure 2, Cricket's core functions and their associated data structures are isolated in the Cricket server where they are protected from client applications. Because of its widespread use, our view is that nobody will take

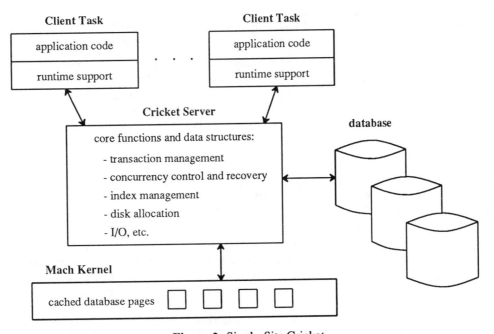

Figure 2: Single-Site Cricket

us seriously if we are unable to support applications written in C [Kern78] or its derivatives. Consequently, separate protection domains are a necessary evil. (One can imagine the damage a buggy C application could inflict if it had access to the disk allocation bitmaps!) In commercial database systems, the application code and the system software typically reside in separate address spaces for the same reason.

Where Cricket departs from a more traditional design is that we let clients directly access regular data via Mach's external pager facilities. (Bitmaps and other meta-data structures are still inaccessible, of course.) Although this compromises protection somewhat, we view it as manageable and worth the extra performance for the types of applications we have in mind. Moreover, because all database accesses filter through Cricket's locking mechanism, which is discussed below, an application can only damage the data pages that it has gained access to anyway. Without direct access to the database, a client application would have to make an explicit request to read data into its address space, and it would have to take analogous steps to have it written back. This would involve added complexity, copying costs, extra buffering (possibly leading to double-paging [Bric76]), and would also destroy the abstraction of a single-level store.

5.1.3. Concurrency Control

By default, Cricket provides transparent, two-phase, page-level locking for client access to the database. This is done using Mach's exception handling facility [Blac88], which allows the exceptions of one task to be caught and handled by another task. In our case, Cricket handles exceptions for client tasks.

When a client first *connects* to Cricket, its exception handler is set to be the Cricket server. Later, when the client executes *begin_transaction*, all the virtual addresses in the client that map to the database are protected against read and write access. Subsequent attempts by the client to access a page in the database triggers an address exception, causing Mach to block the client and send a message to Cricket. The message is received by a Cricket thread, which attempts to acquire the appropriate (read or write) lock for the client, blocking itself if necessary. Once the lock has been acquired, the thread fixes the client's access permissions for the page via a kernel call and then lets Mach know that the exception has been successfully handled. At that point, Mach resumes the client.

The exchange of messages involved in catching an address exception and setting a lock is similar to that shown in Figure 1 for external pager fault handling. As one can imagine, setting a lock is not cheap! But compared to a more traditional design, our scheme is not as bad as it may appear at first glance. In a more traditional design, an RPC would typically have to be sent from the client to the database system to acquire a lock. And, as our preliminary results will show, exception handling in Mach is not drastically more expensive than sending an RPC.[2]

As mentioned earlier, we are also experimenting with different concurrency control options other than simple two-phase, page-level locking. Among other things, we eventually intend to support dirty reads [Moh89a] and also design- or file-level locks. The latter would be used by design transactions, where aborting a long-running transaction due to a deadlock makes little sense. Of course, the smallest granularity of locking that we can transparently provide in Cricket is limited to a page, but for the applications we have in mind that should be sufficient.

It is important to note that using address exceptions to trigger locking is not a new idea. Exceptions were also used in the Bubba database system [Bora90] to set locks. Our scheme differs from theirs in that we perform lock management in a user-level task, whereas locking was performed by the operating system in Bubba. This required special modifications to the operating system. Address exceptions have also been used by Li [Li86] to implement memory coherency in a distributed virtual memory system and in the language ML to trigger garbage collection [Appe86].

5.1.4. Disk Allocation

Cricket uses an extent-based scheme for managing disk space. A disk is partitioned into extents, with each extent containing the same number of pages — usually at least 16 Kbytes worth. Extents and the pages within an extent are allocated in a lazy manner, much like in Camelot. Linear hashing [Litw80] is used to map a virtual address to a physical extent on disk, allowing us to efficiently handle sparse databases. Because hashing is done on an extent basis, the hash table will generally consume very little space.

For allocating persistent data, we provide something similar to Camelot's recoverable virtual memory facility. In contrast to Camelot, however, we take measures to ensure that allocation respects physical page boundaries. The runtime support code provides a *DBmalloc* function for allocating persistent "objects" and a corresponding *DBfree*

---

[2] It is worth noting that we also experimented with an alternative locking scheme where the exception handler ran as a thread in client's runtime support code. When an address exception was caught, this thread would send an RPC to Cricket to acquire the appropriate lock. Because of RPC costs, this turned out to be more expensive than the design we have chosen.

for deallocating them.

DBmalloc takes *size* and *near−hint* parameters. The *size* parameter tells how much space to allocate, while the *near−hint* parameter is a virtual memory address that tells *DBmalloc* where it should try to allocate space. The *near−hint* is used to simultaneously provide both virtual and physical clustering. That is, *DBmalloc* tries to allocate the new object on the same page as the *near−hint*. Failing that, it sends an RPC to Cricket, which tries to allocate the object either within the same extent as the *near−hint* or as physically close to it as possible. (Optimizations to cut down on RPCs are obviously possible here.)

As illustrated in Figure 3, individual disk pages are formatted as slotted pages [Date81]. The slot information at the bottom of a page is used to keep track of the objects and the free space on the page. When all the space on a page is free, it is marked as such in the page-allocation bitmaps maintained by the Cricket server. Large multi-page objects are allocated as runs of pages that are virtually contiguous, but not necessarily physically contiguous. Only the first page of a large object is formatted as a slotted page.

In addition to providing information about the objects on a disk page, the slot array at the bottom of a page also provides a level of indirection for accessing the objects on the page. If that extra level of indirection is always used, then it becomes possible to compact the free space on pages during idle periods. By default, this is not done because it would force applications to distinguish between non-persistent and persistent data access. However, in object-oriented languages that provide encapsulation, it may be possible to hide the extra level of indirection.

5.1.5. Buffer Management

At the moment, we delegate all page replacement decisions for regular data to Mach. Consequently, an LRU replacement policy is used by default. For the types of applications we have in mind, where the working set of an application will typically fit in memory, this is expected to be adequate. As noted in [Eppi89], the beauty of letting Mach buffer regular data is that it effectively provides a buffer pool that dynamically changes its size in response to other system activity.

We examined two alternatives for managing system meta-data such as the page-allocation bitmaps. The first alternative was to maintain a small, wired-down virtual memory buffer pool in the Cricket server, while the second alternative was to map meta-data into the virtual address of Cricket itself and treat it as yet another memory object. We have chosen the first alternative because of the expense associated with using an external pager. Moreover, the abstraction of a single-level store is not particularly important for meta-data.

5.2. Unresolved Design Issues

5.2.1. Files

Although we recognize that files are needed to group related objects, we have not yet settled on a particular implementation for them. Given enough address bits (e.g., 64 bits), it may be sufficient in many cases to simply partition the virtual address space into large fixed-sized segments and treat each segment as a different file. Another alternative is to view a file as a list of (not necessarily contiguous) extents. This would require that all the objects in an extent belong to the same file.

Disk Page Format

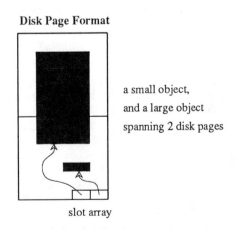

a small object,
and a large object
spanning 2 disk pages

slot array

Figure 3: The Format of Disk Pages

5.2.2. Index Management

Eventually, we would like to include support for indexes such as B-trees in Cricket. An index in Cricket would simply map from some user-defined key to the virtual address of an object in the database. Our view is that indexes need to be managed by Cricket for reasons of protection and also performance.

As far as protection goes, we view indexes as meta-data, and as such they must be protected. An errant client application could cause considerable and potentially unrepairable damage if it were allowed write access to an index. And as far as performance goes, our feeling is that simple two-phase, page-level locking is inadequate for indexes, even in a design environment. Consequently, index pages cannot be treated as regular data. Obtaining adequate system performance usually requires fairly complex concurrency control and recovery algorithms to be used on indexes [Moh89b]. (In general, the same holds true for all meta-data structures.)

Index management presents something of a dilemma because on the one hand we would like to protect indexes from being damaged by client applications, but on the other hand the cost of sending an RPC to the Cricket server for each index access is likely to be too expensive, even if they are batched. To get around this dilemma, we are examining the possibility of giving clients read-only access to index pages. In this scheme, the runtime support code would take care of read operations on indexes (including locking), but updates would be forwarded (perhaps in batch-mode) to the Cricket server.

5.2.3. Recovery

Recovery is another area where we have yet to settle on a particular implementation. In discussing recovery algorithms, one of the key things to remember is that we give response time priority over throughput in Cricket. As a result, we are willing to accept a recovery algorithm that slows down transaction commit somewhat if it significantly improves response time during the execution of the transaction. Another thing to remember is that Cricket is intended to be used in a design environment, where the same set of persistent objects may be updated thousands of times by the same transaction. In such an environment, traditional old-value/new-value logging is clearly inappropriate.

At this point, we have decided that for disk allocation data, indexes, and all other meta-data, we will use the ARIES recovery algorithm [Moh89a], which is based on operation logging. For regular data, we have identified a number of alternatives, all of which require a *no-steal* buffer policy.[3] With a no-steal policy, steps must be taken to ensure that a dirty data page is not written to its home location on disk until the transaction that has modified the page commits. For the types of applications we have in mind, this is not expected to be a problem (especially in a distributed environment, which is briefly discussed below). The advantages of using a no-steal policy are that old-values do not have to be logged and repeated changes are aggregated before being logged at commit.

One alternative for regular data recovery in Cricket is to simply log full pages at commit. Although this sounds like it could generate excessive amounts of log data, the applications that use Cricket may tend to update a large fraction of each page that they modify. If this turns out to be the case, then logging full pages at commit will result in an efficient recovery algorithm. During idle periods, the on-line log can be compressed by removing all but the most recent copy of a given page.

Another alternative is to use a copy-on-write mechanism. When a write lock for a page is granted, the page is copied to a temporary location in memory. Then, at commit, the new version of the page is compared to its original and the changed portions are logged. If log space is a concern, a compression algorithm can be applied to the log records that are generated.

One final alternative is to require all updates to persistent objects to filter through a runtime support function. The support function would record information that indicates which persistent objects have been modified. At commit, the Cricket server would then use the recorded information and its knowledge of which pages were modified to generate new-value log records. The disadvantage of this approach is that persistence is no longer transparent to applications.

5.2.4. Moving to a Distributed Environment

Since a client/server hardware configuration is expected to be the norm for design applications, we naturally plan on moving Cricket to a distributed environment. In fact, that has always been our main goal, and the single-site architecture is really just a stepping stone. Because it has been built on top of Mach, client applications and the Cricket server can already run on separate machines. However, the current design has not yet been optimized for the distributed case.

---

[3] Note that with a no-steal policy, logging is only needed to provide commit atomicity and to support recovery from media failure.

When we move to a distributed environment, we expect Cricket's architecture to look like Figure 4. As illustrated, Cricket will be split into a front-end and a back-end. The front-end will take care of functions that can be handled more efficiently on the local machine, while the back-end will take care of global functions like cache coherency. Note that because we provide a single-level store to clients, this architecture supports what amounts to distributed, transactional, shared, persistent virtual memory (phew!). Although we could use the algorithms described by Li [Li86] to maintain memory coherency across machines, transaction semantics open up the possibility for us to use more efficient algorithms. There has been some work done in this area (see [Wilk90, Dewi90]), but not in the context of a single-level store. Two of Cricket's designers are actively working on this problem already [Fran90].

Some of the interesting problems that surface in a distributed environment include index management, buffering, and the general question of what functionality belongs in the front-end and what functionality belongs in the back-end. We also expect distribution to affect our choice of recovery algorithms. For example, in a distributed environment, it probably makes more sense to offload as much commit processing as possible to the front-end machine. Also note that there is no need to use Mach's external pager facilities in the back-end, as the data pages that are cached there are not directly accessible to clients.

6. Preliminary Performance Results

To get a rough idea of how the single-site version of Cricket can be expected to perform, we ran a series of benchmarks on a DEC MicroVax 3200 workstation with 16 Mbytes of memory. The benchmarks were run in single-user mode on version 2.5 of Mach with the workstation disconnected from the network. We only ran single-user benchmarks, and the average cost of a given operation was calculated by performing the operation several thousand times, and then dividing the measured elapsed time by the number of operations performed. This was done several times to check for stability, and the average observed values are the ones reported here. The Mach real-time clock, which has a resolution of roughly 17 msec, was used to measure elapsed times. The virtual page size in the version of Mach that we were running under was 4 Kbytes.

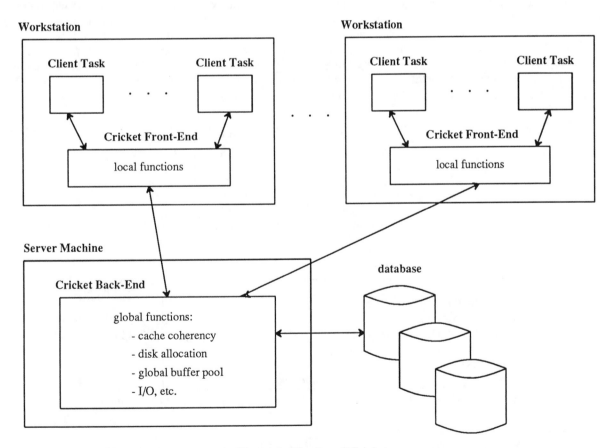

Figure 4: Distributed Cricket

Before running any benchmarks, we measured the CPU costs of various key operations in Mach. This was done to get a general feel for the cost of different operations on the MicroVax. The results are presented in Table 2. *Getpid* (get process ID) is the simplest kernel call that we could think of, while *vm_protect* is the call that Cricket uses to set the access rights on client pages. *Bcopy* is a library function for copying data in memory, and the last three operation costs listed are for sending a null RPC with no arguments, sending a page out-of-line via an RPC, and sending a page in-line via an RPC, respectively.

6.1. The Cost of Using Mach's External Pager and Exception Handling Facilities

The performance of Cricket is largely dependent on the cost of Mach's external pager and exception handling facilities. To measure these costs, we used a simple scan benchmark. In this benchmark, a single client *connects* with Cricket, invokes *begin_transaction* and then sequentially touches the first 1,280 pages (i.e., 5 Mbytes) of the mapped database. All I/O is short-circuited in the benchmark by having the Cricket server pass Mach a pointer to a dummy page in *memory_object_data_provide*. By using the scan benchmark and by turning off all aspects of transaction management in Cricket other than exception handling and external pager requests, we were able to obtain the results shown in Table 3. These results capture the per-page CPU cost of using Mach's external pager and exception handling facilities.

The costs listed in Table 3 are as follows: (1) is simply the CPU cost of handling a page fault for a page that is already cached in Mach kernel memory. (2) is the CPU cost of handling an address exception in Cricket to trigger locking on a database page. (3) is the CPU cost of having the kernel send a *memory_object_data_request* message to Cricket, with Cricket responding via a *memory_object_data_provided* message. (4), which should approximately equal (1) + (2), is the CPU cost that a client incurs on the first access to a database page that is cached in kernel memory. Finally, (5), which should approximately equal (1) + (2) + (3), is the CPU cost that a client incurs on the first access to a database page that is not cached in kernel memory.

As Table 3 clearly indicates, the external pager and exception handling facilities of Mach are not exactly free! Most of the expense presumably comes from context switches, message costs, and management of the kernel data structures associated with memory objects. However, the reader should bear in mind that (4) or (5) will only be incurred on the first access to a page. Furthermore, there are a number of ways that these costs can be reduced. One way is to simply do large block-sized I/O operations for regular data. We simulated the effect that this would have on the CPU costs in Table 3 by providing 16 Kbyte blocks of data to Mach in *memory_object_data_provided*. When this was done, the CPU cost of (5) dropped to 4,954 usec per 4 Kbyte page. Another method to reduce costs is to read data from disk and asynchronously call *memory_object_data_provided* as soon an address exception for an uncached data page is caught.[4] This is in contrast to waiting for an explicit *memory_object_data_request*

Operation	Cost in usec
getpid ( )	108
vm_protect ( )	490
bcopy ( ) a 4 Kbyte page	585
null RPC	1,275
send page out-of-line	1,316
send page in-line	4,493

Table 2: Cost of Various Operations in Mach

Event	Cost in usec
(1) page fault that is handled completely in the kernel	420
(2) address exception	3,180
(3) *memory_object_data_request* & *memory_object_data_provided*	3,221
(4) address exception + page fault	3,605
(5) address exception + page fault + *memory_object_data_request* & *memory_object_data_provided*	6,845

Table 3: Per-Page CPU Cost of External Pager and Exception Handling Facilities

---

[4] This is a rather obvious thing to do, but surprisingly Mach does not currently provide a way for an external pager to determine if a given page of a memory object is cached in kernel memory. Hopefully, this design flaw will be fixed in the near future.

message from the Mach kernel. Finally, large-grained locks can be used to cut down on the number of exceptions generated. To examine the effects of combining these methods, we simulated doing 16 Kbyte block I/O as soon as an address exception was generated for the first page in the block, and we also set the granularity of locking to 4-page units. When this was done the CPU cost of (5) dropped further to 2,248 usec per 4 Kbyte page. In design environments, we may do even better if design-level locks are acceptable.

6.2. Comparing Cricket to a General-Purpose Database Storage System

To determine how Cricket's performance compares to a general-purpose database storage system, we ran a tree-search benchmark on Cricket and also on the single-user version of the EXODUS Storage Manager [Care86]. In this benchmark, a persistent tree is searched in a depth-first manner, and the number of times the tree is searched can be varied. No processing is done on a node other than to follow its edges to neighboring nodes. This benchmark was chosen because it is representative of the types of data access that Cricket applications are expected to make. It is important for readers to realize that this is not really a fair comparison, as the single-user EXODUS Storage Manager does not provide shared access, protection, or locking. Nonetheless, we were still able to obtain some results that we thought might be of interest to other researchers.

In the tree-search benchmark, we used a tree with a depth of 4 and a node fanout of 11 (16,105 nodes total). For uniformity, the nodes in the tree were padded so that data pages in both the EXODUS Storage Manager and Cricket contained the same number of nodes, namely 12. As a result of padding nodes, the tree spanned 1,343 pages in both storage systems. Readers should note that padding the nodes in this manner biases the results in favor of the EXODUS Storage Manager due to the fact that its object identifiers consume 12 bytes, whereas they only consume 4 bytes in Cricket. Therefore, under normal circumstances, the resulting tree would tend to span fewer disk pages in Cricket than than it does in the EXODUS Storage Manager. This would in turn lead to less I/O, smaller buffering requirements, etc.

To measure the effect of doing I/O, we used a version of the tree-search benchmark that read the tree from disk at startup. When we sat down and looked at the numbers that were generated for Cricket, however, they made no sense. In particular, the CPU cost of using Mach's external pager facilities was not showing up. A little experimentation revealed that Mach could not issue I/O requests fast enough to avoid rotational delays (even for sequential reads on a raw disk partition). Since the average rotational delay for the disk we used was 8.3 msec, this meant that Cricket could, on average, do an extra 8.3 msec of CPU processing per page without it ever showing up in a single-user benchmark! This, of course, lead to the strange results. In the near future, we will try to get I/O numbers using some other benchmark.

As a result of the above problems and due to time constraints, we ended up generating only the results shown in Table 4. To ensure that no I/O would take place, the whole tree was read into memory by a separate transaction before the benchmark was run. Although exception handling for locks was turned on in Cricket, the transaction management code associated with locking was turned off to keep the comparison as fair as possible.

The first line in Table 4 shows the cost of searching a non-persistent version of the tree. The values shown there and in Table 3 can be used to validate the results that we obtained for Cricket. For example, the elapsed time for the one-pass search in Cricket is estimated to be 5,631 msec (789 msec for the base cost of executing the search code, plus 4,842 msec for the cost of handling page faults and exceptions on 1,343 pages). This estimate is quite close to the measured time of 5,680 msec. The same holds true for all the results, and therefore we are confident that the numbers we obtained are accurate.

As the results in Table 4 show, even with just 12 nodes per page and with almost no processing on a node, Cricket was still able to outperform the EXODUS Storage Manager. To understand why, it suffices to look at the interface that the EXODUS Storage Manager provides for accessing persistent objects. There, access to a persistent object is obtained via the *ReadObject* procedure call, which locates the object in the buffer pool, pins the page that

| Setting | Elapsed Search Time in msec | |
	One Pass	Two Passes
non-persistent tree	789	1599
Cricket	5,680	6,515
EXODUS	6,122	12,246

Table 4: Results for the Tree-Search Benchmark

contains it, and sets up an indirect pointer that is used to access the object.[5] After the object is no longer needed a *ReleaseObject* call is issued to upin the object. In the tree-search benchmark, *ReadObject* and *ReleaseObject* had to be called once per node per search pass. It was the costs associated with these two procedures (somewhere around 330 usec for the pair) that lead to the slower times in the EXODUS Storage Manager. Given that this benchmark was somewhat biased in favor of the EXODUS Storage Manager, we view these results very positively. To us, they suggest that for its intended applications, Cricket can provide better performance than a general-purpose database storage system.

7. Related Work

The work most closely related to ours is that done by the implementors of the Bubba database system at MCC [Bora90, Cope90]. In Bubba, the kernel of an AT&T UNIX System V kernel was modified to provide a single-level store with automatic, two-phase, page-level locking. Although we have borrowed a number of ideas from Bubba, several differences distinguish Cricket from the approach taken in Bubba. One difference is that Bubba's implementors had to modify the operating system kernel, since they did not have the luxury of using Mach. This, of course, caused problems with portability. Also, their recovery algorithms relied on battery-backed RAM, again causing problems with portability. Furthermore, in contrast to Cricket, the implementors of Bubba were able to ignore protection issues because their applications were written in FAD, which is a "safe" language. Finally, the focus in Bubba was on building a highly parallel database system, whereas in Cricket we are more interested in storage system issues, client/server hardware configurations, and providing support for design environments and persistent languages.

The Camelot Distributed Transaction System [Spec88] is another related work. Camelot also used the external pager facilities of Mach to provide a single-level store. In contrast to Cricket, however, the single-level store that Camelot provides is not meant to be directly accessed by client applications. Instead, it is intended to be accessed only within a "data server" for storing all the persistent data and meta-data managed by that server. It is not clear, however, that the abstraction of a single-level store is all that important in the context of a data server. In contrast to Cricket, Camelot also provides fairly conventional locking and recovery services that must be explicitly invoked by its clients.

The last related work that we need to mention is that done in IBM's 801 prototype hardware architecture [Chan88]. In the 801 prototype, the operating system essentially provided mapped files with automatic concurrency control and recovery. Special hardware was added for both locking and logging. While this is an interesting approach, our view is that it suffers from being too inflexible. In particular, no support was given for anything other than two-phase locking and value-based logging. This, of course, causes problems for indexes and other meta-data structures where two-phase locking is inappropriate. Distribution is also problem. Finally, special hardware support was necessary, which clearly causes problems with portability.

8. Conclusions

In this paper, we have introduced Cricket, a database storage system that is intended to be used as a platform for design environments and persistent programming languages. Cricket uses the memory management primitives of the Mach operating system to provide the abstraction of a shared, transactional single-level store that can be directly accessed by user applications. In the paper, we described our motivation for building Cricket, and we argued that a single-level store is a useful abstraction for many database applications. We also presented a fairly detailed description of Cricket's architecture, outlining a single-site architecture as well as a distributed architecture that we will eventually move to. Finally, we presented some preliminary performance results, which compared Cricket to the EXODUS Storage Manager. A simple tree-search benchmark was used to show that, for its intended applications, Cricket can provide better performance than a general-purpose database storage system.

As far as the implementation status of Cricket is concerned, the single-site version is currently up and limping along. However, much work remains. We have stolen the code for transaction management and locking from the EXODUS Storage Manager, but recovery has yet to be implemented; and likewise for index management. Eventually, of course, we will move to a distributed architecture. That move looks like it will lead to a number of interesting research problems. These include the problem of how to split storage system functionality between client machines and servers, and also the problem of maintaining memory coherency for what amounts to distributed, transactional, shared, persistent virtual memory.

---

[5] The interface of the EXODUS Storage Manager requires all accesses to persistent objects to be made through these indirect pointers. Due to a coding error in our tests, however, the extra level of indirection was short-circuited, and direct pointers were used instead. If the correct interface protocol had been followed, the EXODUS Storage Manager would have fared even worse than it did.

References

[Acce86]   M. Accetta et al., "Mach: A New Kernel Foundation for UNIX Development," *Proc. of the Summer Usenix Conf.*, June 1986.

[Agra89]   R. Agrawal and N. Gehani, "ODE (Object Database and Environment): The Language and the Data Model," *Proc. of the 1989 ACM SIGMOD Conf.*, June 1989.

[Appe86]   A. Appel et al., "Garbage Collection Can be Faster Than Stack Allocation," Computer Science Tech. Report 045-86, Princeton Univ., June 1986.

[Atki87]   M. Atkinson and P. Buneman, "Types and Persistence in Database Programming Languages," *ACM Computing Surveys*, 19(2), 1987.

[Bako90]   H. Bakoglu et al., "The IBM RISC System/6000 Processor: Hardware Overview," *IBM Journal of Research and Development*, 34(1), 1990.

[Bens72]   A. Bensoussan et al., "The Multics Virtual Memory: Concepts and Design," *CACM*,

[Bora90]   H. Boral et al., "Prototyping Bubba, A Highly Parallel Database System" *IEEE Trans. on Data and Knowledge Eng.*, 2(1), 1990. 15(5), May 1972.

[Blac88]   D. Black et al., "The Mach Exception Handling Facility," Computer Science Tech. Report 88-129, Carnegie Mellon Univ., April 1988.

[Bric76]   P. Brice and S. Sherman, "An Extension of the Performance of a Database Manager in a Virtual Memory System using Partially Locked Virtual Buffers," *ACM Trans. on Database Systems*, 6(1), 1976.

[Care86]   M. Carey et al., "Object and File Management in the EXODUS Extensible Database System," *Proc. of the 12th Intl. Conf. on Very Large Databases*, Sept. 1986.

[Chan88]   A. Chang and M. Mergen, "801 Storage: Architecture and Programming," *ACM Trans. on Computer Systems*, 6(1), 1988.

[Chan89]   E. Chang and R. Katz, "Exploiting Inheritance and Structure Semantics for Effective Clustering and Buffering in an Object-Oriented DBMS", *Proc. of the 1989 ACM SIGMOD Conf.*, June 1989.

[Chou85]   H-T. Chou and D. Dewitt, "An Evaluation of Buffer Management Strategies for Relational Database Systems," *Proc. of the 1985 VLDB Conf.*, Aug. 1985.

[Cock84]   W. Cockshott et al., "Persistent Object Management Systems," *Software-Practice and Experience*, vol. 14, 1984.

[Cope90]   G. Copeland et al., "Uniform Object Management," *Proc. of the Intl. Conf. on Extending Database Technology*, March 1990.

[Date86]   C. Date, "An Introduction to Database Systems," Ch. 3., pg. 56, Addison-Wesley, Reading Mass. 1986.

[DBE87]   *Database Engineering*, Special Issue on Extensible Database Systems, M. Carey ed., 10(2), June 1987.

[DeWi90]   D. DeWitt et al., "A Study of Three Alternative Workstation-Server Architectures for Object-Oriented Database Systems," Computer Science Tech. Report 907, Jan. 1990. Univ. of Wisconsin,

[Drav88]   R. Draves and E. Cooper, "C Threads," Computer Science Tech. Report 88-154, Carnegie Mellon Univ., June 1988.

[Duch89]   D. Duchamp, "Analysis of Transaction Management Performance," *Proc. of the 11th Symposium on Operating System Principles*, Dec. 1989.

[Eppi89]   J. Eppinger, "Virtual Memory Management for Transaction Processing Systems," Ph.D thesis, Computer Science Tech. Report 89-115, Carnegie Mellon Univ., Feb. 1989.

[Ford88]   S. Ford et al., "ZEITGEIST: Database Support for Object-Oriented Programming," *The 2nd Workshop on Object-Oriented Database Systems*, 1988.

[Fran90]   M. Franklin, M. Carey, and E. Shekita, paper in progress on algorithms for maintaining cache coherency in a client/server hardware environment.

[Horn87]   M. Hornick and S. Zdonik, "A Shared, Segmented Memory System for an Object-Oriented Database," *ACM Trans. on Office Information Systems*, 5(1), 1987.

[Katz87]   R. Katz and E. Chang, "Managing Change in a Computer-Aided Design Database," *Proc. of the 1987 VLDB Conf.*, Sept., 1987

[Kern78]   B. Kernighan and D. Ritchie, "The C Programming Language," Prentice-Hall, 1978.

[Li86]   K. Li and P. Hudak, "Memory Coherence in Shared Virtual Memory Systems," *Proc. of the 5th Annual ACM Symposium on Principles of Distributed Computing*, Aug. 1986.

[Litw80]   W. Litwin, "Linear Hashing: A New Tool for File and Table Addressing," *Proc. of the 1980 VLDB Conf.*, Aug. 1980.

[Lind87]   B. Lindsay et al., "A Data Management Extension Architecture," *Proc. of the 1987 ACM SIGMOD Conf.*, May 1987.

[Maho86]   M. Mahon et al., "Hewlett-Packard Precision Architecture: The Processor," *Hewlett-Packard Journal*, August 1986, pp. 4-22.

[Maie89]   D. Maier, "Making Database Systems Fast Enough for CAD Applications," in *Object-Oriented Concepts, Database and Applications*, W. Kim and F. Lochovsky, eds., Addison-Wesley, 1987, pp. 573-581.

[Moh89a]   C. Mohan et al., "ARIES: A Transaction Recovery Method Supporting Fine-Granularity Locking and Partial Rollbacks Using Write-Ahead Logging," IBM Research Report RJ6649, Jan. 1989.

[Moh89b]   C. Mohan and F. Levine, "ARIES/IM: An Efficient and High Concurrency Index Management Method Using Write-Ahead Logging," IBM Research Report RJ6846, Aug. 1989.

[Moss88]   J. Moss and S. Sinofsky, "Managing Persistent Data with Mneme: Designing a Reliable, Shared Object Interface," in *Advances in Object-Oriented Database Systems*, vol. 334 of *Lecture Notes in Computer Science*, Springer-Verlag, 1988, pp. 298-316.

[Moss90]   J. Moss, "Working with Persistent Objects: To Swizzle or Not to Swizzle," Computer Science Tech. Report 90-38, Univ. of Massachusetts, May 1990.

[Rich89]   J. Richardson, *E: A Persistent Systems Implementation Language*, Ph.D thesis, Computer Science Tech. Report 868, Univ. of Wisconsin, August 1989.

[Sche90]   H. Schek et al., "The DASDBS Project: Objectives, Experiences, and Future Perspectives," *IEEE Trans. on Data and Knowledge Eng.*, 2(1), 1990.

[Schu90]   D. Schuh et al., "Persistence in E Revisited — Implementation Experiences," *Proc. of the 4th Intl. Workshop on Persistent Object Systems Design, Implementation and Use*, Sept. 1990.

[Spec88]   "The Guide to the Camelot Distributed Transaction Facility: Release 1," A. Spector and K. Swedlow eds., Carnegie Mellon Univ., 1988.

[Ston81]   M. Stonebraker, "Operating System Support for Database Management," *CACM*, 24(7), 1981.

[Ston84]   M. Stonebraker, "Virtual Memory Transaction Management," *ACM Operating Systems Review*, 18(2), 1984.

[Ston90]   M. Stonebraker et al., "The Implementation of POSTGRES," *IEEE Trans. on Data and Knowledge Eng.*, 2(1), 1990.

[Trai82]   I. Traiger, "Virtual Memory Management for Database Systems," *ACM Operating Systems Review*, 16(4), 1982.

[Wilk90]   K. Wilkinson and M. Neimat, "Maintaining Consistency of Client-Cached Data," *Proc. of the 1990 VLDB Conf.*, Aug. 1990.

[Youn87]   M. Young et al., "The Duality of Memory and Communication in the Implementation of a Multiprocessor Operating System," *Proc. of the 11th Symposium on Operating System Principles*, Nov. 1987.

Cache Coherency and Storage Management in a Persistent Object System

Bett Koch, Tracy Schunke, Alan Dearle, Francis Vaughan,
Chris Marlin, Ruth Fazakerley & Chris Barter.

Department of Computer Science
The University of Adelaide
G.P.O. Box 498, Adelaide
South Australia 5001
Australia

{bett,tracy,al,francis,marlin,chris}@cs.adelaide.edu.au

Abstract

A distributed architecture for the support of programs written in the persistent programming language Napier is described. The architecture consists of a central server containing the stable persistent store and a collection of clients, each executing Napier processes. Since each client has a cache of objects, some of which may be shared with other clients, a protocol is required to ensure that the caches are coherent and that any access of an object will be to the most up-to-date copy. This architecture is explicated by following the lifecycle of an object from its 'birth' inside a client, through its life in the persistent store and its migration into other clients. Using this vehicle, the coherency protocol and client/server architecture are illustrated and explained.

1 Introduction

This paper describes a distributed architecture designed to support applications written in the persistent programming language Napier [1]. The Napier programmer views the world as a graph of strongly typed, stable persistent objects known as the persistent store. In this domain of discourse, all the physical properties of data have been abstracted over; examples of such properties include the location of the data, i.e. whether it is on disk or in RAM, and on which machine it resides, and how long the data exists. The Napier programmer has no control over the store — the underlying system manages the creation, movement and garbage collection of all objects.

Here we describe progress on an implementation of a persistent system based upon the well known multiple clients and single server model shown in Figure 1. In this system, a number of clients execute concurrently against a stable persistent store, managed by a single server, using a coherency protocol that guarantees data integrity. Each client corresponds to a single process executing a Napier program. These programs execute in an environment that is robust and guarantees correct execution, regardless of the failure of parts of the system.

Napier programs are compiled into Persistent Abstract Machine (PAM) code and it is an invocation of the PAM that executes the programs. One of the most notable features of the PAM [2,3] is that it is constructed entirely upon a heap-based storage architecture. The persistent store is therefore implemented as one very large heap in which all Napier objects, including process objects, reside. Each client contains a PAM interpreter, and is provided with an area of the persistent store within which to place newly created objects; this area is termed a *local heap*.

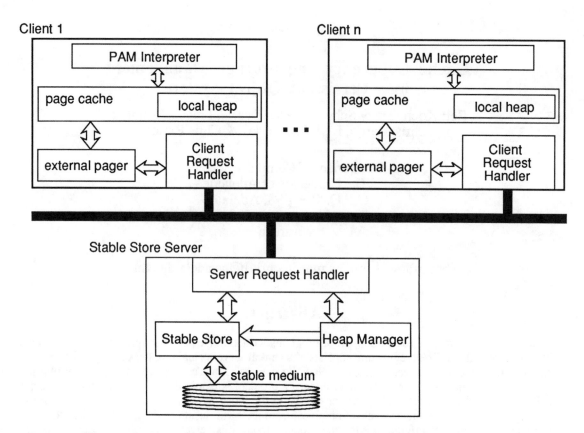

Figure 1. A persistent architecture to support distributed execution

2   The object lifecycle

In this paper, we use the metaphor of the life cycle of an object. We will follow the progress of a Napier object from its 'birth' inside a client, through its life in the persistent store and its migration into other clients. Using this metaphor, the coherency protocol and client/server architecture are illustrated and explained.

The example shown in Figure 2 manipulates two object types, namely *domicile* and *animal*. The program creates an instance of each type, makes some assignments to one of the objects, makes another assignment to some data in the persistent store, and finally makes one of the newly created objects reachable from the persistent store. The program is explained more fully in the following sections.

```
type domicile is structure( name, location : string )
type animal is structure(   name : string ;
                            home : domicile )

let smallPond = domicile(  "pond", "Adelaide" )

let afrog = animal( "tadpole", smallPond )

afrog( name ) := "frog"

use PS() with bigPond : domicile in
        afrog( home ) := bigPond

in PS() let Kermit = afrog
```

Figure 2. A Napier program

2.1. Creating local objects

Figure 3 shows a piece of code which creates an object of type *domicile* named *smallPond*, and another called *afrog* of type *animal*. As a result of running this code on Client A, five objects are placed in its local heap, corresponding to the structures denoted by *smallPond* and *afrog*, and the three strings "pond", "Adelaide" and "tadpole".

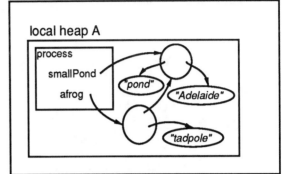

```
let smallPond = domicile(  "pond",
                          "Adelaide" )
let afrog = animal( "tadpole", smallPond )
```

Figure 3. Creating local objects

Local objects are freely modifiable. Assignments may be made to fields of structures; for example, the *name* field of the *animal* object denoted by *afrog*, may be updated as shown in Figure 4 below. Note that this update results in the string "tadpole" being unreachable from the running process. This object will end its life in the local heap.

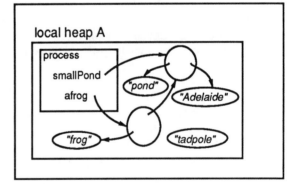

```
afrog( name ) := "frog"
```

Figure 4. Modifying local objects

2.2 Accessing the persistent store

Any Napier program can access objects which exist in the persistent store by calling the predefined function *PS* to obtain the *root of persistence*. Local objects may refer to such objects. If we assume that an object called *bigPond* of type *domicile* exists in the persistent store and is reachable from the root of persistence, the migration of a frog from a small pond to a big pond may be modelled by the language-level assignment shown in Figure 5.

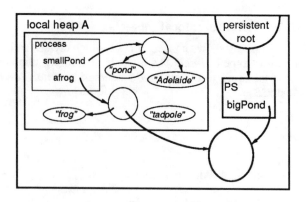

use PS() with bigPond : domicile in
afrog(home) := bigPond

Figure 5. Object field assignments

2.3   Sharing in the persistent store

Independently, within another client, another instance of type *animal* may be created which also contains a reference to *bigPond*. Clients A and B now share references to (and possibly copies of) persistent data.

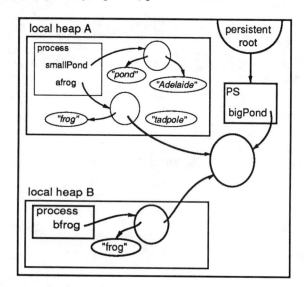

use PS() with bigPond : domicile in
    let bfrog = animal("frog", bigPond)

Figure 6. Shared references

2.4   Making local objects persistent

One way of making a local object available to other users of the persistent system is to make a name, and therefore a reference to that object, public. The declaration of the object *Kermit* in the root environment shown in Figure 7 achieves this.

in PS() **let** Kermit = afrog

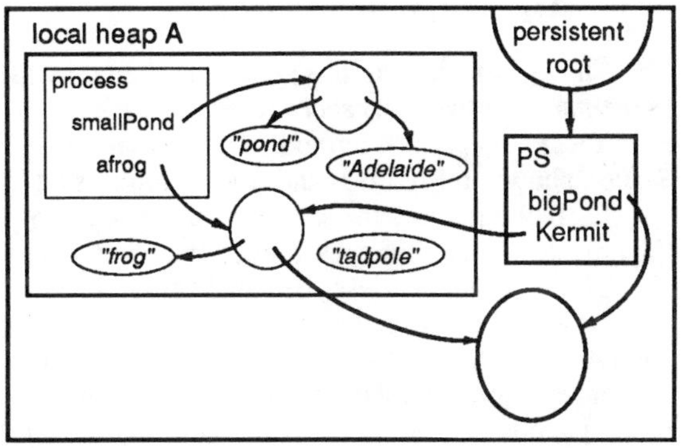

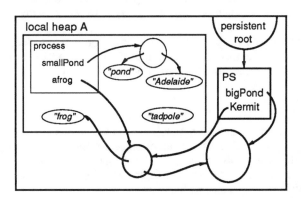

Figure 7. References from persistent to local objects

However, such an assignment causes problems as the isolation of a client's local heap from external references must be preserved. Should another client wish to access the persistent object associated with the name *Kermit*, known as *afrog* in the context of Client A, the object must be removed from its place of origin in Client A's local heap. This mechanism is shown in Figure 8.

Figure 8. Object Migration

3   Characteristics of the architecture

Although the example shown in Figure 2 is obviously contrived, it is however typical of many Napier programs. Firstly, notice that the program constructs a graph, in this case a trivial one; once the graph is constructed, it is linked into the persistent object graph. This kind of behaviour is common in programs written in persistent programming languages. In fact, linking a newly constructed data structure into an existing persistent structure is often the last act of a program before ceasing execution.

If this is typical behaviour for persistent programs, it would suggest that making assignments from persistent data to newly created data is relatively infrequent. Furthermore, it has been shown by Loboz [4] that most objects in persistent object stores are not modified. If the persistent address space is large, we believe it is also safe to assume that most data will not be shared. The strategies described in Section 7 depend on these assumptions.

We have attempted to design a system in which there is only one level of object addressing like that used by Thatte [5]. This contrasts with other persistent systems which use the now well known technique of persistent identifier (PID) translation [6,7]. The benefit gained is the opportunity to exploit address translation hardware.

The strategies used attempt to optimise what we expect to be common access patterns. Whether or not these strategies are advantageous will only be revealed through measurement once the system is complete. The system described in the following sections takes advantage of paging hardware, utilises the external paging facilities provided by the Mach operating system [8] and avoids the use of indirection tables and PID address translation (pointer swizzling) implemented in software.

4   Creating local objects

The object space in this system is shared by all clients and comprises a single 4 gigabyte address space known as the *persistent address space*. Objects reachable from the persistent root are termed persistent, and the pages used to hold these objects are termed *persistent pages*. The persistent address space is maintained by the *Stable Store Server*, shown in Figure 1, and it is within this address space that instances of PAMs execute.

Each client views the same address space of objects within which references may be made by directly addressing the objects. At any time, each client may contain part of the total persistent address space in a *page cache*.

The local heaps described in Section 1 reside inside page caches. Each local heap corresponds to a Napier process and is constructed from a contiguous set of pages from the persistent address space. Local heaps are small enough to always remain resident within the client's page cache during normal execution. Experience with earlier implementations has shown that significant improvements in performance may be obtained if the local heap area is rarely paged. Furthermore, greater locality of reference may be obtained in relation to larger heaps that do not use the local heap model. This can result in improved performance from better page fault behaviour and improved processor cache utilisation.

All objects are created in a local heap. In Figure 3, the object representing the string "tadpole" will be unreachable long before it gains any rights to long-term persistence. In fact, many Napier objects are short lived; this is exacerbated by the fact that Napier is a block retention language [9] and that activation records are allocated by the PAM from the heap rather than from a stack.

If transient objects are confined to a localised area, they may be distinguished from persistent objects resident in the total persistent address space and consequently garbage collected locally at low cost. Local heaps may be safely garbage collected provided that no external references (from other processes or the server) point into them. Fortunately, the creation and export of such pointers are easily detected, making this technique tractable. This is discussed further in Section 7.

The implementation permits, and requires, a single external pointer into local heaps. This pointer is to the *process header* object representing the process executing in the local heap and is used as a root for local garbage collection. Process headers are reachable from the root of persistence making processes restartable in the event of a failure.

5   Accessing the persistent store

The distinguished object known as the root of persistence is stored at a known address and is accessible by any process. A typical Napier program makes use of many objects found in the persistent store; examples of such objects include a browser [10], a window manager [11] and the Napier compiler. A process may traverse the transitive closure of objects reachable from the persistent root in order to access these tools; in so doing, it constructs references to objects that are outside its local heap.

An example of this mechanism is shown in Figure 2, in which the object denoted by *bigPond* is reachable from the root environment. The code fragment in Figure 5 results in the creation of a pointer from the locally created object, denoted by *afrog*, to a member of the persistent heap (*bigPond*). Recall that the objects named *afrog* and *bigPond* reside in the same persistent address space and therefore the reference to *bigPond* from *afrog* is a direct pointer stored within the object.

When an attempt is made to access an object not resident in the page cache, a page fault is generated. Under Mach, the user is permitted to provide a process called an external pager which services page faults. If an external pager is associated with a user process, the Mach kernel will forward page fault exceptions to that external pager, which will return the required data (in the case of a read fault) or may write the data to some stable medium (for a write fault).

The external pager, upon receipt of the page fault, communicates with the Stable Store Server via the *Client Request Handler*. The Client Request Handler handles all communications with other clients and the Stable Store Server. Once the appropriate page is delivered and placed in the client's address space, the access may proceed normally.

6   Sharing in the persistent store

The coherency algorithm addresses the problem illustrated in Figure 6, where persistent page copies are required by a number of clients. Further problems arise when one of those clients attempts to modify such a page. Two finite state automata have been developed to implement a coherency protocol between the clients and the server. These are based on the following principles:

- a page copy may be held by more than one client for read-only access, and

- only one client may hold write permission for a particular page.

To enforce these access restrictions, the Stable Store Server referees all page requests from connected clients. It determines whether pages are available for read or write access and distributes the requested pages accordingly. The server, therefore, maintains the majority of data structures used to ensure coherency. For each page, a data structure records those clients which hold up-to-date copies of that page; this list is known as the V-list (valid list).

If the Stable Store Server receives a request from a client to read a persistent page, it must determine if it is capable of directly supplying a copy of that page. If it can, it immediately sends the page to the requesting client; this is illustrated in Figure 5 where a previously unrequested page is requested by Client A. If the page may have been modified with respect to the server's copy, it must forward the read request to a client with a valid copy of that page. Such a client may be identified by examining the V-list associated with that page.

In Figure 6, the server is unable to supply the page copy as the page is held by a single client which may freely modify the copy of the page in its local page cache without arbitrating with the server for write permission. The server must therefore forward client B's read request to Client A which will, in turn, forward the potentially updated copy of the page to client B.

Note that if a client is known to hold the only copy of a page, it may update that page without requesting permission from the server. However, if the page is unmodified, the client must inform the Stable Store Server of its intention to modify the page. This mechanism will represent a considerable performance increase if the assumptions made in Section 3 are correct.

Copies of persistent pages in clients' page caches are initially write protected. This causes an access exception to be raised if a PAM attempts to modify a shared page. Whenever this occurs the Client Request Handler requests the Stable Store Server for write permission for that page. The server must ensure that all valid page copies are removed from other clients before it grants write permission to the requesting client. The server sends invalidation signals to all V-list members except the client which requested modification permission for the page. Upon receipt of all the invalidation acknowledgements from those clients requested to invalidate, the Stable Store Server informs the original requesting client that write permission is granted.

7   Making local objects persistent

Continuing the progression through the events an object may experience in its lifetime, we now consider the situation where a persistent object, resident in a persistent page cached within a client, points to an occupant of that client's local heap. As illustrated in Figure 7, this arises at the language level when an assignment is made from an object which is already persistent, to data created locally. At the implementation level, this assignment means that data created by the interpreter within the confines of its local heap is now reachable from an external point, other than its process header. For the reasons stated earlier, chief among which is preserving the ability to garbage collect the local heap area independently, it is important to:

- be able to detect the construction of pointers from persistent pages to locally created objects, and

- devise a mechanism whereby no other client will obtain a page while it contains references into local heap areas.

Using a scheme derived from generation-based garbage collection [12], another set of previously unused persistent pages, termed *copy-out pages*, is maintained by a client. In addition, the set of persistent pages which reference local objects is recorded; following Ungar, this set is termed the *remembered set*. New members may be added to this set when an assignment occurs at the machine level. For example, the statement

in PS() **let** Kermit = afrog

results in the addition of the address, representing *Kermit*, to the remembered set.

If a local heap always comprises *contiguous* pages, the interpreter can make a simple check at such a time: if the source address lies outside the range reserved for the local heap, and the assignment target lies within it, the source and its corresponding page identifier are placed in the remembered set. In Figure 9, pages P1 and P2 contain objects which reference the local objects A and D. These represent the instances of animal and domicile structures from Figures 3 to 8. The remembered set records the addresses of the pointers representing *Kermit*, *Muppet* and *Rymill*. The last two references could be the result of the following implementation level assignments:

in PS() **let** Muppet = afrog
in PS() **let** Rymill = smallPond

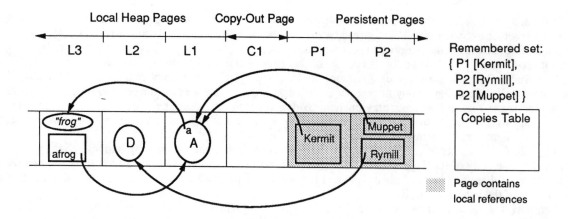

Figure 9. A client's page cache

The copy-out pages are used when an external request arrives at the client for a page belonging to the remembered set. The basic strategy is to copy the local heap object (or objects), referred to by the requested page, into a copy-out page. All references to the objects must eventually be changed to reflect their new locations within the persistent virtual address space. References from other persistent pages may be found efficiently, and updated immediately, by searching the remembered set. However, references from local heap pages may only be detected by traversing the local heap.

Such a traversal is expensive in terms of time, delaying the required page supply; it also necessitates halting the interpreter, which is potentially running concurrently at this time. Instead, this operation is postponed, and another data structure called the *Copies Table* is utilised. This table holds (*old, new*) address pairs for objects which have been duplicated. Once moved, the object itself must be scanned for local addresses among its pointer fields; should any be found, appropriate entries are inserted in the remembered set. The old and new addresses of the object are placed in the Copies Table. The page may now be safely exported since it no longer contains references to the client's local heap.

Figure 10 shows the situation where page P1 has been prepared for export by the above procedure. Object A has been moved into the copy-out page C1, and the two persistent locations which contained references to A, now point to the object A'. Finally, the mapping between A and A' has been entered in the Copies Table.

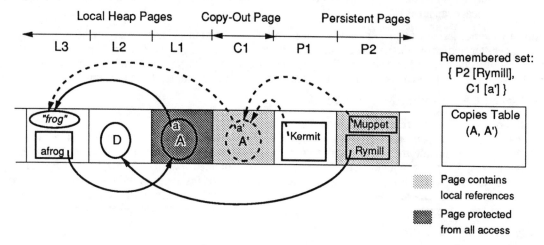

Figure 10. Copying out a local object

The original copy of a duplicated object cannot be classed as garbage until those references to it from within the local heap are altered. To trigger the alteration procedure, the local heap page containing the original copy is completely protected from all accesses. Page L1 in Figure 10 is depicted as protected since it contains the old copy of object A.

If the interpreter attempts to access such a page, the external pager will be invoked with an access exception. Since the interpreter has halted, the local heap can now be fully traversed to find and update all references to copied objects; the relevant entries in the Copies Table can subsequently be deleted. If the interpreter does not attempt to access this page before the next local garbage collection, all references from within the local heap to relocated objects are updated at this time, and the Copies Table becomes empty.

In Figure 11, the pointer from *afrog* has been updated, the mapping (A,A') has been removed, and the protection on page L1 has been lifted. In this way, objects migrate from initial creation as part of a process' local heap, to general availability as part of the shared persistent store.

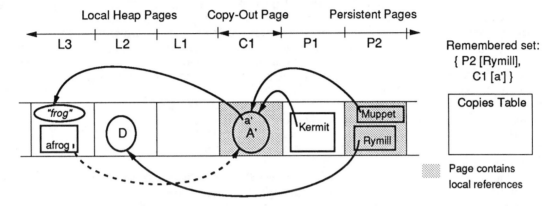

Figure 11. Completing reference updates

Different clustering strategies may be modelled by altering the way in which the copy out process is implemented. Suppose the copy-out page C1 in Figure 11 is required by another client; the procedure described above would be repeated. If object A formed part of a linked data structure, it is highly probable that C1's data would soon be of non-local interest. It may be advantageous, when initially required to copy an object, to immediately copy its transitive closure as well. Such a strategy caters for a depth-first pattern of access to objects.

Alternatively, it may be better to anticipate future export requests for all pages in the remembered set, and, when one such page is requested, move *all* objects directly referenced from this set. Adopting the first option would cause both the structure A and the string object "frog" to be moved if page P1 was requested; adopting the second would result in the relocation of both the structures A and D in a breadth-first manner. Experimentation and further measurements regarding typical object access will be needed to determine an optimal strategy.

8   Stabilisation

We have described a distributed object space managed by a central server. The central server provides a stable store in which a self consistent version of the object space is maintained. To ensure stability may always be achieved, rollback is made possible by writing data to disk using a shadow paging technique [13]. In general terms, this scheme involves maintaining original page versions along with the new. As the final stage in a stabilisation, a single disk-page write updates a mapping, reflecting which version is to be treated as the original henceforth [14]. Until this point, the previous stable state is completely preserved, and indicated by the old mapping.

The Stable Store Server maintains those structures needed to correctly roll back the execution state of interdependent clients should failure occur in any part of the system. Those parts of the system that can continue without jeopardising the store's integrity are unaffected.

A client which holds modified pages may pass copies on to another client as a result of read requests. Thus, clients may become dependent on one another by virtue of having seen the same data, which has been modified with respect to the Stable Store. We term such dependent clients *associates* and a set of mutually dependent clients an *association* [15].

It is important to note that associations are dynamic in nature, with clients being added and associations merging over time. Associations, which are maintained by the Stable Store Server, contain a list of page identifiers, which identifies those pages modified by members of the association since the last stabilise.

Any client may initiate a stabilise operation. At such a time, the server notifies the instigating client's association to stabilise in order to bring the stable store into a new consistent state. Each of the associates must send back copies of all modified pages held in their local cache. It is not necessary to write back pages until this time. Due to the nature of associations (that is, a client may belong to only one association and a modified page belongs to only one association's page list), several independent stabilisation cycles may be in progress at any time.

9   Conclusions

A distributed architecture designed to support applications written in the persistent programming language Napier has been described. Objects are manipulated within caches inside clients, each of which are serviced by a central server; the architecture supports the sharing of objects between clients. Thus, the question of cache coherency arises and a sophisticated cache coherency protocol has been designed for the system.

Alternative schemes for sharing virtual memory between distributed clients have been proposed [16,17]. In [18], the underlying data repository moves between *stable states* through *checkpoint* operations. A checkpoint involves flushing those pages onto disk which have been modified since the last checkpoint. A new stable state is achieved when a known set of such pages has been thus secured, and any record of their original contents, as held in the previous stable state, can be safely disposed. Wu and Fuchs [19] describe a system whereby checkpoints are carried out on individual nodes (i.e. clients), as soon as another node requests the use of any updated data. A major concern of this work has been to limit rollback propagation, so that the failure of any client only affects that client.

The idea of having local heaps originates in architectures such as POMS [6] and CPOMS [7] that perform PID translation. These systems have the advantage of being able to perform local garbage collection, but pay a heavy cost penalty in the form of software address translation.

Our approach to distributed support for persistent objects has been illustrated through the description of the lifecycle of an object from its 'birth' inside a client, through its life in the persistent store and its migration into other clients. Our scheme also shows potential for clustering objects in a page based persistent address space, with all the attendant benefits. The architecture exploits hardware address translation through the external pager mechanism provided by the Mach operating system. This scheme capitalises on the advantages of a local heap. In addition to potentially improving performance through locality of reference, the likelihood of having to perform garbage collection over a large persistent address space is minimised.

Acknowledgements

This work was partially supported by Australian Research Council grant number 4900-6830-1000. We would like to thank the Persistence Project at the University of St Andrews for their continuing cooperation in this work; in particular, we acknowledge the contributions of Fred Brown to whom this work owes a great deal.

We would also like to thank the National Parks and Wildlife Service of South Australia, particularly the staff of the Morialta Falls Conservation Park who erected a billboard showing the life cycle of a frog.

References

[1]   Morrison R., Brown A.L., Connor R. & Dearle A. "The Napier88 Reference Manual". Universities of Glasgow & St Andrews Persistent Programming Research Report 77-89 (1989).

[2]   Morrison R., Brown A.L., Carrick R., Connor R. & Dearle A. "The Persistent Abstract Machine". Universities of Glasgow & St Andrews Persistent Programming Research Report 59-88 (1988).

[3]   Connor R., Brown A.L., Carrick R., Dearle A. & Morrison R. "The Persistent Abstract Machine". In "Persistent Object Systems". Workshops in Computing, Rosenberg J. & Koch D. (eds.) pp. 279-288 (Springer-Verlag, 1990).

[4]   Loboz C.Z. "Monitoring Execution of PS-algol Programs". In "Persistent Object Systems". Workshops in Computing, Rosenberg J. & Koch D. (eds.) pp. 353-366 (Springer-Verlag, 1990).

[5]   Thatte S.M. "Persistent Memory: A Storage Architecture for Object Oriented Database Systems". Proceedings ACM/IEEE 1986 International Workshop on Object Oriented Database Systems, Pacific Grove, California, pp. 148-159 (September 1986).

[6]   Cockshott W.P., Atkinson M.P., Chisholm K.J., Bailey P.J. & Morrison R. "POMS: a Persistent Object Management System". Software Practice and Experience, 14,1 (January 1984).

[7]   Brown A.L. & Cockshott W.P. "The CPOMS Persistent Object Management System". Universities of Glasgow & St Andrews Persistent Programming Research Report 13-85 (1985).

[8]   Acceta M., Baron R., Bolosky W., Golub D., Rashid R., Tevanian A. & Young M. "Mach: A New Kernel Foundation for UNIX Development". USENIX, pp. 93-112 (July 1986).

[9]   Berry D.M. "Block Structure: Retention or Deletion?". Conference Record of the Third Annual ACM Symposium on the Theory of Computing, Shakes Heights, Ohio, pp. 86-100 (May 1971).

[10]   Kirby G. & Dearle A. "An Adaptive Browser for Napier88". University of St Andrews Research Report CS/90/16 (1990).

[11]   Cutts Q., Dearle A., Kirby G. & Marlin C. "WIN: A Persistent Window Management System". Universities of Glasgow & St Andrews Persistent Programming Research Report 73-89 (1989).

[12]   Ungar D. "Generation Scavenging: A Non-disruptive High Performance Storage Reclamation Algorithm". ACM SIGPLAN Notices, 9,5 pp. 157-167 (May 1984).

[13]   Lorie A.L. "Physical Integrity in a Large Segmented Database". ACM Transactions on Database Systems, 2,1 pp. 91-104. (1977).

[14]   Challis M.L. "Database Consistency and Integrity in a Multi-user Environment". In "Databases: Improving Usability and Responsiveness". B Scheiderman (ed.), pp. 245-270 (Academic Press, 1978).

[15]   Vaughan F., Schunke T., Koch B., Dearle A., Marlin C. & Barter C. "A Persistent Distributed Architecture Supported by the Mach Operating System". Proceedings USENIX Workshop on the Mach Operating System, *to appear* (October 1990).

[16]   Li K. & Hudak P. "Memory Coherence in Shared Virtual Memory Systems". ACM Transactions on Computer Systems, 17,4 pp. 321-359 (November 1989).

[17]   Rosenberg J., Henskens F., Brown F., Morrison R. & Munro D. "Stability in a Persistent Store Based on a Large Virtual Memory". University of St Andrews Research Report CS/90/6 (1990).

[18]   Morrison R., Brown A.L., Connor R. & Dearle A. "Napier88 Release1.1". St Andrews University, St Andrews, Scotland (1989).

[19]   Wu K.L. & Fuchs W.K. "Recoverable Distributed Shared Virtual Memory". IEEE Transactions on Computers, 39,4 pp. 460-469 (April 1990).

An Object-Based Memory Architecture*

Ifor Williams
Department of Computer Science
The University
Manchester M13 9PL
U.K.
ifor@cs.man.ac.uk

Mario Wolczko[†]
Department of Computer Science
The University
Manchester M13 9PL
U.K.
mario@cs.man.ac.uk

Abstract

A typical implementation of an object store upon a conventional architecture sacrifices a good deal of performance in emulation overheads. In this paper we describe the design of a high-performance hardware-based object memory. This work forms a part of the MUSHROOM Project, which is constructing a high-performance architecture tailored for symbolic processing and especially object-oriented languages.

Alternatives in the design of an object-based memory system are presented. Each alternative is analysed using the results of simulations based on memory reference traces taken from a Smalltalk-80 system. The best of the alternatives is chosen and used as the basis for the MUSHROOM memory system.

The principal areas described and evaluated are:

- Addressing formats suitable for Smalltalk-like object-based systems,
- The parameters describing the novel object-based cache used in MUSHROOM, and
- Schemes for object address translation.

1 Introduction

As object-based systems become widespread, large object stores will become common. As processor speeds rise, these object stores will need to provide fast access to large collections of persistent objects if they are not to become a bottleneck in system throughput. To date, most object stores have been implemented using stock hardware, by emulation in software. While acceptable as an initial solution, it is possible that large performance gains are to be had by using architectures more suited to the task at hand.

The MUSHROOM Project at the University of Manchester is investigating new architectures for object-based systems. The aim is to design, construct and evaluate a novel architecture which should reclaim the performance lost in software emulation. As part of this project, we have designed a novel object-based virtual memory system. This system aims to meet the twin objectives of high throuput for object accesses together with the scalability to large object stores. In previous work we have described how we intend to improve the performance of the object store by decreasing the number of transfers between primary and secondary memory [WWH87a, WWH87b]. In this paper we report on the design of the MUSHROOM primary memory system, which should also deliver high throughput with low latency.

The basis for all our investigations has been the Smalltalk-80 system. Smalltalk-80 is a good choice for investigations into object-based architectures for these reasons:

- Numerous techniques to improve its performance on stock hardware have been devised, implemented and described (see [Kra83] for just a few; [DS84] describes others). There are unlikely to be more large increases in the performance of Smalltalk-80 on stock hardware.

- It is a *pure* object system; nothing in the computational model does not use the object paradigm. This releases us from having to consider features not germane to object-oriented systems.

---

*This work was supported by Research Grant GR/E/65050 from the UK Science and Engineering Research Council.
[†]Supported by a SERC Research Fellowship

114

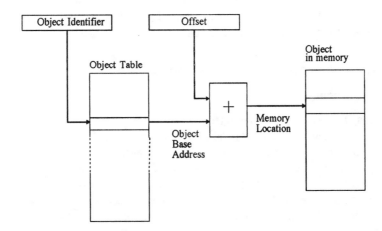

Figure 1: *Object Addressing in Smalltalk-80*   An object identifier is used as a direct index into the object table. The object table contains information about the object, including its location in memory. The address of the memory location to be accessed is determined by adding the offset to the object's base address.

- There are numerous applications available written in Smalltalk-80 which can be monitored to provide realistic data about the behaviour of the system.

In this paper we present the design of the MUSHROOM primary object memory. The design decisions are motivated by analyses of the results of simulations of different designs. These simulations are driven by realistic data taken from an existing Smalltalk-80 implementation.

1.1   Overview

The next section outlines the basic object store model, and describes problems with conventional, software implementations. It also details the requirements of hardware-based implementations, and the problems to be overcome by those implementations. These are threefold, and are described in succeeding sections: object addressing formats, object-based caches, and address translation. In each section we describe the problem, outline candidate solutions and present results of experiments to determine which solution, if any, is best.

2   Object-based storage models

This section describes the storage model used within the MUSHROOM Project. Although it is based on that required by Smalltalk-80, it is sufficiently simple that many of its properties are present in other systems.

In an object-based system, the memory consists of objects. An object contains a number of memory words, each accessed by an integer offset. The valid offsets are contiguous. Objects can contain any number of words; some objects may even change size during their lifetimes.

Objects are referred to by object identifiers. Consequently, an access to a word within an object requires an object identifier and an offset into the object. An object identifier acts solely as the identifier for that object and cannot be affected by operations on the object. Additionally, the object identifier can only be created or modified by privileged system code (for example, arithmetic cannot be performed on object identifiers).

Object addressing (also known as symbolic segmentation) has been used in many machine architectures — the Burroughs B5000 series of computers [LK61] is a classic example. In many such systems, objects are also known as segments.

Figure 1 illustrates the object memory model as used in the Smalltalk-80 virtual machine definition [GR83]. Address translation is performed by using the object identifier as the index into a large table (the *object table*) containing the location of objects. The memory address of the desired word is then formed by adding the offset to the memory address of the first word of the object (the *base address*). Note that in this model there is no requirement to perform any form of access control on each object access, as in some capability-based systems.

2.1   Conventional implementations of object stores

2.1.1   Emulating object memory

On most implementations, the base address of an object will be a virtual address for the virtual memory system of the host machine; this may be mandated by the host operating system. However, for a native implementation of Smalltalk, the base address would either be a real memory address, or a disk address from which the object would be fetched. In this case the memory manager must deal explicitly with the mapping of variable-sized objects onto fixed-size disk blocks. In both cases the memory manager must handle free lists of address space.

Emulation of an object memory is achieved by maintaining an object table in software and performing a lookup of the object table on each object access, again in software. Additionally, the final address is formed by adding the offset to the base address.

2.1.2   Eliminating the object table

In order to avoid such inefficiencies, some implementors have chosen to discard the object table and implement direct addressing. Instead of using object identifiers to index into the object table, the object identifier is also the base address of the object. Eliminating the object table indirection increases performance. For example, Ungar and Patterson have reported that their implementations of Smalltalk-80 would run approximately 25% slower had they implemented a software object table lookup for each object access [UP83, Ung87].

Using base addresses as object identifiers imposes many restrictions on the system. Firstly, it means that if virtual memory is to be used, it must be provided by an underlying system, as the base addresses cannot be real addresses. Also, removing the indirection on every memory access makes it extremely expensive to relocate objects in memory. On a system with an object table, relocating an object only requires that the relevant object table entry be updated. On the other hand, in a system using direct addressing, all memory locations that point to that object require updating. Typically, this requires a sweep of the whole memory space to identify all the references to the relocated object. Note that the indirection provided by an underlying virtual memory system does not help, because it will typically associate whole pages, containing many objects, with a set of real addresses. Individual objects cannot be relocated cheaply.

Prohibitively expensive object relocation can have a large effect on the performance of the Smalltalk-80 system. For example, the `become:` primitive, which exchanges the identities of two objects, typically occurs once every 100,000 bytecodes [Wal83]. Without an object table, the whole object memory has to be swept for references to the participating objects. Sweeping the entire memory space at this frequency will cause substantial performance degradation, proportionately increasing as the virtual memory size increases. Although some of the uses of this primitive can be removed by rewriting parts of the system software, enough uses are likely to remain to cause problems. Every use of `become:` will cause all of virtually memory to be accessed, and will defeat the virtual memory algorithms.

A more far-reaching implication is the limitation imposed on the memory management system. Efficient relocation of objects allows the grouping of related objects to increase locality [WWH87a]. Easy relocation also provides scope for efficient object migration in a distributed environment. Additionally, it eases the task of garbage collection. Direct addressing results in complex memory management systems as sophisticated techniques are employed to minimise relocation costs.

The motivation for direct addressing is to avoid the cost of object table indirection performed in software on every object access. Despite the limitations, this approach has provided significant performance improvements for many Smalltalk-80 implementations (e.g., see [UP83]). However, when considering a new machine architecture to support object-oriented systems, we can start anew and design a virtual memory system that supports the object table in hardware, releasing us from the cost of software emulation.

2.2   A new approach

Before deciding on the broad outline of a virtual memory architecture, it would be useful to identify some of the requirements:

High performance Because the virtual memory system is to be part of a new architecture, MUSHROOM, specifically aimed at yielding high performance for Smalltalk-80, it is essential that it be able to deliver high throughput with low latency. The new system must be competitive with conventional memory systems in these aspects.

Mobility of objects A twin aim of the MUSHROOM architecture is to support large applications in Smalltalk-80, consisting of virtual memory sizes much larger than currently available. As part of our investigations, we have determined that an effective mechanism in the support of object-based virtual memory is the use of dynamic grouping when transferring objects between primary and secondary memory [WWH87a]. To allow effective grouping, the system should be able to migrate objects easily. This can improve virtual memory locality and aid efficient distribution.

A machine directly supporting such an object memory would be the ideal platform for Smalltalk. Previous low-level implementations of object memories have been restricted by the limitations of the underlying hardware. The OOZE system, for example, severely restricted the number and allocation of object identifiers, whilst the the LOOM system on the other hand introduced too much complexity due to the split address spaces [Kae86]. Given current 32-bit architectures, the problems addressed by LOOM and OOZE are not relevant.

In order to achieve the desired performance, the four major concerns of any new implementation of object memory are:

Addressing efficiency On a 32-bit Smalltalk implementation, 64 bits are required to identify a memory location: a 32-bit object identifier and a 32-bit offset. Since the average object size is 77 bytes (20 words) [Ung87], most of the offset representation is redundant. Direct addressing does not suffer from this problem (an access to an object at offset $size + 1$ will return the head of another object if the memory is compacted). Can a more efficient scheme be devised?

Access time As the new object store is to be a central part of a high-performance system, it is vital that it be able to service object accesses quickly and with high throughput. Main memory access times are not sufficiently small to meet the exacting demands. Can a fast object cache be devised?

Address translation performance The object table indirection implies at least two memory accesses for each data access. If a hardware object table were provided, could object address translation be competitive with conventional virtual address translation?

Base-offset addition Having determined the location of the object, an addition must be performed to generate the address of the memory location. Can this addition in a critical path be eliminated?

The remainder of this paper address these problems in a new object-based memory design. The next section outlines an efficient addressing format. After that an object-based cache design is described that can meet the requirements for latency. Finally, an approach to address translation is presented that needs negligible hardware support.

3   Address formats

A 32-bit Smalltalk implementation implies 32-bit object identifiers and 32-bit offsets. However, this is undesirable for a number of reasons. Firstly, it has been observed that the average dynamic object size is only 20 words (77 bytes) implying an average dynamic offset size of 5 bits. Clearly, providing a 32-bit offset to access such small objects is unnecessarily expensive. The second, and more serious implication of 32-bit offsets is the excessive amount of hardware resource which they would consume. For example, address busses would need to be 64 bits wide (object identifier and offset) and caches must handle 64-bit quantities.

Fortunately, we do not need to represent addresses in such a profligate fashion. The vast majority of objects are of fixed size, with many fewer than 256 words; only comparatively few objects are of much larger size. By using the abstraction mechanisms available in object-oriented languages, we can represent large objects by collections of

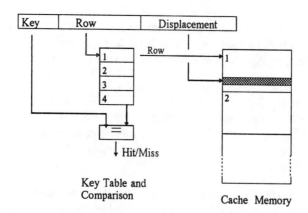

Figure 2: *Schematic of a simple cache*   The cache block is identified from the 'row' bits of the address whilst the least significant bits form an index into the block. The most significant 'key' bits must be associated with the cache block to ensure unique mapping.

smaller objects, just as files are fragmented into disk blocks. This can either be visible to the programmer (i.e., the basic array class can limit the number of elements to 256), or be made transparent in system software.

In [WWH87b] it was shown that 8 offset bits suffice for Smalltalk. In fact, 86% of all memory references could be expressed in using 4 offset bits or less. Using 8 offset bits, only 0.12% of all memory references will require an additional indirection. Consequently, we assume in the rest of this paper that addresses are represented by 32 object identifier bits, and 8 offset bits.

4   Memory caching

Most computer systems contain a hierarchy of storage with higher levels increasing in size and decreasing in access time. Traditionally, the lowest of these levels is the machine registers. Memory caches are typically the second level in the hierarchy and provide an invisible association between memory addresses and their values cached in small, fast memories. Ideally, full association between addresses and memory locations is provided. However, due to the expense of fully associative memory, most caches implement a *pseudo-associative* memory.

A fully associative memory can cache any permutation of memory locations whilst a pseudo-associative memory has restrictions on which locations it may cache. For example, a simple pseudo-associative memory implementation may be unable to cache concurrently two memory locations whose least significant 16 address bits are identical. For a carefully designed cache, however, such restrictions are insignificant for most applications. Additionally, pseudo-associative caches are substantially easier and cheaper to implement than fully associative caches.

Figure 2 illustrates the classical pseudo-associative cache structure. The cache memory is divided into equal-sized *blocks*, each of which caches a contiguous portion of main memory. The location of a block in cache is determined by a hash of the address. Clearly, many addresses may hash onto the same cache block; consequently a key is required to form an unique association between an address and a particular cache block. All cache designs are variants of this theme. Caches vary in the kind of addresses used, the nature of the associativity and in techniques for maintaining consistency with main memory.

In addition to the basic access time when the cache hits, there are two main restrictions on the performance of caches. An application may have many addresses that map onto the same block within the cache. In this case the contention for the block results in excessive purging and filling activity. Such *interference* is particularly apparent immediately after process switching due to new patterns of access [TS87] (separate address spaces per process introduce additional problems). Secondly, the amount of work performed on each cache miss can have a significant effect on overall performance.

Cache interference may be reduced by increasing the *associativity* of the cache. The approximation to a fully associative cache may be improved by replicating the structure illustrated in Fig. 2. Allowing two or four associations to be tested in parallel can substantially reduce interference, at the expense of greater cost and complexity. A compromise may be constructed by replicating the association circuitry and encoding the results to form an address for a single cache memory bank [CLP81]. A cache with an associativity of one is also known as a *direct-mapped* cache.

Cache miss overheads can be reduced by ensuring that the main memory contains an accurate image of the cache memory. This is achieved by *write-through* caches in which all cache updates are also performed on main memory, consequently removing the need to write back the cache contents when purging on a miss. *Write-back* caches are an alternative approach which maintain a *dirty bit* for each cache block to indicate whether the contents of the block have been modified and require writing back when purged. Highly associative caches have multiple association banks; consequently there are several cache locations that could be purged to accommodate a block to be brought into the cache. The choice could be arbitrary, or a sophisticated least-recently-accessed mechanism could be employed. Whatever mechanism is used, care must be taken to ensure it does not have a detrimental effect on performance.

The management of cache misses also affects the performance. Many high-performance systems service cache misses in hardware whilst others rely on microcode or system software to perform cache transfers. The cache block may be cyclically filled from the required memory location allowing the faulted process to be restarted before the cache update is completed. Alternatively, the faulted process must wait until the transfer is complete. Other factors that influence overall cache performance are discussed later.

5   An object cache

The design of caches for conventional memory architectures is well understood and has been the target of much investigation. However, little information exists on the design of storage hierarchies for object-based systems. Memory caching is a critical factor in the design of any high-performance computer, especially so in object-based systems with their inherently high memory management overheads. Consequently, in designing the MUSHROOM architecture much emphasis was placed on the cache design.

The aim was to design a cache which would return a value one machine cycle after it was presented with the object identifier and offset. Given that we notionally needed to translate the object identifier into a real address, add the offset to the real address and access the memory in this single cycle, it was clearly an unrealistic goal! The cache design described in the following sections achieves an average access time of approximately 1.8 cycles with a simple, practical cache.

The first problem to overcome is the addressing. Caches on conventional machines are based on linear address spaces and associate a single address (virtual or real) with a memory location. Object addressing on the other hand uses two elements to identify the memory location — namely the object identifier and the offset. By *concatenating* these two elements together we get the equivalent of a 40-bit "virtual address" that can uniquely identify the memory location. Admittedly these virtual addresses will be sparse, but at least they uniquely identify memory locations.

The important point is that by constructing a cache to associate this 40-bit virtual address with its value, not only is the need for object identifier address translation eliminated, but also the need for offset addition. In terms of cache design there are two overheads, namely the extra memory required to handle the sparse, 40-bit virtual addresses and the overhead of managing object boundaries in cache.

5.1   Object boundaries in an object cache

An object-based cache will require additional functionality to recognise object boundaries. On conventional systems, contiguous portions of physical memory are allocated to pages which contain contiguous portions of virtual memory. Whole cache blocks are read and written back into memory, and are guaranteed not to cross page boundaries. Object addressing, however, complicates memory allocation by requiring variable-sized segments which may be smaller than cache blocks. Also, objects are usually allocated on a 'best fit' strategy into free spaces in physical memory. Thus there are no regular boundaries for cache blocks and care must be taken in organising proper alignment.

Figure 3 illustrates the fetching and purging of objects between cache blocks and main memory. In Fig. 3, an access to object 3 has caused a cache miss. Since the cache block is larger than the object, a portion of object 4 is in danger of being copied into cache. However, only the virtual address for object 3 is associated with the cache block, therefore even if a portion of object 4 is copied into the cache it can never be accessed. Clearly, for efficiency reasons

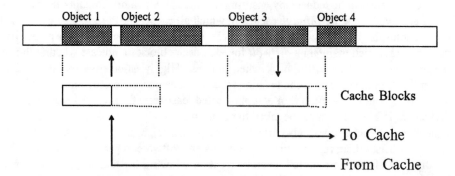

Figure 3: *Filling and purging an object-based cache*   Unlike conventional memory, an object based-memory is not contiguous. Care must be taken to ensure that cache operations on blocks of contiguous memory do not corrupt physically adjacent, but logically separate objects. When writing a block from the cache into main memory, object 2 must not be overwritten by empty words of the cache block containing object 1. Similarly, on fetching an object into the cache, there is no need to copy the head of object 4 into the cache block containing object 3.

it would be best to fetch object 3 only. The cache block purged into main memory contains the whole image of object 1. The remainder of the cache block does not contain sensible data and only object 1 should be written back lest object 2 be corrupted.

5.2   Separate instruction and data caches

High-performance machines of the Reduced Instruction Set Computer (RISC) [Sta86] style of architecture require an instruction every cycle. Additionally, as many as 40% of instructions perform memory accesses [Ste87]. In the MUSHROOM processor, it is anticipated that the memory bandwidth requirements will not be much less than this and estimates indicate a requirement for 1.3 memory accesses per cycle. Clearly, a single cache capable of servicing one access per cycle is insufficient to sustain the processor's performance.

To eliminate the contention between data and instruction accesses to cache, many systems provide separate caches for data and instructions. Because data and instruction accesses exhibit different memory referencing behaviour, the separate caches can be designed to exploit these characteristics. For example, not only does a separate instruction cache provide increased instruction bandwidth, but the cache design can be tailored to instruction fetch patterns. Similarly, the data cache may be designed to maximise data access performance.

The analysis of instruction cache design is similar to that of data cache design [Wil89]. In the rest of this paper only the data cache is considered.

5.3   Cache performance evaluation

It is impossible to choose between the multitude of cache structures without detailed analysis of their performance. The following sections present results obtained from detailed simulations of various cache structures driven by memory reference traces obtained from various Smalltalk-80 applications.

To gather the data, a simulator was constructed capable of simulating a wide variety of cache structures. Numerous options allowed a wide range of cache associativity, block sizes and cache size to be monitored in addition to many purging and consistency strategies. The cache simulator was driven by memory reference traces gathered from a modified Smalltalk-80 virtual machine implementation. The traces represent activity in the Smalltalk object memory while running one of four Smalltalk applications. These applications involve browsing, editing, compiling,

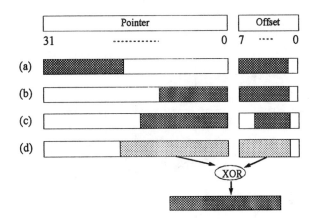

Figure 4: *Four schemes for constructing a hash into the cache*   In the above figures, the dark gray areas represent the portions which form the hash. Scheme (a) would be effective if object identifiers were randomly allocated. However, scheme (b) is more effective when object identifiers are allocated sequentially. Scheme (c) is similar to (b) and takes advantage of the fact that the more significant bits in the offset are rarely used. Long sequential accesses cause problems with (c) because different parts of the same object may map onto the same cache block. To remedy this, scheme (d) uses an XOR hash to achieve a more even distribution.

and running new code, and hopefully are representative of typical Smalltalk-80 usage. The traces vary in length from 22 million to 203 million object references (3 to 19 million Smalltalk-80 bytecodes). In order to improve the accuracy of the figures, accesses to Smalltalk contexts (which are placed in a register-windowed hardware stack in MUSHROOM) were not included in the traces. Also, object accesses to bitmaps during graphics operations (the BitBlt primitive on Forms) was also excluded, as these will be performed by an auxiliary display processor in the MUSHROOM system.

Two main statistics gauge the performance of a cache: the hit rate and the amount of traffic generated between main memory and the cache. The latter figure is of utmost importance in a multi-processor system where a single main memory may be shared amongst many caches. In a multiprocessor system, maximum performance is achieved by a careful balance between the bandwidth requirements and miss rate. However, our primary aim is to maximise the performance of a single processor architecture, and hence multiprocessors are not considered further.

Even on a single processor system, maximising the hit rate does not necessarily lead to the optimal performance. The significance of the hit rate is heavily dependent on the relative service times of cache hits and cache misses. In later sections, an average access time based on estimated hit and miss overheads is used to evaluate performance.

There are many cache structure parameters which affect the overall performance. The number of possible permutations of cache structures is unmanageably large. However, the combinations may be limited by simulating realisable structures and concentrating on the effects of varying a single parameter. For example, the first set of simulations models various hashing mechanisms for a small set of cache structures. The best hashing mechanism is then used in later simulations to determine the best cache structure. Further simulations identify the most promising memory consistency policy.

5.4   Hash construction

Figure 2 illustrates the partitioning of the virtual address into three portions for cache access. The displacement indexes into the selected cache block, the row selector identifies the cache block which may contain the required datum and the key is used to verify that a hit has occurred. Cache interference occurs when more than one address maps onto the same row in the cache. Occasionally, this may occur because of unfortunate permutations of address accesses; however poor design of the row selector hashing will lead to frequent interference.

In the object-based cache, the virtual address is formed by the concatenation of the object identifier and the offset. The lower portion of the offset forms the displacement into the cache block (the size of displacement is dependent on the cache block size) whilst the remainder of the virtual address is partitioned into row selector and key. The row

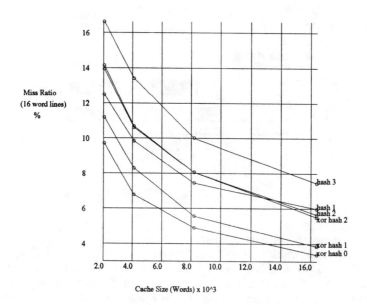

Figure 5: *Miss rates for direct-mapped data cache hash construction*   Varying the number of bits of the offset included in the cache row selector has a significant effect on the cache performance. A simple XOR hash of the object identifier and offset is the most effective. Of the concatenation hashes, including the two bits above the block displacement of the offset provides the best performance. Decreasing the amount of offset in the row selector increases interference. Similarly, including too many of the most significant offset bits has an adverse effect on performance.

selector may be formed from any portion of the virtual address not used by the displacement. The choice of this formation is crucial to the performance of the cache (Fig. 4).

Consider a system where object identifiers are allocated to objects sequentially with object 0 representing the first allocated object. Accessing the cache according to the organisation of Fig. 4 (a) would lead to high levels of interference in the cache as most object identifiers map onto the same row. Although partitioning the hash according to the organisation of Fig. 4 (b) would substantially reduce interference, there would still be some avoidable collisions. Most objects are very small, thus resulting in a large degree of redundancy in the top bits of the offset. Consequently, it is probable that the best hashing for the row selector would consist of the lower portion of the offset not used as a displacement and the lower portion of the object identifier as illustrated in Fig. 4 (c). However, this method of generating the row selector also has its disadvantages. Not using all the offset bits allows different portions of an object to map onto the same cache block. Thus, sequential access to all locations of a large object will cause many cache misses. An alternative approach is to form the row selector by performing a logical XOR of a portion of the object identifier and the offset. The formation of the row selector by the XOR function as illustrated in Fig. 4 (d) does have the disadvantage of increasing the width of the key stored in the cache. Consequently, a scheme whereby only a portion of the offset is XORed with the object identifier was also simulated.

In order to quantify the differences between these alternatives, several simulations were performed using a direct-mapped cache with a range of sizes and 16-word blocks. Set-associative caches were not simulated on the basis that they are effectively multiple direct-mapped caches; thus the best hashing construction for a direct-mapped cache will also be the best for a set-associative cache.

Figure 5 illustrates the hit rates obtained for a variety of organisations for the row selector. The best hashing organisation is the simple XOR hash where the least significant portion of the object identifier is XORed with the whole of the offset. Using smaller portions of the offset in the hash leads to worse performance for all the cache sizes. Hashes formed by concatenating portions of the offset and object identifier were not as effective as the simple XOR hash. The best concatenated hashing is formed by ignoring the two most significant bits of the offset — ignoring either one or

Size (Words)	N-Way	Block Size (Words)			
		4	8	16	32
4K	1	**93.87**	93.62	93.22	91.55
	2	95.29	**95.51**	94.87	93.43
	4	95.83	**95.92**	95.37	93.90
8K	1	95.28	**95.53**	95.09	94.29
	2	96.87	**97.03**	96.73	95.73
	4	97.24	**97.42**	97.03	96.21
16K	1	96.36	**96.64**	96.62	96.06
	2	97.79	**98.21**	98.02	97.42
	4	98.18	**98.48**	98.30	97.67
32K	1	96.89	**97.76**	97.60	97.39
	2	98.34	98.85	**98.89**	98.55
	4	98.66	99.06	**99.08**	98.77
64K	1	97.17	98.14	**98.55**	98.20
	2	98.60	99.06	**99.33**	99.21
	4	98.89	99.32	**99.46**	99.38

Table 1: *Cache hit rates as a function of block size, cache size and associativity*   The highlighted figures are the best for each row. Predictably, the worst hit rate is obtained with the 4K-word, 1-way cache with 32-word blocks. A 4-way set-associative 64K-word cache with 16-word blocks achieves a 99.5% hit rate.

three bits leads to worse performance. Consequently, for the remainder of this paper, all data cache simulations will be based on the simple XOR hash.

5.5   Data cache structure

Having identified the best hashing construction, a full range of cache structures may be simulated. There are three main variables: the cache size, the associativity and the block size. Additional considerations such as differences in purging policies and memory traffic considerations are covered in later sections. Each of the available memory reference traces was used to exercise 48 different configurations for a data cache. Table 1 summarises the miss rates obtained from these simulations for a number of cache sizes, driven by one of these traces. Some of the results are also presented graphically in Fig. 6. A noteworthy point is that the memory accessing profiles of the four traces, when analysed for these and other statistics, were almost identical, despite the traces coming from four very different uses of the system. The authors speculate that this is due to the fact that applications in Smalltalk tend to reuse the same system classes, and actually spend only a small fraction of their time in the "application" code. It would be of interest to investigate this further.

A large, highly associative cache (64K-word, 4-way, 16-word blocks) achieves a 99.5% hit rate. For all cache sizes, increasing the associativity improved the cache performance (as expected). For all configurations, increasing associativity from one to two provides a significant improvement in the hit rate. However, further increasing the associativity from two to four has much less effect, especially for large cache sizes. For the smaller caches, small block sizes are best. As cache sizes increase, the best block sizes also increase, tending towards the average object size (20 words).

5.6   Interpretation of data cache results

Hit rates for various data cache configurations have been presented. Although these provide a reasonable indication of the expected cache hit rates, they do not indicate the impact of cache hit rate on overall performance. For example, a cache with 16-word blocks may exhibit a marginally better hit rate than a cache of similar configuration with 8-word blocks. Assuming block transfers are not performed autonomously, when the increase in miss overhead is taken into

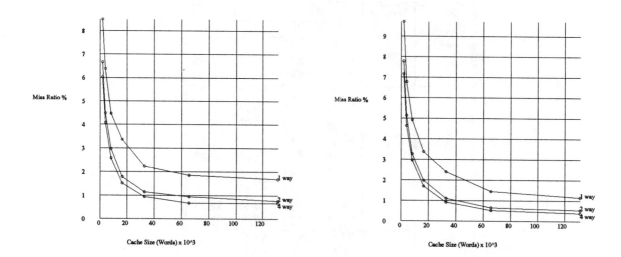

Figure 6: *Cache performance* with respect to associativity and size for an 8-word cache block (left) and a 16-word cache block (right).

consideration, the performance of the 8-word block cache is superior. Table 2 presents the derived performance figures given miss overheads proportional to cache block sizes for write-back caches.

Not all cache configurations have the same access time. For example, small one-way caches can be constructed that service accesses in one cycle[1] whilst larger, highly associative caches may require two machine cycles to operate [Hil88]. Therefore even though a cache excels on hit rate figures, a less effective cache may perform better by virtue of its fast hit service times. Table 2 incorporates assumptions about the access times of direct-mapped and set-associative caches.

The results given in Table 2 change the suggested performance profile given in Table 1, due to differences in access time and cache miss overheads. For all the cache sizes, a single-cycle direct-mapped cache outperforms a multi-cycle set-associative cache. Assuming a difference of one cycle between a direct-mapped and a four-way set-associative cache may be optimistic. However, comparing the performance of the two-cycle direct-mapped cache with that of a four-way set-associative cache will give an indication of how much faster a direct-mapped cache must be in order to be competitive. For both the 16K and 64K word caches, a direct-mapped cache would need to be 20% faster than a 4-way set-associative cache to be of equivalent overall performance. On a 20MHz machine, this translates to a requirement for 20ns reduction in data cache access time from 100ns to 80ns. Given the simplicity of a direct-mapped cache and lack of hit-detect critical paths, this is easily achievable.

5.7   Write-through *vs* write-back caches

A write-through data cache maintains memory consistency by duplicating all cache updates into main memory. The write-through cache results in lower miss overheads since the cache block need not be written back before the new block is fetched. On the other hand, processor performance may be impaired because memory updates are limited by main memory speeds. However, this bottleneck may be reduced by buffering memory updates. Write-back caches write a modified cache block back to main memory on a cache miss. The increased miss overhead may be compensated for by faster updates to the cache. In addition to cache access performance considerations, write-through and write-back policies have an important effect on memory traffic. For caches with low miss rates the write-back policy results in lower memory traffic since a write-through cache would accumulate many memory updates between each cache miss. For high miss rates, the number of memory updates is low compared with the amount of traffic created by writing back each block on a miss.

---

[1] A direct-mapped cache may access the datum in one cycle and check for a hit in the following cycle. Set-associative caches must determine which column has hit before the output can be enabled.

Size	N	Cache Block Size (Words)			
(Words)	Way	4	8	16	32
4K	1a	**3.39**	4.00	5.27	9.03
	1b	4.33	4.93	6.20	9.94
	2	3.79	4.07	5.18	8.18
	4	3.58	3.88	4.87	7.73
16K	1a	**2.42**	2.58	3.13	4.74
	1b	3.38	3.55	4.10	5.70
	2	2.84	2.82	3.23	4.43
	4	2.69	2.70	3.05	4.19
64K	1a	2.10	**1.87**	1.91	2.71
	1b	3.08	2.86	2.90	3.69
	2	2.53	2.43	2.42	2.74
	4	2.42	2.31	2.33	2.58

Table 2: *Average access times for various cache structures*   The rows labelled 1a are for single-cycle direct-mapped caches; 1b for two-cycle, direct-mapped caches; 2 and 4 are for two and four way set-associative caches, respectively (both assumed to be two-cycle). The fastest average access time for each cache size is highlighted. Miss overhead is estimated to be twice the block size plus a 32 cycle latency.

Size	Cache Block Size (Words)			
(Words)	4	8	16	32
2K	1.39	1.15	1.02	0.95
4K	1.57	1.26	1.08	0.98
8K	1.75	1.40	1.16	1.03
16K	2.47	1.54	1.27	1.40
32K	2.71	2.26	1.40	1.17
64K	2.90	2.50	2.03	1.27
128K	3.11	2.67	2.28	1.56

Table 3: *Write-through vs write-back caches*   The ratio of memory traffic in a write-through cache to that in a write-back cache (assuming only dirty blocks are written back).

Table 3 summarises the memory traffic results obtained for a direct-mapped cache simulation. The table presents the ratio of cache-memory traffic observed for a direct-mapped write-through cache relative to the traffic observed for the same cache with a write-back policy. The write-back policy resulted in less memory traffic for all except two cache configurations. As one would expect, a small cache with large cache blocks is not suited to a write-back policy as each modified block is large and cache misses occur often. At the other extreme, the write-back policy in a large cache with small blocks causes approximately 68% less memory traffic than the write-through policy.

6   Address translation

6.1   Size of hardware object table

In translating from virtual to real addresses, a conventional paged virtual memory system uses a set of Translation Look-aside Buffers (TLBs) as a cache of active entries in the system page table. Similarly, in an object-based system, a cache of active entries in the object table can be used to translate object identifiers into real addresses.

While TLBs in conventional systems are widely used and well understood, there are many uncertainties about object address translation. The main area for concern is the number of cached object table entries required to provide an acceptable hit rate for object translations. Objects are usually much smaller than conventional pages (typically by

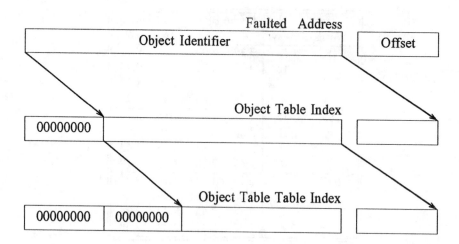

Figure 7: *Generation of an object table address for use with in-cache address translation*   Shifting the identifier 8 bits to the right into the offset and masking the top 8 bits forms an index into the relevant entry of the object table. If this causes a cache miss, the object table table address may be formed in a similar fashion.

a factor of 10–100). Consequently, it might be expected that a hardware object table will contain many more entries than an equally effective set of TLBs.

In a previous paper we reported on simulations to determine the effectiveness of various numbers of cached object table entries [WWH87b]. It was determined that for very low miss rates (10^{-5}) many more entries were required in a hardware object table than TLBs (1000 OT entries compared to 100 TLB entries). As the miss ratio increased, the size of the required object table cache approached the number of TLB entries. For a miss rate of 1%, approximately 4 times as many object table entries were required (80 vs 20); for a miss rate of 10%, the numbers were approximately equal.

6.2   In-cache object table

It has been determined that a small fully associative table provides acceptable hit rates for object identifier address translation. Thus, in principle, such a table could be implemented in hardware to translate object references into real addresses for each memory access. However, the use of a virtually-addressed cache obviates the need for an address translation on every access. In such a system, address translation is only required on cache misses in order to determine the location of the object to be brought into the cache. Given this reduced performance requirement, there may not be a need for hardware dedicated to address translation.

Providing hardware address translation merely for use on cache misses may still be attractive because performing a full software translation on every cache miss can be expensive. However, a compromise between hardware and software implementation of page table lookups has been developed for conventional systems [W+86]. The in-cache address translation mechanism assumes that the system page tables always reside in the same place in virtual memory. On a cache miss, an index into the system page tables is formed and a cache access performed. If the cache hits, the resultant word is the real address of the page containing the data for the cache. In-cache translation works in a similar fashion to conventional associative translation tables except that the existing pseudo-associative data cache hardware is exploited, thereby removing the need for TLB hardware.

The concept of in-cache address translation can also be applied to object-based systems. If the object table is represented by a number of pre-allocated objects, an appropriate index into the table can be generated as required. When a cache miss occurs, the index into the object table is produced by manipulating the object identifier in question (Fig. 7). The cache is then accessed using this newly formed address and, if successful, returns the real address of the object to be fetched into the cache. However, if this access fails, an object table table index is formed in a similar

Cache Size (Words)	Block Size (Words)	Normal Cache % Hit	Dual Cache % Hit	Decrease (%)	First Hash % Hit	Second Hash % Hit
16K	4	96.0	93.8	2.29	71.5	68.7
	8	96.3	94.4	2.03	67.2	69.9
	16	96.3	93.8	2.59	60.1	71.3
32K	4	96.6	94.9	1.74	75.0	67.4
	8	97.5	96.2	1.32	69.2	69.4
	16	97.4	95.9	1.47	67.0	71.2
64K	4	96.9	95.5	1.41	77.8	67.9
	8	98.0	97.0	0.96	73.9	70.0
	16	98.4	97.5	0.96	66.8	69.5
128K	4	97.2	96.0	1.22	79.4	66.8
	8	98.2	97.4	0.76	77.1	69.5
	16	98.7	98.1	0.68	70.3	68.8

Table 4: *Effectiveness of in-cache address translation*   The first two columns are the percentage hit rates for data accesses in a conventional data cache and in a data cache with in-cache translation. Next is the percentage reduction in hit rate. The last two columns are the percentage hit rates for object table and object table table accesses respectively.

fashion and the process repeated. Clearly, this progression must terminate with a root table whose real address is fixed.

6.3   Simulating in-cache object address translation

In order to determine the effectiveness of in-cache object address translation a simulation was constructed using the previously described cache simulator. Direct-mapped caches of various depths and block sizes were simulated implementing this in-cache object address translation scheme. Table 4 presents the results obtained from the simulations. The best translation performance for the object table access was a 79% hit rate observed with a 128K-word cache with 4-word blocks. As cache sizes decrease the translation hit rate decreases. Additionally, as block sizes decrease, the translation hit rate increases. Clearly, the best configuration for object address translation would be a large cache with small blocks.

In-cache object address translation affects the performance of conventional data accesses. In the worst case, the data cache hit rate is reduced from 96% to approximately 94% because of interference between data and translation accesses. Although this is only a 2.3% reduction in performance, the large overhead associated with cache misses compounds the performance degradation.

6.3.1   Limiting interference

The performance of both the data cache hit rates and object translation hit rates are limited by their mutual interference. Furthermore, their performances are also limited by the differing requirements for cache block size — object address translation requires smaller cache block sizes than normal data accesses. Consequently, it may be possible to improve performance by dividing the cache into two sections — one section for data cache accesses and another for object address translation. The sizes of these sections could be varied and the granularity of the blocks in each section can be different.

To determine the feasibility of this idea, a simulation of such a cache structure was constructed. The block size for the data section of the cache was fixed at 16 words, whilst a range of block sizes for the object address translation section was simulated. Three cache sizes were simulated with varying amounts of the cache dedicated to object address translation. Table 5 illustrates the results obtained and contains comparisons with the un-sectioned and normal data caches.

Cache Type	Section Size	Data Hit %	% Translation Hit for Block Size					Access Time (cycles)
			1	2	4	8	16	
32K cache								
Un-sectioned	0	95.9					67.0	2.73
Sectioned	1024	97.7	**55.2**	52.2	54.1	52.4		2.06
	2048	97.8	53.6	51.7	**56.7**	51.2		2.00
	4096	97.2	60.5	58.5	63.9	**67.5**		2.18
	8192	97.4	51.6	50.1	55.2	**58.3**		2.17
	16384	96.3	55.5	53.9	58.7	**61.6**		2.62
64K cache								
Un-sectioned	0	97.5					66.8	2.06
Sectioned	1024	98.2	**61.4**	58.9	57.3	59.8		1.79
	2048	98.5	60.5	59.7	**65.8**	60.6		1.64
	4096	98.3	61.7	61.1	66.3	**68.4**		1.71
	8192	98.0	67.2	67.2	71.8	**74.7**		1.80
	16384	98.2	58.2	57.3	62.0	**65.8**		1.77
128K cache								
Un-sectioned	0	98.1					70.3	1.78
Sectioned	1024	98.4	69.6	69.1	**70.5**	69.5		1.66
	2048	98.5	67.6	66.4	**68.7**	67.0		1.63
	4096	98.8	66.8	66.3	72.5	**75.5**		1.48
	8192	98.7	67.6	68.9	73.7	**76.6**		1.51
	16384	98.3	74.6	76.2	79.3	**81.9**		1.64

Table 5: *Sectioned in-cache address translation performance* Blocks of 16 words were used for the data section of the cache whilst the block size for the translation section was varied from 1 word to 8 words. As the object address translation section increases in size, the size of the data section decreases. Section sizes are measured in words. Figures for data cache hit rates and the un-sectioned translation are included for comparison. The final column gives the effective access time based on the best (highlighted) result in each row, assuming a 32 cycle penalty for a miss.

It is interesting to note that for most cases the hit rates for the sectioned in-cache address translation were worse (or comparable with) the hit rates achieved without sectioning. Only in cases where extremely large portions of the cache were reserved (e.g. 16K words of a 128K cache) did the sectioned in-cache translation perform significantly better. Thus it is evident that the amount of cache available for address translation is more important than the interference experienced from data accesses.

Although sectioning the cache does not benefit object address translation, it does improve the hit rate for data accesses. For all the cache configurations simulated, sectioning improved data access performance over the un-sectioned cache. The performance improvement was more marked on smaller cache sizes — introducing a 1K word translation section into the 32K word cache increased data access hit rates from 95.9% to 97.7%. However, this improvement was achieved at the expense of a reduction in address translation hit rate from 67% to 55.2%. An alternative approach to a sectioned cache might be to control the allocation of object identifiers in software in such a way as to avoid any interference between the two uses. This is the subject of current investigations.

6.4   Interpretation of results

In is important to note that the figures for the fully associative object table translation are not comparable with those obtained for the in-cache address translation. In the former case, translations were performed on every memory access while in the latter example, translations are performed on every cache miss. The large quantity of accesses and the locality of memory references ensures that the hit rate of the fully associative table is high. In contrast, the in-cache address translation services a relatively small number of requests which have poor locality. By implication, if they exhibited good locality there must be some failing in the cache design. The in-cache translation mechanism is extremely effective in that few data accesses require main memory access to perform address translation. For example the 64K-word cache with 2K-word address translation section and 4-word section blocks has an effective translation hit rate of 99.5%.[2] This is equivalent to a fully associative object table with between 100 and 1000 entries.

The figures presented in Table 5 exhibit some interesting characteristics. The hit rate observed for the sectioned portion of the cache is dependent on the size of the data section. For example, with a 1K-word section reserved for address translation and a block size of 1 word, the address translation hit rate increases from 55.2% to 69.6% as the overall size of the cache increases. Clearly, as the cache size increases, the miss rate decreases, consequently the number of address translations also decrease. This will have a beneficial effect on address translation performance.

Table 5 also includes an estimated average access time for the particular in-cache configuration (rightmost column). This was determined by assuming (for simplicity) that each cache miss and each object table miss costs 32 cycles, whilst a hit only costs a single cycle. Additionally, it is assumed that the real address of the relevant entry in the object table table is known. Although the average access time is an approximate measure, it is useful in comparing relative performances. In all cases, the un-sectioned cache performs worse than the sectioned cache configurations. However this difference reduces as the cache size increases. For both the 32K and 64K caches, providing a 2K section for object address translation gives the fastest average access times. As cache size increases, a larger translation section can be afforded.

7   Summary and Conclusions

This paper described the problems inherent in implementing object-based memory on a conventional virtual memory and developed a new object-based memory architecture. It has been shown that object stores can be constructed that are efficient in terms of hardware resource, have small average access times, and high throughput. In all respects, such object stores will compare favourably with a conventional paged virtual memory.

Several issues had to be resolved to achieve a successful cache design:

- An address format was needed that did not require large address busses or wide cache association keys.

- A cache was required that had fast average access times.

- A scheme for virtual-to-real address translation had to be devised that was acceptably efficient, and did not consume large amounts of hardware.

Initially, an efficient addressing format was presented with 32-bit object identifiers and 8-bit offsets. The 8-bit offsets are sufficient to express 99.88% of memory accesses in typical Smalltalk usage and are inexpensive to implement in hardware.

By concatenating the 32-bit object identifier with the 8-bit offset, a 40-bit "virtual address" is formed which uniquely identifies the memory location. This 40-bit virtual address is then used to access a pseudo-associative virtually-addressed cache. This avoids the need for address translation and base-offset addition on the vast majority of memory accesses. Extensive simulations of various cache structures demonstrated that a single cycle, direct-mapped cache with an XOR hash function for row selection was the best option. A 64K-word cache of this configuration achieved an average access time of 1.8 cycles.

With virtually-addressed caches, object address translation is only required on cache misses (compared with every memory access). Consequently, the need for fast address translation is diminished. A novel object address translation scheme was presented whereby the pseudo-associative functionality of the data cache was exploited to translate object identifiers to real addresses. This "in cache" address translation scheme was successful and resulted in an effective address translation hit rate of 99.5% — comparable with separate object address translation hardware.

The results from these initial simulations of the object-based caching are promising. Hardware implementing the object-based cache is being constructed as part of the MUSHROOM processor and further investigations into the management of the caches are being carried out.

---

[2] Effective hit rate is the cache hit rate combined with the translation hit rate for every cache miss, i.e., $98.5\% + ((100 - 98.5\%) \times 65.8\%)$.

References

[CLP81]   D. W. Clark, B. W. Lampson, and K. A. Pier. The memory system of a high-performance personal computer. In *The Dorado: A high-performance personal computer—three papers*, pages 51–80. Xerox PARC, January 1981. Technical Report CSL–81–1 (also in IEEE Trans. on Computers, October 1981, 715–733, number 10, volume C–30).

[DS84]   L. P. Deutsch and A. M. Schiffman. Efficient implementation of the Smalltalk-80 system. In *Proceedings of the Eleventh ACM Symposium on the Principles of Programming Languages*, pages 297–302, Salt Lake City, Utah, January 1984.

[GR83]   A. Goldberg and D. Robson. *Smalltalk-80: The Language and its Implementation*. Addison-Wesley, 1983.

[Hil88]   M. D. Hill. A case for direct-mapped caches. *IEEE Computer*, pages 25–40, December 1988.

[Kae86]   T. Kaehler. Virtual memory on a narrow machine for an object-oriented language. *ACM SIGPLAN Notices*, 21(11):87–106, November 1986. Proceedings of the Conference on Object-Oriented Programming Systems, Languages and Applications.

[Kra83]   G. Krasner, editor. *Smalltalk-80: Bits of history, words of advice*. Addison-Wesley, 1983.

[LK61]   W. Lonergan and P. King. Design of the B 5000 system. *Datamation*, 7(5):28–32, May 1961. (also in Computer Structures: Principles and Examples, D. P. Siewiorek, C. G. Bell and A. Newell (eds), pages 129–134, McGraw-Hill, 1982).

[Sta86]   W. Stallings. An annotated bibliography on Reduced Instruction Set Computers. *ACM SIGARCH Newsletter*, 14(5):13–19, 1986.

[Ste87]   P. Steenkiste. LISP on a reduced-instruction-set processor: Characterization and optimization. Technical Report CSL-TR-87-324, Computer Systems Laboratory, Stanford University, March 1987.

[TS87]   D. Thiebaut and H. Stone. Footprints in the cache. *ACM Transactions on Computer Systems*, 5(4):305–329, November 1987.

[Ung87]   D. M. Ungar. *The Design and Evaluation of a High Performance Smalltalk System*. MIT Press, 1987.

[UP83]   D. M. Ungar and D. A. Patterson. Berkeley Smalltalk: Who knows where the time goes? In G. Krasner, editor, *Smalltalk-80: bits of history, words of advice*, pages 189–206. Addison-Wesley, 1983.

[W⁺86]   D. A. Wood et al. An in-cache address translation mechanism. *Proceedings of the Thirteenth Annual ACM/IEEE International Symposium on Computer Architecture*, 14(2):358–365, June 1986.

[Wal83]   D. Wallace. Making Smalltalk less becoming: Removing primitive becomes from Smalltalk-80. In D. A. Patterson, editor, *Smalltalk on a RISC: Architectural Investigations (proceedings of CS292R)*, pages 213–222. Computer Science Division, University of California at Berkeley, April 1983.

[Wil89]   I. W. Williams. *Object-Based Memory Architecture*. PhD thesis, University of Manchester, 1989.

[WWH87a]   I. W. Williams, M. I. Wolczko, and T. P. Hopkins. Dynamic grouping in an object oriented virtual memory hierarchy. In J. Bézivin, J.-M. Hullot, P. Cointe, and H. Lieberman, editors, *Proceedings of the 1987 European Conference on Object-Oriented Programming, Lecture Notes in Computer Science*, volume 276, pages 79–88. Springer-Verlag, Paris, June 1987.

[WWH87b]   I. W. Williams, M. I. Wolczko, and T. P. Hopkins. Realisation of a dynamically grouped object-oriented virtual memory hierarchy. In *Proceedings of the Workshop on Persistent Object Systems: Their Design, Implementation and Use*, pages 298–308, August 1987. Persistent Programming Research Report, Universities of Glasgow and St. Andrews (PPRR-44-87).

Implementing the O_2 Object Manager: Some Lessons

Fernando Velez   Vineeta Darnis   David DeWitt*   Philippe Futtersack

Gilbert Harrus   David Maier[†]   Michel Raoux

Altaïr[‡§]

BP 105, 78153 Le Chesnay Cedex–France

Abstract

After a three year prototyping period, the version V1 of the O_2 system is operational. We describe in this paper the evaluation of the Object Manager layer of this prototype and present the design choices we made for the new version which is currently under development.

1   Introduction

Altaïr is a five year project which began in September 1986. Its goal is to implement an Object-Oriented Database System, O_2, and its programming environment. The 5 year period was divided in two phases: a three year prototyping phase and a two year development phase. The three year prototyping period ended in September 1989 and version V1 of the prototype is operational as scheduled. A complete description of the prototype can be found in [Deu90]. The V1 prototype supports a set of Database Programming Languages, CO_2 and BasicO$_2$[LR89b], an interactive query language [BCD89], a set of user interface generation tools, LOOKS [PCMP90] and a programming environment, OOPE [BDPT90].

The O_2 Object Manager (OM) is the layer of the system that deals with complex object access and manipulation, transaction management, persistence, disk management (i.e., clustering, access paths, etc), and distribution in a server/workstation configuration. The main design decisions for the V1 prototype are described in [VBD89] and are summarized briefly below.

We entered a new evaluation loop for the whole system before the new implementation effort corresponding to the two year development phase. This paper describes the evaluation of the OM version V1 and presents the design choices that we made for the new version of the OM which is currently under development. Section 2 presents a short overview of the architecture of the V1 version of the OM. Section 3 reports on some problems that we found with its architecture and implementation. In Section 4, we describe the study of three workstation-server architectures. Section 5 summarizes our current experiments and concludes the paper.

---

*On sabbatical with Altaïr. Author's address: Computer Science Department, University of Wisconsin, Madison, WI 53706.

[†]On sabbatical with Altaïr. Author's address: Department of Computer Science and Engineering, Oregon Graduate Institute for Science and Technology, Beaverton, OG 97006.

[‡]Altaïr is a consortium funded by IN2 (a Siemens subsidiary), INRIA (Institut National de Recherche en Informatique et Automatique) and LRI (Laboratoire de Recherche en Informatique, University of Paris XI).

[§]Authors' electronic mail addresses: fernando@bdblues.altair.fr, vineeta@bdblues.altair.fr, dewitt@cs.wisc.edu, futter@bdblues.altair.fr, gh@bdblues.altair.fr, maier@cse.ogi.edu, raoux@bdblues.altair.fr.

2   A Short Overview

The assumptions for the V1 prototype are the following: there are two different target configurations: the *development* configuration in which the programmers design and program the applications and the *execution* configuration in which the applications are run once operational. In development mode, the system runs on a workstation/server configuration. We assumed that there is a single server. Workstations can be with or without disk. The set of workstations can be heterogeneous. The execution configuration is basically the same (single server, multiple workstations) but allows the presence of dumb terminals connected to the server.

2.1   Server/Workstation Architecture

The OM is constructed from a workstation and a server components. Both have (almost) the same interface. The main distinction is in the actual implementation: the workstation component is single user (as a workstation is single-user), memory based; while the server version is multi-user, disk based. The server component is built on top of WiSS, the Wisconsin Storage System [CDKK85]. The server provides persistence, disk management and concurrency control. WiSS provides persistent structures such as record-structured sequential files, long data items and B-tree or hash-based indices. All these structures are mapped to pages, the basic persistence and I/O unit. Concurrency in WiSS is handled by a hierarchical, two-phase locking algorithm on pages and files, and non two-phase lock on indices.

An important problem we faced while designing the system was: given an (execution mode) application in O_2, how do we decide which part runs on the server and which part runs on the workstation? The main goal is (i) to make tasks run efficiently, and (ii) to program distribution as simply as possible. Recall that we are not dealing with a distributed query problem, but with general purpose computations. The ideal would be to make distribution transparent and let the system determine the "best site", but solving this problem is still a research issue.

We decided to make the distributed architecture visible to the application programmer. The programmer is aware of the existence of two machines (the server and the workstation) and may explicitly specify on which of the machines a message passing expression is to be executed. So, for example, a method scanning through a collection and selecting elements according to some criteria may run much faster in the server if the collection is large and the selectivity factor is low, as the transfer of the entire collection to the workstation is avoided. Note that we associate location with message passing and not with methods: the same method could be once run on the server and later on the workstation, if the programmer decides so. For messages without site specification, execution is local.

This decision, and the fact that dumb terminals may be connected to the server, implied that the server component of the OM understands the concept of object and is capable of applying methods to objects. A natural unit of transfer between the server and the workstation is objects, especially if machine heterogeneity is assumed, as was our case. So, each object was encoded before each transfer and decoded at the other side (we used XDR [Mic86] as the presentation protocol). The Orion 1 prototype [K*90] and some pre-release versions of GemStone [CM84] employed an object-server architecture.

The following process layout was adopted: on the workstation, an application and the workstation version of the OM form one unique process and there are as many workstation processes as running applications. For each process running on a workstation, there is a mirror process running on the server. This is because the mirror process has to contain the code that is to be executed in the server in case an execution migration arises.

Both the workstation and the server maintain caches of recently accessed objects. On the server, there are in fact two caches: an object cache and the page cache maintained by WiSS. There were two reasons for this. The first one was that memory formats could be made different from disk formats. This proved to be useful when manipulating temporary components of objects in memory, or varying length data such as strings and sets. The disk format is more compact. The second reason was that the standard interface of

WiSS forces programmers to copy objects when reading them. Both caches are shared among all processes through the use of Unix System V shared memory mechanism.

When the workstation needs to read an object, it first searches its local object cache for the object. If the object is not found it sends a request for the object to the server. If the object is not in the server's cache, the server calls WiSS to retrieve the object from disk; WiSS reads the corresponding page, locks it in shared mode, and the server converts this object and all the other objects in the page into their memory format in the cache. If the object was already in the server's cache (this may happen because it was already converted on a request for another object, or on a request for the same object on behalf of another workstation – recall the server caches are shared), WiSS is called simply to lock the page. Finally, it returns the object to the requesting workstation. When the workstation needs to update a (persistent) object, an explicit exclusive lock request on the page the object resides on is made. This can be done because a persistent object identifier contains the page identifier of the page on which it resides (see Section 2.2).

The architecture of the V1 OM is illustrated in Figure 1.

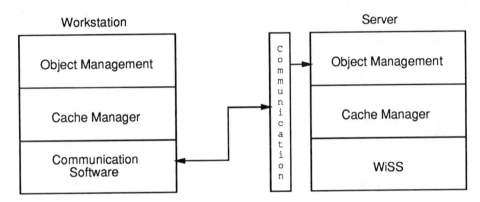

Figure 1: Architecture of the V1 OM

2.2   Addressing Scheme

The O_2 data model [LR89a] distinguishes between *values*, on which we can perform any of a set of predefined primitives, and *objects* which have identity and encapsulate values and user defined *methods*[1]. Values can be *set*, *list* or *tuple* structured, or *atomic*. They do not have object identity, and therefore they cannot be shared by other objects or values.

Persistence is defined in the O_2 model as reachability from persistent root objects or values (which are objects explicitly named by the programmer)[2]. In the OM, objects and values are mapped into a WiSS record if they are persistent, or to records in virtual memory if they are temporary. A WiSS record identifier, i.e., a RID, is coded in 8 bytes: a volume identifier (2 bytes), a page identifier within a volume (4 bytes), and a slot-number (2 bytes) which indirectly addresses a record within a page. Virtual memory records are identified by a pair (virtual memory address, machine tag). We will refer to them as TempIDs in the sequel. A machine tag indicates if the virtual memory address is a workstation address or a server address (recall that methods can be executed on the workstation or on the server).

The design decisions for the mapping of objects and values into records (in disk format) are the following:

1. Non-atomic (i.e., constructed) values are decomposed into records on type constructor boundaries. So for example, a tuple value containing a set valued attribute and an integer attribute will be stored in

---

[1]Up to here, the word "object" referred both to objects and values. From now on, we will follow the precise O_2 meaning.

[2]This is implemented by associating a reference count with each object or value.

(at least) two records (there may be more if the set is large: see below). Atomic values are embedded in their parent record, the only exception being large strings, which are stored in one or more records.

2. List and set values are "small" if their corresponding record fits in one page, otherwise they are "large" and they consume more than one record.

3. An object and (the root of) its value are stored in one record.

RIDs and TempIDs are used as identifiers for objects *and* as physical pointers for constructed values, even though the latter are never shared. In the sequel, we will talk about the "identifier of a value" referring to the physical pointer of its record, and we will refer to object and value identifiers loosely by the term *oid*. To access resident records (those in a cache), we use a table hashed on oid.

Values have a representation that is similar to that of objects, but they behave differently: they have a "copy" semantics. For example, when returning an set-structured value attribute of a tuple object or value, the identifier of a copy of the set value is returned. If the set is itself a set of tuple values, the copy is recursive.

When a temporary record becomes persistent, it is because it is made a component of a parent record. The RID, which is delivered only on insertion of the corresponding WiSS record, is assigned at transaction commit in order to avoid extensive message exchange between the two machines. A WiSS record belongs to a WiSS file. The mapping of objects and values to files is controlled by the cluster trees [BD88], which contain information provided by the Database Administrator. A cluster tree expresses the way in which a composite object and its object or value components will be clustered together (the main heuristic we used to postulate that two objects will be used together frequently is their relationship through composition structure). Cluster trees are traversed at commit time to determine the file into which the record is to be inserted. Furthermore, one has the option of specifying the RID of the parent record r in the insert routine to compel WiSS to try and store the new record in the same page as r or in a nearby page.

3   A Critique of the V1 Prototype

We first analyze the advantages and disadvantages of the V1 OM architecture and our addressing scheme for objects and values.

3.1   On the Object Server Architecture

An important advantage is the server's ability to execute user-defined methods. Initially, we viewed this as an important performance-tuning facility. This ability is most valuable when methods selecting small subsets of a large collection don't find any index that can be used by the selection operation. In addition, one can balance the system workload by moving work from the workstation to the server; however, this is not a real advantage, as technology trends show that most of the computing power will soon end up being concentrated in the workstations and not in the server, so it makes no sense to move work from the workstation to the server.

Another advantage is that this architecture simplifies the design of the concurrency control subsystem as the server knows exactly which objects are accessed by each application. Hence, concurrency control can be almost completely centralized in the server. Furthermore, the implementation of object-level locking is straightforward (but was not implemented, however).

The main drawbacks are the following : first, in the worse case there may be one remote procedure call per record reference (although the hit rate on the workstation's object cache may be high enough to satisfy most requests). In order for the server to transfer more than a single record at a time, it must be capable of figuring out which records belong with one another, replicating the work that the clustering mechanism did when it placed records together on a disk page. Note that an interesting unit of transfer would have been objects instead of records: in this case, all records in an object would get transferred. However, the number of records might get very large in the case of large value subcomponent collections, so the system needs to determine "where to cut". As this appeared to be not too easy to implement, we only sent one record at a time.

The opposite extreme (i.e., the server sending more than required) can also happen, since the software on a workstation simply requests a record from the server without being aware of its size. Large byte strings are implemented in WiSS using the long data item (LDI) abstraction. An LDI is a record that can span multiple pages. As the workstation software does not understands anything about pages, LDIs have to be transferred in their entirety, even if the application needed to access only a few bytes.

Second, records tend to get copied multiple times. For example, a record may have to be copied from the server's page cache into its object cache before it can be sent to a workstation. Further copies are performed at the presentation level of the communication software when dealing with machine heterogeneity.

Third, this architecture complicates the design of the server, as it must be capable of executing arbitrary user methods. This implies addressing potential cache inconsistencies: an updated version of an object may exist in the workstation's cache but not in the server's cache. As the method may operate on this object, the workstation has to flush all the modified records in its object cache back to the server. The same operation has to be performed when the method sends its result, if the latter updates objects. When the number of modified records becomes large, the expected advantage of executing a method in the server is dominated by the overhead incurred in maintaining cache consistency. We therefore concluded that, for such a scheme to work, the system alone must decide the site of application of a method: the programmer may only give hints on whether a message passing expression is worth considering as a candidate to be performed remotely.

3.2   On the Addressing Scheme

Our choice for physical oids for persistent objects and values was largely motivated by performance reasons. Oids could be "logical", i.e., give no information about their location in secondary memory, as in Gem-Stone [MS87], Orion [K*90] and ObServer [HZ87]. With logical identifiers a correspondence table between oids and physical addresses is needed. Moving records in secondary memory is straightforward, but the object table might be very big as it would contain one entry for each record in the database[3]. One disk access is likely to be performed to retrieve the object table entry of the object, and a second to retrieve the record.

To move records on disk, the solution we adopted is to use the forward marker technique implemented by WiSS. When accessing on disk a record which has been moved elsewhere, we will perform two disk accesses: one to retrieve the forwarding RID and the other to retrieve the record[4].

This seems reasonable for persistent records. However, it does not work well for temporary records, as the memory address at which a record is stored at creation time is forced to remain the same until commit time. This has a number of problems: first, promotion of records from temporary to persistent must be delayed until commit. While this seems reasonable on a workstation/server architecture, it is not correct on a single-processor implementation of the system (which exists and is the version that is actually being used by customers). For example, if no cluster tree has been defined for a database (a fairly normal case), nothing should prevent us from performing the promotion of a temporary record to persistent space when it becomes persistent.

Second, it prevents us from using well-known garbage-collection techniques such as generation scavenging [LH83]. So records cannot be freed from memory until commit time unless a temporary reference count

---

[3]Note that, in the case of O_2, one could have logical identifiers for objects and physical pointers for component values, however.

[4]Note that if a record is further moved, there is no need to leave another marker behind, as the only reference to its current physical location is in the original marker.

scheme is built (which we decided not to include because it added complexity to the system). In fact, as a record may be referenced by the O_2 variables of a method (which are, by nature, temporary), even if the reference count of the record is 0, it should exist as long as it is pointed to by a variable. The decision not to include a temporary reference count scheme now appears to be a mistake, as typical applications running on top of the OM create temporary records at a furious rate, and these records never get deleted explicitly before commit.

Third, and more important, the number of temporary records that can be created is limited by the size of virtual memory (this is aggravated by the above point: temporary records never get freed until commit). The reason is that memory addresses are given to the clients of the OM, and this prevents the OM from swapping then to disk when the (Unix) swap space is entirely consumed. This did not seem to be a nuisance, as we thought that virtual memory would be "big enough", but there already have been applications that ran out of virtual memory space, and the programmers were forced to split their applications into smaller transactions.

Finally, and this is specific to the O_2 model, efficient support for values cannot be performed. Recall that values have a copy semantics, as they are not shared. The OM could implement a scheme in which a value could be shared temporarily, and be copied only if it is updated through another composition path, giving the illusion that they are, in fact, never shared. Having a physical addressing scheme for values (temporary or persistent) prevents the OM from doing this kind of optimization. In the applications we have observed until now, most of the "temporary garbage" generated is due to copying of value structures. This not only has an impact on space, but also involves an important CPU cost.

4   A Study of Three Different Architectures

Based on our experience with the V1 prototype, some of the assumptions for the V1 prototype changed, namely (i) machine heterogeneity will be not be incorporated in the first release of the new version of the O_2 system, and (ii) X-terminals will be supported instead of dumb terminals in future releases.

One of the main lessons we learned in implementing the V1 OM is that the design choices that appear in partitioning database functionality between the server and workstation processes are fundamental and have to be carefully studied. To better understand the alternatives, we carried out a study of three alternative architectures for implementing object-oriented database systems in a workstation/server environment. The results are presented in [DFMV90], and we will briefly summarize them here. Then we will mention the choice we made and the implications it has on the overall architecture of the system.

We analyzed three different workstation-server architectures: *object server*, *page server* and *file server*. The object server transfers individual objects between machines (this corresponds to the V1 OM architecture), the page server transfers disk pages, and the file server transfers pages using a remote file service mechanism such as NFS.

We analyzed each architecture qualitatively. The main advantage of the page-server and file-server architectures is the simple design of the server, as most of the complexity of the OODBMS is placed on the workstation, an approach that coincides with the current trend towards very powerful workstations. The main drawbacks are that fine-grained concurrency is not obvious to implement, that non-two phase locking protocols on indices must involve the workstation, and that objects cannot be manipulated in the server. The advantages and drawbacks of an object-server architecture have already been mentioned above.

To compare the performance of the architectures, we built prototypes of all three, using a stripped-down version of WiSS as a starting point. To experiment with sensitivity to data placement and cache sizes, we developed our own object manager benchmark, the "Altair Complex-Object Benchmark". It is similar to the new version of the Sun Benchmark [CS90] but at that point we didn't know about it. We opted against the previous version of the Sun benchmark because it forms complex objects by choosing random objects to relate to one another, so clustering issues were impossible to study. Our benchmark supports experiments that vary both clustering and workstation buffer size. The test suite includes queries for scanning the entire database, traversing complex objects and updating them.

Our main conclusions of these experiments are as follows: The object-server architecture is relatively insensitive to clustering. It is sensitive to workstation buffer sizes up to a certain point, at which point its performance is determined by the cost of fetching objects using the RPC mechanism.

The page-server architecture is very sensitive to the size of the workstation's buffer pool and to clustering when traversing or updating complex objects. While the page-server architecture is far superior on sequential scan queries, the object server architecture demonstrates superior performance when the database is poorly clustered or the workstation's buffer pool is very small relative to the size of the database.

The file server's performance is very good when reading pages of the database using NFS, but, writes are slow. On the update query, and in the combination of all three queries, the file server is very sensitive to the size of the workstation buffer pool (even more so than the page server).

5 Conclusion and Future Plans

We are in the process of experimenting with hybrid architectures to maximize overall performance. A scheme we want to look at is to read pages through NFS and write individual objects back, taking into account a lock protocol for concurrency control. Messages for lock requests are shorter so a round trip to the server is cheaper. Furthermore, the workstation could batch groups of lock requests. The expected benefit has to be weighted against the overhead incurred by keeping an object cache in the workstation.

Concerning the addressing scheme, we are working on a scheme that avoids the problems incurred with temporary records, notably, their being pinned in virtual memory and their inability to promote them to permanent records before commit. The main idea is to come up with a uniform identifier to use in memory that spans both temporary and persistent records, so that:

(i) a record can switch status from temporary to persistent or the converse.

(ii) temporary records can be swapped out to disk if virtual memory space is consumed.

Such an identifier is a temporary handle on objects and values, as we are still reluctant to add the indirection of an object table in secondary storage. The scheme will be described in detail in a forthcoming report.

References

[BCD89]   Francois Bancilhon, Sophie Cluet, and Claude Delobel. "Query Languages for Object-Oriented Database Systems: Analysis and a Proposal". In *Proceedings of the 2nd Intl. Workshop on Database Programming Languages*, Salishan Lodge, Oregon, 1989.

[BD88]   V. Benzaken and C. Delobel. *"Clustering Objects on Disk in an Object-Oriented Database"*. Technical Report, Altaïr, 1988.

[BDPT90] Patrick Borras, Anne Doucet, Patrick Pfeffer, and Didier Tallot. "OOPE: the O_2 Programming Environment". In *Proceedings of 6th PRC–BD3 Conference*, Montpellier, France, September 1990. Also available as Altaïr Technical Report 43.

[CDKK85] H.-T. Chou, David J. DeWitt, Randy H. Katz, and Anthony C. Klug. "Design and Implementation of the Wisconsin Storage System". *Software - Practice and Experience*, 15(10), October 1985.

[CM84]   George Copeland and David Maier. "Making Smalltalk a Database System". In *Proc. ACM SIGMOD. Intl. Conference on Management of Data*, June 1984.

[CS90]   R. G. G. Cattell and J. Skeen. *Engineering Database Benchmark*. Technical Report, Sun Microsystems, April 1990. Submitted for publication in ACM TODS.

[Deu90]   Octave Deux. "The Story of O_2". *IEEE Transactions on data and Knowledge Engineering*, March 1990.

[DFMV90]   David Dewitt, Philippe Futtersack, David Maier, and Fernando Velez. "A Study of Three Alternative Workstation/Server Architectures for Object-Oriented Database Systems". In *Proceedings of the 16th VLDB Conference*, Brisbane, Australia, August 1990.

[HZ87]   Mark F. Hornick and Stanley B. Zdonik. "A Shared, Segmented Memory System for an Object-Oriented Database". *ACM Transaction on Office Information Systems*, 5(1), January 1987.

[K*90]   Won Kim et al. "Architecture of the ORION next-generation Database System". *IEEE Transactions on Data and Knowledge Engineering*, March 1990.

[LH83]   H. Lieberman and C. Hewitt. "A Real-Time Garbage Collector Based on the Lifetimes of Objects". *Communications of the ACM*, 26(6):420–429, June 1983.

[LR89a]   C. Lécluse and P. Richard. "Modeling Complex Structures in Object-Oriented Databases". In *8th Symposium on Principles of Data Base Systems*, Philadelphia, Pennsylvania, March 1989.

[LR89b]   Christophe Lécluse and Philippe Richard. "The O_2 Database Programming Language". In *Proceedings of the 15th VLDB Conference*, Amsterdam, August 1989.

[Mic86]   SUN Microsystems. *"External Data Representation Protocol Specification"*. February 1986.

[MS87]   David Maier and Jacob Stein. "Development and Implementation of an Object-Oriented DBMS". In Bruce Shriver and Peter Wegner, editors, *Research Directions in Object-Oriented Programming*, MIT Press, Cambridge, Massachussets, 1987.

[PCMP90]   D. Plateau, R. Cazalens, J.C. Mamou, and B. Poyet. Building User Interfaces with the LOOKS Hyper-Object System. In *Proceedings of the Eurographics Workshop on Object Oriented Graphics*, Königswinter, Germany, June 1990. Also available as Altaïr Technical Report 40.

[VBD89]   Fernando Velez, Guy Bernard, and Vineeta Darnis. "The O_2 Object Manager: An Overview". In *Proceedings of the 15th VLDB Conference*, August 1989.

Part IV
Types

Chair: Stan Zdonik

Types have been studied extensively in the context of programming language theory and design. In this context, types provide a specification for the behavior of values. Expressions and statements must conform to well-defined typing rules. Some type systems have been defined to ensure that all violations of these rules can be caught at compile-time, while other type systems require that some checking of these rules be done at run-time. In either case, however, typing is aimed at ensuring the correctness of programs.

Type systems have a role in traditional databases as well. In this context of persistence, a type typically describes the format of the elements of a set of data items. For example, in a relational database system, the type Employee tells us something about the form of the records contained in the set of records (i.e., the relation) called Employee. Here, these types are shared by many independently developed programs. Again, the focus is on correctness, but the typing mechanisms are much more concerned with the correctness of the data instead of the correctness of the programs. This is understandable since the programs are outside and not within the control of the database system.

Database type systems have traditionally been unconcerned with compile-time type checking since they do not participate in the compilation process. They tend to do all checking at run-time, whenever the database is updated. These type models can, therefore, be semantically richer. They often include notions like keys (i.e., uniqueness of records within a set) and inclusion dependency (i.e., inclusion of a value in a set of keys).

Persistent object systems are attempting to put these two kinds of type systems together. The papers and discussion in this session were aimed at technical issues that arise from merging programming languages and persistent type systems. Although this workshop is not primarily interested in issues of language design, typing issues that effect the implementation of a persistent object system are considered relevant.

The first paper by Ohori, Tabkha, Connor, and Philbrow, takes a theoretical view of typing as proposed by Mitchell and Plotkin and puts forth a way of adding persistence to such a language. Their model retains the traditional model of typed memory in which a programming language transmits values to an untyped object store. This paper raises some interesting questions about the proper theoretical model of persistence.

The second paper by Connor, Brown, Cutts, Dearle, Morrison, and Rosenberg explores the differences and similarities between type equivalence based on names and type equivalence based on structures. The authors show that the two mechanisms can be viewed as computationally equivalent, although structural equivalence is typically more complex than name equivalence.

Much of the discussion centered around the question of which kind of type checking was more appropriate for persistent object systems. It was argued that structural equivalence is better in a persistent environment because programs are developed independently and will need to be put together later. Name equivalence does not guarantee that two programmers mean the same thing when they both develop a type called Employee. They might each have different definitions for the structure of an Employee.

It was further pointed out that even structural equivalence falls short. Although two programmers might both define a type T with structure (Int X Real), they might use this structure in completely different ways. A participant observed that what we really need is semantic equivalence. Of course, the question of how the semantics of a type should be specified, and how the semantics of two types should be compared, were not answered.

Persistence and Type Abstraction Revisited*

Atsushi Ohori[†]   Ivan Tabkha[‡]   Richard Connor[§]   Paul Philbrow[¶]

Abstract

Existential data types as described by Mitchell and Plotkin are an appealing model for data abstraction. However, they are somewhat restrictive within a persistent type system, as values created by an existentially defined package may not be stored and retrieved in different static contexts. This is because values of an abstract type are type equivalent only in the scope of the same package opening. This allows packages to be used as first-class values, but precludes the kind of dynamic type check associated with the retrieval of a value from the persistent store.

This paper refines Cardelli and MacQueen's analysis of the interaction between persistence and abstract data types and proposes a new adaptation of these types. The resulting type system loses none of the desirable static properties of Mitchell and Plotkin's model, but is more flexible dynamically and allows a value of a witness type to be stored in one context and retrieved in another. An intuitive explanation of the new model is given, along with formal type checking rules and an implementation strategy.

1   Introduction

The usefulness of abstract data types is widely recognized. They serve as a powerful tool for information hiding and modular programming. One way of achieving data abstraction is to hide implementation details by "packing" the concrete structure of its representation and restricting its use within a special open statement, which creates a scope where a particular implementation of an abstract data type is available through a fixed set of explicitly specified interface functions. Mitchell and Plotkin gave [MP88] a formal model for this intuitively appealing idea and showed that this feature can be uniformly integrated in the Girard-Reynolds [Gir72, Rey74] polymorphic lambda calculus. They interpreted a "package" implementing an abstract data type as a *value* having an *existential type*. They called these values *data algebras*. For persistent programming systems, the most attractive feature of Mitchell and Plotkin's model is that such data algebras may be first-class values. This allows the programmer the advantages of orthogonal persistence [Coc83]. This contrasts with the other models of abstract types such as those implemented in Standard ML [HMT88], CLU [LAB+81] and Ada [Ada80]. Mitchell and Plotkin achieved this flexibility by treating the implementation type of a data algebra (sometimes called a *witness type*) as a type which exists only within the scope of the special open statement for the data algebra. This mechanism, however, conflicts with persistence – a mechanism to allow values to survive independently of any particular program activation.

To see the problem, let us examine a simple program in Mitchell and Plotkin's SOL language (with a slight change of its syntax). In the following examples, we assume that $PointADT(\sigma)$ is shorthand for the following record type:

[create:(real*real) $\rightarrow \sigma$, x_val:$\sigma \rightarrow$ real, y_val:$\sigma \rightarrow$ real, move:$\sigma \rightarrow$ (real*real) $\rightarrow \sigma$]

To create a data algebra, say for manipulating "points", we use the primitive **pack** which "packs" the concrete implementation type:

---

*To appear in *Proc. 3rd International Workshop on Persistent Object Stores, Martha's Vinyard, USA. September 1990. Will be published from Morgan-Kaufmann Publishing.*

[†]Supported by a British Royal Society Research Fellowship. On leave from OKI Electric Industry, Co., Japan.

[‡]Supported by ESPRIT II Basic Research Action 3070 – FIDE, and by the Committee of Vice-Chancellors and Principals of the Universities of the United Kingdom.

[§]Supported by ESPRIT II Basic Research Action 3070 – FIDE, and by SERC GRF 02953.

[¶]Supported by ESPRIT II Basic Research Action 3070 – FIDE.

[0]Authors' addresses. Ohori, Tabkha and Philbrow: Department of Computing Science, University of Glasgow, Glasgow, G12 8QQ, Scotland. Connor: Department of Computational Science, University of St Andrews, St Andrews, KY16 9SS, Scotland.

[0]Authors' electronic addresses. {ohori,tabkha,pp}@cs.glasgow.ac.uk, richard@cs.st-and.ac.uk

```
cart_point = pack real*real in
                [create = λx:(real*real).x,
                 x_val = λp:(real*real).p.1,
                 y_val = λp:(real*real).p.2,
                 move = λp:real*real.λd:(real*real).(p.1 + d.1,p.2 + d.2)]
            to ∃t.PointADT(t)
            end
```

where ($\exists t.PointADT(t)$) is an existential type, which intuitively says that there is some type called t whose actual structure is hidden. To use this, the programmer must explicitly open it as:

```
open cart_point as point with
    P:PointADT(point)
in
    . . .
    P.create(0.0,0.0)
    . . .
end
```

Intuitively, this statement creates a "new" type called point and binds the variable P of type $PointADT$(point) to the value of the data algebra cart_point (i.e. a record of four functions). Therefore, in the body of this statement, P.create(0.0,0.0) is a type correct expression yielding a value of type point. One crucial assumption of this model is that the abstract type created in this open statement has no "real existence" and has no connection to any other type in the system. In the type system, this is enforced by treating the type name (point in the example) as a free type variable which will never be instantiated. Without the context of an **open** statement, such free type variables have no independent meaning. This is the mechanism that enables them to treat a data algebra as a first-class value. However, this feature also causes difficulty when we want to make a value having a witness type persist across different program activations, since for a value to persist it must have its own type and meaning independent of any program session. In the example, it is therefore meaningless to export the point P.create(0.0,0.0).

Perhaps Cardelli and MacQueen were the first to consider this problem and sketched a solution [CM88]. In their *abstract witness model* witness types have "real" existence associated with the package that implements them and values of those types are type compatible whenever they originate from the same package. Since packages can exist independently of any program session, this may be used to solve the problem we have just stated. However, as they pointed out, the solution seems to cause a difficulty in static type checking when we want to continue to treat packages as first-class values. They suggested the possibility of an *ad hoc* method to resolve this conflict. It is, however, not entirely obvious that one can develop a sound method without constructing a proper formalism. The goal of this paper is to analyze the problem in the context of a typed functional calculus and to propose one such method. Our proposal is based on Mitchell and Plotkin's model but it could also be adapted to Cardelli and MacQueen's model with a moderate amount of change.

The idea behind our approach is to allow programmers to treat witness types as values so that they may be stored and subsequently "reactivated". Intuitively, this allows the programmer to re-establish necessary bindings from a particular opening of a package. To develop a sound type discipline based on this idea, we are going to introduce a mechanism to treat witness types as values in a restricted way. The major technical contribution of this paper is to show that such a mechanism can be safely introduced in Mitchell and Plotkin's formal calculus.

The rest of this paper is organized as follows. Section 2 sets the basis of our discussion by defining a model of persistence in a paradigm of functional calculus through extending Mitchell and Plotkin's SOL language with persistence. We then identify the problem. In Section 3, we analyze Cardelli and MacQueen's proposal within the above framework. Our major contribution is presented in Section 4 where we present the mechanism to reconcile persistence and abstract data types, first by examples and then by giving a formal system of types. An implementation is described in Section 5.

2   Persistence and Mitchell and Plotkin's Abstract Data Types

2.1   A Model of Persistence in a Typed Functional Language

In a functional calculus, one way to model persistence is to introduce two primitives, denoted here by **get** and **put**, to retrieve and store a value from a store. Of course, a practical persistent programming language should provide more convenient ways to store and retrieve data. However, our main concern here is a type discipline for persistence and this simple model provides us with sufficient detail to analyze the interaction between the type system and persistence. We believe that, with moderate effort, our analysis of a type discipline for persistence can be applied to languages with more elaborate persistence mechanisms.

In order to integrate these primitives in a typed functional calculus, we need to assign them a type and introduce them as term constructors in the calculus. This requires us to type objects that are in a persistent store. As pointed out in [CM88, ACPP89], an *infinite union type* is appropriate. This is the type whose values are a pair consisting of a value and (the description of) its type. A type system with such an infinite union is developed in [ACPP89], where the type is called **dynamic**. Here we call it **any** to avoid confusion with the dynamic types we shall introduce later. **env** in Napier88 [MBCD89] and **pntr** in PS-algol [Per87] can be regarded as infinite union types, the former combined with other features for easy manipulation of persistent stores. Any values can be injected into **any** by:

   inject($M:\sigma$) :   **any**

and subsequently exported into a persistent store. Possible operations on **any** are dynamic inspection of the actual types and projection to a type. In [ACPP89] these are combined in a single **typecase** statement which achieves flexible manipulation of values of type **any**. For our purpose, however, it is enough to assume the following simple projection function:

   project(M,σ) : σ

which projects a value of type **any** onto the specified type σ if the actual type of the value is the same as σ, otherwise it causes a run time exception.

If the type component of a value of type **any** has its own meaning independent of any program session, then we can safely store the value and later retrieve and project back to the type. For this purpose, the type component of a value of **any** is restricted to be a *closed type*, i.e. a type that does not contain type variables. This condition corresponds to the intuition that storable values are those that have their own meaning and existence which is independent of any program session. The meaning of values whose types contain type variables in general depends on the context in which they are used. Under this restriction, we can give the following types to **get** and **put**:

   get :   string $\to$ any
   put :   (string*any) $\to$ unit

where **unit** is a trivial type and the **string** is used as a search key in the persistent store. In examples, we also use the following shorthand:

   intern(s,σ) = **project**(**get**(s),σ)
   extern(s,$M:\sigma$) = **put**(s,**inject**($M:\sigma$))

In the next subsection we extend Mitchell and Plotkin's SOL language with type **any** and the above two primitives. The extended language provides an appropriate medium to study the interaction of persistence and abstract data types. We still call the extended language SOL.

2.2   Mitchell-Plotkin's SOL Language with Persistence

The set of types (ranged over by σ) of SOL is given by the following syntax:

   $\sigma ::= b \mid t \mid [l:\sigma,\ldots,l:\sigma] \mid \sigma \to \sigma \mid \forall t.\sigma \mid \exists t.\sigma$

b stands for base types including **any** and **unit**. *t* stands for type variables. $[l:\sigma,\ldots,l:\sigma]$ stands for labeled record types where $l_1,\ldots,l_n$ are all distinct and there is no significance in the order of the components. We write $\sigma_1 * \cdots * \sigma_n$ as shorthand for $[1:\sigma_1,\ldots,n:\sigma_n]$. In our discussion, the introduction of record types is not essential. They are here for convenience. As was done in [MP88] the desired feature of record structures is easily simulated by product types with appropriate syntactic sugaring. $\forall t.\sigma$ stands for Girard-Reynolds' polymorphic type [Gir72, Rey74] and $\exists t.\sigma$ for Mitchell-Plotkin's existential types. These are binding mechanisms of type variables for which the notion of *free variables* and *bound variables* are standard. We write $\sigma_1[\sigma_2/t]$ to denote the type obtained from σ_1 by replacing all the free occurrences of the type variable *t* by σ_2.

The set of expressions (or terms) is given by the following abstract syntax:

$$M ::= c^\sigma \mid x \mid \lambda x{:}\sigma.M \mid M(M) \mid [l{=}M,\ldots,l{=}M] \mid M.l \mid \Lambda t.M \mid M[\sigma] \mid$$
$$\textbf{pack } \sigma \textbf{ in } M \textbf{ to } \sigma \textbf{ end} \mid \textbf{open } M \textbf{ as } t \textbf{ with } M{:}\sigma \textbf{ in } M \textbf{ end} \mid$$
$$\textbf{inject}(M{:}\sigma) \mid \textbf{project}(M,\sigma)$$

c^σ stands for type constants including the primitive $\textbf{get}^{string \to any}$ and $\textbf{put}^{(string*any) \to unit}$ as well as ordinary atomic constants. $[l{=}M,\ldots,l{=}M]$ is the syntax for record expressions. We write $(M_1,\ldots,M_n)$ as shorthand for $[1{=}M_1,\ldots,n{=}M_n]$. We also write $x_1{=}M_1 ; M_2$ as shorthand for $(\lambda x_1{:}\sigma_1.M_2)(M_1)$ where σ is the type of M_1 and write $x_1{=}M_1;\cdots;x_n{=}M_n$ as shorthand for $x_1{=}M_1;(x_2{=}M_2;(\cdots;x_n{=}M_n)\cdots)$. Assuming that the evaluation is call-by-value, this provides value binding and sequential evaluation.

The expression **pack** σ **in** M **to** σ **end** is used to create a package or data algebra implementing an abstract data type by packing the type σ, representing the intended abstract type. σ is sometimes called a *witness type* [CM88]. A package is opened by the **open** statement: **open** M_1 **as** t **with** $x{:}\sigma(t)$ **in** M_2, which associates the witness type of the package M_1 with the type variable t, binds the variable x to the package value M_1, and executes the body M_2.

The type system of SOL is given as a proof system for *typings*. Since the type of an expression depends on the types of its free variables, the type system is represented as a proof system for *typings* of the form $\mathcal{A} \triangleright M : \sigma$ where $\mathcal{A}$ is a function from a finite set of variables to types, called a *type assignment*. We write $\mathcal{A}\{x : \sigma\}$ for the function $\mathcal{A}'$ such that $dom(\mathcal{A}') = dom(\mathcal{A}) \cup \{x\}$, $\mathcal{A}'(x) = \sigma$ and $\mathcal{A}'(y) = \mathcal{A}(y)$ for all $y \in dom(\mathcal{A}), y \neq x$. Some of the typing rules are shown belows:

$$(\textsc{record}) \quad \frac{\mathcal{A} \triangleright M_i : \sigma_i \ \ (1 \leq i \leq n)}{\mathcal{A} \triangleright [l_1{=}M_1,\ldots,l_n{=}M_n] : [l_1{:}\sigma_1,\ldots,l_n{:}\sigma_n]}$$

$$(\textsc{dot}) \quad \frac{\mathcal{A} \triangleright M : [l_1{:}\sigma_1,\ldots,l_n{:}\sigma_n]}{\mathcal{A} \triangleright M.l_i : \sigma_i \ \ (1 \leq i \leq n)}$$

$$(\textsc{inject}) \quad \frac{\mathcal{A} \triangleright M : \sigma}{\mathcal{A} \triangleright \textbf{inject}(M{:}\sigma) : any}$$

$$(\textsc{project}) \quad \frac{\mathcal{A} \triangleright M : any}{\mathcal{A} \triangleright \textbf{project}(M,\sigma) : \sigma}$$

$$(\textsc{pack}) \quad \frac{\mathcal{A} \triangleright M : \sigma_1[\sigma_2/t]}{\mathcal{A} \triangleright \textbf{pack } \sigma_2 \textbf{ in } M \textbf{ to } \exists t.\sigma_1 \textbf{ end} : \exists t.\sigma}$$

$$(\textsc{open}) \quad \frac{\mathcal{A} \triangleright M_1 : \exists t.\sigma_1 \qquad \mathcal{A}\{x{:}\sigma_1\} \triangleright M_2 : \sigma_2}{\mathcal{A} \triangleright \textbf{open } M_1 \textbf{ as } t \textbf{ with } x{:}\sigma_1 \textbf{ in } M_2 \textbf{ end} : \sigma_2} \quad t \text{ not free in } \sigma_2 \text{ or } \mathcal{A}$$

The rules for the other term constructors are the same as in the second-order lambda calculus [Gir72, Rey74]. The rules for records are standard. The rule (PACK) says that *any* term of type $\sigma_1(\sigma_2)$ can be turned into a data algebra of type $\exists t.\sigma$ by packing the type σ_2. As seen from the definition of the set of types, existential types are first-class types in the sense that they can be freely mixed with other type constructors. The typing rule (PACK) therefore implies that data algebras are first-class values and can be freely mixed with any other expression constructors. Mitchell and Plotkin achieved this very flexible treatment of data algebras by placing proper restrictions on their usage. The rule (OPEN) says that in the body M_2 of the **open** statement, the abstract type implementing the package M_1 must be treated as a free type variable. The constraints associated with this rule prohibit the programmer from making any connection (possibly through type abstraction or other **open** statements) between this type variable and any other types. This condition is a simplified version of the slightly more general one in [MP88]. However, assuming an unbounded supply of type variables, we do not lose any generality. Since free type variables carry no structural information, the compiler can check the type correctness of the program that uses a data algebra without inspecting the structure of its implementation type. Because of this very restrictive treatment of witness types, this model is named the *hypothetical witness model* [CM88]. The type variable t in the **open** construct can be thought of as a name, in the body of the construct, of the hypothetical witness which is supposed to exist.

In order to ensure the conditions for values of type **any** we have defined earlier, we have to constrain the usage of **inject**. To do this in the most general way, we define the notion of *closed expressions*. The notions of free and bound variables are defined as in the second-order lambda calculus. The definition of *bound type variables* in an expression M is obtained from that of the second-order lambda calculus by adding the rule: t is a bound type variable in M if $M \equiv$ **open** M **as** t **with** $\cdots$ **end** and extend it to a general expression in a usual manner. An expression is closed iff it does not contain free variables and free type variables. The desired constraint is then given:

(*) If M is a closed expression then all type variables in its subexpressions of the form **inject**$(M' : \sigma)$ must be bound by Λt.

The rationale behind this condition is that we allow type variables in the specification σ of **inject**(M, σ) only if they will eventually be instantiated (substituted) by some closed types before it is evaluated.

2.3   The Problem of Persistence and Abstract Types

The language we have just defined serves as a formal model for a polymorphic programming language with persistence and abstract data types such as Napier88 [MBCD89]. However, it has one serious drawback in that it cannot express the injection of values having a witness type into type **any**. From a database perspective, this implies that the language cannot provide an abstraction mechanism for values stored in persistent data. This becomes a serious problem since most objects in database programming are persistent ones.

One possible solution, requiring no more material than that of Mitchell and Plotkin's framework, is to use the **pack** statement and create a new package. Suppose we want to create a few points having a witness type, store them, and later retrieve them for further processing. We can achieve this by creating a new package containing the desired points together with any necessary operations, and storing the package as shown in the following example:

```
open cart_point as point with
    P:PointADT(point)
in
    a = P.create(1.0,2.0);
    b = P.create(1.0,3.0);
    c = P.create(1.0,4.0);
    extern("my_point_pack",
            pack point in [a=a,b=b,c=c,create=P.create,
                            x_val=P.x_val,y_val=P.y_val,move=P.move]
            to ∃t.[a:t,b:t,c:t,
                create:(real*real) → t,
                x_val:t → real,
                y_val:t → real,
                move:t → (real*real) → t]
            end:∃t.[a:t,...,move:t → (real*real) → t])
end
```

Then later, we can retrieve the package, open it and continue the computation as in:

```
my_point_pack = intern("my_point_pack",∃t.···[a:t,...,move:t → (real*real) → t]);
open my_cart_point as point with
    P:[a:point, b:point, c:point,
        create:(real*real) → point,
        x_val:point → real,
        y_val:point → real,
        move:point → (real*real) → point]
in
        ···
        P.x_val(a)
        ···
end
```

Since the package has a closed type (i.e. an existential type), this approach immediately gives a sound type system for persistent abstract objects. This solution is effective but it requires the programmer to create one package containing all the related objects and operations. This seems to be problematic when we are dealing with a community of users with a large shared database, since this approach requires the user to have a complete knowledge of the values of the witness type and retrieve all the values at once.

Another way of allowing these values to persist is to embed the persistent store access within the package. For example

```
cart_point_ps = pack ···
                to ∃t.[create:real*real → t,
                        x_val:t → real,
                        y_val:t → real,
                        move:t → (real*real) → t,
                        store:(string*t) → unit,
                        retrieve:string → t]
                end;

open cart_point_ps as point with ··· end
```

thus allowing users of the package to store new values within a context from which they may later be accessed. Although this is at least useful, the persistence involved is no longer orthogonal [ABC+83], as the programmer must invent a different naming scheme for each different abstract package through access functions (such as store, retrieve in the above example). This is a serious restriction for general persistent programming.

The goal of this paper is to propose a mechanism which allows values of witness types to achieve the full range of persistence without losing the desirable properties of Mitchell and Plotkin's model of abstract data types. But before presenting our system, we review Cardelli and MacQueen's proposal.

3   Cardelli and MacQueen's Proposal

Cardelli and MacQueen proposed [CM88] a different view of abstract data types called the *abstract witness model* and discussed the relationship between their model and persistence. In this model, the witness type of a data algebra is "abstract" but is supposed to have a "real" existence. This means that when we create a data algebra, we also create an actual type associated with it. Opening a data algebra no longer creates a new hypothetical witness but only associates a name to the data algebra's witness type. For example, under this model,

```
open M as point1 with P:PointADT(point1) in
   open M as point2 with Q:PointADT(point2) in
      (Q.move(P.create(1.0,2.0)))(3.0,4.0)
   end
end
```

is presumably legal and returns a value of a type associated with the data algebra M.

In this model, an abstract type seems to have its own meaning and existence so long as the associated data algebra exists. In order for a value of a witness type to be persistent, it therefore seems sufficient to make the associated data algebra persistent. For example,

```
extern("point_package",cart_point:∃t.PointADT(t));

open cart_point as point with
   P:PointADT(point)
in
   extern("a",P.create(0.0,0.0):point)
end;

open intern("point_package",∃t.PointADT(t)) as point2 with
   Q:PointADT(point2)
in
   intern("a",point2)
end
```

should presumably be type correct since both `point` and `point2` are the names of the same abstract witness type associated with the data algebra `cart_point`.

This model provides an intuitively appealing solution to the problem we have just described in the previous section. There are, however, several issues which require careful scrutiny. The first problem is to understand their informal description of the model as a formal definition of a type system. Without such a proper formalism, it is not obvious that we can extract some usefulness, such as a type-checking algorithm, out of the model. One well established way of giving a formal description of a model is to formulate the model as a typed functional calculus similar to SOL. The authors found this a non trivial challenge. Under this model, they suggested that the set of types should be extended with the expressions of the form M.`type` which denotes the *abstract witness type* associated with the expression M having an existential type. The **open** statement should then be treated as a shorthand to introduce a local name to the type M.`type` where M is the data algebra being opened in the statement. In order to give a formal account for the model we therefore need to define a type system in which those expressions can be treated as types. In doing this we need to answer several important questions, including the followings. Which class of terms can appear in a type expression of the form M.`type`? When are two types M_1.`type` and M_2.`type` equal? The relationship between the notation M.`type` and Mitchell-Plotkin's open statement was also studied in [CL90] but it does not seem to provide a mechanism needed to represent the abstract witness model. One consistent solution is to follow the proposal of [Mac86] and to introduce *levels* in the type system; the first level of types are types of values and the second level of types are types of data algebras. All second level objects are compiled before the compilation of the first level objects. The expressions of the form M.`type` where M is a second level object are treated as types only in the first level. Under this approach data algebras are compile time objects and the equality of types is simply identity. This is adopted in Standard ML to introduce modules [HMT88] in a higher-order functional calculus. Under this approach, however, data algebras cannot mix with ordinary expressions and therefore it sacrifices most of the flexibility of Mitchell and Plotkin's model of abstract types.

The other extreme alternative is to extend the type of SOL with M.`type` where M may be *any* term having an existential type. The equality of types is the congruence induced by the value equality. An obvious drawback to this approach is that it does not yield a static type checking algorithm. Cardelli and MacQueen suggested that there might be some *ad hoc* way to compromise between the static type checking and the flexibility of treating data algebras as values. They gave the following example of a difficulty with static type checking

$$\texttt{C} = \textbf{if}\ b\ \textbf{then}\ A\ \textbf{else}\ B$$

where A and B are terms having the same existential type. The existence of a conditional statement was also suggested as the cause of the difficulty of static type checking in [DT88]. However, the problem seems to be more fundamental. The least thing we should be able to do with values is to bind names to them. In a functional calculus this is done through lambda abstraction and function application. This mechanism seems to be needed in any attempt to treat objects as values. Note that this also is needed for objects to persist since persistence is a feature that is achieved by special functions. Under this view, any attempt to treat data algebras as values might cause the difficulty with static type checking. Worse yet, there seems to be no existing proposal that enables a desired *ad hoc* method in a consistent way. A detailed analysis of this problem is outside the scope of this paper and here we only suggest the difficulty by examples. Consider the following function application:

$$(\lambda \texttt{x}\!:\!\exists \texttt{t}.\,PointADT(\texttt{t}).\,\lambda \texttt{y}\!:\!\exists \texttt{t}.\,PointADT(\texttt{t})$$
$$\quad \textbf{open x as p1 with } P\!:\!PointADT(\texttt{p1})\ \textbf{in}$$
$$\quad\quad \textbf{open y as p2 with } Q\!:\!PointADT(\texttt{p2})\ \textbf{in}$$
$$\quad\quad\quad \texttt{Q.move(P.create(0.0,0.0))(1.0,2.0)}$$
$$\quad\quad \textbf{end}$$
$$\textbf{end})\texttt{(M)(M)}$$

Under the abstract witness model, at least semantically the application of `Q.move(P.create(0.0,0.0))` is type correct. However, the type consistency is known only at run time: since functions are first class values they should be type checked before each application. Therefore if we maintain static type checking, the type system should reject the above code. Now consider the following example involving persistent store:

$$(\lambda \texttt{x}\!:\!\exists \texttt{t}.\,PointADT(\texttt{t}).\,\lambda \texttt{y}\!:\!\exists \texttt{t}.\,PointADT(\texttt{t})$$
$$\quad \textbf{open x as p1 with } P\!:\!PointADT(\texttt{p1})\ \textbf{in}$$
$$\quad\quad \texttt{extern("mycreate",P.create:(real*real)} \to \texttt{p1);}$$
$$\quad\quad \textbf{open y as p2 with } Q\!:\!PointADT(\texttt{p2})\ \textbf{in}$$
$$\quad\quad\quad \texttt{Q.move(intern("mycreate":(real*real)} \to \texttt{p2)(0.0,0.0))(1.0,2.0)}$$
$$\quad\quad \textbf{end}$$
$$\textbf{end})\texttt{(M)(M)}$$

This example is essentially the same example as the one Cardelli and MacQueen gave in [CM88] and therefore should be type-checked under their model. But according to the obvious model of persistence, the above two examples are essentially the same. These two examples suggest a difficulty in developing a safe and consistent type system with persistence under the abstract witness model. Developing such a type system seems to require a significant extension to the existing system of types for persistence and data abstraction. In the next section, we attempt to construct one such system based on Mitchell and Plotkin's model. This also sheds some light on the abstract witness model as well. We will take up this point again in the next section.

4   Reconciling Abstract Data Types and Persistence

We now present a new mechanism which we believe to provide a satisfactory treatment of persistence without sacrificing the desirable features of Mitchell and Plotkin's abstract data types. We first explain this mechanism through examples and then provide its formal account as an extension of Mitchell and Plotkin's SOL language.

The intuition is that we allow the programmer to store the "hypothetical witness" created in an **open** statement and later "reactivate" it. Since, under our model of persistence, the only objects that can be stored are values that have a closed type, this requires us to treat hypothetical witnesses as values in the language. For this purpose, we introduce the new type `Witness`. This is the type of all the possible hypothetical witness types. The values of this type are themselves types and therefore can be used as types. Different from other types in SOL, however, these types are run time objects and cannot be examined by the compiler. To emphasize this difference, we use the term *dynamic types* for those types that contain values of the type

Witness and distinguish them from the other ordinary types, which we call *static types*. The reader is again warned that the type **any** (which is also named **dynamic** in some literature) is not a dynamic type. As we noted earlier, however, the general introduction of dynamic types would cause conflicts with static type checking. We solve this problem by introducing a mechanism to localize the typing judgements that involve dynamic types. The major technical contribution of this paper is to establish that such a mechanism is possible in the framework of Mitchell and Plotkin's calculus.

The only construct that creates values of type **Witness** is the **open*** statement, whose syntax is

open* M **as** t **with** w:**Witness** **and** x:$\sigma(t)$ **in** N **end**

As in the **open** statement, x is bound to the value implementing the data algebra M and is used in the body N as an expression of type $\sigma(t)$. In addition to this binding, **open*** creates a value of type **Witness** which represents the hypothetical witness associated with this statement and binds the variable w to it in the body N. Since the type **Witness** is a closed atomic type, w can then be used to export the hypothetical witness type into a persistent store using the ordinary primitives. Note that **open*** creates a value of type **Witness**. This reflects the hypothetical witness model of Mitchell and Plotkin. Another possibility would be to extend the language so that the **pack** statement creates a value of type **Witness**. For this purpose, we would presumably need a primitive such as **witness** [Mac86] which takes a value having existential type and returns a value of type **Witness**. By this alteration, we think we could achieve a type system which is faithful to the abstract witness mode. However, we have not yet examined the details of this alternative.

Since w is assigned the same hypothetical witness type associated with the type variable t in the body N, an expression which has a type of the form $\sigma(t)$ can be coerced to the expression having the type $\sigma(w)$. This coercion is embedded in the primitive **inject***. Different from **inject**, σ in **inject***$(M::\sigma)$ is in general a dynamic type. To emphasize this property, we use :: instead of ordinary static typing :. This statement, when evaluated, creates a value of type **any** whose type component is the dynamic type denoted by σ. As seen below our type system guarantees type correctness by maintaining the relationship between t and w.

By these mechanisms, we can safely export values having abstract types. The following is an example of **open***:

```
open* cart_point as point with
   mywitness:Witness and
   P:PointADT(point)
in
   a = P.create(1.0,2.0);
   put("mypt_type",inject(mywitness:Witness));
   put("somepoint",inject*(a::mywitness));
   put("my_y_val",inject*(P.y_val::mywitness → real))
end
```

`a` and `y_val` are injected into **any** as values having dynamic types **mywitness** and **mywitness** → **real** where **mywitness** is the value denoting the hypothetical witness created by the entire statement.

The important difference between ordinary types and types containing values of type **Witness** is that the latter are not compile time objects. To preserve the static type-checking, special constructs are needed to use values having dynamic types. For this purpose, we provide **project*** and **reopen*** statements. **project***(M,σ) projects the value M of type **any** onto a dynamic type σ. Similar to **project**, the entire expression has the type σ. However, since σ is a dynamic type, the type information about the result of this expression is not available at compile time. To indicate this dynamic nature of the typing judgement, we write **project***$(M,\sigma)::\sigma$. This statement can only be verified at run time. The only operation that can use values having dynamic types is the **reopen*** statement, whose syntax is given as:

reopen* M_1 **as** t **with** w:**Witness** **and** x:$\sigma(t)$ **is** $M_2::\sigma(w)$ **in** M_3 **end**

This statement first binds the variable w to the value M_1 of type **Witness** and then dynamically verifies the typing $M_2::\sigma(w)$. If it is verified it then binds the variable x to the value M_2 and executes the body M_3. The important feature of this statement is that the variable x has the *static type* $\sigma(t)$ where t is a type variable associated with the hypothetical witness being reopened by this statement. By this mechanism we successfully localize the dynamic type check. This implies that we can still check statically the type correctness of the body of the **reopen*** statement just as we do that of the **open** statement. The following is an example of **project*** and **reopen***.

```
p = intern("mypt_type",Witness);
reopen* p as mypoint
with
    w:Witness
and
    a:mypoint is project*(get("somepoint"),w),
    y_val:mypoint → real is project*(get("my_y_val"),w → real)
in
    ...
    y_val(a)
    ...
end
```

This "reopens" the hypothetical witness created and stored under the name "mypt_type" in the previous example as the type variable mypoint. To do this, the statement first checks that the type components of the values retrieved by the names "somepoint" and "my_y_val" are respectively the dynamic types p and p → real and then binds the value components of them respectively to the variables a and y_val, and executes the body. As with the **open** statement, the type correctness of the body is established statically.

In the rest of this section, we provide a formal system where **reopen*** is possible by extending the SOL language. We call the extended language SOL^*.

The syntax of the set of dynamic types (ranged over by τ) of SOL^* is given as follows:

$$\tau ::= t \mid b \mid \tau \rightarrow \tau \mid [l : \tau, \ldots, l : \tau] \mid \forall t. \, \tau \mid \exists t. \, \tau \mid Witness \mid w$$

where w stands for variables having the type Witness. The set of static types is the following subset of dynamic types:

$$\sigma ::= t \mid b \mid \sigma \rightarrow \sigma \mid [l : \sigma, \ldots, l : \sigma] \mid \forall t. \, \sigma \mid \exists t. \, \sigma \mid Witness$$

The set of pre-terms of SOL^* is given by the following syntax:

$$
\begin{aligned}
M ::= \; & c^\sigma \mid x \mid \lambda x {:} \sigma. \, M \mid M(M) \mid [l{=}M,\ldots,l{=}M] \mid M.l \mid \Lambda t. \, M \mid M[\sigma] \mid \\
& \textbf{pack } \sigma \textbf{ in } M \textbf{ to } \sigma \mid \textbf{open } M \textbf{ as } t \textbf{ with } M {:} \sigma \textbf{ in } M \textbf{ end} \mid \\
& \textbf{open* } M \textbf{ as } t \textbf{ with } x {:} \text{Witness and } x {:} \sigma(t) \textbf{ in } M \textbf{ end} \mid \\
& \textbf{reopen* } M \textbf{ as } t \textbf{ with } x {:} \text{Witness and } x {:} \sigma(t) \textbf{ is } M {::} \tau \textbf{ in } M \textbf{ end} \mid \\
& \textbf{inject}(M {:} \sigma) \mid \textbf{inject*}(M {::} \tau) \mid \textbf{project}(M, \sigma) \mid \textbf{project*}(M, \tau)
\end{aligned}
$$

As is done for SOL, the type system of SOL^* is given as a proof system of typings. As in SOL, a typing is a triple consisting of a set of assertions, a pre-term and a type. For SOL^* we have two forms of assumptions. One is an assignment of a static type to a variable $x : \sigma$; the other is an association of a type variable to a witness variable $t \leftrightarrow x$. This is needed to type check **inject***. An *environment* $\mathcal{E}$ (which is an extension of type assignment in SOL) is a finite set of the above two forms of assertions. We write $\mathcal{A}\{x : \sigma\}$ and $\mathcal{A}\{t \leftrightarrow x\}$ for extensions of $\mathcal{A}$ with $x : \sigma$ and with $t \leftrightarrow x$ respectively. We distinguish static typings and dynamic typings. A static typing is a formula of the form $\mathcal{A} \triangleright M : \sigma$ and corresponds to a typing in SOL. A dynamic typing is a formula of the form $\mathcal{A} \triangleright M :: \tau$, which has no equivalence in SOL. Dynamic typings are typing judgements which are verified only at run time. The set of rules for SOL^* typings (both dynamic and static) are the ones obtained from that of SOL by adding the following rules for new constructs we introduced in SOL^*:

$$\text{(INJECT*)} \quad \frac{\mathcal{A}\{x{:}\text{Witness}, t \leftrightarrow x\} \triangleright M : \sigma(t)}{\mathcal{A}\{x{:}\text{Witness}, t \leftrightarrow x\} \triangleright \textbf{inject*}(M {::} \sigma(x)) : \text{any}}$$

$$\text{(PROJECT*)} \quad \frac{\mathcal{A}\{x{:}\text{Witness}\} \triangleright M : \text{any}}{\mathcal{A}\{x{:}\text{Witness}\} \triangleright \textbf{project*}(M, \sigma(x)) :: \sigma(x)}$$

$$(\text{OPEN*}) \quad \frac{\mathcal{A}\{x{:}\text{Witness},t \leftrightarrow x, y : \sigma_1(t)\} \vartriangleright M_1 : \sigma_2 \qquad \mathcal{A} \vartriangleright M_2 : \exists t.\sigma(t)}{\mathcal{A} \vartriangleright \textbf{open*}\ M_2\ \textbf{as}\ t\ \textbf{with}\ x{:}\text{Witness}\ \textbf{and}\ y{:}\sigma_1(t)\ \textbf{in}\ M_1\ \textbf{end} : \sigma_2}$$

$(t \text{ not free in } \sigma_2 \text{ or } \mathcal{A})$

$$(\text{REOPEN*}) \quad \frac{\mathcal{A} \vartriangleright M_1 : \text{Witness} \qquad \mathcal{A}\{y{:}\text{Witness}\} \vartriangleright M_2 :: \sigma_1(y) \qquad \mathcal{A}\{y{:}\text{Witness}, x{:}\sigma_1(t), t \leftrightarrow y\} \vartriangleright M_3 : \sigma_2}{\mathcal{A} \vartriangleright \textbf{reopen*}\ M_1\ \textbf{as}\ t\ \textbf{with}\ y{:}\text{Witness}\ \textbf{and}\ x{:}\sigma_1(t)\ \textbf{is}\ M_2 :: \sigma_1(y)\ \textbf{in}\ M_3\ \textbf{end} : \sigma_2}$$

$(t \text{ not free in } \sigma_2 \text{ or } \mathcal{A})$

The reader is encouraged to trace the typing derivation of the above examples using these rules.

5   Implementation

The static type checking of these new existential types is, as required, exactly the same as that of standard Mitchell and Plotkin existential types, and has been fully discussed elsewhere. Here we will give a possible implementation of the dynamic checking associated with the injection and projection of a witness value.

When a value is stored in an infinite union, it must be stored along with a representation of its type. When a projection statement is compiled, the compiler must construct a representation of the type the union is being projected onto, and must cause an equivalence function to be executed over the type representation stored with the value and that constructed by the compiler for the projection statement. The dynamic projection may only succeed if the two type representations are compatible.

The simplest way to arrange this is in a persistent system where the compiler may access the persistent store. When an injection statement is encountered, the compiler may place the type representation in a known location within the store as the program is compiled, and the address of this single representation may be stored with any values which are injected dynamically. When a projection is encountered, again a suitable type representation may be placed once within the store as the program is compiled, and code planted to access this representation dynamically as required. The function which tests two type representations for equivalence must also be at a fixed location within the store.

When a value of a free witness type is injected as a special Witness type, the injection must be slightly different from that described above. In this case, the type representation to be stored with the value may not be created statically by the compiler but must be created dynamically for each invocation of the **open*** statement which performs the injection. Two such type representations may be considered as compatible if and only if they represent the same dynamic invocation of a particular **open*** statement.

In a persistent system with referential integrity this is not hard to arrange; each such new type may be represented by a new object appropriately marked as dynamic for the equivalence algorithm. The equivalence algorithm should allow two objects so marked to pass the equivalence test if and only if they share the same identity. As this identity must in any case be preserved for the lifetime of the system to preserve the referential integrity of the store, no further work need be done for persistent values. Such a scheme is already in operation for abstract data types and polymorphic procedures in the language Napier88 [MBCD89].

Whenever the compiler encounters a definition of value of type Witness at the start of an **open*** statement, it must therefore plant code to construct a new store object appropriately marked for the type equivalence algorithm. It should also make a note of the offset within the current frame at which this new value will be located. When it encounters a special injection operation which uses this value as a type, the code generated to perform the injection must create a new union value which contains the unbound witness value in the value field, and this type representation value in the type field. When the Witness value itself is injected into the infinite union, the type representation stored with it is a simple marker to indicate that the value stored is a witness type representation.

For the **reopen*** clause, this value is first retrieved from the union. The value is then used as the type representation for the projection of all witness types stated at the head of the statement. As long as these values have been injected within the same dynamic scope as the witness type itself, the value of the type representation will have the same identity, and the dynamic type checks will succeed.

As can be seen, this implementation mirrors exactly the intuitive description and justification of the **reopen*** clause, by creating an unforgeable value for each dynamic execution of an **open*** clause which must be presented in order to perform the **reopen*** and achieve access to the same witness type definitions.

6   Conclusion

We have examined the interaction between persistence and Mitchell and Plotkin's abstract data types and proposed an extension to their system which allows values of witness types to achieve the full range of persistence without losing the desirable properties of the original model. In order to do this we introduced a mechanism to treat witness types as values in a restricted way such that the typing judgements that depend on these values are localized.

The language we have described is a variant of a functional calculus that can serve as a core of the type system of practical persistent programming languages. As we have discussed in section 5, an efficient type-checking algorithm can be extracted from our type system.

There are a number of ways to extend the work described here. One of them is to exploit the mechanism introduced that allows the programmer to treat types as values in a restricted way while preserving static type checking. This might be useful when we want to achieve some degree of dynamic manipulation of objects which are usually restricted to compile time, such as database *schemas* (the database system analogue of types).

Acknowledgement

We would like to thank Malcolm Atkinson for his useful comments on an earlier version of the paper and and stimulating discussion on abstract data types.

References

[ABC+83]   M.P. Atkinson, P.J. Bailey, K.J. Chisholm, W.P. Cockshott, and R. Morrison. An approach to persistent programming. *Computer Journal*, 26(4), November 1983.

[ACPP89]   M. Abadi, L. Cardelli, B. Pierce, and G. Plotkin. Dynamic typing in a statically-typed language. In *Proc. 16th ACM Symposium on Principles of Programming Languages*, 1989.

[Ada80]   Reference manual for the Ada programming language. G.P.O. 008-000-00354-8, 1980.

[CL90]   L. Cardelli and X. Leroy. Abstract Types and the Dot Notation. SRC Research Report, Digital Equipment Corporation, March 1990.

[CM88]   L. Cardelli and D. MacQueen. Persistence and type abstraction. In M.P. Atkinson, O.P. Buneman, and R. Morrison, editors, *Data Types and Persistence*, Topics in Information Systems, chapter 3, pages 31–41. Springer Verlag, 1988.

[Coc83]   W.P. Cockshott. *Orthogonal Persistence*. PhD thesis, University of Edinburgh, February 1983.

[DT88]   S. Danforth and C. Tomlinson. Type theories and object-oriented programming. *ACM Computing Surveys*, 20(1), 1988.

[Gir72]   J.-Y. Girard. Une extension de l'interpretation de Gödel à l'analyse, et son application à l'élimination des coupures dans l'analyse et théorie des types. In *Second Scandinavian Logic Symposium*, pages 63–92. Springer-Verlag, 1972.

[HMT88]   R. Harper, R. Milner, and M. Tofte. The definition of Standard ML (version 2). LFCS Report Series ECS-LFCS-88-62, Department of Computer Science, University of Edinburgh, August 1988.

[LAB+81]   Barbara Liskov, Russell Atkinson, Toby Bloom, Eliot Moss, J. Craig Schaffert, Robert Scheifler, and Alan Snyder. *CLU Reference Manual*, volume 114 of *Lecture Notes in Computer Science*. Springer-Verlag, Berlin, 1981.

[Mac86]   D. B. MacQueen. Using dependent types to express modular structure. In *Conf. Record Thirteenth Ann. Symp. Principles of Programming Languages*, pages 277–286. ACM, January 1986.

[MBCD89]   R. Morrison, A.L. Brown, R.C.H. Connor, and A. Dearle. Napier88 reference manual. Technical report, Department of Computational Science, University of St Andrews, 1989.

[MP88]   J.C. Mitchell and G.D. Plotkin. Abstract types have existential type. *ACM Transactions on Programming Languages and Systems*, 10(3):470–502, 1988.

[Per87]   Persistent Programming Research Group. PS-algol reference manual - fourth edition. Technical Report PPRR-12-87, Universities of Glasgow and St Andrews, 1987.

[Rey74]   J.C. Reynolds. Towards a theory of type structure. In *Paris Colloq. on Programming*, pages 408–425. Springer-Verlag, 1974.

Type Equivalence Checking in Persistent Object Systems

Connor, R.C.H., Brown, A.L., Cutts, Q.I., Dearle, A.,[†]
Morrison, R. & Rosenberg, J.[¥]

University of St Andrews, Scotland
[†] University of Adelaide, Australia
[¥] University of Newcastle, Australia

email: {richard,ab,quintin,ron}@cs.st-and.ac.uk
al@adelaide.edu.au
johnr@nucs.nu.oz.au

Abstract

Two common methods of determining type equivalence in programming languages and database systems are by name and by structure. In this paper we will show that both mechanisms are myopic views of the type equivalence required for persistent systems. Methods of representing schema types within a persistent store will be discussed, and two possible implementations will be given. Finally discussion and measurements of the efficiency trade-offs for both representations will be presented.

1   Introduction

Type systems provide two important facilities within both databases and programming languages, namely data modelling and data protection. Recent developments in type systems have greatly increased their expressive power while retaining their traditional safety. These developments include parametric and inclusion polymorphism [CW85], abstract and existential types [MP85,CDM90], bulk data types such as sets, lists and arrays etc.[AM85], classes as type extensions [AGO89] and static constraint checking [SS89,SWB89]. One future goal for persistent programming languages is to develop a type system that will accommodate the structures required for both modelling and protection in less traditional database applications such as scientific programming, engineering applications and office automation, whilst also capturing the type description of more conventional database systems.

Our extended view of type systems allows the traditional database schema to be regarded as a type. We are concerned in this paper with how this schema type is manipulated efficiently by the persistent system. Central to this is how the schema type is represented within the persistent system and how type checking is performed using the schema type.

Traditional type checking within programs and type checking within the persistent store are rather different animals. Type checking within a program may entail a type checker in building a representation of the type, inferring some types, checking for the equivalence of the types and some compatibility checking on the types for coercions and subtype polymorphism, for example. Within the persistent store type checking is generally only concerned with checking the equivalence of two types for which representations already exist. For the moment we restrict this to an exact equivalence check and remark that subtype checking is somewhat more complex [ACP89].

Two common methods of determining type equivalence are by name and by structure. We will define these terms for clarity later in the paper and go on to show that both mechanisms are myopic views of the type equivalence that is required for persistent systems. To do this we will discuss the issues involved in schema type evolution, the distribution of the schema type in a distributed system, the merging of independently developed schema types, late binding to the schema type and how programs partially specify the section of the schema type of interest. We will then discuss the representation of the schema type within a persistent store, and present two suitable methods of representation. A comparison of these methods is given, along with measurements of the efficiency of both representations.

2   Models of Type Equivalence Checking

In database systems and programming languages, two methods of checking type equivalence are common. These are by name and by structure. The definitions of these two mechanisms given below are taken from [ADG89]. They are:

- in name equivalence, two values have equivalent types if the types share the same declaration, and

- in structural equivalence, two values have equivalent types if the types have isomorphic structures.

We will use these definitions to highlight the issues in this paper but note that most systems do not adopt such extreme positions for all their type equivalence checking. Many compromises can be made some of which will be exposed later.

It should also be noticed that the issue of static and dynamic checking is not of importance here. The separation between compile and run time can be obscure in a persistent system and does not affect the work involved in type equivalence checking. We are however still concerned with efficiency. We would prefer our type checking to be fast since depending upon the usage of the system it may have to be performed frequently. It is generally accepted that name equivalence is fast and structural equivalence is slow.

For these equivalence checking categories we will investigate type checking both within programs and within a persistent object store, which may be centralised or distributed.

2.1   Name Equivalence Checking

2.1.1   Name Equivalence Checking within Programs

The programming language Ada [Ich83] is a good example of a system that primarily uses name equivalence checking. An example is the definitions of the types *ANIMAL* and *VEHICLE* given below:

```
type ANIMAL is record
       Age : INTEGER;
       Weight : REAL;
end record;

type VEHICLE is record
       Age : INTEGER;
       Weight : REAL;
end record;
```

In structural terms, *ANIMAL* and *VEHICLE* define the same set of values from the value space, namely the labelled cross product *Age* : INTEGER x *Weight* : REAL. However, in name equivalence terms values of type *ANIMAL* are not type compatible with values of type *VEHICLE*. There are advantages and disadvantages to this.

One disadvantage is that anonymous types are not permissible in name equivalence and indeed Ada has to use an *ad hoc* mechanism to achieve the same effect. For example, it is not possible with strict name equivalence to write a procedure that will accept a parameter of a particular shape, such as a one dimensional array, even if it has a fixed size. The declaration,

```
procedure Add-elements (A : array (1..6) of INTEGER);
```

is achieved in Ada by having an anonymous type mechanism for the structure matching on the array, not by name equivalence. Such a disadvantage is only a minor drawback since it only takes a type definition to resolve the problem. For example

```
type INT_ARRAY_ONE_SIX is array (1..6) of INTEGER;
procedure Add-elements (A : INT_ARRAY_ONE_SIX);
```

At worst strict name equivalence is verbose. However, variable size arrays do cause problems for strict name equivalence checking since a different type name and procedure declaration are required for each size. Ada uses another *ad hoc* mechanism, that of unconstrained arrays, to overcome this.

Subtype checking, as used for inclusion polymorphism in object oriented languages, can be defined in name equivalence systems by explicitly stating the relation of a subtype to its supertype. For example

```
type LEGGED_ANIMAL isa ANIMAL with (No_of_legs : INTEGER);
```

This extends the supertype definition and ensures that *LEGGED_ANIMAL* is a subtype of *ANIMAL*. The mechanism is restrictive in that the structure of the inheritance hierarchy is explicit and costly to reconstruct.

With structural equivalence [Car84] one type is only a subtype of another if it has all the attributes of the supertype and possibly some more. The corresponding common attributes must be in the subtype relation themselves. To check that one type is a subtype of another, the structure of the two types constrained by the subtype relation must be checked. For example, consider the following declaration of *LEGGED_ANIMAL* :

```
type LEGGED_ANIMAL is record
        Age : INTEGER;
        Weight : REAL;
        No_of_legs : INTEGER;
end record;
```

In this case *LEGGED_ANIMAL* is a subtype of *ANIMAL* implicitly. This allows arbitrary construction of the inheritance hierarchy but requires a structural type check to validate that *ANIMAL* and *LEGGED_ANIMAL* are in the subtype relation.

Problems similar to the above occur in languages with parametric polymorphism where the type of the specialised form is deduced from the polymorphic form. This can be regarded as a type coercion or type inference but requires a structural check.

The major advantage of name equivalence checking is that it is efficient. The check involves ensuring that two types have the same declaration, which can be reduced to a single word comparison in most machines. This advantage goes a long way to explaining the popularity of the scheme within many programming languages.

2.1.2 Name Equivalence Checking in a Persistent Object Store

Name equivalence checking within a persistent store is based on a dictionary of type names which contains the schema. Programs producing persistent data extend the schema with the type of the data before placing the data in the persistent store. Programs using this data must reuse the type definition contained in the schema type to ensure compatibility of the types. The dictionary of type names may be one level, tree structured or even a graph depending on the mechanism used for names in the system. Tree and graph name spaces are essentially distributed in nature.

The manipulation of the schema may become a major efficiency bottleneck in these systems especially in the presence of concurrent access. Typical operations on the schema type are:

- adding a type definition,

- removing a type definition,

- altering a type definition,

- using type definitions, and

- merging type definitions.

Adding a type definition to the type schema only causes problems of name clashes within the dictionary. This is most acute in a flat name space but is not a serious problem since the name has to be added before the separate compilation of modules using the type can be performed. Changing the clashing name to an unused one and altering the code for the modules that share the type description solves the problem.

Removing a type definition from the schema type is more difficult since data of that type may exist in the persistent store. Removing the type definition would ensure that the data could not be used again with its original type. Only where the type is abstracted over, such as in polymorphism, could the data be used. If there is no type abstraction, then either the request to remove the type is denied, if data of the type still exists, or the data is removed with the type definition, although perhaps not immediately. This requires the ability to reach all programs and data that use a particular type, from the type schema itself. This may not be trivial where data is encapsulated within objects. One interesting aspect of removing types occurs with mutually recursive types and is similar to the problem of removal of values from mutually recursive classes in Object-Oriented Databases posed by Atkinson [Atk89]. If the type is removed what happens to its mutually recursive partners?

The type descriptions within the schema type are used by compilers to generate efficient code for the manipulation of the data of that type. For example, this may entail generating static offsets for indexing and means that altering the type requires recompilation of the programs and data that use that type. As with removing types, this requires the ability to reach all programs and data that use a type. More interesting, in altering a type definition the system is not concerned that the alteration is performed on the same type, since that is already established by identity, but that the alterations are compatible with the existing data. This requires a structural check.

Using a type description is equivalent to using a name. It depends upon two programs finding the shared name. Although this may be difficult in a large system, software tools such as browsers can be used to help.

As the use of the persistent object store grows, the schema evolves and a need arises for merging definitions. This may occur because mistakes have been made in defining two separate types that are logically the same and building half a system with each definition or it may occur in a distributed environment where separate universes are merged. There are a number of solutions to this problem.

The first point is that merging definitions in a name equivalence scheme requires user intervention. Since there may be many definitions that are structurally the same the system cannot decide automatically which of the definitions have to be aliased. Of course, when the user specifies that two types have to be aliased then the system must check that the types are compatible for all the existing programs and data. This involves a structural equivalence check.

There are two approaches to aliasing. One method is to recompile all the programs which use one type with the definitions of the other. Existing data poses a more severe problem, as it must be read as the old type and re-written as the new. The old type can then be removed.

The recompilation approach to definition merging is only feasible for small object stores since the time for recompilation in large stores may be prohibitive. A second solution to the problem is to alter the equivalence check itself. By using an indirecxtion in the type definition the old value may be overwritten with a new one without altering any of the references to the type.

The problem of name clashes also appears when separate schema types are merged. This is a problem of user perception of how the system works and not a technological problem. One of the names can easily be changed in the dictionary and all problems of referring to the correct type handled by the persistent address translation. The difficulty is that users do not know the new name and worse still the old one exists with a different definition.

Name equivalence checking lends itself to the partial specification of the type schema since only names of interest need be used within programs and not the whole schema.

Late binding of programs and data requires that when the program runs the data has an equivalent type to the one compiled in the program. This is performed by checking the persistent identifiers of the type names of the program and the data. Thus name equivalence checking in a persistent object store may be very efficient.

Examples of name equivalence checking over a single persistent object store can be found in the object oriented database systems ENCORE [SZ86] and O_2 [BBB88] and the persistent programming language Galileo [ACO85].

2.2   Structural Equivalence Checking

Structural equivalence checking poses a different set of problems for the user and system architect from name equivalence. In particular, structural equivalence checking may be complex in terms of time and space and is not even known to be decidable in some cases [Rec90]. Just as we have shown in the previous section that name equivalence schemes require to use a structural check for some activities we will show that structural equivalence schemes can use a naming system to overcome some of the efficiency problems.

First of all we will describe structural equivalence in programs and in persistent stores, highlighting some of the advantages and pitfalls of the mechanism.

2.2.1   Structural Equivalence Checking within Programs

The language Napier88 [MBC88] will be used to describe our examples of structural equivalence since it uses only that form of type equivalence. The type definitions of *ANIMAL* and *VEHICLE* given in Ada earlier would be in Napier88:

> **type** animal **is structure** (Age : **int** ; Weight : **real**)
> **type** vehicle **is structure** (Age : **int** ; Weight : **real**)

These types are equivalent in Napier88 since the type declaration is only regarded as providing a syntactic shorthand for the set described in the type expression. The set of values in this case is the labelled cross product *Age* : **int** x *Weight* : **real**.

The freedom of this mechanism is that it allows type names to be used anywhere a type expression is valid and vice versa. This means that anonymous types, i.e. type expressions, may be used. For example, a procedure may be defined that returns the *Age* field of all records of type *Age* : **int** x *Weight* : **real**. This is given below.

> **let** age = **proc** (x : **structure** (Age : **int** ; Weight : **real**) → **int**) ; x (Age)

In the above the identifier *age* is declared to be a procedure which takes a parameter *x* of type **structure** (Age : **int**;Weight : **real**) and returns an integer result. The body of the procedure is the expression *x (Age)* which is the Napier88 syntax for selecting the *Age* field of *x*. The result is the value of the *Age* field.

The procedure *age* will work for values of type *animal* and *vehicle* as well as any other aliases of the cross product type. Notice that this is not polymorphism nor is there any form of subtyping. It is merely structural equivalence.

Another example of the use of structural equivalence is given in the passing of procedures as parameters. The procedure *integral* is given below.

```
let integral = proc (f : proc (real → real) ; a,b : real ; no_of_steps : int → real)
begin
        let h = (b - a) / float (no_of_steps) ; let sum := 0.5 * (f (a) + f (b))
        for i = 1 to no_of_steps do
        begin
                a := a + h
                sum := sum + f (a)
        end
        h * sum
end
```

In this code fragment the identifier *integral* is declared to be a procedure that takes four parameters and returns a **real** result. It calculates the integral of a function between two limits, *a* and *b*, using the trapezoidal rule with *no_of_steps* intervals. *a*, *b* and *no_of_steps* are given as parameters. The first parameter is the function to be integrated. Its name is *f* and its type is specified by the type expression **proc (real → real)**. *f* is a procedure that takes a **real** parameter and returns a **real** result. Any procedure of this structural form may be used.

Thus integral may be called by,

        integral (sin, 0.0, 3.14159, 10)

or by

        let quadratic = proc (x : real → real) ; (3.0 * x + 4.0) * (x - 3.0)
        integral (quadratic, 1.0, 4.0, 30)

without introducing a common type name for *f*, *sin* or *quadratic*. They are all structurally equivalent by definition.

As mentioned earlier anonymous types also solve problems with array parameters, and structural equivalence facilitates implicit subtyping and implicit inclusion polymorphism, as well as specialisation in parametric polymorphism. These benefits must be balanced against the cost of performing the structural check. This can be substantial, although it is inexpensive where two types are quite different in structure. It is only where two complicated types are equivalent or nearly equivalent that the cost may be significant. Of course, as compiler writers have known for some time, if the user defines a type name and uses that alias instead of an anonymous expression in all cases, the equivalence check can be resolved by name. This possibility is usually checked for by compilers before a full structural check is attempted.

2.2.2 Structural Equivalence Checking in a Persistent Object Store

With structural equivalence checking in a persistent object store there is no requirement for a centralised type schema. Types are stored with the objects and the schema is effectively distributed with the objects themselves. Programs producing persistent objects place them in the persistent store along with a representation of their type. Duplicate type descriptions may occur but this is unimportant for equivalence checking purposes since it is done by structure.

Programs which bind dynamically to existing persistent data may employ two possible methods of operation. In the first, the program defines a type equivalent to that of the data in the persistent store that it wishes to use and the compiler assumes that this assertion is correct. A type check is made as the data is accessed at run-time to validate this assertion. This allows for very late binding of program and data. The second method uses a software tool to browse the persistent store and pick up the type from the data in the persistent store. This will then be included in the program automatically and the system proceeds as above. The advantage of the second method is that the type need not be written down, which may be a considerable saving where complex types are used. Another advantage of the second method is the speed of the equivalence check, since equality can most often be established by identity. This is not name equivalence, since non-equivalence must still be checked by structure, but it achieves the same efficiency in normal use.

Partial specification of the type schema is less easy in structural equivalence systems than name equivalence schemes since the whole structure of the type must be written down. Again this can be overcome by the second method of operation but there are some other solutions. Type **dynamic** of Amber [Car85] and types **env** and **any** in Napier88 are infinite union types with dynamic injection and projection operations. The type structure of any part of the schema need only be specified up to the limit of these infinite unions, which is convenient for partial specification of the type schema.

We will now consider the same operations of the type schema that we considered earlier for name equivalence.

Adding a type definition to the type schema causes no problems. Duplicate representations of types may occur but, as described later, this will only affect performance.

Removing a type definition from the schema is not possible explicitly. Since the schema is effectively distributed then the type may only be removed by garbage collection after all objects bound to that description of the type have disappeared.

Altering a type definition can be accommodated but only through the compiler changing both data and program simultaneously. However, the change is local and does not affect every value of a particular type, only the instances bound to that description of the type. Another method such as an IPSE is required to apply the change to the entire system. Most persistent systems already rely upon a mechanism such as reflection for this, which can also provide genericity [SFS90], browsing facilities [DB88,DCK89], data modelling facilities [CAA87], schema editing and query facilities.

Merging type schema is not a problem with structural equivalence since the schema is already distributed. Adding another part only adds to the distribution. No recompilation is required for this.

The major drawback of structural equivalence is that it is sometimes slow. Checks on vastly different types can be performed quickly. It is only where the types are complex and equal, or nearly equal, that the check may be costly.

There are a number of optimisations that may be made. First of all the compiler can generate code using the persistent identifier of a type identified by some browsing tool. The type environments of Napier88 and Type::Type of Quest [Car88] give a basis for this. In this case the structural check may be shortened to identifier equality without losing the desirable semantics.

Secondly when the pointers to different representations are found to represent equivalent types one of the pointers can be overwritten with the other. Subsequent checks on this pair of pointers will be fast. This method can however be unstable depending on which pointer is chosen for overwriting.

A third speed up is for an autonomous process to scan the persistent store combining pointers for equivalent types. A table of preferred identities can be constructed and thrown away at any time.

These efficiency measures speed up the check for equivalence to identity checks as in name equivalence. However they do not speed up checks for non-equivalence or for equivalence where identity is not assured. Indeed they slightly slow them down since the identity check is performed first.

2.3   A Universal Equivalence Checking Mechanism

Both structural and name equivalence type checking are myopic views of what is required for checking in persistent object systems. Name equivalence schemes require the structure of the data to be retained for code generation and checking in schema merging. Structural equivalence schemes may often achieve the speed found in name equivalence. This is perhaps the holy grail: to find a method of structural checking that is as fast as name checking while retaining its flexibility.

3   Implementation of Structural Type Checking

3.1   Type Equivalence Checking

In a structural equivalence type system, the types consist of sets defined over the value space of a language. Membership of these is defined by some properties of the values themselves. Values are usually of the same type only if they have the same set of operations defined over them. Type equivalence is therefore an implicit property of a value, and values do not need to be constructed with reference to a type definition. To decide type equivalence, a language definition must include a set of type rules. These define the universe of discourse of the langauge and allow the type of any value to be deduced.

The universe of discourse of a type system may be represented by the set of base types and the set of type constructors. Type constructors allow the derivation of new types from other types and perhaps some other information. Where the language is data type complete, the universe of discourse is infinite, consisting of the closure of the recursive application of the type constructors over the base types.

The structural type equivalence relation may be with a similar set of rules. For two types to be equivalent, they must be created with the same type constructor and in an equivalent manner, using types which are themselves equivalent. An equivalence rule must be defined for each different type constructor.

To perform structural type equivalence checking, it is necessary to build representations of types which contain sufficient information to establish the defined equivalence for each constructed type. An equivalence function which traverses two instances of such representations must also be defined. The essential feature of any representation type is that there exists a well-defined mapping from the value space of the representations to the type space of the language. It may be desirable in some systems for different values to represent the same type, as long as the equivalence algorithm used implements an equivalence relation which respects the semantics of structural type equivalence.

3.2 Representing Types

Any type is either a base type or a constructed type. Constructed types are a composition of other types, along with some information specific to the particular construction. This information could consist of, for example, field names in a record type or the ordering of parameters for a procedure type. In general, therefore, a type representation consists of three parts:

- a label, to determine which base type or constructor it represents

- the information specific to the construction of this type, if any

- a set of references to other type representations

The equivalence algorithm for a representation must check that, for any two representations, that the labels are the same, the specific information is compatible, and that the other types referred to are recursively equivalent.

For some type systems there is a requirement that the chain of references may be circular. This is the case in a type system with recursion, where circular references are used to achieve a finite representation. For example, the type of an integer list may be

rec type IntList **is structure**(head : **int** ; tail : IntList)

Also, to represent a type system which includes values of either universally or existentially quantified types, it is essential for any quantifier type to contain a reference to the type to which it is bound, to allow either inference or explicit specialisation to deduce the correct type equivalence rules of values with these types.

These circular references, although not increasing the conceptual complexity of type representations, are the source of serious problems with the efficient implementation of a structural equivalence algorithm.

3.3 Efficient Structural Checking

Types may be represented in a relatively straightforward manner, and a suitable equivalence algorithm is not hard to specify. There is a full discussion of this in [Con88]. However, there are two factors which can cause serious problems with the efficient implementation of structural checking.

A trend in modern programming languages, and particularly database programming languages, is to provide more and more sophisticated type systems which allow more program errors to be detected statically. This is currently pushing knowledge of static type checking to its limits, and there are even systems which need to employ theorem provers within the type checking system. Programmers are encouraged to provide the most detailed type specification possible, as this increases the chance of a programming error being detected before execution. As a consequence of this, type specifications may become extremely large and complex. It may be imagined that the size of a database schema specified statically as a type is considerable. In a system which performs structural equivalence checking dynamically, it must be possible to check types of this complexity without incurring an unacceptable overhead.

The problem of large representations is compounded by the fact that they may contain cycles. In general, an algorithm which traverses a potentially cyclic structure must check at each stage that its area of current interest has not been previously traversed. If this check is not made, then the algorithm cannot be guaranteed to terminate.

The check for cycles must be made on an attribute which is unique to each component of the representation, rather than to the type constructor it represents. This may be, for example, the identity of a node in a graph representation or the starting position within a string representation. The difficulty here is that there is only a small amount of information specific to a particular constructor, most of the important information of the type representation being resident in its topology. It may not be possible to define a useful ordering over the node instances for the purpose of a fast lookup. This depends on the chosen representation and the implementation language. If there is no good ordering, the major cost of the equivalence algorithm becomes a check for equivalent cycles, and its complexity is $O(n^2)$ where n is the number of nodes. This is because during the traversal of the graph, itself of $O(n)$, the cost of checking whether a node has been previously visited is itself $O(n)$.

The performance of algorithms to check equivalence is crucial in a persistent system, as checking may frequently be required during the execution of a program. Complexity of an algorithm is perhaps more important than performance within a conventional system, as it is likely that a persistent system would have custom-built support for an appropriate algorithm. After some more general discussion of efficiency considerations, two different methods which achieve this are described.

3.4   Normalisation

It may be seen that there is a major tradeoff between the cost of constructing type representations and the cost of executing the equivalence algorithm. For example, strings which consist of definitions within a language's type algebra contain sufficient information to perform equivalence checking, but the checking algorithm is complex. As the construction of representations is a task performed during the static checking of the program, and equivalence checking is performed during execution, it is clearly desirable to put as much of the burden as possible into the building of the representations.

For example, consider a type system which includes a structure type which is a labelled cross product. Two such type constructions are considered equivalent if they are constructed over equivalent types using the same labels, but the order of the labels is not significant. Therefore,

structure(a : int ; b : bool)

and

structure(b : bool ; a : int)

are equivalent. In general, as the ordering of the fields is unimportant, representations may be constructed with the fields in any order. In this case, the equivalence algorithm must allow for this during its execution. The fields may however be rearranged by placing them in alphabetical order according to the labels. If this is the case, the equivalence algorithm may then assume that the ordering of the fields is significant. Thus the task of equivalence checking may be simplified at the cost of complicating the task of representation building.

In general, it is possible for many differently "shaped" representations to be constructed for equivalent types. For example, consider the equivalent types:

structure(a,b : structure(c : int))

and

structure(a : structure(c : int) ; b : structure(c : int))

If the algorithm which constructs type representations is written naïvely, then the first of these definitions may result in what is, in some sense, a minimal representation of this type, whereas the second may contain duplicate components. For representations which contain cycles an infinite number of possible representations exist for any one type, although again there is only a single minimal representation.

A normal form is one in which no two component representations are equivalent to each other. The construction of a normalised representation may be highly expensive computationally, as it involves checking every component representation against every other one. This involves the execution of n^2 embedded equivalence checks, where n is the number of nodes. Balanced against this, for some classes of representation the equivalence algorithm for normalised representations may be substantially faster. This will be discussed in more detail later.

3.5   Representing types by graphs

In an implementation language which has a constructor type such as a record or structure, a graph representation of types is straightforward and elegant. It is highly suitable because of the recursive nature of type definitions and the requirement to have circular references between constructor nodes. This makes such representations simple to build and to decompose, and as such they are ideally suited for static type checking purposes. In one implementation of the Napier88 system the following representation type is used:

rec type TYPE is structure(label : int ; specificInfo : string ; references : list[TYPE])

This is sufficient to uniquely represent any type describable by the Napier88 type system using some straightforward mapping rules. The *label* field distinguishes the base type or constructor each node represents. The *specificInfo* field contains information such as fieldnames, concatenated together with markers to form a single string. The *references* field represents all references to other types from this type constructor. This has an implicit ordering which may be used as part of the type information where required.

Type equivalence is a recursively defined algorithm over this structure, and must check only for equality of the *label* and *specificInfo* fields, before recursively checking any representation in the *references* field. The following algorithm would work for type systems where cycles are not required:

```
rec let eqType = proc( a,b : TYPE -> bool )
       a = b or                          !** this means pointer equality (identity)
       (
              a( label ) = b( label ) and
              a( specificInfo ) = b( specificInfo ) and
              eqList( a( references ) , b( references ) )
       )

& eqList = proc( a,b : list[ TYPE ] -> bool )
       ( a is tip and b is tip ) or
       (
              a isnt tip and b isnt tip and
              eqType( head( a ),head( b ) ) and eqList( tail( a ),tail( b ) )
       )
```

As described previously, it may often be the case that the types being checked have the same identity. In this case the equivalence is detected immediately, otherwise the full structural check is necessary. Notice that the test for identity is also performed recursively, which optimises the case of two different representations sharing components.

When the possibility of cyclic structures is introduced, it is necessary to take further steps to ensure the termination of the algorithm for equivalent types. This is done by keeping a note of all pairs of nodes that are traversed in a "loop table". Before any pair of nodes is traversed, a check is made to see whether the same pair has already been encountered. If they have, then either the full recursive check over these nodes has already been performed, or else is in the process of being performed. If the check has already been performed, then the nodes must be equivalent, otherwise the algorithm would have already been terminated with failure. In the case where the test is still in the process of being performed, these nodes may safely be assumed to be equivalent. If they turn out to be equivalent then the assumption is correct and re-traversal of the loop has been avoided. If they turn out to be non-equivalent then the algorithm will in any case end with failure from another branch of the recursion.

The new algorithm looks like this:

```
rec let eqType = proc( a,b : TYPE -> bool )
a = b or
in_loop_table( a,b ) or
begin
       add_to_loop_table( a,b )
       a( label ) = b( label ) and
       ...
```

The use of the loop table not only ensures termination in the case of a cycle in the graph, but also prevents multiple traversals of a shared component within the graph. This adds to the efficiency of the algorithm.

With this representation, recording and looking up pairs of nodes in the loop table may cause a performance problem, as no suitable key is readily available to use for indexing. This would result in long lists of pairs being searched for an identity match. This can be simply solved by introducing an extra field into the node structures. When each type representation is created, this field is initialised with a value which may be used as a key for the node. Each pair of nodes, as encountered, is now tabulated using one of these keys on the first traversal, and the cost of checking for cycles is no longer significant. Another possibility is to use a pseudo-random number instead of a unique key, and to use a hashing algorithm based on this.

The reason for using pseudo-random keys is that the hash table may be preserved between executions of the equivalence function, and will then act as a memo table for all pointer pairs which are compared more than once. The pseudo-random keys reduce the possibility of hash clusters forming.

This persistent hash table has the interesting feature that it is not required to preserve the correctness of the algorithm, and so may be re-initialised at any time. It is important also to note that should the equivalence algorithm fail, all nodes added during that execution must be removed. For this reason, a "shadow-copied" table is used, which may be either preserved or restored depending on the outcome of the equivalence test.

The use of these techniques allows the check for cycles to be performed in constant time, and so the checking algorithm may achieve complexity of $O(n)$ where n is the number of nodes.

3.6   Representing Types by Strings

There are many possible ways of representing types by strings. One possibility is to use strings which consist of type definitions within the type algebra of the programming language, which would normally be sufficiently powerful to provide a representation for any describable type in the language's universe of discourse. However, for a sophisticated type system, any equivalence algorithm over such representations would be inefficient.

A normalised string representation is more useful. An ideal transformation from types to strings would be canonical, so that there is a reversible mapping from strings to types. In this case, the type equivalence relation may be modelled by string equality. This may be implemented in a computer by a block comparison, an extremely fast operation on most machines.

A constructive proof that a canonical string form exists for a particular type system, although not necessarily difficult, is beyond the aims of this paper. A method of construction will instead be outlined.

The method relies upon the assumption that the graph representation and equivalence algorithm outlined above are sufficient to model type equivalence in the system in question. Firstly an algorithm will be described which produces a normal form of any such graph. Normal graphs are canonical representations of types. Another algorithm will then be described, which maps graphs to strings. This mapping is demonstrably reversible, and therefore gives the desired result of canonical strings.

3.6.1 Normalising Graphs

The condition for a graph to be normal is that no two nodes of the graph represent equivalent types. Therefore the type equivalence algorithm may be applied to any two nodes within such a graph, and will always fail unless the nodes have the same identity. The algorithm we will describe to map a graph to its normal form operates by copying the graph, but mapping any equivalent nodes in the original graph to a single new node.

This algorithm relies upon a data structure similar to the loop table of the previous algorithm. In this context we will describe it as a "memo table". Each node traversed is placed in the table as before, but this time it is used to memoise the result which has already been, or is currently being, calculated for the normal form which represents the node. The algorithm to produce the normal form of a node checks in this table to see whether it has previously produced, or is in the process of producing, a normal representation for an equivalent node. The check is thus based upon the equivalence algorithm previously described, rather than simple identity.

The algorithm is as follows:

1. Construct a new memo table

2. To copy a node, first check in the memo table to see if a node with an equivalent type has already been copied. If it has, return the corresponding node stored with it. Otherwise,

3. Create a new node, without filling in the fields.

4. Add to the memo table a pair consisting of the node being copied and the new "dummy" node.

5. Fill in the fields appropriately, including recursive use of this algorithm to fill in the component types.

Notice the way that each new node must be created as a "dummy" so that each pair of identities may be added to the memo table before any recursive calls are made. Notice also that because the test applied to the memo table is equivalence, rather than identity, any nodes in the original graph which are equivalent will be mapped to the copy of the first of these nodes which is traversed during the copy algorithm. The resultant graph is therefore normal. For any type system which may be correctly represented using this graph representation, there exists only a single normal form which represents each type. Therefore there exists a reversible mapping between normal representations and types, and so this representation is canonical. This is achieved at the cost of executing the equivalence algorithm over every pair of nodes within the original graph.

3.6.2 Mapping to Strings

The following algorithm maps graphs to strings. It again uses a memo table, this time to provide unique names for any types which occur more than once in the representation. Again, this deals both with cycles and with shared components in the graph representation.

startSymbol, *endSymbol*, and *separatorSymbol* are mutually distinct characters which do not occur within the strings found in graph nodes.

1. Construct a new memo table

2. Initialise *nextMarker*, a procedure which produces a deterministic series of unique strings, a different string being produced on each call. These strings consist of characters which do not occur within the strings found in graph nodes, and do not contain the characters *startSymbol*, *endSymbol*, and *separatorSymbol*

3.   First check in the memo table to see if the node with this identity has already been traversed. If it has, return the corresponding string stored with it. Otherwise:

4.   Store the node in the memo table, associated with the result of calling *nextMarker*.

5.   The result string is the concatenation of:

- *startSymbol*

- The node's *label* field in string format

- The node's *names* field

- The concatenation of the recursive application from Step 3 of this algorithm to any component types

- *endSymbol*

The reader should be convinced that the above algorithm both terminates and produces a unique form for any graph. The unique markers used within the string for loops in the graph depend upon the traversal order of the graph; as the component types within any node are ordered as part of the normalisation process this order is always significant type information. The nth marker produced by the *nextMarker* symbol corresponds to the nth *startSymbol* which occurs within the string, and so these markers act as explicit references within the string. The string produced may thus be regarded as a normalised set of mutually recursive type definitions.

As these string forms are canonical, the type equivalence relation is implemented by string equality. The important result is that a flattened form may be found, which is implemented by a block comparison. This operation is already optimised in much conventional hardware, and so such a representation may be highly suitable for a prototype persistent system.

3.7   Comparison of Graphs and Strings

3.7.1   Speed

As has been shown, linear complexity can be achieved for equivalence algorithms over both graphs and strings. This would imply that either representation is reasonable to build into a persistent system, as no dramatic slowdown would be associated with a programmer using more complex types in a program.

However, although the complexity may be the same, the hidden constant may be significantly different. The block comparison associated with strings would be faster than the graph traversal, even if both systems were constructed in hardware. In particular, conventional hardware is already optimised to perform block comparisons, and so the string representation should be substantially faster on an existing machine.

3.7.2   Space

Due to its recursive nature, the graph equivalence algorithm uses more space during execution than string equivalence. This temporary space however is not expected to be a significant cost in a persistent system, especially compared with the permanent space required for the type representations.

The overall space occupied by a single representation is significantly greater for graphs than strings. This is because each node in a graph carries the overhead associated with a persistent object, whereas a string may be implemented as a single object. Also, references to other nodes are persistent identifiers, which may be large depending upon the implementation of the persistent store. As the amount of information contained within any single node is relatively small, these overheads will be the major space cost of a graph representation.

The strings however require contiguous space, whilst the graphs do not. There are advantages on both sides of this. For large types, comparing strings may cause a large amount of volatile memory to be used up at one time, whereas the graph nodes may be fetched from non-volatile store in pairs if necessary to use only a small amount of space. On the other hand, fetching the graph requires a large number of object faults, whereas only one is required for a string. The importance of these considerations depends upon the implementation of the persistent store.

As already stated however dynamic checking may be worthy of customised implementation, and it would be expected that both string and graph type representations would be adjusted to have similar characteristics using clustering, compression and fragmentation techniques as appropriate.

3.7.3   Sharing

So that the block comparison may be made over strings, all of the references to other types are converted so that they may be interpreted only within the context of the string. This means, unlike the graph representation, that sharing of common component type representations is not possible. This has serious implications for both time and space complexity.

For example, a program may require two values of related types from the store. This is common in persistent programming, where one procedure may generate an object of a complex type and others may use it in different ways:

```
type aType is ....

let generator = proc( -> aType ) ; ...
let user1 = proc( aType -> int ) ; ...
let user2 = proc( aType -> bool ) ; ...
```

Using graph representations, the type representations of these three procedures may use the representation already constructed for *aType*, and so only a few extra graph nodes are required to represent the more complex types. Using strings, however, complete new strings must be constructed for each procedure type, which duplicate all of the information already in the string constructed for *aType*, as the context-sensitive references may be different. This is because strings are a truly anonymous representation, whereas graphs contain implicit naming information in their store addresses. The difference in space may be significant for programs which use a complex type in many different ways.

Another aspect of sharing components is that any memoisation performed over these components then carries over all types which use them. In the above example, it would be common practice for one program to define the three procedures and place them within the store and for another to subsequently access them. In this case, the memoisation performed by the graph equivalence algorithm will mean that the structural equivalence check is only performed once on the type *aType*, whereas the full structural check is required for each different procedure if a string representation were used. Again, this is a substantial saving for a large class of programs.

3.8   Measurements

To give an idea of the expected performance of these algorithms, we include some measurements taken from the Napier88 system. We have made measurements to indicate space overhead, performance, and complexity of the different schemes.

All measurements were made with the type of a Napier88 abstract syntax tree. This is an extended and revised version of PAIL [Dea87], and is a large, mutually recursive type, consisting of around one hundred and forty definitions.

The measurements of performance are hard to quantify, as they are highly dependent upon the implementation of the Napier88 system within which they were made. Suffice it to say that the best figures we have achieved for checking independently prepared versions of this type are at the rate of several per second for a graph representation, with a substantial speedup to several hundred per second for a string representation.

The complexity measurements confirm the deduction that complexity at least as good as linear may be achieved for checking graph representations, with a suitable size of hash table. It is a reasonable assumption that a large enough table may be employed, as this is a fixed overhead per system. As explained, the table may be re-initialised if it becomes too large. In the case where the table may be large enough to contain all types used within the system, then the resulting memoisation achieves the same efficiency as name equivalence checking.

3.8.1   Space

The graph representation of the Napier88 PAIL type consists of 413 objects, with an average of just under nine words per object. The total size of this graph is 14,466 bytes. The string form of the graph is 2,206 bytes long.

These figures are all taken from relatively naïve representations; we have made no serious effort to compress the representations.

The benefits of space saving by sharing are hard to quantify, as they depend very much upon the manner in which the types are used. However, in our use of the abstract syntax tree type in building a Napier88 compiler, we found that the type is used in 276 different contexts. Each context requires a different string for its representation, as previously explained, but a graph may be shared by different contexts. Even if the system is fully optimised and only a single representation is used for each type, the total amount of store used to represent this type by strings is therefore more than 600,000 bytes, as oppose to a constant 14,466 bytes for the graph representation. Furthermore, each of these 276 representations requires at least one full structural check, whereas the first check using the graph representation acts as a memo for any other check performed while the system is running.

4   Conclusions

Type systems in persistent programming languages are assuming an increasingly important role, and the traditional database schema is now commonly regarded as a type. This leads to a requirement for the efficient manipulation of types in a persistent system to allow provision of the facilities traditionally found in DBMS for schema editing, use and evolution. We have chosen one aspect of schema manipulation in this paper, that of type equivalence checking, and have described the use of the common methods of name equivalence and structural equivalence.

We have shown that while name equivalence schemes are easier to implement and are more efficient they still have to use structural checks to provide important facilities such as schema merging. On the other hand structural equivalence, generally more flexible and less efficient, can often achieve the same performance as name equivalence.

Given that the efficiency of name equivalence is adequate for our needs, we have concentrated on how to improve the performance of structural equivalence checking. We have described how such checking is performed, and shown that there is a balance between constructing efficient representations of types in terms of store and the speed of the equivalence algorithm in comparing two representations.

We have shown how types may be represented by strings and by graphs, highlighting the difficulties in their construction and use. Some preliminary measurements are presented and our main conclusion is that where the type schema is large and involves the sharing of types, the graph representation will be much more efficient in terms of space. It may however be slower in terms of speed of checking depending on its use within the persistent store.

5   Acknowledgements

We would like to acknowledge funding from the following: SERC grant GRF 02953; Esprit II Basic Research Action 3070 - FIDE; SERC Visiting Fellowship GRF 28571 which allowed John Rosenberg to visit St Andrews for a year, and the UK DTI Object-Oriented Awareness Initiative. We would also like to thank Mike Livesey of St Andrews University for his many constructive criticisms.

6   References

[ACO85]   Albano, A., Cardelli, L. & Orsini, R. "Galileo : A Strongly Typed Conceptual Language". ACM TODS 10,2 (June 1985), pp 230-260.

[ACP89]   Abadi, M., Cardelli, L., Pierce, B.C. & Plotkin, G. "Dynamic Typing in a Statically Typed Language". DEC SRC Report 47, (June 1989).

[ADG89]   Albano, A., Dearle, A., Ghelli, G., Marlin, C., Morrison, R., Orsini, R & Stemple, D. "A Framework for Comparing Type Systems for Database Programming Languages". *Proc 2nd International Workshop on Database Programming Languages*, Oregon (June 1989), pp. 203-212.

[AGO89]   Albano, A., Ghelli, G. & Orsini, R. "Types for Databases: The Galileo Experience". *Proc. 2nd International Workshop on Database Programming Languages*, Oregon, (June 1989), pp 196-206.

[AM85]   Atkinson, M.P. & Morrison, R. "Types, bindings and parameters in a persistent environment". *Proc. 1st Appin Workshop on Data Types and Persistence*, Universities of Glasgow and St Andrews, PPRR-16, (August 1985),1-25. In **Data Types and Persistence** (Eds Atkinson, Buneman & Morrison) Springer-Verlag. (1988), 3-20.

[Atk89]   Atkinson, M.P. e-mail barrage on O-O classes and deletion. (1989-90).

[BBB88]   Bancilhon F., Barbedette G., Benzaken V., Delobel C., Gamerman S., Lecluse C., Pfeffer P., Richard P. & Valez F. "The Design and Implementation of O_2, an Object Oriented Database System". Proc. 2nd International Workshop on Object-Oriented Database Systems, West Germany. In **Lecture Notes in Computer Science 334**. Springer-Verlag (1988), pp. 1-22.

[CAA87]   Cooper, R.L., Atkinson, M.P., Adberrahmane, D. & Dearle, A. "Constructing Database Systems in a Persistent Environment". 13th VLDB, Brighton, UK, (September 1987), pp 117-126.

[Car84]   Cardelli L. "A Semantics of Multiple Inheritance", *In Semantics of Data Types*, **Lecture Notes in Computer Science 173**. Springer-Verlag (1984) pp 51-67.

[Car85]   Cardelli, L. *Amber*. Tech. Report AT7T. Bell Labs. Murray Hill, U.S.A. (1985).

[Car88]   Cardelli, L. "Typeful Programming". *1st European Conference on Extending Database Technology*. In **Lecture Notes in Computer Science 303**. Springer-Verlag (1988).

[CDM90]   Connor, R.C.H., Dearle, A., Morrison, R. & Brown, A.L. "Existentially Quantified Types as a Database Viewing Mechanism". *Advances in Database Technology - EDBT90*, Venice. In **Lecture Notes in Computer Science 416**. Springer-Verlag (1990), pp. 301-315.

[Con88]   Connor, R.C.H. "The Napier Type Checking Module". Universities of St Andrews and Glasgow. PPRR-58-88 (1988).

[CW85]   Cardelli, L. & Wegner, P. "On Understanding Types, Data Abstraction and Polymorphism". ACM Computing Surveys 17,4 (December 1985), pp 471-523.

[Dea87]   Dearle, A. "A Persistent Architecture Intermediate Language". PPRR-37-87, University of St. Andrews. (1987).

[DB88]   Dearle A. & Brown A.L. "Safe Browsing in a Strongly Typed Persistent Environment". The Computer Journal 31,6, (December 1988), pp. 540-545.

[DCK89]   Dearle, A., Cutts, Q.I. & Kirby, G. "Browsing, Grazing and Nibbling Persistent Data Structures". *3rd International Conference on Persistent Object Systems*, Newcastle, Australia (1989), pp 96-112.

[Ich83]   Ichbiah et al., The Programming Language Ada Reference Manual. ANSI/MIL-STD-1815A-1983. (1983).

[MBC88]   Morrison, R., Brown, A.L., Connor, R.C.H. & Dearle, A. "Napier88 Reference Manual". Persistent Programming Research Report PPRR-77-89, University of St Andrews. (1989).

[MP85]   Mitchell J.C. & Plotkin G.D. "Abstract Types have Existential type". ACM TOPLAS 10,3 (July 1988), pp 470-502.

[Rec90]   **type** AnyArray[t] **is variant**(simple : t ; complex : AnyArray[**array**[t]])

[SFS90]   Stemple, D., Fegaras, L., Sheard, T. & Socorro, A. "Exceeding the Limits of Polymorphism in Database Programming Languages". *Advances in Database Technology - EDBT90*, Venice. In **Lecture Notes in Computer Science 416**. Springer-Verlag (1990), pp. 269-285.

[SS89]   Sheard, T. & Stemple, D. "Automatic Verification of Database Transaction Safety". ACM Transactions on Database Systems 12, 3 (September, 1989), pp. 322-368.

[SWB89]   Schmidt, J.W., Wetzel, I., Borgida, A. & Mylopoulos, J. "Database Programming by Formal Refinement of Conceptual Design". IEEE - Data Engineering, (September 1989).

[SZ86]   Skarra A. & Zdonik S.B. "An Object Server for an Object-Oriented Database System", *Proc. International Workshop on Object-Oriented Database Systems*, Pacific Grove California (September 1986) pp 196-204.

Part V

System Implementation II

Chair: J. W. Schmidt

It comes as no surprise that initial answers to crucial questions in object store implementation are revised as soon as experiences with first system versions are evaluated. Take, for example, the contribution of Velez et al in the System Implementation I session where major changes in the second version of the O_2 object manager and its implementation technology are reported.

In this sense there is strong commonality between the three contributions of this subsequent System Implementation section. The work reported herein is motivated by the experience within long-term projects that provide the opportunity for an iterative design and implementation effort. These results are considered of particular importance since they contribute to the maturing of object store implementation technology.

The work of Harrison and Powell aims at extending object store technology into distributed environments that evolve over time. The authors suggest a partitioning of the object space into (nested) object scopes. These logical units of addressing, reconfiguration and transmission are mapped onto physical containers attached to network nodes. The paper investigates addressing, transmission and recovery aspects of such a modular persistent store.

There seems to be general agreement that persistence models which are based on the notion of reachability are of particular interest. Object stores based on such models make heavy use of garbage collection to achieve storage reclamation and reorganization. The paper by Kolodner is based on experience gained through the Argus and Mercury projects at MIT and presents a garbage collection mechanism that is tailored to the demands of large, stable and concurrently accessed heaps as found in persistent object stores. The main focus of the work is on the interaction between garbage collection and transaction management. An important property of the proposed algorithm is that it carries out garbage collection "on the fly" thus avoiding long delays at collect time, transaction commit points or during system recovery activities - a prerequisite for interactive applications.

Taken for granted that object stores have to make use of intrinsically expensive garbage collection techniques, there seems to be a general consensus that these costs can–and should–be diminished by backpacking other complex activities on the collection process. Examples of such activities are data clustering, address translation, data transmission in distributed environments or support for integrated approaches to concurrency and version management.

The third contribution, by Brown and Rosenberg, reports on experiences from the Napier88 project and presents a layered architecture for language-independent object stores. The central idea behind their design is to separate persistence and stability issues from object addressing, manipulation and garbage collection as well as object management from particular language characteristics. Brown and Rosenberg demonstrate how this three-level structure can be utilized for three substantially different languages with only minor modifications to the language interface layer. The paper furthermore sketches several language independent techniques to improve the overall performance of their store.

The Napier88 uniform storage model raises, of course, the question to what extent the central operation of storage stabilization is scalable. This issue refers back to the proposal of Harrison and Powell for storage modularization and extension. Another point of discussion is the tradeoff between the gain of language independence by utilizing object stores through abstract machines and the loss of efficiency by not compiling directly into object store primitives.

In summary, the contributions of this section demonstrate that there is, based on a commonly agreed upon kernel functionality of object stores, a lively discussion on functionality extensions and their architectural implications. However, there is also a strong feeling that the community of implementors should develop a common framework for the description and evaluation of their object stores to diminish work duplication and to encourage software exchange and system experimentation.

A Modular Persistent Store

Chris Harrison
&
Malcolm Powell

Department of Computation
University of Manchester Institute of Science & Technology
P.O. Box 88
Manchester M60 1QD
United Kingdom

Abstract

The store described in this paper has been developed in an attempt to address some of the areas in which persistent stores do not perform well for existing applications when compared with the use of conventional file stores. Particular concerns have been the replication of large composite objects, and the ability to construct two or more persistent stores, as a set of totally independent modules, which can subsequently be merged into a single distributed store with minimal reconfiguration of the stored data. It must also be possible to cope with the removal of a module from a composite store, if only because such removal may be the result of a catastrophic failure.

1 Introduction

The following sections introduce two of the fundamental problems which were addressed in the design of the persistent object store described later in the paper. Firstly, there is the problem of providing an efficient means of replicating/transmitting large amounts of information represented by large numbers of small objects. Persistent stores encourage the use of dynamic, often recursive, data structures where linear, contiguously allocated structures are found in more conventional systems, e.g. trees instead of arrays. There are performance problems associated with the replication of complex structured objects and for their transmission over sequential communications systems. These problems are less severe for contiguously allocated structures which may be replicated and transmitted bit-by-bit. Secondly, there is the problem of object addressing in an environment where it is unrealistic to place any upper bound on the number of objects which may need to be addressed. This is the situation which exists if independent object stores are continually created in parallel and incrementally merged together to form larger more complex stores. This will be the commercial situation if persistent stores come into wide spread use in conjunction with individual workstations.

The store architecture presented here is intended to represent the bottom layer of a persistent system architecture. It does not proscribe garbage collection or transaction strategies, programming language structures or the organisation of type domains. However, some bias towards particular ways in which the store might be used has crept in as a result of experience with previous systems, e.g. the Abstract Data Store[10] and the Paradox Environment[11].

1.1 Object Replication and Transmission

The limitations of conventional systems in which two levels of storage, i.e. persistent secondary memory and volatile primary memory, are visible to the programmer, have made the use of contiguously allocated linear data structures, e.g. arrays and files, common place for the storage of bulk information. Such structures have the advantage that they can be replicated or transmitted without a detailed knowledge of their type, i.e. it is only necessary to know how many bits are required for their representation. The generic storage capability of conventional file stores also stems from this fact, i.e. the designer of a file store does not need to know the types of all of the data structures which will ever be stored in it, he only needs to worry about storing sequences of bits.

In a persistent programming environment, the same pressure to use data structures which have convenient contiguous representations does not exist. It is possible to organise persistent data structures which contain object references, and thus use recursive data structures which provide more convenient access to stored information than do the contiguously allocated alternatives. Thus, B-trees become a better choice for many purposes than storing the same information in an array and using a binary search algorithm to access the elements. At a slightly higher level, it will often be more convenient to store the parse tree representation of a program rather than the linear string of characters which represent its source text. The source text can usually be recomputed from the parse tree by unparsing far more quickly than the parse tree can be computed from the text by parsing, and if required the tree can be folded into a graph which reflects the logical identity of the objects it defines.

The penalty to be paid for all this flexibility is that efficient bit-by-bit replication and transmission become much more difficult, and can only be accomplished if a fairly detailed specification of the type of the object to be replicated or transmitted is available. Whereas many programming languages allow the direct replication of objects of any static type, e.g. the assignment of one array to another in Pascal, the replication of recursive data structures usually needs to be defined by the programmer. In a Pascal implementation, a single generic operation can be provided to perform a bit-by-bit assignment operation, as the number of bits to be copied can be determined for any static type. An equivalent operation for recursive data structures must at least be provided with details of the sizes of all the objects involved and the offsets of object references within them, i.e. it must dynamically interpret information associated with the type of each object to be replicated. In the case where graph structures are to be replicated or transmitted, there is the additional problem of avoiding deadlock in the presence of cycles. The Abstract Data Store[10] provides such an operation, but it cannot be made nearly as efficient as bit-by-bit replication, in terms of the total number of bits copied.

1.2 Object Addressing

Many of the persistent object store architectures which have been proposed are organised around a single mapping between object identifiers and object content[3, 4]. A principle design decision in such stores involves the number of available object identifiers. This usually results in a specific decision being made as to the number of bits to be used to represent an object identifier. In a realistic store, this number will depend on the designer's conception of the largest number of objects required by all of the users of the store throughout its expected lifetime. If object identifiers are not reissued when objects are disposed of, the number of bits required to represent an object identifier can be defined in terms of the peak rate of object creation and the expected lifetime of the store[4].

If a store is designed as an object which will inhabit a single locality, e.g. like a disk store in a workstation, it will be relatively easy to decide on the number of available object identifiers required by predicting the uses to which the workstation will be put. An obvious problem with this approach, is that it leads to a world which contains a number of isolated persistent stores with users who will undoubtedly want to move information between them. This implies that there must be some means of moving objects between stores whilst maintaining their integrity. It also implies that objects cannot be accessed remotely without duplicating them in more than one store, i.e. objects must be copied across disjoint address spaces. This causes problems where there are good reasons for not duplicating objects, e.g. where object identity is used as the basis for strong typing and type conformance.

Another approach to this problem is to provide sufficient object identifiers to allow a network address to be incorporated into each one [4], i.e. the locality of an object is encoded into each object identifier. This approach was also employed in slightly simpler form in the Abstract Data Store[7]. Objects can then be accessed across a network of localities without duplication. However, it becomes much more difficult to decide on the required number of object identifiers as the number of localities and the number of uses to which they may be put becomes more difficult to access.

Buhr and Zarnke[2] describe a structured addressing scheme in which memories are organised into a hierarchy. Access to objects stored in the memory hierarchy is accomplished via the use of structured object identifiers, which are the analogue of qualified names in programming languages, e.g. x.y.z. Thus, if two such memory hierarchies are to be merged into one composite memory, one possibility is to create a new "root" and prefix its identity to all existing object identifiers, i.e. object identifiers are of variable size with no fixed upper bound to the number of bits required to represent them. This may represent a significant efficiency problem. Gehringer[6] also describes a hierarchical addressing scheme based on the use of textually represented structured names similar to file store path names.

1.3 A Modular Store

The modular store described in the following sections uses a hierarchical addressing scheme with object identifiers built up out of fixed length segments. Each segment provides access to a set of objects at a particular level in the hierarchy, and each level in the hierarchy has the status of a scope which maintains its own mappings between object identifiers and objects. A number of different ways of mapping object identifiers onto objects are provided including a simple ordinal mapping which corresponds to field indexing, and a sparse mapping which corresponds to the kind of addressing scheme found in single level object stores. Each scope has the status of an object, and may be replicated or transmitted on a bit-by-bit basis without inspecting its detailed internal structure.

2   The Overall Structure of the Store

Each module in the store is associated with a container which can store a finite number of bits. A container may consist of one or more partitions on a physical storage device, or one or more physical storage devices. Where a number of exchangeable storage elements are associated with one or more devices, each element represents a unique container or set of containers, and exchanging elements represents reconfiguration of the store. The organisation of the bits in a container is subject to exactly the same rules as the organisation of the bits which represent any object stored in a container. The following sections describe the organisation of some of the kinds of objects which the store supports.

2.1 Uncommitted Objects

An uncommitted object is the simplest form of object found in the system. It consists of a fixed number of fields represented by a contiguous set of bits preceded by a header which indicates its kind, i.e. an uncommitted object, and the total number of bits needed to represent it. Each field consists of a fixed number of bits, e.g. a whole number of bytes or words. The only operation which the store provides for uncommitted objects is field selection via the presentation of a valid field index. Fields may be read and updated.

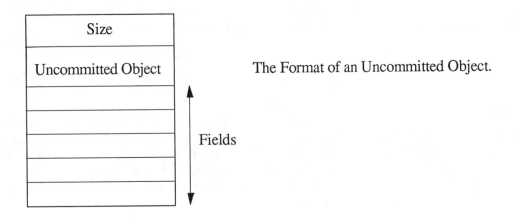

The Format of an Uncommitted Object.

2.2 Sparse Scope Objects

A sparse scope object consists of a header which indicates its kind, i.e. a sparse scope, and the total number of bits needed to represent it. Following the header is a catalogue which maps the identifiers of objects contained in the scope into their offsets within the memory which follows the catalogue.

Size
Sparse Scope Object
Catalogue
Memory

The Format of a Sparse Scope Object.

The catalogue component of a spare scope contains all the information needed to generate new identifiers for objects within the scope and to associatively map such identifiers into the offsets of the objects in the memory component. In addition to providing storage for a set of objects, the memory component contains sufficient information to keep track of the free space available for the storage of new objects. The current implementation of the store uses a bit map representation of the free space in conjunction with a minimum allocation block size which is chosen so that the size of the free space map can be kept below a threshold value. An important aspect of this free space organisation is that all the free space information can be loaded rapidly into the transient memory of a workstation independently of the rest of the scope object. This implies that a minimum size can be defined for the transient memory in all workstations which are to access the store. It also implies that the minimum allocation size increases with the size of the memory component of a scope. However, if the hierarchical organisation of the store is used as intended, the average size of objects will also increase with the size of the memory in which they are allocated, and the percentage of space wasted in any container by rounding up object sizes to be a multiple of the allocation block size will remain small. It is worth noting that this technique is used in a number of file store implementations[1].

New space is allocated and disposed in the map using a next fit algorithm[9] which has been modified so as to achieve near constant average time complexity across stack, queue and heap allocation patterns. The current implementation of the store does not proscribe garbage collection strategies, and so the set of operations applicable to a sparse scope object include allocation of a new object of some kind and size along with the generation of a new object identifier and its insertion in the catalogue, the disposal of an existing object given its identifier, and the dereferencing of an object identifier to provide access to the representation of the associated object.

Object identifiers are currently 64 bits long and are not reused when an object is disposed of. This will allow objects to be created at an average rate of 1 million per second for a period of just over 0.5 million years, provided that the difference between the size of the objects created and the size of the objects disposed of never exceeds the size of the scope in which they are stored during this period. There may be some benefit in concatenating a random number, say 32 bits, to each identifier for security purposes[4] to form a 96 bit address. Alternatively, a 16 bit random number might be incorporated in the existing 64 bits. However, this latter approach reduces the useful lifetime of a scope to only 8 years at an average object creation rate of 1 million objects per second. Although this may well be longer than the lifetime of a workstation in our current throwaway society, it might not be sufficient to provide a personal database for one human lifetime and would undoubtedly be insufficient to support a continuously updated administrative database for a large city over any reasonable length of time.

The object identifier made up entirely of zero bits is never stored in a catalogue and is used to represent a **nil** reference. Dereferencing an object identifier which does not exist in the scope's catalogue causes a reference failure. If all nonexistent object identifiers are regarded as being equivalent to **nil**, then the dangling reference problem disappears, i.e. an attempt to dereference an object identifier associated with an object which has been disposed of will result in a reference failure rather than the selection of an unpredictable object value. This provides facilities similar to those associated with the Abstract Data Store's **shared** type constructor[10], but for all objects irrespective of the organisation of any type domain implemented within the store. The potential disadvantage of this scheme is that the **is nil** operation, which is used for testing for **nil** object identifiers, must be as efficient as possible for all object identifiers. Deliberately slowing the operation down for **nil** identifiers other than the "official zero" identifier, as might be required to defeat systematic probing of a scope in an attempt to break any security measures, would reduce the overall efficiency of the entire store. More experience is required in using this facility of the store architecture to allow the potential tradeoff between security and flexibility to be accessed and to consider alternative ways of achieving the same ends.

2.3 Constructing and Accessing Objects Within a Scope

Although the store supports more than two kinds of object, the normal organisation of information within a single store module can be described in terms of the two kinds of object discussed so far, i.e. uncommitted objects and sparse scope objects. The following description assumes that the available hardware technology provides high capacity persistent storage and low capacity volatile storage at a reasonable cost, such that the access time for a small number of bits of volatile storage is very much shorter than for the same number of bits of persistent storage. Given high capacity, high speed persistent storage at a reasonable cost, the implementation described here would be simplified, but the overall organisation of the store, and in particular the format of the objects stored in it, would not change significantly. The principle reason for this is that in a general distributed implementation of the store there is no way of guaranteeing that a container will be local to every workstation which needs to access it. It will often be necessary to access a container via a communications link with a finite transmission rate. Some local buffering will therefore be necessary whether low cost, high speed, high capacity, persistent memory is available or not.

The normal use of a container will be such that all of its available bits will be used to store a single scope object. In its initial state, this scope object will have an empty catalogue, and all of its memory space will be available for the creation of new objects nested within the scope. The intention is that such a scope should provide the capabilities of a persistent heap which allows objects and their identifiers to be created, objects to be dereferenced so that their fields can be read and updated, and objects which are no longer required to be disposed of so that the memory space they occupy can be reused. All this is possible if the only objects created within the scope stored by a container are uncommitted objects whose fields may be used to represent any kind of information, e.g. procedures, stacks, types, strings, numbers, and object identifiers. The store can provide two different implementations of these facilities, and the implementation used can be selected dynamically to suit the needs of the user. Both implementations involve persistent storage to implement the container, and a volatile memory used as a rapid access cache into which objects are loaded to permit their fields to be accessed.

There are two principle ways in which access can be obtained to an object stored in a scope in conjunction with the use of a cache memory. At one extreme, the entire scope object can be loaded into the cache, and at the other extreme only the object itself is loaded. The principle advantage of loading the entire scope is that, after the initial overhead of moving all of the bits in the scope into the cache, the performance of subsequent operations on the scope will be similar to that of a conventional heap in fast access local memory. The only additional overhead is the indirection inherent in the use of the catalogue to map object identifiers into memory offsets, and this is clearly an area which is amenable to hardware support. A second advantage is that it is possible to commit or abort a set of operations on objects in a scope simply by writing a modified scope back to the container or by deliberately not doing so. Two disadvantages of loading the whole scope are that large scopes require large amounts of cache memory, and that commit and abort operations are more difficult to organise for individual objects within the scope. The latter point is addressed in a later section of this paper.

As scopes are self contained, they can be replicated and transmitted bit-by-bit without a detailed knowledge of their internal organisation. A scope object may therefore be used to store the individual components of a single complex data structure associated with a particular application, in much the same way that a file might be used to store a document associated with a particular application in a more conventional system. A common way of using such a file is to copy all of the bits it contains into primary memory, update them, and then either decide to abandon the changes or to commit them by copying them back into the file store. A scope object may be used in a very similar way, but allows full use of complex recursive data structures to represent the information required by the application. In both cases, the full speed of bit-by-bit transfers between backing store and primary memory can be exploited.

The alternative implementation, which involves loading individual objects into the cache, is slightly more complex than in the former case. The access speed of the container will usually make it imperative to load the catalogue of the parent scope into the cache, and if new objects are to be created or disposed of it will be necessary to place the free space map for the scope's memory into the cache as well (as was pointed out previously, the free space map is represented by a contiguous set of bits with a fixed maximum size). In addition, it will be necessary to maintain information to allow individual objects to be located in the cache and to distinguish objects loaded into the cache from those that are not. It should however be pointed out that this is simply a generalisation of the mechanism required previously to allow a single scope object to be located in the cache. It should also be pointed out that the simple implementation of commit and abort operations exists for independently loaded objects in the same way that it does for independently loaded scopes. This is simply a consequence of scopes being objects.

There are a number of ways in which the decision to load a whole scope, or only individual objects from it, can be made. At one extreme, the decision can be left to the programmer, and at the other extreme, the decision can be made totally automatically. The latter course would appear to be more in keeping with the spirit of persistence as it keeps the two levels of the store completely hidden from the programmer. However, it leaves little room for making the engineering compromises which are necessary in almost all useful systems. A compromise position is to employ an automatic mechanism which makes use of parameters which may be controlled by the programmer. The current implementation of the store achieves this by allowing the size of the largest object to be loaded into the cache to be specified. This size will usually depend statically on the overall size of the cache, but can be varied dynamically. An example of the way in which this works will be given after the organisation of scope hierarchies has been described in the next section.

2.4 Scope Hierarchies

The description of the store given so far has assumed that a single scope object is stored in a container, and that it only contains uncommitted objects. However, as scopes are objects, it is just as easy to create scope objects within a scope as it is to create any other kind of object. This implies that, as object identifiers only have significance within a single scope, it is necessary to provide some way of selecting which scope objects are to be accessed for any particular activity. The store therefore provides an **enter** scope operation which, given a valid identifier for a scope object in the current scope, will make it the current scope. A corresponding **leave** operation restores the previously selected scope, i.e. access to the scope hierarchy is stack ordered. The advantage of this organisation is that object identifiers can be of a fixed size, i.e. structured identifiers of arbitrary size do not have to be formed by the concatenation of identifiers, which are valid in individual scopes, every time it is necessary to access objects stored in the hierarchy. Paths in the hierarchy are always specified incrementally. The disadvantage of this mechanism by itself is that it does not allow objects in any scope other than the current one to be accessed without leaving the current scope and "entering" the scope containing the required object(s). There is therefore a danger that, for many applications, the concatenation of object identifiers might simply be replaced by frequent sequences of **enter** operations containing object identifiers.

In order to overcome this problem, two kinds of object identifiers are recognised by the catalogue operations. These are "local" and "global" identifiers. When a local identifier is dereferenced, the catalogue provides the memory offset of the associated local object in the current scope. When a global identifier is dereferenced, the catalogue provides a further object identifier which is then dereferenced in the enclosing scope in order to provide access to the associated global object. This sequence of dereferences may be repeated an arbitrary number of times, as each stage may generate a global identifier for an object which is global to the enclosing scope. The process is similar to that of following a static link in the implementation of a block structured programming language[12]. New global objects are created by a **new global** operation which takes an existing object identifier, valid in the enclosing scope, and generates a new global identifier to associate with it in the catalogue of the current scope. Thus, an activity which elects to use a particular scope can dereference object identifiers without needing to know which ones are local and which ones are global, and without knowing the identifiers of the scopes which contain the global objects once the global links have been established. If required, global references can be used to build graph structures in the scope hierarchy. A **reset global** operation allows global bindings to be updated.

2.5 An Example

Suppose that a workstation makes available a 4M byte cache and is connected to a 400M byte container. The container stores a scope object that occupies the entire 400M bytes. The system is configured so that the largest object which will be loaded into the cache will occupy 1M byte. When the first access is made to the scope object stored in the container, the system loads just that part of the scope which includes its catalogue and the free space information for its memory. This sequence of operations would occur as the result of applying the **enter** operation to the scope stored in the container. We will assume that the objects stored in this scope represent the top level of the hierarchy of objects available to the user of the workstation, and that one of them represents a "directory" object which contains references to all of the others (this should not be confused with the scope's catalogue). It is likely that this directory object is not very big, i.e. much smaller than the 1M byte loading limit, and therefore an attempt to access it (dereference its identifier) will result in the whole object being loaded into the cache.

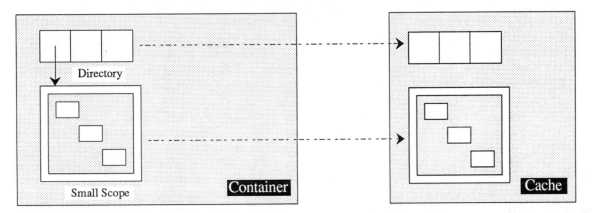

Now suppose that the user causes the **enter** operation to be applied to one of the object identifiers stored in the directory, and that the associated object is a scope object with a total size of less than 1M byte. This will cause the entire scope to be loaded into the cache and all subsequent accesses to objects contained in it will be made without further loading from the container. This situation is illustrated above. One of the important things about this is that, if the user is using a workstation with a smaller cache, and consequently a smaller loading limit, it will still be possible to access the contents of the second scope object provided that none of the objects are monolithic uncommitted objects larger than the loading limit. The individual objects will simply be loaded into the cache one at a time, as illustrated below. Thus, the granularity of object loading may change dynamically from one workstation to another or from one session to another according to the available cache size. As with most conventional systems, the user with the larger cache will get better overall performance, but risks having to recompute more information in the event of a failure which prevents updated objects in the cache from being written back into the container.

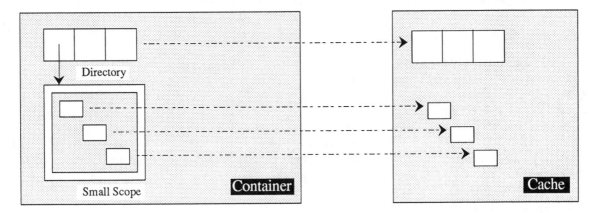

Adjustment of the maximum size of an object to be loaded into the cache can be used to control the tradeoff between access speed and cache size, and access speed and transaction granularity using the simple commit and abort scheme described earlier. A wide range of workstations can load information stored in a single container in a wide range of different sized units. One problem with this is that the use of a small cache and a small loading limit implies the use of a small transaction granularity. However, this problem can be overcome, by a layer implemented on top of the store, by using a shadow object paging technique in conjunction with each scope which is larger than the loading limit, but which must have atomic operations performed on sets of objects contained in it.

2.6 Other Scope Operations

It is possible to store an object identifier which is valid in one scope, in another scope, e.g. its immediate parent. An object identifier used in this way represents a capability for accessing information within the scope it is associated with. However, if this is the only way that access can be obtained to the objects within a scope, then this implies that there must be an extra level of persistent storage, outside of all scopes, which stores the initial access point(s) to the scope hierarchy. In order to avoid this necessity a second special object identifier, in addition to **nil** is provided. This is currently represented by an identifier in which all of the bits are ones. It is referred to as the "public identifier", and a **new public** operation allows an object to be associated it. The dereferencing and disposal operations work with it in the normal way. If no object is associated with the public identifier in a particular scope it has the same status as **nil**. It is the only identifier which is ever reused in a scope, and provides the initial entry point to a scope. It will often be associated with some kind of directory object, as in the previous example, which provides access to other objects within a scope.

One of the design objectives behind the store was to provide a number of ways of representing common structures so that there is some choice to enable engineering compromises to be made to suit particular applications. The ability of the store to load objects with a dynamically adjustable granularity is one result of this which has already been described. Another result of the same thinking is the existence of more than one kind of scope object. The sparse scope objects which have been describe so far are the most general objects supported directly by the store in that they provided a means of grouping together variable sized objects into a dynamic set of arbitrary, but finite, cardinality such that all of the objects which exist in the set during its lifetime can be given unique names. However, this kind of generality is not required for all applications, and represents an overhead if it must be used when it is not required.

"Indexed Scope" objects are provided for those applications which require arbitrary sets of variable sized objects, but do not require each one to be given a unique name during the lifetime of the set. The object identifiers which are used in such a scope are simply natural numbers with zero representing **nil**. When applied to an indexed scope, the **new** operation simply associates an object with an unused index. The dereferencing and disposal operations work in the same way as they do for sparse scopes. Indexed scopes have much simpler catalogues than sparse scopes, and do not need to employ associative searching strategies. Simple indexing suffices to convert an object identifier into an offset in the memory component of the scope. Clearly the dangling reference problem still exists in indexed scopes. Uncommitted objects represent a further simplification of object structure, i.e. at any point in its lifetime an uncommitted object represents a fixed sized set of fixed sized objects, identified directly by their offsets within the object. Thus, an uncommitted object has no catalogue and no free space map. It is the degenerate form of a memory. In effect, the store supports a hierarchy of basic object kinds and provides a uniform interface to them all.

Both sparse scopes and indexed scopes can be used to represent the same information with different degrees of flexibility and security. Any object which is represented by a complex recursive data structure should be created using a sparse scope. However, at some point in its lifetime the number of changes which are made to the object, compared to the number of times that the information it contains is read, may reduce to a low level. The object may even become "finished" and never be changed again. At this point an indexed scope would provide a more efficient static representation for the object. A layer implemented on top of the basic store, which imposes additional structure on objects, perhaps as part of the implementation of a programming language or type domain, might provide an operation called **freeze**, to allow a sparse scope to be converted into an equivalent indexed scope, and an operation called **thaw** to perform the inverse operation. Such operations would need to be able to find any object identifiers stored in the fields of uncommitted objects.

Two operations which apply to sparse scopes, indexed scopes and uncommitted objects are **shrink** and **expand**. **Shrink** reduces the size of the memory associated with an object so that either, all unallocated space is removed, or the memory is reduced to a specified size, whichever happens first. **Expand** increases the size of the memory to a specified size, or leaves it as it is if it is already larger than the specified size. For a scope with a memory of size **n**, the sequence **shrink 0; expand n** compacts all of the free space towards the end of the memory. When applied to uncommitted objects, these operations simply change their overall size. Both operations are supported by the current implementation of the memory and do not need to be able to identify object identifiers stored in uncommitted objects.

3   Configuring a Distributed Store

There is only one kind of node in a distributed system based on the store architecture described here. Each node consists of a store access controller and a set of containers which it administers. The controller may be implemented in software on a conventional workstation (as in the prototype) or might be an independent unit with or without a conventional processor attached to it. Containers are attached to the controller by "channels" along which objects are moved between the containers and the cache. Channels may be implemented by a range of suitable communication mechanisms from SCSI buses for geographically local containers, to ethernet links to remote containers belonging to other controllers. Such remote containers will usually be accessed via their parent controller, and many remote channels may be multiplexed onto one physical channel such as an ethernet. It is the organisation of the channels which establishes the structure of the store, and any reconfiguration of the channels will usually require actions to be taken by the software systems resident in it so that they may continue to function. In this respect, physical reconfiguration of the store is no different to unplugging or relocating memory chips in the store of an individual workstation.

3.1 Joining Two Existing Stores

The controller associated with each workstation provides its users with a sparse scope containing a directory object which contains references to the containers connected to the controller by both local and remote channels. This scope is called a "root scope" and will usually be unique to all of the workstations connected to the store. Each container will appear to exist as an object stored within this scope. This appearance is a result of the physical configuration of the store rather than of any information stored in it in the normal way. It can only be changed by reconfiguration of the store. Entries appear in the scope created by the controller in response to channels being connected to it. This is similar to the way that a conventional workstation might scan its SCSI channels and mount any disk volumes that it finds as part of its file store. The directory object will usually be associated with the root scope's public identifier.

Suppose user A has a controller and one container connected to his workstation, and that user B has a similar arrangement. The root scopes of the two users will initially appear to each user as illustrated below.

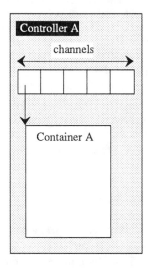 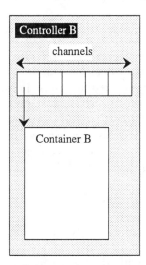

Now suppose that B wishes to refer to objects contained in A's container. With the consent of A (A must provide the connection activity with the object identifier of the container in its root scope), B establishes a physical link between their individual store controllers, and this is configured to provide B's controller with a channel to A's container. A's container will be considered to be local to A's root scope, but global to B's root scope.

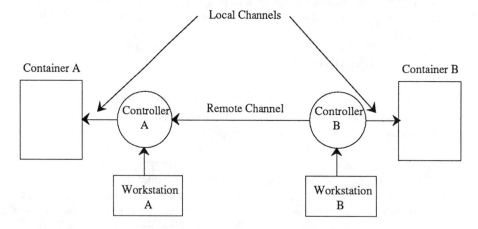

The two root scopes will now appear to their respective users as shown below, i.e. both users share access to container A. At the level described here, the store does not proscribe mutual exclusion or protection mechanisms to control such sharing. Such mechanisms are expected to be defined by layers built on top of this layer of the store.

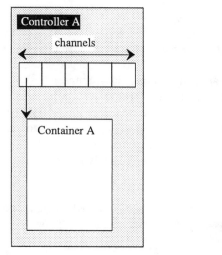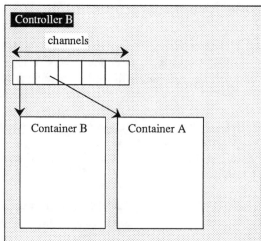

If A had access to more than one container, it could provide B with access to objects in these other containers by using the global reference mechanism described in section 2.4. It is important to remember that a global reference provides access to objects associated with the parent of the scope in which it occurs, i.e. it is the static nesting of scopes, and not the dynamic nesting, which dictates access paths through the store. Thus, in the above example, A could provide B with access to objects in other containers connected to A's controller *even if the containers concerned were not connected to B's controller*. For the same reason, in this example user B cannot create global references in container A which refer to to his own container B, because he does not have access to the scope to which container A is local, i.e. user A's root scope is not accessible to B. Thus, global references are secure and unambiguous, even when two or more users share access to a container.

3.2 A Commercial Information Network Based on a Persistent Store

In a slightly more complex environment that the one described in section 3.1, we might find persistent store users who variously wish to behave as providers of information services, and users of information services. In a commercial world, we will also find agents who wish to make a living by putting users in the former category in touch with users in the latter category. The following example shows how a distributed store may be configured to suit the interactions between these three classes of user. From the agents point of view, all that is required is a workstation, a controller which allows a relatively large number of channels to be connected to it, and a container in which to advertise clients who provide information services. A provider of information services requires a workstation, a controller with a moderate channel capacity, and a container in which to advertise services. A user of information services will require a workstation and a controller, and will probably have their own private container for storing information.

In order to sell a service or services, a provider buys or rents a connection to an agency. This connection is used to implement a channel which gives the agency access to the container in which the client advertises services. Connections might be provided by a packet switching service, high bandwidth telephone lines, or the equivalent of cable TV connections. Potential users also buy or rent connections to agencies to gain access to portfolios of services, which are stored in agent's containers, and contain references to the containers made available by providers.

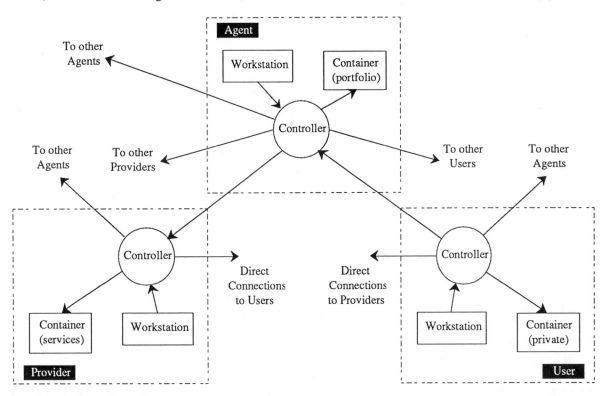

Hierarchies of agents may be constructed if required, and both users and providers may have access to more than one agent. With this arrangement, users can gain access to and communicate with providers. The process is driven by the user, so that neither agents nor providers have direct access to information belonging to the user. The provider's rôle may be passive, i.e. the user browses information stored by the provider, or active, i.e. the provider processes information made available by the by the user. The provider might charge the user for processing activities, and/or for access to stored information. Initial communication will take place via an agent, but once communication has been established, and depending on the flexibility of the underlying network system, a user might buy or rent a direct link to a provider. By doing this, the user avoids any charges levied by the agent for acting as an intermediary. Agents might also prefer this arrangement, as it reduces the required bandwidth of their own controllers through which all communication between users and providers must otherwise pass.

3.3 Channel Failure

If a connection which implements a channel or set of channels is broken, any attempt to access the container to which it provides access will fail. Sometimes the failure will only be detected when the store attempts to use the channel to commit updated objects contained in the cache. The current implementation of the store does not proscribe any means of dealing with this situation, it expects some higher level transaction mechanism to be implemented on top of the basic store. Very often, a failure will be detected when the store attempts to dereference an object which has not been copied into the cache. Under these circumstances all of the identifiers of objects which must be fetched via the broken connection will be equivalent to the **nil** identifier. Thus the physical loss of access to the objects concerned will be directly reflected in the object addressing mechanism. The store provides operations to enable the probable cause of the failure to be identified, and also allows the identity of the inaccessible containers to be established. This information can be used by higher levels of the software running in the store to determine what action should be taken. One possible action is to wait for the connection to be reestablished. A polling action can check for this happening by periodically testing the identifier through which the failure was detected using the **is nil** operation supported by the store. An alternative way of coping with the failure would be to attempt to repair the store by installing substitutes for the inaccessible containers. This might be appropriate if the original containers have been totally destroyed. Means of carrying out such substitutions are discussed in the following sections.

3.4 Object Migration

The global access mechanism allows global identifiers to be rebound by using the **reset global** operation introduced in section 2.4, i.e. the binding between a global identifier and the identifier of an object in the parent of the scope in which it is stored may be updated. This facility may be used in a number of ways. It allows a scope to be treated as an object which provides an interface to its environment containing both access points and dependencies. A directory object, usually associated with its parent scope's public identifier, may provide a segregated list of those object identifiers which are to be directly accessible within the scope, and the global identifiers which must be bound to identifiers in the scope in which it is stored (the **new global** operation will allow a global identifier to be created and bound to **nil** initially). This allows a scope to be cloned, i.e. copied bit-by-bit into another part of the scope hierarchy, and then plugged into its new environment by resetting its global identifiers.

This mechanism also makes it possible to relocate an object, which is global to one or more scopes, and to reset the appropriate global references so as to maintain the integrity of the information contained in the scopes concerned. The effect of this is to separate the issues of object identity and object locality, i.e. objects may be moved around in the scope hierarchy with out effecting their users.

Although it would probably be undesirable to overwork the mechanism which achieves this, there are some circumstances in which it provides great flexibility. A particular example involves the issue of using object identity as the basis for type checking. In one locality, a user may design a programming language or a type system, and store the key objects which define types in a scope that is global to all of the places where instances of objects described by the type system are stored. Within this environment, an object is of type "integer", for example, if and only if its type is described by the single global object which represents the definition of the type "integer". An object identity relation, which returns true if the result of dereferencing two object identifiers gives access to a single object, and false otherwise, may be used to implement such type checking. Notice that this operation is not the same as comparing two object identifiers for equality as they may not be defined in the same scope. The implementation of the object identity relation is described in section 3.6.

Now suppose that another user wishes to make use of objects defined by the same type system, and would like to be able to exchange objects with the originator of the type system via a strongly typed interface. Provided that the scope which contains the objects which define the type system can be relocated to a position in the scope hierarchy where they can be made global to the environments of both users, it will only be necessary to reset the single global reference belonging to the original user. Repeated movement of the type definition objects towards the root of a scope hierarchy makes the single copy of the type definitions available to a progressively larger set of users. It should be noted that the "root" mentioned in this context is not a fixed target, as the hierarchy may grow dynamically as new modules are added to the store. It is also possible to use the same mechanism to join two disjoint hierarchies together so that two independent but structurally identical objects can be replaced by references to a single object, or to split a hierarchy into two components each containing replicas of previously shared objects.

3.5 Object Repair

The facilities described in the last section can also be used to built new objects to replace components of the hierarchy which have been irretrievably lost due to connection failures or container failures. One of the factors which will dictate the difficulty of completing any particular repair will be the extent to which object identifiers have been used to represent capabilities as described in section 2.6. In a scope hierarchy in which all initial entries to scope objects are effected via their public identifiers, there is no requirement to preserve internal object identifiers in scopes which have to be rebuilt as a result of failures. There is a tradeoff in this situation between the requirements of security and ease of repair.

3.6 The Object Identity Relation

The determination of object identity in the store requires that all reference paths, i.e. the sequence of object identifiers required to access a particular object in the scope hierarchy, are "anchored" in uniquely identifiable containers. This is the only reason that containers require unique identities. All of the other operations provided by the store can be implemented with out this. Even with unique container identifiers, there is still the potential problem that it is possible to access a single object via more than one reference path, as the scope hierarchy may be graph structured. Therefore, the direct comparison of reference paths is not a guide to object identity. Fortunately, two or more objects cannot occupy the same physical space in a container, in much the same way that two particles cannot occupy the same place in the physical universe (Pauli's exclusion principle). The combination of the offset of an object within a container and the unique identity of the container represent a unique identity for the object. The offset of an object and the identity of its parent container will always be known by the store as a byproduct of the operations which move objects between containers and the cache. Thus, object identity can be computed with reasonable efficiency without having to compare reference paths.

As has already be stated, the price of implementing this operation is that all containers in a single store must be uniquely identifiable. However, this does not mean that two disjoint stores can never be joined together, as described in sections 3.1 and 3.4, if the sets of container identifiers used in the two stores are *not* disjoint. This is because container identifiers are only used as part of the implementation of the object identity operation, i.e, they are totally inaccessible to normal users of the store. It is therefore possible to change them in one of the stores, so as to avoid conflicts, provided that the updating operation can be made mutually exclusive with the evaluation of any object identity relations in the store concerned. In a store with a single flat address space object identity depends on all objects having unique identifiers. Therefore the problem of joining two stores together may involve changing the identifiers of **all** of the objects in one store which clash with those in the other. The scheme described here reduces the worst case problem to that of changing all of the container identifiers in a particular store. Such a change does not require any changes to the object identifiers stored in the effected containers. However, the problem should never become even this severe. We live in a world in which commercial organisations can ensure that all credit cards have unique numbers. If it becomes commercially important, it should be possible to ensure that the same is true for a sufficiently large set of persistent storage devices. One last point related to this issue is that, in the scheme described here, object identifiers, container identifiers, cache addresses, container offsets and network addresses are all disjoint.

4   Conclusions

It has been suggested[8] that a persistent system will automatically control the movement of data to where it is required and that the programmer is therefore freed from the burden of organising this movement. However, this places a tremendous responsibility on the designer to produce a system which will make acceptable, let alone optimal, decisions about how this should be done under all possible conditions of use, including failure conditions. A compromise position which has been explored in the design of the store described in this paper, is that the system should provide a number of alternative ways of doing the same thing. One of the alternatives will be chosen automatically whether the programmer takes any action or not, i.e. the programmer does not *have* to get involved in the decision making process. However, if after an initial working system has been produced, the programmer wishes to override the automatic mechanism, he can get involved in order to select alternative actions which represent better engineering compromises that the defaults. The selection of an alternative implementation for any operation provided by the store should have minimal impact on the existing structure of the system being constructed.

This paper suggests that the choice of the granularity with which complex structured objects are moved around within the store represents one area in which the programmer might require some control. Choice of locality within a distributed store is another. It is difficult to imagine that a commercial organisation will trust a distributed persistent store to protect confidential information, if there is no control over the geographic locations of the containers in which the information is stored. The need to be able to describe procedures for repairing damaged stores by rebuilding chains of references is another example of an area in which it is unrealistic to expect a totally automatic mechanism to find an acceptable compromise between the needs of efficiency and security for all possible failure modes.

A number of side effects have resulted from pursuing the design objectives described above. These include the mechanism for relocating objects within the store so as to extend the range over which object identity may be defined. It might appear from the frequency with which "containers" have been referred to, that the programmer must be continually aware of the physical organisation of the store. However, for the majority of purposes, containers behave exactly like scope objects, and may even be used to store uncommitted objects if required. In a programming language, scopes might be used to provide the basis for higher level constructs similar to the environments proposed by Dearle[5], i.e. they would not necessarily be directly visible to the programmer. One of the consequences of allowing entire scopes to be loaded down a channel into the cache, is that the average size of the objects moved between the persistent store and the cache is likely to be significantly larger than would be the case in a single level store with a flat address space. This is important, as the extent to which any store has to analyse object structures when they are moved about, as opposed to merely moving sequences of bits from place to place, has a significant effect on its overall performance.

5   Acknowledgments

This work was partially supported by AT&T ISTEL limited. Some related work on a distributed version of the Abstract Data Store was undertaken by ISTEL's John Twigge while at UMIST, and thanks are also due to Dave Blakeman and John Alexander at ISTEL for their suggestions and encouragement, to Bulent Ozcan, for his work on the formal specification of persistent storage mechanisms at UMIST, and to Chris Tan and Alan Florence, also at UMIST, for their related work on the Paradox environment.

6   References

[1].   Apple Computer Inc., The file manager.
        Inside Macintosh, Vol II, Addison-Wesley (1985).
[2].   Buhr, P.A. and Zarnke, C.R., Addressing in a persistent environment.
        Proceedings of the 3rd International Conference on Persistent Object Systems, Newcastle, Australia (January 1989).
[3].   Cockshott, W.P., Atkinson, M.P., Chisholm, K.J., Bailey, P., and Morrison, R.,
        POMS: A persistent object management system.
        Software Practice & Experience, Vol 14, 1 (1984).
[4].   Cockshott, W.P., Design of POMP - Persistent Object Management coProcessor.
        Proceedings of the 3rd International Conference on Persistent Object Systems, Newcastle, Australia (January 1989).
[5].   Dearle, A., Environments: A Flexible binding mechanism to support system evolution.
        Proceedings of the 22nd annual Hawaii International Conference on System Sciences,
        Vol II: Software Track, Ed. Shriver, B.D., Hawaii (January 1989), 46 - 55.
[6].   Gehringer, E.F., Name-based mapping: Addressing support for persistent objects.
        Proceedings of the 3rd International Conference on Persistent Object Systems, Newcastle, Australia (January 1989).
[7].   Hughes, J.W., and Powell, M.S., A strongly typed, distributed virtual memory.
        Proceedings of the SERC Distributed Computing Systems Conference, Ed. Duce, D.A., Peter Peregrinus, (1984).
[8].   Morrison, R., *et al.*, Language design issues in supporting process-oriented computation in persistent environments.
        Proceedings of the 22nd annual Hawaii International Conference on System Sciences,
        Vol II: Software Track, Ed. Shriver, B.D., Hawaii (January 1989), 736 - 744.
[9].   Page, I.P., Analysis of a cyclic placement scheme.
        Computer Journal, Vol 27, 1 (1984), 18 - 26.
[10].   Powell, M.S., Strongly typed user interfaces in an abstract data store.
        Software Practice & Experience, Vol 17, 4 (1987).
[11].   Powell, M.S., A program development environment based on persistence and abstract data types.
        Proceedings of the 3rd International Conference on Persistent Object Systems, Newcastle, Australia (January 1989).
[12].   Tennent, R.D., Principles of programming languages.
        Prentice Hall International Series in Computer Science, Ed. Hoare, C.A.R., Prentice Hall.

Atomic Incremental Garbage Collection and Recovery for a Large Stable Heap

Elliot K. Kolodner
Laboratory for Computer Science
Massachusetts Institute of Technology
Cambridge, MA 02139
kolodner@lcs.mit.edu

Abstract

A *stable heap* is storage that is managed automatically using garbage collection, manipulated using atomic transactions, and accessed using a uniform storage model. Automatic storage management, used in modern programming languages, enhances reliability by preventing errors due to explicit deallocation. Transactions, used in database and distributed systems, provide fault-tolerance by masking failures that occur while they are running. A uniform storage model simplifies programming by eliminating the distinction between accessing temporary storage and permanent storage.

Many applications that could benefit from a stable heap (e.g., computer-aided design, computer-aided software engineering, and office information systems) require large amounts of storage, timely responses for transactions, and high availability. This paper sketches a design for an integrated garbage collector and recovery system that meets these goals and is appropriate for stock hardware with virtual memory. The collector is incremental and atomic: it does not attempt to collect the whole heap at once and it interacts correctly with the recovery system. The time for recovery is independent of heap size, and can be shortened using checkpoints.

1 Introduction

A *stable heap* is storage that is managed automatically using garbage collection, manipulated using atomic transactions, and accessed using a uniform storage model. Automatic storage management, used in modern programming languages, enhances reliability by preventing errors due to explicit deallocation (e.g., dangling references and storage leaks). Transactions, used in database and distributed systems, provide fault-tolerance by masking failures that occur while they are running. A uniform storage model simplifies programming by eliminating the distinction between accessing temporary storage and permanent storage. Stable heap management will make it easier to write reliable programs and could be useful in programming languages for reliable distributed computing [9, 21], programming languages with persistent storage [1, 2], and object oriented database systems [7, 23, 34, 35].

In earlier research [16, 17] we designed algorithms suitable for the implementation of small stable heaps. However, many applications that could benefit from a stable heap (e.g., computer-aided design, computer-aided software engineering, and office information systems) require large amounts of storage, timely responses for transactions, and high availability. The goal of our current research is to design algorithms to implement the large stable heaps necessary to support these applications.

In our earlier work we introduced the notion of atomic garbage collection to provide automatic storage management for stable heaps, and presented an algorithm for it. We also showed how the atomic collector must be coordinated with the recovery system. (A recovery system provides fault-tolerance for transactions.) Since atomic garbage collection is more expensive than normal garbage collection and some of the data in a stable heap is volatile, we described how to divide the heap into a volatile area and a stable area. Storage management in the volatile area is provided cheaply by a normal garbage collector; the more expensive atomic garbage collector is used only in the stable area.

This research was supported in part by the National Science Foundation under grant CCR-8716884 and in part by the Defense Advanced Research Projects Agency (DARPA) under Contract N00014-89-J-1988.

We based our atomic garbage collector on a stop-the-world copying collector; it suspends work on all transactions while it collects and traverses the stable part of the heap. These pauses grow longer as the stable area grows larger. When the pauses become intolerable, the stable area is too large for a stop-the-world collector. The exact size at which this occurs depends on the application and its response time requirements, as well as on hardware characteristics such as processor speed.

Similarly, the recovery system used in our earlier work requires a traversal of the whole stable object graph after a crash. For an application with a large stable area, this traversal delays recovery and reduces the availability of the application. The heap size at which this delay becomes intolerable depends on the application and its availability constraints.

Our current research builds on our previous research; its goal is the design of an integrated atomic garbage collector and recovery system appropriate for a large stable heap on stock hardware. The collector is incremental; i.e., it does not attempt to collect the whole heap in one pause. The time for recovery is independent of heap size and can be shortened using a checkpointing mechanism. The design is for stock hardware with virtual memory, since these are the most common computing machines. We have completed the design of the algorithms, and are beginning an implementation of a stable heap prototype to show its feasibility. The current implementation of Argus [22] serves as the basis for the prototype; we are replacing its existing storage management and recovery algorithms.

In this paper we describe our approach. We begin by reviewing our model of a stable heap. Then we discuss the requirements and issues in the design of algorithms for a large stable heap. We describe an approach that satisfies the requirements and compare the approach with related work. Finally, we summarize and discuss future work.

2   Stable Heaps

Our model of a stable heap is based on the model of computation used by Argus [21], a language for reliable distributed computing. An Argus program is a collection of guardians, each encapsulating a stable heap, that communicate with one another using remote procedure call. We begin this section by describing our model of a stable heap. Then we discuss recovery and our failure model. We review the definition of atomic garbage collection. Finally, we discuss the hardware and operating system for which our design is appropriate.

2.1   System Model

In the model, computations on shared state run as atomic transactions [12] and storage is organized as a heap. Transactions provide concurrency control and fault tolerance; they are *serializable* and *total*. Serializability means that when transactions are executed concurrently, the effect will be as if they were run sequentially in some order. Totality means that a transaction is all or nothing; i.e., either it completes entirely and *commits*, or it *aborts* and is guaranteed to have no effect. A single transaction can observe, modify, and create multiple objects.

A heap consists of a set of root objects and all the objects accessible from them. Objects vary in size and may contain pointers to other objects. In a stable heap, some roots, specified by the programmer, are stable; the rest are volatile. The stable roots are global. The *stable state* is the part of the heap that must survive crashes; it consists of all objects accessible from the stable roots. The *volatile state* does not necessarily survive crashes; it consists of all objects that are accessible from the volatile roots, but are not part of the stable state, e.g., objects local to a procedure invocation, objects created by a transaction that has not yet completed, and global objects that do not have to survive crashes.

Objects shared among transactions must be *atomic*. Atomic objects provide the synchronization and recovery mechanisms necessary to ensure that transactions are serializable and total. Atomic objects can be mutable or immutable. Immutable objects are always atomic because their values never change. For the purposes of this paper, we assume that mutable atomic objects control synchronization using standard read/write locking, and we discuss mechanisms required for recovery.

The programmer sees one heap containing both stable and volatile objects. He can store pointers to stable objects in volatile objects, and can make volatile objects stable by storing pointers to them in an object that is already stable. A volatile object becomes stable when the transaction that makes it accessible from a stable root commits. Transactions share a single address space that contains both shared global objects and objects local to a single transaction; the programmer does not need to move objects between secondary storage and a transaction's local memory, or distinguish between local and global objects.

2.2   Recovery and Failure Model

A recovery system handles recovery from crashes and transaction aborts. It maintains information, typically organized as a log, to undo the effects of aborted transactions and to redo the effects of committed transactions. While the system is up and running, the stable heap resides in virtual memory. Virtual memory uses main memory as a cache for a slower backing store on disk. Main memory is volatile, so the recovery system has to control the movement of pages between main memory and disk to ensure that the information on the disk together with the log can be used to recover the stable state in virtual memory after a crash. The disk is non-volatile, but not stable, so the recovery system must also maintain redo information on a stable storage device. (A stable storage device [18], with very high probability, avoids the loss of information due to failure.) Typically, a recovery system keeps its log on stable storage to avoid storing the redo information more than once.

There are two kinds of crashes: system crashes and media failure. System crashes are either software failures (e.g., inconsistent data structures in the operating system) or hardware failures (e.g., power failures). We assume that when the system crashes, bad information is not written to the disk. Main memory is lost in a system crash; the disk and log survive. The recovery system uses the disk and the log to recover the stable state in virtual memory.

A media failure occurs when information on disk is lost. For simplicity we assume that no information on disk survives a media failure; only the log, which is on stable storage, survives. The recovery system recovers the entire stable state from the log.

2.3   Atomic Garbage Collection

Automatic storage management for a stable heap is complicated by the fact that a garbage collector typically moves and modifies objects. Collectors move objects to improve paging performance; they modify objects to reduce the amount of additional storage needed by the collector itself. The movement and modification of objects during garbage collection requires coordination with the recovery system: the objects modified by the collector must be recoverable, objects must be locatable on disk by the recovery system even though their locations change during a collection, the collector must synchronize with the recovery system, and some of the roots for collection might be in information managed by the recovery system. A collection algorithm for a stable heap that solves these problems is called an *atomic garbage collector*.

2.4   Implementation Platform

The design is for stock uniprocessors with virtual memory; these are the most common computing machines. No special-purpose hardware to support recovery or garbage collection is assumed.

The design requires an operating system that allows a program some control over the virtual memory system. Primitives are needed to control when a page of virtual memory can be written to the backing store and to set protections on pages. The ability to preserve the backing store for virtual memory after a crash is also required. Mach [29] satisfies these requirements and is being used for the prototype implementation.

3   Requirements And Issues

The goal of the research is to design an atomic garbage collector and a recovery system for a large stable heap. This section discusses requirements for the design of the collector and the recovery system. It also discusses the interaction between the two.

3.1   Garbage Collection

Many garbage collection algorithms have been described in the literature. Which is the most appropriate as a basis for atomic garbage collection? Applying system requirements narrows the choice.

The principal requirement is that the algorithm be suitable for collecting a large heap. There are two implications: (1) the pauses associated with garbage collection must be short enough to support interactive response times, and (2) the collector must interact well with virtual memory.

A stop-the-world collector is not suitable for large heaps because the pauses associated with its collections are too long. Two general techniques have been used to shorten garbage collection pauses: (1) incremental garbage collection [3], and (2) dividing the heap into independently collectible areas [4]. Steps of an incremental collector are interleaved with normal program steps such that the pause due to each incremental step is small. An incremental collector is also called real-time if there is a bound on the longest possible pause. To date most incremental collectors have been based on Baker's algorithm [3].

When dividing the heap into areas, either stop-the-world or incremental collection can be used in each area. A good division of the heap into areas leaves few inter-area references and places objects with similar lifetime characteristics into the same area. For programs without persistent storage, an automatic way of dividing the heap without programmer intervention is according to the age of objects; this is called generational collection [19, 25, 33]. Generational collection depends on an observed behavior of program heaps that new objects are more likely to become garbage than old objects; it concentrates its work on the areas containing the youngest objects where the most storage will be reclaimed for the least amount of effort. Generational collection might also be appropriate for persistent heaps; but this can be determined only by studying real workloads. Other ways for automatically dividing the heap into areas also need to be investigated.

For large heaps implemented in virtual memory, one important purpose of garbage collection is to reorganize the heap to provide good paging performance. Reorganizing the heap requires a collector that can move objects, e.g., a copying collector. Copying collectors can increase locality of reference and reduce paging by moving objects that are referenced together to the same page [8, 25].

Both dividing the heap into areas and reorganizing the heap during garbage collection to improve locality are similar to the problem of clustering in object-oriented database systems. Clustering occurs at two levels: (1) partitioning objects into areas, and (2) arranging objects within an area. At the higher level, databases [14, 23] typically provide segments for grouping objects. However, the division into segments is not automatic; the programmer or database manager must decide the proper segment for each object. At the lower level, databases [15, 23] typically provide mechanisms for reclustering objects within a segment; these mechanisms are similar to the ones used by garbage collectors.

The second requirement is that the algorithm must work well on stock hardware. Without hardware assists, Baker's incremental garbage collector is expensive on stock hardware–it requires a comparison on every heap reference. A variant of Baker's collector [5] substitutes a memory indirection for the comparison, but is still too expensive. Ellis, Li and Appel [11] and Zorn [36] have shown how the virtual memory hardware on stock hardware can be used to facilitate incremental garbage collection with lower overhead.

The last requirement is that the algorithm not increase the cost of collection for volatile objects. Atomic garbage collection for stable objects is inherently more expensive than normal garbage collection for volatile objects. Most garbage is likely to be volatile, so we need to manage storage such that the volatile parts of the heap can still be collected cheaply.

3.2   Recovery

There are two principal requirements for the recovery system: (1) suitability for a large heap and (2) ability to find and handle new stable objects as they become accessible from the stable roots. These requirements narrow the choice of recovery algorithms.

3.2.1   Large Heaps

The recovery algorithm must be suitable for a large heap. This requirement has implications both for recovery overhead during normal processing and for recovery overhead after a crash.

First consider recovery overhead after a crash. Crash recovery time is proportional to the number of log records processed and the number of objects touched. A checkpointing mechanism can be used to reduce the number of log records that need to be read. We also want recovery to avoid touching every accessible stable object after a crash. This leads to the additional requirement that no volatile information be stored in a stable object. This is typical in database recovery systems. In contrast, the current Argus system [22] stores volatile lock and version information in the representations of atomic objects. Using that representation, each stable atomic object has to be touched to clear its lock and version information after a crash. This is clearly unacceptable.

Now consider recovery overhead during normal processing. Time overheads include speed of access to atomic objects, time to commit a transaction, and time to abort a transaction. The requirements for these overheads do not differ from other transaction systems. Speed of access to atomic objects and commit should be fast because these are normal operations. Abort is infrequent compared to commit and can be somewhat slower. Note, however, that the requirement for fast recovery slows access to atomic objects since storing volatile information in them would speed access to them during normal operation.

Space overhead includes the space overhead for the representation of an atomic object. For example, the current Argus system allocates a header for every mutable atomic object. This header requires five words of storage and takes up space whether or not the object is active (locked by an active transaction). In a large stable heap, only a small fraction of the stable objects will be active at any one time. Since many objects are small (e.g., in Argus a variant takes up two words), this header becomes very expensive.

As a second example of space overhead, Argus uses versioning to provide recoverability for atomic objects. When a transaction acquires a write lock on an object, a new version of the object's base value is allocated, and the transaction updates the version. When the transaction commits, a pointer from the object's header is updated to point to the new committed version. Versioning creates a lot of stable garbage in the heap; stable garbage is more costly to reclaim than volatile garbage.

3.2.2   Newly Stable Objects

Because the system model defines stability according to accessibility from stable roots, it requires functionality not found in other recovery algorithms. Exceptions are the current recovery system for Argus [28] and PS-algol [2], though PS-algol has a weaker transaction and recovery model, which is discussed below in Section 5.4.

An object becomes stable at the commit of the transaction that made it accessible from a stable root. Once stable, the recovery system must ensure that the object survives failures by maintaining its value on stable storage. For this reason updating a stable object is more expensive than updating a volatile object. The extra expense should be incurred only if the object is stable.

3.3   Interactions Between Garbage Collection And Recovery

The previous two sections have discussed constraints on the design of garbage collection and recovery algorithms for a stable heap; this section discusses the interactions between the algorithms. Some of the interactions concern correctness; others affect the speed of crash recovery.

3.3.1   Correct Interaction

There are four interactions that must be handled correctly for the collector to be atomic; these were originally described in our report on earlier research [16]. First, copying collectors overwrite parts of objects in from-space with forwarding pointers. If a crash occurs while garbage collection is in progress, the part of an object overwritten by the forwarding pointer must be recoverable.

Second, copying collectors move objects. The recovery system records values for objects in the log. The value of an object usually contains the names of other objects. Since collectors move objects, simply using virtual addresses as names is not enough. In the event of media failure, the recovery system needs some way of mapping virtual addresses before a collection to the corresponding addresses after a collection.

Third, garbage collection has to be synchronized with the recovery system. Without synchronization, the collector might process an object in an inconsistent state, miss a pointer in it to a second object, and inadvertently reclaim the second object. This synchronization has to be cheap.

Fourth, for objects being updated by an active transaction, the recovery system keeps track of undo and/or redo information. This information has to be made available to the collector so that it will not reclaim objects that might still be accessible if the active transaction commits or aborts.

3.3.2   Fast Recovery

For fast crash recovery, the garbage collector must inform the recovery system about the progress of the collection. A crash may occur toward the end of an incremental atomic garbage collection. Without information on the progress of the collection, the recovery system may have to redo the entire collection.

3.4   Discussion

So far, we have discussed the requirements on garbage collection and recovery for a large stable heap. From the size requirement, we concluded that the times for recovery and the pauses due to garbage collection must be independent of the size of the heap.

An additional problem, related to size, is that a stable heap may be so large that it may not fit into a single virtual address space. There are several approaches to solving this problem: (1) build machines with larger address spaces; (2) require the programmer to segment his heap, e.g., in Argus the programmer can partition his heap across guardians, each with its own address space; and (3) provide automatic segmentation by the system, i.e., the system divides the heap among several disjoint address spaces and maps the spaces appropriately. Choosing among these approaches is left for future research; in this paper we show how to make recovery and garbage collection independent of heap size.

4   Approach

Our approach divides the heap into volatile and stable areas. Objects are created in the volatile area. After an object becomes stable it is moved to the stable area at an appropriate time. The volatile area can be collected using incremental and/or generational collection. The stable areas are collected using an incremental atomic garbage collector based on the ideas of Ellis, Li, and Appel [11]. Recovery uses a form of update-in-place such that there is no volatile information in stable objects, no space overhead for inactive objects, and no stable garbage due to version management.

4.1   Dividing the Heap

There are several reasons for dividing the heap into stable and volatile areas. First, atomic garbage collection is more expensive than normal garbage collection. The extra expense should be avoided when collecting volatile objects. If the heap is divided, the volatile area can still be collected using a normal collector; only the stable area needs to be collected atomically. Second, most short-lived objects will be volatile. Dividing the heap allows garbage collection work to be concentrated in the volatile area where there is a higher return for the effort. The last reason is to ease the management of disk storage: only disk storage associated with stable objects needs to survive a crash. This is just the disk storage associated with the stable area.

It might pay to further subdivide the volatile and stable areas. Given the reported success of generational garbage collection in collecting volatile program heaps [8, 25, 30, 33], it is likely that this would be a good choice for the volatile heap. The appropriateness of generational garbage collection for the stable area is less certain, and depends on the way the stable objects are used. If they are used for long-lived information, there is no reason to believe that newer information is likely to become obsolete before older information. However, if they are being used to provide fault-tolerance, e.g., a stable output queue, their use is similar to that of objects in volatile program heaps.

There might be other bases (besides object age) on which to subdivide the stable area automatically. One such way might be according to the structure of the stable object graph. The graph might be easily divided into several disjoint sub-graphs or sub-graphs with few inter-graph references. Type declarations and static type checking might provide useful information for this purpose.

A report on previous research describes how to divide a stable heap into a single stable area and a single volatile area [16]. We are using the same method in our prototype. The method is easily adapted to allow several generations in the volatile area. Further sub-division of the stable area is a topic for future research.

4.2   Atomic Incremental Garbage Collection

Atomic incremental garbage collection of the stable area will be based on an idea of Ellis, Li, and Appel [11] (hereafter called Ellis's idea). They showed how the virtual memory hardware on a stock architecture can be used to implement incremental collection. Below, we briefly present their idea and an alternative due to Zorn [36]. Then we discuss an approach to atomic garbage collection and how it addresses the problems outlined earlier.

4.2.1   Read Barrier

Most incremental garbage collectors have been based on Baker's algorithm [3]. As in other copying collectors, Baker divides memory into from-space and to-space. In one collection cycle, the collector copies the objects accessible from the roots from from-space to to-space. As each object is copied, a forwarding pointer is inserted in its from-space copy. The forwarding pointer is used to preserve sharing in the object graph.

A new garbage collection cycle begins with a flip. At a flip, the spaces exchange roles and the collector copies the the root set (including the objects referenced in the registers) to the new to-space. In order to be incremental, the garbage collector runs and does part of its work every time the program allocates a new object. It scans some locations in to-space looking for pointers to objects in from-space, translating the pointers to point to the corresponding to-space objects, and copying objects to to-space as necessary.

The key to Baker's incremental collector is the so called "read barrier". The read barrier prevents the program from seeing pointers into from-space. Baker suggested the following implementation of the read barrier: every time the processor fetches the contents of a memory cell, it checks to see whether the cell contains a from-space address. If it does, the collector returns the corresponding to-space address, transporting the appropriate object to to-space as necessary.

Ellis suggests a cheap implementation of the read barrier. At a flip, the root set is copied to to-space. The collector uses the virtual memory hardware to read-protect the unscanned pages of to-space. When the program tries to access an unscanned page, the collector fields the trap and scans the page, translating all from-space addresses on the page to the corresponding to-space addresses. The program never accesses an unscanned page, so it never sees a from-space address.

Ellis's approach is cheap; it adds little to the overall garbage collection time since there will be at most one trap per page of to-space. However, Ellis's collector might not be as incremental as a Baker-style collector. The distribution of read barrier traps for both collectors will be skewed to be very frequent just after a flip. In the case of Ellis, each trap requires that a whole page be scanned, whereas a Baker trap only requires that a single location be scanned. Thus, the pauses for garbage collection just after a flip might be long and frequent, thereby defeating the purpose of incremental collection.

Zorn describes a different way of using page protection to implement garbage collection. His method is more incremental than Ellis's, but it adds a lot to the overall garbage collection time because it leads to many more traps. Zorn proposes a weaker read barrier. The barrier is weaker because it allows the program to read from-space addresses into its registers, but it does not allow the program to store from-space addresses in memory. To implement the weaker barrier, the pages of from-space are protected and all stores into to-space are checked. Zorn's approach could require a trap per location of to-space; it makes all stores, including those to the stack and to initialize a newly allocated object, more expensive; and it complicates pointer comparisons.

Since Ellis's approach is simpler and cheaper than Zorn's, it is used as the basis for atomic incremental garbage collection. We will use the prototype to measure the length and frequency of the pauses attributable to the read barrier.

4.2.2   Interactions With Recovery

To be atomic, an incremental garbage collector must interact correctly with the recovery system. To allow fast recovery and to avoid redoing the entire collection after a crash, the collector writes extra information to the log. Below, we describe an approach to interaction with the recovery system that addresses the issues outlined in section 3.3.

Changes to Objects.   To deal with the overwriting of objects by forwarding pointers, the atomic incremental collector writes a record to the log every time it copies an object. The record contains the from-space address of the object and the previous contents of the overwritten cell. The collector writes these records using a write-ahead log protocol to ensure that they are in the log before the corresponding change to from-space reaches disk. This guarantees that in the event of a crash, the values for overwritten from-space cells can be found in the log.

Movement of Objects.   There are two approaches to solving the naming problem caused by the movement of objects: (1) the unique object identifier (UID) approach and (2) the virtual address approach. When an object value is written to the log using the UID approach, the pointers in it to other objects are replaced by the UIDs of those objects. For fast recovery from system crashes, the UID approach requires that a map of UIDs to virtual addresses also be available (either in the log or virtual memory) so that objects on disk can be found. When an object value is written to the log using the virtual address approach, pointers in it to other objects remain unchanged. For recovery from media failure, the virtual address approach requires that a map relating object addresses before a garbage collection to addresses after a collection be written to the log. Depending on the recovery algorithms, this map may also be required for system crashes.

Since the collector writes a record to the log every time it copies an object anyway, we choose the virtual address approach. The record containing the object's from-space address and the contents of its overwritten cell is augmented by the object's to-space address and is called a translation record. This way the map relating from-space and to-space addresses is written incrementally to the log during the course of garbage collection.

Synchronization With Recovery.   Each transaction is a sequence of elementary actions that read and update individual objects. An update action updates an object and its corresponding undo or redo information. One approach to synchronization with the recovery system is to require that a flip occur in an action-quiescent state. The system is action-quiescent when no elementary action is in progress. Since the elementary actions are short, the flip is not significantly delayed. Given that a flip occurs in an action-quiescent state, the read barrier ensures that a copying or scanning step of the atomic incremental garbage collector only observes an object in an action-consistent state.

The correctness of the above approach can be seen by viewing the system as a multi-level transaction system with two levels. At the high level, there are user transactions; at the low level, there are elementary actions. An elementary action can be an update action, a read action, a copy action, or a scan action. A user transaction is made up of a sequence of low level read and update actions. The garbage collector uses copy and scan actions: a copy action copies an object from from-space to to-space, and a scan action scans a single location in to-space.

At the level of transactions, a transaction obtains read and write locks that it holds for its duration. The read and write locks ensure serializability at the transaction level. At the level of actions, a synchronization mechanism ensures that only one action accesses a given object at a time, so that an action always observes a consistent object state. Since the garbage collection actions do not change the abstract value of an object, they are invisible to the transaction level: an object can be copied or scanned even while a transaction holds a write lock.

In the approach described above, synchronization between garbage collection actions and the other low-level actions is implemented cheaply by the read barrier. At a flip the collector obtains a "lock" for every stable object at once by protecting the unscanned pages of to-space. As each page of to-space is scanned, the "locks" for the objects in it are released by changing its protection. Restricting flips to occur in an action-quiescent state ensures that the collector obtains the "locks" at an appropriate time.

Roots In Recovery Information.   Dealing with roots in the recovery information depends on the recovery system. Using update-in-place and a write-ahead (undo/redo) log, the undo records for active transactions contain roots for collection. Accessing the undo records in the log during collection might be expensive. To reduce the expense, the collector can delay scanning the roots in the undo records until the end of the collection. Since most transactions commit and are expected to be shorter than the time between flips, this delaying strategy reads few undo records from the log.

Using intentions lists and a redo log, as described below, the recovery information is maintained in the heap and the collector naturally finds it as it traces the object graph.

Speeding Recovery.   To inform the recovery system about the progress of a collection, the garbage collector writes information to the log. A page is the unit of recovery on disk. To ensure fast recovery, recovery systems typically use the log to keep track of which disk pages might need to be restored after a crash [20, 24]. They write a fetch record when a page is read from disk and an end-write record after an updated page is written back to disk. This feature meshes nicely with the incremental atomic garbage collector. After scanning a page of to-space, the collector removes the protection from that page enabling access by the program. At the same time, the collector writes a scan record for the page to the log to inform the recovery system that the page has been scanned. After a crash, the recovery system uses the scan records together with the end-write records to determine which pages have to be rescanned.

4.3   Recovery

The approach to recovery must satisfy the requirements: it must find and handle newly stable objects, and it must be appropriate for a large heap. We have worked out the details for two approaches: (1) write-ahead logging with update-in-place and (2) a variation of intentions lists. We are using intentions lists in the prototype. In this section, we begin by discussing newly stable objects. Then, we discuss the two approaches.

4.3.1   Handling Newly Stable Objects

An object becomes stable at the commit of the transaction that made it accessible from a stable root. To make sure that the extra costs for recovery are paid only for stable objects, the recovery system uses two sets: (1) the Accessibility Set (AS), and (2) the Logged Set (LS). An object is inserted in the AS when the recovery system determines that it is accessible from the stable roots. It is inserted in the LS when its value and the values of all objects accessible from it are also recoverable from the log. Before a transaction commits, the recovery system must ensure that the log contains new values for each object in the AS that the transaction modified, and it must ensure that all objects accessible from the new value are in the LS. Using two sets allows recovery work for several transactions to proceed concurrently.

This approach is based on Oki's earlier work for Argus [28]. His algorithm uses only one set, the AS, but it suffers from a race condition: a transaction may commit before values for all the objects accessible from the objects that it modified have been written to the log. We found this bug as part of this research.

4.3.2   Satisfying The Other Requirements

There are several approaches to recovery that satisfy the requirements: (1) write-ahead logging with update-in-place and (2) a variation of intentions lists. In both approaches the information associated with atomic objects maintained for active transactions is kept in the volatile area separate from the objects themselves. This allows recovery without a traversal of the object graph and lowers the space overhead for stable objects. For both approaches, the location of the committed version in the stable area does not change; it is updated in place. This avoids creating garbage in the stable area and also lowers the space overhead.

The approach to write-ahead logging is the standard approach taken in database systems [12, 20, 24]. When a transaction updates an object, it writes a log record containing enough information to undo or redo the update, and updates the object in place in main memory. The object is prevented from reaching the disk until the log record is physically in the log.

The variation of intentions lists is a combination of the standard intentions list technique [18], the versioning approach used in Argus [21, 22], and the use of the garbage collector to reduce writing to the stable area. In the approach, the system maintains a table of intentions and locks in the volatile area. There is an entry in the table for each mutable atomic object read or updated by an active transaction. There is also an entry for each atomic object updated by a committed transaction since the last garbage collection of the volatile area. When a transaction first obtains a lock on an atomic object, the system finds or creates an entry for the object in the table. Then it records the lock mode in the entry. For a write lock, the system also makes a copy of the last committed value of the object to use as an intention. The transaction updates the copy, which is also called the current version.

To commit a transaction, the recovery system writes new values to the log for the stable objects that the transaction has updated and then writes a commit record to the log to signal the commit point. After commit, the recovery system uses the intentions in the table to update the objects' values in the stable area. In a normal intentions list implementation, the recovery system would update the stable area immediately after writing the commit record; then it would write a log record signaling that the updates had reached the stable area. For an object that is updated frequently, this would entail many writes to the stable area—one after the commit of each transaction that modified the object. To reduce the frequency of writes, we delay writing the committed version to the stable area. Specifically, we delay writing until the next garbage collection of the volatile area; the version would have to be copied during garbage collection in any case.

Both recovery approaches use additional techniques to reduce recovery time after a crash: they write records to the log to determine which pages of virtual memory might have been dirty at the time of a crash, they checkpoint the stable heap in a low-level action-quiescent state while only suspending transactions long enough to construct and write a checkpoint record, and they use the translation and scan records written to the log by the atomic garbage collector. The first two features are not new to write-ahead logging [20, 24]; they might be new for intentions lists techniques.

Without further information about the applications that use the stable heap, it is not clear whether the write-ahead log or the intentions list approach should be preferred. The write-ahead log approach writes undo and redo information to the log for every update, but it is possible to use a partial logging technique such that only the part of the object that changes gets written. The intentions list approach copies the entire object in main memory up to two times for each transaction and writes redo information to the log (partial value logging is also possible). The intentions list approach is preferable when an object is updated many times within a single transaction since no undo information is written to the log. The write-ahead logging approach is preferable when the object is updated one time within a transaction, especially when an update is small compared to size of the object.

For the prototype, we choose the intentions list approach because it is closest to the current Argus implementation and requires less work. It provides fast recovery independent of heap size, and its performance during normal operation should be comparable to the current implementation, except that the cost of accessing an atomic object has been increased. Once the stable heap prototype has been implemented and applications have been written, future research can gather statistics on applications and reevaluate the choice.

5   Related Work

This work draws on previous work done in garbage collection and recovery. Our goal is to design algorithms to efficiently manage a large stable heap; the individual garbage collection and recovery methods that we have chosen are not fundamentally new, but are based on existing ones. For that reason, the discussion of related work concentrates on other attempts or proposals to integrate garbage collection and recovery: previous work on the Argus recovery system [16, 17, 28, 27], a proposal for atomic garbage collection for Avalon [10], and work from the persistent programming community [2, 32].

5.1   Current Argus Recovery System

The approach to recovery and storage management taken by the current Argus implementation [22] is suitable only for small heaps or applications that can tolerate long garbage collection pauses and long recovery times. The recovery system [28, 27] does not differentiate between system crashes and media failures. It always discards the disk backing store of virtual memory and recovers the whole stable state from the log; therefore the time for recovery depends on the sizes of the log and the stable state. For storage management Argus employs stop-the-world garbage collection; all transactions are suspended during a collection.

As mentioned earlier in Section 4.3.1, the algorithm for handling newly stable objects suffers from a race condition that could occur when several transactions call the recovery system concurrently. We correct this bug.

5.2   Atomic Copying Collection

In earlier work [16, 17], we introduced the concept of atomic garbage collection and showed how to provide fast recovery for small heaps. Recovery for a system crash is faster than the current Argus recovery system because it takes advantage of information left on disk in virtual memory and brings that information to a consistent state by reading a small part of the log. However, the approach is still limited to small heaps: it uses stop-the-world collection and during crash recovery it traverses the whole object graph to clear volatile information out of the representations of stable objects.

5.3   Avalon

Avalon [9] is a language for distributed computing built as an extension to C++ on top of the Camelot transaction facility [31]. Dave Detlefs has proposed atomic concurrent garbage collection for Avalon to provide better support for large heaps [10]. He also bases his garbage collection algorithm on the read barrier of Ellis, but he is designing his algorithm for a tightly coupled multiprocessor with a shared virtual memory. His design concentrates on the problems of concurrency, calling for multiple garbage collection threads and extra shared state. One of his goals is to change the Camelot recovery system as little as possible. In contrast, our approach concentrates on the interactions between garbage collection and recovery, and we redesign both algorithms accordingly. We believe that fully understanding the issues in the uniprocessor case will lead to better algorithms for multiprocessors. Furthermore, our design is useful for stock uniprocessors.

Avalon's notion of stability (Camelot and Avalon use the term recoverability in place of stability) also differs from ours. In Avalon, an object is stable because the program creates it in a stable area; in our model, an object is stable because it is accessible from a stable root. Avalon's notion simplifies storage management, and its recovery system does not need algorithms to track newly stable objects.

5.4   PS-algol.

PS-algol [2, 26] is a language for persistent programming. There are many similarities between the system model of PS-algol and the one discussed here: both define persistence according to reachability from a persistent root, and both use transactions to control concurrency and provide fault-tolerance. However, the transaction model of PS-algol is primitive: it restricts concurrency and does not provide for recovery from media failure.

A programmer using PS-algol partitions his data into databases; databases may contain arbitrary object graphs and be interconnected. Read/write locking on whole databases is used for concurrency control. When a program opens a database in read or write mode, the system also opens all of the databases recursively accessible from the opened database in read mode. The first open of a database for write implicitly starts a transaction. The transaction commits and a new one starts when the program calls the commit procedure. At commit, changes are written atomically to the databases open for writing.

The limited concurrency of the transaction model allows a simple recovery system, which uses shadow pages. At commit the changed objects are written to fresh disk pages. Also, newly persistent objects are found as the changed objects are written. The new disk pages then replace their old counterparts in a single atomic step. Notice that commit is expensive compared to typical database implementations because it does not complete until it updates the databases on disk.

There are two kinds of garbage collection in PS-algol: garbage collection of a program heap and garbage collection of the persistent store [6]. Garbage collection of the program heap collects volatile objects; it may occur while a transaction is active. If necessary, it may write changed and newly persistent objects to database shadow pages to make room in main memory. Garbage collection of the persistent store uses stop-and-copy collection to free disk space from databases. This garbage collection occurs offline and all databases must be closed for its duration.

5.5   Persistent Memory

Thatte describes a different approach to providing a stable heap [32] (though he uses different terminology). He proposes to build a stable heap on top of an abstraction he calls persistent memory. Thatte does not address the problem of recovering persistent memory adequately, his approach uses resources inefficiently, and he does not deal with the interactions between garbage collection and recovery.

5.5.1   Approach

Persistent memory provides the abstraction of a virtual memory that survives crashes. The system uses shadowing: it maintains two backing store pages on disk for each active page of virtual memory, using one for swapping and the second for checkpoints. At regular intervals the system checkpoints: first, it writes all dirty pages of main memory to their respective swapping pages; then, it switches the roles of the disk pages in each pair to create a new checkpoint. The checkpoint also saves processor state. After a crash the state of virtual memory and the registers revert to their state at the last checkpoint, after which normal system operation resumes.

All running programs share the same heap built on top of the persistent virtual memory. Some roots of the heap are volatile and some are persistent. An object persists beyond the lifetime of the program that created it if it is accessible from a persistent root. Implementing persistence for objects does not require special garbage collection techniques.

Thatte proposes to build stable objects (which he calls resilient objects) on the persistent heap. Transactions update stable objects in place, keep undo information in the persistent memory for the duration of the transaction, and write redo information to a separate log. After a system crash, persistent memory is restored to its state at the last checkpoint; the recovery system applies the undo information saved by the checkpoint and the redo information written since the checkpoint to bring the stable objects up to date.

5.5.2   Problems

Thatte does not address an important problem adequately–the restart of the processor after a crash. Often system crashes are caused by software and not by faulty hardware. If the processor starts with the same state as existed at the last checkpoint, what prevents it from crashing again? Also, what does it mean to restart a program in the middle of input or output with the external world?

Thatte's approach to shadowing is novel: unlike other schemes, no directory containing indirection pointers must be updated atomically at a checkpoint. Instead, the system stores a timestamp with each page when it writes the page to disk; after a crash, the system uses the timestamps to determine which page of each pair belongs to the checkpoint. However, his mechanism suffers from other problems associated with shadowing [13]: loss of locality for disk storage (adjacent pages of virtual memory do not remain adjacent on disk), and an increased appetite for disk storage.

In addition, the costs for persistence are paid for the whole virtual memory, not just the part that requires persistence. Disk usage is increased because all pages are shadowed, not just those containing persistent data. Similarly, more disk I/O bandwidth is used because the checkpoint must write all dirty pages, not just those containing persistent data. In contrast, the approach proposed in this paper pays the costs of recovery only for stable objects.

In suggesting how to build stable objects on the persistent heap, Thatte neglects to consider the interactions between garbage collection and recovery. In particular, he does not consider the movement of objects during garbage collection and its associated naming problem: the redo log contains the names of objects that move during garbage collection and Thatte does not describe the contents of these names. We discuss the options in Section 4.2.2.

6   Conclusions

In this paper we have described an approach to garbage collection and recovery suitable for large stable heaps running on stock hardware. The approach divides the heap into volatile and stable areas. Objects are created in the volatile area; an object is moved to the stable area at an appropriate time after it becomes stable. The volatile area is collected using incremental and/or generational collection; the stable area is collected using a new incremental atomic garbage collector based on the collector of Ellis, Li, and Appel [11]. Two approaches to recovery were sketched: (1) write-ahead logging and (2) a new variation of intentions lists that uses the garbage collector to carry out the intentions.

Currently we are building a prototype by replacing the storage management and recovery systems in the current Argus implementation [22]. Once the prototype is built, we will use it to evaluate and improve our design.

References

[1] A. Albano, L. Cardelli, and R. Orsini. A Strongly Typed Interactive Conceptual Language. *ACM Transactions on Database Systems*, 10(2):230–260, June 1985.

[2] M. P. Atkinson, P. J. Bailey, K. J. Chisholm, P. W. Cockshott, and R. Morrison. An Approach to Persistent Programming. *The Computer Journal*, 26(4):360–365, 1983.

[3] Henry Baker. List Processing in Real Time on a Serial Computer. *Communications of the ACM*, 21(4):280–294, April 1978.

[4] Peter B. Bishop. Computer Systems with a Very Large Address Space and Garbage Collection. Technical Report MIT/LCS/TR-178, Laboratory for Computer Science, MIT, Cambridge, Ma., May 1977.

[5] Rodney A. Brooks. Trading Data Space for Reduced Time and Code Space in Real-Time Garbage Collection on Stock Hardware. In *Proceedings 1984 ACM Symposium on Lisp and Functional Programming*, pages 256–262, 1977.

[6] Jack Campin and Malcolm Atkinson. A Persistent Store Garbage Collector with Statistical Facilities. Persistent Programming Research Report 29, Department of Computing Science, University of Glasgow, Glasgow, Scotland, 1977.

[7] M. Carey, D. DeWitt, J. Richardson, and E. Sheikta. Object and File Management in the EXODUS Extensible Database System. In *Proceedings of the 12th International Conference on Very Large Databases*, August 1986.

[8] Robert Courts. Improving Locality of Reference in a Garbage-collecting Memory Management System. *Communications of the ACM*, 31(9):1128–1138, September 1988.

[9] David Detlefs, Maurice Herlihy, and Jeannette Wing. Inheritance of Synchronization and Recovery Properties in Avalon/C++. *IEEE Computer*, 21(12), December 1988.

[10] David L. Detlefs. Concurrent, Atomic Garbage Collection. Thesis proposal, March 1989.

[11] John R. Ellis, Kai Li, and Andrew W. Appel. Real-time concurrent collection on stock multiprocessors. Technical Report 25, Systems Research Center, Digital Equipment Corporation, Palo Alto, Ca., February 1988.

[12] James N. Gray. Notes on Database Operating Systems. In R. Bayer, R. M. Graham, and G. Seegmuller, editors, *Operating Systems–An Advanced Course*, volume 60 of *Lecture Notes in Computer Science*, pages 393–481. Springer-Verlag, New York, 1978.

[13] James N. Gray, Paul McJones, Mike Blasgen, Bruce Lindsay, Raymond Lorie, Tom Price, Franco Putzolu, and Irving Traiger. The Recovery Manager of the System R Database Manager. *ACM Computing Surveys*, 13(2):223–242, June 1981.

[14] M. F. Hornick and S. B. Zdonik. A Shared, Segmented Memory System for an Object-Oriented Database. *ACM Transactions on Office Information Systems*, 5(1):70–85, 1987.

[15] Scott E. Hudson and Roger King. Cactis: A Self-Adaptive, Concurrent Implementation of an Object-Oriented Database Management System. *ACM Transactions on Database Systems*, 14(3):291–321, September 1989.

[16] Elliot Kolodner, Barbara Liskov, and William Weihl. Atomic Garbage Collection: Managing a Stable Heap. In *Proceedings of the 1989 ACM SIGMOD International Conference on the Management of Data*, pages 15–25, June 1989.

[17] Elliot K. Kolodner. Recovery Using Virtual Memory. Technical Report MIT/LCS/TR-404, Laboratory for Computer Science, MIT, Cambridge, Ma., July 1987.

[18] Butler. W. Lampson. *Atomic Transactions*, volume 105 of *Lecture Notes in Computer Science*, pages 246–265. Springer-Verlag, New York, 1981. This is a revised version of Lampson and Sturgis's unpublished *Crash Recovery in a Distributed Data Storage System*.

[19] Henry Lieberman and Carl Hewitt. A Real-Time Garbage Collector Based on the Lifetimes of Objects. *Communications of the ACM*, 26(6):419–429, June 1983.

[20] B. G. Lindsay, P. G. Selinger, C. Galtieri, J. N. Gray, R. A. Lorie, T. G. Price, F. Putzolu, I. L. Traiger, and B. W. Wade. Notes on Distributed Databases. Technical Report RJ2571, IBM Research Laboratory, San Jose, Ca., July 1979.

[21] Barbara Liskov. Overview of the Argus Language and System. Programming Methodology Group Memo 40, Laboratory for Computer Science, MIT, Cambridge, Ma., February 1984.

[22] Barbara Liskov, Paul Johnson, and Robert Scheifler. Implementation of Argus. In *Proceedings of the Eleventh Symposium on Operating Systems Principles*, November 1987.

[23] David Maier, Jacob Stein, Allen Otis, and Alan Purdy. Development of an Object-Oriented DBMS. In *Proceedings of the Object-Oriented Programming Systems, Languages and Applications*, pages 472–482, November 1986.

[24] C. Mohan, D. Haderle, B. Lindsay, H. Pirahesh, and P. Schwarz. A Transaction Recovery Method Supporting Fine-Granularity Locking and Partial Rollbacks Using Write-Ahead Logging. Technical Report RJ6649, IBM Almaden Research Center, San Jose, Ca., January 1989.

[25] David Moon. Garbage Collection in a Large Lisp System. In *Proc. of the 1984 Symposium on Lisp and Functional Programming*, pages 235–246, 1984.

[26] Ron Morrison. PS-algol Reference Manual Fourth Edition. Persistent Programming Research Report 12, Department of Computing Science, University of Glasgow, Glasgow, Scotland, February 1988.

[27] Brian Oki. Reliable Object Storage to Support Atomic Actions. Technical Report MIT/LCS/TR-308, Laboratory for Computer Science, MIT, Cambridge, Ma., May 1983.

[28] Brian Oki, Barbara Liskov, and Robert Scheifler. Reliable Object Storage to Support Atomic Actions. In *Proceedings of the Tenth Symposium on Operating Systems Principles*, pages 147–159, December 1985.

[29] Richard F. Rashid. Threads of a New System. *Unix Review*, 4(8):37–49, August 1986.

[30] Robert A. Shaw. Improving garbage collector performance in virtual memory. Technical Report CSL-TR-87-323, Computer Systems Laboratory, Stanford University, Stanford, Ca., March 1987.

[31] Alfred Z. Spector, J. J. Bloch, Dean S. Daniels, R. P. Draves, Daniel Duchamp, Jeffrey L. Eppinger, S. G. Menees, and D. S. Thompson. The Camelot Project. *Database Engineering*, 9(4), December 1986.

[32] Satish M. Thatte. Persistent Memory: A Storage Architecture for Object-Oriented Database Systems. In U. Dayal and K. Dittrich, editors, *Proceedings of the International Workshop on Object-Oriented Databases*, Pacific Grove, CA, September 1986.

[33] David Ungar. Generation Scavenging: A Non-disruptive High Performance Storage Reclamation Algorithm. In *ACM SIGSOFT/SIGPLAN Practical Programming Environments Conference*, pages 157–167, April 1984.

[34] Daniel Weinreb, Neal Feinberg, Dan Gerson, and Charles Lamb. An Object-Oriented Database System to Support an Integrated Programming Environment. Submitted for publication, 1988.

[35] Stanley Zdonik and Peter Wegner. Language and methodology for object-oriented database environments. In *Proceedings of the 19th Annual Hawaiian Conference on Systems Science*, January 1986.

[36] Benjamin G. Zorn. Comparative performance evaluation of garbage collection algorithms. Technical Report UCB/CSD 89/544, Computer Science Division (EECS), University of California, Berkeley, California, December 1989.

Persistent Object Stores:
An Implementation Technique

Alfred Brown
Department of Mathematical &
Computational Sciences,
University of St.Andrews,
North Haugh, St.Andrews.
KY16 9SS, Scotland.
ab@cs.st-and.ac.uk

John Rosenberg
Department of Electrical Engineering &
Computer Science,
University of Newcastle,
New South Wales 2308,
Australia.
johnr@nucs.nu.oz.au

Abstract

This paper presents the design of a layered architecture that can be used to support a persistent object store where the protection is enforced by a high level type system. Inherent in the design of the layered architecture is the ability to conduct cost effective experimentation. Each of the architectural mechanisms required is supported by a distinct architectural layer that conforms to a specific interface. The layer interfaces include facilities to support the efficient use of the available system resources. In order to demonstrate the flexibility of this implementation technique the paper describes an instance of the layered architecture that can be used to support either the persistent programming language Napier88, the functional programming languages Staple or the database programming language Galileo.

1 Introduction

A number of persistent programming systems are supported by some form of layered architecture. Examples of such systems include Galileo [alb85a], Smalltalk [gol83] and the TI Persistent Memory System [tha86], each of which is based on a subtly different concept of persistence [atk83a]. This paper presents the design of a layered architecture that can be used to support a type secure persistent object store where the protection is enforced by a high level type system. This implementation technique has been used to construct the persistent programming system for Napier88 [mor89] and is powerful enough to support languages with similar type systems, for example Galileo and Staple [mcn90].

Inherent in the design of the layered architecture is the ability to conduct cost effective experimentation. Each of the architectural mechanisms required by the implementation technique is supported by a distinct architectural layer that conforms to a specific interface. This allows a new instance of the architecture to be composed from an arbitrary set of implementations, each of which could be prepared in isolation.

As an example of the genericity of this technique, a persistent version of the functional programming language Staple has also been constructed. This was formed by composing a new instance of the architecture with the Staple interpreter as the top layer and an existing implementation of the persistent object store as the lower layers.

Within the layered architecture, the movement of persistent data to and from secondary storage is managed by a stable store. Stability is supported by a combination of shadow paging [lor77,ros83] and checkpointing mechanisms [gra81,ros90] that periodically record a self-consistent version of the system. Following a failure the system is restarted from the last recorded checkpoint. Since the entire system state is preserved, a checkpoint may be initiated at any point during the execution of a user program without jeopardising the integrity of the system.

The implementation technique described is intended to maximise the use of the available system resources. For example, in many systems storage may be allocated from a stack and from a heap. If either the stack or heap overflows then the system may fail even if there is sufficient storage available in the other. This problem is avoided by treating the entire storage as a single heap of objects. Furthermore, the stable store may be dynamically configured to make the best use of the available secondary storage. A major advantage of this technique is that the store is able to determine when the stable memory cannot record any further changes. If that point is reached a checkpoint can be initiated to allow the system to continue operation.

To complement the description of the design of the layered architecture, a description of the particular implementation that supports Napier88 is given. Within the example system the Napier88 compilation system guarantees type security thereby ensuring that the architecture's persistent object store is not misused.

2   A Layered Architecture

A type secure persistent object store is required to exhibit certain perceived properties of the persistence abstraction, namely uniform addressing, unbounded size and absolute stability [bro89]. These properties arise from the desire to abstract over all the physical properties of data including where it is stored, the form in which it is stored, how long it is retained and the physical properties of the underlying storage media. Since the location and storage format of data is hidden a uniform addressing mechanism must be applied to all data. Similarly, by hiding the physical properties of the storage media, the storage capacity of the media and its patterns of failure are also hidden resulting in the requirements of unbounded size and absolute stability. However, it should be noted that in practice these last two properties can not be realised but must be simulated.

There are a wide variety of implementation techniques that may be employed in constructing a persistent object store and simulating the required properties. In this paper we describe a layered architecture that forms a framework within which an appropriate selection of implementation techniques can be combined to form a persistent object store. The layered architecture is a result of analysing the requirements of a persistent object store and identifying the levels of abstraction inherent in the underlying architectural mechanisms. For example, we have noted the many logical levels of addressing mechanism present in computer architectures ranging from purely symbolic addresses to physical memory addresses. We have also investigated the range of possible storage management techniques that may be employed in simulating unbounded size and failure free storage. A full discussion of these implementation techniques and the corresponding levels of abstraction is given elsewhere [bro90].

In order to construct a type secure persistent object store an appropriate protection mechanism must be provided to enforce type security. That is, a mechanism is required to ensure that all operations attempted by a program adhere to some predefined set of type rules. The required checking may be performed at run-time by validating every data access as it occurs. For the purposes of this paper this will be referred to as *low level protection*. Alternatively, a compiler may be used to validate the operation of a program and where necessary generate explicit checks to be performed at run-time. This form of protection will be referred to as *high level protection*. A discussion of these two forms of protection and the trade offs between them is given in [bro90].

As a result of our investigations, we have suggested the following approach to constructing a type secure persistent object store. First, a uniform addressing mechanism appropriate to the desired use of the object store should be selected. A storage management scheme should then be chosen to support the addressing mechanism and the intended applications. Thirdly, a stable storage mechanism should be interfaced with the addressing mechanism and storage management in order to provide the necessary resilience to failures. Finally, an appropriate protection mechanism should be adopted to ensure that applications cannot gain unauthorised access to data or misinterpret the data they can access. Within this approach it is envisaged that each of the four mechanisms should be provided as a distinct architectural layer and that each layer will conform to some predefined interface. In this way, the overall complexity of designing, constructing and maintaining type secure persistent object stores should be minimised, resulting in more robust and potentially more efficient systems.

3   The Architectural Layers

In the previous section we identified the distinct architectural mechanisms required to support a persistent object store. They include a uniform addressing mechanism, a storage management mechanism, a stability mechanism and a protection mechanism. We shall now present the design of a layered architecture that provides the above mechanisms within a set of distinct architectural layers. The architecture supports orthogonal persistence and has been used in implementations of the persistent programming language Napier88 and the functional programming language Staple.

3.1   The Basic Layers

The layered architecture has been designed to support cost effective experimentation with the implementation of persistence. The key to achieving this aim is the separation of the distinct architectural mechanisms into well defined layers. Thus, each architectural mechanism is provided by a distinct architectural layer that must conform to a particular specification. In this way, individual layers may be independently re-implemented without reference to the implementation of the other layers. It is also possible to merge adjacent layers provided that the interface to the top-most layer is preserved.

The architectural layering has been chosen to take advantage of the persistence abstraction by ensuring that programs are not able to discover details of how objects are stored. This divides the architecture between the architectural layers that provide the persistent object store and those facilities that may be programmed by a supported programming language. The architectural layering is shown in Figure 1.

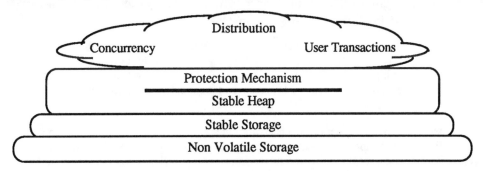

Figure 1: The basic architectural layers

The division has an important consequence for the provision of concurrency, user transactions and distribution. Since these three mechanisms are essentially modelling techniques they may be implemented at the programming language level and need not be primitive facilities provided by the persistent store. This allows experimental implementations to be constructed without the need to redesign the entire architecture. However, once a particular implementation technique has been identified as essential one or more layers of the persistent store may be re-implemented to incorporate the mechanism. If a layer interface is changed the change is only visible to the layer immediately above thereby limiting the required re-implementation.

3.2   The Stable Heap

The layer of the persistent object store which is visible to the programming language level is the stable heap shown in Figure 1. The stable heap layer provides a view of the persistent store that appears stable, is conceptually unbounded in size and may be uniformly addressed. All objects in the stable heap are reachable from a single distinguished root object and conform to a single object format that distinguishes object addresses from non-address data. The interpretation of an object is the responsibility of the higher level architecture. The persistent object store does not support object formats specific to any particular programming language, thereby allowing the persistent object store to operate independently of the supported programming languages.

Within the persistent store, stability is simulated by a simple checkpointing mechanism. This mechanism is provided as part of the stable heap interface for two reasons. Firstly, it may be made available to the programming language level to support user level transactions. For example, a transaction may maintain a log of operations to be performed and may wish to ensure that the log is preserved in stable storage prior to performing the actual operations. Another reason for making the checkpoint explicit is that it allows the higher level architecture to cache data outwith the persistent store. When a checkpoint is required any data held in registers or other special purpose hardware is copied back to the persistent store. Thus specialised code generation techniques can be used without impacting on the implementation of the persistent store.

The stable heap is implemented as a set of object management procedures that organise a single contiguous stable store. To ensure that the heap is correctly used, its interface includes a set of five conventions to which the higher level architecture must conform. They are:

- objects will only be created via the object management procedures,
- addresses will not be manufactured,
- all addresses will be held in the address fields of objects,
- all addressing is performed by indexing object addresses and
- a reachable object will not be explicitly deleted.

These conventions ensure that objects can only be accessed by following object addresses starting from the root object of the persistent store. They also ensure that all object addresses are held in the persistent store and can be located easily. This facilitates the implementation of storage utilities such as garbage collectors that may be used to simulate the perceived property of unbounded size.

Adherence to the five conventions requires the higher level architecture to address the store in terms of indexing object addresses. However, it does not define the level of addressing abstraction employed. Thus, a particular heap implementation may treat object addresses as object numbers and perform all addressing via table lookups to determine an object's address in the stable storage. Alternatively, object addresses may be in the form of stable storage addresses and not require mapping by the heap implementation. In either case the higher level architecture is constrained to address objects using an object address and a separate index.

The stable heap layer forces the higher level architecture to view the persistent object store as a uniform stable store of unbounded size. To extend this view to that of a type secure persistent object store a protection mechanism is required to ensure that the higher level architecture conforms to the specified conventions and correctly interprets the data held in the store. The architectural layering can support both high level and low level protection mechanisms.

Low level protection may be supported by encoding the appropriate checking mechanisms into the stable heap implementation. This may be further complemented by tagged memory locations. For example, the implementation of the architecture on the Rekursiv [bel88] enforces the interface definition using a hardware address translator that only accepts object number, index pairs, and by tagging addresses to prevent their unauthorised manufacture. Similar approaches to store level protection may be employed by alternative implementations of the stable heap layer.

High level protection may be provided by compiling all supported programming languages against a compatible type system with suitable dynamic checks being planted to accommodate those situations that cannot be statically checked. This approach allows the persistent object store to assume that all attempted operations are type correct. However, to achieve an efficient implementation without hardware support an instance of the architecture is constrained to use programming languages that make exclusive use of high level protection. Otherwise, some hardware support may be necessary to implement the run-time checking efficiently.

The provision of a low level protection mechanism must be specified as part of the stable heap interface. For example, if an implementation does not provide a low level protection mechanism then it can only support programming languages that rely on high level protection. Thus, the stable heap interface must specify the supported protection mechanism to ensure that an instance of the architecture is composed from compatible layer implementations.

3.3 The Stable Store

The stable heap layer is directly supported by a single contiguous stable store, see Figure 1. The stable storage layer provides the required stable storage mechanism and also supports a uniform addressing mechanism over the stable storage. In practice the uniform addressing is supported by lower level addressing mechanisms that give access to the non-volatile storage, the main memory and any other physical storage devices provided by the underlying hardware.

The interface to the stable storage has been designed to provide a contiguous range of storage addresses whose associated storage is always in a self-consistent state. This is achieved by implementing a checkpointing mechanism that preserves the current state of the store on non-volatile storage. At any point in time the non-volatile storage contains a self-consistent version of the store. The act of performing a checkpoint replaces the previous recorded state in a single atomic action. When a failure occurs the store is automatically restored to the state recorded by the most recent checkpoint. This simple checkpointing mechanism is sufficient to simulate a stable store [bro89].

Although the semantics of the required checkpointing mechanism are simple, the actual implementation may be quite sophisticated. To accommodate as much flexibility as possible, the interface includes a set of procedures that allow the use of the stable storage to be dynamically configured. For example, an implementation of the stable heap layer may use some temporary data structures that are reconstructed each time the system is restarted. In this case, changes to the storage containing these data structures need not be recorded between checkpoints and the data itself need not be recorded by a checkpoint. In contrast, any changes to user data must be recorded between checkpoints to support the reconstruction of the previous self-consistent state and the new values of the data must be recorded by a checkpoint.

The range of storage uses that are supported include:

• Read-only   This is the default state for all user data.

- **Save-only**   This describes an area of store that must be saved at the next checkpoint but it does not form part of the previous checkpoint.

- **Shadow**   All changes to the specified area of storage must be recorded. It contains data that is part of the previous checkpoint and must be part of the next checkpoint. This requires the allocation of non-volatile storage to record any changes.

- **Scratch**   The specified area of storage is for use by temporary data. The data is not part of the previous checkpoint and need not be protected from store failures.

- **Reserve**   The specified area of storage may be required following the next checkpoint operation. It must be allocated non-volatile storage but the storage may be used for other purposes prior to the next checkpoint.

- **Not-required**   The area of storage is no longer required to contain data. The non-volatile storage allocated to the area may be re-allocated for other purposes.

Given this detailed information on the desired use of the stable storage, the layer implementation may be able to optimise its checkpointing and storage allocation strategies. Thus it may be possible to use the available physical resources to better effect.

4   An Example Implementation

There have been several implementations of the layered architecture described above; the first is described in [bro89]. In this section we shall describe the most recent implementation that is used with Napier88 compiled to native code, with Staple and will be used with Galileo. The description is divided into four parts,

a)   a brief description of Napier88,
b)   a description of the implementation of the stable heap,
c)   a description of the implementation of the stable storage, and
d)   a brief description of how Staple and Galileo map onto the implementation.

4.1   Napier88

Napier88 is a persistent programming language with a sophisticated type system that permits the recursive definition of data structures including abstract data types and polymorphic first class procedures. As far as possible the Napier88 compilation system performs static type checking. That is, the compiler will determine whether or not an attempted operation is type correct. However, in those situations where this is not possible, appropriate dynamic checks are explicitly generated.

4.1.1   The Persistent Abstract Machine

The Napier88 compilation system maps programs onto an abstract machine, the Persistent Abstract Machine [con89]. The abstract machine is based on block retention and is responsible for implementing those primitives necessary to support the polymorphism and abstract data types. In turn, the abstract machine views the persistent object store as a single stable heap that is assumed to be a stable store of unbounded size. Since the abstract machine does not allow direct access to the persistent store it ensures that the compilation system is unaware of the implementation of the object storage, thus separating the use of an object from the way it is stored.

In addition to supporting Napier88, the abstract machine is constrained to use the persistent object store as its only available storage. This requires all the storage used by the abstract machine to be mapped onto persistent objects and it prohibits the use of known addresses to access predefined objects such as error handling procedures or literal values.

To support the use of predefined objects, the abstract machine maintains a special object that contains the address of every predefined object that may be required. When the architecture is first used, the abstract machine creates the special object and places its address in the root object of the stable heap. Thereafter, the special object can be accessed via the root object, whose address is provided by the interface to the stable heap. The predefined objects can then be accessed via the special object.

The combination of the block retention scheme and the persistent object store has an important consequence for the operation of the abstract machine, in that there is no separation of the available storage between a program's data and its dynamic state. In a traditional computer architecture, this division of storage may be in the form of a heap and a stack. When either the heap or stack is exhausted a program will fail even if there is storage available in the other. The advantage of eliminating the division is that a program will only fail when the entire storage has been exhausted.

The other features of the abstract machine are not relevant to the implementation of the persistent object store and are described elsewhere [con89].

4.1.2 Type Security

Within the Napier88 implementation of the layered architecture, all type security is enforced by the Napier88 compilation system. As described above, the compilation system enforces high level protection that either statically determines the validity of an operation at compile time or it explicitly generates an appropriate check to be performed at run-time. Consequently, the persistent abstract machine, the stable heap and the stable storage may assume that all attempted operations are type correct. Therefore no protection mechanisms need to be built into the implementations of these lower architectural layers.

4.2 The Stable Heap

An implementation of the stable heap must address several issues. These include:

a)   How much of the stable store can be modified between checkpoints?
b)   Can the system be stopped for the length of time required for a garbage collection?
c)   Which garbage collection algorithm is best suited to the size of the heap?
d)   Should the heap support direct or indirect object addressing?

The amount of data that can be modified between checkpoints of the stable store is specific to an instance of the architecture and may not be available to an implementor of the stable heap. Consequently, an implementation of a garbage collector must assume that several checkpoints may occur during each garbage collection. Furthermore, it must be able to restart the garbage collection after any of the checkpoints.

Another major issue that must be addressed in implementing the stable heap is the potential size of the heap. This has several consequences for the overall efficiency of the architecture. For example, a particular garbage collection algorithm may perform acceptably for a small heap but prove too slow for a very large heap. This problem would be further aggravated if the system to be supported could not be stopped for more than a few seconds at a time. Such a system would require a garbage collector that could operate concurrently with a user's programs.

The size of the stable heap also affects the choice of direct or indirect object addressing. For example, a very large heap that supported direct addressing may be unable to relocate objects during a garbage collection, due to the high cost of identifying and modifying all the copies of an object's address. Alternatively, an implementation of a small heap may not wish to support indirect addressing due to the space overhead involved.

The implementation we shall now describe was designed to support a potentially very large stable heap. As such, the storage allocation and garbage collection mechanisms were chosen with a view to minimising the costs associated with short lived temporary objects, the costs of storage fragmentation and the costs of modifying stable storage.

4.2.1 The Stable Heap Organisation

The stable heap is organised as two sections. The first section, at the low address end of the heap, contains objects and grows towards high addresses whereas the second section, at the high address end of the heap, contains two words for each object and grows towards low addresses. The second section is used to hold the stable storage address for each object and is known as the indirection table. The organisation of the heap is shown in Figure 2.

When an object is created, it is allocated space from the first section of the heap and a pair of words from the indirection table. Within the stable heap, the logical address of an object is the address of the pair of words in the indirection table. A logical address is known as a key. Indirect addressing was chosen to support object copying during a garbage collection since it allows all references to an object to be changed by a single modification to the indirection table [atk82,atk83b,bro85].

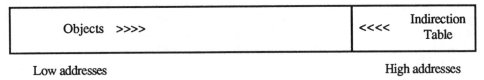

Low addresses   High addresses

Figure 2. The stable heap.

One word of the indirection table allocated to an object is used to hold the stable storage address of the object. The other word allocated to an object is divided between a mark-bit for the object and space reserved to record the progress of a marking algorithm, hereafter referred to as the *mark-stack*. One advantage of this organisation of the indirection table is that a mark-scan garbage collector may be implemented without needing to allocate additional storage to record the progress of a marking algorithm. Another advantage is that the marking of objects only involves modifying a relatively small area of stable storage, the indirection table, thereby reducing the potential overheads in modifying stable storage. Figure 3 illustrates the use of the indirection table and the space allocated to an object.

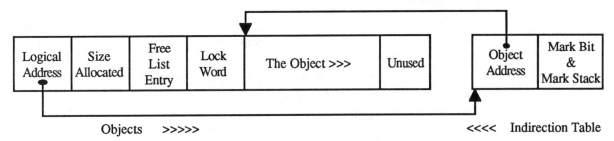

Objects   >>>>>   <<<<   Indirection Table

Figure 3. The layout of space allocated to an object.

4.2.2   Efficient Storage Reuse

One of the most significant factors affecting the overall performance of a system supporting first class procedures is the allocation and reclamation of activation records [bai89]. In a system that is able to statically determine whether or not an activation record must be retained, temporary activation records may be allocated from a stack. Although this technique may be very efficient once a program is running, it does require a separate stack area to be allocated to each active program. Furthermore, mechanisms must be provided to cope with possible stack overflows and any resultant storage fragmentation.

A system that cannot statically determine which activation records need to be retained requires an alternative storage allocation scheme. The storage allocation scheme chosen for the stable heap was designed to support such systems and has been tailored to support the efficient allocation and reclamation of activation records. The scheme is based on the use of free lists and operates as follows:

a) When an object is created it is allocated a multiple of some fixed size unit of storage, in addition to a pair of words from the indirection table. The choice of the fixed size units is made when the stable heap is implemented and should be based on the expected size of activation records. In the case of Napier88 a static analysis of user programs suggested activation records were usually of the order of 20 to 80 words. Consequently, a unit size of 16 words was chosen.

b) The first four words of allocated storage contain the following housekeeping information. The logical address of the object, the size of space allocated, a word for use in constructing a free list and a word to support object locking. The layout of space allocated to an object is shown in Figure 3.

c) When an object is no longer reachable, as determined by the garbage collector or at the end of a procedure call, it is added to a free list containing objects that have been allocated the same amount of storage. There is one free list for each size of allocation up to the expected maximum size of activation record. In the case of Napier88 there are

8 free lists allowing for activation records up to 128 words in size. Objects that do not have a corresponding free list are inserted into the first free list which is ordered in decreasing size.

d) When space is required for a new object its size is rounded up to the next multiple of the fixed size unit. The free list corresponding to the rounded up size is then checked to see if there is an object that can be reused. In the case of the first free list, which contains objects that were allocated different amounts of storage, a *best-fit* algorithm is used to search the list. The first entry may be taken from the other free lists. A new object is only created if a suitable object cannot be reused.

e) When an object is reused it is overwritten by the new object but retains the four prefixed housekeeping words and the pair of words in the indirection table. Thus, the logical address of the new object is the same as the object that is reused.

There are two major advantages of the free list approach just described. Firstly, it can be efficiently implemented. A native code Napier88 program can allocate and reclaim an activation record in 12 machine instructions. Another advantage of this approach is that multiple programs can be run without having to provide each program with its own stack. This reduces the potential fragmentation of the stable storage and the costs associated with starting a new program.

4.2.3   The Garbage Collector

The garbage collector implements a mark-scan algorithm that constructs a set of free lists containing objects that are no longer reachable from the root object. For example, consider the heap shown in Figure 4. It contains the root object and 10 other objects numbered 01 to O10 that are either size X or size Y.

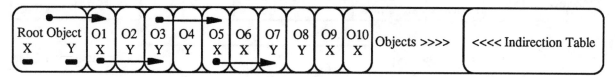

Figure 4. An example heap before garbage collection.

Since objects O1, O3, O5 and O7 are reachable from the root object the garbage collector would transform the heap shown in Figure 4 into the heap shown in Figure 5. After the garbage collection the free list for size X contains objects O6, O9 and O10 and the free list for size Y contains O2, O4 and O8.

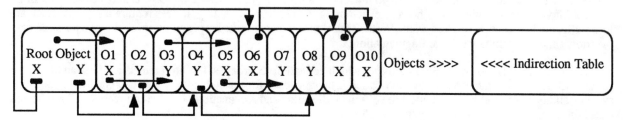

Figure 5. The example heap after garbage collection.

The garbage collection algorithm is composed of the following four steps:

a)   clear the mark-stack,
b)   mark the root object,
c)   mark objects pointed to by objects on the mark-stack, and
d)   construct a set of free lists one for each size of object.

4.2.3.1   Clear the Mark Stack

The words in the indirection table that were reserved for use for marking are cleared. At this point a flag is set in the root object to indicate the first step of the garbage collection has been completed.

4.2.3.2 Mark the Root Object

The root object in the heap is marked as reachable. This is performed by setting the mark-bit in the second word allocated to the root object in the indirection table. The stable storage address of the root object is then written to the first word of the mark-stack and a stack pointer is set to point at that word. It should be noted that writing a stable storage address to a word of the mark-stack will not affect the value of the mark-bit held in the word. Since all objects are word aligned, the two least significant bits of the mark-stack word can be reserved as mark-bits without restricting the maximum size of a stable storage address.

At this point a flag is set in the root object to indicate the second step of the garbage collection has been completed. The value of the stack pointer is always recorded by a checkpoint so that, if necessary, the marking algorithm can be automatically resumed following a failure.

4.2.3.3 Mark Objects Pointed to by Marked Objects

The next step is to scan the mark-stack and mark objects directly reachable from objects that have already been marked. That is, the object whose address is held in the mark-stack word referenced by the stack pointer is itself scanned. Each object address that is encountered is checked to see if it refers to a marked object. If it does not, the corresponding object is marked and its stable storage address is appended to the mark-stack. Once all the object addresses have been checked the stack pointer is moved onto the next word in the mark stack.

This step of the garbage collection continues until the stack pointer is moved past the end of the mark-stack. At this point every object reachable from the root object will have been marked. A flag is then set in the root object to indicate that this step of the garbage collection is complete.

4.2.3.4 Construct the Free Lists

The final step of the garbage collection is to construct a set of free lists. With one exception these free lists contain a list of unreachable objects that have been allocated the same amount of space. The exception is the first free list which contains entries for very small and very large objects. It is organised in decreasing order of size.

This step of the garbage collection is performed by scanning the indirection table and inserting the stable storage address of each unmarked object into the appropriate free list. Once the scanning is complete all unreachable objects will have been allocated to a free list and the garbage collection will be complete. A flag is then set in the root object to record this.

4.2.4 Checkpointing the stable heap

The stable heap is implemented directly on top of the stable storage layer. Therefore the stable heap's checkpoint mechanism can be implemented in two simple steps. Firstly, any data held outwith the stable heap must be replaced. The entire heap will then be held in stable storage. Secondly, the checkpoint procedure provided by the stable store's interface is invoked. This will checkpoint the stable storage and, therefore, checkpoint the stable heap.

4.2.5 Dynamic Configuration of Stable Storage

In order to operate correctly the underlying stable storage must be able to record any changes that may be made between checkpoints. To ensure that the changes can be recorded the stable heap makes use of the dynamic configuration routines described in section 3.3. At no point will an area of stable storage be updated unless the stable storage has given permission for the update to take place.

The cost of interrogating the stable storage prior to every update may be considerable. In order to avoid undue cost, the stable heap takes the following steps.

a) Following a garbage collection, checkpoint operation or system restart, some stable storage is allocated to hold any newly created objects. This storage is marked as save-only since its contents need only be recorded at the next checkpoint.

b) The root object, which holds all the housekeeping information for the stable heap, is marked as shadow so that it may be freely updated whenever a free list is modified.

c) Objects that are reclaimed from free lists must have the area of storage allocated to them marked as shadow since it may need to be restored if a failure occurs. However, any objects that were created since the last checkpoint can be reused without this overhead since they reside in an area of storage already marked as save-only.

d) When an object is reused only the free lists need to be updated. This is because the indirection words allocated to the reused object remain valid. The free lists are held in the root object which is always updatable.

e) Before an existing object is modified it must be marked as shadow. Although this cannot be circumvented, those activation records that form the dynamic chain will normally be newly created objects and already be modifiable. Therefore, a significant extra cost need only be incurred for updates to objects that are not part of the dynamic chain. In the case of the Staple system, the extra cost is estimated to be approximately a 10% performance penalty.

4.3   The Stable Storage

The stable storage provides a contiguous range of addresses whose associated storage that can always be restored to a self-consistent state. It also provides a checkpointing mechanism to change the self-consistent state to which the storage will be restored. The basic technique used to implement the stable storage is to make copies of those parts of the storage that are to be changed.

In the implementation to be described the address space is divided into pages with a page corresponding to a block of non-volatile storage. The stable storage operates by making copies of pages before they are changed. Thus, the state of the storage can be restored by replacing all the changed pages by their copies. To achieve a new self-consistent state, the appropriate changes are made and then all the copied pages are deleted. This prevents the stable storage being restored to a previous state. To ensure that the stable storage cannot be restored to an inconsistent state, the copied pages are deleted in a single atomic action. That is, regardless of when a failure may occur the copied pages will either all be deleted or none of them will.

4.3.1   The Layout of the Stable Storage

The stable storage is divided into 3 areas: a pair of root pages, those pages holding the live data and an area containing copies of pages before they were changed. Hereafter the third area will be referred to as *shadow storage*. The size of the stable storage and its division into the three areas is fixed when the store is created. The organisation of the stable storage is illustrated in Figure 6.

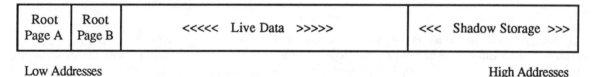

Low Addresses   High Addresses

Figure 6. The organisation of the stable storage.

4.3.2   Modifying Pages of Live Data

When a page of live data is to be modified for the first time, a copy of the page is made in the shadow storage. The modified page will not be written back to non-volatile storage until both the copy and a record of the copying have been written non-volatile storage. Furthermore, the record of the copying will not be written until after the copy is written. This guarantees that if a subsequent failure occurs, the original value of the modified page can be safely restored to its previous state.

When the system is restarted following a failure, the most recent self-consistent state can be restored by scanning the record of changed pages and overwriting them with their copies. Thus, to achieve a new self-consistent state it is sufficient to write all the modified pages to non-volatile storage, as described above, and then destroy the record of changed pages. The new values of the modified pages will then be treated as the most recent checkpoint.

4.3.3   The Root Pages

The record of which pages have been copied is essential to the correct operation of the stable storage. Therefore, to ensure that the record of copied pages is up to date it is protected by a transaction mechanism that operates over the pair of root pages. Logically, there is only one root page and it contains the dimensions of the stable storage, the record of which pages have been copied and housekeeping information that includes two version numbers for use by the stable heap and stable storage implementations. Figure 7 illustrates the format of the root page. The pair of root pages on non-volatile storage represent two different versions of the logical root page that are differentiated by a pair of date stamps. When a new value of the root page is written to non-volatile storage it overwrites the oldest of the pair of pages thereby preserving the previous value in case of failure.

When the system is restarted following a failure both root pages on non-volatile storage are read. The date stamps in each root page are compared to see which page is the most up to date. A further check is made to ensure that both date stamps within a particular root page are equal. If they are not equal then an I/O error occurred while the page was being written and the other page must be the most up to date. Since the most recent copy of the root page is never overwritten, at most one of the root pages should be corrupt.

Stable Store Version	Stable Heap Version	Date Stamp A	Sizes of Non-Volatile Storage	Number of Shadowed Pages	Record of Shadow Pages	Date Stamp B

Low Addresses   High Addresses

Figure 7. A root page.

The record of copied pages is implemented as follows: The root page holds a list of page numbers, the first page number records the page copied to the first page of shadow storage, the second page number records the page copied to the second page of shadow storage, and so on. To complement this, a count of how many pages have been copied is held. At any point in time this count indicates how much of the list of page numbers is valid. Thus, the record of copied pages can be destroyed by simply setting the count to 0.

4.3.4   The Underlying Non-volatile Storage

To support the transactional updates described above certain assumptions are made regarding the operation of the underlying non-volatile storage. Firstly, the non-volatile storage is made up of fixed equal size blocks. Pages in the stable storage correspond to one or more blocks of non-volatile storage. Other assumptions are that, a block can only be corrupted if it is being written to, if a write operation completes it did not cause any corruption, all blocks are written in a specific address order, reading a block never causes corruption and if a read or write fails the architecture halts.

In the implementation being described, the non-volatile storage is provided by a single fixed size disk file. This implementation strategy is based on the assumption that the host file system is block oriented and conforms to the required assumptions. In practice, these assumptions may not be valid but this limitation may be overcome by duplicating the file over several physical devices. In fact, it is possible to provide an arbitrarily stable store by maintaining multiple physically disjoint copies of the file [koh81]. Furthermore, each of the necessary assumptions could be implemented by procedures that would coordinate access to the multiple copies. However, for the purposes of experimentation, a single file supported by regular dumping is sufficient.

4.3.5   Identifying Changed Pages and Dynamic Configuration

In order to minimise the costs of implementing the stable storage, two sets of bitmaps are maintained to record which pages must be protected by copying and which pages have been modified. In the implementation being described these bitmaps are created each time the system is restarted and are discarded when the system halts or fails. Their sole purpose is to optimise the performance of the stable storage implementation.

When the system is restarted and the previous self-consistent state has been restored, the bitmaps are initialised to record the entire stable storage as read only and unmodified. The bitmaps both contain one bit for each page of live data, the *protected* bitmap contains a set bit for each page that must be copied before it is updated whereas the *written* bitmap contains a set bit for each page that has been updated.

When a configuration procedure is called, see section 3.3, the two bitmaps are consulted to determine what actions, if any, are required to support the desired use of the specified area of stable storage. In deciding which actions are appropriate, account is taken of conflicting demands on a single page. The choice of actions will guarantee that if any part of a page contains live data, then the data will be preserved. If necessary the entire page is copied. As a precondition for granting the desired use of an area of stable storage, the configuration procedures will check that the necessary non-volatile storage is available. A configuration request will fail if the necessary physical resources are not available.

4.3.6 Checkpointing the Stable Storage

A checkpoint of the stable storage is performed in two simple steps. Firstly, all modified pages that form part of the next checkpoint are written to non-volatile storage. These pages may be identified from the written and protected bitmaps, they are marked as both modified and protected. Once all these pages have been written to non-volatile storage, the record of changed pages is destroyed. This second step involves setting the count of copied pages to 0, and then writing the root page to non-volatile storage. The checkpoint is now complete and the non-volatile storage contains a new self-consistent state.

4.4 Staple and Galileo

The Staple and Galileo programming languages are both implemented via abstract machines. Staple is compiled onto the CASE machine [dav88] and Galileo is compiled onto the FAM machine [car83]. In order to minimise the cost of re-implementation, both of these programming languages may be mapped onto the layered architecture by interfacing their abstract machines to the stable heap.

Staple uses the persistent store as an enabling technology with which to implement the programming environment. A major advantage of using the persistent store is that the task of implementing name equivalence based type checking is greatly simplified. Since all program modules and types are loaded into the persistent store, equivalent types can be represented by a pointer to the same object.

The Galileo implementation will be used as a base on which to conduct experiments with transactions. The integration of the existing Galileo implementation with the layered architecture will result in a system that is functionally equivalent to the design originally proposed for Galileo [alb85b].

5 Performance

High performance is a desirable property of any computer system. In the case of the layered architecture just described we are investigating techniques that will allow an implementation to achieve high levels of performance while retaining the flexibility offered by the layering. Our initial approach has been to investigate native code generation as an alternative to an interpreted abstract machine.

The code generation technique we have adopted is based on a macro expansion of the Persistent Abstract Machine's abstract code. Macro expansion was chosen for two reasons. Firstly, this localises the re-implementation task to changing the final phase of compilation and providing a relatively simple boot strapping mechanism. Since the compilation system is still generating abstract machine code, the majority of the compilation system and all the higher levels of the architecture remain unaltered. Furthermore, since the native code is functionally equivalent to the abstract machine code the existing object store implementations can still be used.

The second reason for choosing macro expansion is that the resulting native code can be effectively optimised. The Persistent Abstract Machine is stack based requiring a significant number of stack load and assign instructions. If the hardware registers are used as a cache for efficiently accessing the stack then most of the stack based instructions can be compiled away. For example, a stack load instruction may involve copying a word to the top of stack. This operation can be reduced to loading the desired word into a register and then establishing a mapping from the register to the top of the stack. If the desired word is already in a register then the operation can be further reduced to simply re-mapping the register to represent the top of stack. Consequently, the operation would not require any code to be executed at run-time.

To complement the code generator we have also investigated extending the interface to the persistent object store to permit the interface functions to be compiled away. That is, the code generator is given explicit knowledge of how to interpret an object's logical address thereby allowing the native code to access objects at full memory speed. However, all operations attempted by a program will still conform to the object store's published interface.

Another optimisation technique under investigation is to permit programs to manage temporary free lists, separate from those managed by the persistent store, in order to efficiently reuse activation records. In the experimental code generated system for Napier88 this technique allows an activation record to be allocated and reclaimed in 12 machine instructions. Consequently, code generated Napier88 programs can perform procedure calls at about a third of the speed of C.

Finally, we are investigating the use of a fault handler as a mechanism for optimising updates to objects outwith the dynamic chain. When an area of stable storage is updated without specifying the intended use via the configuration routines, then an implementation of the stable storage could generate a write fault. As described in section 4.2.5, updates to objects that do not form part of the dynamic chain can incur a significant overhead. One reason for this is that a check is required to ensure that these objects can be safely modified without exhausting the available shadow storage. The use of a fault handler allows these objects to be modified without the overheads of explicit checks but provides a mechanism for automatically copying an object when it is first modified. In addition, by giving the fault handler explicit knowledge of the code generation techniques, it may be possible to perform an automatic checkpoint if an update to an object would exhaust the shadow storage. This allows improved performance to be achieved without sacrificing functionality.

The initial measurements of code generated Napier88 suggest that naive code generation in combination with the optimisation techniques just described may result in a system whose overall performance is comparable to un-optimised C.

6 Conclusions

We have presented the design of a layered architecture that provides a flexible framework with which to conduct experiments in persistence. The layered architecture has been used in implementations of the persistent programming language Napier88 and the functional programming language Staple. An implementation of the database programming language Galileo is under construction. We have also demonstrated that the architecture can be efficiently implemented while preserving the flexibility of the layering. We are currently working on the application of this implementation technique to the study of large scale distributed systems.

7 Acknowledgements

This work was undertaken at St.Andrews University during the study leave period of Prof. J. Rosenberg of the University of Newcastle, New South Wales. The work was supported by SERC Grant GR/F 28571, SERC Post-doctoral Fellowship B/ITF/199, ESPRIT II Basic Research Action 3070 - FIDE and a grant from the DTI Awareness Initiative in Object Oriented Programming.

8 References

[alb85a] Albano A., Cardelli L. & Orsini R. Galileo: A Strongly Typed, Interactive Conceptual Language. ACM Transactions on Database Systems, vol. 10, no. 2, 1985, pp230-260.

[alb85b] Albano A., Ghelli G. & Orsini R. The Implementation of Galileo's Values Persistence. Proc. First Appin Workshop on Persistence and Data Types. Universities of Glasgow and St Andrews PPRR-16, Scotland, 1985, pp197-208.

[atk82] Atkinson M.P., Chisholm K.J. & Cockshott W.P. CMS - A Chunk Management System. Software Practice and Experience, vol. 13, no. 3, March 1983.

[atk83a] Atkinson M.P., Bailey P.J., Chisholm K.J. Cockshott W.P. & Morrison R. An Approach to Persistent Programming. The Computer Journal, vol. 26, no. 4, 1983, pp360-365.

[atk83b] Atkinson M.P., Bailey P.J., Cockshott W.P., Chisholm K.J. & Morrison R. The Persistent Object Management System. Universities of Glasgow and St Andrews PPRR-1, Scotland, 1983.

[bai89] Bailey, P.J. Performance Evaluation in a Persistent Object System. Proc. Third International Workshop on Persistent Object Systems: Their Design Implementation and Use. Newcastle, New South Wales, Australia, January 1989, pp373-385.

[bel88] Beloff B., McIntyre D. & Drummond B. Rekursiv Hardware. Linn Smart Computing Ltd, 1988.

[bro85] Brown A.L. & Cockshott W.P. The CPOMS Persistent Object Management System. Universities of Glasgow and St.Andrews PPRR-13, Scotland, 1985.

[bro89]   Brown A.L. (Ph.D. Thesis) Persistent Object Stores. Universities of Glasgow and St.Andrews PPRR-71, Scotland, 1989.

[bro90]   Brown A.L., Dearle A., Morrison R., Munro D.S. & Rosenberg J. A Layered Persistent Architecture for Napier88. International Workshop on Computer Architectures to Support Security and Persistence, Universität Bremen, West Germany, May 1990.

[car83]   Cardelli L. The Functional Abstract Machine. AT&T Bell Laboratories Technical Report, TR-107, 1983.

[con89]   Connor R.C.H., Brown A.L., Carrick R., Dearle A. & Morrison R. The Persistent Abstract Machine. Proc. Third International Workshop on Persistent Object Systems: Their Design Implementation and Use. Newcastle, New South Wales, Australia, January 1989, pp80-95.

[dav88]   Davie A.J.T. & McNally D.J. CASE - A Lazy Version of an SECD Machine in a Flat Environment. Staple Project Research Report, Staple/StA/88/2, University of St.Andrews, Scotland, 1988.

[gol83]   Goldberg A. & Robson D. Smalltalk-80: The Language and its Implementation. Addison Wesley, 1983.

[gra81]   Gray J., McJones P., Blasgen M., Lindsay B., Lorie R., Price T., Putzolu F. & Traiger I. The Recovery Manager of the System R Database Manager. Computing Surveys, vol. 13, no. 2, June 1981, pp223-242.

[koh81]   Kohler W.H. A Survey of Techniques for Synchronisation and Recovery in Decentralised Computer Systems. ACM Computing Surveys, vol. 13, no. 2, 1981, pp149-183.

[lor77]   Lorie A.L. Physical Integrity in a Large Segmented Database, ACM Transactions on Database Systems, vol. 2, no. 1, 1977, pp91-104.

[mcn90]   McNally D.J., Joosten S. & Davie A.J.T. Persistent Functional Programming in the Large. Proc. Fourth International Workshop on Persistent Object Systems: Their Design Implementation and Use. Martha's Vineyard, Massachusetts, USA, September 1990.

[mor89]   Morrison R., Brown A.L., Connor R. & Dearle A. The Napier88 Reference Manual. Universities of Glasgow and St.Andrews PPRR-77, Scotland, 1989.

[ros83]   Ross G.D.M. Virtual Files: A Framework for Experimental Design. (PhD Thesis), University of Edinburgh, 1983.

[ros90]   Rosenberg J., Henskens F., Brown A.L., Morrison R. & Munro D.S. Stability in a Persistent Store Based on a Large Virtual Memory. International Workshop on Computer Architectures to Support Security and Persistence, Universität Bremen, West Germany, May 1990.

[tha86]   Thatte S.M. Persistent Memory: A Storage Architecture for Object Oriented Database Systems. Proc. ACM/IEEE 1986 International Workshop on Object Oriented Database Systems, Pacific Grove, CA, September 1986, pp148-159.

Part VI
Architectures

Chair: Ron Morrison

The persistence abstraction is in part a reaction to the late 1960s and early 1970s model of computation based on small, volatile, fast main stores and large, stable, slow rotating technologies. The advent of new hardware technologies with different time, space and cost trade-offs together with the advent of new applications areas, such as office automation, CAD/CAM, CASE, etc. has led to proposals for different models of computation both linguistically and architecturally. Persistence is one such model which allows the complexity of applications construction to be alleviated thereby reducing the cost of designing, implementing and maintaining the uses of long term data.

The persistent abstraction requires

- Programming methodologies to express the development of persistent systems;

- Programming languages in which persistent computations may be expressed; and

- System architectures, both software and hardware, to support the implementations of the methodologies and languages.

The debate on persistent system architectures has so far concentrated on the provision of a persistent store. Some desirable properties of such a store have been identified. They are

- a freedom in binding mechanisms that allows the reuse of components in the store to match the needs of the programmer;

- unbounded capacity to match the conceptually unbounded nature of the stores provided in some languages;

- infinite speed to overcome latency problems; and

- error free semantics.

The properties of persistent stores given above are not realistic in terms of implementations with current technologies. They therefore have to be approximated in such a manner that the persistence abstraction is not totally compromised.

More controversially, other desirable properties of persistent stores have been proposed. These include protection mechanisms, transaction control, version management and concurrency control. The difficulty is that if one mechanism is built in, which one should it be and will it be efficient or even appropriate for all applications? On the other hand building such mechanisms above the store is thought to be inefficient.

The papers in this section concentrate on the mechanisms for providing the components of persistent architectures. There is an underlying debate as to whether the systems should be built out of layers, as in the Monads system, or out of tools, as in "a la Carte".

Layering allows abstractions to be built up in layers and provides a framework for the reuse of the layer interfaces to test experimental systems. Rosenberg describes the Monads architecture in five layers - physical memory, virtual address space, virtual store, object store and abstract machine. This is similar to other work on layering by Balch et al [Software Engineering Journal,4,2,1989] but is based on the description of a real architecture. Each of the layers may be implemented by different modules to provide architectures with different performance characteristics. Rosenberg's paper proposes three methods of mapping Napier88 on to the system at the abstract machine level.

In "Memory Semantics in Large Grained Persistent Objects", Dasgupta and Chen concentrate on the provision of tools for abstracting over four types of storage. These are per-object memory, per invocation memory, per thread memory and the derived per-object/per thread memory. The per object memory is persistent and allows concurrent executions and sharing of data. The other categories control the visibility and extent of the data. Memory systems for all our persistent programming needs may be constructed from the tool set.

The third paper in the group, "A la Carte..." by Drew, King and Bein, describes a framework for tailoring systems out of components in heterogeneous object stores. This consists of a backbone into which the user, with the aid of a software tool, can plug the appropriate components for the application in hand. The work has three objectives

- to specify the framework;

- to design plugable components; and

- to provide a toolkit environment for heterogeneous configurations without immersion in the entire implementations.

The MONADS Architecture
A Layered View

John Rosenberg
Department of Electrical Engineering & Computer Science
University of Newcastle
New South Wales 2308
Australia
johnr@nucs.cs.nu.oz.au

ABSTRACT

The MONADS architecture was developed with three main goals in mind. These were support for orthogonal persistence via a large uniform virtual memory, support for a uniform and secure protection scheme based on capabilities, and support for the construction of programs as independent information-hiding modules with purely procedural interfaces. The MONADS-PC implementation of the architecture was strongly influenced by these goals. Previously we have described the architecture and implementation in these terms, with a strong bias towards the MONADS philosophy. In this paper we give a layered view of the architecture. It is shown that the architecture is far more general than it may first appear and that it is possible to substitute different higher level layers to support other persistence paradigms, either concurrently with MONADS or as a standalone system. As an example, the paper discusses mapping the Napier88 language and environment onto the MONADS architecture.

1 Introduction

The MONADS project has as its central aim the development of a computing environment providing a high level of security and a good approach to software engineering. Such an environment should result in reliable, consistent and secure systems. In order to achieve these aims a new architecture has been developed. The key features of this architecture are:

- support for orthogonal persistence via a uniform virtual memory with very large addresses (128 bits in the latest implementation)

- a uniform and secure protection scheme based on the presentation of capabilities

- support for the construction of programs as independent information-hiding modules with purely procedural interfaces

A subsidiary aim of the project is that these goals should be achieved without loss of efficiency. For this reason the architecture has been implemented using a combination of hardware, microcode and software. There are two implementations. The first is known as MONADS-PC [16] and is a locally designed microcoded processor of which four prototypes are operational. The second, known as MONADS-MM [19], is currently being designed, based on the SPARC chipset [21].

Previously we have described the architecture and implementation in terms of the MONADS philosophy [11, 18]. In this paper we give a layered view of the architecture. It is shown that the architecture is far more general than it may first appear and that it is possible to substitute different higher level layers to support other persistence paradigms, either concurrently with MONADS or as a standalone system. As an example, the paper discusses mapping the Napier88 language and environment [13] onto the MONADS architecture.

2   Layered Persistent Architectures

The specification, design and implementation of a computer architecture is a complex task. This is because an architecture includes many diverse facilities for use by software executing on the machine. Different categories of software make use of facilities at different levels. For example, a user program simply wants to be able to create and manipulate objects and does not want to be concerned with how the memory and/or disk storage in which the objects reside is managed[1]. On the other hand, the operating system must have the ability to directly control the storage and the mapping from virtual to physical addresses.

The usual approach to simplifying the design of complex systems is to employ abstraction. Applying this technique to a computer architecture can result in a layered view of an architecture. That is, the architecture is described as a sequence of layers, each building upon the facilities provided by lower levels and providing a more powerful (and abstract) architectural interface to the layer above. Similar techniques have been applied to the design of communication protocols such as the OSI reference model [9].

Balch et al [1] have previously proposed a general standard for layered implementations of persistent architectures and have applied this standard to a well-known family of microprocessors [4]. Their model has seven layers as follows.

(-2)   *Physical memory*, including disk and RAM

(-1)   *Virtual store*, a non-volatile flat virtual address space

(0)   *Object store*, a layer supporting untyped persistent objects

(1)   *Base types,* elementary types, e.g. integers, reals, instructions, etc.

(2)   *Aggregate types,* type composition rules to form aggregates, e.g. structures and functions

(3)   *Abstract types,* mechanisms for the constructions of new abstract types

(4)   *Applications,* user specific application software

Each layer has an interface defined in a parametric form. Any particular implementation would in addition provide an applied specification which defines the parameters for each layer, including the size of persistent pointers and minimum and maximum object sizes. The intention is that all implementations of object stores would adhere to this standard and this would allow developers of new persistent languages to use existing object stores. In addition it would facilitate the transfer of persistent objects between systems.

While there is virtue in defining standards, it is difficult to ensure that the standard is general enough to cater for all of the needs of future systems. This is particularly the case in a relatively new area such as persistent systems, where concepts and ideas are still being defined. For example, layer -1 assumes a single flat virtual address space. Some systems may wish to partition this address space and have this partitioning visible to higher layers for organisational reasons such as assignment of regions of the virtual address space to particular disks.

Brown has described a layered architecture for the Napier88 system [3]. In that architecture there are four layers as shown below.

---

[1]We exclude efficiency considerations (e.g. requirements for objects to be placed in consecutive locations in secondary storage) at this stage for simplicity.

- *Non-volatile storage*, i.e. disks

- *Stable storage*, a flat stable virtual address space

- *Heap of persistent objects*, possibly incorporating a protection scheme

- *Abstract machine*, supports the Napier88 abstract machine instructions which guarantee type security

The structure is very similar to that of Balch with layers 1, 2 and 3 being incorporated into the abstract machine. The major purpose of the layered structure in Brown's scheme is to facilitate experimentation and software re-use. The layering simplifies the task of experimenting with different implementations, e.g. virtual memory management schemes, heap management schemes, etc. It also makes it easier to transport the software to a new machine, since in general only the lower level layers need be modified.

In the next section we describe the MONADS architecture in terms of layers of abstraction. The techniques used are similar to those described above.

3   The MONADS Architecture Layers

The MONADS architecture can be viewed as consisting of five conceptual layers. The purpose of providing this view is not, however, to achieve portability in the sense of Balch. We believe that an appropriate hardware base is required for efficient persistent systems and are therefore unlikely to move the MONADS system to current conventional architectures. The layered view is provided to support and encourage experimentation, in the same sense as Brown. We are particularly interested in transporting other persistent systems to the MONADS architecture, and in a later section of this paper we discuss the implications of running a Napier88 system on MONADS. Since portability is not an issue we have not restricted ourselves to idealised interfaces, and such entities as registers appear in the layer specifications.

The five layers in the MONADS architecture are:

- *Physical memory*: the physical storage on the machine consisting of primary store (RAM and ROM) and secondary store (disks).

- *Virtual address space*: an addressing mechanism which supports the mapping of a large, flat virtual address space onto primary store addresses.

- *Virtual store*: a non-volatile partitioned virtual store which hides the distinction between different types of physical store, handles page faults and supports multiple concurrent activities, i.e. processes.

- *Object store*: a repository of untyped objects. Each object can contain some data and references to other objects. This layer ensures that only such references are used to access another object.

- *Abstract machine*: this is the layer which imposes a discipline on the management and organisation of the object store

It should be noted that the positions of the layers do not indicate anything about the implementation. In the MONADS-PC system, for example, the first two layers are directly implemented in hardware and the last three layers enlist microcode support. In the MONADS-MM system there is no microcode and much of the abstract machine is implemented in the kernel.

In many cases a particular interface appears in several layers. No new functionality is added in such cases. Usually the outer layer facility is restricted and subject to tighter control in order to guarantee the integrity of the system.

In the remainder of this section we examine each of these layers in more detail. An informal description of each of the interfaces is given. In these descriptions it is assumed that there are certain constant parameters to the architecture which are available to all levels. These include the word size, virtual address size, page size and number of addressing registers.

3.1   Physical Memory

In a sense this is a conceptual layer in that any given implementation will have its own physical addressing structure. However, there are some interesting issues and decisions which must be made at this level. The most important of these is to decide what constitutes memory and what is an input-output device.

The present implementations encompass only primary and secondary store as part of the virtual store. All other devices, including those used for backup, are accessed using conventional input-output techniques and their control blocks are made available as special portions of memory which can then be incorporated into the kernel's virtual address space. Backup devices such as tapes are therefore *not* considered to be an extension of the virtual address space, but rather a special form of replication.

Apart from the obvious ability to read and write memory this layer provides the upper layers with a specification of the memory and input-output device configuration.

3.2   Virtual Address Space

This layer provides a mechanism for mapping large virtual addresses to primary store addresses. It defines no structure on the virtual addresses. It is expected that the mechanism would be hardware-supported for efficiency. The interface is defined below.

- *Read and write byte/half-word/word*: allows reading and writing of a byte, half-word or word of data currently in primary store using a flat virtual address. An exception is raised if the referenced data is currently not in primary store, if the map entry is invalid (see below) or if an attempt is made to write to a page marked as read-only.

- *Probe byte/half-word/word*: returns a boolean result indicating whether the referenced data is currently in primary store.

- *Map virtual page*: maps a virtual page to a specified primary store page. The page may be marked as read-only, which is required to implement certain network paging schemes [8] and stability algorithms [7, 17], and as non-cacheable, which is required for memory-mapped input-output devices.

- *Unmap virtual page*: removes the mapping for the specified virtual page.

- *Get map entry*: returns the map entry, including the primary store page number and status bits, for the specified virtual page, and returns a boolean flag indicating if the page exists.

- *Set/clear invalid flag*: sets or clears the invalid flag for the specified virtual page. Setting the invalid flag for a page does not remove the map entry, but any subsequent access to a byte in the page will cause an exception. This facility is useful for certain memory management algorithms such as second-chance.

- *Set/clear read-only flag*: sets or clears the read-only flag for the specified virtual page. Write access to a read only-page causes an exception.

The distinction between this virtual address space layer and the next layer, called the virtual store, is significant. It allows a clear separation between the translation of virtual addresses to primary store addresses and the management of the secondary store, and therefore facilitates independent experimentation with both addressing and virtual memory management mechanisms. A similar approach has been taken in recent UNIX look-alike systems such as Mach [15] and Choices [20] for portability reasons.

3.3   Virtual Store

The virtual store layer makes use of the virtual addressing mechanism to support a one level store encompassing all primary and secondary store. It is therefore responsible for handling page faults and managing free space in both primary and secondary store. The virtual store is not flat, rather it is divided into regions called *address spaces*. These address spaces are potentially very large (up to 2^{32} bytes on the MONADS-MM system). The reasons for the division are related to flexibility and efficiency. In particular we wish to provide a system which is at least as efficient and flexible as a conventional file system. It is expected that related data will be grouped together in a single address space (in the same sense as a file or a database), allowing memory management parameters to be defined individually for each address space. Such parameters include the disk on which the pages are located and the page replacement algorithm. The latter is chosen from a list of algorithms, including LRU and sequential pre-page, supported by the virtual store layer.

The address spaces are identified by *address space numbers*. Each virtual address is divided into two components, the address space number and the offset within address space. Each new address space created is given a unique number which will never be re-used for another address space in the life of the system. For this reason address space numbers are very large (96 bits on the MONADS-MM system). As a result the complications associated with aliasing problems experienced on some other systems [14] are avoided and garbage collection is simplified since an entire address space may be safely deleted without the risk of an *undetected* dangling reference. The subsequent use of a reference into a deleted address space will cause an invalid address exception.

The virtual store layer is designed to support concurrent processes. It interfaces with a process scheduler via an exception mechanism which allows a new process to be executed while the disk transfer associated with a page fault occurs. Within the process scheduler a process is represented by a process control block (PCB) which is held within the store itself. The PCB contains the values of all working registers (both addressing and arithmetic) for the corresponding process. Since the PCB is held within the store itself, processes automatically persist.

Finally, the virtual store layer provides access to input-output devices including terminals, printers and backup peripherals. The input-output interface is quite conventional and is not described here.

The interface for the virtual memory layer is shown below.

- *Read and write byte/half-word/word*: allows reading and writing of a byte, half-word or word of data at the specified virtual address. An exception is raised if an attempt is made to access a non-existent address.

- *Create address space*: creates a new address space on a specified physical secondary storage device. A maximum size in pages and the page replacement algorithm may also be specified.

- *Create temporary address space*: creates a non-persistent address space. Such address spaces, which are useful for operations creating very large temporary data structures, would usually be held entirely in primary store.

- *Delete address space*: deletes the specified address space and releases all memory (primary and secondary) associated with it. Subsequent use of an address within this address space will cause an exception.

- *Stabilise*: checkpoints a specified set of address spaces onto stable storage. Appropriate schemes for implementing the stabilise operation are described in [7, 17].

3.4   Object Store

The object store layer provides a higher level abstraction of the virtual store. The object store is a repository of arbitrary length objects, called *segments*. Each segment has the same basic structure, consisting of some control information, a data section and a *segment capability* section. A segment must be fully contained within a single address space and the size of the segment is fixed at the time of its creation. The control information contains the length of the data and segment capability portions of the segment and a type/access rights field. This last field may be used by higher layers to differentiate between different kinds of segments, e.g. for protection reasons.

Segment capabilities are references to other segments. These are normally held in a short form which can only refer to a segment in the same address space, since this is the most common usage. References to segments in other address spaces are achieved by an automatic indirection mechanism. An attempt to store a reference to a segment in a different address space causes the creation of an additional hidden indirection segment containing the full virtual address of the target segment.

Each address space has a distinguished segment, called the *root segment*. The root segment is automatically created when the address space is created. During a garbage collection only those segments reachable from the root segment of one of the address spaces being examined will be retained.

The interface to the object store includes a set of addressing registers, called *capability registers*, which are the only means of access to segments. Each capability register contains the virtual address of the referenced segment and a copy of the control information of the segment. All fields of a capability register may be read, but only the type/access field may be written. Access to the contents of a segment is always achieved by specifying a capability register. There is one distinguished capability register called the *code capability register*. The code capability register contains a segment capability for the code of the current procedure.

The interface to the object store layer is shown below.

- *Read and write byte/half-word/word*: allows reading and writing of a byte, half-word or word from the data portion of the segment referred to by the specified capability register. The offset within the segment is specified as an integer. An exception is raised if an attempt is made to access beyond the end of the data portion of the segment.

- *Create address space*: as in the virtual store layer, except that the size and type/access for the root segment are also specified.

- *Create temporary address space*: as in the virtual store layer, except that the size and type/access for the root segment are also specified.

- *Delete address space*: as in the virtual store layer.

- *Stabilise*: checkpoints a specified set of address spaces onto stable storage.

- *Create segment*: creates a segment of specified size and type/access in the specified address space and returns a segment capability for this segment in the specified capability register. An exception is raised if the address space is full.

- *Delete segment*: deletes the segment indicated in the specified capability register. Only the last segment in an address space may be deleted. This is useful for implementing stack address spaces.

- *Get root segment*: loads a segment capability for the root segment for the specified address space into the specified capability register.

- *Load capability register*: loads a segment capability into the specified capability register. The segment capability to be loaded is indicated by a capability register and an offset to the required capability.

- *Store capability*: stores a segment capability from the specified capability register. The destination is indicated by a capability register and an offset to the destination capability within the segment. An indirection segment is automatically created if required.

- *Garbage collect*: causes a compacting garbage collection to take place. A set of address spaces is specified and they are all garbage collected, including cross-address-space references (see below).

The object store layer guarantees that segments are created correctly and that capability registers are only loaded with segment capabilities. However, it does not alone guarantee the integrity of the object store. This is left to the next layer above. Thus if there is a cross-address-space reference and one of the address spaces is garbage collected alone, then a dangling reference can result. It is the responsibility of the next layer to ensure that appropriate address spaces are garbage collected together. In the case of the MONADS abstract machine this is not difficult [18]. For other systems (e.g. Napier88) it may be necessary to garbage collect all existing address spaces together.

3.5   The Abstract Machine

The abstract machine is the outermost layer and is the only layer visible to programs. It is this layer which effectively supports the MONADS philosophy and persistence paradigm and guarantees the security and integrity of data. This level of the MONADS architecture has been fully described in other publications [11, 18] and thus we do not provide the full interface description, but rather only a brief review.

The MONADS abstract machine effectively implements a primitive type system over the data portion of segments. The type/access rights field contains a simple type which then defines the permissible operations on the segment. Only a limited number of abstract machine types are supported. These include *module capability* and *simple data*. Module capability segments may only be manipulated by specific abstract machines instructions whereas simple data segments may be arbitrarily read and written.

The abstract machine supports information-hiding modules as the fundamental software construct. An information-hiding module consists of a set of procedures and some internal data. The data may only be accessed by the corresponding procedures. There may be many instances of any given module type. Each such instance has its own private data and shares the code with all other instances of that type.

When a new instance of a module type is produced a module capability for that instance is provided by the abstract machine. In order to call one of the interface procedures of the module the correct module capability must be produced. Since these are held only in module capability segments they cannot be maliciously or accidentally constructed. A module capability is either obtained by virtue of creating a new instance, or given to the user by another user/program. The latter is easily achieved since module capabilities can be passed as parameters and copied, subject to certain restrictions [10]. A module capability contains a list of the interface procedures which may be called by the holder. Thus it is possible to provide restricted views of modules.

Finally, the MONADS abstract machine layer enforces certain rules concerning cross-address-space references. These rules limit the propagation of segment capabilities and make it possible to safely garbage collect individual address spaces in most cases.

By changing the abstract machine, different persistence paradigms can be supported. Such new abstract machines can enlist microcode support resulting in a more efficient implementation. It is also possible to have multiple abstract machines executing on the same store since mechanisms for enforcing protection between objects are provided at an inner level. Such multiple abstract machines may share common facilities. Of course, if two procedures executing on different abstract machines wish to communicate then they must agree on a suitable protocol.

4   Mapping Napier88 onto MONADS

In this section we consider the mapping of the Napier88 language and environment onto the layered architecture described above. Napier88 is a persistent programming language with a quite sophisticated type system [12]. It supports recursive data structures, first-class polymorphic procedures and abstract data types. As far as possible static type checking is employed. Dynamic type checks are used only for vector indexing operations, for ensuring constancy of constant structure fields, and for projections out of infinite unions.

Napier88 supports first class procedures via a block retention mechanism. A separate object is created for each stack frame so that it can be retained if required, i.e. if there are any references from outside the frame to variables within the frame.

Napier88 has a quite different persistence paradigm from the MONADS abstract machine and thus it is a good test of the flexibility of the architecture. Napier88 does not partition the store or enforce any rules about encapsulation. Arbitrary graph structures may be created between objects and thus the entire store must eventually be garbage collected at once.

The current implementation of Napier88 runs on Sun3 and Sun4 architectures using an object store based on memory-mapped files [3]. The compiler produces an abstract machine code [2] which is then interpreted at run-time. Protection is enforced by this abstract machine in conjunction with the compiler. In order to ensure type security it is essential that only the compiler be able to produce executable objects, i.e. procedures. Mechanisms which can be used to achieve this are described in [5].

There are three basic possibilities for mapping Napier88 onto MONADS. The first is to replace the MONADS abstract machine layer with a Napier88 layer. This would result in a dedicated Napier88 machine. The second is to provide a second abstract machine layer concurrently with the MONADS abstract machine, and the third is to implement the Napier88 abstract machine above the MONADS abstract machine. In the remainder of this section we consider each of these alternatives.

4.1   Replace MONADS Abstract Machine with Napier88 Abstract Machine

This first alternative involves implementing the Napier88 abstract machine directly above the object store layer described above, which does support the required facilities. This would be achieved by defining a new instruction set based on the current Napier88 abstract machine and mapping this onto the available hardware. On the MONADS-PC system this would involve developing new microcode to directly support the instruction set, whereas on the MONADS-MM the Napier88 abstract machine code would have to be translated into the extended SPARC assembly language supported by that architecture. Alternatively, the Napier88 compiler could be modified to produce SPARC machine code. Neither of these alternatives would present any conceptual difficulty. Appropriate support code for basic input-output would also have to be provided as part of the abstract machine. However, much of the code developed as part of the MONADS abstract machine could be re-used for this purpose.

The more interesting consideration is the partitioning of the object store into address spaces. Napier88 does not have any such concept and views the object store as flat. There are two alternatives. The first is to place the entire Napier88 object store in one address space. Since address spaces may be up to 2^{32} bytes, which is considerably larger than any existing object store known to the author, this would not seem to be a severe restriction. If a larger object store is required this can be achieved by using several address spaces. Some management software would be required to determine the address space in which an object is to be created and all address spaces would be garbage collected at the one time.

The partitioning of the store does open up another possibility, namely the support of several independent Napier88 stores concurrently. This is of interest since the Napier88 language designers are currently considering the question of multiple, possibly distributed, object stores.

The approach described in this subsection should produce an efficient Napier88 system. However, the major disadvantage is that the machine would support only the one language.

4.2   Concurrent MONADS and Napier88 Abstract Machines

The second possibility is essentially an extension of the first. This involves supporting both the MONADS and Napier88 abstract machines concurrently, but essentially independently. Each abstract machine layer would be allocated a separate range of address spaces and would manage these independently. There would have to be some co-operation in order to schedule the processor and manage peripherals. In a sense this is the equivalent of the virtual machine approach used on some IBM systems [6].

Such an arrangement will allow a range of languages to be supported under the MONADS environment without compromising the efficiency of Napier88. However, it does potentially compromise the security of the MONADS system, since incorrect use of the object store layer by the Napier88 abstract machine can result in illegal access being gained to MONADS store objects, e.g. if address spaces with cross references are not garbage collected together.

4.3   Napier88 Abstract Machine based on MONADS Abstract Machine

The third possibility is to implement Napier88 above the MONADS abstract machine layer. At first this may seem impossible because of the MONADS enforced encapsulation. However, it can be achieved with only minor modifications and extensions to the MONADS abstract machine and with a restriction of the size of the Napier88 object store to one address space.

The basic idea is that Napier88 runs as a single module under MONADS. The module has one interface procedure which starts the Napier88 system and has the Napier88 object store as its encapsulated data. MONADS places no restrictions on references between objects within a single module and so arbitrary data structures may be built by Napier88 procedures running within the Napier88 module.

Currently the MONADS architecture requires that the code for a module be statically created before any instances of the module are created. In order to support Napier88 this condition would have to be relaxed. New MONADS abstract machine instructions could be provided to allow code segments (procedures) to be created by an executing module. Creation of such a segment would return a segment capability which could then be used to call the procedure. The Napier88 compiler would be a callable procedure within the module and would produce a procedure segment as a result of compilation. The compiler would produce MONADS abstract machine instructions, although for efficiency it might be sensible to add some new instructions specifically for Napier88. Closures could be represented by two segment capabilities, one for the code segment and one for the stack frame. This is similar to their representation within the current Napier88 system.

A major advantage of this approach is that the security of both Napier88 and MONADS are guaranteed. Napier88 cannot directly access any MONADS segment and, since the Napier88 object store is encapsulated within the Napier88 module, type security can be ensured. It is still possible to have multiple Napier88 object stores by having multiple modules. In addition it is possible for Napier88 programs to access MONADS modules by using the normal MONADS inter-module call mechanism. This would require either an extension to the Napier88 language or the provision of some library routines. If type security is to be enforced such inter-module calls should have only value parameters. However, it is possible to pass reference parameters to a restricted section of the object store if that is deemed desirable. It is also possible to pass read-only reference parameters.

5   Conclusions

The MONADS architecture has been fully described in several previous publications. In this paper we have attempted to give a different view based on a series of abstract layers. We have shown that, although the outermost layer imposes a particular philosophy of system construction, the inner layers (including the hardware) are in fact quite general and can be used to implement a number of different persistence paradigms.

As an example we have described three methods which could be used to implement a Napier88 system on the MONADS architecture. Of these three methods we favour the third since it does not compromise the MONADS philosophy but still supports a potentially efficient Napier88 system. It has the advantage that it allows co-operation and communication between Napier88 and MONADS and supports multiple Napier88 systems. It is hoped to proceed with such an implementation shortly.

Acknowledgements

The author gratefully acknowledges the helpful suggestions and comments on earlier drafts of this paper from other members of the MONADS team, particularly Frans Henskens and David Koch. This work was partly undertaken during a study leave period at the University of St Andrews and was supported by SERC grant GR/F 28571. The MONADS project is supported by ARC Grant A48716316.

References

1.   Balch, P., Cockshott, W. P. and Foulk, P. W. "Layered Implementations of Persistent Object Stores", *Software Engineering Journal*, 4, 2, pp. 123-131, 1989.

2.   Brown, A. L., Connor, R. C. H., Carrick, R., Dearle, A. and Morrison, R. "The Persistent Abstract Machine", Universities of Glasgow and St. Andrews, Persistent Programming Research Report PPRR-59-88, 1988.

3.   Brown, A. L., Dearle, A., Morrison, R., Munro, D. and Rosenberg, J. "A Layered Persistent Architecture for Napier88", *Proceedings of the International Workshop on Computer Architectures to Support Security and Persistence of Information*, Bremen, West Germany, ed J. Rosenberg and J. L. Keedy, to be published by Springer-Verlag, 1990.

4.   Cockshott, W. P. and Foulk, P. W. "Implementing Large Persistent Address Spaces on Intel Processors", *Proceedings of the International Workshop on Computer Architectures to Support Security and Persistence of Information*, Bremen, West Germany, ed J. Rosenberg and J. L. Keedy, to be published by Springer-Verlag, 1990.

5.   Dearle, A. "On the Construction of Persistent Programming Environments", Ph.D. Thesis, University of St. Andrews, 1988.

6.   Goldberg, R. P. "Architecture of Virtual Machines", *Proceedings of AFIPS NCC*, vol 42, pp. 309-318, 1973.

7.   Henskens, F. A., Rosenberg, J. and Hannaford, M. R. "Stability in a Network of MONADS-PC Computers", *Proceedings of the International Workshop on Computer Architectures to support Security and Persistence of Information*, Bremen, West Germany, ed J. Rosenberg and J. L. Keedy, to be published by Springer-Verlag, 1990.

8.   Henskens, F. A., Rosenberg, J. and Keedy, J. L. "A Capability-based Fully Transparent Network", University of Newcastle, N.S.W. 2308, Australia, Technical Report 89/7, 1989.

9.   ISO "Information Processing Systems - Open Systems Interconnection - Basic Reference Model", ISO 7498, 1984.

10. Keedy, J. L. "Support for Software Engineering in the MONADS Computer Architecture", Ph.D. Thesis, Monash University, 1982.

11. Keedy, J. L. and Rosenberg, J. "Support for Objects in the MONADS Architecture", *Proceedings of the International Workshop on Persistent Object Systems*, Newcastle, Australia, ed J. Rosenberg and D. M. Koch, to be published by Springer-Verlag, 1989.

12. Morrison, R., Brown, A. L., Carrick, R., Connor, R. C. H., Dearle, A. and Atkinson, M. P. "The Napier Type System", *Proceedings of the Third International Workshop on Persistent Object Stores*, Newcastle, Australia, ed J. Rosenberg and D. M. Koch, to be published by Springer-Verlag, 1989.

13. Morrison, R., Brown, A. L., Conner, R. C. H. and Dearle, A. "Napier88 Reference Manual", Universities of Glasgow and St. Andrews, Persistent Programming Research Report PPRR-77-89, 1989.

14. Organick, E. I. "The Multics System: An Examination of its Structure", MIT Press, Cambridge, Mass., 1972.

15. Rashid, R., Tevanian, A., Young, M., Golub, D., Baron, R., Black, D., Bolosky, W. and Chew, J. "Machine-Independent Virtual Memory Management for Paged Uniprocessor and Multiprocessor Architectures", *Proceedings of the Second International Conference on Architectural Support for Programming Languages and Operating Systems (ASPLOS II)*, Palo Alto, ACM Order Number 556870, pp. 31-39, 1987.

16. Rosenberg, J. and Abramson, D. A. "MONADS-PC: A Capability Based Workstation to Support Software Engineering", *Proc, 18th Hawaii International Conference on System Sciences*, pp. 515-522, 1985.

17. Rosenberg, J., Henskens, F. A., Brown, F., Morrison, R. and Munro, D. "Stability in a Persistent Store Based on a Large Virtual Memory", *Proceedings of the International Workshop on Architectural Support for Security and Persistence of Information*, Bremen, West Germany, ed J. Rosenberg and J. L. Keedy, to be published by Springer-Verlag, 1990.

18. Rosenberg, J. and Keedy, J. L. "Object Management and Addressing in the MONADS Architecture", *Proceedings of the International Workshop on Persistent Object Systems*, Appin, Scotland, 1987.

19. Rosenberg, J., Koch, D. M. and Keedy, J. L. "A Massive Memory Supercomputer", *Proc. 22nd Hawaii International Conference on System Sciences*, vol 1, pp. 338-345, 1989.

20. Russo, V. and Cambell, R. "Virtual Memory and Backing Store Management in Multiprocessor Operating Systems using Class Heirarchical Design", *Proceedings of OOPSLA '89*, New Orleans, Louisiana, pp. 267-278, 1989.

21. Sun Microsystems Inc. "The SPARC Architecture Manual, Version 7", Part No: 800-1399-08, 1987.

Memory Semantics in Large Grained Persistent Objects [*]

Partha Dasgupta   and   Raymond C. Chen
College of Computing
Georgia Tech, Atlanta, GA 30332
partha@cc.gatech.edu
chen@cc.gatech.edu

Abstract

Large-grained persistent objects are persistent encapsulation of code and data that reside in a complete virtual address space. These objects exist in a multi-user distributed system and are accessible by all nodes of the system. Threads are execution paths that execute within the objects. Each object can contain nested (finer-grained) objects that can be persistent or volatile.

In this paper we propose memory structuring semantics for controlling scope and longevity of memory in the large grained objects. We present four types of memory that can be used in such a system and show the functionality, usage and implementation details. These four types of memory are *per-object memory*, *per-invocation memory*, *per-thread memory* and *per-object/per-thread memory*. The per-object (or global) memory supports concurrent executions and sharing of data (or objects) between threads (or processes) and is persistent. The other forms of memory allow storage for variables and objects within more limites scopes during executions and are not shared. We discuss the utility of such memory structures.

1. Introduction

Extending the object-oriented paradigm to encompass a large multiuser distributed system can be done in several ways. However operating system support for objects is essential for a flexible and clean design. The *Clouds* operating system is a native distributed operating system that provides support for large-grained persistent objects (LGP objects). LGP objects are complete, virtual address spaces that are backed by secondary storage thus providing persistence. Since the objects are mapped into memory, they can support computation. Since the objects are passive, they can allow several threads of computation to execute concurrently within them, allowing multithreaded services. Also, the threads that execute within these objects can cross object boundaries and machine boundaries, and thus are distributed computations.

In conventional systems volatile memory comes in several forms: global, stack and heap. In persistent memory systems there are similar needs for memory structures that provide both persistent and volatile objects with varying scopes and longevity. The memory structures that can be supported within these large-grained objects is the focus of this paper. We discuss some properties of these objects, and address programmability needs for writing applications on

---

[*]   This work is supported in part by NSF contract CCR-86-19886

such systems. We first present the attributes of large-grained objects in our model and then present a proposal for additional memory semantics.

2. Persistence in Object Memory

Objects are encapsulations of variables and methods. In persistent objects systems, the object data is long-lived, that is they can survive termination of an application, as well as system crashes. Several persistent object systems have been proposed as well as built. Persistent objects are very often encountered in object-oriented database systems as the storage unit in such systems is the object.

Persistent object systems raise several isses:

- How are the objects stored on long-lived media?

- Is storing/retrieving an object done explicitly or implicitly?

- Is storage and usage orthogonal issues? That is, do the objects have different representations when stored and when used?

- Since objects can be stored and reused, how is concurrent access and/or sharing handled?

- How does one recover state when a program manipulating objects crashes?

A persistent object store can be implemented by providing a "*save*" method in each object [Sh90]. Sending a *save* message to an objects causes the object to save its data space into a file (with appropriate headers) and propagate the *save* message to other objects reachable from this object. The saved image can later be restored by instantiating an object of the appropriate type and sending a restore message to it, which causes it to restore its saved state from a specified file.

It is also possible to partially save some objects in the object tree (or graph) to a file (or Unix pipe) and restore the objects in a different application; allowing passing of object data between processes. In this scheme storage of objects is done explicitly under programmer control; the saved state is different from the usable state and sharing is done by using the save/retrieve mechanism.

A similar approach is used by the Coral3 system [MeLa87] in which Smalltalk objects are stored as persistent objects in a file system. Coral3 uses the concept of "object holders" to store the objects and provides facilities to save and retrieve objects to and from the object holders. Locking is provided by the object holders to allow proper (controlled) sharing of persistent objects across applications.

Distributed Smalltalk [Be87] allows transparent remote invocations of Smalltalk objects. This system allows objects to move and participate in distributed computations as well as provide limited support for object sharing.

Object-oriented databases (such as Orion [Kim*88, Kim90], GemStone [CoMa84, Ma*86, PeSt87]) provide a persistent object store consisting of instances of objects in the database. These objects are retrieved by application programs by copying them out (check-out) of the persistent store (or database manager). The applications may check the objects back into the store after using them. Sharing and concurrency control is performed by the database manager by performing lock/unlock on objects upon check-out and check-in.

Some operating systems implement their own versions of objects at the kernel level. These include Argus [Li*87], Cronus [ScTh86] and Eden [Al*85]. The objects in these systems are modules that run as Unix processes and respond to invocations or messages. The objects can be checkpointed to files on demand. Sharing of data in the objects are controlled by the objects themselves using locks.

The Commandos operating system [MaGu89] provides support for all types of object (fine and large grained, persistent and volatile) in an uniform fashion. The operating system provides management of object types, location, and sharing. The object support is provided by the Commandos virtual machine which supports the virtual object manager (VOM) and a Storage System (SS). Commandos is an operating system that is closely tied to the programming environment and thus is a special purpose, single paradigm system.

Usage of objects in a virtual object space has been used by several systems for varying purposes. The Sloop system [Lu87] provides MIMD support for distributed objects. The objects exist in one or more virtual address spaces in the system. The operations on the objects can support parallel computations. [Ca87] discusses the usage of distributed objects and remote invocations in multimedia applications.

The memory in most of the above systems are private to the process or application using the objects. The objects exist in the global address space of the process executing the application and are copied in or out of the space, as and when necessary. When the process terminates, the memory is lost and the persistent objects have to be saved on secondary storage.

A different approach to persistent object management is used by the *Clouds* operating system [Da*88, Da*90]. The *Clouds* system is is designed for general purpose distributed computing and thus has to support multi-paradigm, multi-language computing. To manage most of the above issues using a simple consistent framework, the *Clouds* system provides support for large-grained objects at the operating system level.

Making the operating system know of, and manage every instance of of every object that every application program uses would be too inefficient and counter-productive. Also, this type of support will be ineffective in dealing with programs that are not inherently object-oriented, and hence is not suitable for general purpose operating systems. Thus the *Clouds* operating system supports only large-grained objects. The operating system recognizes each object as a named address space and provides mechanisms that make these object invocable while providing for transparent-long term storage.

The *Clouds* mechanisms make object storage implicit and transparent; that is programmers do not save/retrieve objects, they are by definition persistent. This is achieved by making the core image of all objects backed by secondary storage. Concurrent access to objects are possible and programmers have the facilities to control concurrently as well as recovery.

The memory in *Clouds* belongs to the objects and not to the processes (or threads). The memory is persistent, global and can be shared by several computations sharing the same objects. In this paper we discuss memory structures for *Clouds* objects.

3.   Large Grained Persistent Objects

A *Large-Grained Persistent object* (LGP object) is a complete virtual address space. This address space contains the code and data that are physically a part of the object. The data space of the object may contain more finer grained objects (like the objects in any object-oriented application program), or may contain flat data. The code in the object are the methods this object responds to. These methods are activated by an external invocation that happens when a thread invokes this object. The object and thread model illustrated in this section are consistent with the type of object implemented by the *Clouds* distributed operating system.

3.1.   Objects

As mentioned, an LGP object, at the conceptual level, is a virtual address space. Unlike virtual address spaces in conventional operating systems, an object is persistent and is not tied to any process. An LGP object exists forever and survives system crashes and shutdowns (like a file) unless explicitly deleted. These objects are intended for storage and execution of large-grained data and programs because invocation and storage of objects bear some non-trivial overhead.

The system-level name of an object, also known as its *sysname*, is unique over the entire distributed system, creating a uniform, flat system name space for objects. User names are added to the sysname scheme using a naming services that translate user specified names to sysnames.

An LGP object is not associated with any server process and hence they are passive unlike objects in some object-based operating systems (such as Argus, Eden, Cronus). The address space of an object is structured. The data in an object is stored in a set of segments, and are accessible only by the code in the object, and not by any other object. The code that is accessible through entry points is known as *operations* (or methods) of the object. Data can be moved between objects as parameters to the entry points (see the discussion on threads).

Each LGP object is composed of several data segments and code segments. The object may contain classes and instances of nested fine grained objects. The data segments contain the data of these objects and the code segments contain the corresponding code. Each data segment contains the static data as well as a heap for allocating dynamic memory. An LGP object is shown in Figure 1.

An LGP object is implemented as a single level store that is demand-paged from a backing store. Thus the objects always appear to be in core. This is somewhat similar to memory-mapped files in Multics. The backing stores are on the network, and hence all machines on the network have access to all the LGP objects. The concept of having a demand-paged backing store for each object makes the objects persistent. As the data in the object changes, it is automatically reflected in the backing store (with some latency [*]). Thus programmers do not have to explicitly save or retrieve the objects.

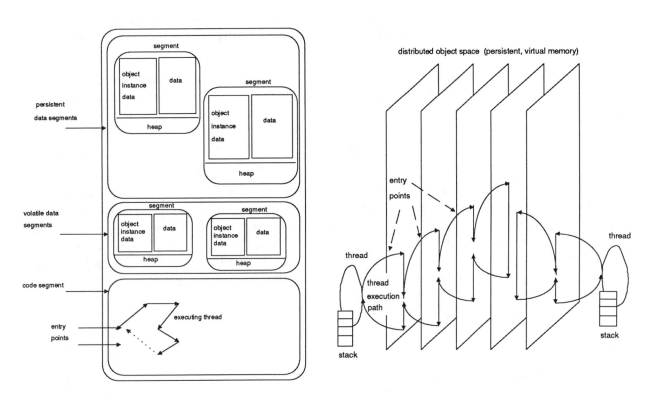

Figure 1: A Large Grained Persistent Object   Figure 2: The Object/Thread Model

---

* Controlling the latency is possible, but a description of the details are outside the scope of this paper.

3.2. Threads

The only form of activity in the LGP object system is the thread. A thread can be viewed as a thread of control that executes code in objects, traversing objects as it executes. A thread executes in an object by entering it through one of several entry points (or methods); after the execution is complete the thread leaves the object. Several threads can simultaneously enter an object and execute concurrently (or in parallel, if the host machine is a multiprocessor). Threads can span address spaces (LGP objects) and machine boundaries; making the distributed system look seamless.

Upon creation, a thread starts up at an entry point of an object. As the thread executes, it executes code inside an object and manipulates the data inside this object. If the code in the object contains a call to an operation of another object the thread temporarily leaves the address space of the calling object, enters the called object, and commences execution there. The thread returns to the calling object after the execution in the called object terminates. The calls to object entry points are called *object invocations*. Object invocations can be nested and/or recursive. An example of two threads executing in a set of objects is shown in Figure 2.

When a thread executing in an object (or address space) executes a call to another object, it provides the called operation with arguments. When the called operation terminates, it returns results. That is, object invocations may carry parameters in either direction. These arguments are strictly data (or sysnames); they may not be memory addresses. This restriction is necessary as the address spaces of objects are disjoint, and an address is meaningful only in the context of the appropriate object.

3.3. The Object/Thread Paradigm

The structure created by a system composed of LGP objects and threads has several interesting properties. First, all inter-object interfaces are procedural. Object invocations are equivalent to procedure calls on modules not sharing global data. They are also equivalent to sending a message to a method in an object.

Secondly, the storage mechanism used in this object-based environment is quite different from that used in the conventional operating systems, and many persistent object systems. Conventionally, memory is tied to processes and files are tied to secondary storage. Since processes are volatile, memory is not persistent and file is the storage medium of choice for data that has to persist. However, memory is easier to manage, more suited for structuring data and essential for processing. The LGP object concept merges these two views of storage, to create the concept of a permanent virtual address space (similar to single-level stores).

Although files can be implemented using objects (a file is an object instance with operations such as read, write, seek, and so on), the need for having files disappears in most situations. Programs do not need to store data in file-like entities, since they can keep the data in the data spaces of LGP objects, structured appropriately. The need for user-level naming of files transforms to the need for user-level naming of objects. Also, *Clouds* does not provide user-level support for disk I/O. In fact, there is no concept of disks or secondary storage. The system creates the illusion of a large virtual memory space that is permanent (non-volatile), and thus the need for using peripheral storage from a programmer's point of view is eliminated. Similarly there is no message support (or IPC), as messages can easily be implemented (if necessary) by a bounded-buffer object.

3.4. LGP Objects and Types

At the operating system level, the objects are not typed. This is because the *Clouds* operating system is a general purpose operating system and should support objects programmed in any language, including those that are not object-oriented or modular. To the operating system, a LGP object is an address space that is a single level store that has entry points.

However, each object is generated by a language module and the language can impose typing restrictions. In one of the programming systems being developed for *Clouds*, a programmer programs a *class* for an LGP object. This class may be inherited from from other LGP class definitions. The class may contain data and or other classes of finer grained objects.

A LGP class is then instantiated, producing one or more LGP objects (or instances). These instances can then participate in a computation by responding to invocations. Each LGP object can contain nested fine-grained classes and nested objects formed by instantiating these classes. However, visibility of objects within an LGP object is constrained to within the LGP object (this restriction may be removed in the future). The internal objects are persistent, if instantiated in the persistent memory of the LGP object; otherwise they are volatile (see discussion of types of memory.)

In this scheme, each object, LGP or not, has a type and the invocations are subject to type checking (static or dynamic, depending on the language conventions). The operating system does not do any type-checking, and this function is left to the compiler for statically bound languages or the runtime system for dynamically bound languages.

4. The Implementation of Clouds

The implementation of the above scheme of objects and threads is the focus of the *Clouds* operating system project. *Clouds* is a native operating system that runs on a network of Sun-3/60 machines. The *Clouds* operating system runs on top of a minimal kernel (called *Ra*) that provides low-level OS support such as virtual memory management, interrupt handling and scheduling. The operating system is built by plugging in a set of system objects to the kernel that performs rest of the operating system services, such as networking, storage, thread management, object management and so on [Da*90].

In brief, the objects are implemented as a set of memory segments. The segments are persistent segments that are mapped into one or more backing stores called partitions. A scheme called *Distributed Shared Memory* (DSM) allows all machines on the network to access any segment (and hence object) using network paging. Threads are implemented using lightweight processes (a PCB and a stack). Object invocation by threads are handled by mapping the address space of the object with the address space of the stack and starting the process at the entry point of the object. Thus threads can easily cross address spaces. Using light-weight processes to implement threads allows us to have concurrency in objects for free. Inter-machine invocations are handled by a *Remote-Procedure-Call* (RPC) mechanism that creates a slave process on a remote machine to perform the invocation. The *Clouds* operating system is in operation and supports all the above facilities. Work is in progress in using the *Clouds* LGP objects for implementing application programming environments.

The complete details of handling distribution, coherence, concurrency control, I/O and kernel mechanisms are beyond the scope of this paper.

5. Memory in Object Systems

In the persistent object model described above, there are two kinds of memory: persistent memory in the object address spaces and stack memory (volatile) on the thread stacks.

The persistent memory is global within the object and shared by all threads that invoke the object. The persistent memory comes in two flavors: static and dynamic. The static part contain all the class and instance variables declared by the object class programmer. The dynamic memory is implemented as a heap in the object. Any thread can allocate memory from this heap and once allocated, the memory becomes part of the persistent object (unless explicitly deallocated).

The stack memory is contained in the private stacks of each thread that invokes the object (recall that multiple threads can execute in the object if they concurrently invoke the object). Since the memory is allocated on the stack at the time of invocation, or when procedures inside the object are activated, the declared local variables of the procedures are resident in this memory. Also, this memory is volatile, since the variables are discarded when at each "return". Thus stack-based memory is private, single threaded and predeclared.

5.1. Drawbacks

The set of memory structures outlined above has one major drawback: *A thread has no global private memory. All global memory is shared and persistent.*

This implies that any thread that needs memory for private computation needs has to either (i) allocate it on the stack (as local variables) and suffer from the fact that this space has to be statically pre-declared; or (ii) allocate memory from the persistent heap, ensure that no other thread uses it and clean it up upon termination.

There are some other problems that can cause programming to be more complex than it should. For example, suppose a thread builds a data structure in an object that it intends to use in a future invocation, but not make public. It has to remove it as an output parameter and then re-import it. This can be a programming nuisance.

5.2. Motivation for Expanded Memory Semantics

In conventional systems, a thread (called a process) is completely tied to exactly one address space, and the longevity of this address space is the lifetime of the process. In such systems the processes address space is divided into several segments, and the use of these segments have some implications. For example, global (static) data is kept accessible by the process at all times. A heap provides dynamic memory allocation and a stack provides for variables local to a procedure. In persistent object systems, more powerful memory scope and longevity semantics are necessary as memory is the *only* storage and communication medium. The semantics must include access restrictions, sharing constraints, longevity specifications, usage paradigms and consistency guarantees. In this paper we present a new scheme for handling persistent memory semantics. We will not cover consistency issues arising from concurrency and failures in this paper. Details are available in [ChDa89].

6. Types of Object Memory

We define four types of memory that are useful for persistent programming. They are:

- *Per-Object Memory:* The global (static and dynamic) part of the object data space is the per-object memory. This memory is persistent and shared.

- *Per-Invocation Memory:* When a thread invokes an object it has need for some privately allocated memory. A private space is allocated for every invocation of an object, called per-invocation memory. There are two classes of per-invocation memory. The static class is allocated upon invocation. The dynamic part is allocated on demand during the invocation. This type of memory is available as global memory to the invocation in progress. This memory is automatically discarded on termination of the invocation.

- *Per-Thread Memory:* A thread may choose to have a private memory space, not tied to any particular object. This memory is accessible from a thread regardless of the object it is currently accessing. The per-thread memory serves as a storage area for temporary computation results generated by this thread. This memory lives as long as the thread does. Some disadvantages of this form of memory leads to the next type.

- *Per-Thread/Per-Object Memory:* A conceptual hybrid of per-thread and per-object memory. The memory is private to both the thread and the object under invocation.

6.1. Per-Object Memory:

Per-object memory is the shared, persistent memory that was defined in our object model. This persistent global address space contains static data that is initially declared by the object programmer as a set of segments and a heap per segment. A segment is a collection of logically related group of variables (user defined). A collection of segments is the entire per-object address space. A segment is also the granule of locking in the automatic synchronization system.

Per-Object memory is shared by all concurrent threads running in the object so there is a need for synchronization. Synchronization is supported by two mechanisms:

- A generalized semaphore scheme where semaphores are explicitly (and *statically*) declared and used by users as a part of the data in the per-object area.

- A locking scheme that performs automatic (user-transparent) locking at the segment level. Thus threads that access segments lock them upon access automatically. We do not discuss the synchronization and recovery issues in this paper.

The programmer defines the set of segments and the variables that are allocated in each segment. This allows him/her to control the locking granularities in case the automatic locking is used. Each segment is a logical collection of data and in some cases may not be allocated as several actual segments.

Dynamic memory allocation is done on a per-segment basis. A thread can choose to extend the limits of any segment by dynamically allocating memory space to it. Allocated memory is persistent and remains a part of the object, until explicitly deallocated.

The per-object memory can contain flat data (ordinary and composed data types), class variables that are shared by several LGP object instances, and instance variables of persistent fine-grained objects instantiated in the LGP object. An LGP object can in fact contain an entire object-oriented application or environment in its persistent memory. This environment can be shared by several computations by invoking the entry points it exports.

The implementation of per-object memory is provided by the implementation of the *Clouds* LGP objects. As mentioned earlier, they are composed of segments that are demand paged from one or more persistent backing stores.

6.2. Per-Invocation Memory:

A thread running in an object needs private memory that lasts as long as the invocation does. A form of this memory can be provided by the per-thread stack in form of local variables (automatic storage). The drawbacks of stack based automatic storage are:

- The variables are allocated and deallocated on procedure entry/exit and not invocation entry/exit.

- The scope of the variables are within the procedure it is defined in, and not global to all the procedures.

- The storage has to be statically declared.

Per-invocation memory is global memory on a per-invocation basis. To an invocation, the memory looks like global per-object memory, but it has limitations on persistence and sharing. This memory is private and not visible to any other thread. It is also non-persistent. A fresh copy is provided when the invocation starts and then discarded when the invocation terminates. Concurrent invocations have separate copies of per-invocation memory.

Per-invocation memory can be statically declared or dynamically allocated. The static part is allocated upon the start of the invocation and the dynamic part is allocated upon demand. Both are discarded upon termination.

The static part of per-invocation memory can be allocated on the per-thread stack (each thread has a private stack). However the dynamic part does not lend itself easily to stack implementations, so we use a per-thread heap for both static and dynamic per-invocation memory.

A thread in *Clouds* has a thread space (called P-space) that is merged with the object space (called O-space) upon invocation. The stack is located in the P-space. Per-invocation memory is implemented by providing a heap in the P-space.

The per-invocation memory can not only contain data, but objects that are instantiated during the invocation. Objects instantiated in the per-invocation memory will exist as long as the invocation does and are hence not persistent.

However they can be copied to the per-object memory. Note that pointers from per-object memory to per-invocation space will lead to dangling references.

6.3. Per-Thread Memory:

This type of memory is presented for conceptual completeness but has some dubious features. However, a hybrid of the per-thread memory (called the per-object/per-thread memory) is quite useful and presented in the next subsection.

Conceptually, per-thread memory is a memory space that is always within the address space of a thread. This memory is a collection of variables associated with a thread and moves with the thread as it traverses the LGP objects in the distributed system. At a first glance, per-thread memory seems to be a better form of private memory than per-invocation memory. However, it has some awkward drawbacks.

First, in a persistent object system, a programmer programs objects not threads. Threads execute in the objects that exist in the system. Since per-thread memory is not a part of any object, but a part of each thread programming access to per-thread variables pose problems:

- How are these variables declared? Where are they declared?

- How are the variables accessed in a program? This is tied to the first problem.

Thus we feel that the per-thread memory concept does not fit well in this paradigm, and should not be used. Since all programs and variable declarations are placed in objects, placing the per-thread variables in objects, in a per-object fashion is more intuitive. This is discussed in the next section.

Second the object encapsulation is lost. A thread T keeps some private data pertaining to object O_1 in the per-thread space; and subsequently invokes object O_2. Now the code in object O_2 can access the data stored by O_1 (in T's private space.)

Per-thread memory can be very useful for user-specified, thread-specific attributes (such as the values corresponding to Unix environment variables). However, since each object invoked by the thread has unrestricted access to the per-thread memory area, usage of this memory must be determined by convention and there is no way to ensure that every object obeys the specified conventions.

We feel that using per-thread memory is not advisable and choose not to implement it. We now modify the scheme to yield per-thread/per-object memory.

6.4. Per-Object/Per-Thread Memory:

This is similar to per-thread memory but is maintained within objects. It can be visualized as belonging to an object on a per-thread basis. That is all the threads executing in an object have their own per-thread space located within this object. The semantics are somewhat cleaner and it provides a useful programming tool.

Per-Object/Per-thread memory consists of a set of data variables or objects, that is allocated when a thread visits (invokes) an object for the first time but is not deleted when the thread exits the object. On subsequent invocations this memory space is re-used along with its contents. The space is deallocated when the thread terminates (even though the termination of the thread may happen in some other object.) This memory is also private to the thread, that is it is not visible to other threads. Every thread has a per-object/per-thread memory space for every object it has invoked.

Note that the lifetime of this memory is the life of the thread and *not* the lifetime of the invocation. Which means, if thread T invokes object O and then returns, T's private space associated with O will still be kept alive. The contents of the memory will be visible to T if it visits O at some future point.

This memory can be visualized as belonging to an object, with copies for every thread that is executing in the system which has visited this object. Or it can be visualized as belonging to the thread with copy for every object it has visited. Though both views are equivalent, it should be conceived as the former (since all variables are programmed into objects) but is implemented as the latter.

The per-object/per-thread space is implemented as a segment that gets allocated on the P-space (and hence "belongs to the thread") when it invokes an object. This segment is mapped into the same place for all objects the thread visits. This is achieved by changing the mappings of the segments in the P-space upon invocation. Thus an object that is being concurrently invoked has a separate set of per-thread memory spaces for each of the threads (just as each thread has a separate stack). Also the position of the space is uniform for all objects and all threads. Since the space is implemented as a part of the thread, it can be re-used when the same thread visits an object again, and is deallocated when the thread terminates (the entire P-space is deallocated).

When a thread is distributed, that is when it has used the RPC mechanism to invoke objects, there are situations when garbage collection is necessary to deallocate the per-thread segments for remote objects. However this produces no added overhead, as this is necessary anyway, to recover the stack segments.

7. Usage

The memory structures discussed above provide powerful storage paradigms for programmers. We sketch some of the usage techniques for each type of memory.

The global *per-object* memory is for global data storage, including long-term storage. Fine grained objects instantiated in this area are also persistent. The data (and objects) can be shared by all threads that access the LGP objects, and thus can participate in distributed computations. Per-object memory was the first type of memory proposed for distributed object based systems.

The *per-invocation* memory is for computational results obtained during a particular invocation. This is a global alternative to "local variables". For example an editor object can store the contents of the files being edited in this space. A compiler can store the symbol tables and other data structures here.

The *per-thread* memory usage can be tricky and is not advised. It is not implemented in out system.

The *per-thread/per-object* is the most complex form of memory to implement, and the usage is quite interesting. This memory allows programmers to keep thread specific information in the object even after the thread has left the object. A simple example is the seed value for a pseudo-random number generator. A thread can call a object containing the randomizing code, and each invocation can return a number based on the previous invocation. Of course the seed can be provided by the caller on each invocation, but this approach makes programming simpler, especially in is situations where more data has to be stored for the thread context.

7.1. Programming LGP Objects

In this section we present some intuitive program skeletons to show how to use the memory structures presented above to program LGP objects. To keep the examples simple we choose not to present the class/instance structure of LGP object, but to treat each LGP object as a program module. Further, the data in the LGP object is treated as flat data (not objects) and static. The program skeletons are in a pseudo C-like language.

Figure 3 shows a program module using two per-object segments called `g1` and `g2`. These are created by the keywords `global segment`. The number of segments used to store the data is up to the programmer. The system will treat each segment as a logical unit and will provide locking on a per-segment basis, and hence grouping related data into one segment has performance implications. The names of the segments can be used to qualify variables if the same name is used in different segments.

Per-invocation segments are created using the keywords `invoke segment` and the program has one such segment called `i1`. Having more than one per-invocation segment does not provide any performance advantages as the per-invocation segments are private and hence there is no need for locking support.

The per-object/per thread segment is programmed into the object (hence visualized to be a part of the object), using the keywords **thread segment**. As in the case of the per-invocation segment, only one segment is needed and in out example this is called **t1**.

We show one entry point, a procedure marked with the keyword **entry**, called **op1**, that takes one integer parameter and returns an integer. **op1** has a local variable called **x** that is allocated on the stack of the thread. The entry point called **constructor** is a initialization routine that is called when the object is instantiated.

When a thread invokes **op1** it can access the variables in **g1** and **g2** as globals. These are persistent variables. Also several threads can concurrently execute **op1** and arbitrarily conflict on updates to variables in **g1** and **g2** unless the programmer uses synchronization mechanisms (semaphores) or opts to use automatic synchronization.

All threads invoking **op1** will get separate copies of **i1** and **t1**. As described before **i1** will be allocated on invocation and deleted on exit (for each thread). but **t1** will be allocated when the thread first makes a call to **op1** and will be reused for all subsequent calls by this thread to **op1** and will be deleted when the thread dies.

Dynamic memory allocation is handled by an allocator called **malloc**. **malloc** takes a segment name as a parameter, and hence will allocate persistent memory or volatile memory of the correct type when called with the appropriate segment name (**g1, g2, i1** or **t1**). Dynamic allocation examples are omitted for the sake of brevity.

We now show another example that uses the per-object/per-thread memory effectively. Consider a file implemented as an LGP object. This file is to be shared by several threads (or computations) that invoke **read** and **write** methods on the file. The **read** method reads **N** characters from the file. A subsequent **read** by this thread will return the next **N** characters.

```
global segment {                    int entry op1(x)
    int i, j, k;                    int x;
    /*per-object,shared segment*/   {
    } g1;                           /* uses the same g1 and g2
                                     * for all threads
global segment {                     *
    char c1, c2, c3;                 * gets a new (private) copy of i1
    /*per-object,shared segment*/    *
    } g2;                            * gets a new copy of t1 on
                                     * first invocation
invoke segment {                     * (re-uses t1 for subsequent
    int temp;                        * invocations)
    /*per-invocation segment*/       */
    } i1;

thread segment {                    operation code ...
    int count;
    /*per-thread/per-object segment*/  /* deletes copy of i1
    } t1;                            * before return
                                     */
                                    }

                                    void entry constructor ()
                                      {
                                         initialize the object
                                      }
```

Figure 3: A Sample Program

```
global segment {
    char store[MAX];
    int size; /* for marking EOF */
} fs;

thread segment {
    int fptr = 0;
    /* file pointer, per thread */
} t;

invoke segment {
    int temp; /* temporaries */
} i;
```

```
entry read (buffer, N);
{
    read "N" characters from
    store[fptr] to store[fptr+N]
    and place in buffer;

    fptr = fptr + N;
    /* should check for EOF */
}

entry write (buffer, N)
{
    /* similar to read */
}

entry constructor()
{
    size = 0;
}
```

Figure 4: A file object.

Figure 4 shows the implementation of this file object. The file storage is placed in the persistent per-object memory as a large array called **store**. Dynamic memory allocation can be used to avoid pre-declaration of maximum file size. The file pointer (**fptr**) points to the location in the file a thread has read data from (or has written data into). This pointer is used to service subsequent read (or write) requests. The file pointer is kept in the per-thread area. The per-invocation area can be used for storing temporary variables that are necessary for servicing the **read** and **write** calls.

Since **store** is shared, several threads can concurrently read and write data to and from the file (similar to Unix files). However as the file pointer (**fptr**) is in per-thread space each the file object "remembers" the pointer for each thread. Though we do not show the usage of per-invocation memory in this example, variables used in **read/write** routines for private computations should be kept in per-invocation space.

8. Conclusions

The persistent object is a powerful concept that is easy to use as it provides a structured storage system. It also eliminates the need for I/O and messages. Programming objects can be made simpler by well defined semantics of memory abstractions in the objects.

In this paper we present a synopsis of a distributed system designed and built around large-grained persistent objects. We describe a scheme to structure memory semantics in the persistent objects.

We currently have a running system that provides per-object memory and a form of per-invocation storage. We are implementing operating system support for the other types of memory as well as language features to effectively use them. Our environment is a modified (pre-processed) C++ language, running on the *Clouds* operating system.

9. References

[Al*85] G. Almes, A. Black, E. Laswoska and J. Noe, "The Eden System: A Technical Review". *IEEE Trans. on Software Engg.*, SE-11, January 1985.

[Be87] J.K. Bennet, "The Design and Implementation of Distributed Smalltalk". *In Proc. OOPSLA-87 Conference,* October 1987.

[Ca87] M. Caplinger, "An Information System Based on Distributed Objects". *In Proc. OOPSLA-87 Conference,* October 1987.

[ChDa89] R. C. Chen and P. Dasgupta, "Linking Consistency with Object/Thread Semantics: An Approach to Robust Computations." *In Proc. 9th Intl. Conf. on Distributed Computing Systems,* June 1989.

[CoMa84] G. Copeland and D. Maier, "Making Smalltalk a Database System" *In Proc. ACM SIGMOD Conference* June 1984.

[Da*88] P.Dasgupta, R. J. LeBlanc and W. F. Appelbe, "The Clouds Distributed Operating System." *In Proc. 8th Intl. Conference on Distributed Computing Systems* June 1988.

[Da*90] P. Dasgupta, R. C. Chen, S. Menon, M. P. Pearson, R. Ananthanarayan, U Ramachandran, M. Ahamad, R. J. LeBlanc, W. F. Appelbe, J. M. Bernabeu, P. W. Hutto, M. Khalidi and C. J. Wilkenloh, "The Design and Implementation of the Clouds Distributed Operating System" *Computing Systems,* Volume 3, No. 1, 1990.

[Kim*88] W. Kim, N. Ballou, H. T. Chou, J Garza and D. Woelk, "Integrating an Object-Oriented Programming Systems with a Database System". In Proc. OOPSLA-88 Conference, September 1988.

[Kim90] W. Kim, "Architectural Issues in Object-Oriented Databases". *Journal of Object Oriented Programming,* March/April 1990.

[Li*87] B. Liskov, D. Curtis, P. Johnson and R. Scheifler, "Implementation of Argus." *In Proc. 11th ACM Symposium on Operating Systems Principles.* November 1987.

[Lu87] S. E. Lucco, "Parallel Programming in a Virtual Object Space" *In Proc. OOPSLA-87 Conference,* October 1987.

[Ma*86] D. Maier, J. Stein, A. Otis and A. Purdy, "Development of an Object-Oriented Database". *In Proc. OOPSLA-86 Conference,* November 1986.

[MaGu89] J. A. Marques and P. Guedes, "Extending the Operating System Support for an Object Oriented Environment". *In Proc. OOPSLA-89 Conference,* October 1989.

[MeLa87] T. Merrow and J. Laursen, "A Pragmatic System for Shared Persistent Objects". *In Proc. OOPSLA-87 Conference,* October 1987.

[PeSt87] D. J. Penney and J. Stein, "Class Modifications in the GemStone Object-Oriented DBMS." *In Proc. OOPSLA-87 Conference,* October 1987.

[ScTh86] R. E. Schantz, R. H. Thomas and G. Bono, "The Architecture of the Cronus Distributed Operating System" *In Proc. Sixth International Conference on Distributed Computer Systems,* May 1986.

[Sh90] J. Shilling, "Implementing Incremental Persistent Objects in C++" Technical Report, GIT-ICS-90   College of Computing, Georgia Tech. August 1990.

A la carte: An Extensible Framework
for the Tailorable Construction of Heterogeneous Object Stores

Pamela Drew*
Roger King**
Jonathan Bein

Campus Box 430
Department of Computer Science
University of Colorado,
Boulder, Colorado 80309

Abstract

To adequately support new application domains, extensible object management facilities are required. Further, more and more frequently, new applications require access to objects that reside in diverse, heterogeneous object stores. To meet these needs, we are investigating *A la carte*, a toolkit for the rapid construction of heterogeneous, persistent object stores. It provides an extensible framework in which object management facilities can be implemented and combined to meet the requirements of a specific environment. Among our experiments to verify the utility of the system is one in which we will construct a heterogeneous object store that has been tailored to requirements of an integrated software engineering environment being investigated by the Arcadia research consortium.

1. Introduction

New and diverse application domains are straining the capabilities of current DBMS and object management technology in several ways. First, these new domains require new types of functionality or specialized data models to optimally, or even adequately, support the nature of the applications' domain. Since these domains place such diverse requirements on a DBMS, it has become apparent that no one set of DBMS functionalities will satisfy every application's requirements [CDF86]. Therefore, researchers have been investigating extensible DBMSs that can be tailored to a particular application's requirements. (Although the phrase "OMS" is sometimes used to refer to fairly simple sets of management facilities that are typically subsumed by the set of functionality found in a "DBMS", we use the terms interchangeably here.) Further, more and more frequently, new applications require access to objects that reside in diverse, heterogeneous object stores. Just as extensibility is useful for tailoring homogeneous object stores, an extensible framework for integrating heterogeneous object management systems would also be useful [Kim89, Pu88].

This requirement for tailorability and extensibility has led us to investigate *A la carte*, a workbench for the rapid construction of heterogeneous, persistent object stores. We define a heterogeneous object store to be one in which several autonomous object stores are integrated through a unified global management system which may include facilities for schema integration, query processing, transaction management, and recovery. *A la carte* provides an extensible framework in which DBMS functionality is implemented and combined in potentially very unusual ways to create a heterogeneous system that has been tailored to a particular set of requirements. It provides a set of *Framework Objects* that model an extensible heterogeneous management system (HMS) architecture, a library of reusable software components that can be used to populate the architecture, and a set of constraints that help control HMS construction and partially ensure the integrity of execution in the resulting system. (Note that the extensible *Framework Objects* from which an *A la carte* user creates a heterogeneous management system should not be confused with the persistent objects that are managed in the heterogeneous environment.) If a desired functionality does not exist in the

---

*This researcher was supported by a fellowship from U S West Advanced Technologies.

**This researcher was supported in part by ONR under contract number N00014-88-K-0559, and in part by a contract from AT&T.

library, the user can add it using object-oriented programming techniques. In this fashion, a user can tailor a heterogeneous management system to best meet the environment's requirements. These requirements can be determined by factors like the type of internal algorithms provided by each autonomous system, the amount of information available from each object store, the nature of the global applications (e.g., whether queries are mostly updates or reads, the likelihood of conflict, and the required degree of sharability), and performance considerations.

We have four main research goals in this work. Our primary goal is to specify the framework of an extensible HMS architecture that can be easily reconfigured to support varied combinations of object management functionality. This framework subsumes, as much as possible, the intricacies of HMS implementation so that the user can concentrate on rapidly constructing a system which best meets the requirements of a particular environment. While our primary focus is the construction of heterogeneous stores, we will also use this same mechanism, in a limited way, to construct autonomous systems from heterogeneous components. A second research goal is to design "pluggable" components that can be easily added and removed from the framework. For example, a user of *A la carte* should be able to easily change the concurrency control mechanism that unites an architecture of several autonomous concurrency managers if the set of autonomous systems changes. Finally, it is our third research goal to provide a toolkit environment in which the user can create heterogeneous configurations and combinations of functionality without having to be immersed in the details of the entire implementation. To this end, *A la carte* provides the object framework and the library of software components from which a user can build a HMS. Example configurations are available to edit and modify to meet specific requirements. *A la carte* also provides the user with a constraint base which helps control the framework population. These constraints can help the user combine and integrate library functionality into a correct, executable heterogeneous object management system. However, it is not a goal of *A la carte* research to provide a complete set of constraints. Instead, we will implement and enforce constraints that we discover in our design experiments. This will provide a limited constraint base upon which users of *A la carte* can build.

This research is restrained in the following ways. First, we focus the primary domain of extensibility supported by *A la carte* to heterogeneous transaction management, concurrency control, and recovery mechanisms. To retain our primary focus of heterogeneous transaction management, we are taking a multidatabase approach to heterogeneous systems integration in which local transactions can access an autonomous system in the presence of global transactions without using a new global schema or query language. This will limit the scope of the research to internal functionality. To further bound the scope of our research, we also exclude other potentially extensible functionality, like query optimizers or security managers, that comprise a large part of production DBMS software.

Although our main research focus lies in the heterogeneous domain, *A la carte* will also support a limited "boot-strapping" process to create heterogeneous architectures. In this boot-strapping process, the user can extend autonomous systems with certain required functionality so that they can be incorporated into a heterogeneous architecture. For example, an environment might require access to objects that are managed by a storage facility that has no native or local concurrency mechanism with which a global transaction manager can communicate. In this case, *A la carte* provides, in a limited way, the ability to construct an autonomous DBMS from disparate components which can then be incorporated into a heterogeneous environment. To achieve this, *A la carte* provides a set of *Autonomous Framework Objects* that model functionality found in autonomous systems including low-level storage management facilities. Using the Autonomous Framework objects, the user can construct an autonomous DBMS from an *A la carte* implementation of a local concurrency mechanism and the given storage manager.

Finally, it is not a goal of the *A la carte* project to produce production heterogeneous management systems. However, we do not expect the software embodied in an *A la carte* management system to be unnecessarily inefficient. In fact, as we shall describe in a section below, the user can create separate runtime systems from the *A la carte* environment. These run-time systems are written in the implementation language, Eiffel [Mey88], which in turn generates optimized "C" delivery packages. Thus, we expect that systems generated from *A la carte* specifications to be as efficient as a coherent modular design allows. Of course, a user could then further optimize the generated software for more performance enhancements; *A la carte* will simply not automate such optimizations.

We are planning to use *A la carte* in an experiment for the Arcadia research consortium [TBC88] which is currently investigating integrated software engineering environments. The Arcadia consortium brings together researchers from several industrial research facilities and universities including the

University of Colorado, Boulder, the University of California, Irvine, and the University of Massachusetts, Amherst. In the *A la carte* experiment, we plan to tailor a heterogeneous object management architecture according to the consortium's requirements, thereby using some "real-world" requirements to drive the construction of an *A la carte* management system. Since this consortium is already using several existing systems, the autonomous components cannot be "massaged" to fit into the *A la carte* Framework objects. It is hoped that this exercise will help verify that the Framework specifications are indeed extensible and tailorable.

So far, we have designed a significant portion of the Framework specifications and library components in the Eiffel programming language. We have also designed and implemented a majority of the internal *A la carte* management facilities which will support the user in the creation of new heterogeneous managers. In order to perform some early experiments, we have populated the Library with various autonomous storage managers first so that we can determine if our current implementation of the internal creation and constraint management systems are feasible solutions. Now, we are extending the Library to include implementations of various transaction management and recovery mechanisms [BST90, Du89b, LiT89, Pu88]. Using this library of components, we intend to experiment with constructing various autonomous object management systems, and then uniting various DBMSs in a multidatabase architecture. When required we will use the boot-strapping process we described earlier to extend existing object stores with any functionality required to incorporate the system into a heterogeneous environment.

This paper is an introduction to the *A la carte* environment and the mechanisms which implement it. Section 2 gives a brief description of some of the relevant work related to *A la carte*. Section 3 then gives an overview of the *A la carte* approach to heterogeneous management system construction and the underlying architecture of the environment. Section 4 gives a more detailed example of how a user might create various heterogeneous management system in an *A la carte* environment. And finally, Section 5 summarizes the paper.

2. Related Work

There are several relatively disparate fields of research that are relavent to the *A la carte* project. First, there is research into extensible DBMSs. Second, there is research into heterogeneous systems from which we will draw our domain knowledge and populate the *A la carte* Library. And finally, there has also been some related research performed in the operating systems community that takes a similar approach to tailorable systems.

Extensible DBMSs

Related research into extensible DBMSs can be divided into two categories. One type of research concentrates on providing an extensible data model in which the user can add new user-defined types and operations [CDV88 , FBC87, LKP88, MaD86, RoS87, SCF86, StR86]. Much of this research investigates extending relational or semantic data models to include support for user-defined procedures. Providing an object-oriented data model* directly, in which user-defined types and operations are intrinsic, has been a way of achieving extensibility in other research projects [AnH87, BCG87, MSO86]. *A la carte* shares this approach by providing an object-oriented data model as a default model for those storage management systems that require a data definition language. It differs from these projects, however, by concentrating on providing extensibility and tailorability for internal heterogeneous management system software.

More closely related to our research are those systems which provide extensible or reconfigurable homogeneous architectures like EXODUS [CDR86, CDF86, CDG90, RiC87], GENESIS [BBG87], Starburst [SCF86], and POSTGRES [RoS87, StR86]. While *A la carte* shares many of the goals of these projects, *A la carte's* focus on supporting tailorable heterogeneous environments sets it apart from each of them. *A la carte* also supports, to a limited extent, the tailorable construction of autonomous systems from heterogeneous components which these projects do not address either. *A la carte* also extends the notion of reconfiguration and tailorability beyond physical storage management issues; *A la carte* architectures include Framework object specifications for other components like concurrency control and transaction management. And finally, *A la carte* provides environmental support, e.g. an internal creation and constraint management system, to aid the user in constructing new configurations.

---

* Here we borrow the classification set forth by Wegner [Weg87] of object-oriented models.

Heterogeneous OMSs

Integration of heterogeneous object management systems is *A la carte's* primary domain of extensibility. The research in this area can be roughly described by two major points of focus. First, there is a set of work which investigates integrating the schemas of systems with different native data models and query processing in a heterogeneous environment. To this end, there are several different approaches. One approach entails creating a global schema and query language which unites all of the autonomous system schemas and translates queries from the global scheme to each local language [LaR82, SiM89, Tem89]. Another approach is the federated database work in which various DBMSs maintain private schemas and use a message-passing and import/export mechanism to share information about schemas and transactions [BDW89, HeM85, LiA86]. *A la carte* takes an approach closer to the federated database approach in that each autonomous system will maintain its own private schema. However, *A la carte* will not provide any message passing to exchange information between the autonomous systems. Global applications access local database schemas and query facilities directly.

The other point of focus are studies which address the issues of heterogeneous transaction management and recovery. Within this domain, basically two approaches have been taken. In one approach, each autonomous DBMS does not need to be modified in order to accommodate the global transaction management system [BST89, BST90, Du89a, Du89b, LiT89]. With this approach, local transactions can execute against the local DBMSs without having any knowledge of the global transactions accessing the database. However, not until recently has any mechanism been proposed with reliable recovery in the event of a failure of the global transaction processing system [BST90], and only then under the limitation that the global and local transactions access disjoint data sets. The other basic approach to this problem is to modify the component DBMSs to provide the information required by the global transaction manager [Du89b, EIL87, Pu88]. Limited support for transaction recovery can be provided with these approaches since the the local DBMSs can share some of the required information with the global transaction management system. This domain of reliable heterogeneous transaction management algorithms will provide the software components for the *a la carte* library. Then, given a particular environment, an *A la carte* user can construct the HMS from these components that will best suit their needs. In Section 5, we will give an example of this process and which algorithms we currently plan to implement.

Tailorable Operating Systems

Finally, the operating systems community has also begun to investigate tailorable operating systems for parallel and distributed computing as seen in PRESTO [BLL88 , BLL88] and Choices [RuC89]. These systems share some of *A la carte's* research goals and, to a certain extent, the paradigm by which extensibility and tailorability is achieved. Each of these systems provide a set of extensible objects which are responsible for a certain type of operating system functionality, e.g. spin-locks and threads. However, the domains that these systems model and that on which *A la carte* is focussed are very different. These systems also do not include any formal mechanisms to help control the tailoring of the operating system objects. *A la carte* will also provide environmental support to aid the user in prototyping experimental HMS software. Nevertheless, the success of these related operating systems gives encouragement that this course of research into extensible HMS architectures is a viable approach.

3. An Overview of A la carte

In this section, we give a brief overview of the basic features of a la carte. We describe the architecture from the user's point of view, the Framework, and the internal management system.

3.1. The User's View

Figure 1 shows the user's view of the *A la carte* architecture. It is composed of four main components: the *A la carte* Design Space, the *a la carte* Tool Set, the object management system constructed by the user, and the run-time system generated from the *A la carte* environment. The arrowed lines in Figure 1 represent user actions. Thus, the user can use the tools provided in the *A la carte* Tool Set to edit, browse, and query the *A la carte* Design Space from which the management system is constructed. In the future, this tool set will also provide monitors and debuggers with which to test the system software. The user can also create, if desired, a "Run-Time" version of an *A la carte* management system. In this fashion, although it is not a goal of this research to create production software, a user of *A la carte* can extract an

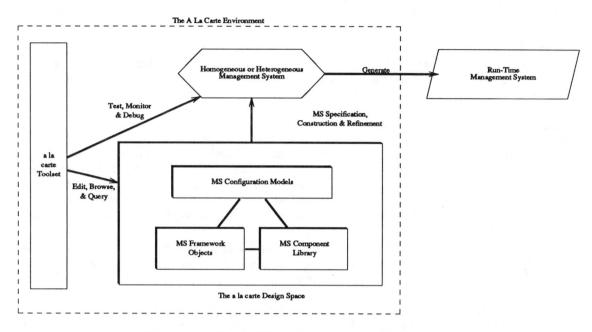

Figure 1 - A User's View of the A la carte Architecture

executable system from the constraints and environmental support provided for the construction phase to achieve better performance.

There are three different views of HMS functionality in the *A la carte* Design Space: the Configuration Models, the Framework Objects, and the Component Library. Each view is responsible for providing the user with a different level of abstraction for HMS construction and each layer is related to the others. The Framework provides an extensible architecture which consists of a set of objects that model a large-grained object-oriented design of the functionalities of a heterogeneous object management system. The Library, which provides a lower level of abstraction, is an object-oriented class library of DBMS functionality. It contains specializations of the Framework Objects which implement a particular type of behavior for that object. For example, a *Concurrency Control* Framework Object might be implemented in the Library as a *"Timestamp" Concurrency Control Manager*.

Both the Framework objects and the Library components include constraints in their specifications that help assure correct execution of the HMS specified by the user and of the run-time executable that could be generated from it. There is also another internal constraint management system, which helps control the construction and combination process, which will be describe in more detail below.

Finally, the Configuration Models provide example configurations of objects from the Framework which can be used as templates for HMS construction. A configuration model represents the communication protocols required between a particular set of Framework objects. It also represents an implemented heterogeneous architecture. Although tailorability is the first and foremost aim of *A la carte*, communication protocols between Framework objects will not vary radically from one configuration to another. That is, a *Recovery Manager*, a *Transaction Manager*, and a *Concurrency Control Manager*, would always require communication between them to coordinate their functionality. Thus, if the required heterogeneous management system were to have all of these functionalities, the communication links between the managers would exist. In fact, the only way that one set of communication protocols can radically vary from one configuration to another is if a particular type of functionality is not included in the specification. There are, of course, limits to which kinds of functionalities can be included or excluded from a particular configuration in order for it to execute correctly. These constraints would be enforced by *A la carte*.

The Configuration Models can guide the user creating new combinations of Framework objects. The Configuration Models can also be refined to meet a particular environment's requirements. Of course, if none of the configurations are close to satisfying the current requirements, the user can always create a new

HMS by combining an all together different set of Framework objects into a configuration with some set of algorithms implementing their respective functionalities.

3.2. The Framework

There are two different sets of Framework objects in the *A la carte* Design Space: the Heterogeneous Framework shown in Figure 2 and the Autonomous Framework shown in Figure 3. The Heterogeneous Framework defines those objects that might be required for the implementation of a heterogenous management system; similarly, the Autonomous Framework defines those objects one might find in a single object management system. While the primary focus of our research is directed toward the heterogeneous managers, we do provide the Autonomous Framework for those cases in which an existing autonomous object management system requires some extension in its functionality in order to be incorporated into a heterogeneous architecture. For example, in some cases a global transaction management system would require some local mechanism with which to communicate in each autonomous object store. Before an object store could be incorporated into a heterogeneous architecture using this type of mechanism, it would have to be extended with a concurrency mechansim if needed. We will see an instance of this scenario in the example of the next section.

There are similarities and differences between the two levels of abstraction. First, there are Framework objects with the same name in each set, e.g. Concurrency Manager, and the functions being performed by these duplicated objects are similar to a certain extent. However, each duplicate function will have very different implementations at each level. Second, it may also be the case that the Framework objects have a different interface at each level. And third, the implementations that can populate them certainly run under different constraint sets. However, it is our premise that the same underlying creation and constraint mechanism will work for both Framework sets. Thus, the remainder of this paper, we will refer to the Framework objects generically, only differentiating between the heterogeneous and autonomous objects when required.

There are two types of objects in the Framework. One type, depicted with the shadowed boxes, are the so-called *Manager* objects. These objects are responsible for the protocols of a particular type of

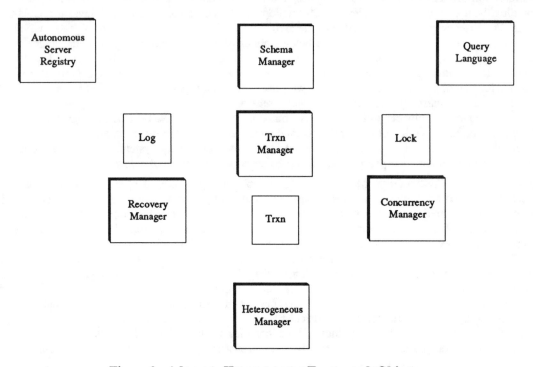

Figure 2 - A la carte Heterogeneous Framework Objects

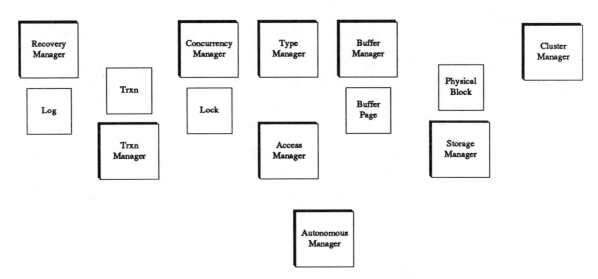

Figure 3 - A la carte Autonomous Framework Objects

functionality. For example, a *Concurrency Manager* is responsible for coordinating the concurrency control of any particular configuration implemented using *A la carte*. The other objects shown in the Framework are those that the *Manager* objects manipulate and coordinate. For example, a *Concurrency Manager* coordinates *Lock* objects according to whatever locking mechanism the user chooses. Notice that this set of objects is skeletal and, possibly, incomplete. As different configurations are created with *A la carte*, new objects may be identified and incorporated into the Framework.

While we cannot give a complete description of each of the Manager objects in the Framework, we will highlight a few of the less intuitive Manager functions. In particular, both sets of the Heterogeneous and Autonomous Framework objects each have an overall manager, the *Heterogeneous Manager* and the *Autonomous Manager* respectively. Each of these managers frequently provides the communication links between the Framework objects that are being used in a particular configuration at their respective level of control. That is, the *Heterogeneous Manager* integrates Heterogeneous Framework objects and the *Autonomous Manager* integrates Autonomous Framework objects. The point of contact between the two sets of objects is the *Autonomous Server Registry* object in the Heterogeneous Framework. This manager provides a local server for each of the autonomous systems that are included in a particular heterogeneous configuration. These local servers understand how to manipulate object references provided by each of the autonomous systems in a heterogeneous configuration.

3.3. The Internal Architecture

As mentioned previously, *A la carte* provides an internal management system which helps control the HMS construction and combination process. This internal manager is composed of two main components: the *Creation Manager* and the *Constraint Manager*. Briefly, the Creation Manager is responsible for the instantiation of a set of Library Components selected by the user. As the construction proceeds, the Creation Manager queries the user for the required input to instantiate each component, and consults the Constraint Manager for the legality of the specification. First, the constraints which govern the internal operations of any particular Manager object selected from the Framework (e.g., a *Recovery Manager*) must be satisfied. Then, constraints which govern the combination of various object management functionalities must be satisfied. For example, if a *Timestamp Concurrency Manager* is specified for a particular configuration, then an *"Optimistic" Transaction Manager* that does not suspend transactions would be required, since, under this type of concurrency control, conflict is determined at commit-time [Ull82].

The Creation manager serves other functions as well. It can be queried by the user for alternative functionality which could be used in the current configuration. Further, these responses are preprocessed according to the constraints that apply to the current configuration. Thus, the alternatives of the design space are narrowed for the user; some of the details of implementation are removed. The Creation Manager also provides the capability to generate the separate executable of a specified configuration.

There several important points to note about the Constraint Manager. First, only those constraints which we identify in our design experiments will be maintained in the system; it is not our intent to identify all of the constraints for every possible functionality combination. Therefore, the user of *A la carte* will be responsible for the correct specification of new constraints. *A la carte* cannot guarantee correct execution of any prototypical management system; the constraints are provided as a service to the user. So far, we have identified two categories of constraint semantics: **coexists(class1, class2, ...)** which declares a dependency between some set of functionalities, and **violates(class1, class2, ...)** which declares that the specified sets of functionality cannot exist in the same executable unless some conflict resolution is provided. Although the Constraint Manager is achieved through an implementation in the Eiffel programming language and serves a more limited purpose, its role in the *A la carte* environment has been influenced by the method combination techniques provided in Flavors [Moo86] and other first-order logic constraint programming languages such as Juno [Lel88 ,Nel84]. Finally, since there may be cases when an existing constraint-base may prevent the user from creating some unusual, experimental architecture, *A la carte* will also provide a mode in which the constraints are turned off to provide as much flexibility as the user requires. If the experiment proves fruitful, the user may then evolve the *A la carte* library and constraint-base to include this new architecture.

4. An Example Experiment

In this section, we give an example scenario of how a user of *A la carte* can create various heterogeneous management systems. First, we will describe the the object management facilities currently being used by the Arcadia Consortium. Some of the goals of the Arcadia object management experiment are providing the requirements for the construction of the first configuration in our scenario. Then, we will show how an *A la carte* user could easily tailor that configuration to meet a new set of requirements. This scenario demonstrates how one can reuse *A la carte's* framework with different tailored implementations of functionality to meet the requirements of a heterogeneous environment.

Object Management in Arcadia

One of the long-range goals of the Arcadia Consortium is to provide an object management infrastructure that supports multiple users with heterogeneous DBMSs. Currently, the Arcadia object management infrastructure provides two autonomous object management systems which differ in several aspects (e.g., models of persistence), and the application's programmer can choose the one which best suits the requirements of the given application. Each system is composed of a low-level storage manager which is then extended with some additional functionality that the Arcadia Consortium has identified as useful for object management in software engineering environments. In one case, EXODUS is being used as the storage manager and, in the other, Mneme is currently being used. Further, the extensions made to each of these systems support different data models, models of persistence, etc. Thus, these two systems represent relatively disparate components which we will attempt to integrate into a heterogeneous architecture using *A la carte*. The scenario that follows explains how an *A la carte* user could integrate this configuration. During the scenario, the reader should keep in mind that the components chosen in this configuration were driven by a long-term requirement that Arcadia object management should ultimately provide reliable global transaction management. As we shall see, this requirement constrains the types of functionality that can be used to implement the autonomous concurrency mechanisms.

A Starting Configuration

A typical *A la carte* session could proceed as follows. First, the user chooses the example template shown in Figure 4 from the existing configuration models. This model contains two autonomous DBMSs comprised of various Autonomous Framework objects and an integrating HMS constructed from the Heterogeneous Framework. The bold lines between the Framework Objects represent lines of communication in the system. The reader should note that, particularly in the case of the autonomous systems, this representation of a configuration model is an abstract view of the underlying implementation. For example, each of the autonomous systems may be a commercial DBMS with those types of facilities provided. In this case, the user would most likely not be able to view the underlying software component that implements each Framework object separately. Nor would the user be able to change a Framework Object implementation since the types of extensibility provided by even the most powerful commercial systems are typically limited to access methods. The rigidity of these systems would be enforced by the *A la carte* constraint base. That is, when an existing object management system, that cannot be broken into its sub-

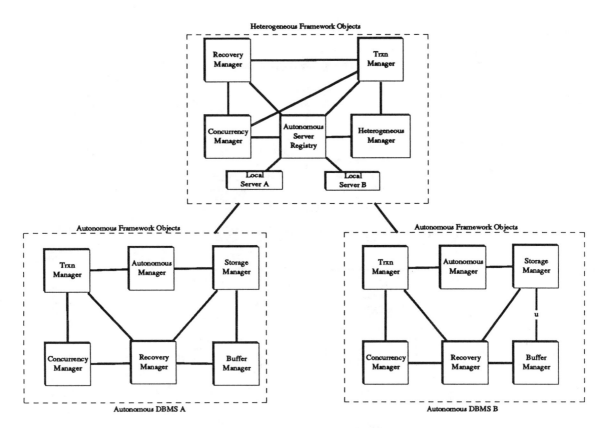

Figure 4 - An Example Heterogeneous Configuration Model

components easily, is incorporated into the *A la carte* library, the **coexists** constraint is used to represent the dependency in the implementation of the Framework for that particular model. For example, the EXODUS Storage Manager [CDR86] supplies an implementation for the *A la carte Storage* and *Buffer Managers* in the Autonomous Framework. So, if a user chose an Exodus implementation for the *Autonomous Buffer Manager* in the creation process, *A la carte* would automatically assign the EXODUS implementation for the *Autonomous Storage Manager* for that configuration.

Figure 5 shows the implementation strategy for this configuration that has been defined for the Arcadia Consortium. There are four major components to this configuration: the heterogeneous object applications shown at the top of the diagram, the heterogeneous object management system to be constructed with *A la carte* shown in the long shadowed box, and the two autonomous object stores, DBMS *A* and DBMS *B*, that will be extended using the *A la carte* Component Library.

Before we detail how the user could change this configuration, we describe how a user could bootstrap the current Arcadia object managers into the heterogeneous configuration shown in Figure 5. In this process, each autonomous system is constructed from disparate components in order to create a system that can operate with a heterogeneous transaction management facility. Autonomous DBMS *A* is implemented using the EXODUS Storage Manager[CDR86], and other components, represented by the solid line boxes, are implemented in *A la carte's* native language. Thus, the Autonomous Framework Object facilities of buffer management and storage management are implemented by EXODUS. The *Autonomous Concurrency Manager* is implemented with a 2-Phase locking scheme, the *Autonomous Transaction Manager* uses deadlock detection and recovery scheme, and the *Autonomous Recovery Manager* implements a write-ahead log recovery mechanism. Each of the concurrency control, transaction management, and recovery managers are native *A la carte* Library components. Similarly, Autonomous DBMS *B* is comprised of disparate components: the same implementations for the *Concurrency Manager*, *Transaction Manager*, and the *Recovery Manager* as Autonomous DBMS *A* are used. However, the *Storage Manager* and *Buffer Manager* functions are implemented by the Mneme storage management system [MoS88]. In

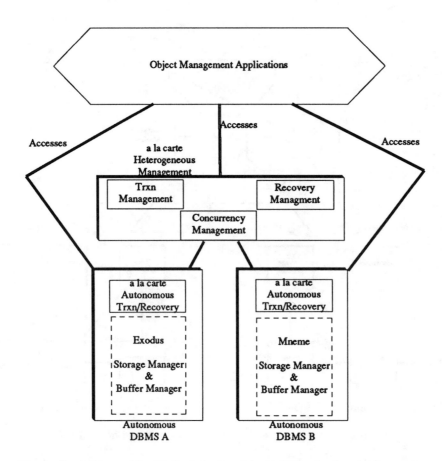

Figure 5 - A View of the Underlying Implementations in the Configuration

this fashion, each of the existing object managers are extended with the appropriate functionality so that they can be integrated into a heterogeneous transaction management system.

We are currently considering implementing the Heterogeneous Framework objects in this configuration with either the reliable heterogeneous transaction management scheme described in [BST90] or a slightly more flexible variation of it. The [BST90] scheme accounts for the failure of global transaction processing as long as the object stores are partitioned so that local and global write sets do not overlap. That is, local transactions and global transactions cannot update the same data. We are currently collaborating with other Arcadia researchers to devise a scheme that will loosen this restriction, but still provide reliable heterogeneous transaction management. This mechanism implements the heterogeneous *Concurrency Manager* with a 2-Phase locking algorithm to operate over global locks. The *Transaction Manager* and *Recovery Managers* implement a variation of a deadlock detection mechanism and a variant of a 2-phase commit protocol that detects and breaks any global deadlocks.

The choice for this particular implementation of heterogeneous management functionality was determined by the requirement for reliable heterogeneous transaction management in the presence of local transactions. Further, the only mechanisms known to us that provide this functionality are the one described in [BST90], and the variation of it which we are currently pursuing. Both of these algorithms require that the autonomous concurrency mechanisms be implemented with 2-phase locking. Thus, the requirement for reliability at the heterogeneous level constrained the choice for the implementations of the *Concurrency Managers* in the Autonomous Framework to 2-phase locking. The *A la carte* constraint-base enforces this constraint.

Tailoring a New Configuration

The configuration just described was one tailored to the requirements of the Arcadia Consortium. Now we will describe how a user could tailor this configuration to another set of requirements. Suppose a user wishes to use a la carte to construct a heterogeneous management facility in a different environment. In this environment, one of the autonomous DBMSs is required to support a timestamping concurrency control algorithm. One way to achieve this goal would be to swap out the 2-phase locking implementation for the *Concurrency Manager* in Autonomous DBMS A. Given this user action, *A la carte* would initiate several other steps. First, the user would be prompted for the required information to create a timestamping *Concurrency Manager*. Once, the user had provided all of the creation input, the *Creation Manager* would check for its legality.

Assuming that the specifications satisfied the constraints which govern its internal operation, the Creation Manager would then consult the Constraint Manager for the legality of the combination of functionality at the autonomous level. At this point, a dependency constraint between the 2-phase locking *Concurrency Manager* and the deadlock detection *Transaction Manager* would be violated since the 2-phase locking *Concurrency Manager* was no longer part of the configuration. Now, *A la carte* would give a message describing the constraint violation and offer a solution. The solution would list a set of *concurrency managers* that operate properly with a deadlock detection *Transaction Manager* and a list of *Transaction Managers* that will operate properly with a timestamped-based *Concurrency Manager* (e.g., an "optimistic" *Transaction Manager* that does not suspend transactions would be required in this case since conflict is not determined until commit time). Now, the user can create the optimistic *Transaction Manager*, and swap it into the configuration in place of the deadlock detecting *Transaction Manager*. In this fashion, *A la carte* supports the user in a rapid reconfiguration of a system by providing reusable Framework specifications that can be easily replaced with tailored implementations, and by constraining the user's options based on the current combination of functionality in the configuration.

Once the user has completed the changes to the autonomous DBMS, the Creation Manager will consult constraints which operate over heterogeneous architectures. At this point, another constraint is violated. The heterogeneous transaction management and recovery mechanism that was implemented in the original configuration depends on the fact that each of the autonomous stores implements a 2-phase locking scheme internally. Now, the user must tailor the implementation of the heterogenous management system to accommodate the new timestamping *Concurrency Manager*. Given no other requirements, there are a number of mechanisms that the user could swap into the configuration which accomodate heterogeneous algorithms in the autonomous systems [BST89, Du89b, LiT89, Pu88]. Currently, the *A la carte* library doesn't supply all of these mechanisms (and probably never will), but some subset will be implemented over the next months. For the sake of argument however, suppose that of a yet to be determined selection, the user chose the mechanism described in [BST89]. This mechanism provides serializable global transactions without having to know anything about the internal implementation of autonomous DBMSs. However, this mechanism does not provide any recovery in the event of failure of the HMS. Thus, as the user swapped out the existing *Concurrency* and *Transaction Managers* and replaced them with this new implementation, another constraint violation would be signaled that the *Recovery Manager* should be removed from the set of heterogeneous managers included in this configuration.

The creation of the second configuration illustrates that the incorporation of a new system or a change in an existing one can have a rippling effect throughout the system. However, although there are several changes in the implementation of one of the Autonomous DBMSs and the Heterogeneous Manager, most of the system's function remains the same. Much of the previous configuration's implementation can be reused, and all of the Framework object specifications can be reused. As long as the underlying constraint-base is not violated, fairly radical changes can be made in a HMS's behavior with relative ease. And, as mentioned preivously, the Constraint Manager can be turned off for those cases where maximum flexibility is required.

5. Conclusion

In this paper, we have introduced *A la carte*, a system which provides a toolkit approach to the implementation of tailorable heterogeneous object management systems. At this stage in the project, we have designed a significant portion of the *A la carte* Framework objects and library component interfaces in in the Eiffel programming language. We have also designed and the implemented a significant portion of the internal *A la carte* management facilities which will support the user in the creation of new heterogeneous management systems. In order to perform some early experiments, we have populated the Library with various autonomous storage managers first to determine our current implementation of the internal management system is a feasible solution. Our future work includes extending the Library to include various transaction management and recovery mechanisms. As we gain more experience with *A la carte*, we expect to better understand whether or not the *A la carte* framework object specifications are adequately extensible and whether or not the current constraint manager is powerful enough to model the complex interactions in a heterogenous object store.

Acknowledgements

We gratefully acknowledge Mitch Smith for his work in the design and implementation of the internal management system. We'd like to thank the Arcadia researchers for providing requirements and input to help shape the *A la carte* experiment. In particular, Dennis Heimbigner and Stan Sutton have been very helpful in defining the use of *A la carte* in an Arcadia environment. Dennis has also been instrumental in discussions about a solution for a new reliable transaction processing mechanism that may be incorporated into the *A la carte* library.

References

[AnH87]   T. Andrews and C. Harris, "Combining Language and Database Advances in an Object-Oriented Development Environment", *OOPSLA87*, 1987, 430-440.

[BCG87]   J. Banerjee, H. Chou, J. F. Garza, W. Kim, D. Woelk, N. Ballou and H. Kim, "Data Model Issues for Object-Oriented Applications", *Trans. on Office Info. Systems 5*, 1 (Jan. 1987), 3-26.

[BBG87]   D. S. Batory, J. R. Barnett, J. F. Garza, K. P. Smith, K. Tsukuda, B. C. Twichell and T. E. Wise, "Genesis: A Reconfigurable Database Management System", *ACM Transactions on Database Systems*, 1987.

[BLL88]   B.N. Bershad, E.D. Lazowska, H.M. Levy, and D.B. Wagner, "An Open Environment for Building Parallel Programming Systems", *ACM SIGPLAN Notices Conference on Parallel Programming: Experience with Applications, Languages, and Systems*, New Haven, CT, July, 1988.

[BLL88]   B. N. Bershad, E. D. Lazowska and H. M. Levy, "PRESTO: A System for Object-Oriented Parallel Programming", *Software - Practice and Experience Vol. 18* (August, 1988), 713-732.

[BST89]   Y. Breibart, A. Silberschatz and G. Thompson, "Transaction Management in a Multidatabase Environment", *Integration of Information Systems: Bridging Heterogeneous Databases*, 1989, IEEE Press.

[BST90]   Y. Breibart, A. Silberschatz and G. R. Thompson, "Reliable Transaction Management in a Multidatabase System", *SIGMOD*, Atlantic City, N.J., May, 1990.

[BDW89]   O. P. Buneman, S. B. Davidson and A. Watters, "Federated Approximations for Heterogeneous Databases", *Workshop On Heterogeneous Databases*, December, 1989.

[CDV88]   M.J. Carey, D.J. DeWitt and S.L. Vandenburg, "A Data Model and Query Language for EXODUS", *Proc. ACM SIGMOD Conf.*, 1988, 413-423.

[CDR86]   M. J. Carey, D. J. DeWitt, J. E. Richardson and E. J. Shekita, "Object and File Management in the EXODUS Extensible Database System", *Proc. of the 11th VLDB*, 1986, 91-100.

[CDF86]   M. J. Carey, D. J. DeWitt, D. Frank, G. Graefe, M. Muralikrishna, J. E. Richardson and E. J. Shekita, "The Architecture of the EXODUS Extensible DBMS", *International Workshop on Object-Oriented Database Systems*, 1986, 52-65.

[CDG90]   M. Carey, D. J. DeWitt, G. Graefe, D. M. Haight, J. E. Richardson, D. T. Schuh, E. J. Shekita and S. L. Vandenburg, "The EXODUS Extensible DBMS Project: An Overview", *Readings in Object-Oriented Database Systems*, 1990.

[Du89a]   W. Du and A. K. Elmagarmid, "Quasi Serializability: a Correctness Criterion for Global Concurrency Control in Interbase", *Proceedings of the International Conference on Very Large Data Bases*, 1989.

[Du89b]   W. Du and A. K. Elmagarmid, "A Paradigm for Concurrency Control Heterogeneous Distributed Database Systems", *Technical Report Computer Science Dpt.-Tech. Rep.-894*, July 1989.

[EiL87]   A. Elmagarmid and Y. Leu, "An Optimistic Concurrency Control Algorithm for Heterogeneous Distributed Database Systems", *IEEE Data Engineering*, 1987.

[FBC87]   D. H. Fishman, D. Beech, H. P. Cate, E. C. Chow, T. Connors, J. W. Davis, N. Derrett, C. G. Hoch, W. Kent, P. Lyngbaek, B. Mahbod, M. A. Neimat, T. A. Ryan and M. C. Shan, "Iris: An Object-Oriented Database Management System", *Trans. on Office Info. Systems 5*, 1 (Jan. 1987), 48-69.

[HeM85]   D. Heimbigner and D. McLeod, "A Federated Architecture for Information Management", *ACM Transactions on Office Information Systems*, July, 1985.

[Kim89]   W. Kim, "Research Directions for Integrating Heterogeneous Databases", *Workshop On Heterogeneous Databases*, December, 1989.

[LaR82]   T. Landers and R. L. Rosenberg, "An Overview of Multibase", in *Distributed Databases*, H. J. Schneider (editor), North-Holland, 1982.

[Lel88]   W. Leler, *Constraint Programming Languages: Their Specification and Generation*, Addison-Wesley, 1988.

[LKP88]   V. Linneman, K. Kuspert, P. Pistor, R. Erke, A. Kemper, N. Sudkamp, G. Walch and M. Wallrath, "Design and Implementation of an Extensible Database Management System Supporting User Defined Types and Functions", *Proceedings of the Fourteenth International Conference on Very Large Databases*, August, 1988, 294-305.

[LiA86]   W. Litwin and A. Abdellatif, "Multidatabase Interoperability", *IEEE Computer*, December, 1986, 10-18.

[LiT89]   W. Litwin and H. Tirri, "Flexible Concurrency Control Using Value Dates", *Integration of Information Systems: Bridging Heterogeneous Databases*, 1989, IEEE Press.

[MSO86]   D. Maier, J. Stein, A. Otis and A. Purdy, "Development of an Object-Oriented DBMS", *OOPSLA86*, 1986, 472-481.

[MaD86]   F. Manola and U. Dayal, "PDM: An Object-Oriented Data Model", *International Workshop on Object-Oriented Database Systems*, 1986, 18-25.

[Mey88]   B. Meyer, *Object-Oriented Software Construction*, Prentice Hall, 1988.

[Moo86]   D. A. Moon, "Object-Oriented Programming with Flavors", *OOPSLA86*, 1986, 1-8.

[MoS88]   J. E. B. Moss and S. Sinofsky, "Managing Persistent Data with Mneme: Designing a Reliable, Shared Object Interface", *Advances in Object-Oriented Database Systems*, September, 1988, 298-316.

[Nel84]   G. Nelson, "How to Use Juno", *Manuscript CGN11*, Palo Alto, California, January, 1984.

[Pu88]   C. Pu, "Superdatabases for Composition of Heterogeneous Databases", *IEEE Data Engineering Conference*, 1988.

[RiC87]   J. E. Richardson and M. J. Carey, "Programming Constructs for Database System Implementation in EXODUS", *Proceedings of the ACM SIGMOD Conference*, 1987.

[RoS87]   L. Rowe and M. Stonebraker, "The POSTGRES Data Model", *Proc. of the 13 VLDB*, Brighton, England, 1987, 83-96.

[RuC89]   V. F. Russo and R. H. Campbell, "Virtual Memory and Backing Storage Management in Multiprocessor Operating Systems Using Object-Oriented Design Techniques", *OOPSLA '89*, New Orleans, October, 1989, 267-278.

[SCF86]   P. Schwarz, W. Chang, J. C. Freytag, G. Lohman, J. McPherson, C. Mohan and H. Pirahesh, "Extensibility in the Starburst Database System", *International Workshop on Object-Oriented Database Systems*, 1986, 85-92.

[SiM89]   M. Siegel and S. E. Madnick, "Schema Integration Using Metadata", *Workshop On Heterogeneous Databases*, December, 1989.

[StR86]   M. Stonebraker and L. Rowe, "The Design of POSTGRES", *Proceedings of the 1986 SIGMOD Conference*, Washington, D.C., May, 1986.

[TBC88]   R. N. Taylor, F. C. Blez, L. A. Clarke, L. Osterweil, R. W. Selby, J. C. Wileden, A. L. Wolf and M. Young, "Foundations for the Arcadia Environment Architecture", *Proceedings of ACM Software Eng. Notes '88: Third Symposium on Software Development Environments*, Boston, November, 1988, 1-13.

[Tem89]   M. Templeton, "Schema Translation in Mermaid", *Workshop On Heterogeneous Databases*, December, 1989.

[Ull82]   J. D. Ullman, *Principles of Database Systems*, Computer Science Press, Rockville, MD, Second Edition 1982.

[Weg87]   P. Wegner, "Dimensions of Object-Based Language Design", *OOPSLA87*, 1987, 168-182.

Part VII

Heterogeneity

Chair: Malcolm Atkinson

The three papers in this section all describe methods of dealing with heterogeneity. Heterogeneity arises naturally as different people and organisations use different methods to organise, manipulate and store their data. Whilst the different concerns and practices motivate the different regimes they all represent aspects of a common world. This commonality suggests that it may be possible to use these disparate systems together in some cooperative endeavour. Frequently, human issues, such as the requirements of merged organisations that have historically chosen different methods, give strong motivation for enabling this heterogeneous collaboration.

Needless to say, trying to provide some technically feasible method of enabling such collaboration is very difficult. It is a challenge to put the disparate components into a common framework, difficult to identify the common features of the components and hard to reconcile their differences. The authors in this section report three different approaches to meeting this challenge. They would argue that this is worthwhile for three reasons:

1. The existing investment in independent programs and data collections is very valuable, and methods are needed to make that investment more accessible and better utilised;

2. Heterogeneity itself is valuable, it will allow people to collaborate who do not wish to conform to a restrictive single model, preserving the investment in their education and experience, allowing the different appropriate choices in different circumstances to be used, and amortising the cost of providing a common harness over many more applications; and,

3. By experimenting to determine the efficacy of methods of coping with heterogeneity we will learn to understand complex systems, and particularly, discover the underlying consistency that may then provide better abstract understanding.

Barbara Liskov and her team from MIT, in *A Highly Available Object Repository for Use in a Heterogeneous Distributed System*, plan to build on their previous software engineering experience with CLU, ARGUS and MERCURY. The paper reports a requirement analysis and initial design for this highly reliable distributed and scalable object server. All the traditional concerns of a homogeneous system have to be dealt with, such as distributed nested transactions, recovery, protection and garbage collection. The heterogeneity comes from allowing many programming languages to be used in conjunction with this store. The common framework depends on these programs accepting a common model of distributed server management. The collaboration between these programs is achieved through a canonical type system and translation to and from this lingua Franca.

Dave Wile from the University of Southern California reported on work with Rick Hull and Tina Widjojo in *A Specificational Approach to Merging Persistent Object Bases*. This work assumes that a user at a work station, say in the home, wants to read data from many different sources (utilities, local government, etc) and wants to see data concerning one common aspect presented according to one chosen schema. The major step is to recognise how to separate this merging process into three reasonably independent phases. First the data pertinent to the common aspect is identified in each source, this is the basis for filtering. Second, the data from each source is transformed to be compliant with a common schema. These separate collections of data that came from each source are now merged to one composite data collection. The problems that arise in this stage are the focus in this paper, for example how to recognise when the data from two sources is about the same thing in the real world and how to deal with data that has conflicting information.

Alejandro Buchmann from GTE Laboratories presented his work on *Modelling Heterogeneous Systems as an Active Object Space*, which is part of the DOM project being undertaken by the team at GTE. The system attempts to bring together into one collaborating framework such disparate systems as HyperCard and relational databases, so it is not possible to even assume that every component has a notion of transaction and recovery, nor that every component is continuously available. The chosen tactic is to model all components as active objects, and to augment their behaviour with rule sets. Strategies for efficiently triggering these rules are considered.

The dominant theme of the discussion was, can we hope to build such complex systems. There was common recognition that these are very ambitious projects to bring to practical use. The authors defended themselves, either by indicating that they have chosen a tractable subproblem, or that they have a quiver full of partial solutions. They also reminded us of the strong motives for undertaking this work, reiterated above. Another challenge was that the same effort might be better expended in our research into how to engineer persistent object systems by concentrating efforts on more confined subproblems. There were two rebuttles to this: the distribution and heterogeneity may force one to deal with issues properly, and subproblems may dodge essential complexity.

A Highly Available Object Repository for Use in a Heterogeneous Distributed System

Barbara Liskov
MIT Laboratory for Computer Science
Cambridge, MA 02139
liskov@lcs.mit.edu

Robert Gruber
MIT Laboratory for Computer Science
Cambridge, MA 02139
gruber@lcs.mit.edu

Paul Johnson
MIT Laboratory for Computer Science
Cambridge, MA 02139
prj@lcs.mit.edu

Liuba Shrira
MIT Laboratory for Computer Science
Cambridge, MA 02139
liuba@lcs.mit.edu

Abstract

This paper describes a new project to design and implement an object repository for use in a heterogeneous distributed system. The primary goal of this work is to provide a convenient medium for sharing of information among programs written in many different programming languages. In addition, the repository will provide highly reliable and highly available storage for objects entrusted to it.[1]

1. Introduction

In the heterogeneous distributed systems of the future, there will be a need for an object repository that allows programs implemented in different programming languages to store and share objects. Although a file system could be used for such a purpose, it will be more convenient, and less error-prone, if the types of the stored objects reflect the kinds of information of interest to the programs that use them. We are working on a project to design and implement such an object repository. In addition to providing a convenient medium for sharing of information among programs written in many different programming languages, the repository will also provide highly reliable and highly available storage for objects entrusted to it.

This paper provides an overview of our approach. It begins in Section 2 by sketching the services provided by the repository to its users. Section 3 describes the system architecture and discusses some aspects of the implementation, including a description of the replication method we plan to use to support our reliability and availability goals. We conclude in Section 4 with a discussion of the properties of our system that distinguish it from other work. Our system differs from other related efforts in three main ways: it will be a distributed system containing replicated components and designed for use in a heterogeneous environment; it will attempt to improve response time and reduce system load by optimizing user requests; and it will provide a programming language that supports type evolution and gives users control of lock granularity.

We are still working on the design of our repository; we do not expect to begin implementation until next year. Our design has been influenced by work in object-oriented databases [18, 21, 30, 27] and distributed and replicated file systems [19, 22, 26].

[1]This research was supported in part by the Advanced Research Projects Agency of the Department of Defense, monitored by the Office of Naval Research under contract N00014-89-J-1988 and in part by the National Science Foundation under Grant CCR-8822158. The research was also supported under a National Science Foundation Graduate Fellowship.

2. Overview

The repository is a distributed system made up of many individual repositories, which we refer to as ORs. The ORs cooperate to provide the repository services to clients. Most of the time, users of the repository need not be aware of the individual ORs, but occasionally this is necessary as discussed further below. Some details of the services the repository will provide to its users are given below.

2.1. The Object Universe

The repository provides a universe of objects that clients can access and share. Each object stored by the repository has a unique name (an *object identifier*, or *oid*) and a value. Clients can identify objects by providing their oids, and objects can refer to one another using oids.

Each object is stored at a particular OR, which is selected by the client when the object is created; therefore, object creation is one of the times when a client needs to be aware of the distributed nature of the repository. Later, a client may chose to move an object to another OR; this is the only other point at which a client must be aware of the ORs. The oids provide a global name space, and clients can access objects without needing to know where they reside. Moving an object does not change its oid, so all references to it will continue to work.

Each object has a type that determines the set of operations that can be applied to it. The repository guarantees that objects are accessed only by means of the operations of their type. Thus, these operations are the only way that the objects' values can be observed or modified.

The repository provides a rich set of built-in types (e.g., integers, booleans, characters) and constructors (e.g., arrays, records, unions). In addition, users can define new abstract types for the repository.

Sets will be provided as a built-in constructor, and clients can cause indexes to be provided for sets, to speed up queries. (We may extend this ability to "set-like" constructors.) We are currently working on a method to allow efficient maintenance of indexes on sets where the objects in the set are of abstract type.

Clients of the repository interact with it by invoking operations on its objects. These calls (from clients to the repository) follow call-by-value semantics. Arguments and results are usually oids. For example, a call to add an employee to a set of employees would take the oid of the set and the oid of the employee as arguments.

However, sometimes actual values of objects are needed. For example, a user may wish to obtain an array of integers from the repository so that it can be manipulated directly by the client program, or may wish to store the array value as the value of an array object in the repository. Therefore, along with oids, it must be possible to use values as arguments and results. For a given type T in the repository, T can have an *external representation*, ext(T); this is a description of the format of the data that a client will receive (when reading the value) or provide (when specifying a value). The external representation is similar to a *message representation* used for communication in distributed system [8, 14]. It differs from the way the object is represented within the repository, and also from the way the value will be represented in the client program. Typically, translations are provided on both ends: the internal representation is *encoded* to produce the external representation by the provider of the value, and the external representation is *decoded* to produce the internal representation used by the receiver.

Within the repository, if the definer of type T provides an encode routine from T to ext(T), it is legal to return result values of type T to client programs. If the definer provides a decode routine from ext(T) to T, it is legal to accept argument values of type T from client programs. The simple built-in types (integers, reals, characters, etc.) will provide encode and decode routines; thus, like most object repositories, simple values can be used as arguments and results. Unlike most other object repositories that use an abstract type approach, (e.g., Encore [27]), values of user-defined type can also be arguments or results, provided the type has the encode or decode routine.

The types of objects in the repository are language-independent and a way is needed for describing them that is independent of any programming language (such as the one used to implement them). This can be accomplished by providing a "type specification" that defines the names and signatures for the type's operations and also the external representation if the type is to be transmitted as a value. The signatures will be defined in terms of other types known to the repository. In addition, the definer needs to give a description of the behavior of the type so that programmers who wish to use objects of the new type can understand its meaning. The important point to notice here is that all of this can be done without defining an implementation for the new type, and the information is independent of the programming language that will be used to implement the type (or any of the languages used by clients). Thus, abstract data types provide a means for programs in different languages to communicate.

Since the repository will provide storage for long lived objects, we need to allow object representations and object types to evolve over time. We will allow each type to have multiple implementations, so that different objects of the type may have different storage representations. We will also provide a mechanism to convert objects of an earlier implementation to a later one, if a client wants this to happen. We will not convert all objects of the old implementation at once; instead the conversion will be done lazily, as the objects are used.

To support type evolution, we plan to provide a type hierarchy and to allow an object of a subtype to be used (e.g., passed as an argument) wherever an object of the supertype is required. It is legal for a type S to be a subtype of type T provided objects of type S behave the same as those of type T when accessed using the T operations [11]. Note that this definition has both a syntactic and a semantic component. The syntactic component is that the subtype must provide the same operations as the supertype and these operations must have compatible signatures; this constraint will be enforced by the repository. The semantic constraint (same behavior) will not be enforced (since this would require a proof of correctness based on formal specifications of the two types); instead when a person declares S to be a subtype of T, he or she is promising that the behavior is proper.

We have not yet decided whether to provide a constraint mechanism. Although we can see the value of the mechanism (especially when the constraints can be guaranteed to be side-effect free), we are concerned about the impact of constraints on modularity and understandability. For example, a constraint can cause an object to not satisfy its specification because some operation that is legal according to its type definition cannot be carried out.

Operations of a type can be both procedures and iterators [17]. An iterator is an operation that returns many results one after another. For example, an array iterator would produce the elements of the array from the low bound to the high bound. Procedures and iterators will not be limited to operations of types, however; they can also be stored at the repository as separate callable units.

We plan to deallocate objects in the universe using garbage collection. Each OR will provide one or more root objects. Objects accessible from the root of an OR are not garbage; all others are garbage and will be garbage collected at a convenient time. Some roots are persistent; objects accessible from them will continue to exist even when there is no active client program that refers to them.

2.2. Client Access

We plan to allow clients to interact with the repository only by means of transactions. We will provide support for nested transactions [15]; nested transactions are useful because they allow for checkpoints (if a subaction does not succeed, the parent action can continue from the state as it was before the subaction began) and concurrency (subactions can run in parallel, and each will be atomic with respect to the others). Special support for single-operation transactions (where each operation invocation is to be run as a transaction) will be provided.

If an application needs to support concurrent users that interact in some other way (e.g., if applications want to provide "transactions" with weaker semantics, such as non-serializable behavior), this new behavior can be implemented as a service that runs on top of the object repository. The repository provides such a service with persistent, highly-available storage, and will guarantee that objects in the repository satisfy consistency constraints since all accesses and modifications occur within transactions.

Within a transaction, a client program calls repository operations; a transaction can contain one or more calls. We plan to allow both calls of a single operation, e.g., to create an object, or to apply one of an object's operations to it, and "combined" operation calls in which the client asks the repository to carry out a program containing many individual calls. The combined operations will provide the repository with information about the immediate future, which we plan to use as a context for doing optimizations. In addition, we will take advantage of iterator calls to stream information to the client; this will allow the client to make use of earlier results in parallel with the fetching of later ones.

A query is a special kind of combined operation. As mentioned, we plan to support indexes as a speedup mechanism for query processing and to allow indexes for sets containing objects of user-defined types as well as for set of objects of built-in type.

Since the repository is independent of the client language, we cannot be sure that client calls to the repository will be properly type-checked. Therefore, we plan to type check these calls ourselves. A client call will be permitted only if the types of its arguments match those of the operation being called.

2.3. Naming and Persistence

Suppose a user runs an application that uses the repository and then terminates, leaving some objects in the repository. The next time the user runs the application, he needs to access the objects left in the repository by the previous run. This requires some way of naming those objects. Oids are not suitable here because they are low level and not user-friendly. Therefore, we plan to also provide high level names.

The requirements for the high level names are not very stringent. High level names are needed just to allow a client program to find its objects when it starts running; after this point objects are referenced using oids. Also, oids, and not high level names, are used inside of objects to refer to one another.

In addition, the naming structure need not be very rich, because additional naming structures can be provided by other objects, e.g., the ones that are obtained by using high level names. For example, these objects might provide associative lookup by means of queries.

Our plan is to provide a simple two-level naming scheme. Each OR within a repository will have a unique high-level string name. This name identifies a directory object maintained by that OR. The directory provides a mapping from strings to objects of arbitrary type.

An OR's directory is the single persistent root of that OR. When a client program stores a mapping to an object in an OR directory, or roots a path to that object in the OR directory, that object becomes *permanent* and will continue to exist even though the client program stops running (unless the path is broken explicitly by some client program).

There will be other roots in addition to the OR directory, e.g., to provide an analog of a program stack, but these are not persistent; they will disappear when the client program they were created for terminates, and at this point the objects reachable from them may be garbage collected.

2.4. Protection

We plan to provide authenticated connections by using the Kerberos authentication server [28]. Therefore, when an OR receives a request, it will know who is making it. This information will be used for access control.

Our plan is to provide access control by means of *domains*. Domains are disjoint, and every object belongs to some domain. A domain defines an access control policy. The policy specifies rules to control access to the domain's objects based on their identity and their type, and also specifies rules that govern how the access control rules can change. Domains do not constrain how objects can refer to one another; an object in one domain can contain oids of objects in other domains.

An object is always in a domain. Whenever a new object is created, it must be created in some domain; later, a user can change its domain if desired. However, although it will be possible for a user to review the policy of a domain, it will not be possible to easily identify all the objects currently in the domain.

There is a special *null domain, D_{null}*, that allows everyone to access all of its objects in all possible ways. D_{null} is useful because for many objects no control is required; this includes both immutable types like integers, and also objects that are encapsulated inside the representation of some abstract object. No checking at all will be done for some types of objects (small immutable ones); for these types, the objects will be required (by the type) to all be in D_{null}. For other objects in D_{null}, the checking will be minimal (just a check that the object is in D_{null}).

For objects that are not in D_{null}, checking will have the same cost as in any system based on access control lists [25]. To speed things up, we plan to provide short-lived capabilities associated with the oids we give to clients. Each capability will contain a "death time". Up to that time the capability can be used without any further checking. When a capability expires, we will attempt to renew it automatically using the access control list; if this fails, the client program will be notified.

2.5. Language Veneers

Client programs that use the repository can be written in various programming languages. To make it possible to use the repository from a particular language, that language needs to be extended. We call such an extension a language "veneer". The veneer must allow the client to begin and end transactions; to make use of oids; to communicate values of objects to the repository (for objects of transmissible type); to call operations on objects and also individual procedures and iterators; and to call combined operations and queries. We expect our previous work on defining language veneers in Mercury [14] to be helpful here.

We plan to investigate how best to use the repository from various programming languages. There are two poles here. The object repository can be treated as a persistent extension [1] of a language's heap (for languages with heaps). Note that the semantics of objects in the repository are similar to the semantics of heap-based languages such as CLU, Lisp, and Smalltalk. Alternatively, the repository can be viewed as a foreign environment (e.g., like a file system).

In either case, it is necessary to specify *associations* between transmissible repository types and language types. Each association links a language type and a repository type, and defines how to translate between the language type to the (external representation of the) repository type. For each call to the repository, the language compiler will cause the translations to occur by means of automatic "stub" generation [7].

In the case of the "foreign environment" approach, we will probably make use of "shadow" associations: For each repository type, there will be exactly one language type that is associated with it. This language type is the shadow of the repository type, since all use of the repository type occurs through the shadow. Calls to the repository will look just like regular calls within the language, but to special procedures, e.g., to start a transaction or call an operation on a repository object. Calls to iterators require adding to the language a data type that can be used to request the values when they are needed; this type is similar to the "promise" type we provided for Mercury [16]. Combined operations and queries require provision of a little "repository language" that can be used to express these; the syntax of this language can be tailored to that of the host language.

3. Architecture and Implementation

As mentioned earlier, the repository is implemented by multiple ORs that together provide what appears to clients as a single object universe. In addition, it also contains *front ends*. These two parts of our implementation are discussed below.

3.1. Front Ends

For any given client, there is an associated *front end*. For clients running on a very small machine, the front end may be non-local. The usual case, however, will be one front end per machine. The front end will handle all of the clients on its machine. Clients will interact with it to carry out all interactions with the repository; the front end will communicate with the ORs as needed to carry out the client request.

The front end serves a number of purposes. First, it isolates the client from the fact that there are multiple ORs. A client simply gives its request to the front end, which in turn communicates with the appropriate ORs. It does this by interpreting the oids given to it by the client.

To maintain the illusion of a single object universe, and to allow object movement, oids are globally unique and location independent. When a client invokes an operation on an object, it simply gives the front end the object's oid. The front end must determine which OR stores the object. To make this determination easy, each oid will contain the identifier of the OR believed to hold the object as a hint. If the object has moved, the hint may no longer be valid. This will be discovered when the old OR is contacted, and a location service [9] will be used to find the correct OR. The client oid's hint is then updated. In this way, the hints in client-held oids will be updated lazily as the oids are actually used.

The high level names are also globally unique. If the client refers to a high level name, the front end will interpret the first part of the name (which names the OR) and then proceed from there.

The second major function of the front end is to offload work from the ORs. The ORs will be a scarce, shared resource that must be used efficiently. One way to reduce the load at the ORs is to run client requests at the front ends. Therefore the front ends will be capable of running the code of an object. This may require first copying that code from an OR that stores it.

The goal of offloading work is closely tied to the third main purpose of the front end, namely, to improve response time as seen by the client. Often it will be faster to perform a client's request locally, e.g., if the objects accessed by that request have local copies. In general, we intend to have the front end decide on an effective way to process each client request. In making this decision, it will consider what objects and code is stored locally. In addition, it will also examine the request. For example, it may decide (based on information about sets and indexes) to ship a query to a particular OR for processing because that OR contains the set that should be accessed first. Or it may decide to process a combined operation locally, but to stream a sequence of read requests to the ORs so that it can do the processing in parallel with the reading. Alternatively, it might send the entire combined operation to an OR for processing.

Clearly, in order to process operations locally, the front end must maintain a cache containing copies of repository objects. This raises questions about how to use and maintain the cache.

We are planning to use "lazy locking" as a way to take advantage of cache objects. Recall that every operation performed by a client takes place within a transaction. If the operation uses an object in the front-end's cache, its transaction will be granted the needed lock without checking with the object's OR; this check will be done asynchronously in the background, or when the transaction commits. If the cache data is stale, or the lock cannot be granted, the transaction will abort. (Our scheme is similar to the locking scheme used in Symbolic's Statice system [4].) We will use a similar scheme for pre-fetched data. The data will be fetched from an OR without setting any locks (since it may not actually be used); if it is used, the lock will be granted locally and the OR will be informed later.

With this scheme, a transaction will abort if it is unable to obtain the locks it needs later. Therefore, having stale data in a cache will not cause any errors, i.e., modifications to repository objects based on stale data will not be allowed. However, we do not want to abort transactions because of stale data very often. Thus maintaining cache consistency becomes a performance issue.

To improve the probability that cached data is fresh, ORs will keep track of what front ends have copies of what objects, and will notify them when those objects change. Note, however, that OR's need not insure that these messages get to the front ends, since inconsistencies will be detected before transactions are allowed to commit.

In addition, we need to be concerned with when object copies are added to, and removed from, caches. Copies can be removed using an approximate LRU technique. Obviously, objects are added to the cache when referenced by a transaction, and they will stay there after the transaction terminates (until the LRU algorithm removes them). Therefore, if an object is used several times in transactions that are close together in time, no further fetching will be needed.

3.2. ORs

Having multiple ORs allows us to support the needs of distributed organizations: each part of the organization can place the objects its uses frequently at an OR that is geographically near it, yet objects belonging to other parts can also be accessed (probably with a slower response time). Note that the need to position frequently used objects at a convenient location leads to a requirement that users be able to control object location, including both an initial location and possibly a different one later. This is one reason why we allow this part of the repository structure to show through to clients (the other reason is replication, which is discussed below). Having multiple ORs also gives us the ability to make the system easily scalable as user load changes, and allows us to support a larger user base than could be accommodated with a single OR.

ORs have the following tasks to perform: First, they must carry out the requests sent to them by the front ends. Sometimes these will just be requests to ship data to the front end with or without setting locks. At other times, the OR will be requested to run some code, e.g., a combined operation, or an operation of some object. In doing such a request, the OR may discover that it needs an object located at a different OR. It will use the same scheme as the front end (OR id as a hint in the oid) to determine what OR is needed.

Second, the ORs must carry out transaction-related work, including lock management and running the two-phase commit protocol when transactions complete. Our plan is to always use an OR as the coordinator of two-phase commit [6], since they are more reliable than front ends at client machines (for example, the client might log out and turn off his machine). As part of doing phase 1 of two phase commit, the ORs need to determine whether needed locks can be granted. To do this, we need to identify object versions so that we can tell whether or not the object copy at the front end is the same as that at the OR.

Third, the ORs need to maintain indexes. As part of committing a transaction, all indexes that are affected by objects modified by that transaction must be updated. It will be able to do this effectively because our index technique will provide very accurate information about what objects affect what indexes.

Fourth, ORs need to keep track of what objects have copies at what front ends. One thing that we believe will help here is the natural locality of applications. Front ends will use objects from local ORs most of the time. Therefore, ORs will usually only be concerned with notifying a few front ends. In addition, to reduce the information at the ORs, we may allow front end copies to "expire"; once a copy has expired, it is the front end's responsibility to refresh it, rather than the OR's responsibility.

Fifth, the ORs need to do garbage collection. Our garbage collection mechanism [10, 13] will allow each OR to do collection locally; it accounts for remote references to its objects at other ORs by means of an extra root that records this information. Inter-OR collection is done by means of a garbage collection service that can be used to determine which non-local references are still valid.

Finally, the ORs provide replication for their objects in order to support our reliability and availability goals. Our replication method is discussed below.

3.3. Replication

Each OR actually consists of a number of replicas, and the numbers of replicas in different ORs may vary. In addition, ORs may be configured differently. For some, all replicas might reside on the same local area net, which makes for fast communication, but also means that there will be events (e.g., a power failure) that will cause all replicas to fail. Others might have geographically distributed replicas; they will be more robust, but slower. ORs can be reconfigured if necessary [9]. The differences between ORs with respect to replication is the other reason why the existence of the ORs must be user-visible.

Replication will be used to provide both high reliability (so that an object stored at the OR will survive failures with high probability) and high availability (so that an object will be accessible to clients with high probability in spite of failures). We intend to use a replication scheme based on Oki's viewstamped replication technique [24]. In our scheme, one of the replicas acts as the *primary* for an object, others are *backups* and still others are *witnesses*. To survive N failures, there must be N backups and N witnesses. The primary and the backups store copies of the object; the witnesses usually do not store data, and are only active when failures occur as discussed further below. For example, for an object to survive a single failure, there must be one backup, and thus the object will have two copies. The single witness can fill in for the primary or backup in case of a failure.

In this scheme, the primary does the most work, the backup does much less, and, when there are no failures, the witness does nothing at all. Different objects at an OR will be assigned to different primaries. For example, if there are three replicas at an OR, each can act as primary for approximately one third of the OR's objects, as backup for another one third, and as witness for the rest. In this way we can spread the work of the OR among the replicas.

In our method, client requests are sent to the primary, which decides what to do and communicates with the backup as needed. Requests to do operations, or to send object copies to a front end, can be done entirely at the primary. However, when a transaction that modifies objects commits, the primary must communicate with the backups. For example, the primary of a participant of two phase commit must do the following during phase 1:

1. It must determine whether all locks needed by the transaction with respect to local objects can be granted. If not, it refuses the commit.

2. It stores the new versions of all modified objects in its local (volatile) log.

3. It sends the new log information to all backups. The backups copy the new information into their (volatile) logs and send acknowledgments to the primary.

4. When all backups have acknowledged the new information, it sends an "ok" message to the coordinator. (A "prepare" record is not needed [24, 23].)

Similarly, a coordinator must force the "committing" record in its log to its backups, and a participant in phase 2 must force the "commit" record in its log to its backups.

Each replica is equipped with an uninterruptible power supply (UPS) that will allow it to write its log to disk (and clean up its other state) in case of a power failure. Therefore it is safe to keeps logs in volatile memory and copy them to disk in the background. This means that the cost of two phase commit is entirely in the message passing, which leads to excellent performance, especially when the replicas are on the same local area net. (We have verified our performance expectations in some experiments using this replication scheme [5].)

In addition to keeping information about modifications in the log, the primary will also modify the objects themselves so that later accesses can be carried out rapidly. The backups may also keep copies of the objects; this would permit quicker recovery from failures.

If a worker (a primary or backup) becomes unavailable, one of the other workers carries out a *view change* [2, 3]. In phase one of the view change, this worker communicates will all other replicas (both workers and witnesses), asking them to accept a new view. A new view can be formed if a majority of all the replicas accept it. Note that this means that at least one member of the old view must accept it. One of the workers of the previous view will be the primary of the new view; the primary of the old view will be the new primary if possible. The backups will be any other remaining workers from the old view plus some *promoted witnesses*. Enough witnesses will be promoted so that there are N backups in the new view.

The state of the new view will contain the modifications done on behalf of all committed and prepared transactions: since this information was forced to all the backups, and since at least one member of the previous view must be a member of the new view, the needed information will persist into the new view. This information is propagated to members of the new view as part of the second phase of the view change.

A promoted witness will have a log in which it maintains only recent information; this includes modifications done in the new view, plus some additional information about what happened at the end of the old view. Since a promoted witness does not have a complete state, it cannot be a primary.

A transaction that does not modify any objects at an OR can be prepared at the primary without communication with the backup. This optimization can lead to a serialization problem if a new view has formed but the old primary doesn't know about it. In that case, for example, a modification made by transaction T that committed in the new view might not be visible to a transaction S committing at the old primary even though S must be serialized after T (because of sharing of an object at another OR).

To avoid this serialization problem, we make use of loosely synchronized clocks [20]. (Synchronized clocks are also needed to support capabilities that timeout and cache items that expire.) Each message sent by a backup to the primary contains a time equal to its clock's time + δ; here δ is on the order of a few seconds. This time represents a promise by the backup not to start a new view until that time has passed. The primary needs to communicate with a backup about a read-only transaction only if the time of its local clock is greater than the promised time - ε, where ε is the clock skew. Each view has a *start time*, which is the minimum of the promised times of members of the previous view who are also members of the current view. The primary of a new view cannot prepare any transactions until the time of its clock is greater than the start time of its view. In this way, we guarantee that there cannot be a transaction that committed in the new view and that should occur before a transaction in an earlier view. Note that when the new primary begins to prepare a transaction, most likely the time of its clock will be later than the view's start time and there will be no delay.

We expect our replication method to provide good response time; we are currently studying its performance in some work on a replicated file system [12]. In addition, repository storage is highly reliable and available. It is highly reliable because repository objects can survive at least N simultaneous disk, hardware, or software failures, and all power failures. Furthermore, an OR can provide service as long as no more than N replicas are down or inaccessible. In addition, view changes will be fast. When a witness is promoted, all that is needed is to send it the recent log entries. When a worker rejoins after being disabled, it must be brought up to date. This might take a long time, but it can be done before the view change occurs, while work is still going on in the current view.

4. Discussion

There are three main ways in which our work differs from other, similar projects. The first is our plan to provide a distributed implementation with replication, intended for use in a heterogeneous environment. The second is our use of sophisticated front ends to off load work from the ORs and to do analysis (especially of combined operations and remote iterators) to improve performance. The third is the programming language we will provide for implementing the repository types.

The language has a number of interesting features, some of which have been mentioned earlier. As mentioned, operations on objects can be procedures and iterators; in addition, procedures and iterators can be provided as independent modules that are not linked to particular types. Iterators are important because they can help the system do a good job of prefetching. For example, a graph type can provide an iterator that follows the "standard" path over a graph object; this can be invoked to do prefetching and then terminated if it turns out that another path is needed.

The repository language will be strongly typed and will support a type hierarchy in order to support type evolution. Types will be defined by providing specifications that give the names and signatures of all operations and identify any supertypes. Each type will be implemented by a module, and, as mentioned, there can be several modules that implement the same type. The compiler will check that a module implements all the operations required by its type, and that the operations have the proper signatures. The language will not support an inheritance mechanism. For example, the module that implements a type will be completely independent of modules that implement supertypes of that type.

The language will allow programs to use transactions. Of most interest here is the ability for users to define their own atomic data types. We plan to borrow heavily from our work on Argus here [15], although some changes may be needed to accommodate our lazy locking approach. As in Argus, the locking and version management that is needed to implement transactions will be provided by the objects those transactions use. Atomic data types provide the needed locking and versions; all objects shared by users of the repository must belong to atomic types. The repository language will provide some base atomic types such as atomic records and atomic arrays (which are like regular arrays and records, except that they also provide locking and versions). User-defined atomic types can easily be implemented from these types, but sometimes a different granularity of locking, or a different version management scheme, is needed. In this case, users can implement atomic types using nonatomic objects, using a mechanism similar to what Argus provides [29].

References

1. Atkinson, M. P. et al. "PS-Algol: An Algol with a Persistent Heap". *SIGPLAN Notices 17*, 7 (July 1982), 24-30.

2. El-Abbadi, A., and Toueg, S. Maintaining Availability in Partitioned Replicated Databases. Proc. of the Fifth Symposium on Principles of Database Systems, ACM, 1986, pp. 240-251.

3. El-Abbadi, A., Skeen, D., and Cristian, F. An Efficient Fault-tolerant Protocol for Replicated Data Management. Proc. of the Fourth Symposium on Principles of Database Systems, ACM, 1985, pp. 215-229.

4. Gerson, D. *Private communication.* 1990.

5. Ghemawat, S. Automatic Replication for Highly Available Services. Tech. Rept. MIT/LCS/TR-473, MIT Laboratory for Computer Science, Cambridge, MA, 1990.

6. Gray, J. N. Notes on Data Base Operating Systems. In *Lecture Notes in Computer Science*, R. Bayer, R. Graham and G. Seegmuller, Eds., Springer-Verlag, 1978, pp. 393-481.

7. Hayes, R., and Schlichting, R. "Facilitating Mixed Language Programming in Distributed Systems". *IEEE Trans. on Software Engineering SE-13*, 12 (December 1987).

8. Herlihy, M. P., and Liskov, B. "A Value Transmission Method for Abstract Data Types". *ACM Trans. on Programming Languages and Systems 4*, 4 (October 1982), 527-551.

9. Hwang, D. Constructing a Highly-Available Location Service for a Distributed Environment. Technical Report MIT/LCS/TR-410, M.I.T. Laboratory for Computer Science, Cambridge, MA, January, 1988.

10. Ladin, R. *A Method for Constructing Highly Available Services and a Technique for Distributed Garbage Collection.* Ph.D. Th., M.I.T. Department of Electrical Engineering and Computer Science, Cambrige, MA, May 1989.

11. Leavens, G. Verifying Object-Oriented Programs that Use Subtypes. Technical Report MIT/LCS/TR-439, M.I.T. Laboratory for Computer Science, Cambridge, MA, February, 1989.

12. Liskov, B., Gruber, R., Johnson, P., and Shrira, L. A Replicated Unix File System (Extended Abstract). To be published in the Proc. of the Workshop on Fault Tolerant Support in Distributed Systems held in Bologna, Italy.

13. Liskov, B., and Ladin, R. Highly-Available Distributed Services and Fault-Tolerant Distributed Garbage Collection. Proc. of the 5th ACM Symposium on Principles of Distributed Computing, ACM, Calgary, Alberta, Canada, August, 1986.

14. Liskov, B., Bloom, T., Gifford, D., Scheifler, R., and Weihl, W. Communication in the Mercury System. Proc. of the 21st Annual Hawaii Conference on System Sciences, IEEE, January, 1988, pp. 178-187.

15. Liskov, B. "Distributed Programming in Argus". *Comm. of the ACM 31*, 3 (March 1988), 300-312.

16. Liskov, B., and Shrira, L. Promises: Linguistic Support for Efficient Asynchronous Procedure Calls in Distributed Systems. Proc. of the ACM SIGPLAN '88 Conference on Programming Languages Design and Implementation, ACM, June, 1988.

17. Liskov, B., and Guttag, J. Chapter 6, Iteration Abstraction. In *Abstraction and Specification in Program Development*, MIT Press and McGraw Hill, 1986, pp. 118-130.

18. Maier, D., Stein, J., Otis, A., and Purdy, A. Development of an Object-Oriented DBMS. OOPSLA '86 Proceedings, ACM, September, 1986, pp. 472-482.

19. Mann, T., Hisgen, A., and Swart, G. An Algorithm for Data Replication. Report 46, DEC Systems Research Center, Palo Alto, CA, June, 1989.

20. Mills, D.L. Network Time Protocol (Version 1) Specification and Implementation. DARPA-Internet Report RFC-1059. July 1988.

21. Moss, J. E. B., and Sinofsky, S. Managing Persistent Data with Mneme: Designing a Reliable, Shared Object Interface. Tech. Rept. COINS Technical Report 88-67, University of Massachusetts, Amherst, July, 1988. Also in the Proc. of the Second International Workshop on Object Oriented Data Bases, Germany, September 1988.

22. Nelson, M., Welch, B., and Ousterhout, J. "Caching in the Sprite Network File System". *ACM Trans. on Computer Systems 6*, 1 (February 1988), 134-154.

23. Oki, B. M., and Liskov, B. Viewstamped Replication: A New Primary Copy Method to Support Highly-Available Distributed Systems. Proc. of the 7th ACM Symposium on Principles of Distributed Computing, ACM, Aug., 1988.

24. Oki, B. M. Viewstamped Replication for Highly Available Distributed Systems. Technical Report MIT/LCS/TR-423, M.I.T. Laboratory for Computer Science, Cambridge, MA, August, 1988.

25. Saltzer, J. H. "Protection and the Control of Information Sharing in Multics". *Comm. of the ACM 17*, 7 (July 1974), 388-402.

26. Satyanarayanan, M., et al. Coda: A Highly Available File System for a Distributed Workstation Environment. Tech. Rept. CMU-CS-89-165, Carnegie Mellon University, School of Computer Science, Pittsburgh, PA, July, 1989.

27. Shaw, G. and Zdonik, S. A Query Algebra for Object-Oriented Databases. Proc. of the Sixth International Conference on Data Engineering, IEEE, February, 1990.

28. Steiner, J.G., Neuman, C., Schiller, J.I. Kerberos: An Authentication Service for Open Network Systems. Project Athena, MIT, Cambridge, MA, March, 1988.

29. Weihl, W., and Liskov, B. "Implementation of Resilient, Atomic Data Types". *ACM Trans. on Programming Languages and Systems 7*, 2 (April 1985), 244-269.

30. Weinreb, D., Feinberg, N., Gerson, D., and Lamb, C. An Object-Oriented Database System to Support an Integrated Programming Environment. Symbolics, Inc., Cambridge, MA, 1988. Submitted for publication.

A Specificational Approach to Merging
Persistent Object Bases[†]

Surjatini Widjojo

isssw@nusvm.bitnet

Richard Hull[‡]

hull@hpai23.isi.edu

Dave Wile

wile@vaxa.isi.edu

Computer Science Department

University of Southern California

Los Angeles, CA 90089-0782

and

USC/Information Sciences Institute

Marina Del Rey, CA 90292

Abstract

We examine the problem of *merging* persistent object bases (POBs) and the attendant problem of determining when two objects are *equivalent*. In particular, two or more *source* POBs are combined in a single *target* POB in which physically different objects in the sources may be merged into a single object in the target. Although persistent object base research has not focused on these problems in the past, any attempt to model (portions of) the real world in an object base butts up against them. In fact, the object-centered nature of POBs is consistent with and almost motivates our two-phase solution to the problem, in which an 'object identification' phase precedes a 'constraint resolution' phase. *Families of keys* are used to identify objects, after which various mechanisms are used to merge the remaining data. For example, *preference specifications* are used to resolve constraints violated in the target – by preferring facts from one of the sources over the others.

1 Introduction

One of the features touted by persistent object base researchers is the *lack of need for object identification* in POBs[FBC+87, PSM87, Gro87, DCBM89]. In essence, persistent objects have persistent Identifiers (IDs) which make them distinct from all other objects simply by the way they are created. In fact, this feature is shared with the programming language freedom to create arrays, vectors, records and other structures, arbitrarily, without regard to or fear of their possible equivalence to other such structures that just happen

---

[†]Sponsored by Defense Advanced Research Projects Agency, Information Science and Technology office, ARPA Order No. 6096, issued by Defense Supply Service (Washington) under contract no. MDA903-87-C-0641.

[‡]This author is supported in part and by NSF grant IRI-87-19875.

to be around in the address space. The 'seamless' integration of persistence into such frameworks lends considerable support to the notion of persistent IDs as being a 'good idea' [DCBM89].

But POBs are in many cases used to model some part of the real world. In making that connection one does *not* have the freedom to create objects indiscriminately, but often must rely on *key* attributes to identify objects. The modelled world would be inconsistent if duplicate objects with the same key attributes exist, for fidelity to the real world would be lost, and predictions based on the model would be inaccurate. We emphasize that much – maybe most – persistent data is private, scaffold-like data whose structure and identity are understood by programs alone, but for that data which is shared with the real world, and/or other programs and persons, an object identification scheme is necessary. Furthermore, as POBs take on more database functionality, e.g., in the context of database programming languages, the quantity of real world data in POBs will increase.

The simplest of identification schemes involves matching printable attributes of objects; e.g., one identifies a **person** by his **social-security-number** or (**first-name, last-name**)-pair. A more complex scheme might allow other, previously-identified objects to participate in the identification; e.g., to let **home-owner (a person)** partially identify **property**. The spectrum of possibilities is quite broad, going through chains of composed attributes and ending with subgraph isomorphism; e.g., "his wife is the CEO of the corporation of which his brother is the personnel manager".

Identifying a real-world object with an implemented object is only half of the problem; *merging* the information from two different sources may also be difficult. For example, in the real world the **age** attribute may be 15, but in the modelled world, 14. Naturally, we tend to *prefer* the information from the real world in such a situation. However, if the data to be merged comes from different POBs, the situation is not so clear-cut. Suppose we want to merge **telephone number** attributes from object bases describing **employment data** and **personal data**. We may want to prefer data from one source over another, or we may want to perform some complex function to compute data to resolve conflicts between the source POBs. For example, we may wish to use the **maximum** of a **person**'s **salary** attribute in the source POBs as the value in the target POB.

Unfortunately, the problems of object identification and merging become very complex when we consider sharing data *between* POBs, for objects may be *represented* differently in different POBs. In fact, all manner of inconsistencies can arise: objects in one POB may be represented as attributes in another, attributes may map to printables in one and objects in another, multi-slot relationships with the same name may disagree in number, type, count restrictions, etc.

Despite these problems, we believe the problems entailed by the use of a single, uniform POB to hold all objects in the real world are far more difficult than dealing with the sharing of idiosyncratic POBs. The research described in the current paper forms part of the larger WorldBase project [WWH90], which incorporates a number of functionalities for attacking this problem in its full generality. In WorldBase information from different POBs is extracted and merged through a three stage process. In the first stage the data from separate POBs is filtered and aggregated into conceptually focused clumps (worth sharing and merging), called 'worlds' [WA89][1], which are materialized. In the next stage, data in these worlds is transformed using the language ILOG$^{\pm}$ [HWW90] from their respective schemas into compatible schemas. Finally, in the third stage, which is the focus of the current paper, the data from the separate worlds is merged to form a new (materialized) world. This last stage involves two phases: First, (possibly merged) objects and their key relationships are placed into the target world. Second, the remaining data is merged and incorporated into the target, perhaps with some massaging via preference statements and/or computations.

In the balance of this section we state more completely the general problem of merging POBs having compatible schemas, and describe the range of issues and alternative strategies raised by this problem. Section 2 describes the approach taken in our research, and Section 3 compares it with other approaches described in the literature. In particular, this section indicates the differences between the work described here, and research on database schema integration. Due to space limitations in this paper, the exposition is terse, and many details are omitted. More details may be found in [WWH90].

---

[1] Interestingly, a similar aggregation technique — aptly named 'semantic clustering' — is proposed in the present volume to cluster data for *efficient access* [SS90].

1.1   Schemas and Merging

A POB can be viewed as a triple $\langle S_i, C_i, I_i \rangle$, where S_i refers to the structure or *schema* of the object base, C_i refers to the set of *constraints* of the object base, I_i refers to the *instance* of the structure S_i that is constrained by C_i, i.e., the object base itself. We view merging (denoted by $\oplus$) of two POBs as a mapping onto a third POB: $\langle S_1, C_1, I_1 \rangle \oplus \langle S_2, C_2, I_2 \rangle \Rightarrow \langle S_3, C_3, I_3 \rangle$. We separate the schemas from the constraints because we want to allow the target POB to have the same structure but different constraints.

To merge two POBs, one first has to decide if the two POBs are structurally *compatible*. If they are, they may be merged without any transformation of the POBs. The notion of *schema compatibility* varies depending on the model and merging methodology supported. In a relational model, schema compatibility may be stated in terms of correspondence of relation names and column names of two schemas. In a graph-based or semantic model, schema compatibility may be stated in terms of subgraph properties. For example, we could define S_1 and S_2 to be compatible if both are subschemas of some schema S_3.

In traditional database merging, if the constraints on the schemas to be merged are not equal, there is a conflict and the databases may not be merged. When they are equal, the merged database typically has the same constraints, i.e. if $C_1 = C_2$, then $C_3 = C_1 = C_2$ or the merging process will be aborted if the merged data violates C_3. An alternative pursued here is to relax the impact of constraints on merging POBs, i.e. to allow $C_3 \neq C_1$ or C_2. If some constraint in C_3 is violated, mechanisms must be provided to resolve it in the merged POB.

1.2   Determining Object Equivalence

As mentioned above, we take a two-phase approach to merging POBs – phase 1 focuses on determining object equivalence, and phase 2 focuses on merging the remaining data. We differentiate the notion of objects vs. values. A *value* is something whose meaning is universally understood; an *object* is something whose meaning is understood only by its relationships to other objects and values in the database[Bee89]. There are several ways to determine the equivalence of objects from different POBs. The most common method is through *keys*. Keys are single valued properties of objects (associated with the object type) that uniquely identify an object. An example of a key for objects of type **person** would be **social-security-number**, or (perhaps) the pair $\langle$ **last-name**, **first-name** $\rangle$. Keys might map to other objects rather than values (or printables). However, it is usually appropriate to prohibit circularity of keys.

This example demonstrates that an object may have more than one valid key associated with it. We call the set of keys for a type a *key family*. Each element of the key family is either a single property or a set of properties which uniquely identifies objects of the type. Key families are useful when merging overlapping object bases, where only a subset of information about an object overlaps. If the intersection of key families for a particular type is nonempty, the objects may be merged.

Another method for merging different object bases is to use a *look-up table*. The object bases to be merged may be disjoint, but there is a look-up table that determines the equivalence of the objects in the two object bases. For instance, we may have an object base of Michelin tire types, and a similar one for Goodyear tire types. A lookup table to indicate equivalence of the various types of tires from the two object bases could be provided to determine equivalence.

In some cases, object equivalence is not determined by an exact match of keys. For the purpose of determining if a car could be fitted with equivalent sized tires, the diameter of Michelin and Goodyear tires that differ by 1 cm might be considered equivalent. In merging two objects with such *fuzzy keys*, one also has to decide what the value of the merged key is.

When dealing with merging overlapping object bases, one sometimes has to deal with relationship values that may be undefined. This is especially true if we merge using key families. Since we use only a subset of the key family to determine equivalence, an object from one object base which has no corresponding match may not have the remaining keys in the key family defined. One way of dealing with this is to change the key constraints of the merged object base to be that of the subset. Another way is to allow *optional keys*, i.e. key relationships that may be undefined (missing). Optional keys allow for a more flexible merging, but one may not be able to tell if two objects are equivalent if none of their defined key relationships overlap.

A different way of identifying objects is to simply use global object identifiers as the key, i.e. two objects are distinct if they have no keys associated with their type. With respect to their relationships, the objects are indistinguishable except by their object identifiers (OIDs). However, these objects may be identified when certain relationships are defined for them, e.g. if they are classified into certain subclasses. An example is an object base for chips. Each class of chip contains an indistinguishable set of chip objects of the same type (with class attributes). However, chips which are used have a **board** and **position** relationships defined. Used chips may be identified by their **board** and **position** properties. This problem is similar to optional keys, but here some of the objects have no defined key.

Another tool for determining equivalence of objects is *negative keys*. Intuitively, a negative key helps in deciding if two objects are *not* equivalent. Negative keys may be stated and implemented as constraints. For instance: "No employee has more than one office" or "No person has more than one city for a primary address". In the multiple keys model, key relations that are defined but not used in the merging process can act as negative keys. Negative keys may also be used for deciding non-equivalence of objects in object bases with incomplete information. If there are no overlapping keys that may be used to decide if two objects are equivalent, but they have negative keys that are specified and are different, we may safely assume that the two objects are *not* equivalent.

Perhaps the most complex approach for determining equivalence is based on *subgraph isomorphism*. Two objects are equivalent if there is an isomorphism between selected subgraphs of the respective object bases which maps the first object to the second. An example would be the query: "a husband and wife team where the husband is the chairman of the company, and the wife is the vice chairman whose father is in the board of directors of the same company". Keys can be viewed as a special case of subgraph isomorphism, typically without circularity. The problem, in this case, is finding a feasible implementation to decide subgraph equivalence, since the general problem is NP-complete.

The mechanism for POB merging described in this paper incorporates key families as the method for object identification (see section 2.1).

1.3   Merging the Remaining Data

Once all the equivalent objects are identified, *relationships* and non-key attributes may be merged. Recall that we consider merging only in the case where the schemas are compatible. We assume the source POBs do not violate their own sets of constraints. If the target non-key relationships are unconstrained, the union of the relations is taken as the final result. If the target relationship is constrained, the resulting merged instance may violate the constraints.

Although the user may include arbitrary constraints in C_3, if C_3 is not some combination of constraints in C_1 and C_2, a method must be provided to deal with converting instances I_1 and I_2 to be consistent with C_3. For example, if C_1 includes the constraint: relation **has-phone** is single-valued, and C_2 includes the same constraint, then C_3 can either constrain **has-phone** to be single-valued and provide methods to deal with cases when the relationship violates this constraint (such as when two phones exist for a single person, one from each source), or have **has-phone** be multi-valued.

For each C_1 and C_2 to be merged (for compatible schema), there generally exists a set C_3', containing the most "natural" constraints automatically satisfied by the merged POB. We denote this constraint set $mnm(C_1, C_2)$, for *most natural merge*. Intuitively, the most natural merge is the most restrictive family of constraints such that no method need to be provided to deal with any constraint violation when forming the merge of instances satisfying C_1 and C_2. There may be cases where the instances from source POBs match exactly or are disjoint (properties of the data), and thereby produce a merged POB that satisfies a more stringent set of constraints than the mnm. Also, it remains open whether the concept of most natural merge is unambiguously defined for all families of constraints.

The target POB may always be constrained by a more relaxed set of constraints (denoted $C_3 \geq$

$mnm(C_1, C_2)$). For the target to have a more restricted set of constraints - the normal case -, mechanisms must be provided to deal with constraint violations. There is a spectrum of mechanisms possible, ranging from simple preferences, to filtering mechanisms, to allowing user-defined computations.

A *preference mechanism* allows the user to indicate which source POB he prefers to take certain relationships from when constraint violations arise. As well as allowing for a more restrictive set of constraints for the target, the preference mechanism can be used to indicate general preference. For instance, even if both the sources and the target constraints agree that a relation is multi-valued, one may still state a preference that only relationships from a preferred source be present in the target. For instance, the relationship **has-phone** may be multi-valued in the source POBs and the target POBs, but the user may prefer **has-phone** values from I_1, e.g. if he knows that I_2 is an older version of the object base, and I_1 contains the newer information.

A *filtering mechanism* removes relationships and objects that violate constraints so that the resulting object base conforms to a set of constraints. For example, a filter could be used to remove all objects in the merged object base which have 2 phone numbers. The result is a valid instance that correctly models its schema and constraints. There are two kinds of filters: one acts on the merged POB and has access to where the instances come from; the other simply acts on a single POB, and removes only that data which violates certain conditions without regard to its source. The second filtering mechanism can also be used to preprocess source POBs to conform to a more restricted set of constraints.

The third mechanism allows the user to specify *computations* or functions to deal with constraint violations. This may be specified in terms of ⟨condition:action⟩ pairs. There are two kinds of computations. The first involves computation of a target relationship based on the conflicting source relationships. An example is to allocate **salary** of an **employee** to be the sum of all salaries associated with an employee. The second type of computation involves computing a *new* relationship based on some other relationships being merged. An example is the computation of **average-salary**, a weighted average that depends on the source POBs the relationships are from.

The mechanism discussed below focuses on the preference mechanism we have invented for resolving constraints.

2   WorldBase Merging

This section outlines the approach taken by WorldBase to support object base merging. First, we describe the WorldBase data model for the object bases and define the notion of keys and key families in this model. The emphasis is on that part of a POB which models real world objects, and so a simple semantic data model is used. We concern ourselves with the structure of the objects and ignore the methods associated with them. Next, we introduce the notion of schema compatibility and object base mergeability in our framework, and outline our algorithm for merging object bases. Finally, we briefly describe our preference mechanism, one of the techniques we provide for dealing with constraints.

2.1   WorldBase Data Model

The WorldBase Data Model (WDM) is a modified Entity Relationship model[Che76] that includes specialization (ISA) relationships (in the sense of [AH87, HK87]). The notational and diagrammatic conventions used in this paper are borrowed heavily from IFO[AH87].

Entity types include *abstract types*, *subtypes* and *printable/value types*. *Relations* range over subsets of n-ary cartesian product of entity types. The *ISA* (or specialization) relationship relates subtypes to abstract types or subtypes. Directed cycles of ISA relationships are not allowed in a WDM schema. Also, all maximal directed paths of ISA relationships from a given subtype end at the same abstract type. We do not differentiate the notion of attributes from binary relations in that we allow both entity types and printable types to participate in relationships. The WDM is capable of simulating the structural portion of essentially all object-oriented database systems in the literature.

Members of abstract types are called *abstract objects*; these correspond to physical or conceptual objects in the world. In some implementations these are represented internally using "object identifiers" (OIDs); in other implementations, these are represented by physical addresses over which the system programmer has no control.

In the formal model, we assume for each abstract type T there is an infinite disjoint set $potdom(T)$ of *potential abstract objects* of type T (these correspond to OIDs); and for each printable type V there is a (finite or infinite) set $dom(V)$ of printable objects of type V. It is assumed that all of these sets are pairwise disjoint. A *weak instance* is a mapping from each abstract type T to a disjoint finite set of OIDs in $potdom(T)$; from each subtype p, where there is a path of ISA edges from p to an abstract type node q, to a subset of instances in $potdom(q)$; from n-ary relation nodes to set of n-tuples; and from printable types to values. An *instance* is a weak instance which satisfies (i) all set inclusions implied by the schema (via ISA relationships and tuple-range restrictions), and (ii) all explicitly specified constraints. Two weak instances are *OID equivalent* if there exists a permutation of OIDs that maps one to the other. In the current paper, we follow the usual convention of blurring the distinction between instances and their associated equivalence classes (explicated in [HY90]).

For the purpose of merging, we restrict ourselves to three kinds of constraints: *key constraints*, (restricted) *cardinality constraints* and *disjointness constraints*. At present, we support keys only on abstract types.

Definition: For an abstract type T, a *key dependency* on T is an expression $k = T : \langle R_1 \ldots R_n \rangle$ where each R_i relates T to some other type. (To simplify the notation, we assume that the first coordinate of each R_i has type T). An instance I satisfies k if

(a) for each $o \in I(T)$, there is exactly one x such that $(o, x) \in I(R_i)$, which we denote as $R_i(o)$;

(b) for each pair $o_1, o_2 \in I(T), \langle R_1(o_1), \ldots, R_n(o_1) \rangle = \langle R_1(o_2), \ldots, R_n(o_2) \rangle \Rightarrow o_1 = o_2$

Assertions about keys cannot be deduced or discovered from more basic principles; they are decided when the schema creator designs the type after deliberation about their data and constraints. Let K be the set of keys on a schema S. If T is an abstract type in S, the *key family* of T, denoted $K(T)$, is the set of keys in K for T.

Let C be the set of cardinality constraints and disjointness constraints for S. Cardinality constraints in C, denoted C^{card}, are of the form: $R[p, q]$ or $R^{-1}[p, q]$ where R refers to the binary relation name being constrained, $p \in \{0, 1\}$, $q \in \{1, \omega\}$, where ω denotes the first infinite ordinal. (For simplicity, we will deal only with cardinality constraints for binary relations in this paper; the extension to multiple-slot relations is a topic of future study.) The cardinality constraint is interpreted as follows: the number of tuples selected with a fixed domain element is at least p and at most q. For instance, **last-name**$[1, 1]$ states that every person must have exactly one last-name; **last-name**$^{-1}[0, 1]$ states that every last-name is assigned to at most one person; **takes**$[1, \omega]$ every student takes at least one course; **takes**$^{-1}[0, \omega]$ that a course is taken by zero or more students (unrestricted). Keys imply certain cardinality constraints.

Disjointness constraints in C, denoted C^{disj}, are specified as `disjoint`$(T_1, .., T_n)$ where each T_i's are subtypes of the same abstract type.

A *constrained schema* is a three-tuple $\langle S, K, C \rangle$, where S is a WDM schema, K is the set of key constraints defined on S, and C is a set of cardinality and disjointness constraints for S. $\langle S, K \rangle$ refers to a *key-constrained* schema. A persistent object base is a four-tuple $\langle S, K, C, I \rangle$ where I refers to the object base (instance). This notation is used throughout the next three sections.

2.2 Schema Compatibility and Object Equivalence Specifications

In this section, we describe when a pair of schemas are compatible using the notion of *subschema* defined below. Only when two schemas are compatible can the instances be merged in our automatic merging mechanism. We also define desirable key properties of the merged target.

Definition: A schema S is a *subschema* of S' if there exists an embedding of S into S' where

  (a) each type A in S maps onto type A in S';

  (b) each subtype B in S maps onto subtype B in S';

  (c) if B ISA C is in S, then[2] B ISA$^*C$ is in S';

  (d) all relations $R[T_1, .., T_n]$ in S map onto $R[T_1, .., T_n]$ in S'.

More relaxed notions of subschema could also be explored.

Definition: Two schemas, S_1 and S_2 are *compatible* if there exists a valid WDM schema S_3 such that S_1 is a subschema of S_3 and S_2 is a subschema of S_3.

When forming the merge $\langle S_1, K_1, C_1, I_1 \rangle \oplus \langle S_2, K_2, C_2, I_2 \rangle$ into schema S_3, a combination K_3 of the keys in $K_1 \cup K_2$ is used. We now describe the properties that K_3 must satisfy.

The first property concerns the relationship between K_1, K_2 and K_3.

Definition: Let $\langle S_1, K_1 \rangle$, $\langle S_2, K_2 \rangle$, and $\langle S_3, K_3 \rangle$ be key-constrained schemas where S_1 and S_2 are subschemas of S_3. K_3 is *implied by* K_1 and K_2 if

  (a) If T is an abstract type of S_1 and S_2 then $K_3(T) \subseteq K_1(T) \cap K_2(T)$.

  (b) If T is an abstract type of S_1 but not S_2 then $K_3(T) \subseteq K_1(T)$.

  (c) If T is an abstract type of S_2 but not S_1 then $K_3(T) \subseteq K_2(T)$.

The second property of K_3 will make it possible to determine equivalence of objects from the two source POBs in an efficient manner. To define this, we need some preliminary notions.

An abstract type T *directly depends* on abstract type or value type T' in K if there is some R in a key on T relating T to T' or one of its subtypes. K is *acyclic* if there is no cycle of direct dependence of types in K. K is *stub-free* if for all types T, T', if T directly depends on T', then T' is a value type or $K(T') \neq \emptyset$. Given $\langle S, K \rangle$, K is an *object equivalence specification* if k is acyclic and stub-free. When we merge POBs, we insist that the set of keys for the target is an object equivalence specification.

Definition: K_3 is a *valid object equivalence specification* for $\langle S_1, K_1 \rangle$ and $\langle S_2, K_2 \rangle$ if K_3 is an object equivalence specification and is implied by K_1 and K_2.

Note that K_3 might be empty even though $K_1(T) \cap K_2(T) \neq \emptyset$. In this case, no objects in I_1 and I_2 of type T will be equivalent, and a disjoint union of these objects will be formed in the merged POB.

A merged POB $\langle S_3, K_3, C_3, I_3 \rangle$ is formed from two source POBs $\langle S_1, K_1, C_1, I_1 \rangle$ and $\langle S_2, K_2, C_2, I_2 \rangle$ in two phases. In the first phase, a merge of objects and key relationships from the two instances are computed and its non-key relationships added to produce a weak instance, call it I_{3-weak}. The second phase uses various mechanisms provided to discriminate the sources of the relationships and to resolve conflicts in I_{3-weak} to produce a valid I_3. Section 2.3 focuses on the first phase, and section 2.4 describes the second phase.

---

[2] $*$ denotes closure.

2.3   Algorithm to Compute the Weak Merge of Two Object Bases

We now define the notion of object *equivalence* in terms of key families.

Definition: Two values are equivalent if they are equal in the primitive equality given for values, i.e. $v_1 = v_2 \Rightarrow v_1 \equiv v2$.

Definition: Let S be a WDM schema, and k is a key for T. Two objects x from I_1 and y from I_2 are *equivalent* (relative to k), denoted $x \equiv_k y$, if x and y are objects of type T, and $k(x)$ is equivalent to $k(y)$.

A *weak merge* is the result of the merge of compatible POBs without considering the non-key target constraints. The weak merge exists only if, for each T, for each $x \in I_1(T), y \in I_2(T)$, if $x \equiv_k y$ for some k in $K_3(T)$, then $x \equiv_{k'} y$ for each k' in $K_3(T)$. A weak merge *may* violate other constraints in C_3. Two object bases are *strongly mergeable* if there exists a weak merge and it does not violate constraints in C_3.

In our approach, we first create a copy of I_1 as initial I_{3-weak}, then I_2 is "added" on to it using the object equivalence semantics. The algorithm to merge a POB instance (I_2) onto an existing one (I_{3-weak}) is given as a single long transaction described below.

Not all types in a WDM schema need to have their keys defined. Objects that do not have keys defined for their type are considered distinct and separate from other objects of the same type and are not merged with any other objects. We do not support the notion of indistinguishable sets of objects with keyed subtypes mentioned in 1.2. We also do not yet support fuzzy keys, optional keys, or negative keys.

Algorithm to compute the weak merge of I_1 and I_2:

(a) Compute a topological sort of abstract types in S_3 based on the direct dependence relationship of keys in K_3 – types that directly depend on value types come first.

(b) For each abstract type T (according to the sorted order) do:
Let $k \in K_3(T)$. For each object y in I_2 of type T, if there is an $x \equiv_k y$ in I_{3-weak}, and if $x \not\equiv_{k'} y$ for some $k' \in K_3(T)$, then abort [In this case, I_1 and I_2 do not have a weak merge relative to K_3]; Otherwise, set $\hat{y} = x$. If no equivalent object is found in I_{3-weak}, then let $\hat{y}$ be a newly created object and insert $\hat{y}$ into I_{3-weak}. Also, insert all key relationships for $\hat{y}$. [The ordering of the keys ensures that all objects being depended on are already merged, before being used as the key for deciding the equivalence of other objects.]

(c) Populate all abstract type nodes T without keys in K_3 by creating a copy $\hat{y}$ in I_{3-weak} of each corresponding object y in I_2.

(d) If $y \in I_2(T)$ for some subtype T, then add $\hat{y}$ to T in I_{3-weak} (and to each supertype of T in I_{3-weak}).

(e) For each relation R not in K_3 and each tuple $\langle y_1, .., y_n \rangle$ in $I_2(R)$, add $\langle \hat{y}_1, .., \hat{y}_n \rangle$ to $I_{3-weak}(R)$.

2.4   Enforcing the Constraints

A *constrained merge* (e.g. I_3) is the result of the merge of compatible POBs that satisfies the target's constraints (C_3) relative to the mechanisms specified (preference, filtering, and computations[3]). If a target (non-key) relation is unconstrained, the constrained merge is formed from the union of the source relations. If the target relation is constrained, the resulting merged relation may violate it. In this subsection, we study the relationship of cardinality and disjointness constraints between the target and the sources, and preference mechanisms to deal with the constraints while merging object bases.

Table 1 describes some of the ways that cardinality constraints in C_1 and C_2 on a given binary relation can be combined to yield a constraint in C_3. The third value in each box in table 1 gives the most natural cardinality constraint implicitly and automatically satisfied by simply asserting all source relations into the

---

[3] We focus here only on the preference mechanism.

merged object base. The set of these resulting constraints forms the most natural merge (*mnm*). For instance, the box for [1,1] in I_1 and [1,1] in I_2 results in [1,ω] and not [1,1] because the relation values for a merged object from different object bases may differ. These constraints may seem overly conservative: recall that not every object is present in both object bases.

R(T)[?,?]	I_2			
I_1	[0,1]	[1,1]	[0,ω]	[1,ω]
[0,1]	[0,1] prefer I_1 [0,1] prefer I_2 [0,ω]	[0,1] prefer I_1 [0,1] prefer I_2 [0,ω]	[0,ω] prefer I_1 [0,ω] prefer I_2 [0,ω]	[0,ω] prefer I_1 [0,ω] prefer I_2 [0,ω]
[1,1]	[0,1] prefer I_1 [0,1] prefer I_2 [0,ω]	[1,1] prefer I_1 [1,1] prefer I_2 [1,ω]	[0,ω] prefer I_1 [0,ω] prefer I_2 [0,ω]	[1,ω] prefer I_1 [1,ω] prefer I_2 [1,ω]
[0,ω]	[0,ω] prefer I_1 [0,ω] prefer I_2 [0,ω]	[0,ω] prefer I_1 [0,ω] prefer I_2 [0,ω]	[0,ω] prefer I_1 [0,ω] prefer I_2 [0,ω]	[0,ω] prefer I_1 [1,ω] prefer I_2 [0,ω]
[1,ω]	[0,ω] prefer I_1 [0,ω] prefer I_2 [0,ω]	[1,ω] prefer I_1 [1,ω] prefer I_2 [1,ω]	[0,ω] prefer I_1 [0,ω] prefer I_2 [0,ω]	[1,ω] prefer I_1 [1,ω] prefer I_2 [1,ω]

Table 1: Merging of Constraints

The preference mechanism allows the user to specify a slightly more constrained target (see Table 1). Stating preference of a preferred source implies that when objects from different sources are merged, the values from the preferred source are taken as the resulting values of the target. Relationships from the other source are removed after the merge, unless the relationship from the preferred source is undefined. For instance, suppose relation **has-phone** is constrained [0,1] from I_1 and [0,ω] from I_2, and we constrain the relation to "[0,ω] prefer I_1" in the target. If o is a merged **person** object whose **has-phone** value is "397-1441" in I_1, then the target has the same value and nothing else, even if o has a phone value of "822-1511" from I_2. All **has-phone** values from I_2 are removed from the target. However, if p is a merged **person** object which has no **has-phone** value in I_1, then *all* the **has-phone** tuples from I_2 are put into the target.

A preference may be stated for each *relation* for possible constraint violation or to indicate choice of source(s) of relationships for the new target POB. A set of preference statements may be provided with the merging operation. The preference mechanism decides which relationship(s) to remove from the merged POB to resolve a constraint violation or discriminate source choice. There is no interaction of cardinality constraints for the different directions of a given relation in the most natural merge case (e.g. if R relates T to T' and $R[1,\omega]$ and $R^{-1}[0,1]$ in S_1, $R[1,1]$, and $R^{-1}[1,\omega]$ in S_2, then the natural merge will include the constraints $R[1,\omega]$, and $R^{-1}[0,\omega]$). However, if different preferences are used for the same relation, the preference mechanism may result in different output I_3, depending on the order the preferences are evaluated. For this reason, we do not allow a user to have more than one preferred source per relation.

Disjointness constraints are also checked for in the target. A simple preference mechanism may be used to weed out those that violate the constraints. The mechanism also propagates preferences to removal of relationships concerning the removed objects. For example, assume that F and G are disjoint, R is a relationship on G not on F, and a is an element of both F and G, thus violating the disjointness constraint. If we prefer F to be true of a, then we have to remove the relationship R on a when we remove a from G. The preference mechanism checks the disjointness constraints before the cardinality constraints and the relationships to be removed (via propagation) inherit the preference of the disjointness constraints.

2.5 Prototype

The merging mechanism is implemented as part of a system called *WorldBase* [Wid90, WWH90] that provides an environment for sharing multiple, possibly inconsistent, possibly overlapping databases. Each POB, called a *world* database (or simply a world), contains a cluster of related information and is a basic unit for sharing information across a network. WorldBase provides support for *selecting* information from worlds and underlying databases; for *transforming* data from one schema to another; and for *merging* the data in two or more worlds to create a new world. With these functionalities, a user is provided with the tools needed to share his information.

A prototype of WorldBase is implemented in AP5[Coh87, Coh86, Coh89], a database programming language which extends Common Lisp. The prototype is tested on small personal databases.

3   Related Research

We mention here three streams of research which involve the issues of object equivalence and POB merging; all have been investigated primarily in the context of databases.

One stream is focused on issues of object equivalence, in the context of a single object-oriented database. Investigations such as [KC86, DKV89, SZ89] have introduced notions of equivalence between complex database objects, based on isomorphism to different depths of the trees representing these objects. The investigation reported in [Mas89] takes a different tack, observing that some other forms of equivalence are needed to differentiate real-world (or conceptual) object equivalence from object-identifier (OID) equivalence, since the same real-world (or conceptual) object may be represented by different OIDs. The notions of object equivalence developed in these investigations are used primarily in the context of query processing. In the data model used in the current paper, the focus is on associations between OIDs, rather than component-subcomponent relationships. As a result, the complex object perspective of the investigations described above does not naturally apply to the context that we are studying.

A second, recently introduced direction [PG88] is focused on the boundary of a POB, specifically in the context of inserting data into the POB. The problem here is to devise an appropriate mechanism whereby users can identify the objects already in the database. As with our approach, the approach of [PG88] is based on the use of stub-free, acyclic sets of keys. However, [PG88] does not permit multiple keys for a given type; and we do not require all objects to have keys defined.

The third stream, which has a longer history, is that of schema integration, which has generally been conducted in the context of semantic models. One of the main foci of this work, as described in the survey article [BLN86], is the problem of constructing a schema, or *superview*, which subsumes two or more existing schemas. This aspect of schema integration is related to the transformation stage of the WorldBase approach (see [HWW90]); and the current paper has assumed that the POBs to be merged already have compatible schemas. One aspect shared by some of the schema integration investigations and the investigation reported here is the issue of selecting the constraints to be associated with the superview (respectively, target schema). The current investigation extends the schema integration literature in this area, by exposing more completely the interaction of constraints in the sources, constraints in the target, and the use of various mechanisms during the schema population phase.

The second focus of the schema integration research is on translating queries against the superview into queries against the underlying database schemas. Such translation requires an explicit specification of how the underlying databases are used to populate (actually or virtually) the superview; essentially the same problem investigated in the current paper. One of the most detailed and rich mechanisms for performing this population is given in [DH84]. The MultiBase project [LA86] also addresses this issue in the context of the relational model. There is considerable overlap in the approaches of [DH84], [LA86], and the one taken here; including the use of keys for object identification, and the use of preference and computation mechanisms. In both [DH84] and [LA86] a relatively rich language is provided for specifying how the underlying databases are to be merged.

A key difference between the schema integration research and the research described here is that in schema integration, the superview is considered to be a *virtual* database, whereas the merged databases formed here are *materialized*. (Such materialization does not have prohibitive space needs in our context, because the world mechanism permits users to focus on reasonably small, self-contained data sets.) In the schema integration literature, if a merging mechanism is introduced, then it must be incorporated into the query translation algorithm – this has had the ultimate effect of restricting the richness of the merging mechanisms investigated. Our context can support a much richer set of merging mechanisms. For example, our key sets may include multiple keys for the same type, and we offer considerable flexibility in the selection of the key set for the target schema. Also, our context allows us to support a much more intricate interaction of constraints in the source schemas with constraints in the target schema, and richer mechanisms for massaging the merged data.

A final contribution of the current work is that we have articulated a family of relatively orthogonal abstractions for specifying object base merges. In many cases, this will make it easier to specify a desired merging protocol. Also, it provides a modular perspective on the various components of a merging protocol, making it more amenable to debugging, modification, and formal analysis.

References

[AH87]   S. Abiteboul and R. Hull. IFO: A formal semantic database model. *ACM Trans. on Database Systems*, 12(4):525–565, Dec. 1987.

[Bee89]   C. Beeri. Formal models for object oriented databases. In *Proceedings of the First International Conference on Deductive and Object-Oriented Databases*, pages 370–395, 1989.

[BLN86]   C. Batini, M. Lenzerini, and S.B. Navathe. A comparative analysis of methodologies for database schema integration. *ACM Computing Surveys*, 18(4):323–364, December 1986.

[Che76]   P.P. Chen. The entity-relationship model – toward a unified view of data. *ACM Transactions on Database Systems*, 1(1):9–36, March 1976.

[Coh86]   D. Cohen. Automatic compilation of logical specifications into efficient programs. In *AAAI*, June 1986.

[Coh87]   D. Cohen. Ap5 reference manual. Technical report, USC/Information Sciences Institute, 1987.

[Coh89]   D. Cohen. Compiling complex database transition triggers. In *Proceedings of the ACM SIGMOD International Conference on Management of Data*, pages 225–234, 1989.

[DCBM89]   A. Dearle, R. Connor, F. Brown, and R. Morrison. Napier88 – a database programming language? In *Proceedings of the Second International Workshop on Database Programming Languages*, pages 179–195, June 1989.

[DH84]   U. Dayal and H.Y. Hwang. View definition and generalization for database integration in a multidatabase system. *IEEE Transactions on Software Engineering*, SE-10(6):628–644, 1984.

[DKV89]   Scott Danforth, Setrag Khoshafian, and Patrick Valduriez. FAD, a database programming language. Technical Report ACA-ST-151-85, Rev. 3, MCC, January 1989. to appear in ACM TODS.

[FBC+87]   D. H. Fishman, D. Beech, H. P. Cate, E.C. Chow, et al. Iris: An object-oriented database management system. *ACM Transactions on Office Information Systems*, 5(1):48–69, January 1987.

[Gro87]   Persistent Programming Research Group. PS-Algol reference manual. Technical report, University of Glasgow, Department of Computing Science, University of St Andrews, Department of Computational Science, 1987.

[HK87]   R. Hull and R. King. Semantic database modeling: Survey, applications, and research issues. *ACM Computing Surveys*, 19(3):201–260, September 1987.

[HWW90]   R. Hull, S. Widjojo, and D. S. Wile. A specificational approach to database transformation. Technical report, USC/Information Sciences Institute, February 1990.

[HY90]   R. Hull and M. Yoshikawa. ILOG: Declarative creation and manipulation of object identifiers. Technical report, Computer Science Dept., University of Southern California, 1990. to appear in VLDB 1990.

[KC86]   S. Khoshafian and G. Copeland. Object identity. In *Proc. ACM Conf. on Object-Oriented Programming Systems, Languages, and Applications*, pages 406–416, 1986.

[LA86]   W. Litwin and A. Abdellatif. Multidatabase interoperability. *IEEE Computer*, Dec 1986.

[Mas89]   Y. Masunaga. Object identity, equality and relational concept. In *Proceedings of the First International Conference on Deductive and Object-Oriented Databases*, pages 170–187, 1989.

[PG88]   N. W. Paton and P. M. D. Gray. Identification of database objects by key. In *Proceedings of Second International Workshop on Object-Oriented Database Systems*, Bad Munster am Stein-Ebernburg, FRG, September 1988.

[PSM87]   Alan Purdy, Bruce Schuchardt, and David Maier. Integrating an object server with other worlds. *ACM Transactions on Office Information Systems*, 5(1):27–47, January 1987.

[SS90]   Karen Shannon and Richard Snodgrass. Semantic clustering. In Al Dearle, Gail Shaw, and Stanley Zdonik, editors, *Implementing Persistent Object Bases*. Morgan Kaufmann, December 1990.

[SZ89]   G. M. Shaw and S. B. Zdonik. An object-oriented query algebra. In *Proceedings of the Second International Workshop on Database Programming Languages*, pages 103–112, June 1989.

[WA89]   D. S. Wile and D. G. Allard. Aggregation, persistence, and identity in Worlds. In *Proceedings of Workshop on Persistent Object Systems: their design, implementation and use*, Jan 1989.

[Wid90]   S. Widjojo. *WorldBase: A Distributed Information Sharing System*. PhD thesis, Computer Science Department, University of Southern California, Los Angeles, CA, 1990. in progress.

[WWH90]   S. Widjojo, D. S. Wile, and R. Hull. WorldBase: A New Approach to Sharing Distributed Information. Technical report, USC/Information Sciences Institute, February 1990.

Modeling Heterogeneous Systems as an Active Object Space

A. P. Buchmann
GTE Laboratories, Inc.
40 Sylvan Road
Waltham MA 02254
buchmann@gte.com

Abstract

The Distributed Object Management (DOM) project at GTE Labs. attemps to provide intelligent interoperability among heterogeneous computing systems with data repositories of various kinds. An interesting way of viewing such a federated, heterogeneous system is to model it as a collection of active objects that are capable of monitoring their state and the object space and reacting autonomously and asynchronously to conditions becoming true. The notion of active objects is defined and compared with various forms that have appeared in active object-oriented languages and in active database systems. Commonalities between the two currents are explored and a particular approach to active objects in a heterogeneous, persistent object space is proposed.

1 Introduction

The Distributed Object Management (DOM) project at GTE Labs. has the goal to provide intelligent interoperability among heterogeneous computing systems with data repositories of various kinds. An interesting way of viewing such a federated, heterogeneous system is to model it as a collection of active objects that are capable of monitoring their internal state and that of the active object space, and can react autonomously and asynchronously, when predefined conditions become true. Active objects appear to be a useful paradigm, since they provide a mechanism for modelling autonomous systems that are interacting, and are capable of performing many system tasks autonomously and transparently to the user. For example, they can control translation between heterogeneous systems, consistency enforcement, access control, and caching or staging of data at remote nodes.

The federated heterogeneous systems we are considering consist of attached application systems that may have their own data repositories and provide a variety of functionality, not necessarily that of a DBMS. Furthermore, attached systems are often closed and may not be modified in order to integrate them, although it is valid to assume that a system that participates in the federation will signal certain events, for example, power up. An example of such an attached application could be a Hypercard system in which data that are available in other materializations across the object space are replicated in form of stacks of cards. A Hypercard system, while offering persistence, does not support any database primitives, such as transactions. Interaction with the data can be either through the attached systems or through a global system interface. Conceptually we can represent such a system as shown in Figure 1.

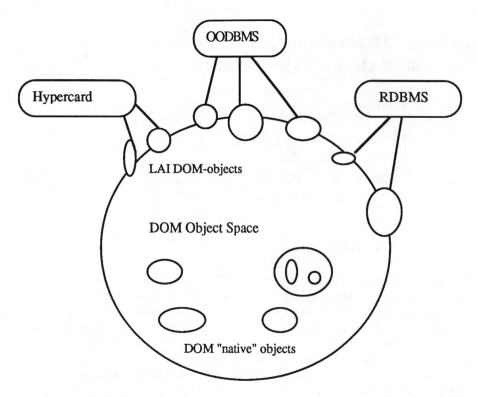

Figure 1: Schematic representation of a heterogeneous object space

Objects may be either native, meaning that they have full functionality and persistence in the object space, or they may be Local Application Interface objects, which are placeholders for objects that are transferred between environments, and from which the functionality of attached applications can be invoked. Let's assume we have an active LAI-object that represents persons maintained in a stack on Hypercard. When Hypercard is powered up in the morning it sends an event signal to its active counterparts in DOM. These react to the "powered-up" event from the external system and fire the proper rules, which now enforce consistency by executing those updates that occurred on the global system while the Hypercard node was unavailable. Consistency may also be enforced through periodic updates, triggered by temporal events, or on access by the Hypercard to DOM-controlled objects and viceversa. Consistency within the DOM object space is always maintained according to the semantics of DOM's transaction model. Across the boundary, different levels of consistency may be maintained, and the active objects within the DOM object space can be used to compensate for the shortcomings of the attached systems. Although we exemplified active behavior across the boundary of the DOM object space, the same behavior is useful for supporting a multitude of mechanisms within the DOM object space, such as access control, prefetching data, and policy-driven consistency enforcement.

The idea of active objects has appeared in various forms in different object-oriented programming languages, such as the Actor-based languages Act1 [LIEB87], Act2 [THER83], Act3 [Agha87a,b] and their derivatives, for example, ABCL/1 [YONE86, YONE87, SHIB87]; other languages are KNOs [CASA88, TSIC87], Hybrid [NIER86, KONS88], and Orient84/K [ISHI86, ISHI87]. Unfortunately, the definition of active object has been vague and the term is appropriated for many different underlying concepts. The actor based languages support a rather primitive notion of active object, not much more than the object notion of other (passive) object-oriented programming languages but with asynchronous messages, while Orient84/K combines in a single language (and its objects) the notions of daemons, declarative or logic-based programming, and procedural programming. Wegner [WEGN88] has tried to analyze objects independently of a specific language based on the internal degree of concurrency they provide, more in the sense of threads running through an object. Manola [MANO89] has used that concept as the basis for his view of active objects.

Parallel with the work on active objects in programming languages the notion of active database systems has evolved [STON88, DAYA88, CHAK89, KOTZ88, CHUN88, HSU88]. Active databases are no longer passive data repositories that only respond to external commands. Instead, they monitor the state of the database and allow the definition of conditions and actions that are to be executed if a condition becomes true. These active databases, often object-oriented, support transaction and execution models that provide more robust concurrency control than most of the programming languages. However, their notion of active object is frequently incompatible with that used in the active object-oriented languages.

In this paper we propose a set of criteria for persistent active objects that is intended as a working hypothesis and basis for discussion. We analyze a set of prominent active object languages, and relate them to the execution models of representative active database systems. We propose the integration of the concepts from the programming languages with active databases as the active objects required for modelling heterogeneous, federated systems. We place special emphasis on the capabilities required for autonomous execution (monitoring) and asynchronous responses (coupling). We identify some of the problems associated with active objects, and propose some mechanisms for their experimental implementation.

2 Active Objects - a Working Hypothesis

Informally, *active objects* will be understood as objects that have the capability of executing *autonomously* and *asynchronously* actions in response to the detection of *events*.

As a working hypothesis we offer a preliminary set of criteria for active objects that was derived from an analysis of both active object languages and active database systems. We state them up front as a frame of reference for the following discussion.

1) An active object is capable of reacting autonomously to events in its surrounding environment, as well as to changes of its internal state.

2) An active object is capable of executing multiple activities concurrently, of which one is necessarily an event detection activity.

3) An active object has to include the capability for defining what events to monitor, how to react to them, and what the behavioral semantics of the object will be.

4) An active object is cognizant of its internal organization and degree of activity in order to manage it. Intra- and inter-object synchronization may be achieved by different mechanisms but have to be subject to compatible correctness criteria.

5) An active object has to provide persistence if so required by its clients.

3 Implications for Languages and Database Systems

The ability to react *autonomously* to changes in state of an object or to external events is one of the main capabilities that sets active objects apart from other object oriented systems.

Interaction among passive objects occurs via imperative messages. A message typically consists of a selector and a list of parameters and/or keywords. The selector is the name of an operation, i.e., an action, to be performed by the recipient of the message. The recipient performs that operation transparently to the invoker but has no autonomy to decide what action to perform. In the case of active objects, the control lies with the recipient of a message (either an event message or a "conventional" message from which the recipient extracts the event). An active object may react just like a passive object to an imperative message, but can execute additional operations and can respond to event messages.

The condition of autonomy eliminates all passive object-oriented languages and DBMSs and many of the existing, so-called active systems that use the term "active" in the sense of objects in the process of executing a method. The languages with a primitive notion of active object do not support the active monitoring of events. Most active object languages only support the monitoring of changes in the internal state of a single active object but do not allow for the monitoring of external events, or conditions over multiple objects. Active databases do allow for the definition of conditions over multiple objects. However, these objects are passive objects encapsulated in a single, large active object, i.e., the active database.

The second condition, multiple concurrent activities of which one is necessarily an event detection activity, is met only by those objects that support multiple concurrent threads within an object, thus eliminating all object languages that provide for only one thread within an object. The intermediate case, objects which support multiple threads of which only one can be active at any given time, may be able to approximate true active behavior by alternating the activation of the threads. Obviously, the need for event detection does not eliminate or interfere with the "normal" object-oriented behavior in response to arbitrary, imperative messages.

Active objects have to provide the mechanisms for defining the events that are to be monitored, the conditions that have to be fulfilled, and the corresponding actions. Active database systems provide mostly for database events, such as accesses or updates. The most general event mechanism is the one defined in HiPAC [DAYA88c, CHAK89], allowing for database, temporal and arbitrary events. Languages that provide for a monitoring part, such as Orient84/K, do so for very specific events and in a rather inflexible manner. For example, Orient84/K provides for the definition of priorities and prioritizes the execution of methods, and also provides for the definition of objects and classes from which messages will be accepted. However, it appears that no general mechanism is provided that could be used for the enforcement of integrity constraints or the triggering of a translation routine for communication among heterogeneous systems.

The fourth condition determines when a given activity is to be performed and how multiple activities are to be synchronized. Active objects are characterized, among other things, by their ability to execute actions *asynchronously*. This implies that active objects are capable of managing their own resources and provide support for internal, as well as external synchronization mechanisms.

Internal synchronization is needed to avoid conflicting invocations of methods within an object. Most active languages that provide for multiple active threads within an object provide as a minimum the guarantee of mutual exclusion. The big difference is between systems that provide the notion of a transaction and those that don't. Therefore, it is possible to encounter the situation in which intra-object synchronization is performed by one mechanism, and inter-object synchronization by another. In the case of inter-object synchronization among heterogeneous active objects it becomes necessary to provide for explicit definition of the assumptions and correctness criteria. An active object language for the integration of heterogeneous systems has to provide for the specification of multiple correctness criteria and the mapping to the corresponding enforcement mechanisms. Finally, the need for coordination between user-generated tasks, and those generated by the system requires much more robust execution models

system / feature	Actl	ABCL/1	Hybrid	KNOs	Orient84/K	HiPAC
Monitoring internal state	through script	through script	programmed obj. using delay queues, delegation	condition-action triggers on single objects	demons	event-condition action rules
Monitoring state of object space	no notion of global obj. space	no notion of global obj. space	multiple objects in single obj. space	no	no	in single DB + expl. rule firing
Multiple threads	no	no, single thread w. express messages	yes (activities) only one active per domain	no	yes	yes
Event detection	reception of message	in coming message, express messages	in coming message via delay queues	in coming message check all triggers	in coming message access, priorities	DB, temporal, generic signal
Event definition	hardcoded as part of an object's script	message arrival, express messages	complex events over multiple objects in single object space via delay queues and delegation	none	preestablished for priority exec. and access control; KB demons, method	DB, temporal, generic signal
Conditions		patterns in script		LISP expression returning boolean	KB demons, variable demons, exceptions	DB queries
Arbitrary actions		yes		method or set of LISP statements	yes	yes
Resource management		queue managmt, objects decide w. messages to serve	thread manager, activity controller, delay server queues	objects decide which messages to service	priority scheduling, knowledge-based query processing	as provided by any DBMS
External commitments	via futures	via futures		no	no	timing constr., coupling modes
Transactions	no	no transactions, atomic grouping	pseudotransactions, via domains, atomicity	flat transactions, 2PL, no abort	no	full nested transactions
Synchronization	asynchronous message passing futures	past (send, no wait), now (send and wait), future (reply later)	RPC blocking sends delay queues (deadlock possible) activity interleaving within domain	asynchronous message passing, synch. execution simulated via queues, triggers	priority-based method execution, suspend, abort of suspended methods in consistent states	coupling modes: immediate deferred detached
Correctness criteria	single message, asynch. interob., no preservation of msg. ordering	send-order preservation, message at a time op. atomicity	mutual exclusion, message at a time, asynch. inter-domain proc.	no notion of consistency outside single object	mutual exclusion: activate, deactivate methods	serializability
Persistence	no	yes (type unspecified)	shadow objects, workspace to file	yes (type unspecified)	bulk image only	persistent type

Table 1: Active Capabilities in Active Object Oriented Languages and Databases

than those provided by simple transactions. This is particularly true if the system is to trigger rules that have complex conditions (possibly defined over distributed objects) and that can fire arbitrary actions in response to the condition becoming true. If this requirement is to be combined with the need for asynchronous response, a complex execution model with a variety of coupling modes, such as the one proposed for HiPAC [HSU88a], will be required.

The notion of persistence is somewhat orthogonal to the issues of autonomy and asynchrony discussed above. However, many of the solutions proposed for so-called active object-oriented languages do not work in the presence of persistence with strict correctness criteria. We view a federated system as a system that can have both native objects (that may have persistence), and imported objects (for which the system may have to provide temporary persistence), in addition to objects which may be stored in external persistent storage. This is true for application objects, as well as metadata used for the operation of the federated system. This requirement makes it difficult to specify a single kind of persistence [ZDON89]. Instead, a variety of persistence mechanisms have to coexist, e.g. metadata may be instantiated from persistent types, while imported application objects have to be coerced into persistence through explicit messages. The requirement of persistence makes the other conditions more difficult to comply with.

We summarize in Table 1 the characteristics and behavior of selected active object languages and active database systems. Act1[LIEB87], ABCL/1[YONE86, YONE87, SHIB87], KNOs [CASA88, TSIC87], Hybrid [NIER86, KONS88], and Orient84/K [ISHI86, ISHI87] are analyzed and compared with HiPAC [DAYA88a, DAYA88b, CHAK89] according to the criteria outlined above. In [RIOS90] we have shown that HiPAC subsumes the execution models of several other active database systems, namely POSTGRES [STON88, STON89], CPLEX [HSU88b], and Taxis [BARR82, CHUN88].

4 Active Object Capabilities for Heterogeneous Systems

It is our intention to define active, persistent objects that combine the strengths of existing active object languages and active database systems. We have the following design goals:

1) To identify basic constructs that ought to be directly supported by an active object model for integration of heterogeneous systems.

2) To provide a high degree of flexibility and generality while providing economy of concepts in a truly object-oriented model.

3) To preserve the symmetry between the language concepts and the transaction execution model.

At present we are experimenting with extensions to an experimental Distributed Object Management System (DOM) to add active object behavior. Some of the design and implementation issues are discussed below.

4.1 Representation of active behavior

Two basically different approaches to describing the active behavior are found in the analyzed systems. One group of languages uses a descriptive mechanism based on *scripts*. These are fully defined within an object and are essentially hard-coded instructions that are triggered by the reception of a new message. Another group provides production rules of different flavors, be it the condition-action rules of KNOs, the demons of Orient84/K or HiPAC's ECA rules. Within this group the Orient84/K demons are the most task-specific, with specialized KB demons, method demons, variable demons, access control demons, and exception handling demons. The KNOs and HiPAC rules are similar but differ in scope. KNOs condition-action triggers are defined on single objects and any reference to the state of another object has to be embedded explicitly in the trigger as a message to the foreign object. This is done to preserve encapsulation but has the disadvantage of making triggers with conditions defined over multiple objects very cumbersome and difficult to program.

We have opted for a rule mechanism based on Event-Condition-Action (ECA) rules. Rules are first class objects and can be attached to any object in the form of rule-sets. It is a natural extension of our model in which properties and methods of an object are kept as a Property-set and a method-set, respectively. Complex objects are defined by pointing to the component subobjects. Rules become thus subobjects which may be shared among multiple objects. By defining rules as separate objects we can define rules with conditions that span multiple objects. They can be triggered by modifications in multiple objects of different types without having to repeat the body of the rule within the objects.

Rules can be explicitly enabled or disabled, can be dynamically inserted and deleted from an object, and can be explicitly fired. They can be defined either at the type level, in which case they apply to all the instances of the class, or they can be defined for individual objects. The rule set is kept as a set of pointers to the rule objects. If the rules are defined only at the type level, then the rule set is the same for all the objects and only one structure is required. If individual rules have been defined or disabled for a particular object, i.e., exceptions exist, then the generic pointer structure is cloned and tailored for that object. An object can behave like any passive object if there are no rules defined for it. In that case the pointer to the rule set is simply set to nil. The overhead for checking for an object's activity is minimal.

Rules control the timing of their execution relative to the events that triggered them. To guarantee correctness of their execution, they have to follow a well-defined execution model.

4.2 Threads, Transactions and Rule Execution

We are specifying multiple threads within objects, with the possibility of multiple threads being active. This is particularly important for rule objects, since rules are defined for multiple objects and their execution should not be blocked because they were fired by another object. A separate thread for monitoring, independent of the main execution thread, is also part of our proposed model. Multiple threads and inter-object synchronization call for a well-defined execution model, a major shortcoming of most active object languages. Even languages that claim to have a transaction model often appear to provide only incomplete, and therefore unsafe, portions (e.g. the use of 2PL and no abort mechanism in KNOs) although in many experimental systems this may be a consequence of incomplete implementations.

We developed a transaction model [BUCH90] that combines the semantics of the HiPAC execution model for rule execution [HSU88a] with Saga-like open nesting for subtransactions that make partial results visible and therefore require compensation [GARC87, GARC90]. The latter is necessary in a heterogeneous environment in which no centralized control is possible over subtransactions that are executed as independent transactions on attached systems. For rule execution, which occurs strictly within the DOM framework, the hierarchically nested transactions specified as part of HiPAC appear to be adequate at this time.

In the current experiment we are assuming that every activity on objects in the object space occurs within a transaction. Events are always detected and evaluated immediately. The condition and action parts of a rule may be coupled to the triggering transaction in one of four coupling modes: *immediate* (essentially an in-line expansion of the triggering transaction), *detached* (a totally independent transaction), *deferred* (a subtransaction of the triggering transaction that is evaluated at the end of the triggering transaction), and *causally dependent detached* (a detached transaction that may not commit until the triggering transaction has committed).

4.3 Event Monitoring

Events that can trigger a rule evaluation may be of different types. They may be derived from a given operation, or they may be a signal that something has occurred elsewhere in the system. Setting a property value is an example of the former, a "power-up" event signalled by an attached component is an example of the latter. At the cost of some indirection, most events can be reduced to operation-related events by registering the events and writing them into the persistent object space. For example, the event BOT signalling the beginning of a transaction can be modeled as an event associated with the creation of a new transaction object. Events may further be simple, or composed.[1] Simple events are easy to monitor at the object level. Composed events, since they mostly involve multiple objects, are better composed outside the object in which the individual component events are detected, i.e., composition is best performed by the rules themselves.

We have opted as a first attempt for the following implementation in two stages: Upon receipt of any message the event monitor checks whether the object is active, i.e., the rule-set pointer is not null, and if so it extracts the event, composes an event message and multicasts it to all the pertinent, enabled rules in the rule-set and blocks for the propper responses. This first communication is done in a manner that guarantees that any rule that has to be fired gets executed with the proper timing, i.e., before processing in the object continues. Rule objects check the incoming event message against the pattern of their own event and either fire the rule according to the proper coupling modes, or they return a negative acknowledgement, so that processing can continue. This mechanism can handle composite events, i.e., each rule accumulates the subevents until they form the necessary triggering event. There appears to be always a trade-off between the generality of the event monitor and the necessary message traffic. A more primitive event handler that has no knowledge of what events a given rule can respond to is rather flexible but has to multicast the detected event to all the rules that are enabled for a given object, thereby incurring a possibly large communication overhead and waiting period for the negative acknowledgements. How large this overhead is depends on the number of rules defined on an object, and the cost of communication. Interpretation of the event at the point where it is detected makes it possible to forward it only to those rules that may be triggered by that event. It requires the storage of the relevant events with the pointers to the rules, and could be viewed as a compromise of encapsulation. In the absence of experience modeling with active object systems, what the average number of rules is, and whether events are mostly simple or composed we cannot judge the trade-off. However, the potential savings make local event discrimination and a lower message volume worthwhile. Therefore, we chose this approach.

Another issue in event monitoring is whether a rule should be fired before or after execution of an operation or method execution. For example, for security enforcement, pre-triggering is better, for consistency checks post-triggerng is needed. We can achieve this simply by separating the rule set into a set of pre-triggered rules and a set of post-triggered rules.

---

[1] The composition operations defined in [DAYA88] are disjunction, sequence, and closure. We are using the same composition operations but are restricting the sequence and closure operations to events occurring within the same transaction, or at least children of a common transaction.

Temporal events are monitored by a specialized temporal event monitor that has a list of pairs of temporal events and the rule objects that are to be fired in response to the occurrance of temporal events. An example of such a clock in ABCL/1 is defined in [YONE86].

4.4 Message Types

An issue under consideration is the kind of messages that ought to be supported. Let us consider for example the temporal event monitor mentioned above, which is a continuously running process. Let's say we want to interrupt the clock to add another event to be monitored, and the object has been implemented with a single thread, then the only way of interrupting it is via express messages. This is the approach taken by ABCL/1. KNOs introduces several levels of priority. It is not clear at present whether express messages will be needed in the presence of multiple threads. It isn't clear either what the effect of express messages would be on the correctness of the execution model.

The message passing modes that are supported must be in accordance with the activities to be performed. In our case this means that we require symmetry between the execution model of the active objects and the message passing modes supported in a language. This symmetry is best illustrated by examining a concrete example. An analysis of the communication mechanisms of ABCL/1 shows that its message passing modes (past, now, and future) are exactly symmetric to the HiPAC coupling modes (detached, immediate, and deferred) for execution of event-condition-action rules. The *past* mode is a totally asynchronous message passing mode, i.e. "send, no wait". This is equivalent to the *detached* execution of a rule in a separate transaction. The *now* mode is a synchronous "send and wait" message passing mechanism, which is equivalent to the *immediate* execution of an ECA rule. Finally, the *future* message passing mode (reply later) is equivalent to a *deferred* execution of an ECA rule in which the evaluation process has to return a value before committing the transaction. We view the symmetry of the message passing paradigm and the transaction execution model as a major benefit, since this reduces the mismatch and need for ad-hoc patches.

5 Status

The ideas presented here correspond to research in progress. We are experimenting with them as extensions to the DOM prototype previously developed at GTE Labs [HORN90]. This breadboard provides a basic object model, and type-based persistence. Multiple threads have been recently added, and the rule and transaction mechanisms are being implemented. We derived a set of desirable features, initially from an analysis of existing active object languages and active database systems, that will be refined through our current experimentation. The next step is to develop a persistent active object language with these features.

Acknowledgements

Many ideas presented in this paper evolved from initial discussions with Daniel Rios Zertuche. Further discussions with Frank Manola, Mark Hornick, Vivek Virmani, and Dinesh Desai are gratefully acknowledged.

References

AGHA87a Agha, G., Hewitt, C.; "Concurrent Programming Using Actors", in "Object-Oriented Concurrent Programming", A. Yonezawa and M. Tokoro (Eds.), MIT Press, Cambridge, 1987.

AGHA87b Agha, G., Hewitt, C.; "Actors: A Conceptual Foundation for Concurrent Object-Oriented Programming", in "Research Directions in Object-Oriented Programming", B. Shriver and P. Wegner (Eds.), The MIT Press, Cambridge, 1987.

BUCH90 Buchmann,A., Hornick,M., Markatos,E., Chronaki,C.; "A Transaction Model for DOM, a Heterogeneous, Distributed Object Management System", submitted for publication.

CASA88 Casais, E.; "An Object Oriented System Implementing KNOs", in "Active Object Environments", D. Tsichritzis (Ed.), Universite de Geneve, 1988.

CHAK89 Chakravarthy,S., Blaustein, B., Buchmann, A., Carey, M., Dayal, U., Goldhirsch, D., Hsu, M., Jauhari, R., Ladin, R.,Livny, M., McCarthy, D., Mckee, R., Rosenthal, A.; "HiPAC: A Research Project in Active, Time-Constrained Database Management". *Final Tech. Report*, Xerox Advanced Information Technology, July 1989.

CHUN88 Chung,K.L., Rios-Zertuche,D., Nixon,B.A., Mylopoulos,J.; "Process Management and Assertion Enforcement for a Semantic Data Model", in Advances in Database Technology, Lecture Notes in Computer Science No. 303, J.W.Schmidt, S.Ceri, M.Missikoff (eds.), March 1988

DAYA88a Dayal, U., et al "The HiPAC Project: Combining Active Databases and Timing Constraints," SIGMOD Record 17, No. 1, March 1988.

DAYA88b Dayal, U.; "Active Database Management Systems", *Proc. 3rd Int. Conf. on Data and Knowledge Bases*, Jerusalem, Israel (June 1988).

DAYA88c Dayal, U., Buchmann, A., McCarthy, D.; "Rules are Objects Too: A Knowledge Model for an Active Object-Oriented Database System," Proc. 2nd Intl. Workshop on Object Oriented Database Systems, Bad Muenster, Germany, Sept. 1988

ELLI89 Ellis, C.A., Gibbs, S.J.; "Active Objects: Realities and Possibilities", in W. Kim and F. Lochovsky (eds.) "Object-Oriented Concepts, Databases, and Applications, ACM Press, 1989.

GARC87 Garcia Molina,H., Salem,K.; "Sagas," Proc. SIGMOD 87, San Francisco, May 1987.

GARC90 Garcia Molina,H., Gawlick,D., Klein,J., Kleissner,K., Salem,K.; "Coordinating Multi-transaction Activities", Princeton University Tech. Rep. CS-TR-247-90, Feb. 1990.

HORN90 Hornick, M.; "An Initial Object Model and Prototype for DOM", GTE Technical Memorandum (in preparation)

HSU88a Hsu, M., Ladin, R., McCarthy, D.; "An Execution Model for Active Database Management Systems,", *Proc. 3rd Int.Conf. on Data and Knowledge Bases*, Jerusalem, Israel, June 1988.

HSU88b Hsu, M., Cheatham, T; "Rule Execution in CPLEX: A Persistent Objectbase," Proc. 2nd Intl. Workshop on Object Oriented Database Systems, Bad Muenster, Germany, Sept. 1988

ISHI86 Ishikawa, Y., Tokoro, M.; "A Concurrent Object-Oriented Representation Language Orient84/K: Its Features and Implementation", Proc. OOPSLA86, Portland, Ore., Sept. 1986.

ISHI87 Ishikawa, Y., Tokoro, M.; "Orient84/K: An Object-Oriented Concurrent Programming Language for Knowledge Representation", in "Object-Oriented Concurrent Programming", A. Yonezawa and M. Tokoro (Eds.), MIT Press, Cambridge, 1987.

KONS88 Konstantas, D., Nierstrasz, O., Papathomas, M.; "An Implementation of Hybrid: A Concurrent, Object-Oriented Language", in "Active Object Environments", D. Tsichritzis (Ed.), Universite de Geneve, 1988.

KOTZ88 Kotz,A.M., Dittrich,K.R., Mulle,J.A.; "Supporting Semantic Rules by a Generalized Event/Trigger Mechanism", in Advances in Database Technology, Lecture Notes in Computer Science No. 303, J.W.Schmidt, S.Ceri, M.Missikoff (eds.), March 1988

LIEB87 Lieberman, H.; "Concurrent Object-Oriented Programming in Act1", in "Object-Oriented Concurrent Programming", A. Yonezawa and M. Tokoro (Eds.), MIT Press, Cambridge, 1987.

MANO89 Manola, F.; "Object Model Capabilities for Distributed Object Management", GTE TM-0149-06-89-165, June 1989.

NIER87 Nierstrasz, O.M.; "Active Objects in Hybrid", Proc. OOPSLA 87, Orlando, Florida, Oct. 1987.

RIOS90 Rios Zertuche, D., Buchmann, A.; "Execution Models for Active Database Systems: A Comparison", GTE TM-0238-01-90-165, Jan.1990.

SHIB87 Shibayama, E., Yonezawa, A.; "Distributed Computing in ABCL/1", in A. Yonezawa and M. Tokoro (Eds.), MIT Press, Cambridge, 1987.

STON88 Stonebraker,M., Hanson, E., Potamianos,S.; "The POSTGRES Rule Manager," *IEEE TSE*, Vol 14, No. 7, July 1988.

STON89 Stonebraker, M., Hearst, M., Potamianos,S.;"A Commentary on the POSTGRES Rules System, "*SIGMOD RECORD*, Vol 18, No. 3, Sept., 1989.

THER83 Theriault, D.G.; "Issues in the Design and Implementation of Act2", MIT Artificial Intelligence Laboratory Tech. Rep. 728, June 1983.

TOKO86 Tokoro, M., Ishikawa, Y.; "Orient84/K: A Language with Multiple Paradigms in the Object Framework", Proc. 19th Hawaii Int. Conf. on System Sciences, Honolulu, Jan. 1986.

TSIC87   Tsichritzis, D., Fiume, E., Gibbs, S., Nierstrasz, O.; "KNOs: KNowledge Acquisition, Dissemination, and Manipulation Objects", ACM TOIS, Vol. 5, No. 1, January 1987, pgs. 96-112.

WEGN88   Wegner, P.; "Granularity of Modules in Object-Based Concurrent Systems", SIGPLAN Notices, 1988.

YONE86   Yonezawa, A., Briot, J.P., Shibayama, E.; "Object-Oriented Programming in ABCL/1", Proc. OOPSLA'86, Portland, Ore., Sept. 1986.

YONE87   Yonezawa, A., Shibayama, E., Takada, T., Honda, Y.; "Modelling and Programming in an Object-Oriented Concurrent Language ABCL/1" in A. Yonezawa and M. Tokoro (Eds.), MIT Press, Cambridge, 1987.

ZDON89   Zdonik, S., Maier, D. (Eds.); "Readings in Object-Oriented Database Systems", Morgan Kaufmann, 1989.

Part VIII
Transactions

Chair: David Stemple

Transactions represent one of the mechanisms used to impose an atomic event and serial time abstraction on the complexity of interleaved and occasionally failing computations. An ordinary database transaction can conveniently model an event that makes an indivisible change to state of the modelled world, even though several aspects of the world are changed by the event. The birth of a child is an example of such an event: a new person comes into the world and two other persons become parents. Sound implementation of transaction semantics while allowing interleaved access to data shared between transactions is quite complex, especially in the presence of failures. The main goal is to prevent one transaction from accessing intermediate values of shared data from another transaction while allowing as much overlap of processing as possible.

The correctness of an interleaved execution of a set of transactions is defined by the concept of serializability: an interleaved or *concurrent* execution of a set of transactions is serializable if the result of the computaion on the shared data is equivalent to the result of some serial execution of the transactions. Serializability can be achieved by avoiding *conflicts* among transactions' constituent actions, typically reads and writes of shared data. Approaches to avoiding conflicts can be characterized as pessimistic – the avoidance of conflicts, or optimistic – delayed checking for conflicts and correcting the data when conflicts are detected. The first paper in this section describes a mixed, *varimistic*, approach in a distributed setting.

Much thought has been given to ways of avoiding strict serializabilty as a criterion of correctness for interleaved execution in the cases where computations on shared data are not independent. Another issue that has been a topic of concern in persistent object processing is that of maintaining consistency of data. Indeed, serializability owes much of its appeal to the fact that the serializable execution of a set of transactions maintains consistency if each of the transactions would maintain consistency individually. While this connection between serializability and consistency is important, most concurrency control mechanisms do not include any mechanism for handling consistency predicates. The second paper in this section presents a consistency management scheme that includes the ability to choose serializability selectively as well as the means to control both the points at which consistency predicates on the state of data are checked and the amount of recovery effected when predicates are violated.

The third and fourth papers in this section deal with the implications of a locking scheme that allows cooperation between "transactions." This scheme allows one computation to be aware of selected intermediate states of data from another computation. This means that the computations are not the independent, atomic computations captured by the original transaction concept, and that their interleaved execution will not be serializable in general. The need for such interdependence is generally accepted for application areas where there is cooperation between different agents using separate but not entirely independent programs. Large computer-aided design environments are the prototypical example of such application areas.

The third paper describes an implementation of the cooperative locking scheme. A use of this scheme in an application is also given.

The fourth paper deals with the recovery problems that arise when non-serializable interleaving is allowed. The recovery problem in the serializable case is relatively simple due to the control of interdependence implicit in the transaction concept. When complex interdependencies arise naturally as part of the progress of a joint computation, recovery becomes very complex. In this paper, a means of limiting the allowable interleaving when serializability is too strict is used to direct and limit the extent of recovery whenever a failure occurs.

Distributed Varimistic Concurrency Control in a Persistent Object Store

Mike Livesey
Department of Computational Science
University of St. Andrews
North Haugh
St. Andrews
Scotland, KY16 9SS
mjl@cs.st-andrews.ac.uk

Abstract

Concurrency control mechanisms are broadly classified into pessimistic (using locking) and optimistic (using runahead and rollback). There is a need for some type of generalised concurrency control mechanism that allows a mix of optimism and pessimism appropriate to the degree of transaction conflict within a system. This paper describes such a "varimistic" mechanism. Varimism is introduced via the notion of *anchoring* a transaction: ensuring at some appropriate point during the transaction that it will suffer no further rescheduling, and therefore that its view of the world will not change again.

1 Introduction

This paper presents a novel distributed concurrency control mechanism. It is intended to be especially suited to the needs of the kind of persistent object store [5] that underlies persistent programming environments [14,15] and object-oriented programming environments and databases [24,18]. We begin by setting the scene with a description of the underlying models of distribution and concurrency control upon which the algorithm is based.

1.1 A Virtual Time Model of Distribution

There are two central features of our approach to the problem of distributed concurrency control:

- An asynchronous message passing model of interaction.
- The use of explicit message timestamps[1] to control synchronisation.

Timestamping has the effect of decoupling the ordering of events in the system from real time, introducing instead a *virtual time* axis against which to measure computational progress. The term "virtual time" appears to originate in [8], although the idea goes back at least to [11] where Lamport looks at the problem of attaching virtual times to events in a distributed system in a manner consistent with the system behaviour. The problem exists because there can be no assumption of a *global clock* in a truly distributed system. The use of virtual time as a **control** device reverses this view: a system behaviour must be found which is consistent with a given virtual time ordering. Nevertheless, the same logical relationship between the behaviour of the system and the virtual time order underlies both views, so we begin with a brief resumé of Lamport's work.

1.1.1 Causality and the Clock Algorithm

Lamport defines the *causality* ordering amongst the events in a system of processes communicating by message passing. Every event is private to some process, and belongs to one of two types:

- Internal events, marking local process actions
- External events, marking the transmission or reception of messages.

Each process has a *local clock* which imposes a total ordering on all its own events. The causality ordering is the transitive closure of all these local event orderings together with the (send, receive) event pair for every message.

Lamport goes on to describe the *Clock Algorithm*, which uses the local process clocks to assign a virtual time to every event in the execution of the system, thereby totally ordering the events. The *Clock Condition* asserts that the virtual time ordering extends the causality ordering, and is thus a statement of the correctness of the Clock Algorithm. The Clock Algorithm imposes three conditions: that a local clock always tick between any two events;

---

[1] In general timestamps can be arbitrary (though probably non-negative) real numbers. In many cases they will be integers.

that outgoing messages are stamped with their transmission times; and that the clock at a message destination is set to an upper bound of its current local time and the incoming message timestamp.

Later, we shall need to incorporate process spawning into this model. A slight problem arises if we think of the parent process as directly spawning the child in a single birth event, because the birth would belong to both processes. To avoid this problem, we shall imagine the child to appear from under a gooseberry bush, to be activated subsequently by a message from its parent. We shall refer to the transmission and reception of the activation message as the *conception* and *birth* respectively of the child process.

1.1.2 Rollback

In order that timestamps can be generated meaningfully, the global virtual time axis must have some semantics common to the whole system. This semantics will derive from the particular application in hand. For example, an application cited in [8] is distributed simulation, where virtual time represents real time in the object system. However, although virtual time has a global significance, distribution precludes the existence of a global **clock** for virtual time.

Virtual time is therefore advancing independently for each process in the system. To respect the global semantics, each process is required to handle its incoming messages in virtual time order. The timestamp of the message currently being handled by a process acts as measure of that process's *local virtual time* (LVT). But the very independence of the various LVTs means that messages will certainly not arrive in virtual time order[1]. Furthermore, a process cannot know at any point what the next highest incoming message timestamp will be. It is therefore inevitable that processes sometimes progress too eagerly (*run ahead*), and later be required to *roll back*. Specifically, rollback will be caused by the arrival of a message whose timestamp pre-dates the process's LVT. The process must be rolled back to the earlier virtual time. Obviously the process's earlier local state must have been *backed up* in order to be available for reinstatement. More fundamental are the following two problems:

- Once one process rolls back, all its work since the rollback point is obsolete, including all the messages it has sent to other processes. The recipients of those messages may now also have run ahead; if so, they must be rolled back in turn. Rollback must be propagated coherently throughout the entire system.

- Interactions with the outside world cannot be rolled back—it is difficult to unlaunch the missile! Such interactions cannot be *committed* until it is known that they can never again be subject to rollback. This corresponds to the system having made global progress relative to the outside world. Some means of assessing such global progress is therefore needed, to provide control over commitment.

These problems have been solved by a mechanism called Time Warp [8], developed at the University of Southern California, originally as a distributed simulation system. The concurrency control mechanism we describe in Section 2 derives from Time Warp, but carries certain important modifications. To provide the necessary background to the understanding of Section 2, we outline here the essential features of Time Warp and its solutions to the above problems.

1.1.3 Time Warp

The basic device used by Time Warp to impose the virtual time order is for every process to queue its incoming messages in their timestamp order rather than their arrival order. In this way, a process can be thought of as working along its *input queue*, increasing its LVT to the timestamp of each message as it gets to it. When a message arrives whose timestamp is smaller than the process's LVT, the message lands in that part of the queue already processed, thereby causing the rollback.

Time Warp solves the first of the above problems by "unsending" messages. Each real message has a corresponding *antimessage* which, when sent to the same destination as the original *positive* message, serves to annul it. It is crucial that the antimessage carry the same timestamp as its positive, because the arrival of the antimessage must invalidate any work performed by the recipient from that time on, and cause the recipient to rollback to that point if necessary. Should the recipient roll back in response to the antimessage, it will send more antimessages to yet other processes. In this way the rollback will propagate to the other affected parts of the system as desired (see Fig.1).

One consequence of using antimessages is that a process must remember all its output messages in case they need to be unsent. To achieve this, each process holds an *output queue* of the messages it sends, in their virtual

---

1 Not even if the underlying communication medium preserves message order (is *monotonic*). It is therefore possible to relax monotonicity, which is especially relevant to "store and forward" networks.

send-time order. Should rollback occur, the negative versions of all the messages in the output queue after the rollback point are sent; the queue can then be truncated at the rollback point.

Time Warp solves the second problem via the notion of *Global Virtual Time* (GVT). A virtual time is *committed* if no process can be rolled back to or before it. GVT is the supremum of all the committed times; when an external interaction has a timestamp less than GVT it can be committed. It is shown in [8] that GVT can be calculated from within the system, but to do so requires knowledge of all LVTs and the timestamps of messages in transit. Such a requirement would seem to run counter the distributed nature of the system. The GVT-based commitment mechanism is one of the components of Time Warp which we shall discard.

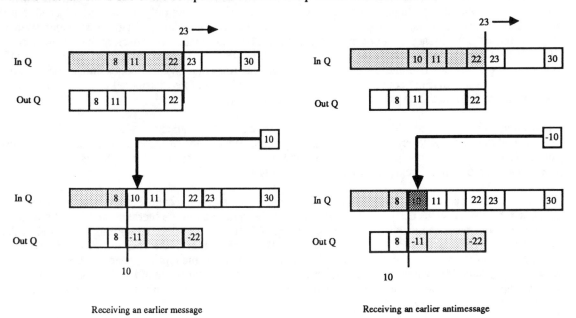

Receiving an earlier message   Receiving an earlier antimessage

Fig.1 Rollback in Time Warp

1.2 Distributed Concurrency Control Requirements

There is a plethora of distributed database concurrency control algorithms in the literature (see [4] and references therein). However, each addresses or emphasises a slightly different set of criteria. In this section we have tried to identify the important criteria, with particular regard to the needs of persistent object stores. These *Concurrency Control Requirements* (CCRs) are as follows.

- *Correctness.* This is the safety requirement that the database remain consistent. We adopt the standard *serialisability* model of consistency [16]. Transactions acting concurrently on the database become interleaved at the level of their component Read (R) and Write (W) *actions*. Such an interleaving is called a *schedule* or *history*. In the special case that the interleaving is simply a concatenation of the transactions, the history is called *serial*. It is assumed that the individual transactions treat the database correctly, whence serial histories do also. To guarantee that an arbitrary collection of concurrent transactions behaves correctly it is sufficient to require that they interleave in a manner which is equivalent in its effect to some serial history. Such a history is called serialisable. Since not all histories are serialisable, a concurrency control algorithm is needed to ensure that only serialisable histories do occur.

- *Liveness.* Every transaction must terminate in the presence of any other transactions, provided it would terminate by itself. The enforcement of serialisability may result in conflict between transactions. The loser will suffer some sort of setback (e.g. rollback, abortion). If a transaction repeatedly loses conflicts, there arises the possibility of indefinite setback and consequent loss of liveness.

- *Minimal interference.* There should be as little re-ordering of histories as possible. In particular, no serial history should be re-ordered.

- *Unboundedness*. The persistent object store is a dynamic data structure, formed by a web of cross-referencing amongst the objects. Moreover, objects may contain code from which new processes can be spawned dynamically, so the number of coexisting transactions is also unbounded. This latter unboundedness tends to be ignored by conventional distributed database concurrency control mechanisms. It raises problems for liveness, because one transaction may suffer defeat in a series of conflicts with opponent transactions that arise each from a different process.

- *Distribution*. The need to support distribution is becoming pressing in modern database and persistent object store environments. It is particularly important to support distribution not only of the data (objects), but also of the processing (transactions), in order that the distributed system is not simply a widespread centralised system. To this end, the concurrency control algorithm must itself be distributed. Moreover, at the application level the algorithm must be able to support the notion of conceptual context [13] or transparent distribution [12], and unboundedness makes a one-one correspondence between entities and physical nodes unrealistic anyway. It is therefore important that the concurrency control mechanism should be distributed at the level of its logical components in order not to prejudge the issue of physical distribution.

- *Interaction*. The system should support foreground transactions originating from an interactive user, as well as background transactions generated by a running program. Rescheduling of incomplete transactions is acceptable for background transactions, but generally not for foreground transactions. It should also be possible for an interactive user to abort a foreground transaction explicitly.

- *Varimism*. This requirement does not have the same status as the preceding ones, because it has not been addressed by any previous design. Nevertheless, it has been mooted in the literature and forms a major design objective of our proposed mechanism. In [10], Kung and Robinson present an optimistic method of database concurrency control as an alternative to locking. They comment that in the case of a database system where transaction conflict is rare, but not rare enough to justify optimism, some type of generalised concurrency control mechanism (preferably adaptive) is needed that will provide the right mixture of locking and rollback, which we call *varimism*. In a sense, varimism gives a concurrency control mechanism *scheme*, rather than a single mechanism.

The remaining sections of the paper are as follows:
2. The proposed varimistic algorithm.
3. The algorithm in the context of a persistent object store.
4. Comparison with other methods.
5. Conclusion.

2   Varimistic Distributed Concurrency Control

We begin by describing how the general model of Section 1 may be applied in the context of distributed database concurrency control. We consider in turn each of the two characteristics of the model.

- *Asynchronous Message-passing*. All the entities within a distributed database or persistent object store will be viewed as autonomous, and correspond to processes in the model. These entities are of two kinds: the *transactions*, and the individual *grains* of data (the *objects*) that constitute the units of access to the database. Hence both transactions and grains are to be thought of as sending messages to each other. In fact, the system is completely bipartite: transactions communicate only with grains, and vice versa. A point of terminology: we shall not continue to refer to the transactions and grains as "processes", but reserve that term for the running programs that generate transactions.

- *Virtual Time*. Every transaction will be allocated a virtual time band [8,9] in which to operate. The bands are made mutually disjoint in order to guarantee serialisability. The allocating of bands is most easily effected by assigning a unique *Transaction Sequence Number* (TSN) to each transaction and ordering its constituent events separately within the TSN, which avoids the problem of predicting the width of each band. However, the uniqueness requirement raises a problem in conjunction with the Distribution CCR, because every process, since it can generate transactions, must also be able to generate virtual time bands. We return to this question below.

Time Warp has already been used for database concurrency control [9], and for version and currency control [19]. However, it does not meet all the CCRs, and for that reason our control mechanism incorporates certain changes. We now look at how Time Warp stands with respect to the CCRs as a background for discussing these changes.

2.1 Time Warp and the CCRs

As mentioned above, Correctness is guaranteed by the allocation of separate virtual time bands to transactions, which forces serialisability. With regard to Liveness, conventional schemes [6,11,17,22] employ some kind of priority with respect to which any given process is guaranteed eventually to come to the top. In Time Warp the virtual time band of a transaction acts as its priority. Liveness is then guaranteed subject to the *groundedness* condition that for any given transaction there is a bound on the number of possible older transactions. This condition is normally ensured by the system comprising a bounded number of processes (one process in the extreme case of central control), which bounds the number of sources of timestamps [11]. However, the combination of Unboundedness and Distribution creates the potential of an unbounded number of processes. Nevertheless, we shall show below that groundedness does still hold under certain reasonable conditions.

The Minimal Interference and Interaction CCRs require the major modification. Time Warp has the property that transactions are forced to occur in their timestamp order whenever they share objects, even if they are separated in real time and there is no actual conflict—the ordering is enforced simply by their potential to conflict. This behaviour contravenes Minimal Interference, which would require that a younger transaction can complete before an older one in the absence of actual conflict. In other words, the timestamp on a transaction has no intrinsic ordering significance, and should not be treated as though it did. Moreover, a transaction can never commit explicitly in Time Warp, but only implicitly by going beyond the commitment horizon.

Minimal Interference is achieved in our mechanism by the introduction of an explicit commitment mechanism, using special lock messages. These are sent to the relevant objects at the end of a transaction, and, if all the objects are successfully locked, the transaction commits. This locking corresponds to the validation phase in the optimistic algorithm of [10]. However, locking can in fact occur at *any* point during a transaction, giving rise to the idea of *anchoring* a transaction at any stage during its execution. It is this capability that provides for Varimism. Insofar as conventional locking corresponds to pre-transaction anchoring, and optimism to post-transaction anchoring, any intermediate anchoring position corresponds to an intermediate degree of optimism. Finally, anchoring also provides a direct answer to the Interaction CCR, as we shall see below.

2.2 The Varimistic Mechanism

We start from the point where each transaction has been assigned its unique TSN T. To perform an action, the parent transaction must generate a *request* message in its output queue for transmission to the relevant grain. Each request has an additional within-transaction *request number r*. We shall refer to a pair (T,r) as a *Request ID* (RID). The RIDs will be taken to be ordered lexicographically r within T. Requests are placed in the input queue of the grain in their RID order, of course, not their arrival order.

Each grain performs the requests in its input queue. Consecutive R-requests can be performed simultaneously (to achieve read-concurrency), but in the case of conflicting pairs of requests (RW, WR, WW) the earlier must complete before the later is begun. Upon completion of a request, the grain will generate an ACK message in its output queue (carrying the result in the case of an R action) for transmission back to the transaction that issued the original request.

When a request causes rollback at a grain, by virtue of being out of order, to a point prior to the currently active message, the grain must send the negative versions of the over-eager ACKs. We shall refer to a negative ACK as a NAK message. Similarly, when a transaction suffers rollback it must send the negatives of the requests (the *unrequests*) for every action beyond its rollback point to the grains concerned. For reasons we explain below, a grain must NAK every unrequest upon arrival, whether it arrive in the grain's virtual future or virtual past.

In the remainder of this Section we examine those aspects of the varimistic mechanism that concern its design and its divergence from the pure Time Warp mechanism.

2.3 Granularity

Since there is no absolute notion of an atomic item of data (other than the bit), there is some choice of how much data a single grain of the database holds. This is the question of the *granularity* of the database, which lies on a spectrum from *coarse* (few large grains) through to *fine* (many small grains). Generally speaking, fine grain increases throughput but incurs higher administrative overheads by comparison with coarse grain. However, there is considerable dependence here on the particular control mechanism used. Certainly fine grain should increase throughput, because a transaction can tailor its "footprint" more precisely, thereby the better avoiding conflict and the resulting rollback. However, in the case of a locking mechanism, fine grain means that a transaction must obtain more locks. In the optimistic mechanism of [10], fine grain means larger read- and write-sets to maintain, and the associated increased time overhead. In both these cases rollback is always abortion, so that more work will be lost should rollback occur.

In our scheme fine grain carries a greater queue space penalty, but the queues are individually smaller. Since the control is distributed over the grains, the corresponding time overhead will be reduced, but this reduction will be offset by the increased message activity. There is also an effect from the "temporal granularity" of a transaction—whether it consists of many short actions of a few long ones. Because our rollback is decremental rather than abortive, fine temporal grain should generally enable rollback to be less severe. Notice that message activity depends only on the volume of traffic and not its destination, and that volume is determined by the temporal, rather than the spatial, grain. Nevertheless, coarse spatial allows coarse temporal grain, whereas fine spatial grain will tend to force fine temporal grain.

2.4 Request Numbers

If a transaction rolls back, then forward again, how are the new request numbers generated? For example, suppose a transaction has made requests 1,2,3,4,5 when it rolled back to its state between numbers 2 and 3. What number is its next request? If the request number were part of the state, the answer must be 3. However, action 2 may have been a read, with action 3 being conditional upon the result of that read. It is then quite possible that the second action 3 be different from the first, yet have a request that bears the same RID. Such a situation is unacceptable, so it appears that request number must remain outside the transaction state and persist across rollbacks, incrementing continually. Thus the action following the rollback in our example would be number 6, not number 3.

For this reason, when a grain is rolled back by a queue-jumping request, all the requests behind the new one in the input queue are now obsolete. The grain will mark them as such and ignore them as it rolls forward again. Also, when a transaction is rolled back, some of the actions beyond its rollback point it may already have unrequested; these are not unrequested again.

2.5 Commitment

We argued above that an explicit commitment mechanism was necessary, and mentioned briefly that it is achieved by the introduction of special messages. We now describe the mechanism in detail.

Upon completion of its last action, a transaction T knows all the grains it has touched. It may then send each a *lock* message. A lock has an RID like any other request, but it does not cause rollback because there is no change in the grain's data state associated with it. When the grain processes the lock, it will be accepted (ACK) or rejected (NAK) according to whether or not T *dominates* the grain, i.e. owns the action at the front of the grain's input queue. The rationale is that the transaction which dominates a grain currently has priority over all other transactions waiting at that grain, so may possibly be able to commit. By contrast, no other transaction at the grain is a candidate for commitment.

An accepted lock forms a barrier in the queue. It stops older transactions from ousting the locked transaction, effectively starting a new queue behind the lock. A rejected lock causes the issuing transaction to unlock all (deadlock avoidance requires all) its already accepted locks. An unlock cancels the lock and the protection it affords, so that the queue becomes one again with a possible consequent reshuffle. This will in turn result in the issuing transaction being rolled back if there were older transactions behind the lock. A conventional rollback may occur during locking, at a grain that is still unlocked; this will also cause the already accepted locks to be unlocked in the same way.

When all its locks are accepted the transaction is *anchored*, and may issue a *commit* message to every grain concerned. It is now impossible for the transaction to suffer any further rollback, so "uncommit" messages are not needed. On receipt of the commit, the grain will back up its new state, discard the old one and remove the transaction from its input queue. The transaction will die when all its commits have been issued.

One effect of commitment that must be guarded against is the possibility of *orphaned* messages, whose source transaction has committed, and *homeless* messages, whose target transaction has committed. Orphans will arise as obsolete requests or unrequests from a transaction that has since rolled back and taken a different computation path to commitment. If an orphan arrives at a grain after that grain has committed the dead transaction, it will be treated as a new transaction. If its antimessage is yet to arrive they will eventually cancel, but otherwise the orphan creates a ghost transaction that may change the grain state, and which never commits. Homeless messages will be ACKs or NAKs in response to obsolete requests. They constitute straightforward dangling references.

To avoid these effects, each entity must know exactly what messages to expect. Now a request may be cancelled by its unrequest in the queue of some grain before or after the grain has processed it, i.e. before or after it has been ACKed. A transaction therefore does not know whether to expect an ACK to an obsolete request. To counter this problem, we shall require that **all** requests be ACKed, either when processed or when cancelled. A transaction will then not remove an obsolete request from its queue until it is both ACKed **and** NAKed. And a grain will not remove an obsolete request from its queue until it has been unrequested, but simply mark it as obsolete. Given these conventions, we can formulate the following rules about commitment:

(1) A grain must not remove obsolete requests from its input queue when committing a transaction (their negatives exist and will eventually cancel).
(2) A transaction must not commit with outstanding obsolete requests.

2.6 Varimism and Interaction

The mechanism described so far is optimistic. A transaction goes ahead in the eternal hope of committing without rollback, but is never safe until it has committed. Indeed, the locking phase can be viewed as a representation of the validation phase of [10]. We have already mentioned that varimism is meant to provide a technique for mixing locking and rollback, but there is another important reason for providing it, which relates to the Interaction CCR. Rollback of a background transaction is acceptable because the only external effect is to delay commitment—or rather, reduce potential eagerness. However, in the case of a foreground transaction the situation is very different, as the following scenario shows. One evening you take your favourite corner of the database home for a candlelit supper followed by a spot of updating. Imagine your chagrin when you return next morning to find that the transaction has been rolled back and the grain values that you lavished your affection upon the night before are now passé! (This "offlining" of transactions is exactly the method used by [10].)

This is where varimism comes to the rescue. Suppose that a transaction is allowed to issue a lock at any point during its lifetime, which may be accepted or rejected as described above. As soon as the transaction has had a lock accepted at every grain it is ever going to touch, immunity from further rollback is again guaranteed just as in Section 2.5. The only difference is that now there will be more requests from the issuing transaction. Such requests must follow the lock in the queue but precede any requests from other transactions queued behind the lock. Hence we must separate logically the lock itself from the barrier it induces in the queue. The effect of this procedure is to anchor the transaction at the point where all its locks were installed.

Thus we get a complete spectrum of optimism ranging from fully pessimistic anchoring at the start of the transaction (which is only possible if all the grains needed can be predicted) through to fully optimistic anchoring just prior to commitment. In the example above, the transaction presumably consists of distinct read and write phases. Locking would be performed between the phases, and you would not take your grain values home until the anchoring was complete.

The Interaction CCR also requires the ability to abort a transaction explicitly. Such a capability is obviously necessary in foreground transactions, and our mechanism provides for it trivially. To abort a transaction it suffices simply to roll it back to the beginning, then commit it. This "null" commitment amounts to no more than making sure that all the relevant NAKs have been received, since there are no grains involved.

2.7 Optimisations

In this subsection we briefly describe two possible optimisations to the basic algorithm.

* *Rollback.* In general when rollback occurs, there will not be a backed up state corresponding exactly to the rollback point. Since rollback of one entity drags others with it, rolling back further than necessary is obviously undesirable. Rather than propagating rollback from the youngest backed up state preceding the required rollback point, the entity concerned can run forward privately from the backup point to the rollback point, thereby regaining the exact state at the rollback point, and then propagate the rollback. Failure recovery is a special case of this, equivalent to doing zero rollback but without the current state. The failing entity can recover privately without invoking any public rollback.
* *Reading.* The algorithm has so far not taken the usual account of the fact that a read action performs the identity state transformation. It is easy to do so using a similar technique. When a read request causes rollback, it is necessary to discover the state at the rollback point in order to return the correct value, but it is not necessary *actually* to perform the rollback because no subsequent states are altered. Indeed, this optimisation applies also to read unrequests, which likewise involve no correction to the state.

2.8 Recovery

It is well known [7] that a distributed asynchronous system cannot be made resilient against arbitrary failure of even one entity. Certain kinds of failure, though, may look exactly like ordinary rollback—say if a grain or transaction were temporarily to "black out" without losing its queues, then wake up to its most recently backed up state and continue to work correctly. Indeed, such failure is actually a null rollback, so by the comments in (2.7), recovery is simply a matter of using the input queue as a log and rolling forward again. However, there are two hidden requirements:

- Roll forward cannot take place unless the input queue remains intact during the failure.
- It essential to the correct functioning of the system that messages do not vanish. An entity must therefore continue to accept messages even while down.

We can meet these requirements in the following way. Suppose that each entity has, in addition to its input queue, an extra *arrival queue*. The arrival queue buffers the incoming messages in arrival order, prior to their being incorporated into the input queue in virtual time order. We now assume that the arrival queue of an entity is unaffected by the failure, and will continue to accept messages throughout. We also assume that these messages are **not** incorporated into the input queue, because then they would effectively vanish by virtue of being made to look like old messages that had already been processed. The input queue itself we shall assume to be affected by the failure and require that it be kept up to date by being backed up at every change. This backup must be done carefully to avoid not only loss but also apparent duplication of messages.

2.9 Spinning Transactions

A word of caution is in order about spinning transactions. Liveness can only be guaranteed under the assumption that every individual transaction will terminate. For example, a transaction may attempt to pop an empty stack, then decide to spin until the stack changes state and the pop becomes enabled. This will result in a series of requests which all have the same TSN, and will therefore always enter at the same place in the grain's queue, repeatedly causing rollback if the grain has run ahead. If the requested action is still disabled when the transaction in question eventually becomes the oldest, *the grain state will never again change* and the transaction will spin indefinitely. Now the transaction will presumably have protected itself with a timeout, but the danger lies in the fact that should it not have done so, not only is the transaction itself blocked, but so is the grain and any other transaction that tries to touch it. The correct way to spin is, of course, *between* transactions, so that every request in the series has a different TSN.

2.10 Correctness

As mentioned above, safety involves both the serialisability of transactions and freedom from deadlock of the system. Serialisability takes on a very simple guise in the present context, for the following reason. Because of the deliberate use of runahead to produce read-concurrency, it is not sensible to ascribe an order to adjacent reads at a grain. And because the grains are distributed, it is not generally sensible to ascribe "unforced" orders between actions at different grains [4,23]. In other words, the behaviour of a distributed system needs to be described by a notion of "distributed history" [16], which we capture as an equivalence class of sequential histories, the equivalence in question being insensitivity under interchange of adjacent independent actions. We shall write this as ~ (it is ~* of [16]).

Now a history h is *conflict serialisable* precisely when $h \sim h'$ for some serial history h'. Hence for us, serial and conflict serialisable are identical; we shall therefore refer to them simply as serial. Associated with each ~-class, H, of histories is its *conflict relation (graph)*, C(H), defined as the set of transaction-grain-transaction triples (T,x,T') such that an action of T on grain x precedes one of T', with the actions not both reads. The importance of C(H) is that it is acyclic precisely when H is serial.

THEOREM. Only serial histories can occur.

PROOF. Notice first that an action of a transaction actually happens at its last attempt (after the last rollback affecting it) prior to the commit. Then, if C(H) has a cycle, it must have consecutive edges of the form (T, x, T') and (T', y, T") with T < T' > T", and the queues at the two grains look like ("l" denotes a lock)

    x: ... T ... T' ...
    y: T'l ... T" ...

But this is impossible, because T' will attempt to lock x, fail, lose its lock at y, and be ousted there by T".   ¶

THEOREM. Deadlock cannot occur.

PROOF. Let T_0, x_0, T_1, x_1,..., T_{n-1}, x_{n-1} be a sequence of transactions and grains with each T_i waiting on T_{i+1} at x_i. Now T waits on T' at x iff either

(a) T > T', or
(b) T' > T but T' locked x before T touched x.

In case (b) T' is trying to commit. If it dominates each grain of interest to it when it tries to lock that grain the commitment succeeds; otherwise it fails and rolls back. Either way T is not blocked at all in (b). Hence the cycle must be a >-cycle, contradiction.   ¶

THEOREM. The system is live (i.e. every transaction eventually commits).

PROOF. Any transaction T has a finite initial <-segment, so there are only finitely many older transactions, whence T is eventually the oldest. By (b) above, it can only be held up by at most one younger transaction at each grain it touches. So T eventually dominates every grain it touches, and must therefore eventually commit.   ¶

Notice that without commitment, a transaction never commits explicitly, but does so implicitly by virtue of eventually becoming the oldest and never thereafter suffering rollback.

3   The Persistent Object Store

As we have already mentioned, the persistent object store is interwoven with cross-references. We are therefore viewing the persistent object store as an *abstract heap*: each grain is an *abstract location* whose content is the current grain data state (the object), and a reference to a grain from within an object is an *abstract pointer*. The heap is "abstract" because the grains do not generally correspond to physical locations. Indeed, there is no limit in principle to the complexity of data that may be stored in a single grain.

In a physical store, such complex values must obviously themselves be built from locations. It is important to keep these two levels of location distinct. And not only must the physical representation of a grain provide for the stored object, it must also carry the necessary server to implement the concurrency control algorithm. The overall appearance of a grain in the physical store will therefore look like Fig.2. We shall refer to the internal physical pointers as *links*.

There is a particularly important consequence of this dichotomy of physical pointers with regard to the implementation of the basic R and W actions on grains. Suppose that an object is to be read from one grain and written to another. Since the links comprising the object have no independent external significance, but serve only to represent complex structure, they cannot be shared between grains. They must therefore undergo structural copy when the object is written to the target grain. By contrast, an embedded pointer to another grain is a scalar value with public significance, which should be written verbatim into the target grain. Briefly, links are subject to *deep copy*, while grain pointers are subject to *shallow copy*.

Another aspect of the dichotomy concerns the backing up of objects. After an object has been backed up and reinstated, not only may the links be different, the whole representation may be completely different (say a single contiguous block). In contrast, the pointers that represent the grains themselves must persist, because the objects are backed up independently of each other and the cross-references must remain meaningful after reinstatement. A full discussion of persistent object store implementation issues can be found in [5].

3.1 Unboundedness

Languages that manipulate a persistent object store allow the programmer to create new objects and, if closures are first class values, spawn new processes. In order to make new objects persist, it must also be possible to create new grains. The persistent object store is therefore *unbounded*; there is no prior limit on the number of grains or processes that it might contain. To avoid dangling references, the reverse capability is not provided; nevertheless entities do die of natural causes, rendering them inaccessible thereafter. For example: there may be no chain of references to a grain from any process; a transaction may commit; and an act of creation may be rolled back over, thereby destroying all memory that the entity ever existed. So the instantaneous population of the system may be bounded; then the system is *dynamically bounded*. Unless it is, it cannot be physically realised indefinitely.

Unbounded systems raise problems of allocating resources to the entities in the system in a way that respects certain constraints. In general the allocation cannot be done beforehand (statically), because there is no uniform method of identifying the entities. Indeed, the problem of giving unique IDs to entities is just one particular allocation problem, which may not be easy to solve even when there is an infinite supply of IDs, as we shall see below. Most resources are in finite supply, and then they must be dynamically *reused* in some way. This is typified by the space allocation problem, whose constraint is that contemporary entities occupy disjoint blocks of physical memory. The reuse here is the responsibility of the garbage collector. In our system it is necessary that both grains and transactions be allocated IDs "unique enough" to enable them to communicate. This problem in fact reduces to the space problem.

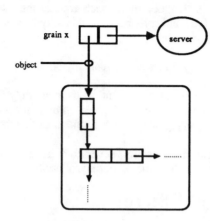

Fig.2 Grain Structure

A trickier allocation problem concerns TSNs. Even given an infinite supply of TSNs, it is not trivial to perform a distributed allocation of TSNs which satisfies the two conditions of respecting causality and being grounded. In Section 1 we saw how Lamport's Clock Algorithm uses local process clocks to allocate a timestamp to each event in a process (for the rest of this section we shall refer to the processes simply as "clocks"). In a bounded system, statically determined process IDs are used to resolve clashes and force uniqueness. This is done by using a rational timestamp, where the process ID is appended to the original timestamp as a "fractional" part. Can the same technique not be used for unbounded systems, given that the identification problem can be solved? There are three types of clashing to be considered:

- *Bounded*: there is a bound on the number of transactions with the same timestamp. In this case, which is the only one possible for a bounded system, the crucial factor is that the ordering remains grounded.
- *Finite unbounded*: there are only a finite number of transactions with the same timestamp, but arbitrarily many. Such clashing can only be resolved with infinitely many IDs.
- *Infinite*: there can be an infinite subset of transactions all having the same timestamp. Here clash resolution needs infinitely many IDs, but even then the ordering becomes ungrounded because there may be infinitely many fractions within one integer.

We shall now show that, under reasonable assumptions, the structure of our system precludes infinite clashing. Consider the graph of the immediate causality relation. There is an arc from event a to event b when either (i) a immediately precedes b in the same clock, or (ii) a is a conception and b the corresponding birth. Since a uniquely determines b in (i), and b has no local predecessor in (ii), the graph is a binary forest—the *lineal chart* of the system.

The clocks containing the roots of the lineal chart we shall call *protoclocks*. In order to establish that all clashing is bounded, we still need a version of boundedness. But instead of boundedness over all time, we now need only initial boundedness, viz:

(B) The number of protoclocks is finite.

Then we have:

THEOREM. The set T_t of transactions with timestamp t is finite.

PROOF. The Clock Condition and (B) imply that every branch of the lineal chart has strictly increasing timestamps. By König's Lemma, there is a depth d below which every event has timestamp > t. And any schedule must eventually consist of events at depth > d.   ¶

Moreover, because clashes only occur between different branches of the tree, dynamic boundedness will imply bounded clashing. In this case the unique transaction ID *can* be used to resolve clashes exactly as for a bounded system.

So far we are allowing the timestamps to be arbitrary integers. Now consider bounding the size of the timestamps also. If we can guarantee that the *range* of contemporary timestamps is bounded (say $\leq M$) we can argue as follows. If there is a transaction with timestamp T, then $T - M$ is the smallest possible extant timestamp. So every extant transaction can deduce that every extant timestamp exceeds $T - 2M - 1$, which can therefore be reused. The obvious way to implement the reuse is with a cyclic clock of at least $2M + 1$ states. (This is very similar to the reuse of frame sequence numbers via a send window in the selective retransmission protocol.) The existence of the bound M is the temporal analogue of dynamic boundedness—the latter limits the instantaneous "width" of the system, whereas the former limits the instantaneous "height".

One final comment is in order here. It might be thought that the TSN allocation problem would reduce to the ID problem, in that the ID server could provide a central global clock. However, IDs can be disseminated throughout the system via a hierarchy of localities, which obviates the need to to invoke the central server for every ID allocation. On the other hand, to obtain a unique TSN from the server would involve access to it at the creation of every transaction. Indeed, the ID allocation is consistent with distribution, whereas the latter kind of TSN allocation would be undoubtedly centralised.

4   Comparison with Other Methods

The Time Warp mechanism has been applied to the database concurrency control problem in [9]. This approach uses "pure" virtual time, without commit. As we have mentioned, transactions then occur in strict virtual time order, with possible violation of the Minimal Interference CCR. Commitment disrupts the virtual time ordering in the input queues of grains. It also obviates the need for fossil collection, and the calculation of GVT, by allowing all reuse to be done by the garbage collector.

Another difference in our system is that after rollback, there is no point in re-running the same actions, because the continuous request numbering makes them obsolete and therefore themselves subject to eventual rollback. However, pure Time Warp would give rise to such redundant runahead, thereby generating a lot of unnecessary message traffic.

The motivation for our approach derives from the comment in [10] quoted above, so, as might be expected, at the optimistic end of the spectrum there are certain similarities. For example, as we pointed out earlier, their validation is analogous to our post-transaction locking. However, there are also some important differences:

- Their method is inherently centralised, while ours is inherently distributed.
- Their optimism derives from caching, while ours derives from run-ahead.
- Although their transaction numbers look like timestamps, they are generated differently and do not naturally provide for liveness, which must be grafted on in a rather ad hoc fashion. Indeed, locking is advocated in [10] as a means of ensuring liveness.

There are many other approaches based on timestamps [3,20,21,19]. However, these methods use timestamps with exactly the opposite priority significance: younger transactions have priority over older ones! This actually favours processes with fast-running clocks, and prevents the timestamp mechanism being used directly to ensure liveness because the timestamp ordering is no longer grounded.

5   Conclusion

We began by stating some requirements that should be satisfied by a concurrency control algorithm for a persistent object store. We then presented a particular algorithm—or rather, because of the varimism, a class of algorithms—that does satisfy those requirements. The algorithm is based upon the notion of virtual time and the Time Warp mechanism. However, it differs therefrom in a number of important respects, most notably the presence of explicit commitment. We have proved the basic correctness properties of the algorithm and discussed some implementation issues. These include the generation of the TSNs, which are crucial to the functioning of the algorithm, and the algorithm's tolerance to some degree of failure.

The obvious next step in this work is to study the performance of the mechanism, along the lines of [1,2]. A major advantage of varimism for evaluation purposes is its *orthogonality*, in that the degree of optimism in the algorithm is decoupled from its other properties. This will enable a direct comparison of the relative merits of different degrees of optimism in any given situation, in terms of the trade-off between improved concurrency and increased rollback. For example, [2] points out that there are conflicting conclusions about the merits of optimism as presented in [10]. It is necessary to decide to what extent these conflicts are a result of optimism per se or of the particular algorithm in [10].

Acknowledgements

I am indebted to Ron Morrison, Richard Connor and Fred Brown for many perceptive comments and illuminating discussions.

References

[1] AGRAWAL R. & DEWITT D.J., Integrated concurrency control and recovery mechanisms: design and performance evaluation, *ACM TODS* 10, 4 (Dec 1985) 529–564.
[2] AGRAWAL R., CAREY M.J. & LIVNY M., Concurrency control performance modeling: alternatives and implications, *ACM TODS* 12, 4 (Dec 1987) 609–654.
[3] BERNSTEIN P.A. & GOODMAN N., Timestamp-based algorithms for concurrency control in distributed database systems, *Proc. 6th Intern. Conf. Very Large Databases*, Oct 1980.
[4] BERNSTEIN P.A. & GOODMAN N., Concurrency control in distributed database systems, *ACM Computing Surveys* 13, 2 (June 1981) 185–221.
[5] BROWN A.L., Persistent Object Stores, PPRR 71-89, Universities of Glasgow & St.Andrews, 1989.
[6] CHANDY K.M. & MISRA J., The drinking philosophers' problem. *ACM TOPLAS* 6, 4 (Oct 1984) 632–646.
[7] FISCHER M.J., LYNCH N.A. & PATERSON M.S., Impossibility of distributed consensus with one faulty process, *JACM* 32, 2 (April 1985) 374–382.
[8] JEFFERSON D.R., Virtual time. *ACM TOPLAS* 7, 3 (July 1985) 404–425.
[9] JEFFERSON D.R. & MOTRO A., The Time Warp mechanism for database concurrency control, U.S.C. Dept. of Computer Science Tech. Rep., U. of Southern California, Los Angeles, June 1983.
[10] KUNG H.T. & ROBINSON J.T., On optimistic methods of concurrency control, *ACM TODS* 6, 2 (June 1981) 213–226.
[11] LAMPORT L., Time, clocks, and the ordering of events in a distributed system, *CACM* 21, 7 (July 1975) 558–565.
[12] MARQUES J.A & GUEDES P., Extending the operating system to support an object-oriented environment, *Proc. OOPSLA 89*, New Orleans, Louisiana, October 1989, 113–122.
[13] MORRISON R., BARTER C.J., BROWN A.L., CARRICK R., CONNOR R., DEARLE A., HURST A.J. & LIVESEY M.J., Language design issues in supporting process-oriented computation in persistent environments, *Proc. 22nd Ann. Hawaii Inter. Conf. on Sys. Sci. (Vol 2)*, Hawaii, Jan 1989.
[14] MORRISON R., BROWN A., CONNOR R., DEARLE A., The Napier88 Reference Manual, PPRR 77-89, Universities of Glasgow & St.Andrews, 1989, 736–744.
[15] O'BRIEN P.D., HALBERT D.C. & KILIAN M.F., The Trellis programming environment, *Proc. OOPSLA 87*, Orlando, Florida (Oct 1987), 91–102.
[16] PAPADIMITRIOU C.H., The serialisability of concurrent database updates. *JACM* 26, 4 (Oct 1979) 631–653.
[17] PARK D., Reasoning with fairness constraints (abstract). *Proc. Intern. Conf. on Foundations of Computer Theory* Bergholm, Sweden, Aug 1983. Lecture Notes in Computer Science **158**, Springer-Verlag.
[18] PENNEY D.J. & STEIN J., Class modification in the GemStone object-oriented database, *Proc. OOPSLA 87*, Orlando, Florida (Oct 1987) 111–117.
[19] RAO K.V.B., GAFNI A. & RAEDER G., The design of Dynamo: a general-purpose information processing model with a time dimension, *Advances in Object-Oriented Database Systems*, Lecture Notes in Computer Science **334**, Springer-Verlag (Sep 1988) 286–291.
[20] REED D.P., Naming and synchronisation in a decentralised computer system, MIT/LCS/TR205, MIT 1978.
[21] REED D.P., Implementing atomic actions on decentralised data. *ACM TOCS* 1, 1 (Feb 1983) 3–23.
[22] THOMAS R.H., A solution to the concurrency control problem for multiple copy databases, *Proc. 1978 COMPCON Conf. (IEEE)*, New York, 1978.
[23] WEIHL W., Local atomicity properties: modular concurrency control for abstract data types, *ACM TOPLAS* 11, 2 (April 1989) 249–282.
[24] ZDONIK S. & WEGNER P., Language and methodology for object-oriented database environments, *Proc. 19th Ann. Hawaii Inter. Conf. on Sys. Sci.*, Hawaii, Jan 1986.

A Flexible Consistency Model
for Persistent Data
in Software-Process Programming Languages

Stanley M. Sutton, Jr.
Department of Computer Science
University of Colorado
Boulder, Colorado 80309-0430
sutton@boulder.colorado.edu

July 24, 1990

Abstract

Software-process programming is the modeling of software development processes using formal languages. Software-process programming languages (SPPLs) must facilitate management of the persistent objects which comprise a software product. An important aspect of software object management is consistency management, including transaction management.

FCM is a flexible consistency model for SPPLs. Consistency is defined with respect to predicates over objects. Predicates can be optionally enforced like constraints; however, their default enforcement can be turned on and off dynamically. The scope of a predicate and its enforcement may be global or local. FCM also includes five composite statements: the serial, atomic, suspend, enforce, and allow statements. These provide specialized combinations of serializability, atomicity, and local control over predicate enforcement. They can be composed to achieve the effects of various higher-level transaction models, such as nested transactions. These features also enable FCM to accommodate inconsistency as a natural rather than exceptional condition.

1 Introduction

This paper presents a consistency-management model for persistent data in software-process programming languages. Software-process programming is the modeling of software development processes using formal languages [12]. Software-process programs are, in effect, meta-programs which guide software development processes. Process programming is receiving increasing attention [15,20,5,7,9]. This approach to the formalization of software processes offers many potential advantages, including increased consistency of execution, the ability to analyze, test, and debug, the possibility of automation, and greater opportunity for the reuse, communication, and evolution of software processes.

Process programs may represent all phases of the software life-cycle. They serve to control and integrate project-specific development activities and also environment support functions. These activities and functions include software-object management, i.e. the management of the persistent objects that comprise the intermediate and final products of software development: requirements, designs, code, test cases, analysis results, project-management data, and so on. Among the requirements for software object management are appropriate capabilities for transaction and consistency management [21,8,14,15,16].

The conventional database transaction model is widely recognized as inadequate for software-object management and other design activities [3,4,13,14]. It provides necessary but insufficiently flexible control over serializability, atomicity, and constraint enforcement, and it is intolerant of inconsistency. Flexible support for transaction and consistency management is needed when transactions are long lasting and prone to errors and the criteria for consistency are process-dependent, evolving, and difficult to maintain. The flexible consistency model presented here addresses these conditions. It includes global and local predicates by which the consistency of persistent data can be specified and tested, mechanisms for optionally enforcing predicates to achieve the effects of constraints or assertions, and several transaction-like constructs for local control over predicate enforcement, serializability, and atomicity.

The flexible consistency model is intended to support the management of persistent data through a software-process programming language (SPPL). The model has been designed as part of the definition of APPL/A, a prototype SPPL which is being developed in conjunction with the Arcadia project [20]. APPL/A is an extension of Ada [1]. It provides persistent relations with programmable implementations and derived attributes, triggers on relation operations, predicates over relations, and several transaction-like control constructs for composite operations on relations. The predicates and control constructs are based on the model presented here. The details of APPL/A are beyond the scope of this report; more information can be found in [17,19]. A more complete discussion of the consistency model is available in [18].

The remainder of this paper is organized as follows: Section 2 discusses consistency in software processes and identifies some capabilities for a flexible consistency model. Section 3 presents the flexible consistency model "FCM." Section 4 presents a concise example of many of its features and shows how these can be combined to achieve various effects. Section 5 discusses several issues raised by the model, and Section 6 reviews related work. Section 7 summarizes the paper.

2   Consistency in Software Processes

The consistency of objects is usually judged relative to predicates, either explicit or implicit. The goal of consistency management is to assure that selected predicates are satisfied at appropriate times. This is usually achieved by enforcing those predicates as constraints. Conventional databases provide a simple model of consistency based on serializable, atomic transactions. Constraints on data are assumed not to apply during a transaction. Serializability assures that one transaction cannot see the incomplete or inconsistent results of another (or interfere with the work of another). Atomicity assures that transactions with results that are incorrect or inconsistent have no net effect on data, thus preserving consistency. The capabilities of conventional transactions are necessary but insufficient for consistency management in software processes. This section presents arguments in favor of a more flexible model of consistency for software object management.

Flexibility in Determining *When* Predicates are Enforced: It is impractical to strictly enforce all predicates at all times, e.g. during composite updates. The conventional transaction model provides for the suspension of all constraints during a transaction. However, the serializability associated with conventional transactions makes them impractical for long-term development processes. Additionally, the conventional transaction model does not allow for representation of the longer-term evolution of consistency. It is not selective with respect to the enforcement of constraints, and it does not recognize that some constraints are not relevant during some phases of development. A more appropriate approach would enable constraints to be enforced only when relevant. Such optionally-enforcible constraints would allow the criteria for consistency to evolve over time and it would free processes from the burden of maintaining constraints that are irrelevant.

Flexibility in Determining *Where* Predicates are Enforced: A similar argument suggests that software processes would also benefit from flexible control over the scope of predicate enforcement. In the conventional model, constraints apply over the whole database and hence equally to all processes that operate on the database. This model of global, process-independent constraints is inadequate for software processes. It does not address the case in which some but not all constraints should be suspended for a process. Neither does it address the case in which an unenforced predicate should be treated like a constraint, for example, as a precondition to or assertion on a specific process. In an environment where concurrent processes generally require different constraints, it is not effective to enforce all indicated constraints on all processes. Thus it should be possible to locally suspend or enforce selected constraints.

Functional Specialization: Conventional transactions provide a combination of concurrency control, suspension of constraint enforcement, and atomicity. A criticism of conventional transactions with respect to software object management is that they provide all of these kinds of functionality where more specialized capabilities may be sufficient, e.g. serializability without atomicity. In [13] it is suggested that separate units of concurrency control and consistency should perhaps be provided for software object management. Taking this suggestion further, it may be hypothesized that software processes require a variety of kinds of "units" for object management and consistency maintenance.

Flexibility to Accommodate Inconsistency: Inconsistency is a common occurrence in software processes. One cause of inconsistency is that not all constraints are known in advance; new constraints are discovered during development. When new constraints are imposed they may not be satisfied by existing objects. Another cause of inconsistency is that software processes are relatively prone to error compared to conventional transactions. Many large-scale software processes, such as the specification of requirements or the development of designs, are lengthy, open-ended, and proceed by trial and error. All of these factors tend to promote results which are, for substantial periods, incorrect, inconsistent, and incomplete. Yet another cause of inconsistency in software processes is conflicts between processes. While a project overall may have a single, well-defined goal, the various subprocesses may have competing subgoals. In this respect the criteria for consistency are process-relative. These considerations imply that inconsistency is inherent in software processes. If inconsistency is inescapable then software processes may be well served by a consistency model in which inconsistency can be *accommodated*. The accommodation of inconsistency is called for in [2].

Capabilities for a Flexible Consistency Model: The paragraphs above argue that several kinds of flexibility are needed for consistency management in software processes. The following capabilities address that need:

1. The ability to specify predicates on data that may be enforced both globally, i.e. for all processes, and locally, i.e. for individual processes.

2. The ability to "turn on and off" the default enforcement of both global and local predicates.

3. The ability to locally and (more or less) independently control serializability, actual predicate enforcement (to override default enforcement), and atomicity (with respect to consistency and/or completeness of work).

These capabilities would enable inconsistency to be accommodated in several ways. For example, the ability to turn off predicate enforcement globally or locally would allow processes to proceed in the face of inconsistency; this would enable inconsistency to be ignored and/or repaired. Conversely, the ability to turn on predicate enforcement can assure that processes proceed only when consistency obtains.

These capabilities would give SPPLs a degree of flexibility in consistency management that is alien to conventional persistent object systems. They provide the basis for the flexible consistency model defined in the next section.

3   FCM: A Flexible Consistency Model

This section presents a flexible consistency model for software processes, "FCM." FCM is described in terms of a persistent process-programming language. However, the concepts in FCM should be adaptable to software environments and persistent object systems generally, and they should also be useful in other applications with complex requirements for consistency management.

This section begins with a description of the execution model presumed by FCM. FCM itself is then presented in two parts: predicates and consistency, and transaction-like statements for concurrency control, atomicity, and control of predicate enforcement.

3.1   Execution Model

The execution model of FCM includes nesting and concurrency as in the nested transaction model of Moss [11]. It also includes subroutines and user-defined abstract data types. In FCM subroutines can be called from transactions as a kind of dynamic subtransaction. User-defined abstract data types have non-primitive operations, i.e. operations that are implemented in terms of operations on other types. Those other types may themselves be abstract, so that one abstract type may be implemented in terms of others. The operations on an object, whether of a primitive or abstract type, are assumed to be atomic and serializable with respect to other operations on that object. An execution model which includes not only concurrency and nesting but also subroutines and abstract data types is essential for process programming.

3.2   Predicates and Consistency

This section defines the FCM model of consistency in terms of predicates and their enforcement.

Predicates   In FCM the consistency of software objects is judged with respect to predicates. Predicates are distinguished class of boolean functions over (possibly selected classes of) software objects. Predicates are defined separately from objects. In APPL/A, for example, predicate units represent predicate logic expressions over separately defined relations. (Two predicates in APPL/A syntax are shown in Figure 1 as part of the example of Section 4.1.)

Predicate Enforcement   A predicate can be *enforced* with respect to a process, in which case no operation by that process on the objects to which the predicate applies is allowed to terminate in violation of the predicate. Any such operation is undone and results in the raising of an exception. However, an enforced predicate need *not* be satisfied *during* an operation on an object to which the predicate applies. By analogy with conventional transactions, each operation on an object is regarded as a unit of consistency and atomicity with respect to predicates enforced on that object. The (default) enforcement of predicates (except for global predicates declared enforced) is optional and can be changed dynamically.

Predicate Extent   A predicate has an extent, which is either global or not. A predicate can be declared global. The extent of a global predicate automatically subsumes all programs which use objects to which the predicate refers. A predicate that is not declared global is called *local*. A local predicate may be included optionally in any program but it need not be included in any; its extent is restricted to those programs in which it is explicitly included.

Default and Actual Enforcement; Enforcement Setting Contexts   A predicate is potentially enforcible throughout its extent. Whether a predicate is actually enforced at a given point in the execution of a process depends on the *default enforcement* of the predicate or the applicability of an *enforcement-setting* context.

- Each predicate has a default enforcement. The default enforcement is represented by a boolean attribute of the predicate (discussed below). If the value of this attribute is **true** then the predicate is enforced by default; otherwise, it is not.

- There are two kinds of enforcement-setting contexts. One is operations on objects. Within an operation on an object the predicates that apply to that object are not enforced. The other includes special block statements (described in Section 3.3). These mandate or suspend the enforcement of designated predicates, regardless of their default enforcement.

When no enforcement-setting context applies the actual enforcement of a predicate is determined by the default enforcement. Otherwise the actual enforcement is determined by the (statically or dynamically) applicable enforcement-setting context for the predicate.

Extent of Default Enforcement   The extent over which the default enforcement of a predicate applies depends on whether the predicate is global or local. A global predicate has a *collective* default enforcement which applies uniformly across all of the programs within the extent of the predicate. At any given time the predicate is enforced by default in either all or none of these programs. A local predicate has a non-collective or *individual* default enforcement for each program in the extent of the predicate. A local predicate is enforced in any one program independently of whether it is enforced in any other program.

Predicate "Enforced" Attributes   The representation and control of the default enforcement of a predicate also depends on whether the predicate is global or local. A global predicate has a single boolean attribute **enforced** which determines whether or not it is enforced by default; this single attribute is visible to all programs within the extent of the predicate. A global predicate can also be declared enforced, in which case the value of its **enforced** attribute is always **true** and cannot be changed. Such predicates are always enforced by default. A global predicate which is not declared enforced has an assignable **enforced** attribute. The default enforcement of such predicates can be changed by assignment to this attribute.

   A local predicate has one boolean attribute **enforced** for each program in which it is used. Each such program sees a separate value for this attribute, and that value determines whether the predicate is enforced by default within that program. Local predicates cannot be declared enforced. The value of each **enforced** attribute is assignable by the program in which it is visible.

Statement	Serializable	Enforcement-Setting	Atomic
Serial	yes	no	no
Suspend	yes	suspends[1]	yes[3]
Enforce	no	enforces[2]	no
Atomic	yes	no	yes[4]
Allow	yes	suspends[1]	no[5]

Notes:
1. Suspends enforcement locally for designated predicates.
2. Requires enforcement locally for designated predicates.
3. Rollback for violation of suspended predicates on termination.
4. Rollback for propagation of an exception.
5. Allows *existing* predicate violations to be perpetuated.

Table 1: Summary of Capabilities for FCM Consistency-Management Constructs

Control over assignment to **enforced** attributes is beyond the scope of FCM. In APPL/A a capability mechanism is defined for this purpose. Assignment to an **enforced** attribute is illustrated in Figure 2 (of Section 4.1) using this approach.

3.3   Control Constructs

As stated above, operations on objects are assumed to be individually serializable, atomic, and consistent with respect to predicates enforced on the object. However, some mechanism is needed to group individual operations into composite operations which have transaction-like properties. This section defines five composite statements that serve that purpose, the *suspend, enforce, allow, serial,* and *atomic* statements. These are referred to below as the consistency-management statements, or "CM" statements.

3.3.1   Overview

The CM statements are block statements which provide various combinations of serializability, atomicity (rollback), and control over predicate enforcement. The statements provide more specialized control over these capabilities than do conventional transactions. The suspend, enforce, and allow statements control the local enforcement of predicates, the suspend and atomic statements are atomic (i.e. may roll back), and all but the enforce statement are serializable for operations on some set of objects. These capabilities are summarized in Table 3.3.1.

As indicated in the table, some of the CM statements provide combinations of capabilities and some capabilities are not available individually. The statements thus provide a middle ground between several constructs with completely orthogonal capabilities and one construct that integrates all capabilities. One could argue that the availability of completely orthogonal constructs would further increase the flexibility of FCM. Thus the design of the statements deserves some justification.

The initial impetus for the design of the CM statements was to separate capabilities found in conventional transactions. This approach is a generalization of the suggestion in [13] that units of consistency and concurrency control be separated. However, to follow this approach to the extreme could lead to serious problems in object management. For example, if atomicity is not coupled with serializability, then concurrent processes may reference data in a state which is subsequently rolled back, leading to inconsistency or cascading rollback. A similar argument applies to the suspension of predicate enforcement: A process which suspends predicate enforcement may create inconsistency; if this process does not hold serializable access to the affected objects then it may interfere with concurrent processes that depend on the consistency of those objects. In order to avoid these conflicts, serializability is associated with those statements that may roll back or that suspend predicate enforcement.

3.3.2   The Consistency Management Statements

This subsection describes the five CM statements. The descriptions apply to the base case in which the statements are not composed with one another.

The Serial Statement   Simple serializable access to objects can be obtained with the serial statement. The serial statement includes a "read-write list" which designates objects to which serializable read or write access is desired (other kinds of access could be added). A serial statement is used in Figure 2.

The serial statement does not affect the default or actual enforcement of predicates. Within a serial statement any operation that violates an enforced predicate is individually rolled back; there is no rollback for the statement as a whole.

The Suspend Statement   The suspend statement provides a context in which the actual enforcement of designated predicates is temporarily and locally suspended. The suspend statement provides serializable write access to the objects to which the suspended predicates apply. Write operations on these objects are logged. Upon completion of the suspend statement any of the suspended predicates which are enforced in the surrounding scope must be satisfied or the logged operations are rolled back. A suspend statement is shown in Figures 2 and 3.

The suspend statement does not affect the actual (or default) enforcement of predicates that are not suspended. The violation of an enforced predicate within the suspend results in the undoing of the violating operation and the raising of an exception. The results of the suspend statement are rolled back if and only if the statement terminates (normally or abnormally) in violation of a suspended predicate which is enforced in the surrounding scope.

The Enforce Statement   The enforce statement provides a context in which the actual enforcement of designated predicates is temporarily and locally imposed rather than suspended. Any operation within the scope of the enforce statement that violates an enforced predicate is individually undone as it occurs. Consequently, there is no need for rollback for the statement as a whole. Because there is no need to protect concurrent processes from rollback or consistency violations, the enforce statement is not serializable. (However, if desired, serializable access to objects can be obtained by nesting an enforce statement within a serial statement.) An enforce statement is used in Figures 2 and 4.

The Allow Statement   The allow statement also creates a context in which the enforcement of predicates is suspended. Any designated predicate that is violated upon entry to the allow may be violated by operations within the allow *and also upon exit from it*. This allows an *existing* predicate violation to be perpetuated and thereby admits the possibility of partial repair of the violation. No other enforced predicates may be violated within or upon completion of the statement. The violation of any other predicate by an operation in the allow statement causes that particular operation to be undone (although a suspend statement can be nested within an allow statement to suspend the enforcement of other predicates). There is no rollback for the statement as a whole. However, because it suspends the enforcement of violated predicates, the allow statement is serializable with respect to operations on those predicates.

The Atomic Statement   Serializable recoverable access to objects can be obtained with the atomic statement. The atomic statement has a read-write list of objects to which serializable access is requested. Write operations on these objects are logged. The atomic statement does not affect predicate enforcement. However, the propagation of an exception from the atomic statement does cause rollback of the logged results of the statement. Because the atomic statement may entail rollback it is serializable. An atomic statement is used in Figures 3 and 4.

3.3.3   Composition of the Statements

The CM statements can be nested arbitrarily like conventional block statements. A CM statement may also occur in a subroutine called from another CM statement or from an operation on an object. The composition of CM statements and operations in these ways enables the construction of composite operations which combine capabilities or which have a more complicated structure than the basic statements. (Some combinations are described in Section 4.2.)

The condition in which one CM statement or data operation is nested within or called from another is referred to as the "composition" of the constructs. Two general approaches to composition are possible:

- **Combined composition**: the nested/called construct is functionally a subtransaction of the nesting/calling construct with respect to concurrency control and recovery.

- **Separate composition**: the nested/called construct is functionally a separate transaction from the nesting/calling construct with respect to concurrency control and recovery.

The combined approach is the default in FCM, but separate composed transactions can be explicitly designated. In the discussion below, "transaction" is used to refer to both serializable and recoverable statements and data operations (recall that data operations are assumed to be individually serializable and atomic). A nested/called transaction is referred to as a subtransaction of the nesting/calling transaction.

The rules for concurrency control and recovery for composed transactions in the combined case are essentially those defined by Moss for nested, concurrent transactions [11]. The serializable/recoverable access held by a nesting/calling transaction is passed to its subtransactions. Subtransactions can obtain access that is not held by a nesting/calling transaction; upon termination of the subtransaction that access is assumed by the nesting/calling transaction (to preserve serializability and recoverability). Subtransactions can obtain serializable/recoverable access with respect to concurrent subtransactions. When a subtransaction commits its results become available within the nesting/calling transaction. The rollback of a subtransaction does not entail the rollback of the nesting/calling transaction or sibling transactions (although these may rollback conditionally if desired). The rollback of a transaction does entail the rollback of its subtransactions.

Within a separate subtransaction the rules for concurrency control and recovery are the same as they are for a combined subtransaction. However, with respect to serializability and recovery, a separate subtransaction is functionally distinct from the transaction which lexically nests or calls it. The separate transaction does not inherit any access from the nesting/calling transaction. Serializable/recoverable access held by a separate transaction is released when the transaction terminates and is not assumed by the nesting/calling transaction. A separate transaction commits or aborts its results upon termination independently of the nesting/calling transaction. In particular, the final commitment of the separate transaction is not dependent on the final commitment of the nesting/calling transaction, and the separate transaction may commit even if the nesting/calling transaction aborts. Thus a separate transaction is logically a top-level transaction even though it is lexically composed with another transaction.

The general advantages of combined composed transactions include the subdivision of labor, encapsulation of potential failures, and opportunities for concurrency and distribution. In the context of software processes, a combined composed transaction can be used to coordinate related or cooperating subprocesses, for example, several programmers working as a team on a single implementation task.

The principal advantages of separate transactions are that they enable a single lexical transaction to commit (or abort) various results independently and to acquire and release serializable access to objects differentially (thus promoting concurrency and data sharing). Separate transactions also provide a lexical mechanism for the synchronization of transactions that are functionally distinct. In the context of software processes, separate composed transactions can be used like combined composed transactions to coordinate subprocesses, including subprocesses that are not necessarily cooperative. Separate composed transactions also have two special applications in software processes. One is the persistent logging of process activity, where the information logged is committed even if the including transaction is aborted. This information can be especially useful for process control and debugging. The second is in the "savepointing" of the intermediate results of a transaction so that not all of the work of the transaction is lost in the event of rollback. This is especially important in software processes (and other design activities) where transactions may be very long and difficult to redo.

4   Examples

This section has two parts. The first is an example of consistency management in a simple analysis process. The second discusses how the CM statements can be nested to achieve various transaction-like effects. Several more examples are found in [18].

```
global enforced predicate At_Most_One_Parent is
-- Test whether any node in the tree has more than one parent
    every t1 in Bin_Tree satisfies
        if t1.left_child /= ''none'' then
            no t2 in Bin_Tree satisfies
                ((t2.left_child = t1.left_child or
                  t2.right_child = t1.left_child) and t2 /= t1)
            end no
        end if
    and -- similarly for t1.right_child
        ...
    end every;
end At_Most_One_Parent;



predicate No_Dangling_Children is
-- Test whether all named children exist
    every t1 in Bin_Tree satisfies
        if t1.left_child /= ''none'' then
            some t2 in Bin_Tree satisfies
                t1.left_child = t2.name
            end some
        end if
    and -- similarly for t1.right_child
        ...
    end every;
end No_Dangling_Children;
```

Figure 1: Predicates in an APPL/A-like Syntax

4.1 Consistency Management in an Analysis Process

This example illustrates several of the features of FCM using an APPL/A-like syntax. The example is based
on the relation **Bin_Tree** (not shown) which represents a binary tree. **Bin_Tree** has attributes **name** (the
name of a node), **data** (the data for a node), and **left_child** and **right_child**, the names of the children
of a node. Two predicates (shown in Figure 1) characterize the structure of the tree; a third predicate
(**Data_OK**, not shown) characterizes the data at a node. The procedure **Analyze_Bin_Tree_Data** (sketched in
Figure 2) represents an (unspecified) analysis of data in the tree. It references the predicates and controls
their enforcement by means of predicate **enforced** attributes (using the capability mechanism defined in
APPL/A). It also makes use of several of the consistency management statements. Additional comments
are provided in the figures.

4.2 Some Combinations of Consistency-Management Statements

The consistency management statements can be combined to obtain composite effects, some of which are
conventional while others are not. Some useful combinations are described in the following paragraphs.
Many other combinations are possible.

Conventional Flat Transactions: A suspend statement for predicates that apply to a given object can
be nested within an atomic statement that writes to that object to achieve the effects of a conventional
transaction, i.e. a serializable, consistent, and complete unit of work with respect to the object. An example
is sketched in Figure 3.

```
with Bin_Tree;                          -- shared binary-tree relation
with No_Dangling_Children, Data_OK;     -- optional local predicates
-- Data_OK applies to data stored in tree nodes
-- global enforced predicate At_Most_One_Parent implicitly
-- included and enforced

procedure Analyze_Bin_Tree_Data is
    i:  integer;    -- represents a capability to set predicate enforcement
begin
    -- acquire No_Dangling_Children to turn on its enforcement
    i := No_Dangling_Children'acquire;          -- get the capability
    No_Dangling_Children'enforced(i, true);     -- set the predicate
    -- now must satisfy No_Dangling_Children and At_Most_One_Parent both

    serial read Bin_Tree;        -- exclude writers during analysis
    begin
        if not (No_Dangling_Children and At_Most_One_Parent) then
            -- repair tree structure prior to analysis
            suspend No_Dangling_Children, At_Most_One_Parent;
                -- serial write access to Bin_Tree within suspend
                Bin_Tree.update(...);   -- needn't satisfy either predicate
                ...                     --   within suspend;
            end suspend;                -- must satisfy both upon completion
        end if;                         --    or rollback ensues

        -- perform the analysis
        enforce Data_OK;            -- must also satisfy Data_OK within enforce
        begin
            -- analyze data
            ...
        end enforce;
    end serial;
end Analyze_Bin_Tree_Data;
```

Figure 2: Consistency Management in an Analysis Process

Conventional Nested Transactions: Several suspend statements that apply to an object can be nested sequentially and/or concurrently within an atomic statement that writes that object to achieve the effects of the nested concurrent transactions of Moss [11].

"Assertion" Transactions: An enforce statement for predicates over an object can be nested within an atomic statement that updates that object to achieve an effect complementary to conventional transactions. The enforced predicate becomes an assertion on the transaction. The violation of that predicate by any individual operation within the enforce statement raises an exception. That exception indirectly causes the whole construct to be rolled back (when the exception is propagated through the atomic statement). An example is sketched in Figure 4.

"Repair-Enforce" Statements: An enforce statement a predicate can be nested in the latter part of a serial statement that writes to objects referenced by the predicate to construct a "repair-enforce" statement. A construction like this is used in Figure 2. The initial part of the serial statement is used to repair predicate violations free of interference from other processes. Following the repair operations the enforce statement assures continued satisfaction of required predicates.

```
atomic write O;           -- object O
begin
    suspend P;            -- predicate P applies to O
    begin
        -- operate on O here, unconstrained by P
        ...
    end suspend;          -- check P:  if violated, then rollback
                          -- operations in suspend and raise an
                          -- exception
end atomic;       -- rollback if any exception is propagated
```

Figure 3: Sketch of a "Conventional Flat Transaction" in FCM

```
atomic write O;           -- object O
begin
    enforce P;            -- predicate P applies to O
    begin
        -- operate on O here, constrained by P; violations
        -- of P cause an exception to be raised
        ...
    end enforce;
end atomic;       -- rollback if any exception is propagated
```

Figure 4: Sketch of an "Assertion Transaction" in FCM

5   Discussion

This section includes a statement of the FCM approach to alternative transaction models, discussions on the accommodation of inconsistency and the evolution of consistency, and comments on the complexity of the model and the feasibility of its implementation.

5.1   Alternative Transaction Models

The transaction model presented here consists of relatively "low level" constructs. This potential limitation is mitigated in that the constructs are relatively specialized and can be combined in general ways, in process programs, to implement "higher-level" transaction models.

Many advanced object management systems have incorporated higher-level transaction models directly. Two popular approaches are persistent versions [8,21] and long-term transactions with check-in and check-out [15,16,6]. The attitude taken in FCM is that these approaches are process-dependent and should not be embedded in an SPPL. Instead, an SPPL should provide mechanisms by which such high-level transaction models can be programmed. Low-level transactions are necessary in both of the above cases, e.g., for copying persistent versions or for implementing check-in and check-out operations. These functions can be supported by the CM statements of FCM. In APPL/A, features such as persistent relations and triggers provide additional support for the programming of systems based on persistent versions, check-in/check-out, or other high-level transaction models.

5.2   Accommodation of Inconsistency

The consistency model of conventional transactions is intended to assure that no transaction leaves the data in an inconsistent state. In effect this model prohibits constraint-violating operations on data. Balzer [2] has proposed a consistency model in which inconsistency is accommodated. In this model inconsistency (apparently) arises directly as a result of predicate-violating operations on data. Predicate violations must be repaired by transactions that can operate in the inconsistent state.

FCM also accommodates inconsistency. However, by analogy with the conventional model, no CM statement or operation is allowed to leave the data in violation of an enforced predicate. (The one exception is the allow statement, the purpose of which is precisely to enable an *existing* violation to be perpetuated while precluding the violation of additional predicates.) Instead, inconsistency typically arises when a predicate is newly enforced on existing data. Inconsistency can also arise when one process violates a predicate that is enforced locally in a second process; however, that second process is still constrained by the enforced predicate even if the first process is not. Thus the CM statements are required to preserve consistency, while the criteria for consistency may change from time to time and vary from place to place.

When inconsistency occurs, it can be handled straightforwardly and unexceptionally. The default enforcement of a violated predicate can be turned off indefinitely by setting its enforced attribute to false. This removes the prior constraint for all affected processes. Alternatively, the actual enforcement of the violated predicate can be suspended locally and temporarily within a suspend or allow statement. The constraint still applies outside the statement, but within the statement work can proceed despite the violation. Either of these approaches can be used to repair the violation so that the predicate will be satisfied when and where it is enforced. These approaches (except for the suspend statement) also enable work other than repairs to be performed in spite of the violation.

Despite the availability of mechanisms which enable inconsistency to be tolerated, processes which require consistency are still protected from inconsistency. When a violated predicate is not suspended for a process, that process cannot perform work on the data to which the predicate applies (or an exception is raised). In this case the predicate still acts like a constraint, and the process is prevented from executing. Conversely, the process is able to execute only when required conditions obtain.

5.3 Evolution of Consistency

FCM facilitates the evolution of consistency in several ways. The model is neutral with respect to the addition and deletion of predicates, however both of these actions can be accommodated. The addition of an enforced global predicate may strengthen constraints on data, but any inconsistency introduced by the predicate can be handled as described in the previous subsection. The deletion of an existing global predicate can only weaken constraints. This is not generally a problem, except for processes which depend on conditions implied by the predicate for their correct execution. In this case an affected process may introduce a new local (i.e. non-global) predicate. That predicate can be enforced locally to assure that an exception will be raised in the process if the condition is not met. However, since the predicate is only local, it cannot be enforced on other processes, and so they are unaffected. The introduction of a local predicate has no immediate effect because such predicates are not initially enforced by default. The deletion of a local predicate has only a local effect which can be countered, if problematic, by reintroducing the predicate. FCM does explicitly represent the evolution of default enforcement for predicates using assignable `enforced` attributes. Changes in default enforcement are similar in effect to the introduction or deletion of a predicate and can be handled similarly.

In FCM the evolution of consistency is also facilitated by controls which enable operations to be made either independent of or dependent on global predicates (and thus on changes to those predicates). The suspend, allow, and enforce statements can be used to encapsulate operations in contexts in which the actual enforcement of predicates is specified independently of the surrounding context. In this case the encapsulated operations are insulated from changes to enforcement in the surrounding context. Alternatively, operations can be abstracted in an ordinary subroutine which can be called from various contexts. Predicate enforcement in the subroutine is determined by enforcement at the point of call; hence, changes to enforcement at the point of call directly affect enforcement in the subroutine.

5.4 Complexity of the Model

FCM provides flexibility in consistency management but at the cost of some complexity. This complexity derives largely from the the intended domain of application for the model, software development processes, in which the management of consistency is inherently complex. Some of the complexity derives from the decision to provide specialized rather than monolithic constructs and to include both global and local controls over consistency. However, this approach seems essential to obtaining needed flexibility.

The model may seem too complex for use by "ordinary" programmers. In fact, though, the language is intended for use by software engineers who have responsibility for the complex problems of consistency management in software processes. (The model should also be useful to design engineers in other areas where consistency management is complicated.) Elements of the model may still be readily adopted by less sophisticated programmers; for example, it is straightforward to program simple transaction-like operations using the consistency-management statements (as described in Section 4.2).

5.5 Implementation Feasibility

FCM, because it is different from conventional transaction models, raises certain implementation issues. It relies largely on the same basic capabilities as conventional transaction management systems, i.e. logging, concurrency control, and recovery. However, it also requires the ability to manage predicates and to trace the dynamic relationships among nested and called transactions. The former requires support for runtime changes to predicate `enforced` attributes and automatic evaluation of predicates. The latter requires the ability to thread the runtime stack and to supplement stack frames with additional information for transaction and predicate management. In both cases the underlying mechanisms are conceptually straightforward.

An architectural design for transaction management of the CM statements has been developed in conjunction with the effort to implement APPL/A. The design includes algorithms for logging and recovery and assumes standard locking for concurrency control. The design depends on the use of the runtime stack to store and retrieve information about transactions and predicates, and it assumes basic services for logging, recovery, concurrency control, and predicate management. Based on these assumptions, each CM statement can be translated into standard Ada supplemented with calls to store and retrieve needed information and to invoke required services. The underlying capabilities are individually well understood; the translation demonstrates that these capabilities can be orchestrated to provide the desired combination of effects. The design thus indicates that an FCM implementation in APPL/A is feasible.

6 Related Work

As discussed above, Balzer [2] has advocated the accommodation of inconsistency in data management systems. He has proposed a rule-based approach in which predicates are represented as data. In FCM, in contrast, predicates are represented by program units, i.e. code. Balzer's model, like FCM, allows some processes to operate in an inconsistent state but prevents others.

Some systems, for example HiPAC [10] and the software environment proposed in [16], provide for the enforcement of *implicit* constraints by triggers. This approach provides flexibility for consistency maintenance but puts the burden of maintenance on the programmer of the triggers. A problem with this approach is that the constraints are not explicit. It can be difficult to extract a characterization of consistency from the triggers or to be assured that desired constraints will be enforced. Another problem is that inconsistency persists while the triggered operations are under way, so that it can be difficult to tell when a consistent state obtains.

Pu, Kaiser, and Hutichinson [14] define split-transaction and join-transaction operations which respectively enable parts of a single transaction to be committed separately and separate transactions to be committed together. These operations may lead to non-serializable behavior with respect to the original transactions but they preserve the serializability of the committed transactions. An important aspect of their model is that transaction operations are controlled dynamically by users. This is more dynamism than is admitted by the FCM model, in which transaction structure is static. The split/join model is strictly a transaction model; it does not deal with constraints or consistency management otherwise.

Korth and Speegle [8] introduce a model of correctness without serializability. Their model includes nested transactions based on Moss's model [11], predicates which define a database invariant and pre- and post-conditions for transactions, and persistent versions. The role of predicates in their model is somewhat different than in FCM, but similar effects can be achieved in both models. Their model does not allow predicate enforcement to be turned on and off, but, like FCM, it provides a uniform mechanism for expressing and enforcing consistency throughout a hierarchy of nested transactions. In Korth and Speegle's model, unlike FCM, persistent versions are used to enhance concurrency. Each update of an object creates a new version of it, but old versions are retained; transactions which require potentially conflicting access to an object can be given concurrent access to separate copies of it. This model admits more classes of concurrency than does FCM, but it entails the problem of merging separate versions when a single result is desired from concurrent transactions.

7   Summary

FCM is a flexible consistency model, including a flexible transaction model, for the management of persistent data in software-process programming languages. Consistency in FCM is defined with respect to predicates over data. Predicates can be enforced within a process, in which case they have the effect of postconditions on operations by that process. The default enforcement of predicate can be turned on and off dynamically. The scope of a predicate and its enforcement may be global or local.

FCM also includes five block statements with various transaction-like properties: the serial, atomic, suspend, enforce, and allow statements. These statements provide various combinations of serializability, atomicity, and control over predicate enforcement. They can be composed to achieve the effects of conventional transactions, nested transactions, "assertion transactions", and other constructs.

FCM accommodates inconsistency in a natural way. When inconsistency arises it can be ignored or repaired by turning off the enforcement of the violated predicate or by using a suspend or allow statement to perform work regardless of the violation. Processes can protect themselves from inconsistency by controlling the enforcement of predicates and by serializing access to data.

Taken together the features of FCM provide great flexibility in consistency management. They provide global and local control over when and where predicates are enforced, they support serializable access to data under a variety of conditions, and they allow inconsistency to arise and be handled in a natural way. When embedded in a general-purpose process-programming language FCM should enable the construction of process-dependent higher-level transaction and consistency models. FCM should thus greatly enhance consistency management for software process programs.

8   Acknowledgements

This research was supported by the Defense Advanced Research Projects Agency, through DARPA Order #6100, Program Code 7E20, which was funded through grant #CCR-8705162 from the National Science Foundation. Support was also provided by the Naval Ocean Systems Center and the Office of Naval Technology.

The design of APPL/A has been supervised by Lee Osterweil and Dennis Heimbigner. With respect to the present work the author wishes especially to thank Frank Belz for his reading of the first draft; Frank, Christine Shu, Lolo Penedo, and Sandy Schreyer at TRW comments on presentations of later material; and Dennis Heimbigner for his reading of a later draft and discussion of many of the ideas included here. Thanks also to other members of the Arcadia consortium who have provided comments on this material and on related work in APPL/A.

References

[1] *Reference Manual for the Ada Programming Language.* United States Department of Defense, 1983. ANSI/MIL-STD-1815A-1983.

[2] Robert Balzer. Tolerating inconsistency. In *5th International Software Process Workshop – Preprints*, October 1989. Kennebunkport, Maine, October, 1989.

[3] F. Bancilhon, W. Kim, and H. Korth. A model of CAD transactions. In *Proc. of the Eleventh International Conf. on Very Large Databases*, 1985.

[4] Philip A. Bernstein. Database system support for software engineering – an extended abstract. In *Ninth International Conference on Software Engineering*, pages 166–178, ACM, 1987.

[5] Thomas E. Cheatham. Process programming and process models. In *5th International Software Process Workshop – Preprints*, October 1989. Kennebunkport, Maine, October, 1989.

[6] Klaus R. Dittrich, Willi Gotthard, and Peter C. Lockemann. DAMOKLES – a database system for software engineering environments. In *International Workshop on Advanced Programming Environments*, IFIP WG2.4, 1986.

[7] Takuya Katayama. A hierarchical and functional approach to software process description. In Colin Tully, editor, *Proc. 4th International Software Process Workshop*, pages 87 – 92, Moretonhampstead, Devon, U.K., May, 1988, 1988. ACM SIGSOFT Software Engineering Notes, v. 14, n. 4, June 1989.

[8] Henry F. Korth and Gregory F. Speegle. Formal model of correctness without serializability. In *Proc. of the ACM SIGMOD International Conference on the Management of Data*, pages 379 – 386, 1988.

[9] Yoshihiro Matsumoto, Kiyoshi Agusa, and Tsuneo Ajisaka. A software process model based on unit workload network. In *5th International Software Process Workshop – Preprints*, October 1989. Kennebunkport, Maine, October, 1989.

[10] Dennis R. McCarthy and Umeshwar Dayal. The architecture of an active data base management system. In *Proc. of the ACM SIGMOD International Conf. on the Management of Data*, pages 215 – 224, 1989.

[11] J. Eliot B. Moss. *Nested Transactions: An Approach to Reliable Distributed Computing*. PhD thesis, Massachusetts Institute of Technology, May 1981.

[12] Leon J. Osterweil. Software processes are software too. In *Proc. Ninth International Conference on Software Engineering*, 1987.

[13] Maria H. Penedo, Erhard Ploedereder, and Ian Thomas. Object management issues for software engineering environments – workshop report. In *Proc. ACM SIGSOFT/SIGPLAN Software Engineering Symposium on Practical Software Development Environments*, pages 226 – 234, ACM, 1988.

[14] Calton Pu, Gail E. Kaiser, and Norman Hutchinson. Split-transactions for open-ended activities. In *Proc. of the Fourteenth International Conf. on Very Large Data Bases*, pages 26 – 37, 1988.

[15] Jayashree Ramanathan and Soumitra Sarkar. Customized assistance for software lifecycle approaches. *IEEE Trans. on Software Engineering*, 14(6):749–757, June 1988.

[16] Soumitra Sarkar. *Data Model and Persistent Programming Language Features for Integrated Project Support Environments*. Technical Report OSU-CISRC-6/89-TR22, Computer and Information Science Research Center, The Ohio State University, Columbus, Ohio, 43201, June 1989.

[17] Stanley M. Sutton, Jr. *APPL/A: A Prototype Language for Software-Process Programming*. PhD thesis, University of Colorado, August 1990.

[18] Stanley M. Sutton, Jr. *FCM: A Flexible Consistency Model for Software Processes*. Technical Report CU-CS-462-90, University of Colorado, Department of Computer Science, Boulder, Colorado 80309, March 1990.

[19] Stanley M. Sutton, Jr., Dennis Heimbigner, and Leon J. Osterweil. Language constructs for managing change in process-centered environments. In *Proc. of the Fourth Symposium on Practical Software Development Environments*, 1990. Irvine, California.

[20] Richard N. Taylor, Frank C. Belz, Lori A. Clarke, Leon J. Osterweil, Richard W. Selby, Jack C. Wileden, Alexander Wolf, and Michal Young. Foundations for the Arcadia environment architecture. In *Proc. ACM SIGSOFT/SIGPLAN Software Engineering Symposium on Practical Software Development Environments*, pages 1 – 13, ACM, November 1988.

[21] J. Walpole, G. S. Blair, J. Malik, and J. R. Nicol. A unifying model for consistent distributed software development environments. In *Proc. Third ACM SIGSOFT/SIGPLAN Symposium on Practical Software Development Environments*, pages 183 – 190, November 1988. Special issue of SIGPLAN Notices, 24(2), February, 1989.

An Implementation of a Co-operative Locking Scheme for a Persistent Programming Language.

Richard Cooper, Andrew Roberts and Francis Wai
Dept. of Computing Science,
University of Glasgow,
17 Lilybank Gardens,
Glasgow G12 8QQ,
Scotland.

Abstract

Fernandez and Zdonik [ZF89] proposed a mechanism for managing transactions which groups users in order to permit them to work co-operatively. This paper reports an implementation of these ideas in the distributed persistent language, DPS-algol. The system as implemented provides support for many concurrent users on many applications. Users request access to database objects with a variety of locks available - from totally restrictive locks to completely unrestrictive. The paper describes the implementation and experience with using the system on a sample application.

Introduction

Database Management Systems (DBMS) support multi-user access to large amounts of distributed data. In traditional database applications, the pattern of concurrent data usage has been such that simultaneous users are expected to compete for data resources. An airline booking system must function so that only one Travel Agent can book a particular seat and therefore if a second attempt is made to book the seat during the first booking, the second Travel Agent is locked out having essentially lost the competition for the seat. Similarly, in a banking system, two transactions on a single account must proceed serially since otherwise one of the updates may be lost. Database systems which cater for applications of this kind therefore use a fairly simple mechanism for locking data. A query requests a shared lock, so that many enquiries on data can proceed simultaneously (restrictive read), while an update requests an exclusive lock, so that no other transaction can make use of the data item while the update is proceeding (restrictive write).

Extending database systems to cover more complex applications, notably design applications, means having to deal with different kinds of transaction, ones which are potentially long and may need to access data co-operatively. If two designers are modifying parts of a large and complex design, each may wish to view the other's changes and even to commit possibly overlapping changes. Where there is a conflict, these changes must be resolved by discussion. To support such applications successfully a modern DBMS must supply the ability to request more sophisticated locks, which permit co-operative working, and the ability to resolve potential conflicts by use of the communication channels which will already exist to provide distributed systems.

Fernandez and Zdonik [FZ89] propose an environment for supporting such methods of working. Their system provides support for many concurrent users on many applications. Users are arranged into a hierarchy of groups within which lock protocols are determined. They request access to database objects with a variety of available kinds of lock - from totally restrictive locks to completely unrestrictive. Access is requested from the parent group, which passes the request upwards eventually to a group which controls all access to the database the user's application maintains. The communication mode chosen by the user upon logging in determines what happens when a lock clash occurs, i.e. whether or not the user is informed. Inter-user communication will then enable the resolution of conflicts.

The Persistent Programming Paradigm provides an alternative methodology for designing database applications to the use of a traditional DBMS backed up by using one or more programming languages to describe any computation [AM85]. A Persistent Programming Language (PPL) is one within which the whole of the application can be described - the language supplying persistence and computational completeness. PPL's such as PS-algol [PS85] and Napier88 [MB89] contain sufficient constructs to enable data modelling, data storage, user interface design and the building of complete application development systems to be constructed on top of a small and simple core language [Co90].

However, PS-algol and Napier have been designed as single node languages and have not concentrated on the problems of managing distributed databases with many concurrent users. DPS-algol [Wai89] is a language which does tackle this area. The language adds to PS-algol a construct for describing multi-entry processes which may be started off on one node and then be accessed from other nodes of a network. Such processes can therefore intercommunicate and so provide a basis for building systems with inter-communicating applications and data management systems with a client-server architecture.

Given such a language, it becomes possible to attempt an implementation of Fernandez and Zdonik's ideas. This paper describes such an implementation, which allows the creation of a hierarchically structured set of Transaction Groups (TGs) containing users as leaves. Each TG is implemented as a DPS-algol process and there is one process which manages user access to the system. Applications are also installed as processes which are initiated when a user logs onto the system.

The paper proceeds by revisiting the original proposal and then DPS-algol is described, before the main section discusses the implementation work. There follows a description of a sample application, before the paper ends with the conclusions to be drawn from this work, including proposals for future systems.

1.   Transaction Groups - The Original Proposal

The design of Fernandez and Zdonik for the ObServer system [HZ87] contains proposals for non-restrictive locks, communication modes and a transaction group mechanism to control the communication. These aspects will now be described.

As an extension to the usual two kinds of lock available in most DBMS systems (restrictive read and restrictive write), six kinds of lock may be requested when accessing a data object.

null	This is used when a user wishes to monitor changes to an object.
nr-read	Non-restrictive read which permits other users to read or write to the object.
r-read	Restrictive read which prevents other users from writing to the object being read.
m-write	Multiple write which permits many users to simultaneous update the object.
nr-write	Non-restrictive write which permits others to request a simultaneous non-restrictive read.
r-write	Restrictive write, which provides exclusive access to the object.

In order for the non-restrictive modes to function effectively, communication must be established between co-operating transactions in order that they can be notified when possible conflicts occur. Therefore, when a transaction requests a lock, it must also suggest a communication mode from the following:

n-notify	No notification is given.
u-notify	The transaction is informed when the object is updated.
r-notify	The transaction is informed that another transaction cannot acquire a read lock.
w-notify	The transaction is informed that another transaction cannot acquire a write lock.
rw-notify	The transaction is informed that another transaction cannot acquire a read or a write lock.
ur-notify	Combination of u- and r-notify.
uw-notify	Combination of u- and w-notify.
urw-notify	Combination of u- and rw-notify.

Many of the combinations of lock and communication modes are meaningless and so [FZ89] gives the a table of valid modes. To this we add one additional communication mode has to permit a distinguished user to be set up which creates a log of all database accesses.

	null	nr-read	r-read	m-write	nr-write	r-write
n-notify		√	√	√	√	√
u-notify	√	√		√		
r-notify				√	√	√
w-notify		√	√	√	√	√
rw-notify				√	√	√
ur-notify				√		
uw-notify		√		√		
urw-notify				√		
monitor	√					

ObServer also provides complex facilities for broadcasting changes to objects. A transaction may keep hold of an object, but broadcast changes by *registering* the object, or it may make the change permanent in the database by *committing* the object or it may *abort* the changes. The last two operations release any locks held on the object. A transaction therefore has the ability to broadcast changes about an object which it then does not make permanent. Unrestricted use of such a system could produce chaos since users could get hold of ephemeral versions under the illusion that this committed data. Therefore the notion of a *transaction group* is proposed as a scoping mechanism.

A Transaction Group (TG) is a set of users or other TGs within which a particular sort of co-operation or competition is expected to occur. A group of designers in one department may well wish to broadcast non-permanent changes to each other, but not wish to allow others to see such changes. As the members of a TG are either users or other transaction groups, a hierarchy of TGs is created. Several aspects of transaction groups are described:

lock filter - this determines the set of locks which its members may request.
operation filter - this determines which database operations the members may execute.
lock translation - this determines a TGs relationship to its parent and indicates any strengthening of locks that the TG must perform in order to pass lock requests up the hierarchy.
object propagation - this determines when changes to an object are made public outside of the group.

Using these, various kinds of co-operative and competitive groups can be set up which do not interfere with the expected pattern of behaviour of each other.

2. An Example

Figure 1 presents a proposed set of transaction groups to maintain the events database of the Glasgow 1990 Year of Culture. Events will be continually added to the database and removed in the case of cancellations. The events included major festivals, such as MayFest, and one-off events. The database is to be made available to booking and information agencies and will not include booking information which will be held in a separate database which can operate in traditional competitive fashion.

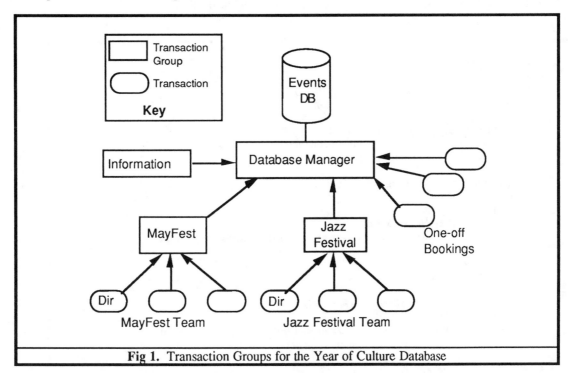

Fig 1. Transaction Groups for the Year of Culture Database

The following transaction groups are required:

Database Manager - a TG which controls all permanent changes to the database. It is the top of the tree of TGs and has as its members other TGs representing groups designing various major festivals, a TG which makes event information available and various ad-hoc transactions which affect information regarding one-off events. It has the following features:

Lock Filter - permits nr-write and nr-read locks. Thus the current state of the DB can be investigated at any time, but only one member can be updating a given event at any time. In general, members would request u-notify locks to check if a given venue is booked by another member.

Operation Filter - commit and abort transaction.

Lock Translation - no parent group.

Object Propagation - puts all committed data into the database.

MayFest - a TG for setting up the MayFest schedule. It contains various co-operative design transactions. The other major events would be implemented similarly. The features are:

Lock Filter - all non-restrictive locks. A designer can get a single writer lock on an event or a multiple writer lock within the group.

Operation Filter - all operations. A designer can abort, commit or register a change within the context of the group.

Lock Translation - all requests are translated into non-restrictive access.

Object Propagation - objects are propagated upwards when the director commits the change.

Information - a TG for ticket agencies which read the database. The features include:

Lock Filter - only nr-read locks are allowed.

Operation Filter - no updates allowed.

Lock Translation - no translation required.

Object Propagation - not required as this group does not update the database.

```
let eventManager= process
  with
    retrieve = entry( string, string -> string )
    book = entry( string, string, string )
  begin
    structure event( string venue, date, act )
    let events = a vector of events with suitable venues and dates ...
    let Nevents = ... the number of events

    let retrieve = entry( string where, when -> string )
      begin
        let answer := ""
        for  i = 1 to Nevents do
            if events(i)(venue) = where and events(i)(date) = when then
                answer := events(i)( act )
        answer
      end

    let book = entry( string where, when, who )
        for  i = 1 to Nevents do
            if events(i)(venue) = where and events(i)(date) = when then
                events(i)( act ) := who

    while true do accept retrieve || book
  end
```

Fig 2. A DPS-algol Process

3. DPS-algol - A Distributed Persistent Programming Language

PS-algol [PS85] is a member of the algol family which supports orthogonal persistence, first-class functions and graphical types. It is designed to be used in a non-distributed way with a single persistent store being held at a particular site and multiple users gaining access to the database by use of the communication protocols available for the system on top of which the language is installed. It has a competitive notion of concurrency control with extremely course granularity in that the unit of locking is the PS-algol database and only restrictive read and write locks are available. There is no method for users communicating with each other except by leaving items in the persistent store, which may only be accessed serially. However, it is possible to build transaction protocols on top of this which permitted atomic locking of finer granularity [Co90].

DPS-algol [Wai89] is a distributed extension of PS-algol which adds a construct for communication in the form of the multi-entry **process**. A process may be started at a given node and this makes available a set of entry-points which may then be called from any other site. As an example, the code fragment on the previous page shows a process which maintains access to a set of event objects, containing a venue, a date and a performer (null if no booking has yet been made). It provides two entries:

> *retrieve* returns the name of the act booked for a given time and place;

and   *book* sets the act for a given venue on a given date.

This process may then be started by the command:

let *dummy* := **start** *eventManager* **as** "eManager" **at** "vanuata"

Now another program on the same or another node can use the information as in:

```
for eventMan = "eManager" at "vanuata"
   with  book = entry( string, string, string )
   do eventMan @book( "Renfrew Ferry", "12 May", "Tracy Nelson" )
```

Some features of the language:

i) An entry call synchronises the two communicating processes.

ii) The **accept** command has the effect of a non-deterministic selection of one of the entries given - i.e. the first one which is called.

iii) The **for** command introduces a local process handle for the server process and only requires the naming of those entries which are going to be used.

iv) Each DPS process is independent from the others. That is, processes may start and kill each other, but there is no parent-child relationship (as is the case for instance in the UNIX™ fork command).

This mechanism is sufficient to permit programs on various machines to inter-communicate and is a suitable implementation platform for the scheme described above.

4. The Implementation

The system as implemented permits sets of applications, transaction groups and users to be registered within the architecture shown in Figure 3. Each application is implemented as a process which controls all interaction with it by users. Each group is also installed as a process, with the groups being arranged into a hierarchy with a system installed Root Group at the top and every other group being installed as the child of some previously installed group. A user is registered as a child of some group and is attached to a particular application - in this sense a particular user id is associated with a rôle rather than with an individual. A database holds the code of all applications as well as the pairings of users to applications. When the user logs on with a particular id, a copy of the associated transaction process will be started up. There are in addition, three distinguished processes: a user access Manager; the Root Group from which all other groups and users are spawned; and a Monitor application which logs attempts to access the database. The system runs on Sun 3 machines and each process may be run on any machine in a network in which the UDP/IP protocol is supported.

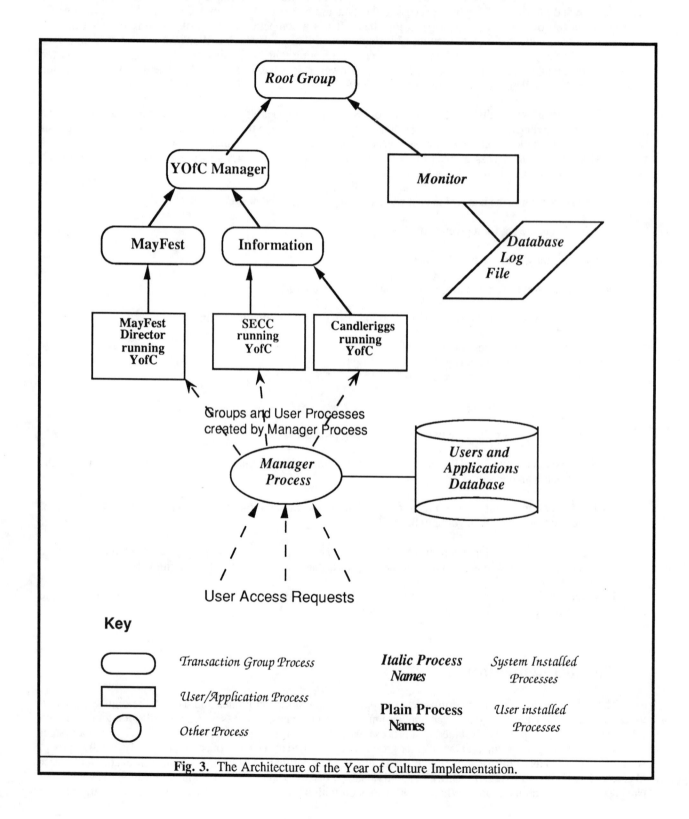

Fig. 3. The Architecture of the Year of Culture Implementation.

The software provided with the system includes:

a program for installing the Root Group and Monitor processes, as well as such system information as the lock/communication mode table given above;

a program for installing new groups and users;

a template for applications;

a program for starting the Manager process;

and   a program for logging users onto the system.

This section will deal with the algorithms for initiating and maintaining each of these. The next section will discuss a sample application. The final section will then discuss the implications of the implementation.

The system is initiated by invoking a program which starts the Manager Process and this has two entry points:

User.Request: This entry is called by any user wishing to access the system. Users access this by running another program called Logon which communicates with the Manager. The entry starts a process running for the user, which is a copy of the process for the user's application. If this is the first user on the system, the entry also starts the Root Group and Monitor processes. Finally, in order to maintain the correct access paths, the entry ensures that every group in the chain from the Root Group to the user is also active by starting their processes if they are not already active.

Process.Shutdown: This entry is called to log a user or a group out of the system. When all users and groups are logged out, the Root Group and Monitor are also killed.

Group processes (including the Root Group process) have several entry points, which can be divided into the following sets:

object access: there are entry points to request and release locks on objects, re-read objects and to register and commit changes;

inter-application communication: three entry points permit one application to find another, to request communication with another and to send a message (these remain unimplemented at present);

database control: there are entries to create and delete objects and to list object identifiers;

user control: there are two entries to permit application users to attach themselves to and detach themselves from groups;

parent communication: finally, there are a set of entry points for communicating with the parent group - these allow requests to passed up the group hierarchy.

Groups have several attributes which may be set when they are installed and are maintained during the lifetime of the group:

group persistence - should the group be automatically killed if all its children are?

operation filter - can the group cause a commit or register the data?

lock filter - which locks can the group can request?

main database - is the group the main controlling group of a particular database?

translation table - a table of how lock/communications mode of the group are translated for its parent.

machine - the machine the process is running on.

users - the set of group users which are currently active

and   items - a set of local copies of data items currently being used by members of the group.

All application processes (including the Monitor) must have at least the entry points:

Startup: This entry makes the application active in the system.

and   Receive.Notification. This entry allows communication with the application.

A notification in the system is a quintuple containing the identifier of the item being used, the user, the application, the lock requested and the reason for the notification.

The Monitor is a trivial application which logs all the notifications it receives into a file. In order to permit the Monitor to function an additional communication mode was devised. This is created to be used with NULL-locks and is created for use with the whole database. This means that any time any part of the database is touched, the Monitor process is informed via its Receive. Notification entry point. The latter will either be an indication that the item has been created, inserted into the DB, deleted, edited or accessed by another user or it will be the reason that a lock request has failed.

Applications are installed into the Users and Applications database using a template program which must be merged with the normal application as follows:

template	application
globals for holding applications	
	globals specific to the application
header for the application process	
	initialisation of constants and variables
definition of Startup and Receive.Notification entries connection of user with parent group	
	code for handling notifications
process startup accept Receive.Notification *in parallel with* commit process to the database.	body of application

The application code is modified so that every access to the database is replaced by a call to an entry in the parent group to request a lock, register and item, etc. Otherwise the code remains unchanged. The notification handler receives notifications as described above and can use them in whatever way is most appropriate to the application.

5.   A Demonstration Application.

To test out the system sample applications were produced. One of these was an implementation of the Year of Culture design system described above. This application recognises a number of classes of users: inquirers who belong to the Information TG; team directors; team designers; and one-off bookers. All of these access a screen that is split into three panels as shown in Figure 4. The upper panel holds scrollable lists of data; the centre panel permits queries and updates to be entered; and the bottom window displays any notifications which are received by the user. By setting up the TGs with various parameters, it is possible to prevent inquirers from gaining access to the update commands; to allow teams designers merely to register changes; and to allow directors and one-off bookers to commit changes.

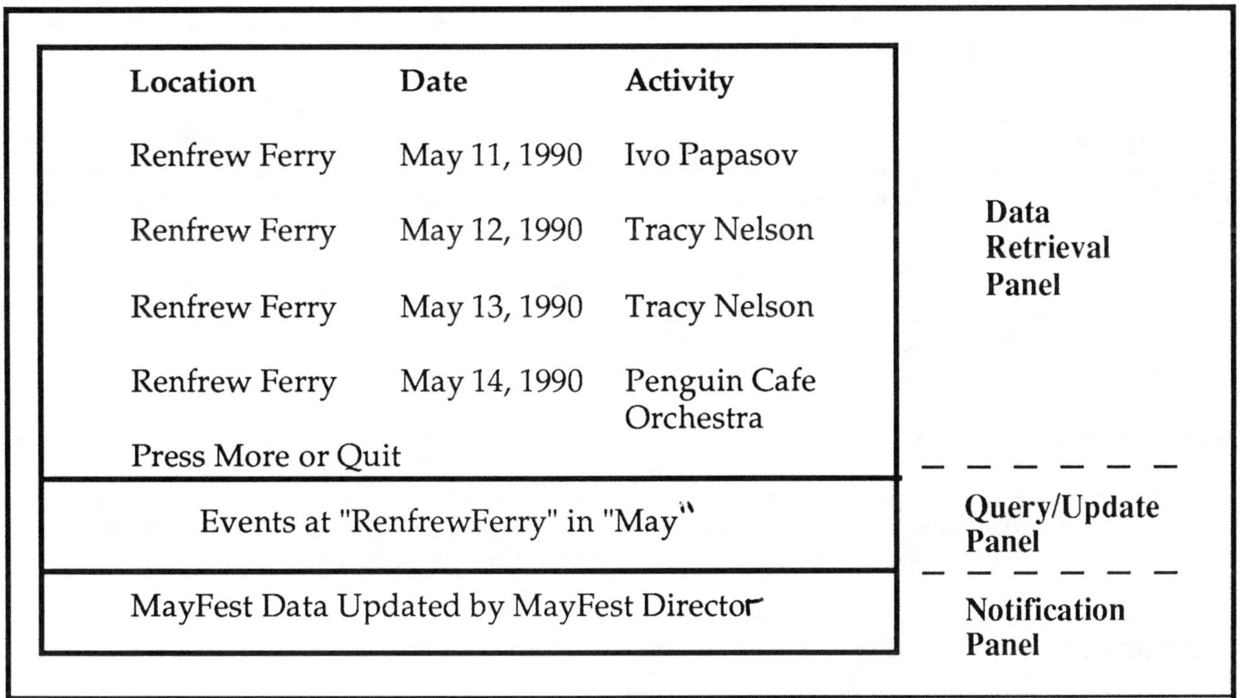

Location	Date	Activity	
Renfrew Ferry	May 11, 1990	Ivo Papasov	**Data Retrieval Panel**
Renfrew Ferry	May 12, 1990	Tracy Nelson	
Renfrew Ferry	May 13, 1990	Tracy Nelson	
Renfrew Ferry	May 14, 1990	Penguin Cafe Orchestra	
Press More or Quit			
Events at "RenfrewFerry" in "May"			**Query/Update Panel**
MayFest Data Updated by MayFest Director			**Notification Panel**

Fig 4. A Users Window from the Year of Culture Application.

6. Conclusions

The system described implements most of the proposal in [FZ89] for a multi-user, multi-application environment. In the interest of speed of implementation many crucial, but well understood database activities have not been realized, for instance security (there is no user authorisation), backup and recovery. Neither has any attempt been made to optimise data location. Presumably, a given user will be interested in a particular part of the database and it would be useful for this information to be available to the system, so that the data can be relocated. The design of DPS-algol includes support for localities, and although yet to be implemented., this would be of use in creating this feature.

There is a requirement for a sophisticated system management tool available for a DBA. This would include a facility for editing the user and group hierarchy. There could also be system observation tools available to managers to monitor database access and the amount of time spent on each project.

Although there are slots in the system for inter-user communication, time prevented these from being completed. When they are completed, we wish to explore the notion of "multi-user commit". That is we will produce a plan by which agreement by a set of users are required for a commit to take place. A given user will initiate a commit command in the context of a group. All the other members will then be consulted using the communication channels before the commit is performed. Indeed, a more sophisticated control mechanism for synchronisation is required. One approach to this is described in [NSZ90].

It would also prove useful to permit one user to maintain a window which essentially eavesdrops on the activities of another user. That is, all changes on one node are immediately visible on another. This has been achieved for a drawing package program as described in [Wai89] in which two artists as separate users can draw pictures and each sees the other. To support this, no addition to the underlying model is required with a TG being required with total notification only allowed. An entry point which disseminates all notifications to all members may be added to the TG process and the application would need to register all changes.

The current system includes lock and operation filters which essentially mean that the operational aspect of the user's environment are filtered appropriately. To this, it would be useful to add a view mechanism to filter the database aspect of the user's environment. When a group or user is registered with the system, it should be possible to specify a part of the database which is all that the group/user can modify and another (larger) part which the group/user can query.

Developing applications presently relies on the programmer filling in slots in a template. A more sophisticated environment for such development is required. This would comprise an editor built around the template, the ability to run the application in "stand-alone" mode and support for testing the communication protocols from the stand points of all potential users.

Finally, some mechanism will be required to overcome node crashes. All users may need to be notified when this happens in order to prevent problems. Shared commits and TGs which include crashed users will need to be insulated against such problems.

Acknowledgements

The authors would like to acknowledge the support of the ESPRIT Comandos Project (Number 834) in carrying out this work and also the important part played in the design of DPS-algol by Malcolm Atkinson. We would also like to thank Paul Philbrow and Moira Norrie for useful comments on the work

Bibliography

AM85

M.P. Atkinson and R. Morrison, "Integrated Persistent Programming Systems", *Proceedings of the 19th Annual Hawaii International Conference on System Sciences*, (ed. B. D. Shriver), vol IIA, Software, 842-854, January 1986.

Co90

R.L. Cooper, "On The Utilisation of Persistent Programming Environments", Ph. D. Thesis, Departmental Report CSC 90/R12, Department of Computing Science, University of Glasgow, April 1990.

FZ89

M.F. Fernandez and S.B. Zdonik, "Transaction Groups: A Model for Co-operating Transactions", *Persistent Object Systems, Newcastle, Australia 1989*, (J. Rosenberg and D. Koch eds), Workshops in Computing, Springer Verlag, 341-352, 1990.

HZ87

M. Hornick and S.B. Zdonik, "A Shared, Segmented Memory System for an Object-Oriented Database", *ACM Transactions on Office Information Systems*, Vol 5, No. 1, 70-95, January 1987.

MB89

R. Morrison, A.L. Brown, R. Connor and A. Dearle, "The Napier88 Reference Manual", *Persistent Programming Research Research77*, Universities of Glasgow and St Andrews, 1989.

NSZ90

M.H. Nodine, A.H. Skarra and S.B. Zdonik, "Synchornisation and Recovery in Co-operative Transactions", *Proceedings of the Fourth Workshop on Persistent Object Systems: Their Design, Implementation andn Use, Martha's Vineyard, Massachusssetts*, September 1990.

PS85

"The PS-algol Reference Manual - Fourth Edition", *Persistent Programming Research Report 12*, Universities of Glasgow and St. Andrews, 1987.

Wai89

HWF Wai, "Distributed PS-algol", *Persistent Object Systems, Newcastle, Australia 1989*, (J. Rosenberg and D. Koch eds), Workshops in Computing, Springer Verlag,126-140, 1990.

Synchronization and Recovery in Cooperative Transactions[†]

Marian H. Nodine
Department of Computer Science
Brown University
Providence, RI 02912
mhn@cs.brown.edu

Andrea H. Skarra
Department of Computer Science
Brown University
Providence, R.I. 02912
ahs@cs.brown.edu

Stanley B. Zdonik
Department of Computer Science
Brown University
Providence, R.I. 02912
sbz@cs.brown.edu

Abstract

Traditional atomic transactions do not work well in databases used by design applications. A typical design task is divided into parallel subtasks that are interdependent. We relax the constraint of atomicity in these situations to allow *cooperative transactions* to work together in groups to accomplish design tasks in the database. These groups may be arbitrarily nested to form a *cooperative transaction hierarchy*.

We examine the notions of correctness, synchronization, and recovery within a single group in the cooperative transaction hierarchy. Each cooperative transaction in a group maintains only partial consistency in the database, and shares data with other transactions in the group in a way that may violate the atomicity of each. We define a programmable mechanism to allow a database administrator to specify and enforce the correctness of the cooperative transactions in a group. We also define a mechanism for recovery when a cooperative transaction aborts or fails.

1 Introduction

With the development of semantically rich data models such as object-oriented models, there has been more demand for databases that support interactive and design applications. These include hypermedia applications, CASE and other computer-aided design tools, and interactive programming environments.

Traditional databases were developed to support on-line data processing applications for businesses, banks, etc. Transactions in these applications are independent, atomic, and usually short. Each maintains global consistency across the database. Traditional database mechanisms for concurrency control and recovery are tailored to these applications and do not perform well for the kinds of transactions that characterize design applications.

Consider the requirements that a design application might place on an underlying database. For example, we will examine a CASE tool being used in writing a simple word processing system. The word processing system has three modules, as shown in Figure 1. The *Display* module manages the user interface, the *Processing* module maintains the document in its internal format, changing it according to the commands received from the *Display* module, and the *Storage* module deals with the disk I/O. Each module has a single designer responsible for designing and programming it. The objects in the database include design specifications for each module, the interfaces between modules and the internal format of the document; also header and source files containing the code.

[†]Support for this research is provided by IBM under contract No. 559716, by DEC under award No. DEC686, by ONR under Contract N00014-83-K-0146, by Apple Computer, Inc., and by US West.

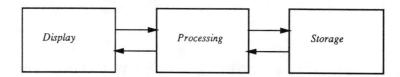

Figure 1: Word Processing System Design.

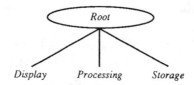

Figure 2: Word Processing Hierarchy.

In this example, the specification for the interface between the *Display* and *Processing* modules may be manipulated by more than one designer. The *Display* module designer may change it as he gives the users new capabilities. The *Processing* module designer may need to change it to provide more information to the *Display* module. In the word processor design, each designer completes only part of the design task and maintains only partial consistency in the database. For instance, the part of the interface discussed above that is in the *Display* module is maintained by the designer of that module, and similarly for the part of the interface in the *Processing* module. However, the two parts of the interface design are interdependent, because the two designers corporately implement the interface, and therefore must agree on any changes made to it. The interactions between the two designers are structured according to the task they are working on; using the example in the previous paragraph, if the *Display* module designer changes the interface, the *Processing* module designer must ensure that the changes are reasonable from his perspective. The two designers also may iterate through several refinements or changes in the initial design as they work, so the task itself is open-ended. Because of the complexity of the design process, the individual designers dynamically determine what is necessary to complete their part of the task.

From the point of view of the database, each designer starts a *cooperative transaction* for each major design change he participates in. In the above example, each of the *Display*, *Processing*, and *Storage* module designers starts up a cooperative transaction. A cooperative transaction issues a sequence of operations that is determined dynamically as the design task progresses. Each cooperative transaction is a *member* of some *transaction group* [FZ89]. The transaction group and transactions for the example are shown in Figure 2.

Because cooperative transactions in the same group may need to read and modify the same set of objects, they may read or overwrite each others' uncommitted object versions (as in the interface example above). Consequently, concurrent cooperative transactions may be interdependent, and atomicity may be too strict a requirement for correct execution. In this paper we define a new method for specifying correctness for a concurrent history of cooperative transactions. This method allows us to tailor the correctness specification in the database according to the nature of the underlying task, and to support and control the interactions among the cooperative transactions working together on the task. We also provide a synchronization and recovery scheme that enforces a particular correctness specification. To simplify matters, in this paper we examine this method only as it applies to a single transaction group with a set of member transactions. Extending these ideas to an arbitrary hierarchy is straightforward [NFSZ90]. Furthermore, we consider only histories that contain nonnested *read* and *write* operations.

Recovery in cooperative transactions is complicated by the fact that the failure of design transactions may be expensive. This is because they generally are long-lived and open-ended. They are long-lived because the design task is slow and complex. They are open-ended because the design task is iterative. Another complication in recovery is that there may be complex transaction interdependencies. These characteristics also indicate that atomicity may not be an appropriate requirement for cooperative transactions; aborting a whole transaction and every transaction that depends on it would eliminate a lot of useful work just to maintain correctness. Instead, we want to restrict the effects of an abort as much as possible.

The new measures for correctness in a database provide the flexibility and the control required for cooperative transactions. Each transaction group explicitly defines the sequences of operations *(patterns)* required for the correct execution of its members and the operations that are prohibited at any specific place in a pattern *(conflicts)*. Thus, the patterns and conflicts define the constraints imposed on the history of the transaction group for it to be correct.

The notion of patterns and conflicts influences the notion of synchronization and recovery in the database. For synchronization, operations requested by cooperative transactions must conform to the pattern and conflict specifications, and are checked as they are requested. The recovery process undoes only the work that is actually invalidated by a failure, and allows each transaction the option of completing the recovery in the forward direction. This is because the *undo* or *invalidation* phase of recovery undoes only the operations that form the parts of the patterns that are no longer valid, rather than undoing whole transactions. To do this properly, the recovery scheme uses *logs* that record the necessary information about the operations in the history, the versions they create, and the dependencies among the operations.

Once all of the operations affected by a failure have been invalidated, we allow the cooperative transactions to work together to recover. We define a set of steps that can be taken during this *recovery* phase. We also show that the history of operations in the transaction group will remain correct after invalidation and recovery.

2   Related Research

We have seen various approaches to making transactions more flexible, to better support long-lived and interactive transactions. These include augmenting traditional locking protocols, specifying a longer transaction as an envelope that contains a sequence of shorter transactions, and nesting the transactions.

ObServer [SZR86, HZ87] augments its locking protocol by supporting non-restrictive read and write locks to allow nonserializable interleaving of concurrent transactions. The locks are associated with a message-passing scheme. Limitations of this approach include the inability to limit the visibility of intermediate results and the inability to define correctness for a history of concurrent transactions.

Examples where long transactions are broken up into sequences of shorter atomic transactions include sagas [GMS87] and group transactions [KSUW85]. Group transactions are defined for design environments, but fail to provide the means for structuring or restricting ways that the users in a group can cooperate. With sagas, we can imagine each saga to be associated with a single designer. In addition to having the same failings as group transactions, sagas must be defined in advance and are consequently not open-ended.

In nested transactions [Mos85], a transaction may be decomposed hierarchically. However, since nested transactions preserve serializability among their subtransactions, they can neither cooperate nor share data. The constraint-based models [KKB87] relax serializability, allowing subtransactions at lower levels in the hierarchy to cooperate as long as each subtransaction preserves its consistency constraint. While this approach weakens serializability, it is not as expressive as our model. For example, a transaction can never read an object while another transaction is modifying it. Multilevel atomicity [Lyn83] allows the specification of a hierarchy of breakpoints within the operation sequence of a transaction that states how other transactions can interleave their operations. However, it is not clear how to specify the breakpoint hierarchy for an interactive or open-ended transaction before it has executed.

When atomicity is relaxed, there still must be constraints on the allowable transaction interleavings. For example, path expressions [CH84] can be used to synchronize concurrent operations on an object. However, they can neither constrain these operations based on the transactions that invoked them nor define the synchronization of a set of operations on multiple objects. Skarra [Ska89] presents a concurrency control scheme for object-oriented systems using *patterns* and *conflicts*, which provides a basis for this work.

Other approaches to increasing the flexibility of design transactions that are unrelated to the approach in this paper include the NT/PV model of Korth and Speegle [KS90], operation transformation for groupware systems by Ellis and Gibbs [EG89], and the flexible transaction model of Kaiser [Kai90].

Another weakness of many of these approaches is the failure to discuss recovery. Of the examples mentioned above, [GMS87] discusses forward recovery using compensating transactions, and [Mos85] and [KKB87] discuss how long transactions can be restarted when a short transaction fails or is aborted.

3   The Model

In our model, cooperative transactions work together in natural groups (*transaction groups*) to do some logical unit of work (*task*), such as a single piece of a design. The cooperative transactions in a single group are called its *members*. The groups may be nested, with the nesting following the natural decomposition of the overall task into subtasks. In the nested situation, a transaction group may have members that are transaction groups, as well as members that are cooperative transactions.

The members of a transaction group work together to do some design task. The transaction group is responsible for ensuring that its members maintain consistency in the database. In this section we present our notion of a cooperative transaction, a definition of correctness, and a model for concurrency control (synchronization) and recovery within a single transaction group.

3.1   Cooperative Transactions

A cooperative transaction is responsible for some particular aspect *(subtask)* of a task. It maintains a local state and issues read and write operations related to that subtask. A cooperative transaction need not be atomic. It may communicate with other cooperative transactions, either directly using messages or indirectly through the sharing of intermediate versions of objects in the database. An individual cooperative transaction may not preserve global consistency in the database, though the set of cooperative transactions in a group does.

Cooperative transactions are delimited by the *begin* and *terminate* primitives. A cooperative transaction operates on the database by issuing *read* and *write* requests. As soon as a cooperative transaction has written an object, other cooperative transactions in its group can read the new version, provided that the read is consistent with the group's notion of correctness. To make the effects of operations visible outside the group, a cooperative transaction *checkpoints* its operations. If the cooperative transaction is not a member of the root transaction group, a checkpoint is equivalent to writing the new object versions created by the operations to the parent of the cooperative transaction's group. The checkpoint proceeds only when both the operations complete the set of patterns associated with the transaction's subtask and the write operations are allowed by the group's parent's notion of correctness. A checkpointed operation still may be revoked if any earlier operations on which it depends are revoked. Once all the operations it depends on have been checkpointed, it cannot be revoked. At this point, we call the checkpoint *complete*. A cooperative transaction may also *abort* specific uncheckpointed operations, removing their effects from the database.

The checkpoint and abort primitives do not terminate the cooperative transaction; that is done separately using the *terminate* primitive. A cooperative transaction cannot terminate unless all of its known operations are checkpointed.

3.2   Transaction Groups

A transaction group oversees a particular *task*, and that task is done corporately by its *members* (in this case, a set of cooperative transactions). The correct operation of its members is specified within the transaction group, and thus the group is responsible for ensuring that the operations in the history conform to its correctness specification. It is also responsible for coordinating recovery when one of its members fails or aborts an operation.

Transaction groups are also delimited by the *begin* and *terminate* primitives. The correctness specification is defined by the database administrator when the transaction begins. Also, transaction groups may *checkpoint* when some aspect or iteration of the task is complete. A transaction group may only *terminate* when everything done by its members is checkpointed.

3.3   Correctness

Traditionally, serializability has been the measure of correctness of an execution of concurrent cooperative transactions. The basic premise behind serializability is that each transaction completes a single, independent task that preserves global consistency in the database. Its result may be based on the results of only those transactions that have already committed. Serializability defines the result of an interleaved execution of a set of transactions to be correct if it is equivalent to some non-interleaved execution. This model of correctness limits concurrency in the execution of transactions that depend on each others' output.

The criteria of global consistency and serializability establish correctness uniformly for all transactions. Our notion of cooperation allows transactions to form dependencies by allowing one transaction to read uncommitted writes from another. We achieve global consistency through the combined effects of several partially consistent transactions. We replace serializability with the requirement that each set of cooperating transactions conforms to a correctness specification tailored to their particular task. This correctness specification defines which dependencies may be allowed at a given time and which are prohibited. It is provided by the administrator who begins the transaction group.

We need to structure the allowable interactions among the cooperative transactions in each group according to the structure of the underlying task. Skarra [Ska89] proposes *patterns* and *conflicts* as a form of correctness specification for concurrent cooperative transactions. In particular, patterns specify sequences of operations on the objects that are required in a correct execution. Conflicts are defined within the context of patterns, and specify operations that are prohibited at a specific points. Many patterns and conflicts may be defined for a particular task, each constraining a different aspect of the cooperative transaction interactions. For example, a pattern might state that if anyone modifies the specification for the interface between the *Display* module and the *Processing* module, the *Display* transaction must modify the corresponding implementation in the file *display.c* as well. A conflict might state that if the interface specification has changed but the code hasn't been updated yet, no other cooperative transaction can modify the specification. This pattern/conflict pair ensures that *display.c* is modified in lock-step with the interface specification. A second pattern may force *Display* to read the latest version of *display.c* before writing it. An operation conforms to the concurrency specification when it is acceptable according to all patterns and conflicts at the time it is executed.

A *history* for a transaction group is the partial order of the read and write operations executed by its cooperative transactions. It does not contain the operations that have been aborted. A *correct history* for a transaction group is one that contains all the operation sequences required by the patterns that apply to the history, and none of the sequences prohibited by the conflicts. We ensure that a history produced by a transaction group is correct by delaying or refusing operations that do not conform to its correctness specification. We also prevent a cooperative transaction from terminating until all of the patterns defined for its associated task are complete in the history.

3.4 Recovery

Recovery takes a history that was correct before some failure and transforms it into a history that is correct after the failure. Operations fail either because they are aborted by the cooperative transaction that issued them, or because the system fails. The failure invalidates some set of operations in the history. Operations are also invalidated when they depend on other invalid operations. We record information about a history and its dependencies in a log, with one log entry per operation. Invalidating an operation undoes its effects in the database and removes its entry from the log.

We assume that the cooperative transactions that remain after the failure may participate actively in the recovery process. A cooperative transaction whose operations have been invalidated either compensates for the failure by initiating a new set of operations or aborts its operations in turn. The compensating operations are generated either by running an intelligent compensating program or by user intervention. As with the original operations, a cooperative transaction may interact with other cooperative transactions during the recovery process.

3.4.1 Invalidation and Dependencies

Since cooperating transactions may read each others' uncommitted changes, their transaction dependency graph may be cyclic. Recovery makes use of dependencies among *operations*, because operations are atomic and can only depend on prior operations. If concurrent execution of operations that depend on each other is prevented, the dependency graph for operations is acyclic.

In the context of cooperative transactions, a failure directly invalidates some number of operations. To invalidate an operation, we remove its entry from the log and remove any object versions it created from the database. We also invalidate the set of operations that transitively depend on the failed operations. The dependencies that exist between operations by members of a single transaction group include *pattern dependencies* and *reads-from dependencies*.

Patterns describe sequences of operations that depend on each other for correctness. For each pattern that applies to a particular history, we can isolate the subsequence of operations in the history that realizes the pattern. This is called the *traversal* of the pattern in the history. In a single traversal, each operation depends on the operation before it. Since an operation may be a part of any number of traversals, it may have any number of *pattern dependencies*.

Pattern dependencies ensure that, when one of the operations that participates in a pattern is invalidated, all operations that follow it in the traversal associated with that pattern also are invalidated. For example, consider the pattern described above, which states that if the interface specification is modified, the code in *display.c* is modified as well. Say the *Processing* cooperative transaction has changed the specification, and *Display* has read the change and modified the code in *display.c*. Invalidating the write of the specification requires that the write of the code also be invalidated, otherwise the pattern might not be realized in the history.

Reads-from dependencies also exist between operations. When a cooperative transaction reads an object last written by another cooperative transaction, the read operation depends on the validity of the earlier write operation. Each read of an object is dependent on the most recent write to that object.

3.4.2   Recovering Correctly

When the operations of one cooperative transaction are invalidated as a result of some failure or abort by another cooperative transaction, it is notified so that it can recover from the failure. The history that remains after recovery must be correct. We allow the cooperative transaction to recover by issuing a sequence of compensating operations, each of which must be correct according to the patterns and conflicts in the correctness specification for its task. These compensating operations are either coded into the cooperative transaction or generated by some user interacting with the cooperative transaction. For example, consider given the patterns above what would happen if the *Processing* transaction aborted its last write of the interface specification. The *Display* transaction would then have its subsequent reads and writes of the specification invalidated. To compensate, it must reread the interface specification to determine what is the current definition of the interface, and possibly also rewrite the code in *display.c*.

Because we recover using the same concurrency specification as was enforced for the original operations, we maintain correctness during the recovery phase. The cooperative transactions remaining after a failure can cooperate in the recovery process in the same manner that they cooperated before the failure.

4   Synchronization and Correctness

Synchronization protocols for a transaction group restrict both the concurrent access of objects by its members and the order in which different objects are accessed by different members. We use *patterns* and *conflicts* to specify required and prohibited operation sequences in a transaction group's history. In this section, we present a user-definable synchronization mechanism called an *operation machine* for expressing and enforcing patterns and conflicts in a transaction group.

4.1   Operation Machine Definition

An operation machine ($\mathcal{M}$) is a tuple defined by:

$$\mathcal{M} = < K, \Sigma, \Delta, s, c, F >$$

> K is a finite set of states.
>
> Σ is an alphabet.
>
> Δ is a transition function from $K \times \Sigma \rightarrow K$.
>
> $s \in K$ is the initial state.
>
> $c \in K$ is the current state.

$F \subseteq K$ is the set of final states.

Each transition in an operation machine includes the alphabet symbols which define the transition functions. A symbol σ in the alphabet Σ is a tuple

$$\sigma = <M, o, O, P>$$

$M \in \{any, m_i, \overline{m_i}\}$ is some member, where any is any transaction, m_i is an identifier
   for some member i, and $\overline{m_i}$ is any member except m_i.

$o \in \{r, w\}$ is an operation, where r is read and w is write.

O is the object identifier of the target object.

$P \in \{a, r, q\}$ is a return value, where a is accept, r is refuse and q is queue.

In an operation machine, the start state represents the beginning of a pattern. Machine transitions represent operations on an object by some transaction. They are annotated with return values that are either a (accept) if the operation conforms to the pattern, r (refuse) if the operation conflicts, or q (queue) when the operation conflicts now, but may conform to the pattern if done later. The lack of a transition for an operation from some state indicates that the operation is not relevant to the pattern at that time, therefore the pattern cannot cause the operation to be queued or refused. The final states of an operation machine indicate when its pattern is complete in the history. A database is consistent if every member checkpoints only when every machine associated with it is in a final state.

4.2   Operation Machine Templates

Operation machines may be defined directly or instantiated from *operation machine templates*. An operation machine template is defined in the same way as an operation machine, but the transition functions may have variables for the member and object identifiers. A machine template is instantiated by making a copy of its definition and binding the variables in the copy to specific object and member IDs.

4.3   Traversals

A *traversal* of an operation machine is a sequence of operations associated with consecutive traversals of accept arcs for the machine, beginning at the start state and ending at the current state. That is, a traversal is a (possibly empty) sequence

$$\{t_i \mid (from(t_1) = s) \land (to(t_i) = from(t_{i+1})) \land (return\_val(t_i) = a)\}$$

For example, given the operation machine shown in Figure 3(a), the operation sequence (1) in Figure 3(b) is a traversal. The operation sequence (2) is not a traversal because the third operation causes the traversal of an arc that returns refuse. Sequence (3) is not a traversal because the first operation does not cause an arc traversal at all, though it would be accepted by the machine. A *complete traversal* ends at a final state, e.g. the sequence (4). The null traversal of this machine is correct, though it is only complete because the start state is also a final state.

4.4   Operation Machine Functions

Operation machines can be used for various functions in a cooperative database. *Synchronization machines* define the patterns that enforce the underlying concurrency control mechanism (e.g., cooperative, serializable). Each transaction group has one synchronization machine template with variables M for a single member identifier and O for a single object. For each $<member, object>$ pair where the member is currently interacting with the object, there is an instantiation of the synchronization machine template with M bound to the *member* and O bound to *object*. Figure 4 gives two examples of synchronization machine templates. Figure 4(a) shows a machine that enforces serializability via two-phase locking. If the transaction is in the lower middle state the object is basically read-locked. Similarly, if the transaction is in the upper middle state, it is basically write-locked. The locks persist until the member is no longer interacting with the object

(a)

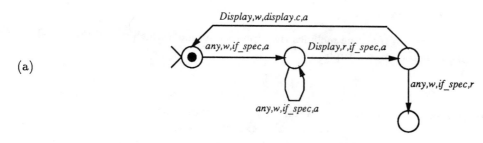

(b)

1. $\{< Processing,w,if\_spec >,\ < Processing,w,if\_spec >,\ < Display,r,if\_spec >\}$

2. $\{< Processing,w,if\_spec >,\ < Display,r,if\_spec >,\ < Display,w,if\_spec >\}$

3. $\{< Processing,r,if\_spec >,\ < Processing,w,if\_spec >,\ < Display,r,if\_spec >\}$

4. $\{< Processing,w,if\_spec >,\ < Display,r,if\_spec >,\ < Display,w,display.c >\}$

Figure 3: Operation machines and traversals

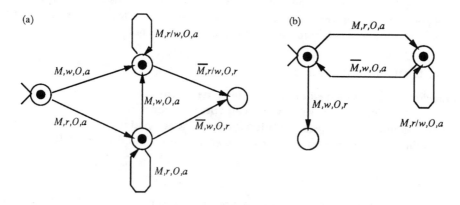

Figure 4: Synchronization machines: (a) serializable; (b) cooperative.

(i.e. the member terminates). At that point, the operation machine is removed. Figure 4(b) shows a synchronization machine template to enforce one type of cooperation. Before member M can write the object, it must have read it. Furthermore, if some other member writes the object, then member M must read the written changes before it can write the object again. This machine prevents a member from overwriting another member's changes.

Pattern machines define the sequences of operations needed to do some current task. For example, the machine defined above in Figure 3(a) forces *Display* to read the interface specification *(if_spec)* after the last write before it can actually make the corresponding changes in the its module *(display.c)*. It also forces *display.c* to be current with *if_spec* before the task is complete. These machines put a general form on the allowable executions consistent with the transaction group's task. They do not necessarily restrict the transactions to conform to one specific execution, though they may.

Protection machines are used to prohibit specific transactions from doing specific operations on an object. They are implemented using refuse arcs.

4.5   Correctness

Since we use operation machines to enforce the patterns and conflicts defined at any given point in an operation sequence, we can formalize our definition of correctness in terms of operation machines.

We defined a *traversal* in Section 4.3 as a sequence of operations associated with consecutive accept arc transitions in an operation machine. A *complete traversal* is a traversal in which the corresponding path in the operation machine ends at some final state. For each operation in a history, we know which arcs were traversed when it was executed. Define the sequence Π_{OM} associated with operation machine OM as

$$\Pi_{OM} = \{op \mid \text{operation } op \text{ caused an arc traversal in machine } OM\}$$

That is, Π_{OM} is the projection of the pattern defined by the machine OM from the history. These operations were acceptable according to the pattern specification *at the time they were executed*. A history is *correct* when all sequences Π_{OM} for the machines OM that were active during the history are traversals. Correctness is an ongoing notion, and implies that there are no conflicts in the history thus far. However, there is no guarantee that the work thus far preserves global consistency. A history is *complete* when all the sequences are complete traversals. A complete traversal is not only correct, but also is globally consistent. A member can only checkpoint when its group's history is complete.

5   Operations

An operation defines an atomic read or write action on a single object by a single member. Each operation progresses chronologically through the following four states, unless it is aborted.

1. *REQUESTED* – A member has requested the operation.

2. *SUBMITTED* – The operation was accepted by all the operation machines that are currently bound to the object, and subsequently was executed.

3. *PENDING* – The operation has been checkpointed by the member. The member no longer can abort the operation.

4. *COMPLETE* – Any operations on which this one depends, either because of pattern or reads-from dependencies, also are in the *COMPLETE* state. The effects of this operation cannot be revoked by any abort by any other member.

An operation request is a tuple

$$\mathcal{R} = <I, M, o, O, V>$$

I is a request identifier unique to the requesting member.

M is the identifier of the member requesting the operation.

$o \in \{r, w\}$ is the operation, where r is read and w is write.

O is the object identifier of the target object.

V is the new version if this is a write operation.

A requested operation must be accepted by the operation machines before it can be executed. The object O specified in the request may be associated with many machines, each of which enforces a different pattern for the members interacting with it. Each such machine may be relevant to the requested operation. Together, the machines enforce the overall correctness of the operations.

We guarantee that an operation is correct at the time it executes by ensuring that the operation causes no traversal of an arc whose predicate returns q (queue) or r (refuse). There may be several operation machines bound to the object O and member M specified in the operation request. For each such machine, the arc labeled either $< M, o, O, P >$ or $< S, o, O, P >$ (where $M \in S$) from the current state in the operation machine defines how this operation participates in the associated pattern. There are four cases:

1. $P = a$ (accept). This operation is a correct continuation of this traversal at this time.

2. $P = q$ (queue). This operation does not correctly continue the traversal at this time, but may be accepted later.

3. $P = r$ (refuse). This operation cannot correctly continue the current traversal.

(a)   (b)

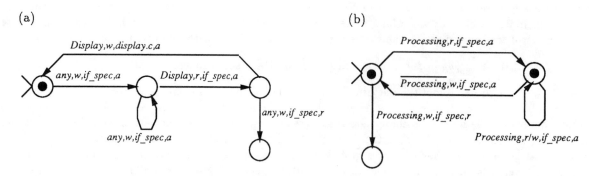

Figure 5: Operation machines bound to *if_spec*: (a) pattern machine, (b) synchronization machine.

4. There is no transition in this machine. This operation does not participate in this machine's pattern. This is an implicit accept.

If any machine returns r (refuse) for the requested operation, it is immediately refused. Otherwise, if any machine returns q (queue), the request is queued. If no machine returns r or q, the operation is accepted.

As an example of this, consider the *if_spec* object and the cooperative transaction *Processing*. Assume that the *if_spec* object has two operation machines associated with it, as shown in Figure 5. The machine in Figure 5(a) is the pattern machine shown previously, and the machine in Figure 5(b) is an instantiation of the operation machine template described earlier for cooperative synchronization machines. Assume the current state is the start state in both machines. The operation request $< Processing, w, if\_spec >$ would be refused, because the transition in machine (b) returns r. The operation request $< Processing, r, if\_spec >$ would be accepted, because it is not relevant to machine (a) and the transition in machine (b) returns a.

Once the operation has been accepted, we know that its execution at this time does not conflict. Therefore, we do the operation by executing the following steps atomically:

1. Read or write the object, as specified in the request.

2. Update each operation machine to reflect the new current state by traversing appropriate accept arcs.

3. Insert a record of the operation (*log entry*) in the log, with the state set to *SUBMITTED*. It should include both pattern and read-write dependencies.

If the member does not abort the operation in the interim, the operation checkpoints the next time the member checkpoints. At this time, the operation's state in its history entry is set to *PENDING* and checkpointing begins. Once all operations on which it depends complete, its state in the history is set to *COMPLETE* as well.

6   Histories, Logging, and Operation Dependencies

A *history* is the partial order of operations executed in a transaction group by its members. The operations in the history, along with other information needed for recovery, are recorded in a *log*. The log for a transaction group is updated as the members execute their operations. Operations that execute simultaneously may be recorded in any order. The log also records the dependencies between operations. When an operation fails or aborts, the log is used to determine which operations are affected by the failure, both directly and indirectly.

6.1   Histories

A history is a partially-ordered sequence of operations. An operation is represented in the history as a tuple $<M,o,O>$ with the fields as in the operation request. The history is partially ordered according to a *happens-before* ordering ($<$), where if *op1* and *op2* are operations, and if *op1* executes before *op2*, then *(op1 $<$ op2)*.

The history conforms to the following constraints:

1. It contains exactly one entry for every operation that has executed and has not been aborted.

2. It contains no operations that either have not executed or that have been aborted.

3. Any operation *op1* in the history that depends on some operation *op2* has *(op2 $<$ op1)*.

6.2   Operation Dependencies

In Section 3.4, we noted that dependency information is recorded at the granularity of operations rather than transactions. We defined *pattern dependencies*, which form between operations that participate in the same pattern. For each pattern defined for a transaction group, there is a corresponding operation machine that executes the pattern. The projection of the pattern from the history is a *traversal* of the corresponding operation machine.

When an operation is invalidated, all subsequent operations in each traversal that contains the operation also become invalid. Thus, each traversal defines a dependency chain, with each operation dependent on the previous operation in the traversal. These dependencies are computable if we keep a record of the last operation executed in each traversal. We also keep *reads-from dependencies*, which occur because a read of some version of an object depends on the correctness of the operation that wrote that version. We can compute these if we keep a back pointer from each version to the operation that created it.

Figure 6 shows an excerpt from the history of the root transaction group containing traversals of the operation machines from Figure 5. To the right of the operation sequence are three columns of dependencies. The leftmost column shows the pattern dependencies associated with the pattern machine in Figure 5(a). The middle column shows the pattern dependencies associated with the synchronization machine in Figure 5(b). The rightmost column shows the read-write dependency associated with the *display.c* object. This set of dependencies is by no means complete, in that there are other machines associated with the members and objects in the history that we have not shown, and therefore we have not shown the dependencies associated with their traversals as well. An example of a machine not shown is the synchronization machine for the *Display* transaction's interaction with the *display.c* object.

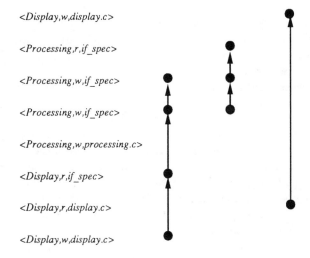

Figure 6: History excerpt with dependencies.

6.3   Logs

A log records the history of a transaction group and other information needed for recovery. There is one entry in the log per operation in the history. In addition to recording the operation, the log records any new object version created by the operation, and the dependencies among the operations. An entry in the log is a tuple $\mathcal{LE}$, defined by:

$$\mathcal{LE} = <I, M, o, O, S, V, D>$$

> I is M's unique identifier for the operation as specified in the operation request.
>
> M is the identifier of the member that did the operation.
>
> $o \in \{r, w\}$ is the operation, where r is read and w is write.
>
> O is the object identifier of the target object.
>
> $S \in \{SUBMITTED, PENDING, COMPLETE, INVALID\}$ is the operation state.
>
> V points to the (possibly null) version created by the operation. Versions are used for recovery only.
>
> D is the set of log entries for operations on which this operation depends. These may be either pattern or reads-from dependencies.

Log entries are identified uniquely by $< I, M >$ pairs. They are totally ordered in the log, with their order consistent to the happens-before order in the history.

7   Invalidation and Recovery

Recovery is a two-phase process. In the *invalidation phase*, all operations that depend on some invalid operation are also invalidated. Any version written by an invalidated operation is also invalidated. In the *recovery phase*, members whose operations are invalidated work together to compensate for the failure. The invalidation and recovery phases preserve the correctness of the history.

A member may abort any of its uncheckpointed operations at any time. The abort process invalidates the aborted operations by marking the log entries as *INVALID*, and invalidating the versions created by them. It then finds the operations that transitively depend on the aborted operation using the *pattern* and *reads-from* dependencies in the log, and invalidates them in the same way.

Once all affected operations are invalidated, any object that has had some version invalidated is restored to its state at the time just after the last valid version was written. The invalidation of an operation breaks each traversal that the operation participated in. Thus, each operation machine is restored to whatever state it was in just before the first invalid operation in its traversal was executed.

The log entry for each write operation points to the version it created. We invalidate a version when we invalidate the write operations that created it. After the invalidation phase, the latest valid version of each object is the most recent version created by some traversal in the history. Thus, all effects caused by invalidated operations are purged from the database.

Figure 6 from the previous section showed an an excerpt of a history containing dependencies associated with the traversal of the pattern machine from Figure 5(a). If *Processing* aborts the second operation in the traversal, the operations $<Display,r,if\_spec>$ and $<Display,w,display.c>$ are also invalidated because of pattern dependencies. The pattern machine is reset to be in the initial state, and the versions created by the two write operations in its traversal are invalidated. The synchronization machine is backed up one transition because the last operation in its traversal is invalidated. The last valid version of the *if_spec* object is the one created by the first write. The last valid version of the *display.c* object is the one that was current just before the write operation $<Display,w,display.c>$. No other operations are invalidated because of dependencies shown in Figure 6, but there may be other operations invalidated because of pattern or reads-from dependencies not shown in the figure.

The database is left in a correct state after the invalidation phase. Assume that the database was correct before the abort occurred. The abort breaks some traversals relevant to the history. For each such traversal, the first invalidated operation is called the *break point*. Because of the pattern dependencies, all operations in the traversal after the break point also are invalidated. The only part of the traversal left in the history is the part preceding the break point. Thus, for each pattern in the history, we are left with a correct traversal ending just before the break point.

The reads-from dependencies show places where one member's read depends on another member's write. The read operation becomes invalid when the write operation is invalid. Thus, other traversals may be severed because of the reads-from dependency. Invalidations may also cascade from traversal to traversal when an invalidated operation participates in more than one pattern. Correctness is maintained because the use of pattern dependencies guarantees that all operations in a traversal that follow its break point will be invalidated as well. We limit the performance penalty due to this cascading with proper definition of the patterns. In particular, we do not define patterns over a set of operations that are not related by data- or application-specific constraints.

Once the invalidation phase is complete, members are notified of any of their operations that have been invalidated, and the recovery phase begins. Since the members may cooperate on a task, we allow them to cooperate in the recovery process. This process is cooperative in the same sense as the initial work, and is governed by the same synchronization protocols. However, other members may wish to take responsibility for some of the changes that would otherwise be invalidated. Therefore, we allow members to do the following during recovery:

1. Abort any uncheckpointed operations. A traditional *abort* operation can be mimicked by immediately aborting all uncheckpointed operations and then terminating. This option also is useful when the member that initiated the invalidated operations has failed.

2. Reread any invalid object versions previously read by the member. This allows the member to remember what it has seen, in case it wants to incorporate some of the invalid data into a new version. The read of the old versions bypasses the synchronization mechanism.

3. Request compensating operations. These operations are scheduled and processed in the normal manner, to ensure that the history remains correct.

Given the example above, *Display* could recover after the invalidation phase by rereading the *if_spec* object, adjusting the code for the part of the display module that implements the interface appropriately, and writing the new *display.c* object.

The recovery phase maintains correctness. This is shown by proving that each action a member can take during recovery is individually correct. If abort requests are issued during recovery, we know from the previous argument that the subsequent invalidation phase maintains correctness. Assume by induction that the recovery phase also maintains correctness. This is acceptable because there are only a finite number of operations. Therefore, even if all members decide to abort, we eventually reach cases where a member that has an operation invalidated has no valid operations left to abort. If a member reads an invalid version that it has already seen, this is equivalent to the situation where it kept a copy of the invalid version. Therefore, the read does not give the member any new information. Since this read is not a part of the history, it does not affect it. If compensating operations are issued, they must be accepted by the operation machines. Since the invalidation phase leaves each machine in the state it was in immediately before its traversal's break point, these operations continue existing traversals correctly. Therefore, they maintain correctness as well, so the recovery phase as a whole is correct.

8   Summary

The design process is an iterative one, and may involve groups of designers cooperating to complete a particular task. The concurrency control and recovery protocols used in traditional databases may get in the way of such iterative, cooperative processes. We have defined a more flexible mechanism for design applications, called a *cooperative transaction*. Cooperative transactions are not necessarily atomic, nor must they individually maintain global consistency. Instead, they work together in *transaction groups* to accomplish specific tasks. We define a way to program the correctness of a transaction group in terms of the interleaving of operations of the group's members. *Patterns* specify sequences of operations the members of a group are required to submit to accomplish a task. *Conflicts* are prohibited operations, and are defined in the context of patterns.

Operation machines are augmented finite state automata, each of which defines a pattern and its associated conflicts. We use collections of operation machines to support and control the interactions among the members of a transaction group. Correctness is defined in terms of collections of operation machines, where each operation machine enforces a particular pattern and its associated conflicts. Thus, the collection of operation machines corporately enforces all patterns associated with the transaction group.

We also define dependencies among operations based on the actual traversals of operation machines in a given history. We use these dependencies during recovery to limit the amount of information that is invalidated as a result of an abort or failure. Only the specific operations that transitively depend on other invalidated operations are invalidated.

The invalidation of an operation breaks the traversals that contain the operation. Each affected traversal must be undone back to the point where the first invalid operation occurred. Recovery can then be done cooperatively by simply allowing the transactions to continue normally from the point where the failure occurred. The recovery mechanism preserves as much prior work as possible and encourages the transactions to recover forward using compensating actions rather than backward by continuing to abort.

References

[CH84]   R. H. Campbell and A. N. Habermann. The specification of process synchronization by path expressions. In *Lecture Notes in Computer Science*, volume 16, pages 89–102. Springer-Verlag, 1984.

[EG89]   C. A. Ellis and S. J. Gibbs. Concurrency control in groupware systems. In *ACM SIGMOD Proceedings*, 1989.

[FZ89]   Mary Fernandez and Stanley Zdonik. Transaction groups: A model for controlling cooperative transactions. In *3rd International Workshop On Persistent Object Systems*, January 1989.

[GMS87]   Hector Garcia-Molina and Kenneth Salem. Sagas. In *ACM SIGMOD Proceedings*, pages 249–259, 1987.

[HZ87]   Mark Hornick and Stanley Zdonik. A shared, segmented memory system for an object-oriented database. *ACM Transactions on Office Information Systems*, 5:70–95, January 1987.

[Kai90]   Gail E. Kaiser. A flexible transaction model for software engineering. In *Proceedings of the 6th International Conference on Data Engineering*, 1990.

[KKB87]   H. Korth, W. Kim, and F. Bancilhon. On long-duration CAD transactions. *Information Systems*, 13, 1987.

[KS90]   Henry F. Korth and Gregory D. Speegle. Long-duration transactions in software design projects. In *Proceedings of the 6th International Conference on Data Engineering*, 1990.

[KSUW85]   P. Klahold, G. Schlageter, R. Unland, and W. Wilkes. A transaction model supporting complex applications in integrated information systems. In *ACM SIGMOD Proceedings*, 1985.

[Lyn83]   Nancy A. Lynch. Multilevel atomicty - a new correctness criterion for database concurrency control. *ACM Transactions on Database Systems*, 8(4), December 1983.

[Mos85]   J. Eliot B. Moss. *Nested Transactions: an Approach to Reliable Distributed Computing*. MIT Press, 1985.

[NFSZ90]   Marian H. Nodine, Mary F. Fernandez, Andrea H. Skarra, and Stanley B. Zdonik. Cooperative transaction hierarchies. Technical Report CS-90-03, Brown University Computer Science Department, February 1990.

[Ska89]   Andrea Skarra. Concurrency control for cooperating transactions in an object-oriented database. *SIGPLAN Notices*, 24(4), April 1989.

[SZR86]   Andrea H. Skarra, Stanley B. Zdonik, and Steven Reiss. An object server for an object-oriented database system. In *Proceedings of the International Workshop on Object-Oriented Database Systems*, 1986.

Part IX
By the C

Chair: Gail Shaw

The title of this session reflects the workshop location as well as the theme of the papers included in the session. The three papers in this session are all related to the implementation of persistence in C-based languages. The first and third papers report on implementation results in C^{++}-based persistent systems, the second paper discusses a persistence mechanism that has been integrated into Ada and C^{++}.

Dan Schuh, in the first presentation, discussed in technical detail the E Persistent Virtual Machine (EPVM). This is work done with Mike Carey and David DeWitt as part of the EXODUS project at the University of Wisconsin. Dan noted that access to persistent objects in E is based on pointers containing object identifiers (OIDs) with storage information. Persistent objects are created using the persistent storage class on a variable or through explicit insertion in a persistent collection. The EPVM provides access to persistent objects via C function calls. These functions handle pointer access to database objects, pushing pointer access complexity into the run-time system. A limited form of pointer "swizzling" (alternating between disk-based pointers and memory pointers) is implemented; the kinds of pointers that can be swizzled are limited to local pointer variables.

This system was compared to the approach described by Joel Richardson (in the Optimization session). Dan noted that EPVM is good for repeated pointer traversals, while Joel's technique gives results that are about the same as swizzled pointer access and is good when the range of a pointer is limited. Dan also discussed in detail the costs of some of the primitive operations performed by the EPVM interpreter as implemented on a DecStation 3100/R2000 based system.

In the second presentation Alex Wolf (AT&T Bell Labs) discussed his work in supporting the addition of persistence to an existing language through the abstraction mechanisms of that language. Alex pointed out that adding persistence in this manner tests the abstraction mechanism of a language, since persistence interacts with such abstraction facilities as extensibility, typing, modularity, information hiding and program construction.

The persistence model used in this work is essentially that described by Peri Tarr in the Language Mechanisms session. Alex quickly reviewed this model, then discussed the addition of persistence to Ada, through a repository manager package which knows about classes, and C++, through a PersistentObject supertype. Alex concluded by noting that he also wants to explore the addition of persistence to ML. He feels that the addition of persistence will be supported by the fact that ML offers type identity (i.e., type *dynamic*) and uniform physical representation of objects in primary memory.

The final speaker for the session was Tom Atwood of Object Design, Inc. presenting work done with Scott Hanna of Eastman Kodak. Tom pointed out that there are two orthogonal issues involved with integrating persistence with a programming language: 1) using an application program interface (API) with class libraries vs. implementing a data manipulation language, and 2) persistence built on top of a language (using inheritance) vs. persistence built into a language (via storage classes). For example, Tom noted that Alex's approach, and Kodak's, fall in the API/inheritance quadrant (of the space defined by the above alternatives), and E (Dan's talk) and CLU fall in the storage class category. Tom pointed out that a comparison of the approach to implementing persistence in his database product and his co-author's product led to the conclusion that the second issue is the important one, and that the better way is to implement persistence through storage classes.

This final talk led us into an active discussion period, initiated by Alex Wolf pointing out that the library approach limitations experienced by Kodak were peculiar to the particular implementation and not to the approach in general and that, although the storage class approach might give extra efficiency, the approach requires changes to the language which could be expensive. This led to a discussion of whether a persistent language implemented with storage classes could use standard C compilers, as well as a question and answer session on Object Design's product implementation.

Persistence in E Revisited — Implementation Experiences

Dan Schuh, Michael Carey, and David Dewitt

Computer Sciences Department
University of Wisconsin
Madison, WI 57306
schuh@cs.wisc.edu

ABSTRACT

This paper discusses the design and implementation of the E Persistent Virtual Machine (EPVM), an interpreter that provides support for persistent data access in the current version of the E programming language. Included are descriptions of both the EPVM interface and the major implementation tactics employed within EPVM. A novel pointer swizzling scheme that has been investigated in the context of E and EPVM is also described. Finally, a performance analysis of the key EPVM primitives is presented.

1. INTRODUCTION

This paper discusses the current implementation of access to persistent data in the E programming language. E is a persistent, object-oriented programming language that was developed as an extension of C++ [Stro86] for use in the EXODUS project at the University of Wisconsin [Care89a]. The E language was originally designed for use in constructing database management system software; an overview of the design and motivation for E can be found in [Rich89a]. Basically, three main innovative features distinguish E from C++: persistent data, generator classes, and iterator functions. Support for persistent data allows program-level data objects to be transparently used across multiple executions of a program without requiring explicit input and output operations. Persistent data in E programs is stored using the EXODUS storage manager [Carey89b]. The current version of E (E 2.0) is based on AT&T C++, version 2.0. The E language processor was built by extending AT&T's C++ 2.0 preprocessor, so it produces C code which is then compiled by a native C compiler to produce object modules and executable programs.

The design and initial implementation of persistence in E, which was the basis for persistent data in E 1.2, is discussed in [Rich89b]. A substantially improved approach to persistence for E 1.2, based on compile-time analysis of E programs, is described in [Rich90]. The topic of this paper is a new approach that is currently employed in E 2.0. The current approach is based on an underlying interpreter for persistent object accesses. This interpreter, called the E Persistent Virtual Machine (EPVM), is invoked through a small set of function calls in the C code that the E 2.0 compiler generates. The interpreter is primarily used to access persistent data; most non-persistent data access and computation in E is compiled into C code and later into the native instruction set of the host computer.

The current approach to persistence in E has several advantages relative to our earlier approaches. Compilation of persistent code is quite simple, and the generated code is compact. The interpretive approach also allows a great deal of flexibility in the underlying implementation strategy. For example, it allows statistics gathering, stronger error checking, and debugging support to be implemented without impacting the normal execution efficiency of E code by simply loading a different version of EPVM. Moreover, the E compiler is no longer tied to the semantics of the underlying storage manager, and could thus be more easily adapted to other storage managers or to different uses.

The advantages discussed above are useful, but they are relatively peripheral in comparison to the main advantage of the interpretive approach — which is the ability of the EPVM implementation to maintain global context over the lifetime of a given program execution. The EPVM interpreter is able to maintain information on all currently accessible objects in order to reduce the number of calls to the underlying storage manager. As such, the interpreter can adapt its behavior based on dynamic (runtime) access patterns. While in principle a pure compiled approach could be based on a global analysis of access patterns, practical considerations usually limit the analysis

---

This research was partially supported by DARPA under contract N00014-88-K-0303, NSF under grant IRI-8657323, and donations from Texas Instruments and Digital Equipment Corporation.

that can be performed to the scope of a single function or procedure. Also, an approach based on compilation must base its code generation decisions on a static analysis of program behavior. The main disadvantage of taking an interpretive approach is runtime inefficiency. However, we believe that the advantages and simplicity of this approach may outweigh its execution time penalty for a broad class of programs. In fact, for programs where a complex global analysis would be required to make the compilation approach perform well, the interpretive approach may well win in terms of performance.

The remainder of this paper is organized as follows. Section 2 discusses the EXODUS storage manager, which is the underlying mechanism used to store persistent objects in E. We give a general overview of its functionality and discuss in detail the most relevant portions of its interface. Section 3 presents a brief overview of the design of persistence in E. Included in the discussion are the E type system, its interaction with persistence, and the various means by which persistent objects are created, destroyed, and addressed. We then turn our attention to EPVM, the runtime interpreter for persistent object accesses. Section 4 describes the EPVM interface and gives examples of its use in C code generated by the E compiler. Section 5 discusses the implementation of the interpreter, showing how it interacts with the EXODUS storage manager; this section also describes extensions to the compiler and EPVM that facilitate a limited version of pointer swizzling in order to allow certain accesses to bypass the EPVM interface. Section 6 contains a detailed cost analysis of the EPVM approach. Finally, in Section 7 we compare our approach with some of the alternatives, reflect on why the approach described here was chosen, and discuss ideas for future work.

2. THE EXODUS STORAGE MANAGER

The EXODUS storage manager (ESM) is the underlying repository used to store and manipulate persistent E objects. ESM manages the allocation of storage for persistent objects, both on disk and in main memory, and it controls the transfer of objects between disk and memory. In this section we provide a brief overview of the ESM programmer's interface. We begin with a brief overview of addressing issues as they apply to ESM storage objects, and follow with detailed descriptions of the key routines used to pin, unpin, and modify objects in the buffer pool. Further details can be found in [Care89b].

2.1. Addressing

There are two forms of persistent object addresses that concern us here. The first is the (permanent) address of an object stored on disk, and the second is the (temporary) address of an object in main memory. Every ESM storage object is identified and accessed though the use of a unique object identifier (OID). An OID is a 12-byte quantity that consists of a 2-byte volume identifier, a 4-byte page number, a 2-byte slot within the page, and a 4-byte unique field. The volume number, page ID, and slot number together specify the physical location of the object in secondary storage, while the unique field is used to prevent reuse of identical OIDs (i.e., to make OIDs safe as unique IDs). The data structure representing an OID is depicted schematically in Figure 1. Finally, ESM supports addressing of subportions of objects; an arbitrary byte within a given object can be addressed by combining its 12-byte OID with a 4-byte offset from the start of the object.

To address storage objects in the main memory buffer pool, client programs depend on user descriptors. A user descriptor is a structure that contains a pointer to a portion of an EXODUS storage object that currently resides in the ESM buffer pool. The user descriptor structure is shown in Figure 2. ESM allocates user descriptors from a pool that it maintains, and calls to access ESM objects return pointers into this pool. Thus, ESM users always

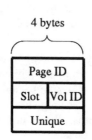

Figure 1: OID Format.

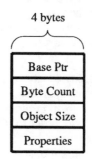

Figure 2: User Descriptor Format.

access objects in the buffer pool through two levels of indirection, first dereferencing a user descriptor pointer to the user descriptor itself, and then dereferencing the user descriptor's data pointer to obtain the actual data in the buffer pool. This form of address is sometimes referred to as a "handle" (though in this case the user descriptor pointer also points to certain other data that may be inspected by the programmer). Since objects are intended to be accessed indirectly through user descriptors, ESM is free to relocate an object within the buffer pool (if needed) by adjusting any affected pointers in the user descriptor pool. When no user descriptors point to a particular object in the ESM buffer pool any more, the object is said to be unpinned and may migrate out to disk.

2.2. EXODUS Storage Manager Interface

The programmer's interface to ESM consists of a set of function calls to support operations on individual objects and collections of objects (files). ESM provides routines to create and destroy objects, to read and overwrite portions of objects, to extend and shrink the size of existing objects, and to sequence through files of objects. Also, ESM provides facilities to enable sophisticated client programs to influence policy decisions such as object clustering and buffer management.

For the purposes of implementing access to persistent objects in E, the key ESM routines are those that bring objects into main memory, update them there, and release them for migration back to disk. These routines are sm_ReadObject, sm_WriteObject, and sm_ReleaseObject, respectively. We discuss each of these routines in more detail below, as they are central to the operation of E as a persistent programming language.

The first routine, sm_ReadObject, provides the interface for establishing a memory reference to an object given its OID. Given an OID and a byte range specified by an offset and a length, sm_ReadObject brings the desired portion of the object into ESM's buffer pool (if it is not already buffer-resident) and returns a pointer to a newly allocated user descriptor to the calling program. The user descriptor itself contains a pointer to the requested portion of the object in the buffer pool. The requested data is considered "pinned" in the buffer pool until it released via an sm_Release call, and the user descriptor pointer remains valid for this duration. Again, it is important to remember that what sm_ReadObject returns is a user descriptor pointer, and that ESM reserves the right to relocate the actual data in the buffer pool as long as it updates the user descriptor's data pointer. As a result, data in ESM storage objects must always be accessed indirectly via the user descriptor.

The next routine, sm_WriteObject, is used whenever a storage object is to be updated. Before an object can be updated, it must first be pinned in the buffer pool by calling sm_ReadObject. For the purpose of updates, objects are addressed by user descriptors, not OIDs. The update itself is requested by passing sm_WriteObject a user descriptor, a specification of the range of pinned data that is to be updated, and a pointer to the data to be copied into the object. Objects may not be directly overwritten in memory because ESM uses a recovery scheme that requires it to be given an opportunity to record both the old and new values for updates to objects. Finally, updating an object does not result in the object being unpinned in general, but an option is provided to allow simultaneous unpinning if it is desired.

The third routine, which was already mentioned, is sm_ReleaseObject. This routine accepts a user descriptor pointer and unpins the associated object region, freeing the user descriptor for subsequent reuse. This routine is needed since sm_ReadObject pins a region of the target object in the ESM buffer pool, and both the buffer pool and the user descriptor pool are finite resources.

Note that no explicit disk I/O is specified by clients in the ESM interface. While the sm_ReadObject call requires that the specified object region be in the buffer pool when the call returns, this does not necessarily imply a disk operation. Similarly, sm_WriteObject and sm_ReleaseObject do not require that the referenced data in the buffer pool be written to disk. Although disk I/O must take place sometime, the interface allows ESM considerable flexibility in scheduling the actual disk operations.

An important point of this section is the relationship between addresses specified using OIDs and those specified via user descriptors. An OID is always a valid specifier for an object; it is valid for the object's entire lifetime and across all programs that have access to the storage volume that contains the object. However, there is no permanent relationship between an OID and an object in memory. To access an object in main memory, a user descriptor must first be established. This descriptor is then a valid means of addressing the specified object, but only until the user descriptor is explicitly freed.

3. TYPES AND PERSISTENCE IN E

This section reviews the semantics and usage of persistence in the E language. Persistence of objects in E is based on the method of allocation used when creating an object. Details of the type system limit the set of program data references that may be persistent. In what follows, we describe the E type system as it relates to persistence. In particular, we attempt to clarify four key topics — the database type system, the persistent storage class, dynamic allocation of persistent objects, and the role of ESM files.

Persistence of an object in E is dependent on a combination of the static type of a declared object and on the storage class or method of allocation of the object [Rich89a, Rich89b]. In particular, E uses a dual type system with a concept of database (db) types to statically distinguish the types of objects that may possibly persist from those types that describe objects that are sure to be transient. In E, all primitive types and type constructors of the native type system of C++ have an analogous db form. The declaration of a db type is determined by prepending ''db'' to the C++ type keyword. For example, the primitive C++ types int, float, and double have the db counterparts dbint, dbfloat, and dbdouble, respectively. Similarly, classes and structs of db types are declared using the keywords dbclass and dbstruct. Pointers to db types are also db types, as are arrays of db types. Structures and classes of db type may only contain data members that are also db types. Pointers are the only non-composite type in which a db type differs in its physical representation from a native type. The db type system was made distinct from the native C++ type system so that variables that are not declared as db types can be treated uniformly as transient, main memory objects, and can thus be manipulated with the same efficiency as is possible in C++.

The fundamental distinction between db types and native C++ types in E lies in the treatment of pointers to these types. For any non-db type, a pointer to an instance of that type is a simple (e.g., 4-byte) memory pointer and is treated as such by the compiler. In contrast, a pointer to a db type object is always a 16-byte db pointer (which is an OID, offset pair). Any pointer that is declared as pointing to a db type object may potentially point to a persistently allocated object, although it may also be used to point to a non-persistent instance of a db type. The treatment of values other than pointers in E's db type system is just as efficient as the treatment of native C++ values. However, the treatment of pointer values incurs the additional overhead of moving additional bytes around. The treatment of references through db pointers is the most important distinction between db types and non-db types.

For an object to be persistent in E, it must be declared as a db type. This is a necessary but not sufficient condition for persistence. To persist, the object must also be allocated persistently. For named objects, i.e., those directly declared in E programs, this is accomplished using the persistent storage class. This storage class is analogous to other C++ storage classes such as extern, static, and auto. If an object is declared to be persistent, the state of the declared object is maintained across different program runs using the same compiled module and ESM volume. Also, the storage class distinction between persistent and non-persistent db type objects allows transient objects to be created and used efficiently within the db type system; even within the db type system, temporary variables and other objects can be created which do not require the overhead of space allocation and deallocation through ESM.

The other method of creating persistent objects in E is dynamic allocation. Db type objects can be dynamically allocated as either persistent or transient objects. If a db type object is allocated using the standard C++ syntax for dynamic allocation, the allocated object will be a transient memory object. The lifetime of the object will then extend until the object is explicitly deleted or until its creating program terminates, whichever is sooner. Dynamic allocation of persistent objects is also possible, and is supported by allowing db type objects to be allocated within collections. Collections are the principle persistent storage management abstraction provided by E, and they are implemented using ESM files. At the simplest, a collection can be viewed as a class that implements a persistent heap. If a db type object is allocated within a persistent collection, its lifetime extends until it is explicitly or implicitly destroyed. An object may be destroyed explicitly by using the delete operator, or it may be destroyed implicitly by destroying the collection that contains it.

Consider the three db type objects allocated in the E code fragment shown in Figure 3. In the absence of explicit destruction by the delete operator, each of these objects will have a different lifetime. The lifetime of the object that `obj1` points to extends until the program that created the object terminates. This object only exists in the transient heap of the program. In contrast, `obj2` points to an object that will exist for the lifetime of the collection that it was created in; this collection will persist for the lifetime of the ESM storage volume on which it resides. This object will thus be maintained on disk across program executions. Finally, the object pointed to by `obj3` is also a ''persistent'' object of sorts, but its lifetime is limited by that of the transient collection that it was allocated in; when the non-persistent program variable `temp_collection` goes out of scope, all of the objects that it contains will be destroyed as well.

In summary, the key points of this section are (i) the notion of db types, (ii) the distinction between objects and references in db types and native C++ types, and (iii) the conditions under which an object may be persistent. There are no persistent values of native C++ types, and references to such types are simple, main memory pointers. Objects of db types may be, but are not necessarily, persistent; a persistent object must be of some db type. References to db type objects are always treated as if the referenced object may be persistent since all pointers to db types are capable of storing a persistent address. The persistence of named db type objects is determined by their declared

```
dbclass vcollection : collection[dbvoid];
persistent vcollection pers_collection;

{ dbchar *obj1, *obj2, *obj3;
      obj1 = new dbchar[10];
      obj2 = in (pers_collection) new dbchar[10];
      vcollection temp_collection;
      obj3 = in (temp_collection) new dbchar[10];
};
```

Figure 3: Object Lifetime Example.

storage classes, while the persistence of dynamically allocated db type objects depends on their method of allocation. Finally, db type values are handled by E just like native C++ values when they are not accessed via pointers, but all such values are treated as potentially being persistent when accessed via pointers.

4. E PERSISTENT VIRTUAL MACHINE INTERFACE

The E Persistent Virtual Machine (EPVM) provides a set of C function calls. The EPVM interface corresponds to a limited portion of the instruction set of a conventional computer. In this section we describe three main types of functions that EPVM provides. The first type is analogous to the load instructions in an instruction set architecture. These functions read a value from persistent storage given a location which is specified as a db pointer and an offset. The second type is analogous to the store instructions of an instruction set architecture. These functions accept a db pointer, an offset, and a value as parameters and store the value at the indicated persistent address. The third type of functions manipulate persistent pointer values, performing operations like pointer arithmetic and pointer comparisons that would be handled via integer arithmetic on address values in a conventional instruction set architecture. The functions listed in this section comprise the major part of the EPVM interface. There are a number of other auxiliary functions, not listed here, which were added to allow more efficient implementation of certain E language constructs. However, the functions listed here are sufficient to implement all accesses to persistent objects in E.

4.1. A Simple Example

We begin by considering a simple code E fragment that illustrates the three main uses of db pointers that the E compiler and EPVM need to handle, which are (i) dereferencing a pointer to obtain a value, (ii) assigning a value to a location specified via a pointer, and (iii) testing pointer values. The E source code for our example is given in Figure 4. The function shown there sets the elements in a linked list of integers to a sequence of integer values beginning at 1. It returns the length of the list, which is assumed to have been created elsewhere. The linked list element type is a db type, so persistent linked lists may be created and operated upon using this code.

```
dbstruct ilist {   /* simple integer linked list */
      dbint i;
      ilist * next;
};

dbint set_list(ilist * lpt) {
      dbint index = 0;
      while (lpt) {
            index++;
            lpt->i = index;
            lpt = lpt->next;
      }
      return index;
}
```

Figure 4: Pointer Uses in E.

The utility of EPVM can be illustrated by examining the C code that the E compiler would produce as output when presented with the E code of Figure 4. Figure 5 shows the code produced by the E compiler.[1] Since the E variable `lpt` is a pointer to a db type, all uses of it are interpreted through the EPVM interface. In this example, the interpretation is done through calling the functions dbNotNull, dbLongAssign, and dbPtrEval. There are three lines in the E source code that must be translated. First, the condition in the while statement, which tests `lpt` for being null, must be interpreted since db pointers are not the same as simple C pointers. Next, the assignment of the `index` value to the linked list element field is implemented through a call to dbLongAssign. Finally, the pointer `lpt` is reset to point to the next item in the list via a call to dbPtrEval, which extracts the value from the `next` field of the list element and uses it to replace the current value of `lpt`. Note that the variable `index` is of a db type, yet it is treated as a normal C variable in the compiled code since it is not accessed through a pointer.

4.2. Load/Store Function Addressing Format

As described in Section 3, persistent pointers are 16-byte quantities that consists of a 12-byte OID and a 4-byte offset within the object. Because of the size of these addresses, they are passed into the EPVM routines by reference; that is, we always pass in the memory address of the C language variable or expression that contains the persistent pointer. It is also common for a pointer dereference to specify an address at an offset from the pointer variable that the dereference is based on. This is illustrated by the following E code fragment:

```
dbint i;
dbint * j;
    ...
i = j[5];
```

Here, it is necessary to add an offset of 20 to the pointer contained in the variable `j` to compute the address of the value to be assigned to `i`. Rather than creating a new db pointer with the adjusted offset to pass to EPVM, all EPVM functions accept persistent addresses as a (DBREF *, offset) pair. Although the DBREF value contains an arbitrary offset already, the additional offset argument lets the compiler avoid creating copies of pointer values in many cases.

4.3. Load Functions

There are seven EPVM functions that "load" values from persistent memory. Each accepts a persistent address (specified by a db pointer) and an integer offset and returns a value derived from the data stored at the specified address. These functions are specified as C function prototypes in Figure 6. Each of these routines returns a value

```
struct ilist {      /* sizeof ilist == 20 */
        int i ;
        struct DBREF next ;
};

int set_list( lpt )
struct DBREF lpt ;
{
        int index ;
        index = 0 ;
        while ((dbNotNull ( & lpt , 0 ) ))
        {
                index ++ ;
                dbLongAssign ( & lpt , 0 , index ) ;
                dbPtrEval ( & lpt , & lpt , 4) ;
        }
        return index ;
}
```

Figure 5: Pointer Uses in C + EPVM.

[1] Variable and data member names have been cleaned up somewhat for human consumption.

```
char        dbCharEval(DBREF *, int);
short       dbShortEval(DBREF *, int);
long        dbLongEval(DBREF *, int);
float       dbFloatEval(DBREF *, int);
double      dbDoubleEval(DBREF *, int);
DBREF *     dbPtrEval(DBREF *, DBREF *, int);
void *      dbArbEval(DBREF *, int, int);
```

Figure 6: EPVM Load Functions.

of the indicated type. Note that the types of the values returned are a subset of the primitive data types of E. This subset is sufficient to cover all of the primitive types with additional casting. For example, unsigned integers would be evaluated with the call:

```
(unsigned int)dbLongEval(...)
```

For the first five functions, the value returned is the value that currently resides at the persistent address indicated by the (DBREF *, int) pair passed in as parameters. The interface for returning DBREF values is somewhat different, however. Since a DBREF value is a large, 16-byte C structure, we chose to return the value for dbPtrEval through a pointer rather than as the function return value. Thus, the first parameter of dbPtrEval is the memory address where the db pointer value will be placed, and this parameter is also returned as the value of the function. Finally, the function dbArbEval is used for cases not covered by the set of primitive values returned by the other six functions (e.g., structure values).

4.4. Store Functions

There are six functions that accept a persistent address and a value argument representing data to be stored in persistent storage. These functions store the value at the indicated address. Figure 7 specifies the interface to these EPVM functions. The first five of these functions each take a persistent address (specified by a db pointer and an offset) and a primitive value as arguments; they store the value into persistent storage at the specified address. They also return the value for convenience, allowing C-style chained assignment statements to be handled via nested function calls. For example, the E statement

```
*a = *b = 3;
```

would compile into the following C code fragment:

```
dbIntAssign(&a, 0, dbIntAssign(&b, 0, 3));
```

The dbPtrAssign function differs from the first five only in that its pointer arguments, which are db pointers, are passed and returned by address rather than by value.

4.5. Pointer Manipulation Functions

Although many of the operations on pointer values are simple enough to be compiled directly into C code, for modularity and abstraction we chose to implement the manipulation of these values as primitive EPVM operations as well. Their function prototypes are shown in Figure 8. The function dbCmpPtr returns a truth value (0 or 1) based on the comparison of two db pointers. The sense of the comparison is specified by the argument op, which specifies one of the 6 comparison operators of C (<, <=, >, >=, ==, !=). For example, consider the E code fragment at the top of the next page:

```
char        dbCharAssign(DBREF *, int, char);
short       dbShortAssign(DBREF *, int, short);
long        dbLongAssign(DBREF *, int, long);
float       dbFloatAssign(DBREF *, int, float);
double      dbDoubleAssign(DBREF *, int, double);
DBREF *     dbPtrAssign(DBREF *, int, DBREF *);
```

Figure 7: EPVM Store Functions.

```
dbchar *p1, *p2;
   ...
if (p1 < &p2[12]) { .... }
```

This would generate the interpretive EPVM call:

```
DBREF p1, p2;
   ...
if ( dbCmpPtr(&p1, 0, &p2, 12, CMP_LT) { .... }
```

Here, CMP_LT is a literal constant defined by the compiler. The next pointer manipulation function, dbNotNull, returns 1 if the address specified by its arguments is not null and 0 otherwise; i.e., it returns 0 if the persistent pointer indicates transient memory address 0, returning 1 otherwise.[2] The function dbPtrVal is used to copy a memory-resident db pointer value to another memory location with an optional adjustment of the offset portion of the address. The function dbMemPtr is use to create a db pointer from a main memory pointer. Finally, dbPtrSub performs C pointer subtraction, scaled by the appropriate data type size.

5. IMPLEMENTATION OF THE EPVM INTERPRETER

In Section 3, on persistence in E, we noted that all access to persistent objects involves access through db pointers. In the E 2.0 version of the E language, dereferencing of db pointers is totally encapsulated by the EPVM interpreter functions. Thus, the key to a usable implementation of E is an efficient implementation of the EPVM functions on top of the EXODUS Storage Manager (ESM).

A naive EPVM implementation would pin and release the byte range necessary to satisfy each persistent data reference in each of the Eval and Assign functions described in Section 4. In fact, the initial implementation of EPVM took this approach. However, the minimal costs for the ESM pin and unpin instructions are hundreds of machine instructions, so another approach was needed. The current approach is based on maintaining a cache of the storage object regions that are known to be buffered in ESM's buffer pool. In particular, EPVM maintains a table of active user descriptors through which it can access each buffered object region, and it performs a simple hash lookup into this table in order to map each persistent address into a corresponding user descriptor. User descriptors are established on demand, when a particular object region is first accessed; once a user descriptor has been established, it is used for all subsequent accesses to the region of the target object that it is valid for.

In the remainder of this section of the paper, we describe the methods used to establish new user descriptors in this table and to map db pointers into user descriptors. We also describe an enhancement that allows the OID to user descriptor mapping operation to be bypassed in certain cases.

5.1. What to Pin

Before we can access any data in an ESM object, we must decide what to pin. The sm_ReadObject interface permits arbitrary byte ranges within objects to be pinned in the buffer pool. In making this decision for EPVM, we wanted to choose the region to pin in such a way as to maximize the usability of the user descriptor established by the pin call. At the same time, though, we wanted to avoid making ESM perform excessive disk accesses for data that may never be used. For small objects, the decision was easy — since the underlying ESM I/O calls are page-based, small objects are alway buffered in the ESM buffer pool in their entirety. Thus, EPVM always pins the entire small object, which allows it to use a single user descriptor to perform any allowable access to the object.

ESM supports storage objects that may be almost arbitrarily large, so it is unreasonable to pin entire objects in all cases. Large objects are therefore handled using a paging scheme that works as follows. The EPVM interpreter

```
int        dbCmpPtr(DBREF *, int, DBREF *, int, op)
int        dbNotNull(DBREF *, int)
DBREF *    dbPtrVal(DBREF *, DBREF *, int);
DBREF *    dbMemPtr(DBREF *, void *);
int        dbPtrSub(DBREF *, offset, DBREF *, offset, scale);
```

Figure 8: EPVM Pointer Manipulation Functions.

---

[2] Transient memory addresses are denoted using OIDs with a disk volume of 0.

is compiled with a maximum object size that it will pin entirely. This size is also used as a block size for objects bigger that the maximum, and large objects are pinned by the EPVM in chunks equal to the block size (always beginning at an offset within the object that is a multiple of the block size). A separate user descriptor is established for each object block when it is accessed, and the hash table used to map from persistent addresses into user descriptors is based on both the OID and the offset. Of course, this makes the mapping process somewhat more complex; each reference must establish a block number based on the offset of a given reference within an object, and this block number is then used together with the unique field of the OID in calculating the hash function and matching the hash table entry for a given reference.

5.2. OID to User Descriptor Mapping

Given these simple policy decisions on how objects are pinned as they are accessed, we can now describe how EPVM maps persistent addresses to previously established user descriptors and thus how persistent values are accessed and updated. The process used to extract a value from a persistent address specified by a db pointer and an offset is illustrated in Figure 9. First, the internal and external offsets are combined and the result is split into an object block number and an offset within the block (step 1). Next, the block number and the unique field of the OID are used to compute an index into the interpreter's user descriptor hash table (step 2 in diagram). Then, the OID and block number of the hash table entry specified by this index are compared to those of the specified database address (step 3 in diagram). If these match, the user descriptor pointer in the hash bucket is used to get the correct base pointer for the object region (step 4), and the base pointer is combined with the object block offset to form the address of the requested data in the ESM buffer pool (step 5). Finally, this address may be used to obtain the requested data value. In step 3, if the comparison fails, EPVM repeats the comparison for any other entries in the same hash chain. If all of the comparisons fail, or if there was no initial entry in the hash table, a fault handling routine is called to establish a user descriptor for the requested address. For updates, the user descriptor pointer and object block offset are used as parameters and the sm_WriteObject call is used to update the object.

5.3. Buffer Management Policy

So far we have explained how object pages are pinned in the buffer pool and how persistent addresses are mapped to established user descriptors. Since the persistent object space maintained by ESM is potentially much larger that its buffer pool, however, the buffer pool may eventually become full. If a program accesses more objects and object blocks than the buffer pool can hold at one time, at some point EPVM will be unable to pin a newly accessed object. This condition is handled by releasing currently pinned objects and object blocks until sufficient space becomes

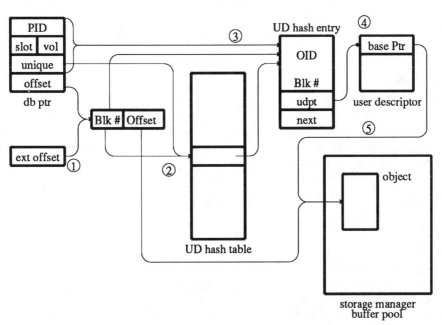

Figure 9: Access Through a Persistent Pointer.

available to handle the new request. The policy currently used by EPVM for releasing objects is a Clock-based LRU approximation based on reference bits kept in the hash table entries. When space is exhausted, EPVM sequentially scans all entries in the user descriptor hash table, freeing entries that have a previously cleared reference bit, and clearing any set reference bits, until sufficient space has been made available.

5.4. Pointer Swizzling

The general idea of ''pointer swizzling'' is to maintain two distinct forms for addressing persistent objects, one for disk-resident objects and another for memory-resident objects [Cock84, Maie86]. Pointers are transformed back and forth during the course of program execution. For example, a pointer in disk format could be transformed to memory format at its first use within a given program run, or all the pointers contained in a disk-based object could be transformed to the memory form when the object is first read from disk into main memory. (Note that the second method requires either a transitive closure reachability analysis or memory protection tricks to work properly, though.) Of course, if a persistent object contains pointers that are transformed into main memory form, its pointers must be transformed back to disk form before the object may be written back to disk.

Certain aspects of the design of the E language make a comprehensive pointer swizzling scheme difficult to implement. One problem is that the type system of E is based on C++, and ultimately C, making it difficult to determine what portion of an object represents a pointer. Union types can result in ambiguity about whether a particular data area represents a pointer or not, and casts can result in arbitrary data areas being treated as pointers regardless of their declared type. These issues could be reasonably dealt with by language restrictions and by maintaining additional data structures indicating the location of valid pointers.

A more difficult problem arises if one wishes to do incremental unswizzling. A fundamental goal of EXODUS is to reasonably handle object spaces that are larger than physical or even virtual memory, and to allow programs to access such spaces without restrictions. Thus, we did not wish to restrict the number or size of objects that a program may access. This implies that EPVM must be able to unpin objects in the buffer pool at rather arbitrary points during program execution in order to allow buffer pool space to be reclaimed. In order to unpin a particular object under a pointer swizzling scheme, it would be necessary to keep track of all valid pointers that could possibly point to the object so that they can be unswizzled (or marked invalid) when the object is unpinned or flushed to disk. While this may be possible in principle, the practical difficulties of doing this in a C-based language are considerable.

Another problem with pointer swizzling in E lies in the indirect nature of the ESM interface to buffered objects. Recall that when the sm_ReadObject call is used to pin an object or a region of an object in the buffer pool, ESM returns a pointer to one of its internal user descriptors rather than a direct pointer into the buffer pool. Because of this, it is impossible to transform persistent E pointers into direct memory pointers. Instead, their swizzled form contains the user descriptor pointer returned by ESM, and references through a swizzled pointer must indirect through the associated user descriptor.

5.4.1. What to Swizzle

Due to the considerations discussed above, rather than attempting a general solution, we implemented a limited form of pointer swizzling in EPVM. The solution implemented is based on transforming a limited set of persistent pointers — local variables which are db pointers. Space for keeping track of these variables is allocated from a global array of db pointers, with a simple stack discipline being employed at function entry and exit. To illustrate the approach, consider the following simple E code fragment:

```
f() {
    dbint *ipt, *ipt2;
    ...
    ipt = ipt2;
}
```

At function entry, a runtime support routine is called to allocate space in the global array for the db pointer variables ipt and ipt2. A main memory pointer is then used as a frame pointer for accessing the db pointer variables. In the example above, space must be allocated for two db pointers, and they will be accessed using the frame pointer with an appropriate compiler-assigned index. The resulting C code is shown in Figure 10. There, references to the variables ipt and ipt2 have been replaced by indirect references through the memory pointer variable _db_fpt. This variable acts as a frame pointer for the portion of the db pointer stack active in this function.

By restricting the location of db pointers that may be swizzled to a single fixed size array, we simplify some of the problems associated with pointer swizzling. The set of currently active local pointer variables is easily

```
/* internal globals for db pointer stack */
DBREF _db_pstack[MAX_DBSTACK];
DBREF * _db_stacktop = _db_pstack;

f() {
    DBREF * _db_fpt = _db_stacktop; /* set frame pointer */
    _db_stacktop += 2; /* make room for 2 local pointers */
    ...
    _db_fpt[0] = _db_fpt[1];  /* ipt = ipt2 */
    _db_stacktop = _db_fpt; /* release stack space on exit */
}
```

Figure 10: Managing Local Db Pointers.

determined from the bounds of the allocated portion of the pointer stack. If object release becomes necessary due to buffer pool overflow, the problem of invalidating pointers to released objects is reduced to scanning the active portion of the pointer stack for references to those objects. The pointer stack can also be used as a hint indicating what objects are likely to be accessed as the program continues execution. Lastly, all EPVM routines are passed memory addresses for their db pointer arguments, so EPVM routines can easily determine whether their arguments are candidates for swizzling by checking to see if the address of the pointer lies within the range of the local pointer stack. This allows the swizzling operation to be handled easily within the normal EPVM pointer interpretation code; no special code needs to be generated by the compiler.

5.4.2. Swizzled Pointer Format

As mentioned earlier, due to the indirect nature of the ESM interface, the swizzled form of a 16-byte db pointer contains a user descriptor pointer that can be used to access the data that the swizzled pointer refers to. When a pointer is swizzled, the 4-byte unique field in its OID is replaced with the user descriptor pointer, and the volume ID field within the OID is used as a tag to indicate the swizzled state of the pointer. In addition, the page ID field of the OID is used to store a pointer to the user descriptor hash table entry that corresponds to the user descriptor. As a result, swizzled pointers always contain sufficient information to be directly converted back into their unswizzled form.

5.4.3. Using Swizzled Pointers

The process for accessing data through a swizzled pointer under this scheme is shown in Figure 11. First, the volume ID field of the OID is tested. If its value is 0 (the transient memory volume ID), the user descriptor pointer stored in the unique field of the OID is used to obtain the address of the object in the ESM buffer pool (step 1). The offset portion of the pointer is then added to the address obtained in step 1, along with any external offset (step 2). The resulting address can then be used to obtain the referenced data. The swizzled form of a db pointer provides a direct enough access path so that the compiler can reasonably generate inline code to access objects in the ESM buffer pool if desired, rather than always using the EPVM interpretive interface. For example, consider the following E code fragment:

```
dbint i;
dbint * ipt;
 ...
i = ipt[3];
```

Given our stack-frame-based approach to allocating local db pointers, the assignment expression can be compiled into C code as follows:

```
_db_fpt[0].volid ==0 ?
    (*(long *)_db_fpt[0].udpt->basePtr + _db_fpt[0].offset + 12) :
    dbLongEval( &_db_fpt[0], 12);
```

In this example, if the pointer is not in the swizzled form, the EPVM function dbLongEval is called to get the value (as if no swizzling were being done). If the pointer can legally be swizzled, swizzling will take place as a side effect of the dbLongEval call. Pointers are transformed into the swizzled form by the first access using the unswizzled form of the pointer; they are transformed back to unswizzled form only when the object that the pointer refers to needs to be released from the ESM buffer pool. Finally, even if inline code generation (a compile-time option) is

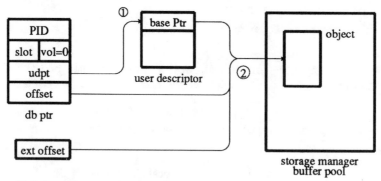

1) follow udpt to get base ptr

2) add offsets to form buffer pool address

Figure 11: Access Through a Swizzled Pointer.

not enabled, swizzled pointers allow improved efficiency within the EPVM interpreter itself as well.

5.4.4. Swizzling Limitations

As previously stated, pointer swizzling in E 2.0 is limited to local pointer variables. In some cases, this limitation can be overcome by the programmer though the use of explicit temporary pointers if efficiency is especially critical. There is another serious limitation of pointer swizzling in this environment, however, which arises when EPVM has not cached an entire object. Recall that large objects are cached in blocks, and that user descriptors for large objects point to blocks rather than whole objects. Since a db pointer may point to an arbitrary offset within an object, the range of bytes accessible from a swizzled large object pointer is limited by the block boundaries that surround the location indicated by the pointer. Since this can vary arbitrarily at runtime, pointer swizzling is not implemented for pointers into large objects. Pointers to large, multi-block objects are always kept in their db form and are not swizzled.

6. EPVM PERFORMANCE

In this section we present a detailed, low-level analysis of the performance we have obtained using the EPVM-based approach to persistence described here. We give the costs of the basic interpreter functions under best case conditions, which is when a reference is made to an object that was previously cached by the interpreter when no hashing collisions occur. The costs are presented in terms of execution cycles for a MIPS-based processor; for the most part, one cycle corresponds to the execution of a single machine instruction. The results presented here were obtained using the "pixie"-based profiling facility on a DECstation 3100. One cycle corresponds to 80 nanoseconds of clock time on a 12.5 MHz machine.

6.1. Access Function Costs

In the preceding section, we described the implementation of EPVM in terms of the mapping of db pointers to ESM user descriptors. As we shall see, this mapping is the most significant cost in the current EPVM implementation, but the cost of accessing ESM's buffer pool through user descriptors is also significant. We begin our analysis by discussing the cost of executing a single evaluation function in the interpreter, dbLongEval. This cost is typical of the set of functions that provide access to persistent data. The cost was measured at 47 cycles, including both call setup and function execution, broken out as indicated in Table 1.

Of the 47 total cycles, we estimate that about 9 cycles (address computation and dereference, tests for non-persistence) are costs that would occur in some form under any implementation using the user descriptor based interface of ESM. The marginal cost associated with EPVM is thus about 38 cycles per reference. This marginal cost is considerable, and thus needs to be justified. The main justification for this cost is that it is relatively small compared to the ESM costs for establishing and releasing user descriptors. The minimal cost measured for this pair of ESM operations was 497 cycles, not including call setup costs. Viewed another way, avoiding one ESM pin/unpin operation pair is sufficient to compensate for the overhead of about 13 EPVM object value accesses using this interface. The cost of using the EPVM interface and implementation is clearly justified compared to the naive alternative of creating and deleting a user descriptor for every access; of course, this is a strawman argument. We

Operation	Cycles
Call setup	3
Function entry and return overhead	7
Test for non-persistence	2
User descriptor hash lookup	26
Set reference bit	2
Address computation and dereference	7
Minimal reference cost	47

Table 1: Access Function Costs.

do note, though, that for a working set that fits entirely in the ESM buffer pool, each object will be pinned and unpinned exactly once by EPVM. Under these conditions, neglecting the cost of the initial pin operation, any approach based on dynamically establishing user descriptors would have to, on average, use each user descriptor for at least 13 accesses in order to be more efficient than the EPVM implementation.

The analysis above shows that the dominant cost in EPVM is that of the hash-based OID to user descriptor mapping process. As such, we analyze this cost in more detail. As mentioned previously, the object caching scheme handles both entire small objects and blocks of large objects; the address mapping scheme must therefore consider both the OID and the offset within an object when translating a particular reference. Moreover, this cost is incurred for both large and small objects, as a db pointer by itself does not indicate whether it points to a small or large object. If the large/small object distinction were eliminated, and objects were always cached in their entirety, the cost of the hash lookup would be reduced to 19 cycles. In the limit, the best possible performance would be obtained by using 4-byte OIDs instead of the current 12-byte OIDs. We estimated the performance of such a best-case system by modifying EPVM to utilize only the unique field of the OID when hashing. This reduced the cost of the user descriptor hash lookup to 12 cycles. Thus, paging large objects and using 12-byte OIDs each impose a 7-cycle cost in interpretation relative to the simplest possible scheme.

6.2. Update Function Critical Path Costs

The basic costs of the assignment functions include all of the basic costs of a typical access function, plus the cost of calling ESM to update the referenced data and executing some additional code to distinguish persistent and non-persistent references. For dbLongAssign, which is typical, the total cost is 63 cycles in the function interpreter plus an additional 109 cycles for the ESM update routine. The additional 19 cycles here, as compared to dbLongEval, reflects the cost of setting up the ESM update call as well as the cost of passing an additional argument. As can be seen from the cycle counts quoted above, the cost of calling ESM to update the referenced object is considerably greater than the costs associated with the functional interface. Moreover, the overhead of updating objects is likely to increase considerably with the forthcoming ESM release (with concurrency control and recovery); the relative cost of using the EPVM interface is thus not likely to be the performance bottleneck for updates.

6.3. Costs Using Swizzled Pointers

We can now compare the costs just discussed with the cost of references using the limited form of pointer swizzling described in Section 5.4. We consider four methods of accessing a persistent value here — dereferencing a swizzled db pointer using inline code, dereferencing a swizzled db pointer using the EPVM interface, dereferencing an unswizzled pointer and swizzling it via the EPVM interface, and dereferencing an "unswizzleable" pointer. The total cost for each of these cases is listed in Table 2.

The 11-cycle cost for the inline dereference of a swizzled pointer is a clear improvement, though it does carry a cost in terms of added code size. The additional cost associated with using a swizzled pointer within EPVM reflects function call overhead; this correlates well with the estimate of the call overhead made in Section 6.1. The difference between the swizzled and unswizzled reference costs using the EPVM interface also correlates with our previous estimate of the cost of the hash-based user descriptor lookup used for persistent pointers. The 56-cycle cost for an initial access reflects the cost of both the unswizzled access process and the swizzling operation on the pointer used for the access. Thus, the additional cost for performing the swizzling operation is seen to be 9 cycles. The additional 1-cycle cost for the unswizzleable case here, relative to the cost of 47 cycles in the non-swizzling case in Section 6.1, is due to a failed test for swizzleability that does not take place if swizzling is not used at all.

Operation	Cycles
Inline dereference of swizzled pointer	11
Interpreted dereference of swizzled pointer	20
Interpreted dereference and swizzling of unswizzled pointer	56
Dereference of unswizzleable pointer	48

Table 2: Swizzled Pointer Costs.

6.4. Faulting Costs

The cost of actually reading an object into memory from disk is difficult to estimate, as it is highly dependent upon the state of ESM at the time. We thus did not try to estimate that cost here. Instead, we estimated a minimal cost for performing the pin and unpin operations that establish and release a user descriptor. This was done by measuring a simple test program that called ESM directly, repeatedly pinning and then unpinning the same small object via calls to sm_ReadObject and sm_ReleaseObject. After the initial call, the object is resident in the ESM buffer pool, so the only costs involved after that should be the bookkeeping needed to manage the user descriptor. The simplest sm_ReadObject/sm_ReleaseObject pair was measured as taking 497 cycles, as mentioned earlier. The additional cost in the EPVM interpreter for establishing a hash table entry for a new user descriptor was measured at 77 cycles (in addition to the normal cost of the EPVM call creating the fault). Thus, the minimal cost for establishing an OID to user descriptor mapping is 574 cycles.

6.5. Discussion

From these discussions, we conclude that the cost of accessing persistent objects through the EPVM interface is moderately expensive but not prohibitive. Without pointer swizzling, on a 12.5 MHz MIPS architecture processor such as the DECstation 3100, the cost can be as low as about 4 microseconds per access to persistent storage. The cost of using the functional EPVM interface for persistent pointer evaluation is expensive, but the overhead is not unreasonable compared to the cost of using user descriptors for access, especially when compared to the ESM costs for establishing user descriptors and updating objects. The cost of translating OIDs to user descriptors is the dominant cost in the current implementation of EPVM; this cost could be reduced if the OID format used by ESM were simplified. Finally, swizzling pointers can also reduce access costs considerably, although indirect access through user descriptors still imposes a significant additional cost compared to a normal main memory pointer access. We expect the current implementation of E to be reasonably efficient for applications that operate on threaded, persistent data structures with sufficient locality of reference that a reasonable working set can be kept buffer-resident.

7. CONCLUSIONS

We have described in detail one approach to implementing persistent data access in the E programming language. This approach, which is based on interpretive access to persistent objects though a functional interface, is quite general. Implementation of compiler support for this approach was straightforward; the efficiency of the implementation depends largely on the efficiency of the underlying interpreter. We described the design, implementation, and initial performance measurements of an EPVM interpreter that is reasonably efficient as compared to the underlying EXODUS storage manager. We argued that the costs of EPVM interpretation are reasonable given the complexity of the underlying persistent object store. Finally, we also showed that pointer swizzling techniques can improve performance markedly, even given the indirect nature of the EXODUS storage manager interface.

The approach that we have described here is somewhat similar in flavor to the abstract machine approach used in the implementations of PS-Algol and Napier [Atki83, Dear88], but EPVM is much more limited in scope. The abstract machines for PS-Algol and Napier implement many aspects of their languages, and they interact much more strongly with the language type systems and programming environments. EPVM is primarily restricted to providing access to persistent storage. The implementation of E depends on support provided by the underlying C compiler for code generation, and on the Unix linkers and debuggers for programming environment support; most type-dependent issues are handled statically by the E compiler.

It is also interesting to compare EPVM to the approach taken by Richardson in the 1.2 E compiler [Rich90]. In 1.2 E, the compiler generated explicit pin and unpin calls to establish the user descriptors corresponding to each pointer value used by an E program to access data. The goal was to use static analysis techniques to establish the minimal number of user descriptors possible, and to be able to amortize the cost of pin and unpin operations over many accesses through each user descriptor. It is easy to construct examples where this approach is clearly superior, but one can also construct examples that traverse threaded data structures and require many pin and unpin operations relative to the number of persistent accesses performed. For example, under the 1.2 E approach, a traversal of a list of persistent objects, where the list is linked by db pointers, would likely require one pin and unpin operation for each node traversed. Under the EPVM approach, the first traversal of the list would also need to pin all of the objects on the list; however, subsequent traversals would require no pin or unpin operations. If few data accesses were made on each traversal, the pin and unpin overhead might be the dominant cost. We conjecture that the class of problems handled reasonably well by the EPVM-based implementation of E is somewhat broader than that which would be handled well, at least without interprocedural analysis, by the 1.2 E approach.

Despite these arguments, it is clear that the cost of persistent object accesses using the techniques described here is quite high compared to that of normal memory accesses. Even our pointer swizzling costs did not come close to memory access costs. In contrast, a virtual memory based approach offers the possibility of performing accesses to persistent storage with a relatively small marginal cost per accessed object [Shek90]. However, such approaches have other problems, such as address space limitations and the difficulty of managing a shared, persistent address space. We feel that the approach shown here may prove to be a reasonable compromise, and it also offers a flexible environment for further research.

REFERENCES

[Atki83]   M. Atkinson, M., *et. al*, "Algorithms for a Persistent Heap," *Software — Practice & Experience*, Vol. 13, 1983.

[Care89a]   M. Carey *et. al*, "The EXODUS Extensible DBMS Project: An Overview," in *Readings in Object-Oriented Databases*, S. Zdonik and D. Maier, eds., Morgan-Kaufman, 1989.

[Care89b]   M. Carey *et. al*, "Storage Management for Objects in EXODUS," in *Object-Oriented Concepts, Databases, and Applications*, W. Kim and F. Lochovsky, eds., Addison-Wesley, 1989.

[Cock84]   W. Cockshott, *et. al*, "Persistent Object Management System," *Software — Practice and Experience*, Vol. 14, 1984.

[Dear88]   A. Dearle, *On the Construction of Persistent Programming Environments*, Ph.D. Thesis, Computational Science Dept., University of St. Andrews, St. Andrews, Scotland, June 1988.

[Maie86]   D. Maier, "Why Object-Oriented Databases Can Succeed Where Others Have Failed," *Proc. of the 1st Int'l. Workshop on Object-Oriented Database Systems*, Pacific Grove, CA, Sept. 1986.

[Rich89a]   J. Richardson, M. Carey, and D. Schuh, *The Design of the E Programming Language*, Technical Report No. 824, Computer Sciences Dept., University of Wisconsin, Feb. 1989.

[Rich89b]   J. Richardson and M. Carey, "Persistence in the E Language: Issues and Implementation," *Software — Practice & Experience*, Vol. 19, Dec. 1989.

[Rich90]   J. Richardson, "Compiled Item Faulting," *Proc. of the 4th Int'l. Workshop on Persistent Object Systems*, Martha's Vineyard, MA, Sept. 1990.

[Shek90]   E. Shekita and M. Zwilling, "Cricket: A Mapped Persistent Object Store," *Proc. of the 4th Int'l. Workshop on Persistent Object Systems*, Martha's Vineyard, MA, Sept. 1990.

[Stro86]   Stroustrup, B., *The C++ Programming Language*, Addison-Wesley, Reading, MA, 1986.

An Initial Look at Abstraction Mechanisms and Persistence

Alexander L. Wolf

AT&T Bell Laboratories
600 Mountain Avenue
Murray Hill, NJ 07974
wolf@ulysses.att.com

Abstract

One approach to supporting persistence in a language is to treat persistence as just another bit of functionality to be implemented in the language, rather than somehow making persistence a genuine part of the language. This is particularly useful for languages that already exist but do not have a notion of persistence. Success, not to mention the quality of the result, depends heavily upon the abstraction mechanisms available in the language, since it is the abstraction mechanisms that are used to simulate extension of the language. I have been involved in the design of a persistence mechanism that has been integrated in this manner into Ada and C++, languages having rather different abstraction mechanisms. This paper discusses the interaction between the languages' abstraction mechanisms and the persistence mechanism. In addition, it gives some initial thoughts regarding the integration of the persistence mechanism with ML, a language with yet another set of abstraction mechanisms.

1   Introduction

For the past several years I have been involved in research aimed at the development of object management systems for next-generation software environments (e.g., [12]) and other such design support systems. Object management systems are distinguished from other kinds of information repositories by such things as the complexity of the objects they are to manage, the complexity of the relationships among the objects, the variety in the sizes of the objects, the non-traditional access methods required, the non-traditional concurrency and transaction disciplines that are encountered, and so on [5, 15].

One key aspect of object management systems is persistence. While at the University of Massachusetts, I participated in the design of a model of persistence for use in software environments [14]. The main features of this model include: orthogonal and transparent persistence, the use of side-by-side name spaces, dynamic persistence by instance (i.e., persistence can be determined on an instance-by-instance basis during execution), and persistence by reachability from other persistent objects. In addition, the model provides the notion of a repository that is responsible for coordinating persistence as well as coordinating concurrent access to persistent objects. While all aspects of this model may not be appropriate for all applications, it appears from our experience to be quite suitable for software environments.

To gain practical experience with the model, we developed a system called PGRAPHITE. PGRAPHITE is essentially an implementation of the model for Ada and for one particularly complex and common type of object, the directed graph. While the predominant methods of incorporating persistence into a language have involved the development of a completely new language (e.g., Galileo [2], Napier [6]), the modification of an existing language in some substantial way (e.g., PS-Algol [3], E [9], O++ [1]), and/or the use of a language that has at most dynamic type checking and at worst no type checking at all (e.g., WORLDS [13]), we chose to take a different tack. That tack was to use the inherent abstraction capabilities of an existing strongly typed, statically type-checked language, in this case Ada, as the means of providing a persistence mechanism to developers of applications written in that language [10]. PGRAPHITE has been profitably used for several years in a wide variety of software environment tools.

Since joining Bell Laboratories I have been pursuing a generalization and expansion of the model of persistence provided by PGRAPHITE that are aimed at two goals. The first is to add facilities such as querying, indexing, and deletion. The second goal is to better understand the interaction of the model of persistence with the abstraction mechanisms of a variety of programming languages. Thus, going beyond Ada, I have implemented the extended model of persistence for C++ and begun to investigate persistence for ML. The C++ implementation, a library called Persi, has been used in the construction of a number of systems, including a persistent representation of semantically analyzed C++ code and several tools that share and manipulate that representation.

This paper reports on initial results of the second goal mentioned above. It describes a set of relevant issues to consider about abstraction mechanisms and then shows how the abstraction mechanisms available in Ada and C++ affected the designs of PGRAPHITE and Persi. It also gives initial thoughts on an integration of the model with ML.

2   Issues

The abstraction mechanisms of a language form the foundation for such things as extensibility, type consistency, modularity, and information hiding. In addition, they are used to aid program construction itself (e.g., libraries, inheritance, etc.). Part of the challenge in any particular language's design is to provide abstraction mechanisms of suitable power that achieve these somewhat conflicting goals.

A facility for managing the persistent objects of programs written in some language can be viewed simply as any other application to be programmed in that language. It is a particularly interesting one, of course, since it places especially heavy demands on abstraction mechanisms. As such, it is a good test of those mechanisms. Here we concentrate on the issues associated with five, not necessarily independent, aspects of the problem:

1. *Extensibility.*

   A goal of language design has been to support the expression of programming solutions in terms appropriate to the application domain. For general-purpose languages, this means allowing the programmer to extend, or appear to extend, the language with new "primitive" concepts, presumably relevant to the application. For persistence, this means the ability to add notions of persistent object, access to a persistent object, repository for persistent objects, and access to a repository (including, perhaps, management of concurrent access and recovery from failures). Moreover, it means the ability to add the persistence property to (arbitrary) application objects.

2. *Typing.*

   There are really three dimensions to this aspect of the problem.

   (a) *type vs. shape vs. value*

      The type of an object has to do with how that object can be manipulated. Typically, this is expressed in terms of the set of operations that can be applied to the object. The shape of an object has to do with how the object is physically represented, both in primary and secondary storage. The value of an object reflects its state (i.e., what fills its shape).

   (b) *static vs. dynamic establishment*

      Generally, by static we mean prior to execution of a program or at creation time of an object, whichever is relevant, and by dynamic we mean during execution of a program or during the lifetime of an object, again whichever is relevant. It is possible for each of type, shape, and value to be either statically or dynamically established. Some examples: subtyping is a common mechanism for dynamically changing the type of an object while leaving its shape and value alone; an object's shape may change when moving between primary and secondary storage or between one machine and another; finally, object values may be mutable or immutable.

   (c) *static vs. dynamic discovery*

      Information about the type and shape of an object can be "discovered" either statically or dynamically. (Of course, if type or shape are established dynamically, then the information cannot be discovered statically.)

   Typing issues for persistence revolve around the following questions:

- Is the type of an object bound by the persistence mechanism? For example, is there some restriction on the interface to an object, such as the operations that are permitted?

- Is the shape of an object bound by the persistence mechanism? For example, must there be a particular layout in primary storage?

- Is the persistence mechanism bound by the type of an object or can it "violate" the type? Typically, violation of a type means being given direct access to the shape and value of an object, which may increase efficiency, but reduce optimization (e.g., the entire value of an object may not need to persist, but this fact may not be evident simply from the shape).

- Is there a uniformity to the type and/or shape information that can be taken advantage of by the persistence mechanism?

- Does the language provide access to type and shape information and, if so, statically or dynamically?

- Is the type and shape information captured as objects that can themselves persist or is the information captured in some other way? The assumption here is that type and shape information must be available in some form as long as an object of that type or shape exists.

3. *Modularity.*

People have proposed many different ways to organize a software system that results in a "modular" design. The basic idea is to isolate concerns within cohesive pieces of code, or modules, and to minimize interactions among those modules. A language can minimally support modularity by providing features to clearly demarcate modules and indicate their points of contact. Modularity and typing are related in that modules are often used in languages as the means to define the type and shape of objects. Modularity and extensibility interrelate in the following way: It is desirable to be able to extend a language by simply adding modules. For persistence, this means adding modules that realize such things as the persistent object and persistent store abstractions. Of course, those additional modules would have to interact with other modules, both old and new. A laudable goal is that no changes should be required of modules to support those new interactions. Specifically, existing modules should not change to accommodate the persistence modules, new modules should not be specially designed to interact with the persistence modules, and the persistence modules should not have to change to accommodate new modules that would make use of the persistence modules. Not surprisingly, this can be a very difficult goal to achieve absolutely, but clearly one worth striving toward.

4. *Information hiding.*

Information hiding is essentially a technique for enforcing modular interactions among system components. Typically, it is based on a delineation of the public portions of a module; those public portions serve as the interface to the module. In effect, the public portions define a protocol through which modules can interact. One question for persistence, as alluded to above, is whether typing is enforced. Another is whether the language itself provides public entities to access type and shape information. (One could argue that compilers must have these entities available in order to do their work, but in many languages these entities are not then made available to application programs.)

5. *Program construction.*

Given the ability to extend a language with a persistence mechanism, what is involved in actually writing programs that make use of the mechanism? In particular, the following questions seem relevant:

- If the type and/or shape of an object must be tailored to accommodate the persistence mechanism, how is that tailoring performed?

- If the modules implementing the persistence mechanism must be tailored to accommodate particular persistent object (types), how is that tailoring performed?

3   The Model of Persistence

The model of persistence being used here is described in [14]. For those unfamiliar with the model, this section provides a brief review of its key features.

Orthogonal and Transparent Persistence

The persistence property of a type is orthogonal to other properties of that type [3]. In fact, persistence is a property of instances, not of types, such that there is no restriction on what kinds of types can have persistent instances and any given type may have instances that persist and instances that do not persist. Moreover, persistence is transparent in that programmers need not be aware of the mapping to, or the existence of, secondary storage representations of persistent object instances; from the programmer's perspective, all objects of a given type have the same appearance (i.e., interface) even though some may be persistent instances and others not. An object's persistence property is something that a programmer may choose to pay attention to or choose to ignore.

Side-by-side Name Spaces

Every language provides some way of referring to instances of types. But in most languages, this mechanism turns out to be somewhat restrictive. In particular, the validity of such references is typically not guaranteed outside of a single program execution. Moreover, the references form a name space that is normally not controllable by anything other than the run-time system of the programming language. There are sound reasons for these restrictions, mostly concerning efficiency. In order to achieve a name space of object references that is valid within and between separate program executions, one must gain control over the name space in one of two ways: by modifying the run-time system of the language or by custom-building a name space on top of that which is already provided by the language. The complexity and threat to portability of the former are prohibitive in most settings, while the latter usually results in a severe efficiency loss due to the unavoidable translations that then must occur between the custom-built name space and the language's primitive name space upon each and every object access.

Our model of persistence, rather than assuming a "single" name space, is based on two, *side-by-side* name spaces and translations between them. Fortunately, this translation process can be made to occur quite infrequently. One of the name spaces is made up of the "normal" references to objects provided by the run-time system of a language. We call such references *non-persistent references* (NPRs), since they themselves cannot be preserved. The other name space is used to refer to persistent objects in a more "enduring" way. We call references in this name space *persistent identifiers* (PIds).

When application programs manipulate objects, they use NPRs (i.e., the primitive reference mechanism provided by the language) to refer to those objects, whether or not those objects persist. If one or more other programs need to refer to an object at some, perhaps indeterminate, time in the future, a PId for the object must be requested. This has the effect of guaranteeing that the object will persist. The PId must then be translated back into an NPR again before the object can be manipulated.

Dynamic Persistence by Instance

Our experience in the area of software environments and tools has led us to conclude that the persistence of a given object is something that occasionally cannot be determined until after that object has been created. Therefore, the persistence mechanism must allow types whose instances may or may not persist and allow the persistence of a given instance to be determined at arbitrary times. This implies that the persistence mechanism must also provide a means to explicitly designate an object as persistent. In fact, this is accomplished as a side-effect of requesting a PId for an object; an object persists if a request is made for an "enduring" way of referring to the object.

Persistence by Reachability

One can imagine that dynamic persistence by instance could be inconvenient if every persistent object would have to be explicitly designated. The model therefore provides a way of implicitly designating persistent objects through reachability from some other (explicitly or implicitly designated) persistent object. Indeed, all objects reachable from a persistent object are necessarily persistent.

Repositories

The store for persistent objects is modeled as a collection of what we call repositories. A repository can be thought of as the second name space described above, within which the names of persistent objects are

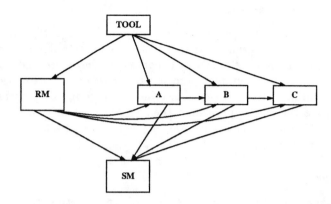

Figure 1: PGRAPHITE/Ada Implementation Architecture of the Persistence Model.

guaranteed to be unique and unchanging. Although the name of an object cannot change, the value of that object can be modified. In other words, objects in repositories are mutable. This permits the modeling of both mutable and immutable stores, since immutability can be achieved by building an appropriate interface on top of the mutable store, one that does not permit modification of objects in a repository.

We distinguish two levels of access to a repository. Both these levels must be passed through before persistent objects can actually be manipulated. The first level is delineated by open and close operations, which broadly indicate a period of time during which access is desired, much like the open and close operations associated with files in a file system. Within that period of time, a finer grain of access to a repository must be indicated using operations to begin and end what we call a session; several sessions may occur during the time between the opening and closing of a repository. The session is a notion concerned with issues of concurrency and reliability, serving as the unit of consistency for concurrency control and transaction management. The advantage of having two levels of access is that opening and closing might involve time-consuming actions, such as establishing and breaking network connections, whose costs could then be amortized over several sessions.

4   Ada and PGRAPHITE

As mentioned above, PGRAPHITE is an implementation of the persistence model for directed-graph objects in Ada. It has been well documented in the literature; the reader is referred elsewhere for details [10, 14]. (Recent extensions and enhancements, which are not considered here, are described in [11].)

Figure 1 shows the gross architecture of the PGRAPHITE implementation of the persistence model, in which tools communicate[1] with a repository manager (RM) and some number of types of objects (A, B, and C).[2] Communication between tools and the repository manager is for the purpose of creating and deleting repositories, open and closing repositories, and beginning and ending sessions. Tools communicate with objects to perform the normal activities associated with those objects. They additionally communicate when a tool requires a PId or an NPR. Other communication links exist between the repository manager and (secondary) storage manager (SM), between the repository manager and all types, between all types and the storage manager, and between some types (i.e., if objects of type X make reference to objects of type Y, then X and Y must communicate; in the figure, this relationship holds only between A and B and between B and C).

Extensibility

Ada supports the definition of user-defined abstract types through the package construct. In PGRAPHITE there is a repository-manager package as well as packages, called interface packages, for each type of persistent

---

[1] Communication is indicated in the figure by an arrow between two boxes.
[2] Note that in Ada, types are essentially packages and that communication with objects is really through packages.

object. An interface package provides the persistent-object abstraction for that particular type in addition to the "normal" abstraction associated with that type.

Typing

Ada does not provide run-time type or shape information. The type information is needed to guarantee type consistency of shared, persistent objects, while the shape information is needed to understand the format of objects for conversion of NPRs to PIds.[3] PGRAPHITE compensates for these shortcomings by capturing type and shape information for itself as code in interface packages. There are several ramifications of this:

- As long as all access to persistent objects is through interface packages, then type consistency can be guaranteed.

- Interface packages completely determine the shape of their objects in primary memory. However, the storage manager may require a different shape, which implies a certain amount of translation.

- Interface packages manage secondary storage for their own objects. This means that repository managers do not require access to shape information. However, it does mean that interface packages must communicate among themselves if an object of one type contains an NPR to an object of another type so that the NPR/PId conversion can take place.

The need to capture type and shape information, as well as the need for communication between a repository manager and interface packages and communication among interface packages, implies that persistent types must be special (i.e., specially written). Thus, arbitrary types cannot have instances that persist.

Modularity

Ada supports a reasonably good modularization for the implementation of the persistence mechanism. The repository abstraction is encapsulated within its own module and all interactions with secondary storage are encapsulated within a storage-manager package. On the negative side, however, the persistent-object abstraction is spread across all interface packages. In addition, each interface package must on its own communicate with the storage manager. Finally, the repository manager is limited to handling a fixed set of types; it must be rewritten in order to add a new type of object to a repository.

Information Hiding

As mentioned above, type and shape information are managed locally by each interface package so that the persistence mechanism, in the guise of the repository manager, does not require access to that information. However, since each interface package must communicate with the storage manager, the external format of objects must be known to all interface packages. (Alternatively, each interface package could have its own storage manager based on a specialized format. This would seem, however, to introduce needless complexity.)

Program Construction

As should be clear from the preceding discussion, the two major difficulties in using the persistence mechanism in Ada are that (*i*) interface packages must be specially written to communicate with other interface packages, repository managers, and storage managers; and (*ii*) repository managers must be written to handle particular types. Recognition of these difficulties led to the development of two processors, one to construct interface packages for directed-graph objects[4] and the other to construct repository manager packages. It also led to the development of a standard interface to storage managers to insulate components from changes to storage managers.

---

[3] Recall that primary memory pointers (NPRs) must be converted to PIds for placement in secondary storage.

[4] A recent enhancement automates construction of relation and relationship objects as well [11].

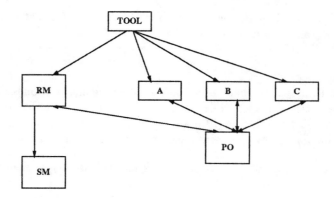

Figure 2: Persi/C++ Implementation Architecture of the Persistence Model.

5   C++ and Persi

Where PGRAPHITE is strongly oriented toward an Ada-like type model and currently provides automated support only for a few kinds of objects, Persi applies the persistence model within the context of C++'s richer ("object-oriented") type model and to arbitrary user-defined types. Continuing the tack of using only the inherent abstraction capabilities of the implementation language, Persi provides a persistence mechanism to developers of C++ applications without requiring any modifications to either the language processor or the run-time system. (Such changes were made for E and O++.)

C++ offers a quite different set of abstraction capabilities from those available in Ada. These capabilities turn out to admit to a very different, indeed better, implementation architecture for the model of persistence (see Figure 2). Heavy use is made of classes, inheritance, subtyping, and dynamic function binding (i.e., virtual functions, in the C++ terminology). Briefly, a persistent object must be an instance of a class that is derived from the Persi library class PersistentObject. In addition to the particular abstraction that it defines, the object's class provides implementations for certain simple virtual functions declared in PersistentObject. The virtual functions define a protocol for communication between repositories and persistent objects. Use of this protocol is invisible and irrelevant to application programs. The store for persistent objects is defined in the class Repository, abstracting away low-level details of storage management, concurrency control, index maintenance, and the like. An important departure from PGRAPHITE is the fact that Repository also provides the persistent-object abstraction of PIds and NPRs, rather than depending on each object type to provide that abstraction.

Referring to Figure 2, notice that as in PGRAPHITE, tools communicate with a repository manager and some number of types (classes) of objects.[5] The Persi/C++ architecture, in contrast to that of PGRAPHITE/Ada, requires only that the repository manager and storage manager communicate, and the repository manager and abstract supertype of all persistent objects, PersistentObject (PO), communicate.

Extensibility

C++ supports the definition of user-defined abstract types through the class construct. In Persi there is a repository-manager class as well as classes for each type of persistent object. The abstract supertype of all persistent objects, PersistentObject, serves to encapsulate the properties of objects that make them suitable for persistence.

Typing

As in Ada, C++ does not provide run-time type or shape information, with one important exception. The run-time information available is the shape information associated with dynamic binding of virtual functions; a virtual function invoked through PersistentObject will be bound to the implementation of that function in the appropriate subclass. This turns out to be quite helpful, but nonetheless insufficient. Persi compensates

---

[5] Actually, in C++, communication is with instances of classes, but the distinction is not important here.

by capturing type information for itself as code in classes and shape information as a special kind of object called a class descriptor.

The fact that the repository manager handles all interaction with the storage manager implies that there must be a standard shape for all objects in primary memory. Actually, this is not true. What is standard is the format of information communicated between the repository manager and classes; classes are free to use any shape internally. The format is based on the one developed for Mneme [8], which segregates pointers to other objects from raw data.

The need to capture type and shape information, as well as the need for persistent object classes to be subclasses of PersistentObject, means that persistent types must be special. Thus, as in Ada, arbitrary types cannot have instances that persist. Instead what develops is a parallel class hierarchy of persistent and non-persistent object types (as in E). On the other hand, through appropriate use of multiple inheritance and subtyping, the existence of these parallel types can be well hidden from applications.

Modularity

The modularity of the Persi/C++ architecture is superior to the PGRAPHITE/Ada architecture primarily because of the decreased coupling of modules (i.e., types do not need to communicate with each other or the storage manager, and the repository manager does not need to communicate with types) and the centralization of the persistent-object abstraction. Moreover, unlike PGRAPHITE, the repository manager can handle any persistent object type without having to be rewritten. This improved modularity is a direct result of the availability of subtyping and inheritance in C++. In particular, PersistentObject establishes a protocol for interaction between types and the repository manager that hides details of object types from the repository manager. In addition, any shape requirements on object types are captured in PersistentObject[6] and inherited by persistent object types.

Information Hiding

Information hiding in C++ is essentially the same as in Ada. Notice, however, that the better modularization possible in C++ has the effect of hiding more information associated with the persistence mechanism.

Program Construction

Program construction in C++ is considerably easier than in Ada. While persistent object types must be specially written as in Ada, the task is almost trivial; the persistent-object abstraction does not require implementation in each type, there is no interaction with a storage manager, and much of the code can be inherited from PersistentObject.

6   An Initial Look at ML

The abstraction mechanisms in ML contrast strongly with those of Ada and C++. ML, while similar to both Ada and C++ in that it is strongly typed and statically type-checked, is based instead on type inferencing, polymorphism, and parameterized modules. Absent are notions of inheritance and subtyping.[7]

The current approach to persistence in ML is typical of other interactive, single-user implementations of languages: a copy of the heap is made and saved on secondary storage in a file. One wrinkle in the ML implementation is that persistence is more like a garbage-collection process in that only reachable objects from a designated root are saved. (This was the same mechanism used in GRAPHITE [4], the predecessor to PGRAPHITE.) A problem with this approach is that upon retrieval, any sharing is lost. Semantically, this does not matter for immutable objects, but it certainly causes problems for mutable ones. In response to this and other, related problems, Harper [7] proposes some changes to ML to support a form of persistence.

The prospect of integrating a persistence mechanism into ML by instead using the abstraction mechanisms of that language is a more attractive approach. There are two characteristics of ML that should aid in this. First, ML objects in primary memory have a uniform shape, in particular, one that distinguishes pointers from other data. This means that the persistence mechanism can be implemented once to handle arbitrary ML objects. Second, while complete information about types is not available at run time, there is

---
[6] PersistentObject defines a small number of instance variables.
[7] There are, however, proposals in this direction.

a notion of run-time type identity that can be used for type-checking purposes.[8] Called type *dynamic*, its role is to wrap together a value and its type. If such a structure were made persistent, then type checking shared, persistent objects would become possible.

Acknowledgments

My work on persistence has benefited from discussions and collaborations with Jack Wileden, Peri Tarr, Lori Clarke, Eliot Moss, Emden Gansner, Dave MacQueen, and Jerry Schwarz.

References

[1] R. Agrawal and N.H. Gehani, *Rationale for the Design of Persistence and Query Processing Facilities in the Database Programming Language O++,* **Proceedings Second International Workshop on Database Programming Languages,** June 1989, pp. 25–40.

[2] A. Albano, L. Cardelli, and R. Orsini, *Galileo: A Strongly-Typed, Interactive Conceptual Language,* **ACM Transactions on Database Systems,** vol. 10, no. 2, June 1985, pp. 230–260.

[3] M.P. Atkinson, P.J. Bailey, K.J. Chisholm, P.W. Cockshott, and R. Morrison, *An Approach to Persistent Programming,* **Computer Journal,** vol. 26, no. 4, November 1983.

[4] L.A. Clarke, J.C. Wileden, and A.L. Wolf, GRAPHITE: *A Meta-Tool for Ada Environment Development,* **Proceedings of the IEEE Computer Society Second International Conference on Ada Applications and Environments,** April 1986, pp. 81–90.

[5] L.A. Clarke, J.C. Wileden, and A.L. Wolf, *Object Management Support for Software Development Environments,* **Proceedings of the International Workshop on Persistent Object Stores,** Appin, Scotland, August 1987.

[6] A.D. Dearle, R. Conner, F. Brown, and R. Morrison, *Napier88—A Database Programming Language?,* **Proceedings Second International Workshop on Database Programming Languages,** June 1989, pp. 179–195.

[7] R. Harper, *Modules and Persistence in Standard ML,* **Data Types and Persistence,** M.P. Atkinson, P. Buneman, and R. Morrison (eds.), Springer-Verlag, Berlin, 1988.

[8] J.E.B. Moss and S. Sinofsky, *Managing Persistent Data with Mneme: Designing a Reliable, Shared Object Interface,* **Proceeding of the Second International Workshop on Object Oriented Data Bases,** September 1988, Springer-Verlag.

[9] J.E. Richardson, M.J. Carey, and D.H. Schuh, *The Design of the E Programming Language,* **Computer Sciences Technical Report #824,** University of Wisconsin, Madison, February 1989.

[10] P.L. Tarr, J.C. Wileden, and A.L. Wolf, *A Different Tack to Providing Persistence in a Language,* **Proceedings Second International Workshop on Database Programming Languages,** June 1989, pp. 41–60.

[11] P.L. Tarr, J.C. Wileden, and L.A. Clarke, *Extending and Limiting* PGRAPHITE-*style Persistence,* **Proceedings Fourth Workshop on Persistent Object Systems,** September 1990 (to appear).

[12] R.N. Taylor, F.C. Belz, L.A. Clarke, L.J. Osterweil, R.W. Selby, J.C. Wileden, A.L. Wolf, and M. Young, *Foundations for the Arcadia Environment Architecture,* **Proceedings SIGSOFT '88: Third Symposium on Software Development Environments,** December 1988, pp. 1–13.

[13] D.S. Wile and D.G. Allard, *Worlds: An Organizing Structure for Object-Bases,* **Proceedings of the ACM SIGSOFT/SIGPLAN Software Engineering Symposium on Practical Software Development Environments,** December 1986, pp. 16–26.

[14] J.C. Wileden, A.L. Wolf, C.D. Fisher. and P.L. Tarr, *PGRAPHITE: An Experiment in Persistent Typed Object Management,* **Proceedings SIGSOFT '88: Third Symposium on Software Development Environments,** December 1988, pp. 130–142.

[15] J.C. Wileden and A.L. Wolf, *Object Management Technology for Environments: Experiences, Opportunities, and Risks,* **Proceedings International Workshop on Environments,** Chinon, France, September 1989 (to appear).

---

[8] This feature is not currently in "standard" ML, but is very likely to appear soon.

Two Approaches to Adding Persistence to C++

Thomas Atwood

Object Design, Inc.

Burlington, MA 01803

tom@odi.com

Abstract

Several OO-DBMS designers — Object Design, AT&T, and Texas Instruments — have designed and implemented high-level DML interfaces to an OO-DBMS. Several others — Objectivity, Versant, and many of the in-house DBMS efforts at end-user organizations — have opted for a lower-level interface based on class libraries. This paper attempts to develop the comparison between the two by looking closely at one example of each — the DML binding developed by Object Design (called OQL), and the class library interface developed by one of its corporate partners. The basic conclusion is that the DML versus Class Library discussion has masked a more important distinction — the distinction between persistence defined on top of the language, through inheritance from a virtual base class (PfVBC), and persistence defined at the level of the language, as a storage class (PasSC). PasSC is simpler (in fact it is completely transparent to the programmer), faster, has lower resident memory requirements, and is upward compatible with C++. PfVBC is more complex, takes more resident memory, is slower at dereference time, and places restrictions on the way the programmer can use C++ in dealing with persistent objects. On these grounds the author recommends PasSC. In closing, I comment briefly on the class library versus DML distinction, again from what I hope is the relatively unbiased ground of having both available commercially.

1 Introduction

The design space for programming language bindings to an OO-DBMS has two orthogonal axis as shown in Figure 1 below— class library versus DML and persistence inherited from virtual base class (PfVBC) versus persistence as a storage class (PasSC):

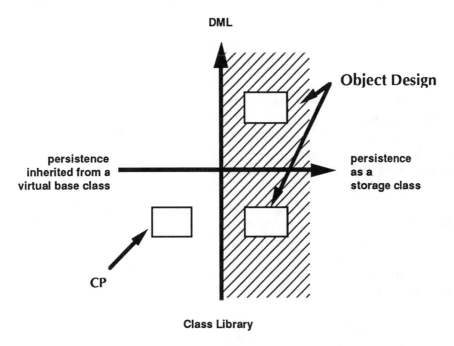

Several OO-DBMS developers — Object Design [Atwood90], TI [Thompson90] and AT&T [Agrawal89] — have defined interfaces between C++ and an OO-DBMS that fall in the upper right quadrant. Several others — Objectivity, Versant, and many of the in-house OO-DBMS efforts at end-user organizations— have opted for a C++ interface that falls in the lower left quadrant. This paper attempts to develop a comparison between the design choices implicit in these opposite quadrants by looking closely at example systems from each. In an effort to remove the competitive marketing issues, we have chose to two systems developed 'among friends' — the DML binding develop by Object Design (called OQL), and the class library interface developed by one of Object Design's corporate partners, CP (names changed to protect the innocent). We look at each system from the vantage point of the programmer writing code that uses it, rather than from the vantage point of the the DBMS developer.

Section 2 outlines a small application that will serve as our example. Section 3 shows the declaration of the classes and the implementation of a particular function method using the PasSC/DML approach used by Object Design. Section 4 shows the same classes using the PfVBC/class library approach used by CP. Section 5 summarizes the differences, and partitions them into those that were due to the persistence-as-virtual-base-class versus persistence-as-storage-class approach, and those that were due to the class library versus DML approach. Section 6 reports on the state of both implementations.

2   Example Application

Our example application is a simple one taken from the domain of CASE systems. We use a database to keep track of which modules call which other modules, and conversely which modules are called by which other modules. The only object type (or 'class' in C++ jargon) in the database is the type MODULE. It has two relationships — callers and calls — each of which is a 1:n relationship which takes as its value a set of other modules.

The sample application consists of a single function that creates a new module, adds it to the list of extant modules, and links it to the modules it calls.

3   Persistence as Storage Class; DML binding

The Object Design implementation is shown in Figure 2:

```
01      class module
02      {
03          char *name;
04          set <module *> callers inverse_member calls;
05          set <module *> calls inverse_member callers;
            };
06      database *current_db
07      persistent <current_db> set <module *> modules;

08      void create_module_as_caller (char *new_module_name,
09          set <char *> existing_module_names)
10      {
11          module *new_module,
12          module *existing_module;
13          char *new_name;
```

```
14              current_db = database::open ("/usr1/atwood/module_db");
15              transaction
16                {
17                   new_module = new (current_db) module;
18                   new_name = new (current_db) char [strlen (new_module_name)+1];
19                   strcpy (new_name, new_module_name);
20                   new_module->name = new_name;
21                   modules =+ new_module;
22                   foreach (char * emn, existing_module_names)
23                     {
24                        existing_module = modules [strcmp(name,emn)==0];
25                        new_module->calls =+ existing_module;
26                     }
27                };
28          };
```

Figure 2: Persistence as Storage Class / DML Combination

Lines 1-5 declare the class module. Module has a character valued attribute name, and two relationships callers and calls, both of which take as their value a set of modules. Line 6 declares a name that will be bound to the database at open time. Line 7 declares a persistent set of modules. Lines 8-28 show the function used to create a new module as a caller of a set of existing modules. Line 14 opens the database. Line 15 starts a transaction. The scope of the transaction is indicated lexically. Lines 17-20 create the new module. Line 21 inserts it in the list of all modules. Lines 22-26 iterate through the list of names of existing modules passed in as an argument to this function. These are the names of the modules that the new module calls. The body of the loop (i) does an associative lookup to retrieve an existing module based on the module's name and then (ii) adds that module to the set that is the value of the calls relationship defined on the newly created module. This insertion automatically builds the inverse links from the existing modules to their new caller based on the inverse_member declarations in class module. Normal exist of the scope of the transaction declaration at line 27 commits the transaction, writing its updates atomically to the database.

The code shown in Figure 2 is C++ with an embedded DDL/DML called OQL. OQL was designed around a small set of premises:

1. OQL should embed a full OO-DBMS data model into the target programming language

2. Persistence should be orthogonal to type

3. The embedded DML should respect the syntactic idiom of the base programming language

The remainder of this section elaborates on these premises and illustrates them using the DDL/DML embedded within the code fragment shown in Figure 2.

3.1   Premise 1—Full OO-DBMS functionality

The first design premise for OQL was that it should introduce into C++ the major data modeling and functional capabilities of a language-independent OO-DBMS. These fall into 3 groups:

1. formal model of object state as well as object behavior — attributes of objects; relationships between objects.

2. associative identification of objects (queries)

3. guarantees of atomicity and integrity (transactions)

The first of these recognizes that C++'s notion of an object is somewhat weaker than the formal semantic models used by object-oriented databases. An OO-DBMS model distinguishes between the specification of an object type and its implementation. The specification may contain attribute declarations, relationship declarations and operation declarations. The implementation is a set of data structures and procedures that implement the operations defined in the specification in terms of those underlying data structures. The data structures are not visible to the caller of the type. Although there may in some cases be a direct mapping between an attribute and a specific field within the data structures, there is no guarantee that this is the case. Having a formally distinct notion of attribute allows the implementation of that attribute to be replaced with a function without the user of the type being in any way affected. Similarly for relationships. There is a formal distinction between a relationship and an object-valued C++ pointer. The deletion of semantics of the two are different. A pointer takes as its value an address. A relationship takes as its value an object. If you delete the data structure at the address refered to by the pointer, it is still legal, in C++, to dereference the pointer. You get whatever is currently at that address — regardless of whether it makes any sense to your program. In the case of a relationship, if you delete the object referred to, a subsequent attempt to cross the relationship will cause an exception to be raised. The system will not blindly give you whatever new object (or part of an object) is at the old address. Similarly, relationships are always bidirectionally traversable. Creating a relationship between two objects implies that you can always get from one to the other. This is not true with a pointer. It only allows one direct of traversal. This means that even a 1:1 relationship would have to be implemented using a pair of pointers that are automatically kept consistent. Higher order relationships, 1:n and n:m, with different requirements for ordered traversal, have more complex representations. We can see both attribute and relationship declarations in the class module. Name is an attribute. Callers and calls are relationships. The inverse_member declarations are used to tell the OO-DBMS preprocessor that if module A refers to module B as its caller, then B will refer to A as one of the modules it calls. ObjectStore does not currently support attributes of attributes, or attributes whose value is determined on demand by a function, so there is currently no syntactic distinction between an attribute in the public portion of a C++ class definition and a literal valued data member. ObjectStore does support relationships — 1:1, 1:n and m:n. Relationship declarations may be distributed as they are here to the class definitions of the object types that serve as the two ends of the relationship, or they may be cast in a centralized form if the relationship itself has attributes or supports unique operations.

An example of associative instance identification (queries) can be seen at line 24. The available syntactic forms are:

object = set [predicate], and
set = set [:predicate:]

The expression set [predicate] returns a single object (or an exception indicating that there is more than one object in the set that satisfies the predicate). The expression set[: predicate :] returns the subset of the base set that satisfies the predicate. If there is nothing that satisfies the predicate it returns the null set. If there is only one object that satisfies the predicate, it returns a set containing one object. Note that this is formally distinct from the object itself.

Finally, a transaction can be seen in our example at line 15. Transactions can be specified either lexically, using the bracket form shown (lines 16 and 27), or dynamically using explicit begin, commit and abort functions defined on the type transaction.

3.2 Premise 2—Persistence should be orthogonal to type.

The notion of persistence orthogonal to type is one that was first introduced by Malcolm Atkinson and his group at the University of Edinborough [Atkinson83]. It is not a notion that has historically been embodied in programming languages or database DDL/DMLs. In both the Codasyl and Relational eras, the DML/programming language combination had two distinct type systems, one that of the programming language, the other that of the DBMS. All instances of programming language types were transient, and all instance of DBMS types were persistent. The lifetime of an object was determined by whether it was an instance of a type defined in the programming language or the database DDL. This awkward amalgam of two distinct type systems had several unfortunate consequences [Thompson90]:

1. Users were forced to write code to map between the two type systems. When they had an instance of a programming language type that they want to make persistent, they had to explicitly write it to the DBMS or file system.

2. Type safety was lost at the interface between the programming language and the DML.

3. There was no symmetry. Set-based associative selection operations (queries) could only be applied to persistent (database) objects, not to objects whose lifetime was limited to that of the process in which they were created. You could not, in fact, do associate queries against sets of persistent objects once they had been retrieved into the program's virtual memory; queries could only be done against objects still on disk (in the database).

4. The DBMS query language came with its own set of built-in functions. The user could not extend this set by defining his own functions and expect these to be usable in a query.

5. Conversely, query expressions could not be freely used wherever an expression could appear within the base programming language. Query expressions could only occur within the rigid context of a query language statement.

Persistence orthogonal to type is achieved in OQL by introducing persistence as another lifetime — or in older programming language terminology as a 'storage class'. Note C++'s heritage of mixing concept (lifetime) with implementation (storage class).

C++ has two forms of variable declaration — dynamic and static. Variables are created dynamically using the new statement. The syntax of the new statement in C++ is:

object = new (*placement_arg*) *class*

An object created with this syntax is allocated out of the heap. Heap storage is available for the life of the process. It is not deallocated on exit from the procedure in which the allocation occured. ObjectStore allows this same syntactic form to be used to request the creation of objects that outlive the process in which they were created. We use the optional *placement_arg* clause to specify the database in which an object is to be created, and to provide directions to the storage subsystem about how to cluster objects into segments and pages. Segments and pages are the units of transfer from disk to main memory in ObjectStore, and clustering has two effects on efficiency: (1) higher hit rate for pages/segments in main memory; (2) smaller working set of pages/segments that need to be brought into memory for the application to run without faulting to portions of the database still on disk.

C++ also provides a means for the programmer to request creation of objects automatically, when the process enters the scope of the declaration. Two forms are available in C++:

syntax	lifetime	allocation	done by
module m	procedure	stack frame	programming language runtime
static module m	process	static	programming language runtime

The first causes storage for the object to be reserved in the stack frame that is created when flow of control enters a procedure. However, when the procedure returns, the stack frame is deallocated, and any storage used for the representation of objects in that stack frame is lost. If the programmer wants to have an object that outlives the procedure in which is was declared, he must add the keyword 'static'. This causes the object to be allocated out of a portion of the program's virtual memory image known an 'static storage'. Unlike heap storage, static storage is not reusable. It is reserved at compile time for objects that are created the first time the process enters the scope of their declaration. These objects are inaccessible outside the scope of their declaration, but their state is not lost. On subsequent reentry into the scope of their declaration, their current state will again become visible. To provide similar automatic allocation functionality for persistent objects that outlive the process that created them, we have added a DDL form which looks very much like its C++ counterparts:

syntax	lifetime	allocation	done by
persistent module m	procedure	stack frame	OO-DBMS runtime

This syntactic form, as well as the arguments to the new function, are processed by a DDL preprocessor which reads the source form of the application program containing the declarations. It strips the DDL declarations out (in this case the line containing the keyword persistent) and substitutes calls to the DBMS runtime system that will be linked with the application before it can be run, and then passes the resulting program on to the C++ or C compiler that is standard on the platform in question. The compiler generates object code files that are linked with the OO-DBMS runtime (again using the standard system linker) to generate an executable program image.

The ObjectStore DDL/DML preprocessor is strong enough to allow the object m to be used freely in any expression or statement within the program, just as an object of process or procedure lifetime could be. The only restriction is that persistent objects cannot, at transaction commit time, refer to objects of shorter lifetime. This is consistent with the notion that objects whose lifetime is process cannot safely refer to objects whose lifetime is a procedure. The reason is the same — the stack frame based storage allocated to store the procedure objects will go away at procedure return. If process-life objects retained pointers to the virtual memory addresses at which those objects had originally been allocated, that storage might well have been reused for something else by the time the program attempted to dereference those pointers. Pointers from transient objects to persistent objects are always permitted.

3.3   Premise 3—Minimalist syntax

The third design premise for OQL was that it should be syntactically minimalist. This is in direct contrast to the tack taken with SQL. SQL attempted to be both an interactive end-user query language and an embedded DML. Like most things designed for two purposes it served neither well. It never succeeded as an interactive end-user query language. It was replaced by application-specific GUIs that generated SQL. It became something analogous to a compiler's intermediate language. But its heritage from this past was that SQL was a complete self-contained language. It had its own definition of variables, expressions, and statements. When DBMS programmers attempted to embed SQL in programming languages like COBOL and PL1, this led to syntactic clash. COBOL had its own definition of variables, expressions, and statements, and they were different from SQL's. Similarly for PL1.

In the object era we have chosen not to attempt to force fit a syntactically complete DML into several programming languages with very different syntactic forms. Instead we expect to develop a family of query languages — OQL[C++], OQL[Ada], OQL[COBOL], ... Although OQL will embody the common semantic model of the OO-DBMS, the syntactic forms through which it will be embedded in each programming language will use the expression and statement forms contained in the base programming language rather than introducing gratuitously different forms.

If we review again the examples of relationships, queries, and transactions seen in our code fragment, we can see the minimalist principal at work.

 o At line 20 the normal C++ syntax is used to refer to the name attribute of the persistent object new_module and to assign a value to it.

o   At lines 4 and 5 the now-standard C++ parameterized type syntax is used to declare 1:n relationships.

o   At line 25 the normal C++ arrow syntax (new_module->calls) is used to refer to the set of objects that are the value of a 1:n relationship.

o   Also at line 25 the normal set insertion operator += is used to add a module to the set of modules which constitute the value of the calls relationship defined on the newly created module.

Query expressions are implemented with a syntax modeled on the array reference in C++ — *array [element_number]*. The array slot is generalized to allow sets or other collection classes rather than just arrays. And the selector is generalized from an ordinal position to allow arbitrary boolean predicates. The predicates are made up of normal C++ variables and normal C++ boolean operators. The other alternative we considered was to introduce an extended SQL notation, but that seemed syntactically foreign to C and C++. It may be a more appropriate syntactic choice for OQL[COBOL].

Since query expressions can return sets, we have the same problems of 'impedance mismatch' in embedding OQL in C++ that Relational DBMS designers had embedding set-at-a-time relational data manipulation sublanguages into one-at-a-time programming languages like COBOL and PL1. The solution that both we and the AT&T OO-DBMS group [Agrawal89] have reached is to introduce a foreach iterator. The foreach iterator at line 22 in our code fragment binds the loop variable emn to successive members of the set existing_module_names each time through the iteration. When it has exhausted the set, the iteration closes. Just as standard C++ variables, expressions, and operators were used in the predicate of the query expression, so standard C++ statements can occur within the body of the foreach block. There is no SQL-like restriction that only SQL statements occur within the loop.

We mentioned above that in Atkinson's dictum, persistent objects should be usable wherever transient objects are. They can be embedded in expressions, passed as arguments, appear on the left and right-hand sides of assignment statements, be returned in exceptions, etc. Ideally the reverse is also true — the associative instance identification (or 'query') capability traditionally provided for persistent objects should be usable with transient objects as well. Although our code fragment does not contain an example of this, it is true in Object Design's implementation of OQL[C++]. Query expressions may be defined over any set, persistent or transient. Similarly for the data model. Relationships may be defined between transient objects as well as persistent ones.

The net of these premises of full DBMS support, persistence orthogonal to type, and syntactic minimalism is a very powerful but simple DML that fits into C++ in ways that make it very familiar to the C++ programmer.

4   Persistence Inherited from a Virtual Base Class; Class Library Binding.

The CP Persistent Object Store (POS) implementation of our sample application is attached as Appendix A.
Lines 5-35 are the definition of the class module. Lines 36-63 are the definition of the class modulelist. Lines 65-90 are a function that creates a new module, filling in references from it to the module it calls and vise-versa. The function at line 72 opens the database. Line 73 starts a transaction. Lines 74-81 iterate through the list of modules until it finds the module whose name was passed into the create_module_as_caller function as the name of the existing module. Line 82 creates the new module. Lines 83-85 create a persistent string (see below) to hold the module name and insert a reference to that string into the name field of the new module. Lines 86-88 create the relationships between the new module and the existing module it calls. Line 88 adds the new module to the list of extant modules. Line 89 commits the transaction.

The approach in all persistence-inherited-from-a-virtual-base-class (PfVBC) implementations is to build a base class (called Pobj in POS) that defines virtual functions for creating, deleting, and referencing persistent objects. Any class that has persistent instances then includes this class in its list of superclasses, and inherits the requisite operations. The implementor of each such class must then supply the actual code to implement each of these virtual functions. In POS these functions are:

o   a constructor
o   an optional destructor
o   a fetch function that checks to see if the referenced object is already in memory, and if not gets it.
o   an optional preMemoryRelease function
o   an option postFetch operation

If we look at the definition of module we see the constructor at lines 10-18. Pobj provides a constructor inherited by each of its subclasses that adds a three field header to the memory representation of each potentially persistent object. The first field is a flag. 1 means that the object is persistent; 0 means that it is transient.

The fetch function defined on module can be seen at lines 23-35. It calls a global function to determine if the object referenced is present, and if not calls malloc to reserve heap space for the object, then calls PobjFetch to bring it in from disk.

The dereference operator is –> is normally overloaded in PfVBC-based implementations to check whether the object referenced is already in memory and if not to call the fetch operation defined on the class; the fetch function allocates storage for the object and calls the generic fetch function defined on the virtual base class. The overloading of the dereference operator can be seen at line 19 — although in POS it is done a bit less efficiently. In POS the –> operator always calls the fetch function, and it is the fetch function that checks to see if the referenced object is in main memory and directly addressable. This puts an extra function call in the dereference path, even when the object is in virtual memory.

Since virtual memory pointers from one object to another are not guaranteed to remain valid when an object leaves memory and returns, classes that contain data members that take as their values potentially persistent objects need to be defined so that they take special objRefs rather than pointers. ObjRefs are automatically defined by POS for each class defined. Class module has the objRef moduleref. Class modulelist has the objRef modulelistref. Notice the use of these objRefs in lines 7-9. Class module defines one 'attribute' an two 'relationships' that are carried by each of its instances. The attribute name takes a value of type Pstringref; and the relationships calls and callers both take values of type modulelistref.

Potentially persistent classes in POS are not upward compatible with C++. There are several restrictions that the author of a potentially persistent class must observe in its definition:

1.   Data members that refer to other potentially persistent objects cannot be constructed using pointers. They must use objRefs as noted above.

2.   Instances of potentially persistent classes cannot be embedded as class members within instances of other potentially persistent classes. ObjRefs must be used instead.

3.   Static member variables are not allowed in potentially persistent classes.

There are also restrictions on how potentially persistent objects interact with other types, e.g., in passing operations defined on potentially persistent classes as function parameters. These incompatibilities raise havoc with attempts to link in existing C libraries with POS code.

Three more subtle problems endemic to the PfVBC approach can be seen in POS also:

1.   the lack of symmetry in handling persistent built-in types;
2.   performance overhead, and
3.   storage overhead.

The only things that can be persistent are instances of classes that inherit from Pobj. This implies that there is no way to create persistent instances of the built-in types, (e.g., INT, CHAR, ...). Instead the programmer has to define a parallel set of types, Pint, Pchar, ...) as subtypes of Pobj. Note the use of a Pstring as the name of a module (line 7) and its creation in the process of creating a new module (line 84). Unfortunately this means that applying the "+" operator to a Pint now becomes a function call. It could be inlined, but it would still be a large body of in-line code; it would have to do everything that the fetch method does. The problem is worse for variable size built-in classes like char*.

Performance for interactive applications is slow in PfVBC systems. The dereference operator, instead of one virtual memory operation, requires several instructions in this architecture. In the pre-release used for this example, POS also faults individual objects into memory one at a time. This will mean that applications that use lots of small objects will do an inordinate number of disk IOs before they build up a usable working set. This could be handled by letting the user explicitly request faulting of a complex object, or the transitive closure of reachable objects, but this is difficult to define declaratively since the optimal aggregates might be different for one program than they are for another. To the extent that the specification of aggregates to read in has to be done at runtime, the system's ability to transparently overload the —> operator is circumscribed. We are back to explicit user knowledge of a two level store. The PfVBC approach also requires the programmer to notify the storage system that he has updated objects so that it can save changes at transaction commit. In POS that is done by calling updateObj() each time an instance is modified. This is an inline operation that sets a bit in an in-memory object table noting that the object has been changed and that it has to be written to disk when the transaction commits. This adds overhead for every update operation.

The storage overhead for objects in a PfVBC architecture is also high. In a system designed to work with CFRONT each instance of a class that inherits from Pobj will carry a two-word Vtbl entry for each node along every path to the base class Pobj. This is a function of the way CFRONT allocates Vtbl entries in the face of multiple inheritance and virtual functions, and not something the OO-DBMS implementor can do anything about. PfVBC implementations also have to maintain an object table to keep track of which object are in memory, where they are, whether they have been modified, and whether they are locked. Additional mapping tables are also required to find objects on disk. If average object size is small (e.g., 4-6 words) and object-ids are long (80 bits in POS, 96 or 128 bits in most distributed implementations) these tables can occupy up to 50% of physical memory and cause thrashing if they are allowed to become unbalanced.. The maintenance code (for rebalancing B trees or reorganizing hash tables) takes additional instructions that have to be amortized over object references, increasing the effective cost of an object reference even further.

5   Comparison

The comparison between Object Design's OQL and CP's Persistent Object Store is perhaps most simply summarized by noting that the sample application required 30 lines in OQL, 90 lines in POS. However, OQL and POS embody opposite choices on two axis of choice — PasSC versus PfVBC and DML versus class library. See Figure 1. OQL is in quadrant 1 — PasSC and DML. POS is in quadrant 3 — PfVBC and class library. *The central message of this paper is that the most important differences turn out to be those between the PfVBC and PasSC approaches, rather than those that have to do with the level of the language binding — class library or DML.*

5.1   PfVBC versus PasSC

There are four problems incident to the persistence-inherited-from-a-virtual-base-class approach:

1. Complexity. The programmer generally has to write at least 4 functions for each object class defined in his application — a construction, a destructor, a fetch and an operator –> method.

2. Poor performance. Interpretive dereference of object id's in software can make this approach nearly an order of magnitude slower for the interactive portion of the application than implementations based on persistence-as-storage-class.

3. Not fully upward compatible with C++.

4. Incompatible with C. No easy migration path for existing C code.

Conversely, the advantages of the persistence-as-storage-class approach are:

1. Simplicity: no additional code for programmer to write

2. High performance for the interactive portion of the application.

3. Full upward compatibility with C++

4. Support for persistent C data structures as well as persistent C++ objects. This allows easy migration of existing C libraries into the new environment.

We comment briefly on each of these four issues.

Complexity

The fact that a significant amount of the complexity of the POS approach was incident to its choice of persistence model, rather than its choice of an class library level binding, was brought home to us by the availability of a PasSC/class library implementation from Object Design. The PasSC/class library implementation fits in quadrant 2 of Figure 1. The implementation of the sample program using the Object Design class library, while longer than the implementation using the Object Design DML, was still only 2/3rds the length of the CP PfVBC class library based implementation.

Performance and Single-Level-Store

The PfVBC model is generally implemented by overloading the member selection operator —>. If a normal C++ object A refers to an object B as the value of a member named parent, an attempt to get from A to B using the expression A—>parent will be compiled into a single instruction that dereferences a virtual memory pointer using the hardware MMU. If A is a persistent object in a PfVBC-based system, the same reference would be expanded into a code sequence that follows the initial pointer to a surrogate object, checks the surrogate to see whether the object B has already been mapped into virtual memory, and if so goes there; if not, calls a fetch method defined on the class of B; this method (or a type-specific method that overrides it) will locate the object on secondary storage, allocate storage for its virtual memory representation, and construct that representation from the on-disk representation of the object (and potentially other information about related objects already moved into virtual memory). This code sequence, even for the case where everything has already been mapped into virtual memory, moves the time of a single object dereference from 1 instruction to 5-10 instructions. This can significantly slow down the interactive portion of an application.

Introducing persistence as a storage class, with the class of an object determined at the time the object is created, can take advantage of much faster implementations that impose no additional overhead on the dereference operations that dominate the interactive portion of the application's execution. The Object Design OO-DBMS 'ObjectStore' has such an implementation. Object-id dereferences are extremely fast — close to the single VM instruction times of a C pointer dereference. This means that ObjectStore can, as a practical matter of fact, as well as in principal, be used to give the programmer the abstraction of a *single level store*. The application does not need to explicitly read in its data structures from large container objects on disk (files, blobs, or large objects) and build up the in-memory graphs of small objects that it uses to represent the design and to derive the visual image painted on the screen that the designer/author interacts with. It can simply store these graph-based representations directly in the database, without flattening them, and when the program is invoked again, simply reference these data structures as though they were already in virtual memory. This can radically reduce the amount of code to be written and therefore reduce both time to market and schedule risk.

If the OO-DBMS is not fast enough to support the single-level-store illusion, then the application program cannot use the DBMS's high level object model. It is forced to use the database as little more than a file system that provides container objects into which the application can pack the small objects it uses during execution and from which it can unpack them when it begins execution the next time. So performance, in an indirect way, becomes the key to the simplicity gains of the high-level object data model and the single-level-store abstraction. And it is really only a part of the performance equation that is critical in this way. I/O performance and query time against disk resident data are not critical for this class of interactive design application. What is critical, is whether the OO-DBMS runtime can give the application programmer access to persistent objects that have already been mapped into memory in time close to that of virtual memory access to transient C++ data structures. If not, the programmer will explicitly copy his database objects into C++ objects, do all of the interactive portion of his application using these C++ objects, then explicitly copy his in-memory data structures back to database objects when he is done. The visual analogy that comes to mind is a child picking tinker toys out of a toy box. He puts the tinker toys together into a helicopter, but when he is done he has to take the helicopter apart, and put each of the individual sticks and nodes back into the toy box. The nodes are like C++ objects, the sticks are inter-object references. An OO-DBMS implemented with the PfVBC model may be so slow that its object-ids cannot be used to model inter-node relationships within the helicopter. It can only be used to model relationships between the toy boxes. What you get is again a two-level-store — main memory is used one way; disk another. An OO-DBMS whose performance is such that it forces the programmer to use it as a two level store, has little advantage over a relational DBMS with blobs or even a modern distributed file system with transaction-based atomic write protocols. The real win is getting an OO-DBMS fast enough to permit the programmer to work in world that appears to him as a shared, single level store. The PasSC model permits this.

Strict C++ Compatibility

The PfVBC approach also introduces a set of restrictions on the use of C++ for objects that have inherited persistence from the virtual base class, and/or restrictions on how persistent and non-persistent objects can be intermixed. A typical example that came up in our sample application was the use of character strings in persistent objects. In the PfVBC approach it is not possible to use the normal string library; a separate type called Pstring has to be written for use with persistent objects. A more serious restriction is the loss of support for virtual functions in some PfVBC implementations. The representation of C++ objects in CFRONT uses a table called a Vtbl to locate the functions that can be applied to the object. The pointers in the Vtbl are virtual memory pointers, and cannot be reconstructed by a language-level function when a persistent object is brought in from the disk and placed in virtual memory. These tables are part of the language runtime and are inaccessible to functions written in the language. If persistence is introduced as a storage class, i.e., as part of the language, then the implementor has access to the runtime structures that support the storage class abstractions. If you attempt to build it on top of the language you simply have no way of getting at these structures. Inheritance is a big part of the object model, and it is arguable that the lack of virtual functions cripples inheritance. Consider as an example an application that does a valuation on a portfolio of securities. The portfolio may contain securities of several different types, each with its own valuation function. If the OO-DBMS implementation supports virtual functions on persistent objects, then value can be defined as a virtual function on the type Security, and the code for portfolio written as

```
foreach (Security s in thePortfolio) { thePortfolio.totalvalue = thePortfolio.totalvalue + s.value}
```

Each subtype of Security, e.g., Bond, Stock, ... will supply its own implementation for the virtual function, and the portfolio code can simply iterate through the elements of the portfolio, treating each as simply a security, knowing that its call on the value function will be deflected to the appropriate implementation for each specific subtype of security it encounters within the portfolio. Without virtual functions, the code deriving the total value of the portfolio would have to be written as a set of nested if statements:

```
foreach (Security s in thePortfolio)
  {
      if s.type == Stock then { ...}
      else if s.type == Bond then { ...}
      else ...
  }
```

The principal problem with this approach is its lack of modularity — and the maintenance nightmare lurking therein. If a new subtype of security is added to the system, the programmer has to not only code the valuation function for that type of security, but find every other program that iterates through portfolios this security might become part of, and add a new clause in the if statement to handle the new subtype of security.

A second problem is that the if statements used as the workaround for virtual functions cannot be written without extending C++. C++ does not make the type of an object available to the program at runtime. The irony is that the PfVBC proponent who descries adding a new storage class to C++ ends up extending the language somewhere else to compensate for the lack of virtual functions on persistent objects.

C   Compatibility

In the PasSC model it is possible to develop a runtime in which the in-memory representation of an object reference is a 32-bit virtual memory pointer without compromising the full 2*128 bit addressability required for objects in wide-area-networks. The Object Design product ObjectStore has such an architecture. Given that C++ objects are referenced with a 32-bit virtual-memory pointer, and that persistence is orthogonal to type, it was fairly straightforward to go ahead and allow persistent C data structures as well as persistent C++ objects. This gives the PasSC implementation a significant practical advantage, at least in today's world. Although C++ is rapidly becoming the language of choice for new application development, existing code is largely C not C++. The PasSC implementation used by ObjectStore allows the application builder to link existing C code with his new C++ code, reusing existing C libraries and even whole applications. A development shop can make the transition from C to C++ gradually, without throwing away their previous code.

5.2   Class Library versus DML

From a technical vantage point, a DML-based interface is higher level and simpler. Both of these translate into less code that the application programmer has to write.

From a management point of view, the DML-based approach also has an advantage that is very real business issue for most would-be users of OO-DBMS technology at this early stage of the technology's development. The DML-based approach is the 'low risk' solution in an era in which OO-DBMS standards have yet to emerge. To the extent that it exposes lower-level interfaces, class library based implementations put large applications at greater risk. An application written to a class library based OO-DBMS implementation may have thousands of lines of application code that are intimately dependent on the low level semantics of the particular DBMS system the application was written to use — which classes are supported and what functions are defined on them.

Although there has been some discussion that a DML-based interface locks the application developer in to the supplier of the preprocessor that recognizes the DML, in actual fact the points of dependency on the OO-DBMS supplier are identical for both the class library and DML-based interfaces. What has not always been clear is that class library based systems still require the developer's C++ class definitions to be run through a DDL preprocessor unique to that DBMS vendor before these classes can be used by the class library. The DDL preprocessor has to deal with a smaller grammar than a full DDL/DML preprocessor, but the bottom line is that with either approach the application builder is dependent on both the DBMS vendor's tools and the runtime that supports the abstractions presented by the class library or in the DML. The only difference is a quantitative one, and since the level of the interface is lower in a class library based OO-DBMS, the application writer's exposure is greater. He has more lines of code that depend on the continued existence of the OO-DBMS vendor chosen, and because his application code interacts with the OO-DBMS as such a low level he may be more sensitive to the specific idiosyncrasies of his OO-DBMS vendor's implementation. His code may 'see' the form of OIDs, buffer management, index maintenance, and lock management. It may even 'see' (or be restricted to) some limited set of representations into which the DBMS maps the data structures the application builder chooses as representations for his C++ types.

5.3   Conclusions

The basic conclusion we drew from our work was that casting the argument over the best binding of C++ to an OO-DBMS as DML versus class_library_interface obscures a more deep-seated and important difference. There are two distinctly different axes on which an interface to an OO-DBMS can be placed — PfVBC versus PasSC, and class library versus DML. And it is the distinction between PfVBC and PasSC that is the most important. Introducing persistence as a storage class at the level of the language is much simpler and cleaner than attempting to introduce it 'on top of' the language by inheriting storage management routines from a virtual base class. With the PasSC approach:

o   There is no need for the programmer to write save, restore, and pin functions for each type that can have persistent instances.

o   There are no artificial restrictions on what objects — database objects or programming language objects — can be used in which expressions, or can/cannot have virtual functions, or can be used with iteration functions defined for database objects. The PasSC approach supports a single, unified type system, with the ability to freely intermix references to persistent instances and transient instances into expressions, assignment statements and function calls. The programmer does not have to be ever-vigilant about the fact that he is using two intermixed, but separate sets of functions — those for transient programming language objects, and those for persistent database objects. In a PasSC-based implementation, persistence is truly orthogonal to type.

6. State of the Implementations

The PfVBC/class library-based system discussed in section 4 was developed by one of CP's research labs in 1989 and 1990. Work on the system was discontinued in late 1990. The CP engineering team has since begun work on developing class libraries that will provide a generic base of support for a broad range of image-based applications. They are also helping Object Design understand the demands of image and voice data on the storage levels of an OO-DBMS. This is data which may have its own compression/decompression algorithms, special alignment requirements in main memory dictated by graphics processors, and type-specific storage media.

ObjectStore, meanwhile, has moved through 3 Beta releases, one each quarter during the first 3 quarters of 1990. It will be released as product in early Q4 1990 with both an class library level and a DML bindings to its PasSC model. A/B tests with existing C-based design applications, before and after they were ported to ObjectStore, indicate that the system is fast enough to support the single-level-store abstraction in practice. The DML level binding discussed in section 2 above has been outlined in a position paper presented to the ANSI OO-DBTG. A reference implementation is available on Sun workstations. We expect to make the actual code available to compiler writers at the major workstation companies in an effort to help a high-quality DDL/DML standard for object-oriented databases take shape. Both the class library and DML level bindings will be ported to the other major Unix workstation platforms during 1991.

References

[Agrawal89]   Agrawal, R., and Gehani, N.H., "ODE (Object Database and Environment): The Language and the Data Model", SIGMOD '89, 18:2, June 1989, 36-45.

[Atkinson83]   Atkinson, M.P., et al, "An Approach to Persistent Programming", The Computer Journal, 26:4, 1983, Cambridge University Press.

[Atwood90]   Atwood, T.M., Orenstein, J., "Notes toward a Standard Object-Oriented DDL and DML", OO-DBTG meeting, Atlantic City, NJ, May 1990

[Thompson90]   Thompson, C.W., Alashqur, A.M., and Blakeley, J., "Strawman Reference Model for Object Query Languages", OO-DBTG meeting, Atlantic City, NJ, May 1990

Appendix A — the POS Implementation

```
01      #include "PobjStd.h"
02      #include "PobjControl.h"
03      int   persistent = 1;
04      int   nonpersistent = 0;

05      class module:Pobj
06        {
07          Pstringref name;
08          modulelistref calls;
09          modulelistref callers;
10          module (int persist,
11              Pstringref myName,
12              classNumberType myClass=moduleclassnumber)
13              :Pobj (persist, myclass)
14            {
15              name = myName;
16              calls = NULLREF;
17              callers = NULLREF;
18          ...};
19          moduleref operator|-> ()
20            {
21              fetch (this).contents;
22            };
23          moduleref fetch (moduleref reference)
24            {
25              if (PobjObjectPresent (reference)
26                {
27                  return reference;
28                }
29              else
30                {
31                  temp = malloc (sizeof (module));
32                  PobjFetch (reference, temp, sizeof(module));
33                  return (moduleref) temp;
34                }
35            };

36      class modulelist:Pobj
37        {
38          moduleref first;
39          modulelistref rest;
40          modulelist (int persist, moduleref myfirst, modulelistref myrest,
41              classNumberType myClass=modulelistclassnumber)
42              :Pobj (persist, myclass)
43            {
44              first = myfirst;
```

```
45                    rest = myrest;
46                };
47        modulelistref operator|-> ()
48          {
49             fetch  (this).contents;
50          };
51        modulelistref fetch (modulelistref reference)
52          {
53             if (PobjObjectPresent (reference)
54               {
55                  return reference;
56               }
57             else
58               {
59                  temp = malloc (sizeof (modulelist));
60                  PobjFetch (reference, temp, sizeof(modulelist));
61                  return (modulelistref) temp;
62               }
63          }
64        modulelistref modules;

65        void create_module_as_caller (char *new_module_name,
66            char *existing_module_name)
67          {
68             moduleref new_module;
69             moduleref existing_module;
70             char *new_name;
71             char *temp;
72             PobjCntrl->connect ("george", password);
73             PobjCntrl->startTransaction();
74             existing_module = NULLREF;
75             for (m=modules; m!=NULLREF; m=m->rest)
76                if (strcmp (existing_module_name, (char *)(m->first->name) == 0)
77                  {
78                     existing_module = m->first;
79                     break;
80                  };
81             if (existing_module == NULLREF) error ("no existing module");
82             new_module = module(persistent, Pstringref (NULLREF));
83             new_module->name->contents = makePstring (strlen (new_module_name) + 1);
84             temp = (char *) (new_module->name->contents);
85             strcpy (temp, new_name);
86             new_module->calls= modulelist (persistent,existing_module,NULLREF);
87             existing_module->callers = modulelist (persistent, new_module, existing_modules->callers);
88             modules = modulelist (persistent,new_module,modules);
89             PobjCntrl->commit();
90          };
```

Part X
Clustering and Tools

Chair: J. Eliot B. Moss

The opening and closing sessions of the workshop both contain papers addressing issues of performance and practical use of persistent object systems. This is fitting, and illustrates a significant development in research on persistence: the research is mature enough that the community is directing increasing attention to performance issues in addition to concepts and functionality. While the opening session, titled Optimization, considered compile-time methods for improving performance, the focus was on saving CPU cycles. In contrast, the first two papers of this session are concerned with ways to reduce the I/O time of a persistent application. Clearly, optimal clustering for one application could be drastically bad for another, so clustering almost always involves tradeoffs between different modes of use for the same collection of objects.

The term "clustering" in this context refers to how objects are grouped into larger units for storage and retrieval on persistent media (generally assumed to be magnetic disks). In almost every case performance will suffer if we fetch and store one object at a time. Shannon and Snodgrass consider several methods for clustering objects and, through a combination of actual performance measurements and a simple cost model, compare the alternatives. A "strawman" case is grouping objects of each type together as was done in the LOOM system; an ideal, minimal cost can also be computed, and several techniques are examined that offer intermediate performance. The unique aspect of their work is *semantic clustering*, in which individual objects are split into pieces called fragments, with the more rarely used fragments grouped and stored separately. Under some conditions this offers improved performance, suggesting that the programmer's view of objects and the lower level system view (e.g., as a contiguous range of bytes) might usefully be distinguished. The authors also consider the cost of checking object residency, and converting between internal and external formats (swizzling), and charge each scheme according to only the overheads it incurs.

Benzaken and Delobel consider essentially only a single *style* of clustering, which then offers a specific set of alternatives for any given schema (type system). Based on some analysis of the source of the applications, information is fed into a cost model; the model is then used to evaluate alternative clusterings. The authors show that the cost model is generally effective in achieving minimal (or at least good) I/O times across the clustering alternatives considered. The particular clustering technique is called *placement trees*. This works by identifying subtrees of the object type graph. If two object instances are joined by an edge (pointer) corresponding to an edge included in a placement tree, then the instances are placed in the same clustering unit, whenever possible.

It may be helpful to consider the commonalities and differences between the papers; I now summarize a comparison kindly provided to me for this purpose by Rick Snodgrass. First, the common features of both approaches include: clustering is specified using annotations to the schema (type graph), which insures data independence and allows clustering to be changed without reprogramming (but recompilation *may* be necessary); instance clustering is accomplished by partial transitive closure (partial reachability) in the instance graph; clustering of new objects is performed at transaction commit time; clustering is ultimately decided by the database adminstrator (DBA); and both approaches are founded on similar type models. Now here are their differences. Semantic clustering allows objects to be fragmented, which sometimes can improve performance (by reducing the volume of data transferred to and from main memory). Semantic clustering faults segments, which may vary in size (one or more pages) and works best for large clusters, by reducing the number of disk seeks and I/O requests. In the O_2 system (Benzaken and Delobel) physical units (pages) are fixed in size and will tend to work best when desired clusters fill exactly one page. O_2 provides a cost model and a tool to evaluate alternatives according to that model; semantic clustering could take advantage of such a tool, but does not currently have one to offer. Semantic clustering groups data in main memory, too, reducing virtual memory paging overhead, and, since its groupings are more rigidly enforced, it admits more compile-time optimizations, which work best only when there are not many cross pointers from one cluster to another. Incremental reclustering is possible for either scheme, but can be done only when reading in the case of semantic clustering (since the compiled code's assumptions must be met). I feel the papers make complementary and useful contributions to the clustering problem.

The third paper in the session is rather different, and concerns a CASE tool, built with persistent systems techniques, that is in everyday use in a telecommunications systems development organization. In addition to illustrating the practical import of persistent systems, the paper indicates the utility of a simple sequential (i.e., temporal) versioning scheme in an actual application. Though the tool is currently limited to a single user at a time, it is encouraging to see reports of progress of persistent object systems ideas into the "real world".

The first part of the discussion consisted of some comparisons of semantic clustering and the O_2 scheme, as well as some general indication of situations that tend to give problems to any clustering algorithms with a static basis, such as recursive data structures and sets of wildly varying size. It was also observed that the reachability based techniques considered all assume (probably correctly) that existence dependencies (usually represented as pointers in object systems) correspond to paths of access. It was also noted that reachability clustering *may* be easier to accomplish than the equivalent in relational database systems. An earlier session contained a paper by Wile on WorldBase, which also involves clustering, but the clustering in WorldBase is related to meaning, whereas the clustering of this session is related only to performance.

At the end of the discussion there were exchanges about the practicality of the temporal versioning (history) kept by a system as described in the final paper. There were concerns about the volume of history information generated, but it was argued that in practice, much of the history is readily pruned and garbage collected, by the identification of significant points in time that should be remembered, with intermediate history discarded.

What was to me one of the more significant points of discussion concerned differing points of view on whether clustering decisions could and should be automated. One camp believed that the complexity of existing database systems, which was stated to be less than the complexity of the object systems we are trying to build, already outstrips our capacity to make good clustering decisions, and thus that automated tools are essential. The other camp felt that the DBA or programmer is frequently in the best position to make a good decision, because they have the best comprehensive knowledge of the behavior of the applications. However, my characterization of these points of view as two camps is really artificial, since it is quite reasonable to give a human (the DBA or programmer) ultimate authority **and** to provide automated tools to suggest a good clustering decision, which the human can accept or modify as desired.

Semantic Clustering

Karen Shannon
Department of Computer Science
University of North Carolina
Chapel Hill, NC 27599-3175
shannon@cs.unc.edu

Richard Snodgrass
Department of Computer Science
University of Arizona
Tucson, AZ 85721
rts@cs.arizona.edu

Abstract

Appropriate clustering of objects into pages in secondary memory is crucial to achieving good performance in a persistent object store. We present a new approach, termed *semantic clustering*, that exploits more of a program's data accessing semantics than previous proposals. We insulate the source code from changes in clustering, so that clustering only impacts performance. The linguistic constructs used to specify semantic clustering are illustrated with an example of two tools with quite different access patterns. Experimentation with this example indicates that, for the tools, object sizes, and hardware configuration considered here, performing any clustering at all yields an order of magnitude improvement in overall tool execution time over pure page faulting, and that semantic clustering is faster than other forms of clustering by 20%–35%, and within 25% of the (unattainable) optimal clustering.

The most salient aspect of a tightly coupled persistent object store is that it blurs the distinction between data stored in main memory and data resident on secondary storage. Objects are accessed in a program using such an object store with little or no regard to where the object actually resides [Balch et al. 1989]. If in fact the object has not been cached in main memory, the first access to the object results in an *object fault*, in which the object is read in from disk and made available for access. Generally, objects are *clustered* on disk into segments, and an object fault transfers an entire segment from disk to main memory. We don't consider here objects whose size is greater than the smallest segment, in part because such objects won't benefit from any clustering scheme.

In this paper we present a new approach to clustering that exploits more of a program's data accessing semantics than previous proposals. This approach retains the user's lack of concern for whether an object is cached in main memory, while significantly increasing the performance of the program by simultaneously reducing CPU overhead and disk I/O time.

The next section introduces the tradeoffs inherent in clustering and summarizes previous approaches. We present an overview of our approach, termed *semantic clustering*, in Section 2, with a detailed example appearing in Section 3. Section 4 presents the results of experiments that indicate several performance advantages to semantic clustering. The last section briefly examines how we plan to put this approach into practice in a fairly large programming environment.

1 Implementing Object Faulting

The data model supported by a persistent object store is a (potentially very large) collection of objects, each containing uninterpreted data along with references to other objects. Programs start with a designated root object, traverse some of the embedded references, and make changes to some of the objects encountered. When the program commits, all changes become visible to other programs that use the object store. The runtime system is responsible for moving objects between main memory and secondary storage, and for converting between alternative representations. To the program, all objects are equally accessible; it is the runtime library's responsibility to maintain this fiction in the presence of disparate main memory and disk access speeds.

There are three policies the runtime system must implement. First, how should objects be grouped into segments? Second, when should each object or segment be transferred to or from disk? And third, when should the representation of each object be converted from external form to internal form, and vice versa?

The most obvious implementation simply brings in only the relevant object when it is first accessed by the program. With this approach, termed *strict object faulting*, objects reside in main memory only if they are actually needed, minimizing main memory usage [Straw et al. 1989]. Another advantage is that locking, which is the usual method of concurrency control, can be easily applied to individual objects. Strict object faulting has several disadvantages. Each access to an object must check for *cache residency*. Such checks add significant overhead. Weddell has shown that in a main memory object-oriented DBMS which closely approximates a tightly-coupled persistent object store, a cache residency check on each access can slow computation by as much as 20% [Weddell 1989]. Alternatively, cache residency checking may be done in hardware, say via a virtual memory mechanism. However, such a mechanism may significantly increase the cost of an object fault, since two context switches are generally involved. In either case, each object fault stops the program for disk I/O, increasing turnaround time. Each object fault results in approximately one disk seek, so the number of disk seeks approaches the number of objects cached in main memory. Memory and disk allocation are complex, due to variable object size. Finally, a cached object table is needed to record which objects are cached in main memory and where such objects are located.

At the other end of the spectrum is a much simpler approach, termed *big inhale* [Conradi & Wanvik 1985], in which all possibly accessible objects are read at program initialization. The advantages and disadvantages trade places relative to strict object faulting: once the objects have been read in, the program runs at full speed, with no cache residency checks or disk reads; a cached object table is not needed; and disk I/O is quite efficient, with few seeks. The disadvantages are all performance related: excessive main memory usage, excessive I/O, and excessive locking.

Clustering has been proposed as a compromise. With clustering, the unit of transfer is a *segment*, containing multiple objects. The advantages are that I/O is somewhat more efficient, since segments are generally a multiple of a fixed page size, and memory and disk allocation (and perhaps locking) are simplified. These advantages depend on an assumed correlation of *temporal locality* and *spatial locality*: objects referenced together in time reside together in the same segment. In any case, there are still significant disadvantages: each segment fault stops the program and causes a disk seek, a cached object table is still generally needed, and cache residency checks are still required.

The fundamental issue concerning clustering is assigning objects to segments to obtain a high temporal/spatial correlation. Various approaches have been proposed. One is to cluster on object creation, either by the program specifying another object with which the newly created object is to share a segment (OB2, ObjectStore), or by defining logical clusters and manually inserting newly created objects into them (OB2, ObjectStore, ObServer [Hornick & Zdonik 1987], Versant). The primary disadvantage here is that the clustering decision is localized to the program which creates the object, and is thus hard to implement or change. Another approach is to cluster by object type (PS-Algol [Cockshott et al. 1984], ObServer), with the disadvantage that such clustering generally results in a lower temporal/spatial correlation. Clustering by total closure, in which all objects reachable from some designated object are placed in the same segment (OB2), generally results in excessively large segments. Finally, clustering by segmenting an embedded tree (termed *syntactic clustering*) results in poor performance for programs that don't walk the embedding tree.

All of the proposed clustering schemes still suffer from several drawbacks. First, entire objects are always transferred, even when only a few attributes are needed by the program. Secondly, all accesses must perform cache residency checks, though syntactic clustering obviates the need for such checks across attributes defining the embedded (abstract syntax) tree. Third, clustering is system-wide, and cannot be configured on a program by program basis. Finally, in most realizations of these clustering schemes, the program source code must be changed if the clustering is modified.

We have developed a new approach to clustering that addresses all of these drawbacks, allowing more of the advantages of both the big inhale and strict object faulting to be simultaneously realized. The basic idea behind our approach is to utilize the semantics of persistent data access by individual programs in determining clustering.

2   Semantic Clustering

In this section we introduce a new approach to clustering; the next section will apply it to an example. Many of our design decisions will become clearer when this example is presented.

Semantic clustering is specified manually by the programmer, who is in the best position to know how the program(s) access data. Of course, the programmer can use statistics on attribute access in clustering the data. Clustering is by *partial closure*: a subset of attributes are specified, and all objects reachable from a designated object, termed the *root* of the cluster, via those attributes are placed in the same *cluster instance*. Particular attributes are designated *cut attributes*; the object referenced by such an attribute becomes the root of a separate cluster instance. The attributes are thereby partitioned into *internal* attributes, whose referent object is guaranteed to be coresident in the same cluster as the object containing the attribute, and *external* attributes, for which no such guarantee is possible. This clustering defines an integrity constraint: no two internal attributes of objects in different cluster instances can reference the same object. It has been our experience that defining appropriate internal attributes is straightforward; often the internal attributes form an embedded tree. Also, it turns out that checking this integrity constraint is almost free during the write operation. Note that clustering determines in which cluster instance each object resides. Interestingly, the concepts of cut attributes, internal attributes, and partial closure for clustering also appear in a different guise, and for a different rationale (logical organization verses performance), in the WorldBase system [Wile & Allard 1989, Widjojo et al. 1990].

Clusters are then *fragmented* by specifying a sequence of sets of attributes. All attributes in the first set are placed in the first fragment type. Those remaining attributes that are in the second set are placed in the second fragment type. This continues until all the attributes in all of the object types have been placed into a fragment type. Hence, an object is represented by a collection of one or more *object fragments*, each in a different fragment instance, termed a *segment*. The first object fragment is termed the *identity fragment*; all references from other objects point to this fragment. The identity fragment points to all other fragments of that object, and they all contain pointers back to the identity fragment. In this way, a cluster instance is composed of potentially many segments, each containing some of the attributes of each object in the cluster instance.

Clustering is specified both for the main memory of each program accessing persistent data and also for the data stored on disk. Clustering defines the fragment types to be present in each location, with the runtime system effecting a translation of the data from one clustering arrangement to another as a result of a segment read operation (translating from disk clustering to main memory clustering on input) or an explicit commit operation by the program (translating back to disk clustering on output). The main memory and disk clusterings are designed together to ensure high performance. Generally, a program's main memory is clustered similarly to the disk data, so that minimal translation is needed.

Each program is associated with one or more input and output *ports*, each of which is itself associated with a set of relevant attributes. Programs access stored data through ports, which appear to the program as routines that may be invoked with object identifiers. Invoking an input port causes all objects reachable from the provided object via the port attributes to be logically read into main memory; in practice the objects are faulted in as needed as the program executes. Invoking an output port causes the port attributes of all objects reachable from the provided object via the port attributes to be updated in the store.

When a port routine is invoked, only the relevant segment(s) containing the root object are read in. Access through internal attributes is always permitted. Access through an external attribute requires a cache residency check, which determines whether the object identifier is a *non-persistent reference* (NPR), i.e., a pointer (which must be an even value), or a *persistent identifier* (PID, which we represent as an odd integer). If the latter is the case, an *object fault* occurs, and the runtime system determines whether the segment containing the object is resident in main memory. If not, a *segment fault* occurs, and the cluster instance containing the object is retrieved from disk. In particular, only the relevant segments are retrieved, i.e., those containing attributes of interest to the program. Some segments may not yet exist, if their attributes have not yet been computed, in which case new segments are initialized so that all of the relevant attributes are available to the program. The PID is *swizzled* into an NPR (actually, all internal attributes in the just input segment(s) are swizzled, termed *eager swizzling* [Moss 1990]) and control returns to the program.

At the same time that the indicated cluster instance is retrieved during a segment fault, additional cluster instances may also be retrieved, as specified when the program was clustered. The advantages are two-fold. First, objects in these other segments presumably will be needed later by the program, so they might as well be read in now, potentially saving disk seeks. Second, pre-paging other segments allows more attributes in the program to be designated as internal, reducing (sometimes dramatically) the number of cache residency checks and object faults performed at runtime.

During the write operation though an output port, the port attributes determine which objects, and thus which cluster instances, are written. Additionally, the programmer can assert that certain clusters or fragments are not modified by the program; the output port need not update these segments, saving disk write operations. In order to further reduce I/O time, the programmer can also specify the order the segments are laid out on disk, potentially decreasing the number of disk seeks.

Sets of attributes are used extensively to specify clusters, fragments, ports, pre-paging, and read-only portions. We utilize *structures*, which are collections of object declarations, as a linguistic device to aid in the expression of clustering. Structures can be derived from other structures in various ways, permitting sets of attributes to be expressed indirectly in terms more natural to the user. One additional benefit of these specifications is that they are language-independent, so that multiple programming languages can be made persistent, and can even share data.

The analysis of structure specifications and of clustering specifications, the designation of internal and external attributes, and the generation of code and tables for attribute access, attribute modification, object creation, object faulting, and object output during commit is performed by a data structure compiler. The data structure compiler is responsible for the exact layout of data both on disk and in main memory.

Finally, it is important that clustering not change the semantics of programs; clustering should only impact performance. Since all aspects of data access, modification, and I/O must be moderated, application programs are processed by a preprocessor that inserts the appropriate code to effect the specified clustering. Clustering is easily altered as new insight is gained into how the programs access data, *without* necessitating any changes to the source code of the application program. This property permits graceful evolution of closely cooperating persistent programs [Snodgrass & Shannon 1990].

3   An Example

To illustrate the effectiveness of semantic clustering, we examine an application appropriate for persistent data stores, namely a programming environment. This highly simplistic environment for a functional language contains two tools, among others: a semantic analyzer and a cross referencer, communicating through a central data store, termed a *repository*. We focus on the semantic analyzer, because its algorithms (name resolution being top-down and type resolution being bottom-up, both computing new attributes) and accessing strategies (both traverse the abstract syntax tree) are fairly typical of analysis tools found in a software development environment. We focus also on the cross referencer because its accessing strategy is *not* oriented around the abstract syntax tree, yet is also fairly typical.

We first specify the input and output data structures. We give the actual specifications in their entirety. The details of the specifications are less important than their general flavor. The tool code is given elsewhere [Snodgrass 1989]. Instances of the `abstract_syntax` structure, shown in Figure 1, are created by a parser tool (not described here) and read by the semantic analyzer. The root object, of type `functions`, contains an attribute `syn_funcs`, which is a sequence of `function` objects, each with a name and a body. The function return type is a *class* containing two members, the `int` and `real` types. Similarly, `expression` is a class containing the object `parameterRef` and the classes `constant` and `operation`. The `Enumerated` representation uses integers for the unattributed types `int` and `real`.

Instances of this structure are processed by the semantic analysis tool, which creates instances of the `attributed_syntax` structure, also shown in Figure 1. This structure is derived from the previous structure, and in this case adds three attributes. Name resolution records with each parameter reference the defining occurrence of the parameter, which will have the same name. It also adds each parameter reference to a sequence attached to the parameter; this sequence will be useful during cross reference generation. The `Threaded` representation is a linked list, with each `parameterRef` containing an internally generated attribute that points to the next `parameterRef` in the sequence. Type resolution involves determining the type of each expression. Since `expression` is a class, each member will inherit this attribute. A partial instance of `attributed_syntax` is illustrated in Figure 2.

Finally, we declare two tools and a central repository, and specify their interactions. The input ports are designated with `Pre` and the output ports with `Post`. The output of `CrossRef` is not specified; presumably it is textual output to the screen, to a file, or to a printer. Tools and repositories both have ports. These ports can be connected, with the result that data in the form of structure instances flow out of a tool or repository via an output port, through a connection, and into another tool or repository via an input port. Only two tools are shown; a fully realized programming environment could contain many such tools,

```
Structure abstract_syntax Root functions Is
    functions => syn_funcs: Seq Of function;

    function => syn_name: identifier,
                syn_header: functionDef;
    identifier => lex_token: String,
                  lex_pos: Integer;

    functionDef => syn_ret_type: types,
                   syn_parameters: Seq Of parameter,
                   syn_definition: expression;
    parameter => syn_name: identifier,
                 syn_param_type: types;

    types ::= int | real;
             int =>;  real =>;
    For types Use Representation Enumerated;

    expression ::= constant | parameterRef | operation;
    constant ::= integer_constant | real_constant;
    integer_constant => lex_value: Integer;
    real_constant => lex_value: Rational;
    parameterRef => syn_name: identifier;

    operation ::= binary_operation | unary_operation;
    binary_operation => syn_op: binaryoperator,
                        syn_left: expression,
                        syn_right: expression;
    binaryoperator ::= plus | minus | times | divide;
          plus =>; minus =>; times =>; divide =>;
    unary_operation => syn_op: unaryoperator,
                       syn_argument: expression;
    unaryoperator ::= unaryplus | unaryminus;
          unaryplus =>; unaryminus =>;
End

Structure attributed_syntax Derives abstract_syntax Is
    -- name resolution
        parameterRef => sem_entity: parameter;
        parameter => sem_cross_uses: Seq Of parameterRef;
        For parameter.sem_cross_uses Use Representation Threaded;

    -- type checking
        expression => sem_type: types;
End
```

Figure 1: The abstract_syntax and attributed_syntax Structures

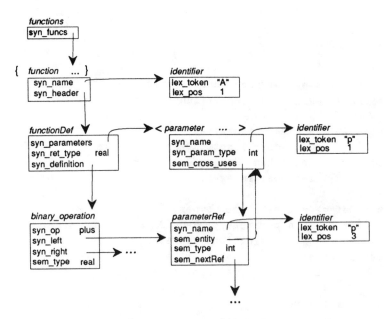

```
function A(p:int; q:real):real = p + q;
```

Figure 2: An Instance of attributed_syntax

connected either to each other or to one or more repositories.

```
Tool SemanticAnalyzer Is
    Pre insyn: abstract_syntax;
    Post outsem: attributed_syntax;
End

Tool CrossRef Is
    Pre insem: attributed_syntax;
End

Repository Rep Is
    Pre insyn: abstract_syntax;        -- computed by parser
    Post outsyn: abstract_syntax;
    Pre insem: attributed_syntax;
    Post outsem: attributed_syntax;    -- sent to optimizer
End

Connect Rep.outsyn To SemanticAnalyzer.insyn;
Connect SemanticAnalyzer.outsem To Rep.insem;
Connect Rep.outsem To CrossRef.inSem;
```

   The unclustered environment executes correctly, but is not particularly efficient. We specify additional statements to cluster the data to increase efficiency. While these changes do not impact the tools' source code, they do change the underlying data organization, yielding very efficient object access and modification. We exploit our knowledge of how the tools access and modify data stored in the repository. The semantic analyzer reads in the **functions** object, searches for a **function** of a given name, then makes two passes over the body of the function: a top-down pass to resolve parameter names and a bottom-up pass to type each expression. To avoid reading the bodies of all the functions, we specify that the **syn_header** attribute of **function** is a cut attribute, implying that the **functionDef** object will be the root object of a cluster. The cross referencer tool similarly searches for a function of a give name, iterates through the sequence of parameters searching through one of a given name, then iterates through the

sem_cross_uses sequence, touching all references to this parameter. To make this operation efficient, we gather **parameterRefs** together in a cluster to separate them from the rest of the function body.

To specify this clustering, we first define a *view*, or subset, of the **attributed_syntax** structure containing the attributes useful to the cross referencer. The most important omission is the **syn_body** attribute of **functionDef**.

```
Structure TopSem Views attributed_syntax Is
        functions => syn_funcs: Seq Of function;
        function => syn_name: identifier,
                    syn_header: functionDef;
        identifier => lex_token: String,
                      lex_pos: source_position;
        functionDef => syn_ret_type: types,
                       syn_parameters: Seq Of parameter;
        parameter => syn_name: identifier,
                     syn_param_type: types,
                     sem_cross_uses: Seq Of parameterRef;
        types ::= int | real;
                int =>;  real =>;
        parameterRef => syn_name: identifier,
                        sem_entity: parameter,
                        sem_type: types;
End
```

We group all objects reachable from the **functionDef** object in a cluster, which we partition into two subclusters, one containing those objects needed by the cross referencer (as specified in the **TopSem** structure), and one containing the remaining objects. We then fragment these latter two clusters into the syntactic and semantic attributes, the former computed by the parser and read by the semantic analyzer; the latter computed and written by the semantic analyzer. The cross referencer tool will read a subset of these segments. We refine our repository to effect the desired clustering.

```
Repository Rep Refines Rep Is
    Cluster Invariant Is
        Cluster A At function.syn_header Via attributed_syntax Is
            Cluster B At functionDef.syn_parameters Via TopSem Is
                Fragment Between abstract_syntax And attributed_syntax
            End;
            Cluster C At functionDef.syn_definition Via attributed_syntax Is
                Fragment Between abstract_syntax And attributed_syntax
            End
        End
    End;
    -- Order the segments on disk
    Order A, B.1, C.1, B.2, C.2;
End
```

The **At** construct specifies the cut attribute, the **Via** clause specifies the attributes that determine object membership in the cluster, and syntactic nesting specifies cluster containment. The **Order** clause will reduce the number of required disk seeks. Figure 3 illustrates the segments that comprise the stored data for the example function shown in Figure 2. We label each object with a PID; the **functions** object has a PID of 1. Sets of objects (denoted with "{ }") and sequences of objects (denoted with "< >") are themselves objects. Objects can appear in several segments if they are fragmented (an example is the **parameter** object with PID 4, whose attributes are located in segments 3 and 4). Object references are eventually represented in main memory as pointers; in the figure we show pointers to objects in other segments with an oval containing the segment number and PID within that segment (e.g., reference 2.8 in the top **function** object points to the **functionDef** object in segment 2). The first segment of a cluster

Segment 1 (Cluster Invariant)

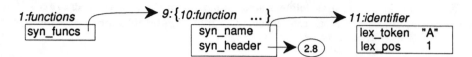

Segment 2 (Cluster A)

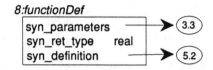

Segment 3 (Cluster B, 1st Fragment)

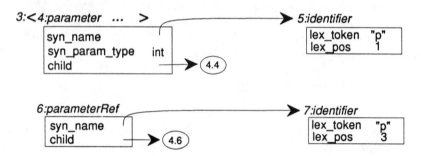

Segment 4 (Cluster B , 2nd Fragment)

Segment 5 (Cluster C, 1st Fragment)

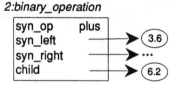

Segment 6 (Cluster C, 2nd Fragment)

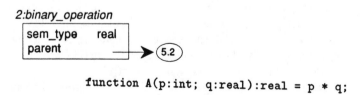

```
function A(p:int; q:real):real = p * q;
```

Figure 3: The Layout of the **attributed_syntax** Instance on Disk

is always the identity fragment; it points to the other segments for that cluster (via generated `child` attributes), and the other segments point back to it (via generated `parent` attributes). The parser creates segments 1, 2, 3, and 5; segments 4 and 6 are computed by the semantic analyzer.

We refine the `SemanticAnalyzer` tool, specifying a clustering identical to that of the repository, in order to minimize data format conversions during reading and writing.

```
Tool SemanticAnalyzer Refines SemanticAnalyzer Is
    Cluster Invariant Is
        Cluster A At function.syn_header Via attributed_syntax Is
            Cluster B At functionDef.syn_parameters Via TopSem Is
                Fragment Between abstract_syntax And attributed_syntax
            End;
            Cluster C At functionDef.syn_definition Via attributed_syntax Is
                Fragment Between abstract_syntax And attributed_syntax
            End
        End
    End;
    -- Read and write Clusters B and C at same time as Cluster A
    Use Cluster A Segments;
    -- Specify which portion of output port structure won't change
    For outsem Use No Write Of abstract_syntax;
End
```

We specify that the required segments reachable from cluster `A` should be transferred during I/O. We need these segments anyway, and this clause will reduce disk seeks, residency checks, and object and segment faults. Finally, we assert that the syntactic attributes will not be modified by the semantic analyzer. Conceivably the preprocessor could figure this out, but it affords more type checking to have the programmer explicitly state this assertion. Note that the length of the cluster specification is roughly independent of the length or complexity of the underlying structures. For example, the clustering for the invariant of an Ada semantic analyzer would be very similar to that above.

We cluster the cross referencer tool in a similar manner.

```
Tool CrossRef Refines CrossRef Invariant TopSem Is
    Cluster Invariant Is
        Cluster A At function.syn_header Via TopSem Is
            Cluster B At functionDef.syn_parameters Via TopSem Is
                Fragment Between abstract_syntax And attributed_syntax
            End
            -- No Cluster C needed
        End
    End;
    -- Read Cluster B at the same time as Cluster A
    Use Cluster A Segments;
End
```

This clustering differs from that of the semantic analyzer in three ways. First, this tool does not need all of the attributes in `attributed_syntax`; it only requires those in `TopSem`. Hence, we specify the global data structure within the tool (termed the *invariant*) to be `TopSem`. Second, no cluster `C` is specified, as the attributes in that cluster are not of interest to this tool. Third, since there is no output port, we need not specify the read-only portion.

4   Performance

To determine how effective semantic clustering is in relation to other proposed clustering methods, we ran experiments on six configurations, the preliminary results of which are described here. The source code remained the same in all configurations; only the policy decisions about how to group objects, when to read or write objects, and when to swizzle were varied. One obvious configuration, strict object faulting, was not included because others have found its performance to be substantially worse than page faulting in the presence of adequate main memory [DeWitt et al. 1990, Stamos 1984].

Configuration 1, termed *pure page faulting*, does not employ application dependent clustering. Instead, objects are grouped on pages based solely on their type. We make the optimistic assumption that the objects of a particular type for each function were grouped together on pages. This assumption, not generally borne out in practice, will minimize the I/O traffic. It also provides a lower bound on the performance of page-based static grouping strategies [Stamos 1984]. In pure page faulting, each access through an attribute that may reference an object is subject to a residency check. If the reference is a PID (this involves simply checking the low-order bit), an object fault occurs, and the PID is looked up in a resident hash table. If the PID is not found there, a page fault occurs, a single page is read in, and all of the objects on the page are placed in the resident hash table. The original attribute is then swizzled. Configuration 2 uses *manual clustering*, where the objects are clustered by executable statements in the parser, which creates the objects. This code arranges that all objects reachable from each `functionDef` object are clustered together in the same segment, which is transferred in whole. Residency checks, object faults, and lazy swizzling (swizzling on access [Moss 1990]) still occur, since the runtime system doesn't know how objects are clustered. However, I/O time is reduced considerably, compared with pure page faulting, since most I/O here is sequential, at least for reasonably sized functions.

In the remaining configurations, the programmer specifies the clustering declaratively in various ways, and the runtime system utilizes this information to increase performance. In the third configuration, syntactic clustering, residency checks and object faults are needed only at the boundaries between segments. As a result, very few residency checks or object faults occur. Configuration 4 uses semantic clustering without fragmentation, here termed *basic semantic clustering*. Compared with syntactic clustering, the partitioning is more sophisticated, as it does not rely on the embedded syntax tree for cluster definition. Configuration 5 uses semantic clustering *with* fragmentation. The clustering statements given in the previous section generate configuration 5; if the `Fragment` clauses are omitted, then configuration 4 results. Configuration 6 assumes an *optimal* clustering strategy that brings in during initialization only those attributes and objects that will accessed. No residency checks are needed; no object faults occur, and no swizzling on input or deswizzling on output is required. Such a strategy is clearly impossible to implement, but provides a convenient lower bound for comparison. Only one seek for read and one for write is needed; the rest of the I/O is sequential.

We instrumented both the semantic analyzer and the cross referencer. We assumed that the repository holds many functions. The tools were executed over five randomly generated function instances stored in the respository; these functions contained from 10 to 100,000 objects. All identifiers in these instances were single characters. The primary metric was total time in seconds to execute the tool. This time may be broken down into the following components: the algorithm, residency checks, processing object faults, reading and writing pages, and swizzling attributes on input and deswizzling attributes on output. Our initial investigations indicated that attribute swizzling/deswizzling in no case totaled more than 2% of the aggregate run time. Hence, we focused on the other components. A somewhat less critical metric is the amount of disk and main memory space required by each configuration.

We ran our tests on an otherwise unloaded NeXT workstation with a 25MHz MC68030 cpu and 16MB of main memory running Version 1.0 of the Mach operating system. All experiments used a local Maxtor 448 MB (formatted) disk, which has an average seek time of 16.5 msec and a raw transfer rate of 4.8 MB/sec, and buffered file I/O. We ensured a cold cache, and flushed the cache to ensure that all modifications were written back to the repository. The source code is in C, and was compiled with GCC. All experiments were run a sufficient number of times to achieve a 95% confidence level of plus or minus 7%.

The algorithm time is not dependent on configuration. To measure it, we loaded the entire database in main memory, swizzled all of the object references, then ran the algorithm multiple times. To measure residency check time, we first measured the number of residency checks performed by each tool in each configuration for each input size, then measured the cost of a single residency check (2.7 μsec). We computed object fault time in a similar manner (a single object fault, which requires a lookup in the object hash table, takes 36 μsec).

I/O time depends on two aspects: the number of seeks and the number of pages read or written. The latter depends on the number of objects transferred, the sizes of the objects, and the page size. We used

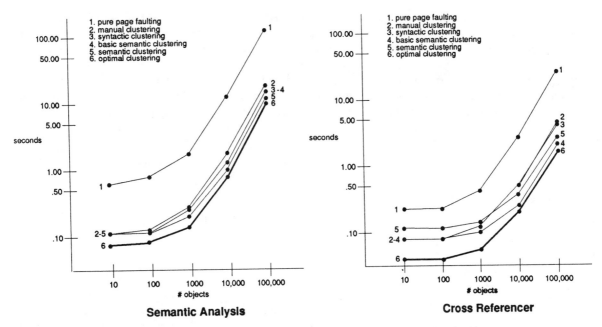

Figure 4: Total Execution Time for the Various Configurations

a page size of 1K bytes; segments consist of an integral number of pages. We measured sequential read and write times (2.2 msec and 2.7 msec, respectively) and random read and write times (38 msec and 37 msec), and determined the number of each required by each configuration to arrive at the total I/O time.

Figure 4 shows how the total time varies over function instance size. All runtimes are in seconds. Both axes are logarithmic. The relative difference between approaches is fairly constant across a wide range of number of objects. Below about 1,000 objects, the minimum number of seeks dominates. The optimal case is shown with a darker line.

The following table gives the breakdown for 100,000 objects for the semantic analyzer.

	Page Faulting	Manual Clustering	Syntactic Clustering	Basic Semantic	Semantic w/Fragmentation	Optimal
Algorithm time	6.89	6.89	6.89	6.89	6.89	6.89
# Residency checks	426,977	426,977	2	2	2	0
Residency check time	1.15	1.15	0	0	0	0
# Object faults	100,000	100,000	2	2	2	0
Object fault time	3.59	3.59	0	0	0	0
# Input disk seeks	1,684	2	2	2	2	1
# Input pages	1,684	1,664	1,664	1,665	1,502	873
Input time	63.3	3.6	3.6	3.6	3.3	1.9
# Output disk seeks	1,684	1	1	1	2	1
# Output pages	1,684	1,663	1,663	1,663	791	477
Output time	61.7	4.5	4.5	4.5	2.2	1.3
Total time	137	19.9	15.2	15.2	12.5	10.3

Pure page faulting is by far the slowest, due primarily to the number of disk seeks performed. Each object fault to a non-resident page causes a random page to be read, preceded by a disk seek. Recall that this number is a lower bound, since we assumed each page contained only objects relevant to the algorithm, which the runtime system had no way of ensuring. Manual clustering effects almost an order of magnitude improvement, as the number of seeks decreased to 3, independent of the size of the input. However, the time to perform residency checks and objects faults becomes more important; this time approaches that of the algorithm, and accounts for almost one-fifth of the total time. Syntactic clustering informs the runtime system of the clustering, reducing residency checks and object faults from an amount linear in the number of objects to 2, independent of the size of the input. Basic semantic clustering in this case takes exactly as long as syntactic clustering, because the accessing patterns of the two configurations are identical. Fragmentation cuts the time down by another 18%, because the semantic attributes are not read and the syntactic attributes are not written. The optimal (and unattainable) clustering is faster still, by 18%, in part because fewer seeks are required (one input and one output, verses two of each). More importantly, fewer attributes, and hence fewer pages, need to be transferred: the values of constants and the operator attribute of operation objects are not needed, and so are not transferred in this configuration, and various internal pointers such as those employed between fragments also are not needed.

The following table gives the breakdown for the cross referencer tool, again for 100,000 objects.

	Page Faulting	Manual Clustering	Syntactic Clustering	Basic Semantic	Semantic w/Fragmentation	Optimal
Algorithm time	0.74	0.74	0.74	0.74	0.74	0.74
# Residency checks	4,640	4,640	2	2	2	0
Residency check time	0.01	0.01	0	0	0	0
# Object faults	4,638	4,638	2	2	2	0
Object fault time	0.17	0.17	0	0	0	0
# Input disk seeks	665	2	2	2	3	1
# Input pages	665	1,664	1,664	656	820	491
Input time	25.0	3.65	3.65	1.48	1.87	1.09
Total time	25.9	4.57	4.39	2.22	2.61	1.83

Cross referencing takes an order of magnitude less time (in large part due to the `sem_cross_uses` sequence so conveniently created during name resolution). Interestingly, pure page faulting has an advantage when used with the cross referencer tool, because the tool touches objects of only a few object types. Hence, the data is accidentally clustered. However, seek time still dominates. Compared with syntactic clustering, basic semantic clustering is significantly faster, because it avoids reading the body of the function. Fragmentation increases the size of objects slightly to accommodate pointers connecting objects in different segments, resulting in slightly lower performance (the increase is more the compensated by the decrease observed in semantic analysis).

The differences in the space requirements aren't as dramatic. The following table how much disk space in MB is required to store a 100,000 object function instance, and how much main memory is used by each of the tools for each configuration. Basic semantic clustering reduces the main memory usage as compared with the other clustering approaches, and semantic clustering with fragmentation generally trades disk space for execution time. The disk space overhead imposed by fragmentation is accentuated by the small objects used in this experiment. If somewhat larger objects were used, then the relative overhead of the additional pointers required by fragmentation would be less.

	Page Faulting	Manual Clustering	Syntactic Clustering	Basic Semantic	Semantic w/Fragmentation	Optimal
Disk space	1.68	1.66	1.66	1.67	2.29	1.65
Sem. analy. main mem.	1.68	1.66	1.66	1.67	2.29	1.35
Cross ref main mem.	0.67	1.66	1.66	0.66	0.82	0.49

This experiment indicates that the following factors may be ranked as follows according to their contribution to the total execution time of each tool: disk seeks (35 msec), pages transferred (2.2–2.7 msec), object faults (36 μsec), and residency checks (2.7 μsec). We now discuss strategies to minimize each in turn.

Minimizing disk seeks is difficult when multiple tools exhibit different accessing patterns. Pure page faulting suffered because page faults were to random pages, requiring a seek for each page read (a total of 3368 seeks in semantic analysis and 665 in cross referencing). Increasing the page size would substantially improve the performance of this configuration for large functions. A page size of 32K bytes would for example cut the semantic analysis execution time to approximately one-fourth and the cross referencer time to one half for functions of 10,000 objects, at the cost of significant wasted main memory (416KB of main memory needed to store 171 KB of data). However, pure page faulting even with this change would not be competitive with the other configurations. Larger page sizes would probably not substantially help the other configurations. Preliminary studies by others have yielded the same conclusion [DeWitt et al.

1990].

The other five configurations required from 1 to 4 seeks for both tools, independent of the number of objects transferred. Semantic clustering minimizes disk seeks in three ways: segments are defined in such a way as to select exactly those objects and attributes of interest to each tool, entire segments are transferred at a time, and the segments are manually ordered on disk to allow several segments to be read in one sequential pass. Even though fragmentation increases the number of segments required (manual, syntactic, and pure semantic clustering required one segment per function, while fragmentation required four), the number of disk seeks required by fragmentation were comparable, and in some cases identical, to these other configurations.

Minimizing pages transferred involves not transferring unneeded objects and attributes. Syntactic clustering suffered in the semantic analyzer because it had to read the uninitialized semantic attributes; it suffered in the cross referencer because it had to read the entire function body, much of which was never used. Fragmentation is the key to minimizing the number of pages read and written, effecting a time savings of 20% for the semantic analysis tool.

Minimizing object faults and residency checks requires knowledge by the runtime system of what objects will be co-resident. In pure page faulting the time to perform these two bookkeeping tasks approached that required to execute the semantic analysis algorithm (disk I/O time still overwhelmed these other components). In manual clustering these bookkeeping tasks accounted for a quarter of the total time. The other configurations all performed exactly two residency checks and two object faults, independent of the number of objects. This low count is due in part to the simplicity and small number of the tools; we envision that other tools may require somewhat more checks. Semantic clustering offers flexibility in clustering objects, and also allows enclosing clusters to be simultaneously read or written by a tool, permitting more attributes to be internal and thus not subject to residency checks or object faults.

As processing speed continues to improve at a faster rate than disk access speed, this ranking of factors should continue to hold, and in fact the goal of reducing the number of disk seeks and page transfers will become increasingly important.

5   Summary and Future Work

In this paper we introduced a new approach to clustering in a persistent object store. Semantic clustering differs from other proposed clustering methods in the following ways.

- Clustering is by partial closure, via a subset of the attributes.

- Objects are then fragmented in a controlled fashion, splitting attributes across segments.

- The program's main memory is clustered to eliminate most residency checks and to effect prepaging of objects.

- The ordering of segments on disk and the portion of main memory objects that are modified by a tool can both be specified; this information is used to reduce I/O time.

- Structures are utilized as a declarative linguistic device to aid the specification of clustering.

- We insulate the source code from changes in clustering, with the result that the clustering impacts performance only (the tool developer need not be concerned with clustering).

We presented results of experiments on a semantic analyzer and a cross referencer, which exhibit quite different object access patterns. While semantic clustering exploits knowledge of these access patterns, it should work well with all of the tools that access the repository. The total execution time for both tools is shown below, along with the overhead imposed by making the tool persistent (calculated as total time minus algorithm time).

	Page Faulting	Manual Clustering	Syntactic Clustering	Basic Semantic	Semantic w/Fragmentation	Optimal
Both tools	163	24.5	19.6	17.4	15.1	12.1
Persistent Overhead	155	16.9	12.0	9.8	7.5	4.5

This experiment indicates that, for the tools, object sizes, and hardware configuration considered here, performing any clustering at all yields almost an order of magnitude improvement in overall tool execution time over pure page faulting, and that semantic clustering is faster than other forms of clustering by 20%–35%, and within 25% of the (unattainable) optimal clustering.

The drawbacks of semantic clustering are (a) the clustering must be correctly specified by the programmer (a bad clustering is often worse than none at all), (b) new or modified tools may be inconsistent with the current clustering in place, resulting in either slow tools or repository reorganization (this tradeoff may be managed by effective tools [Snodgrass & Shannon 1990]), (c) fragmentation requires more disk and main memory space to store cross pointers between segments, and (d) the runtime system is somewhat more complicated than pure page faulting, but similar to that needed for syntactic clustering,

We have developed a formal semantics for the clustering constructs, and are now implementing a runtime system that fully supports semantic clustering. We will then apply this clustering to a large programming environment [Snodgrass 1990]. This environment includes a data structure compiler of the form mentioned in Section 2, as well as a window-based debugger, an assertion checker, an unparser, and a cross reference generator. The dozen programs contain some 20 persistent tools, for a total of approximately 100K lines of source code. This code will require few changes to use the new runtime system, and will provide an opportunity for a much more complete evaluation of this approach. We also plan to apply semantic clustering to specific persistent languages such as Modula-3 [Hosking & Moss 1990] as alternatives to the language-independent constructs illustrated in Section 3.

6   Bibliography

[Balch et al. 1989] Balch, P., W. P. Cockshott and P. W. Foulk. *Layered Implementations of persistent object stores. Software Engineering Journal*, Mar. 1989, pp. 123-131.

[Cockshott et al. 1984] Cockshott, W., M. Atkinson, K. Chisholm, P. Bailey and R. Morrison. *Persistent Object Management Systems. Software–Practice and Experience*, 14 (1984), pp. 49-71.

[Conradi & Wanvik 1985] Conradi, R. and D.H. Wanvik. *Mechanisms and Tools for Separate Compilation.* Technical Report 25/85. The University of Trondheim, The Norwegian Institute of Technology. Oct. 1985.

[DeWitt et al. 1990] DeWitt, D.J., P. Futtersack, D. Maier and F. Velez. *A Study of Three Alternative Workstation-Server Architectures for Object Oriented Database Systems*, in *Proceedings of the Conference on Very Large Databases.* 1990.

[Hosking & Moss 1990] Hosking, A.L. and Moss, J.E.B. *Towards Compile-Time Optimizations for Persistence*, in this proceedings.

[Moss 1990] Moss, J.E.B. *Working with Persistent Objects: To Swizzle or Not to Swizzle.* COINS Technical Report 90-38. Department of Computer and Information Science, University of Massachusetts. May 1990.

[Snodgrass 1989] Snodgrass, R. *The Interface Description Language: Definition and Use.* Rockville, MD: Computer Science Press, 1989.

[Snodgrass 1990] Snodgrass, R. *IDL Toolkit Release 4.2.* Department of Computer Science, University of Arizona, Tucson, AZ, 1990.

[Snodgrass & Shannon 1990] Snodgrass, R. and K. Shannon. *Fine Grained Data Management for Evolving Tools in a Software Development Environment*, in *Proceedings of the Symposium on Software Development Environments.* Irvine, CA: Dec. 1990.

[Stamos 1984] Stamos, J.W. *Static Grouping of Small Objects to Enhance Performance of a Paged Virtual Memory. ACM Transactions on Computer Systems*, 2, No. 2, May 1984, pp. 155-180.

[Straw et al. 1989] Straw, A., F. Mellender and S. Riegel. *Object Management in a Persistent Smalltalk System. Software–Practice and Experience*, 19, No. 8, Aug. 1989, pp. 719-737.

[Weddell 1989] Weddell, G.E. *Efficient Property Access in Memory Resident Object Oriented Databases.* Technical Report CS-89-49. University of Waterloo. 1989.

[Wile & Allard 1989] Wile, D.S. and D.G. Allard. *Aggregation, Persistence, and Identity in Worlds*, in *Proceedings of the Workshop on Persistent Object Systems.* Jan. 1989.

[Widjojo et al. 1990] Widjojo, S., R. Hull, and D.S. Wile. *A Specificational Approach to Merging Persistent Object Bases*, in this proceedings.

Enhancing Performance in a Persistent Object Store: Clustering Strategies in O_2

Véronique Benzaken

Claude Delobel

Altaïr

BP105

78153 Le Chesnay Cedex

E-mail vero@bdblues.inria.fr claude@bdblues.inria.fr

July 17, 1990

Abstract

We address the problem of clustering complex data on disk to minimize the number of I/O operations in data intensive applications. We first focus on the problems related to the design and implementation of clustering strategies. We then propose a set of clustering strategies as well as an algorithm which implements them for the O_2 system.

1 Introduction

New developments, both in the database field and in the programming languages field, have led to the design of new database management systems [Ba88], [Ki88]. These systems have the following characteristics: a complex object model [LR89a], a persistent programming language [AB87], and an object management system [VBD89]. Object management systems have to fulfill the following requirements: (i) efficient management of large amount of (large) objects; (ii) object sharing and versioning; (iii) and usual database functionality such as transaction management, concurrency control and recovery. In this paper, we are interested in how clustering can improve performance of such systems. Consider, for example, a complex object o_1 consisting of two components o_2 and o_3. If each component object is stored in a different page, we may have to perform up to three disk accesses when we want to retrieve the entire object! A clustering strategy might suggest how to place these objects as close to one another as possible on disk memory.

We shall describe the clustering strategies adopted in the O_2 system. We propose a set of flexible strategies which rely upon the inheritance hierachy as well as on the structural information given by the object types. Our strategies are flexible in the sense that we will not try to cluster all the components of an object together; instead, we try to define grouping strategies which take into account the operations performed on the database (i.e, the methods).

We first list the problems which arise when designing clustering strategies. We then describe the strategies that have been implemented in the O_2 system and we show how methods are taken into account and informally give a cost model which allows us to derive an optimal clustering scheme. We detail the implementation of the clustering module and give a set of early measurements which have been performed in the O_2 system in order to evaluate the impact of clustering. Finally, we give some concluding remarks.

2 Issues in the Design of a Clustering Algorithm

The objective of a clustering algorithm is to group objects which are co-referenced as close to one another as possible in physical memory. We list here after the critical problems one must answer when designing a clustering algorithm:

- What are the tradeoffs between static versus dynamic clustering?

- What is the input to the clustering algorithm?

- What are the different kinds of clustering algorithms?

- What are the relationships between clustering and architecture configuration?

2.1   Static versus Dynamic Clustering.

In the *static* case, clustering is done at the time objects are created and no reorganization is implied when the links between objects are updated. *Dynamic* clustering is done at run time when objects are accessed concurrently and becomes attractive in an environment where the write operations dominate the read operations. Here the cost of reorganization is identical to the cost of clustering. In a dynamic environment, when the objects are transferred from the disk to the main memory their physical page locations are not necessarily the same after a write operation. In object-oriented database systems object identity and referential integrity to objects are part of the model. If object identity is implemented as a logical reference then a dynamic clustering algorithm is probably better suited.

2.2   Input to a Clustering Algorithm

The inputs to a clustering algorithm are usually access patterns of objects, given by the user, providing information about the frequency of accesses from an object to another. The higher the frequency the more effective the grouping has to be. This information can be stored at two different levels: object level or type level. At the object level, the access frequency is stored together with the reference "pointer". The overhead of this solution is the cost of updating the access frequency every time we navigate through a link between two objects. If recorded at the type level (and therefore recorded within the schema), the interactions between objects are derived from the type of the objects at creation time.

2.3   Clustering Algorithms

The problem of clustering can be seen as a graph partitioning problem. The nodes of the graph are the objects, and the edges are the links between objects. This problem is NP-complete. However, as the graph of objects represents the database state, all is needed is an incremental solution where new objects are placed at the "right place". Most of the algorithms used can be classified as greedy algorithms: they scan the objects according to their links, and try to place them into the same cluster unit. Thus the cost of clustering has no major impact on the overall system. What are the parameters which are used to control a clustering algorithm? We enumerate below the most important steps that must be considered.

- Obviously the input information is part of the control and determines a possible cluster of objects.

- Once a cluster has been defined, the algorithm must look for a candidate page to insert this new cluster. Different strategies can be used to find the page : the cluster algorithm may use only the pages available in the buffer pool, thus avoiding any I/O; the algorithm may search for a page on the disk; alternatively, it may open a new page if it considers that there is no good candidate. If it also splits pages after reorganzation, the cost of splitting has to be lower than the cost of searching for the best candidate page. This previous step assumes that the search for a page does not consider the available space into the page.

2.4   Clustering and Architecture Configuration

A classification of object servers has been proposed in [DFMV90]. Two basic architectures are retained: the *smart* server architecture and the *dumb* server architecture. In the smart architecture the server understands all the concepts of the object-oriented approach and is decomposed in three layers: I/O, buffer and object layer. The transfer unit between the server and the workstation is the object and thus the effect of clustering is visible only at the server and not on the workstation. Furthermore, clustering can be performed only at the server since it is the only place where the concept of page is understood. Consequently, when a transaction executing on the workstation commits, all the persistent objects have to be returned to the server before applying the clustering algorithm. In the dumb architecture the server is only composed of two layers: I/O and buffer. The concept of object is known to the workstation only. The transfer unit between the server and the workstation is the page and thus if clustering has worked properly, great part of the objects contained within the transferred page will be used without any additional transfers. As the page concept is understood at the workstation, the clustering decisions can be taken at this site.

2.5   Options Taken in the O_2 System

The choice made in O_2 to use physical object identifiers was largely motivated by performance reasons; therefore the O_2 clustering strategies we present in this paper are *static*. Nevertheless, we shall show how our solution may be extended in order to dynamically reorganize clusters. These strategies are defined at the *type level* by the database administrator and could be applied in the context of logical identifiers as well. They are independent, from a logical point of view, of the O_2 system: they could be used in any system managing complex objets with inheritance. The *clustering algorithm* which implements them is a greedy tree-pattern-matching algorithm (with no page splitting). Last, our strategies have been implemented in the context of a *smart* architecture.

3   The O_2 Clustering Strategies

The clustering strategies designed in the O_2 system rely on the concept of *placement trees*. The following section describes these trees.

3.1   Placement Trees

Intuitively, the type structure of a class in the O_2 system may be represented as an infinite tree (in case of recursive types) [AK89]. A placement tree is any finite subtree extracted from this infinite tree. A *clustering strategy* for the system classes is a set of placement trees. Given a clustering strategy, each class in the system is the root of at most one placement tree. We have chosen a finite tree for operational reasons. A placement tree for class c expresses the way in which components of an instance of c are to be clustered. Notice that the definition of a placement tree allows us to handle type recursiveness at the physical level. Figure 1 shows examples of clustering strategies.

In the first alternative for the Restaurant class, the placement tree states that menu (which is an instance of class Menu), the type customers and each of the "customers" elements will be grouped with the corresponding instance of Restaurant. This means that, in a single cluster, we shall store the "menu" object, its atomic components, the value customers, the elements of the corresponding set and the atomic values which compose them. An instance of Courses may be shared by a Chef or a Menu. Therefore, a Course object may either be clustered with a Chef or with a Menu. Unlike the Orion system [KBC87], such a decision is only taken at run time and is not part of the database schema. The placement tree for the class Person for the second alternative reduces to a single node. Indeed, instances of this class are only composed of atoms and we assume that atomic values are stored with the instance to which they are related. Placement trees are the inputs of the clustering algorithm. They only indicate how objects may be stored, they are not part of the schema (there is neither a class placement tree nor instances of placement trees). The definition of placement trees is orthogonal to the schema, thus data independence is insured by such strategies.

Objects are placed in logical clusters using placement trees associated with the class of which they are instances and according to their identifiers (disk or memory). A logical cluster is composed of a root object and a set of objects which are grouped with it. We assume that the size of a logical cluster is unlimited. The algorithm presented here is a greedy tree pattern-matching algorithm. There exist different alternatives for this algorithm based on either depth first or breadth first traversals of placement trees.

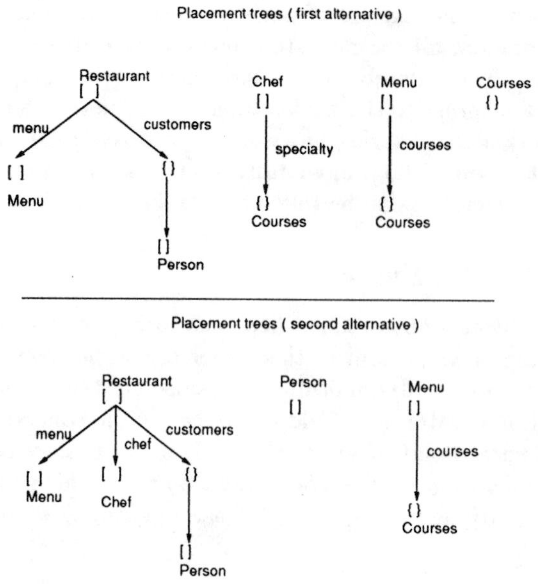

Placement trees (first alternative)

Placement trees (second alternative)

Figure 1: Placement Trees

4   Implementation

4.1   Global Architecture of the System

The setting of the O_2 system [VBD89] consists of a server and a network of workstations. On the server, the object manager is built on top of WiSS [WiSS85]. WiSS provides basic support for persistency, memory management and transactions as such it provides record-structured sequential files, unstructured files, indices and long data items (LDI's). Records may vary in length and are uniquely identified by a RID (Record IDentifier) which describes its physical address (i.e a volume number, a page number and a slot number). WiSS directly controls the physical location of pages on disk and does its own buffering. The clustering algorithm executes at the server level while the definition of placement trees is performed at the workstation level. For the sake of brevity, we do not detail the definition language of placement trees, its syntax is very similar to those of O_2 class definitions [LR89b].

4.2   Object Identifiers Allocation

In the O_2 system, objects are uniquely identified and accessed by object identifiers (oid's). For performance purposes, oid's are physical and correspond to a RID. With physical identifiers and a smart workstation/server configuration, a decision has to be taken upon when to assign oid's to newly created objects. Objects are created in the workstation and persistent physical identifiers containing RID's are only delivered on insertion of the corresponding WiSS record. Identifiers are assigned at transaction commit. In addition, this solves the problem of having to change the identifier of a newly created object when the system decides to cluster it afterwards (but before transaction commit) with another "owner" object. The clustering algorithm is responsible for the assigment of physical identifiers, and thus is viewed as a persistent identifiers server.

4.3   Logical Clusters and Physical Clusters

In the O_2 system, objects are mapped to records. Therefore, a physical cluster is a set of records. WiSS offers the possibility to perform clustering, since a record can be stored near another one (there is a WiSS primitive to do it). WiSS then tries to store the record in the same or in a neighbor page. We have chosen to map a physical cluster to a page (i.e, a page may contain several clusters). The size of logical clusters was considered unlimited. Of course, the size of a physical cluster is bounded to the page size. Therefore there will be some clusters (larger than a page) which will overlap several (contiguous) pages. Large objects (i.e, with large atomic values) will be stored as WiSS LDI's.

4.4   Initial Placement and System Adaptability

Initially, when instances of a given class are created, the placement tree associated with this class generates a first organization on secondary memory. The problem of system adaptability arises in the two following cases:

- Some placement trees have been modified.

- No placement trees are modified but some links between objects have changed.

4.4.1   Placement Tree Modifications

At any time the DBA has the ability to modify placement trees. Neither the clustering module nor the access object module will be affected by such modifications since oid's are physical identifiers. The clustering algorithm will take into account the new grouping scheme. The execution of transactions will not be disturbed. Indeed, only the physical placement of objects is modified (for the newly created objects). This certainly will have some consequences on the performance but not on the behavior of transactions. On the other hand, the physical organization on disk will be modified. The following alternatives thus arise.

- We do not update the old clusters. New placement trees will be taken into account in the future. The objects which have already been placed keep their location on disk.

- We can restructure the database.

For the second alternative a complete study should be performed in order to evaluate at which time we consider that the physical organization is too chaotic. The number of modified placement trees, the number of classes concerned in such modifications might be parameters to be taken into account. In addition to this, for each class whose placement tree has been modified, we can measure the number of instances which have been grouped according to the first PT and to the second one. If the ratio is lower than a given level we can restructure the whole extension of the class. This is an open problem which has not been implemented.

4.4.2   Cluster Reorganization

Different approaches for record clustering and reorganization have been proposed [YLSS85], [SPO89]. Record clustering algorithms usually focus on finding an optimal strategy by rearranging records on pages in the buffer area and writing new pages back to the disk space. Evidently, such approaches are applicable in the case where oid's are logical. We suggest the following solutions to solve the problem of system adaptability in the context of physical oid's. The following cases are taken into account:

- the size of an object increases within a page;

- some logical links are modified.

The first case is automatically managed by WiSS. Indeed if the size of an object increases in such a way that it cannot fit into the page any longer, Wiss allocates a new page and the forwarding pointer allows the system to retrieve the (moved) object.

The second case occurs when among the links which reference an object (o), one link is deleted. We adopt the following strategy: when an object which references o is accessed, thereafter, if there is enough space, we shall re-cluster o with it (if the corresponding PT allows it). We thus assume that we have full control of the forwarding mechanism of WiSS.

For both alternatives the problem of updating the references arises. As we do not want to manage backward pointers, we shall update, incrementally, only the references for future accesses. Indeed it is possible, at this time, to detect the forwarding pointer and thus to update the new reference. However we need to know when the forwarding pointer could be garbaged. We propose the following solution. First,

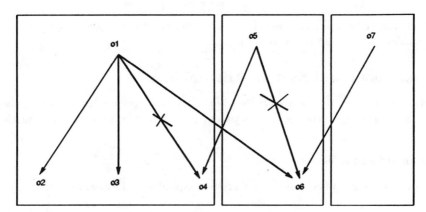

Figure 2: Cluster Reorganization

recall that a reference count of an object is stored in the header of the record containing the object. Assume that the objects have been grouped as in Figure 2. The links (o_1, o_4) and (o_5, o_6) are privileged because they correspond to shared objects which have been grouped. Each time such a link is deleted the corresponding object is not at the right place anymore. We are faced with two alternatives:

1 the reference count is equal to one (it is the case for o_4). When we dereference o_4 through o_5, if there is enough space in the page of o_5 we re-cluster o_4 with o_5. If not nothing is done.

2 the reference count is greater than two (it is the case for o_6). When we dereference o_6 (through o_1 for example) we shall try to store o_6 close to o_1. We then replace the (old) record of o_6 with a special forwarding record which contains: the new address of o_6, a dereferencing count initialized to one (this count will be incremented at each new dereferencing) and the value of the reference count of o_6. As soon as the dereferencing count is equal to the reference count, the forwarding record will be deleted.

4.5   Performance Evaluation and Measurements

The problem of choosing, for a given class, the "best" placement tree arises. We thus have to take into account the most frequently performed operations against the database. We have detailed a cost function [Be90] which takes into account object faults and main memory waste according to the call frequencies of the methods. It also takes into account set-structured components of an object by assigning an average cardinality to each set and an average number of accessed elements (in the set) per method. This cost function is fully described in [Be90]. With respect to this cost function, one placement tree is optimal. Though our cost model relies on some simplifying assumptions, we have a means to help the database administrator in choosing placement trees.

4.6   Early Measurements

The class we have studied is described in Figure 3 and corresponds to the class Restaurant slightly modified. The methods defined for Restaurant are characterized as follows: method m_1 accesses the **menu** component and the **chef** component of class Restaurant, m_2 accesses the component **menu** then the component **course** and the component **chef** of class Restaurant, m_3 accesses the **menu** and **course** components and m_4 accesses the **chef** and **specialty** components of class Restaurant. The four methods have a call frequency of 25%.

Our experiments took into consideration the variation of the following parameters:

- The placement trees for the class Restaurant. Table 2 gives, for each placement tree, the classes it groups.

- The sizes of objects. Table 1 gives the different configurations (A, B, C) of measurements. The values reported denote the sizes (in bytes) of the instances of each class. The size of instances of Courses varies from 10 integers to 1000 integers in the set.

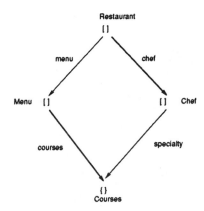

Figure 3: Class Restaurant

- The number of generated objects which varied from 1000 to 10.000.

Configurations	Restaurant	Menu	Chef	Courses
A	42	34	34	128
B	42	34	34	848
C	42	34	34	4048

Table 1: **Configurations of measurements**

	Restaurant	Menu	Chef	Courses
1	●	●	●	●
2	●	●		●
3	●		●	●
4	●	●	●	●
5	●	●	●	●
6	●	●	●	
7	●	●		
8	●		●	

Table 2: **PT's for Restaurant**

The scenario of each experiment is the following. We generated a database according to each placement tree for Restaurant. Each time a database was generated, we executed each method on the whole extension of Restaurant and measured the object faults. We have chosen to penalize an object fault twice as much as main memory waste. The best placement tree according to the cost function is described in Figure 4.

The results for the optimal placement tree are reported in the fourth column of Table 3. The results obtained are the following. In four out of the five sequences, the optimal tree was effectively the best tree (the one which led to fewer object faults). However, the third sequence (configuration C) led to other placement trees as best trees. For this sequence, the simplifying assumptions of the model were violated. Indeed, each cluster (for the tree n° 4) overlapped three or two pages. Notice that an implementation without any clustering leads in this case to the best results. For the trees n° 6, 7 ,8, the number of clusters overlapping several pages was very low (4 for tree n°6 and zero for the other two). The size of logical clusters is thus a crucial parameter with respect to the benefits of clustering.

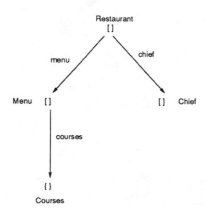

Figure 4: Optimal Placement Tree

		1	2	3	4	5	6	7	8	WC
1000	A	32	27	32	**26**	32	32	32	32	32
	B	112	65	114	**62**	112	118	118	118	118
	C	412	414	414	412	412	*219*	*219*	*219*	*218*
10.000	A	212	*145*	210	**145**	212	211	211	211	211
	B	1012	533	1032	**512**	1012	1078	1078	1078	1078

Table 3: **Impact of PT's on the transaction (without sharing)**

However, we achieved our objective to provide the DBA with a tool to help the choice of the most adequate placement tree. When a cluster fits into a page, the model predicts the placement tree which leads to fewer object faults. When a placement tree leads to clusters whose average size is greater than the page size, such a tree must be rejected. The point is now to find a means in order to select the best placement tree among the remaining ones. We thus shall design, in future work, a cost model which will take into account the sizes of objects.

While the evaluation performed is sound, it could have been more thorough. Further measurements are currently performed in order to evaluate the benefits of clustering [HBD90]. We use a standard object-oriented benchmark (the Tektronix Hypermodel Benchmark) as the basis of the evaluation.

5   Related Work and Conclusions

Most of the prototypes already developed [ZH87], [KBC87], [At85], [MSOP86], [HK90], attempt to perform clustering. In all such systems the segment or the page is the clustering unit and clustering is done when the object is created. The approach adopted in Orion [KBC87] defines the unit of clustering as the composite (exclusive/dependent) object. This is done at the schema level. We think instead that the user should not need to worry about physical issues: the clustering information has to be transparent from an user point of view. Furthermore, if the concept of cluster (via the notion of composite object) is part of the schema, when we want to modify the placement in secondary storage we have to perform a schema update! Data independence is not insured anymore.

In [CK89], it is shown that clustering exploits structural information such as composition hierarchy and inheritance properties. A simulation model has been developed which gives a comparative evaluation of different clustering strategies. The clustering algorithm studied in [CK89] chooses an initial placement for newly created objects which depends on the most frequently used composition links between instances.

The grouping strategies presented in the Encore system [ZH87] seem flexible and powerful (in particular the clustering-by-value feature). In Encore, the following clustering rules may be chosen: (i) ability to store one object per segment if it is large, (ii) ability to store components of a complex object together, (iii) ability to group all the instances of a given class in the same segment, (iv) grouping by value properties (e.g, all blue cars will be stored together). The power of these strategies relies on the fact that, in Encore, objects are shared by means of copies. However, in an environment where update operations are frequently performed, managing such copies seems penalizing with respect to performance.

The approach adopted in the PRIMA project [HMMS87] uses the concept of *type-molecule* as a clustering mechanism for complex objects [SS89]. This concept allows the description of flexible clustering strategies. The main drawback of this approach is that some objects have to be duplicated between several complex objects and that clustering is update dependent.

Design decisions about the clustering are under the control of the Database Administrator. Nevertheless, to help the Database Administrator in taking his decision we have established a link between the access patterns of the methods of a class and the "optimal" placement tree for this class. Our technique is similar of the one proposed by [Sc77] for the hierarchical data model. The idea of Schkolnick is to partition a hierarchical tree structure into subtrees and to find the best partition according to some access patterns inside the hierarchical structure. Our strategy follows the same idea, but differs in the following: (i) the data model is not the same (objects can be shared, inheritance relationship), (ii) clustering is done at commit time as well as persistency, (iii) clustering is transparent to the programmer, thus placement trees can be modified at any time without affecting programs.

Placement trees provide a mechanism for the database administrator to specify exactly how the instances of the classes of a database's class hierarchy are to be clustered on disk. By separating the clustering mechanism from the schema, the database administrator is provided a significantly more powerful mechanism than if clustering was associated with one particular type constructor. In addition, this separation makes it possible for the database administrator to tune the overall performance of the system by modifying the placement trees used for a particular database. Since this can be accomplished without modifying the schema or any applications, data independence is insured.

References

[AB87]   M.Atkinson, P.Buneman, "Types and Persistence in Database Programming Languages." *ACM Computing Surveys*, June 1987.

[AK89]   S.Abiteboul, P.Kannelakis, "Object Identity as a Query Language Primitive" *In Proc Int Conf ACM Sigmod* Portland 1989.

[At85]   T.Atwood, "An Object Oriented DBMS for Design Support Applications" *in proc IEEE COMPINT* Montreal 85.

[Ba88]   F.Bancilhon, "Object-Oriented Database Systems" *Proceedings of the ACM PODS conference*, 152-162 1988.

[Be90]   V.Benzaken, "An Evaluation Model of Clustering Strategies in the O_2 Object-Oriented Database System" *to appear in proc. of the 3rd ICDT conf.* Paris, Dec 1990.

[CK89]   E.E.Chang, R.H.Katz, "Exploiting Inheritance and Structure Semantics for Effective Clustering and Buffering in an Object Oriented DBMS" *in proc ACM SIGMOD conference* Portland 1989.

[DFMV90]   D.DeWitt, P.Futtersack, D.Maier, F.Velez, "A Study of Three Alternatives Workstation/Server Architectures for Object-Oriented Database Systems" *to appear in the proc., of the VLDB'90 conf.* Brisbane, Australia, August 90.

[GR83]   A.Goldberg, D.Robson, *Smalltalk 80 : The language and its implementation*, Addison Wesley, 1983.

[HBD90]   G.Harrus, V.Benzaken, C.Delobel, "Measuring Performance of Clustering Strategies: the CluB-0 Benchmark" *Altaïr internal report* 90.

[HK89]   S. Hudson, R. King, "Cactis: A Self-Adaptative, Concurrent Implementation of an Object-Oriented Database Management System." *ACM TODS, vol 14 n° 3* September 89.

[HMMS87]   T.Harder, K.Meyer-Wegner, K.Mitschang, A.Sikeler, "PRIMA: A DBMS prototype supporting engineering applications" *Proceedings of the VLDB'87 conference*, Brighton 87.

[K*87]   J. Banerjee et al. "Data Model Issues for Object Oriented Applications" *ACM TOIS*, Vol 5 no 1, Jan 87.

[KBC87]   W.Kim, J.Banerjee, H.T.Chou. "Composite Object Support in an Object-Oriented Database System", *OOPSLA '87 Proceedings.*

[KBG89]   W.Kim, E.Bertino, J.Garza, "Composite Objects Revisited" *in Proc ACM Sigmod conf* Portland 1989.

[KCF87]   S.Khoshafian, M.J. Carey, P.Franklin, "Storage Management for Persistent Complex Objects" *Technical Report MCC 87.*

[Ki88]   W.Kim, "A Foundation for Object-Oriented Databases", *Technical Report MCC 88.*

[LR89a]   C.Lécluse, P.Richard "Modeling Complex Structures in Object-Oriented Databases." *Proceedings of the ACM PODS conference*, Philadelphie 89.

[LR89b]   C.Lécluse, P.Richard "The O_2 Database Programming Language" *in Proc., of the VLDB'89 conf.*, Amsterdam, August 89.

[MSOP86]   D.Maier, J.Stein, A.Otis, A.Purdy, "Development of an Object Oriented DBMS" *Technical Report CS/E-86-005* 1986.

[Sc77]   M. Schkolnick, "A Clustering Algorithm for Hierarchical Structures", *ACM Transactions on Database Systems*, Vol 2, n°. 1, March 77.

[SPO89]   P.Scheuermann, Y.C.Park, E.Omiecinski, "Heuristic reoganization of clustered files" *Proceedings of the 3rd FODO conference* Paris 89.

[SS89]   H.Schoning, A.Sikeler, "Cluster mechanisms supporting the dynamic construction of complex objects" *Proceedings of the 3rd FODO conference* Paris 89.

[St84]   J. Stamos, "Static Grouping of Small Objects to Enhance Performance of a Paged Virtual Memory", *ACM Transactions on Computer Systems* Vol 2 no 2 May 84.

[VBD89]   F.Velez, G.Bernard, V.Darnis, "The O_2 Object Manager : an Overview", *Proceedings of the VLDB 89 conference* Amsterdam 1989.

[WiSS85]   H.T. Chou, D.J.Dewitt, R.H.Katz, A.C.Klug. Design and implementation of the wisconsin storage system. *Software - Practice and Experience*, 15(10), October 1985.

[YLSS85]   C.Yu, K.Lam, M.Siu, C.Suen, "Adaptative record clustering", *ACM TODS* vol 10 no2 85.

[ZH87]   M. Hornick, S. Zdonik, "A Shared Segmented Memory System for an Object-Oriented Database", *ACM TOIS* vol 5 no1 Jan 87.

Version and Variant Control for a Commercial Application of Persistence

David Blakeman,
AT&T ISTEL Limited,
PO Box 5, Prospect Hill,
Redditch, B97 4DQ,
United Kingdom

Abstract

The Abstract Data Store is a software tool for specifying persistent strongly-typed objects, together with a mechanism for specifying user interfaces for these objects. This paper describes the addition of type constructors to the abstract data store to allow the specification of versions and variants of objects. These new constructors enable the ADS to support arbitrary historical views of objects. They also enable the provision of concurrency mechanisms for the persistent store, and have implications for the support of changing types of objects within the persistent store. This paper uses a real-world example, the provision of a JSD CASE tool, to illustrate the principles described.

1   Introduction

Within the author's organisation exists a highly effective software development group. This group has been using Jackson Structured Programming (JSP)[1] for the last eight years, and Jackson Systems Development (JSD)[2] for the last five years. Over this time our application of JSD has evolved substantially. The motivation for this is the delivery of high quality software applications to the customer, through more rigorous functional specifications. The rigour of these specifications is such that code generation is possible, and is now in regular use. Prototypes have shown that the generation of entire complex applications is possible. However, the development group is now severely constrained by the existing low-capability tools.

Due to the lack of commercially available toolsets of appropriate focus, the decision was taken to produce our own toolset to support our application of the JSD method. The platform chosen for the toolset was the Abstract Data Store (ADS)[3, 4]

One of the major requirements for the toolset is the ability to handle version control - that is the logging and maintenance of changes to specifications over *time*. Firstly, this permits the recording of changes to specifications and the reasons for these changes. Secondly, it enables the recording of specification decisions which have been made and then later rejected - this forms a vital but frequently ignored information base for the analyst. Thirdly, it allows us to regenerate earlier versions of an application at any time (for example, generated code may become corrupted or lost, and the customer may not yet be prepared to take on board a later version of the application). Finally, the provision of versions enables the handling of concurrency, which is a requirement of the toolset.

An additional requirement is the provision of variant control. A variant is defined as a branch of a specification which differs from its root. The creation of a new variant is a major event, but work upon different variants of a specification is a frequent activity.

413

It is important to emphasise that this project is not concerned with the maintenance of traditional source code and object code; these are outputs of the toolset, but are not stored within it. These components are the outputs of a code generator, and are not for human consumption.

The ability to generate entire applications without manual intervention after the specification stage has profound implications for the software development cycle. The author believes that one of the major reasons for the cost of maintenance being so great is the lack of a clear specification of an application at its installation. At the day of release the implementation of the application is often substantially removed from its specification, and as time passes these two components diverge to such an extent that the specification becomes useless for maintenance purposes. At this point maintenance becomes a task of huge proportion.

Given the ability to generate software from a specification without manual intervention, it is possible to modify the specification of the software, and regenerate a new version from the modified specification. Thus the specification always remains in step with its implementation. Given this situation, the only time when maintenance becomes a problem is when the problem area changes to such an extent that the specification no longer addresses the problems faced by the customer. This requires major specification rework, and it is debatable whether this activity should be classed as 'maintenance'.

Typically, specifications occupy substantially smaller amounts of storage than their implementations, and thus a comprehensive specification version management system need be far less concerned about such matters than source code version management systems.

2   The Abstract Data Store

The ADS allows the interactive specification of types, and then allows the user to create instances of these types. These types are equipped with operations (specifying the semantics of the object), and with views (specifying one or more concrete appearances of the object). The types and their instances are automatically persistent, without the user being aware of this fact. The ADS possesses type constructors based on those described by Hoare[5]. Simple type constructors are provided for subrange, enumeration, string and two other primitive types, document and diagram. As well as these, the following 'structured' type constructors are provided:

Record   - the cartesian product of its components

Union   - the discriminated union of its components

List   - a sequence of zero or more values of its component

Array   - a complete mapping of domain values to their ranges

Map   - a partial mapping of domain values to their ranges

Strict   - the union of its component and the empty value.

In addition, a **Shared** type constructor is provided allowing the creation of secure graph structured objects. A form of reference count garbage collection is provided. Operations to link shared objects are provided as a part of the default user interface. These constructors are described in more detail by Powell[6].

As an example of a type, consider the following (simplified) structure for a JSD role (entity life history).

```
role       = RECORD
                  name     : identifier
                  structure: structure
             END

identifier = STRING[20]

structure  = UNION
                  leaf
                  sequence
                  selection
                  iteration
             END

sequence   = LIST of component

selection  = LIST of component

iteration  = RECORD
                  desc: component
             END

leaf       = identifier

component  = RECORD
                  label    : identifier
                  elements: structure
             END
```

This example illustrates the power of a relatively simple type declaration. This declaration can now be augmented with views, which specify the appearance of the role to the user. (The formatting syntax is slightly different from that described by Powell[6]).

```
role              = display(downwards)
                       justify(centred)
                       spacing(2)
                       display(rightwards)
                         enclose(rectangle)
                         start_line(hook)
                         <name>
                       end
                       <structure>
                    end

identifier        = display(rightwards) <value> end

structure         = display(rightwards) <component> end

sequence          = display(rightwards) <head>(' ') <tail> end

selection         = display(rightwards) <head>('o') <tail> end

iteration         = display(rightwards) <desc>('*') end

leaf              = display(rightwards) <value> end

component (sym)   = display(downwards)
                       justify(centred)
                       spacing(2)
                       display(rightwards)
                         enclose(rectangle)
                         line_to(hook)
                         start_line(hook)
                         display(rightwards) <label> sym end
                       end
                       <elements>
                    end
```

As an example, the screen below is the above view of an instance of the role describing a library book.

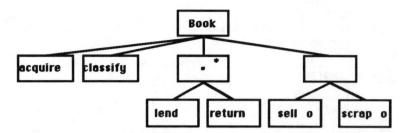

An unusual inheritance mechanism exists; objects inherit operations from their type constructors, and these constructors inherit operations from the root object, *system*. This approach is extremely powerful, general and easily taught. Typically a useful system emerges immediately after creating an instance of a type. The developer need then only be concerned with elaborating the types to add additional semantics, and to modify the user interface. This is the closest the developer ever gets to 'programming'.

3   The ADS User Interface

The ADS allows the user to directly manipulate objects. The user interface appears as shown below:

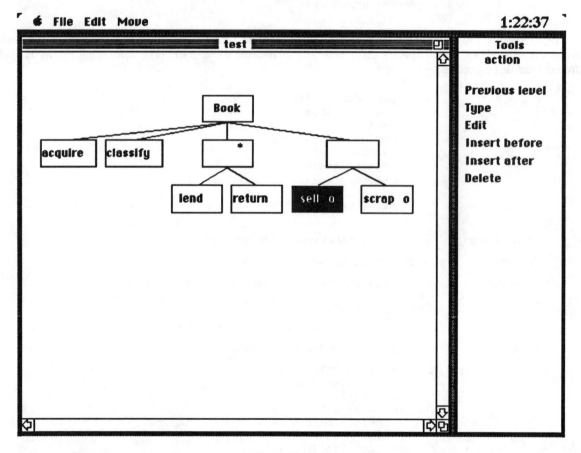

There are three areas to the screen: the menu bar, the work area and the palette. The menu bar (shown at the top of the screen) allows the user to perform standard functions such as quitting from the system and adjusting user preferences. The work area (the large window) contains the currently selected object (which is highlighted) within its context. The palette (the small window) displays the set of operations available to the user on the selected object.

The prompts displayed on the palette are associated with operations on the object, allowing operations to be hidden from the user or redefined.

The system has four categories of user. 'Browsing' users are allowed read-only access to ADS applications. 'Editing' users have read/write access to ADS applications, but no access to types. Application developers have access to application types, operations and views. Finally, ADS developers have access to all system objects, and additional utilities.

The user selects an object by clicking the pointer device over the screen representation of an object. If that object is *selectable*, the object is made the current selection, and is highlighted to indicate this. The palette menu is updated to reflect the prompts available to the user for the current selection. Clicking again on the current selection allows the user to 'zoom in' to that object, if it is *explorable*. Clicking on a palette operation invokes that operation on the currently selected object, as shown below:

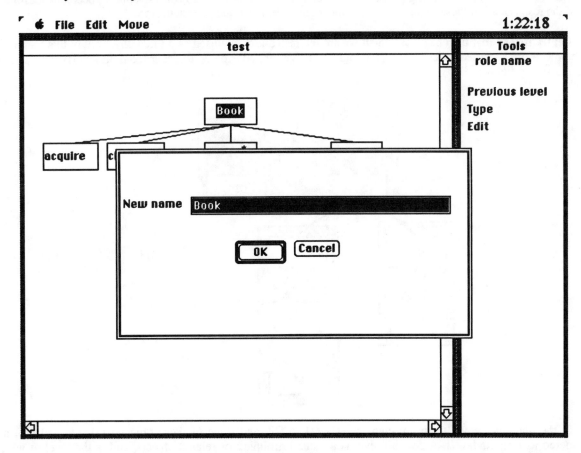

Having been given this prompt, the user may then either enter a value, or cancel the operation. It is important to emphasise that all of these facilities are derived from the strongly-typed nature of the ADS. There is never any need to resort to conventional 'programming'.

A special operation, 'Previous Level', is available to all categories of user. This allows the user to 'zoom out' of the current selection. Application developers and ADS developers also see another special operation, 'Type', which zooms in to the type of the current selection.

4   Versioning

There are two ways in which the problem of versioning can be addressed. Firstly, every change which occurs to the persistent store can be recorded individually in a 'log file' [7]. This approach is often used with conventional databases. If an error occurs in the database, the last reliable copy of the database is taken and the log file reapplied until just before the point where the error occurred. However, this has the disadvantage that the database cannot be inspected for previous versions of objects without substantial (usually impractical) effort.

Secondly, *sets* of related changes can be recorded. In this case, a logical change to a specification may involve a number of small, related changes to the database. This approach is not usually practical with conventional databases, as they have no support for such mechanisms. However, the ADS has the ability to represent hierarchies and graphs of arbitrary complexity. Typically, one logical change occurs in a small area of the hierarchy. For example, a change to a JSD role may involve changing perhaps 50 objects. However, as these objects are small it becomes feasible to record the result of all of these changes as an atomic *logical change* to the persistent store.

Let us assume that the objects in which we are interested are organised as a hierarchy. Within this hierarchy, some objects are specified as levels at which logical changes are considered to occur (commit levels). This state of affairs is shown below:

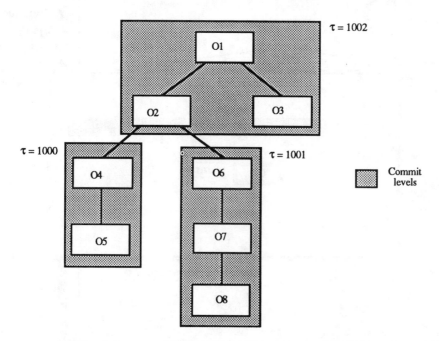

In the diagram above, there are eight objects O1 to O8, and three of these objects (O1, O4 and O6) are considered as *commit levels*. A commit level is a natural grouping of related objects, and is the level at which changes to the persistent store are recorded. For example, O1 may be an entity role, and O4 and O6 may be actions within that role. The other objects above are considered to be subcomponents of the commit level, ie O2 and O3 are subcomponents of O1. Any committed change or group of changes to O1, O2 or O3 results in a new version of O1 being created. O4 and O6 are considered to be external references of O1. A change to O4 or its subcomponent results in a new version of O4 being created, but has no effect on its parent, O1. The same applies to any other external reference (in this case the reference to O6). Commit levels may be nested within other commit levels to arbitrary depth.

Commits are considered to occur sequentially, and the commit is considered to be instant. Thus commits are *totally ordered*. Whenever a commit succeeds a revision clock is incremented and the change is allocated a *revision-time* (τ). The revision clock is completely independent of real-world time, and is used to maintain the total ordering of changes.

Firstly, a user indicates that he intends to work on an object. This creates a temporary copy of the object, and prevents other users from modifying that object. The user operates on the object and its subcomponents until he decides to commit or cancel the changes to that object. Committing the changes forces the temporary copy to supercede the current version. Cancelling the changes 'rolls back' to the previous version, leaving it unaltered.

For example, a user may edit O1 and its subcomponents O2 and O3, this creates a temporary copy of O1. If the user finally commits these changes, the new version of O1 is committed. When this occurs, a unique revision-time is generated for the change, and the new version supercedes the original version. Notice that the subcomponents of O1 may be dynamic structures such as lists. Deleting an item from a list does not affect the original list, but a modified copy of the object supercedes the original version. Thus data is never lost, it is merely relegated to a previous version of the object. This is shown below:

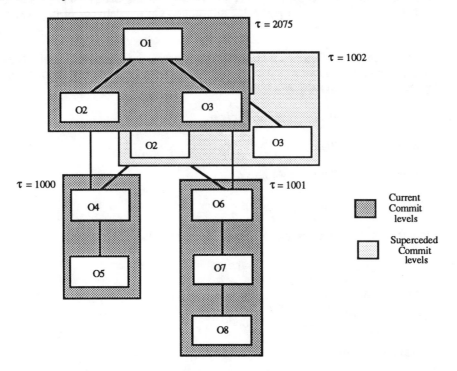

Commit levels are considered to be permanent records of the state of the persistent store at specific points in time. Although this may appear to be an extravagance, the value of such version histories should not be underestimated. In the case of JSD specifications, the version history is a record of the entire specification process. Recovering such information through conventional methods (word of mouth) often takes days or weeks. Further, a technique for reducing the storage requirements is given later in this paper.

Whenever a new version of an object is created, any external references to other commit levels are duplicated. As commit levels may never be destroyed, the integrity of these references is guaranteed. A further constraint is that we must make every object in the system belong to a commit level. This is easily achieved by making *root* (the root of the system) a commit level.

We now need a way of specifying where the commit levels occur in the hierarchy. One way of achieving this is to provide a new type constructor, *versionset*, which specifies that it is a commit level, and therefore a version history of its component is required. As an example, we could specify that the role shown earlier is a commit level as follows:

```
role history = VERSIONSET OF role
```

This states that a role history consists of a set of versions of role. Role retains the definition given earlier.

An instance of a versionset can be in one of two states: *stable* or *transient*. Usually the versionset is in a stable state. However, when an object is subjected to an uncommitted change, the state of the versionset becomes transient. This transient state remains in force until the new version is either committed or cancelled, at which point the state again becomes stable.

5   Using Versionsets

Having described commit-levels and revision-time, it is useful to consider how to use this information. Versionsets allow a *slice*[8] to be cut through an object so that we can inspect the state of its components at a particular time ('last Tuesday at 2pm') or at a particular milestone ('On the delivery of component 6a of Project P11').

To enable a historical view to be taken of a set of objects it is necessary to establish a relationship between the revision clock and real-world time. This may be done through a mapping from the real time to the latest revision-time allocated at that moment. This can be shown as follows:

```
Real time            Latest revision-time

11.00  21/6/90       10045

12.00  21/6/90       10789

13.00  21/6/90       11067
```

Similarly, a mapping from project milestone to revision-time is needed. For example:

```
Project                      Latest revision-time

VIPEUR deliverable 1.1.7     9045

ORDERLINK deliverable 2.2.4  10009

ORDERLINK deliverable 3.6.7  11031
```

The user is now given the facility to invoke a 'historical view'. This allows the user to inspect the objects within the system from a historical perspective, either by specifying a time and a date, or by specifying a project milestone. True to life, it is not possible for the user to change history, but it is possible for him to study it, and copy details from it. This has implications for quality assurance, where a history of the dynamics of change may be used to provide an indication of the problematic areas of a specification.

When a user invokes a 'historical view', he provides the system with an indication of the time or milestone in which he is interested. The mappings described above are used to convert this real-world time into a corresponding revision-time, τ. As objects are accessed, the version which was valid at or before τ is returned. This object may consist of subcomponents to which the same criteria is applied. This technique provides a slice across the specification at the stated revision time. As a special case of this, τ may be given a special value, *latest*, which returns the latest version of the specification.

6 Concurrency

The versionset constructor allows multiple users to concurrently access the ADS. Most access to the ADS is read-only, and this presents no problem. However, when updates are allowed a form of exclusion needs to be provided to prevent two or more users from changing the same object concurrently. The versionset mechanism provides this facility automatically. The moment a versionset becomes transient, as one user attempts to modify it, no other user may create another transient version of that versionset. All other users refer to the stable version of the object, which never changes. When the transient version is finally committed, other users may access the new version of the object. This corresponds to the conventional database approach of locking[6].

The user interface of the ADS provides closures in the form of 'layers' of objects, and ADS applications are organised such that a discrete task is performed at each layer. This approach appears well-suited to a multi-user ADS. When a user explores an object, they are given the latest stable version. If another user then creates a transient version of the object, this is of no interest to the first user. When the other user commits that object, the first user of the object is informed that it has been changed, and given the new version. In the worst case situation, a user (user1) may be working on a branch of the specification. Another user (user 2) may be working above that branch, as shown below:

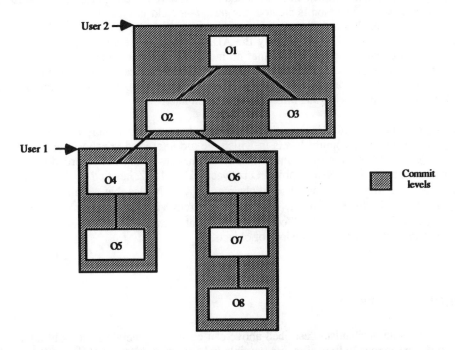

User 2 may now decide that he wishes to delete the reference to object O4 even though user 1 is inspecting it. In this case, a new version of O1 is created. When user 1 returns to the level above, he sees that the object in which he was interested has disappeared! Although the versionset mechanism guarantees that a user will never be left 'dangling' and unable to move back up through the hierarchy, other mechanisms need to be introduced to ensure that work is not 'lost' in the sense of being made inaccessible from the current version. The use of exclusions[9] may be used to solve these problems. In this case, a set of ADS users is maintained. Each user has an 'explore path', which is the path from the user's current position to *root*. Any attempt to modify an object within which a user is working is prevented if that modification would affect that user in any adverse manner.

7   Implementation of a simple versioning mechanism

This section describes one approach to implementing the version mechanism in the ADS. As has been shown above, we need to implement a mapping from τ (revision-time) to version. This is described below:

```
versionset      = RECORD
                       transient: transient
                       versions : versions
                  END

transient       = STRICT creator_id

versions        = MAP OF revision_time TO version_info

version_info    = RECORD
                       id: revision_time
                       (* usual object details *)
                  END
```

Sparse mappings are currently implemented as linked lists. New versions are created by inserting a new entry at the head of the list. When a new version is created, the *transient* field is set to the identifier of the user who has created the transient version. When the version becomes committed, the transient field is set to <undefined>, committing the new version. This field is used by the ADS to indicate whether the head of the map contains a committed or uncommitted version, and ensures that no more than one new version of any object can be created concurrently. Operations are provided to create new versions, commit or cancel versions, and to access a version at or prior to τ. In this simple implementation of versionsets, the identity of the person who committed the new version is not preserved. A means of preserving this information is given later.

In some situations the amount of information captured using versionsets may be more than is required. For example, it may be that the only commit levels in which we are interested are those which directly precede the completion of a project milestone. Let us assume that a set of changes have been recorded between milestones M1 and M2. Let us say there are n changes to an object O between M1 and M2, labelled $C_1..C_n$. If we are only interested in O at milestones M1 and M2 then we can discard changes $C_1..C_{n-1}$. Notice that we must always leave the change C_n in place to ensure that M2 remains complete. This process of removing changes must be applied across the entire specification to ensure self-consistency. The effects of this removal of changes are reduced storage requirements and a small increase in access speed to previous versions of objects.

8   Augmented Versions

The simple versioning mechanism described above can easily be generalised to hold additional information against each version. Unfortunately, it is often not possible to know in advance all of the attributes which need to be stored, and what is desirable in some development groups may be highly undesirable in others. For example, one group may wish to know who made the last change to this component of the specification. However, in another group this information may be unwanted.

A simple solution to this problem is to allow each entry in the versionset to be augmented with additional information. The addition of this extra information means that the size of an augmented versionset will be larger than the simple versionset given above. This space trade-off is for the designer of individual ADS applications to resolve. (In some cases the version information may include full details of change requests, and references to documents containing further details of these requests).

9 Changing Types

It is useful to be able to change a type in the persistent store whilst instances of that type exist. The ADS treats types as first class objects, and so types can themselves be versioned objects. Thus, if a type is changed, its previous definition is not destroyed but merely superceded. We can determine the revision-time of any object in the system, by looking at its parent versionset. Knowing the revision-time of the instance, we can determine the type which was active at the time the instance was declared. This type can then be used to access that instance. Thus several instances may exist each depending on different versions of the type, as shown below.

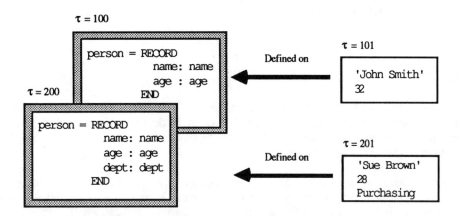

This has some interesting implications. Values are considered to be bound to their type at the time of their creation. Types can now evolve without the problems associated with 'inventing' values for previously unavailable fields. Likewise, if the bounds of a type change (e.g. a subrange) are changed then there is no need to decide how to coerce values which are now out of range. This is an extension of the approach described by Zdonik[7]. Notice that the technique of removing intermediate versions of objects should not be used with versioned types, as values may depend on different versions of the same type.

10 Variants

Variants are branches of a core specification. When generating applications from their specifications, it is useful to be able to specify variants of a specification. Again, because we are dealing with specifications there is no need to consider the maintenance of multiple implementations of the same specification. The approach which we are taking is the generalisation of core specifications, and then extending or overiding these specifications for specific systems. This requires the provision of *variant* management. There is a major difference between variants and versions. Changes to variants may occur in *parallel*, whereas changes to versions occur in *sequence*. We may need to keep several variants of each specification, each of which has a version history. Thus a mapping is required from a variant-id to a variant of the object. This can be achieved by providing an additional type constructor, *variantset*. For example:

```
role variants = VARIANTSET OF role version
```

Role version retains the definition given earlier. Historical versions are recorded against each allocated variant. The first variant which is allocated is the core object, and subsequent variants are created by copying the core object to the new variant and allocating the new variant. Notice that the core object may not be modified when other variants are defined upon it. Variants may then be modified independently of one another. Operations are provided to allocate a new variant and to access a variant from a variantset. The ADS user is provided with facilities to specify which variant of the specification he wishes to use, and that variant-id is used to ensure that the user will always see the variant of the specification in which he is interested. A mapping from variant name to variant-id is maintained to support this, as shown below:

```
Project variant        Variant-id

ADDER                  1

RATTLESNAKE            2
```

At present, variants are focussed on the management of large objects, such as specifications. No facilities are currently provided to merge variants together, as this is done by generalising the core specification instead. This task is probably the most difficult facing the analyst today, and the author does not believe that it will be possible to automate this process in the near future.

11 Summary

We have described work which is under development at AT&T ISTEL. We are working towards the maintenance of software through specifications, and in order to do this, version and variant management is an essential requirement. An additional benefit is the provision of concurrency for the ADS, and the provision of the ability to change types beneath existing data.

A production version of the ADS in now in full-time use at AT&T ISTEL supporting our JSD CASE tool. Prototypes of the version management system and concurrent system are under development. The ideas on concurrency have already been proven in the generation of concurrent applications. The reliability of both the ADS and applications written within it is extremely high, and it is the author's belief that this reliability is a result of the overall simplicity of the ADS. The enhancements described in this paper are made in the same spirit.

12 Acknowledgements

The author wishes to thank Michael Newman, Jonathan Twigge and Malcolm Powell for many useful discussions and comments on the subject matter.

13 References

1.   M.A. Jackson, *Principles of Program Design*, Academic Press, 1975.

2.   M.A. Jackson, *Jackson Systems Development*, Prentice Hall, 1983.

3.   J.W. Hughes and M.S. Powell, *'Rapid Prototyping using an Abstract Data Store'*, in J. McDermid (ed), *Integrated Project Support Environments*, Peter Peregrinus, 1985.

4.   M.S. Powell, *'Adding Programming Facilities to an Abstract Data Store'*, in *Proceedings of the First International Conference on Persistent Object Systems*, Appin, Scotland, 1985.

5.   C.A.R. Hoare, *'Notes on Data Structuring'* in O.J. Dahl, E.W. Dijkstra and C.A.R. Hoare *Structured Programming*, Academic Press, 1972.

6.   M.S. Powell, *'Strongly Typed User Interfaces in an Abstract Data Store'*, Software Practice and Experience, Vol 17, pp 241-266, April 1987.

7.   C.J. Date, *'An Introduction to Database Systems*, Volume II, Addison Wesley, 1985.

8.   S.B. Zdonik, *'Version Management in an Object-oriented Database'* in *Advanced Programming Environments*. Ed. Redier Conrad, 1986.

9.   S.T.Tye, *'A Prototype Abstract Data Store'*, Phd. Thesis, University of Manchester, 1985.

Concluding Remarks:

Perspectives on
Persistent Object Systems

In thinking back to the First International Workshop on Persistent Object Systems (POS1) at Appin, we see some contrasts with the most recent meeting. At the first meeting there were only a handful of running examplars; at this workshop there were reports on over two dozen operational prototypes. Many papers at POS1 were just reports on designs; at POS4 some of those designs had been implemented and measurements were beginning. At the first workshop, people were trying hard to make single-machine, single-user systems work. At this latest workshop we have papers on distribution, heterogeneity and concurrency models.

But the greatest strides have been conceptual. We now have the terminology and shared understanding to easily communicate our problems and proposed solutions to each other. This heightened knowledge hasn't put an end to debate and discussion, but has rather served to make it more efficient and productive. We are starting to see consensus on what persistent object systems should provide, but we are far from agreement on how to provide it. The theme of the workshop might have been "alternatives"–most problems were addressed by several presenters, but there were no "best" solutions acclaimed by the participants.

Few disagreed that the movement of objects between main memory and backing store should be managed automatically by the system. The question was how to make it fast. We saw proposals based on compiler technology, on hardware support, on virtual memory mechanisms and on physical storage organization.

Everyone imagines a layered architecture for their persistent system, but nobody agrees on what features belong at the lowest level. Should it provide a transaction model, or just synchronization primitives? Should it provide objects with uninterpreted state, concrete types or abstract types? Should it mask heterogeneity of underlying platforms, or export it? Should it provide large objects or small? Should it implement a single address space or impose some further structure on it?

Nearly every system described provided some kind of system-managed object identifier. We saw short OIDs and long OIDs and systems with both. We saw OID resolution handled by hardware, hash tables and swizzling. We saw OIDs with information about origin of objects or physical placement, and others that were completely logical.

What is to be retained or borrowed from database models and type theory? Should relations be added as structural approximations or axiomatic analogues with constraints and algebraic operators? Do type abstractions just get in the way when it is necessary to introduce a type defined in one scope into another?

Many attendees desired that garbage collection be handled automatically, but we have still to agree what is an acceptable overhead, whether transient and committed objects should be handled in the same way, and how to avoid creating "gratuitous" references to objects. Particularly interesting was Kolodner's proposal to combine concurrent garbage collection and recovery.

One unit of granularity for atomicity, visibility, integrity and recovery was widely held to be too restrictive a model for transactions. We saw proposals for nesting atomic actions, permitting visibility among cooperating transactions, programming integrity checks and replication for high availability. Do any of these techniques work together?

What is the best way to extend existing languages such as C++ to include persistence? Is it through libraries of persistent classes, additions to the type system, or creation of new storage classes?

What are the challenges over the next five years? Certainly there is the gathering and weighing of evidence on the alternatives set forth above. There is a need to package these systems to get them accepted and tested by a wider user community. Much of the work now is directed at a single layer of a multi-layer architecture. Candidates for the different layers must be brought together and harmonized to provide a platform robust enough to support large applications being written that will persist for more than a few months. Persistent object systems are intended to be a component technology for building final systems, not an end in themselves. We can only be sure of our success when those final systems exist, are reliable and are maintainable. To inform our designs of persistent object systems we need the evidence from well planned experiments running realistic loads. Such realism depends on our systems being well engineered and well presented, so users other than the developers are attracted to build applications on them, and thus generate those loads. We may hope for reports on such experiments at POS5.

Many in the field are promulgating the view that persistent storage layers will be the only persistent memory needed in future systems, yet there are many areas where we have not yet demonstrated they are up to the challenge. We have yet to see a multi-user recovery system built upon a stable store. We are pre-occupied with incestuous applications of our software–building database systems or supporting CASE tools. We end up looking at worlds where most data structures look like a parse tree and most accesses are characterized as graph walking. What will we be able to provide for the ordered data types common in scientific and engineering applications: matrices, time series, finite-element grids, molecular sequences and the like? We dwell on pointers and pay little attention to indexed addressing; we consider associative selection from sets, but say little about the bulk operations on ordered types. We have yet to consider continuous media such as audio and motion video; none of our systems have the hooks to support the resource reservation paradigms necessary to retrieve and render these data types.

Surely we should continue to refine, test and measure what we have created so far, but we must also broaden our vision in choosing what comes next. Inevitably, individual researchers may concentrate on one of these to achieve progress, but it is to be hoped that at POS5 we will hear of considerable progress on both fronts.

Long term persistence means that a persistent system will need to support continuous and sometimes radical change. Physical and logical definitions change, usage changes, and supporting technology evolves. If we are really to support data over any lifetime, then support for extended lifetimes requires management of change. Little work exists at present, but the problem was recognised and we may hope at least for proposed solutions by POS5.

Malcolm Atkinson and David Maier

SUBJECT INDEX

programming environments, 62
programming languages, database, 141
programming, software-process, 305
protection, 199, 215

R

reachability, partial, 389
reconfigurable architectures, 239
reconfigurable persistent store, 171
recovery, 89, 185, 305, 329
reference failure, 171
reliability, 255
repairable persistent store, 171
residency checking, 389
rules, 279
runtime library, 389

S

schema integration, 267
scoping, 43
security, 215
segmentation, 389
segmented memory, 114
semantic clustering, 389
serialisability, 293
shadow paging, 199
shared memory, 226
single-level store, 89, 369
Smalltalk, 17
software engineering, 305
software environment databases, 239
software-process programming, 305
SOL, 141
specification, 31
stability, 199
stable heap, 185
stable storage, 62

STAPLE, 62
static type checking, 141
store, single-level, 89, 369
strongly-typed, 31
subtyping, 17
superview, 267
symbolic architecture, 114
syntactic clustering, 389

T

threads, 279
timestamp, 293
transaction groups, 319, 329
transaction management, 131
transaction model, 279
transactions, 43, 185, 293, 305
    atomic, 255
    cooperative, 329
    design, 329
triggers, 305
type, 31
type checking, static, 141
type completeness, 141
type
    changing, 413
    existential, 141
    language-independent, 255
    subtyping, 17
    user-defined atomic, 255
typing, 43

V

variant control, 413
version control, 413
views, 389
virtual memory, 114, 215, 226
    distributed, 89
virtual object store, 226
virtual time, 293

429

AUTHOR INDEX